Benjamin Wisner Bacon

The Triple Tradition of the Exodus

A Study of the Structure of the Later Pentateuchal Books

Benjamin Wisner Bacon

The Triple Tradition of the Exodus
A Study of the Structure of the Later Pentateuchal Books

ISBN/EAN: 9783337143701

Printed in Europe, USA, Canada, Australia, Japan

Cover: Foto ©Lupo / pixelio.de

More available books at **www.hansebooks.com**

THE TRIPLE TRADITION OF

THE EXODUS

A STUDY OF THE STRUCTURE OF THE LATER
PENTATEUCHAL BOOKS, REPRODUCING
THE SOURCES OF THE NAR-
RATIVE, AND FURTHER
ILLUSTRATING THE
PRESENCE OF

BIBLES WITHIN THE BIBLE

BY

BENJAMIN WISNER BACON, M. A., D. D.

Author of " The Genesis of Genesis."

"The books of the Old Testament in their present form, in many instances are not, and do not profess to be, the original documents on which the history was based. There was (to use a happy expression employed of late) " A BIBLE WITHIN A BIBLE," an " Old Testament before an Old Testament was written." To discover any traces of the lost works in the actual text, or any allusions to them even when their substance is entirely perished, is a task of immense interest."
STANLEY.

HARTFORD
THE STUDENT PUBLISHING COMPANY
1894

BY THE SAME AUTHOR.

THE GENESIS OF GENESIS:

A Study of the Documentary Sources of the First Book of Moses in accordance with the results of critical science, illustrating the presence of BIBLES WITHIN THE BIBLE. Hartford, THE STUDENT PUBLISHING COMPANY, 1893.

CRITICAL NOTICES.

" The fruit of a vast amount of patient research." *The Congregationalist.*

" A popular and interesting contribution to one of the most important and puzzling questions raised by modern Biblical critics." *New York Tribune.*

'' We heartily commend this book to any of our readers who desire to get, in a clear, intelligible and simple form, the modern view of the composition of Genesis." *The Christian Union* (now *The Outlook*).

'' The author neither declaims nor disputes, but instead sets before the reader page after page of internal evidence, which leads with the force almost of a mathematical demonstration to the conclusions of modern critical science." *The Christian World*, London, Eng.

" Man wird gestehen müssen, dass ein Katechismus der Methode alttestamentlicher Wissenschaft von so hohem Unterrichtswerthe bisher nicht annähernd geboten ist." *Schürer's Theologische Literaturzeitung,* Leipzig, Germany.

Prof. T. K. Cheyne of Oxford, England, writes, in his *Founders of Old Testament Criticism,* N. Y. 1893, p. 246, " Mr. Bacon strikes me as the ablest of our younger Hexateuch critics."

Pres. W. R. Harper of Chicago University says : " The best thing in English on the subject."

Prof. K. Budde of Strassburg, declares it '' superior to the German works of the class."

Prof. G. F. Moore of Andover says : " It is the fruit of long and thorough study of the text, and of intimate acquaintance with recent criticism. A more competent guide through the labyrinth of the analysis would be hard to find."

Rev. Julius H. Ward, D. D.: " A very scholarly and thoughtful work."

The *New York Sun* commends it in a four column review.

The *New York Evening Post* gives an editorial to " Changed Popular Conceptions of the Bible," speaking of this work as " written in a style that everybody can understand," and adds : " Books of that sort are destined to increase and to have a powerful influence."

Prof. Oort of Leiden in the *Theol. Tijdschrift,* Prof. Toy of Harvard in *The New World,* Canon Driver of Oxford, and other eminent critics speak of it in similar high terms.

BIBLES WITHIN THE BIBLE.

PREFACE.

It is now some eight years since I undertook a typographical exhibit of the sources of the Hexateuch. The work, at first planned to present the sources, from Genesis to Joshua, was found too voluminous and reduced for "The Genesis of Genesis," (Student Pub. Co., Hartford, Ct., 1892) to include only Genesis and the first twenty chapters of Exodus. Even this was found to be too long, and the material prepared on the first half of Exodus remained over. At the same time the series of critical discussions on Genesis published in *Hebraica*, Oct., 1890, and subsequently, was continued by a similar series in the *Journal of Biblical Literature* (vols. ix–xii.—1890–1893) on " JE in the middle Books of the Pentateuch." The surprisingly cordial welcome accorded me by critics at home and abroad, and the excellent account given by the publisher, have suggested a new volume, independent indeed of the " Genesis of Genesis," but of similar form and character, continuing the analysis to the end of the Pentateuch. We reach thus, with the death of Moses, a convenient stopping-place, though by no means the conclusion of the documents. The period between this event and the death of Joseph, includes the whole Story of the Exodus in its three great divisions, Deliverance from the Bondage of Egypt, Constitution of the Nation, and Wandering in the Wilderness. If occasion serve, the analysis of the three sources may be continued throughout the book of Joshua, and of the two older through Judges and part of Samuel down to the founding of the monarchy, under the title, " The Conquest of Canaan."

For the present only the Triple Tradition of the Exodus, a three-fold account of Israel's beginnings as a nation, engages our attention ; and herein is not included that mass of ritual law which forms the bulk of the Priests' Code, nor the code of Deuteronomy. Neither is susceptible of analysis beyond a division into earlier and later elements of the same documents P^1, P^2, P^3, D, Dp, Dh, and from the nature of the material the codes are easily detachable from the narrative. The present volume concerns itself therefore not with the *Law*, but the *Story* of Israel from the death of Joseph to the death of Moses.

Part I. of "The Genesis of Genesis" was devoted to explaining the nature of the higher criticism in its two branches of source analysis and historical criticism, vindicating its right in the field of sacred literature, and exhibiting its general results in the Hexateuch. What was said there it is the less needful to repeat, for the reason that the intervening years have witnessed the appearance of several works in English, admirably presenting these same results, among which I need here mention only Canon S. F. Driver's "Introduction to the Literature of the Old Testament," Scribners, New York, 1891, and Mr. W. G. Addis' "Documents of the Hexateuch," Putnams, New York, 1893.

Neither do we need to add to the manifold and still unrefuted refutation of the Rabbinic tradition of Mosaic authorship. The ground is cleared ; the facts are in evidence which show the extrication of sources in Genesis to be no illusion nor impossibility ; the presupposition must now be that they are also extricable in the further course of the same composite narrative. Indeed the concessions of the most extreme defenders of tradition as to the earlier portions of Genesis, and the more important admissions of the school represented by Principal Cave, that the results of the documentary analysis are to be accepted in the main up to Ex. vi., decidedly alter the conditions of the controversy. The burden of proof henceforth should rest upon those who admit that the Pentateuch is analyzable in part, but wish to draw the line at Gen. xii., or at Ex. vi., or at some other arbitrary point.

This disposition on the part of the supporters of tradition to come as far as Astruc, who in 1753 gave forth his theory in the title of his book, "*Conjectures sur les Mémoires originaux dont*

s'est servi Moyse pour composer le livre de la Genèse," is one reason
for adopting a somewhat different method from that employed
in Genesis. Another and more weighty reason appears in the
relative incompleteness of the science itself in Exodus and the
following books. This is due to several causes. Partly it is
because more time and effort have been spent on Genesis, the
earlier attempts setting out with Astruc's assumption, that the
documents were compiled by Moses, which implied their limitation to Genesis ; partly because popular interest has chiefly
attached to this book. Principally it is because the analysis
becomes more difficult from Ex. iii. onward. Here in fact one
of the principal discriminating features of the document E disappears, and in Ex. vi. the same becomes true of the document
P. A phenomenon of Genesis, which was almost the sole reliance of Astruc for his analysis, is the uniform employment of
Yahweh as the divine name in one series of narratives, and of
Elohim, El, or El Shaddai in another. Its explanation appears
in Ex. vi. 2f., where P relates the *revelation* to Moses of the name
Yahweh : "And God spake unto Moses, and said unto him, I
am Yahweh : and I appeared unto Abraham, unto Isaac and
unto Jacob as El Shaddai, *but by my name Yahweh I was not known
to them."* Of course then P did not use Yahweh in Genesis,
and of course he now begins to use it as uniformly as Elohim
or El Shaddai before. The justification to the analysis was
invaluable, but it came at the cost of losing the then most
important means of discriminating P from J. Moreover P
does not relate this revelation to Moses on his own authority.
He copied both it, and the practise it logically implies as to the
name Yahweh, from the story of E in Ex. iii. Fortunately E is
less systematic than P in his subsequent narrative, and often allows the name Elohim to stand in long passages of his material.
Wherever this is not the case, however, the clew for analysis
mainly relied upon in Genesis disappears, as in P, and hence the
mere use of " Yahweh " no longer serves, as in Genesis, to prove a
passage Yahwistic or redactional. This is not the only increase
of difficulty. The taking up of Deuteronony into the prophetic
history JE necessitated a revision ; but this of course would

scarcely affect the patriarchal narratives, xxvi. 5 being the
only clear trace of Rd in Genesis, whereas the whole of JE from
Exodus on has undergone more or less systematic revision of
this character, the alteration being especially marked in passages dealing with legislation, as *e. g.* in J's law of Passover, in
both J and E at the Sinai-Horeb chapters, and where, as in
Joshua, account had to be taken of a new legislation by which
the history was supposed to have been controlled.

The comparatively backward state of the science has necessitated a far larger proportion of pioneer work on my part than
in the previous volume.   In "The Genesis of Genesis" I could
content myself generally with exhibiting the consensus of critical
opinion as to the analysis, presenting my reasons for the independent work done in the case of difficult and disputed chapters
in the series of articles on "Pentateuchal Analysis" published
in *Hebraica* VII. 1 (Oct. 1890)—x.   In the present volume I am
obliged to take the attitude of an independent critic.   The
separation of P throughout from JE is now indeed a matter of
general agreement among critics : but the analysis of JE is
quite otherwise.   Its present relative incompleteness is well
illustrated in the work of Addis above referred to, in which the
distinction of type between J and E is carried to the end of
Genesis, but employed after Ex. i. only in those portions of JE
where the strands are traceable with exceptional clearness.   As
to the early chh. of Exodus, Kuenen says ("Hexateuch" § 8, n.
11) : "In Ex. iii. 16–xii. we may find abundant points of support for a critical analysis ; but here we cannot separate two
distinct documents, as we have done in Jacob's biography and
elsewhere, and assign its share to each with confidence.   The
most we can hope for is to determine whether it is E or J that
lies at the basis of the narrative, and sometimes even this is
doubtful. . . .   It appears that in Ex. i. *sqq.* the simple interweaving of the authorities with the retention of the special
characteristics of each gave way to their free use, and their
intimate blending and recasting."   Wellhausen advises relin-
quishment of the attempt at precise analysis of most of the
Plague narratives, declares that JE is more correctly to be re-

garded as the author (Verfasser) of the Horeb-Sinai section than mere compiler (Redaktor) (*Comp.*, Berlin, 1889, pp. 69 and 97), and has perhaps not wholly withdrawn his theory of a "second source of JE" in Numbers.* The French critic Bruston, imitates the example of Wellhausen by assuming a fourth source as a solution of the difficulties, the *deus ex machina* this time being a "second Jéhoviste." It has been my effort to show that no such "Hülfshypothesen" are necessary. JE does not change his method, nor is there a new source introduced. The sources are J, E and P, precisely as in Genesis, and combined in the same way. What is required is not unfounded assumptions to explain our comparative inability to analyze, but more care, more patience, more determination to be guided not by preconceptions but by phenomena. It will be seen, however, from the above, that the problem was by no means the same as in Genesis, and different conditions have made necessary a difference in method of treatment.

To adapt the present volume to the new conditions imposed by the altered problem and somewhat altered circle of readers to which it is addressed, it has seemed best to put in place of the general Introduction of "The Genesis of Genesis" a series of briefer Introductions prefixed to each subdivision of the narrative, the Prolegomena before each § setting forth to the reader in large type the general distinguishing features of each document P, E, J, as they appear in that section, an Analysis in smaller type before each subsection discussing the phenomena of the text as it stands, and stating as briefly as possible the bulk of the evidence for its composite structure, together with the grounds of analysis, and theory of compilation. In addition a few pages at the beginning of the Prolegomena to § § i., v. and vii., are devoted to something more in the nature of historical criticism, discussing the history and significance of the tradition itself. A brief general Introduction sums up the data of the Prolegomena and presents the bearing of the facts derived from the study of the documents in Exodus, Numbers and Deuteronomy upon the Documentary Theory as a whole.

*Cf. Wellhausen's *Comp.*, p. 102 with the *Nachtrag* in the same volume. p. 339, in reply to Kuenen's criticism.

It may also be noticed, that no such systematic attempt has
been made in the present volume as in " The Genesis of Genesis " to distinguish between J¹ and J², E¹ and E². This is not
because of any doubt in my mind that such strata exist ; for of
this I am much more firmly convinced than before my study of
the later historical books was completed. My conclusions are
presented in the Introduction following. It seems to me, however, that the introduction of such questions should properly
await a more advanced condition of the analysis.

Certain minor improvements have been attempted upon the
former work as *e. g.* the entire abandonment of Hebrew type
in favor of transliteration where needful ; the adoption (except
as to P¹ = H) of Cornill's nomenclature ; the use of '   '
for characteristic expressions of J, E and P in Part II.,
and the abandonment of the attempt to reproduce in English
anything of the rhythm of Hebrew verse. If that part
devoted to reconstruction of the documents is thus improved in
any degree, it will be the better able to bear the loss of Prof.
G. F. Moore's kindly, correcting hand in the translation.
Faults and mistakes due to my deficiencies as a linguist will
doubtless appear, but in all essentials I am fortified by the
authority of such scholars as Dillmann and Kautzsch. In addition I must acknowledge my great indebtedness to Budde's
admirable articles on the legislative parts of JE, besides his
personal kindnesses, and to C. H. Cornill's *Einleitung in das Alte
Testament, 2 Aufl. Freiburg i. B.* 1892. Other standard works
will be found referred to in the body of the work.*

In conclusion let me urge the general reader to remember
that while the devotional and scientific treatment of the Bible
are widely different, they are neither incompatible nor independent. For the very reason that devotional exposition
must take as its point of departure some account of its documentary data, either scientific or assumed to be such, it has a
natural inclination to conservatism, an impatience of criticism
and change, and a disinclination to readjust itself to a new
basis. Sometimes it undertakes to decree : " La République

_____
*Wildeboer's *Letterkunde des Ouden Verboords*, Groningen 1893, sent me by
the author's kindness, arrives, unfortunately, too late for present use.

n'a pas besoin de savants," and then its folly soon becomes
manifest in its own destruction. In the nature of the case there
is nothing but indolence and timidity of mind to prevent as excellent a structure of devotional thought and edifying exposition
being reared upon the critical conclusions of modern special-
ists as upon the fantastic legends of those rabbis of whom
Jesus said, " They have made the Scripture of none effect by
their traditions." Practically a dispassionate examination of
the results will show that the former basis gives vastly larger
and more excellent opportunity to set forth the God and
Father of our Lord Jesus Christ as He is revealed in this history of histories, and is far more consistent with Christian
ideas, than the latter. The edifice reared upon it has the
additional advantage of being founded upon tested and proved
rather than untested material. The present work is not intended primarily for devotional reading, but it endeavors to do
its part in substituting for the crumbling foundations of Rabbinic tradition, which have thus far been almost the sole reliance of Christian scholars in formulating their doctrine of
Sacred Scripture, an " impregnable rock " of that true and
divine science of biblical theology whose motto is, " The Truth
without fear or favor."

We stand to-day, as Paul stood, between two opposing cur-
rents of religious thought, both earnest and both devout :
" Jews " that require a sign, and " Greeks " that seek after wisdom. Whatever tends to minimize the miraculous by seeking
the manifestion of God in the normal rather than the abnormal,
is to the " Jew," " destructive criticism." The " Greek " is too
apt to linger amid the lotus flowers of sweet reasonableness. The
present work is " destructive " of nothing but that which stands
in the way of better, and which would not be destructible if it
were not worthless. It is " constructive," at least in purpose,
of a Bible which by the illuminating grace of the Holy Spirit will
be more truly than ever a manifestation " to Jew and Greek "
of both " the power of God and the wisdom of God."

BENJAMIN WISNER BACON.

Parsonage, Oswego, N. Y., December, 1893.

TABLE OF CONTENTS.

PART II. SOURCES RECONSTRUCTED.

INTRODUCTION.

INTRODUCTION.

Our study of the Book of Genesis showed it to be, like all the historical books of the Bible, and like Oriental histories generally, a compilation. The fact is now generally conceded that the documents underlying it admit to a greater or less extent of extrication, though advocates of the traditional authorship necessarily limit the documents to a period earlier than Moses. It is our purpose to test the validity of this limitation, and, if the documentary analysis be found practicable in the later books, and the traditional account of authorship thus becomes untenable, to derive from the documents themselves an inductive theory of their origin, purpose, character, and relation to the progress of religious thought, *i. e.* of divine revelation.

A review of the three documents found to underlie the Book of Genesis, J, E, and P, reveals a very strong presumption in each case that they were continued at least to include the story of the conquest of Canaan. The document P, known as the Priestly Law-book, and generally assigned by critics to the fifth century B. C., is made up in Genesis of ten *toledoth* (approximately = " genealogies "), generally mere pedigrees, or tables of statistics of births, marriages and deaths, of the stock of Israel from Adam to Joseph. These extend to the collateral branches and follow an exact chronology (necessarily artificial) beginning from the Creation, of which the very days of the week are specified. At intervals this slender stream widens out to a broad pool, when the writer proceeds to give in incredibly minute detail *the origin of Israel's religious institutions,* among which the divine covenant to give them *the land of Canaan* occupies perhaps the foremost position. Thus the " Genealogy of the Heavens and the Earth " employs the story of Creation to trace to it the divine origin of the *Sabbath ;* a pedigree of ten generations introduces the "Genealogy of Noah," which employs a version of the Flood-story to trace the origin of the Noachic covenant and *law of blood-shed* and meats ; a second ten-linked pedigree introduces the "Genealogy of Terah," father of Abraham, signalized by the revelation of the name El-Shaddai, *covenant of the Land* to Abraham's seed, and institution of *circumcision*, ch. xvii., and by the acquisition of the first foothold in Canaan, the Cave of Machpelah, ch. xxiii. The subsequent genealogies only depart from the tabular form to record briefly how Jacob was sent by his parents to Mesopotamia to secure a wife of Abrahamic stock, unlike the Canaanite wives of Esau ; how God reiterated the *covenant of the land* to Isaac and Jacob, and how Joseph, having become governor of Egypt, brought his father and brethren thither with all their great wealth. P's story of the patriarchal age concludes with the blessing of the dying Israel, who charges his sons to bury him in the Cave of Machpelah with his fathers, and tells Joseph particularly, in blessing his sons as separate tribes, how El-Shaddai reiterated to him at Luz the blessing of Abraham and the covenant of the land, saying : " Behold I will make thee fruitful and multiply thee, and will make of thee a company of peoples ; and will give this land to thy seed for an everlasting possession." We are thus left looking forward for the redemption of this promise, and for the sequel to this beginning of an account of Israel's religious institutions.

It is conceivable that the narrative stopped short at this point. But in point of fact we find the story proceeding without a gap, first a table of the sons of Israel in Egypt, in the same peculiar style as heretofore, then, after a brief statement of the Egyptian oppression, a " Genealogy of the sons of Levi " introducing Aaron and Moses, and relating how :

"God spake unto Moses and said unto him, I am YAHWEH, and I appeared unto Abraham, unto Isaac and unto Jacob as El Shaddai, but by my name Yahweh, I was not known to them. But I established my covenant with them to give them the land of Canaan . . . and I have heard the groaning of the children of Israel whom the Egyptians keep in bondage ; and I have remembered my covenant. . . I will rid you out of their bondage . . .and will bring you in unto the land concerning which I lifted up my hand to give it to Abraham, to Isaac and to Jacob, and I will give it you for an heritage; I am Yahweh."

The narrative then proceeds to relate the carrying out of this promise. Under the same rigid chronological and genealogical system we are told the story of the Plagues and Exodus, which serves to introduce *the law of the Passover and Feast of Mazzoth*. After a brief account of the miraculous passage of the Red Sea a *table of wilderness stations* begins, as a supplement for the genealogical chain, and carries on the chronology. On the fifteenth day of the third month (the *sacred calendar* has been enacted in connection with the Passover legislation) Israel comes to Sinai. Here is placed the revelation of *the entire Priestly Law and the origin of all Israel's religious institutions connected with sacrifice, the priesthood, and the sanctuary*. After an elaborate *census of the people* the journey is resumed " in the second year, in the second month, on the twentieth day of the month," a brief account of the manna signalizing the march to the wilderness of Paran. A version of the spying out the land and murmuring of the people leads to the 40 years' wandering, to which attach, besides the incidents of the rebellion of Moses and Aaron at the rock of Meribah and the death of Aaron, only the story of the *origin of the priestly castes* (rod of Aaron), and a brief allusion to the plot of Balaam. Yahweh covenants the priesthood to the house of Phinehas. Then a new *census* is taken, preparatory to the *distribution of the inheritances*, accompanied by minute regulations of land-tenure. Moses gives to Reuben and Gad the land of Gilead, taken from Midian, and dies, committing his trust to Joshua. A few words tell how the latter sweeps the land of Canaan, and the final chapters of Joshua relate the *allotment of the promised land to the tribes*, minutely describing the boundaries "according to their inheritances."

Were it possible to enumerate here the extraordinary peculiarities of style and language in which all the latter part of this narrative minutely agrees with the story of Genesis, which it thus brings to its expected conclusion, it is hard to believe that any competent or candid mind could reject the overwhelming probability that we have here not two separate writers, one beginning where the other left off, referring constantly to his predecessor, using identically the same style and language, system, purpose, material, and occupying the same standpoint; but one and the same hand. But even apart from these important criteria it is safe to leave the question of the continued identity of the document distinguished as P^2 in Genesis to simple perusal of the sequel herewith afforded to the source as extricated in Genesis. Whether this document stands alone in Exodus—Joshua, or whether, as in Genesis, it has been more or less incongruously associated with other material will appear in the process of analysis.

There is no indication in this document P that its purpose is not fully attained and its subject matter exhausted with the establishment of Israel in the Land of Promise " according to their inheritances," and in full possession of all their peculiar institutions. Neither is there the least trace in the books of Judges, Kings and Samuel of any further fragments. The story of these books is indeed rewritten in the priestly sense in a later work, which in many respects has a striking resemblance to P, viz., the Book of Chronicles—Ezra—Nehemiah. But the compiler of this work makes a new beginning with " Adam, Seth, Enosh, Kenan, Mahalalel, Jared, Enoch, Methuselah," etc., and is clearly independent of P, though controlled by his ideas. There is, in short, every reason to believe that P, as analyzed from Genesis to Joshua, is a complete work from which scarcely anything is missing. As extricated by practical consensus of criticism it could, therefore, be already characterized to some extent, in "the Genesis of Genesis" (p. 55ff.), though we may have somewhat to add in our present discussion of the documents, as their individuality emerges upon further analysis.

The Analyses prefixed to each subsection of the present volume aim to show that the internal discrepancies of Genesis continue to appear throughout Exodus, a considerable part of Numbers,

and a smaller part of Deuteronomy. Hereafter there may be
occasion to show that the same is true of Joshua. Are then
these *stories of the Exodus*, with which the Priestly Lawbook has
been filled in, a continuation of the documents J and E already
extricated in Genesis, and which in their combined form, JE,
served as source to P? To answer this question we must
apply the same tests as applied just now to P.

The analysis of Genesis gave a document known to critics as
E, attributed by all to the Ephraimite monarchy. This work
seems to begin with the career of Abraham as a " prophet "
(Gen. xx. 7) called by God out of the midst of a heathen ances-
try to the " land of the Amorite," which God promises to his
descendants when, after four generations of oppression "in a
land that is not theirs," they should come thither again, and
" the iniquity of the Amorite should be full." A few stories of
Abraham's relations with the Philistines, duplicating those
related by J of Isaac, explain in E the origin and names of the
sacred wells of the Negeb ; while one regarding Hagar and
Ishmael and the birth of Isaac, likewise a duplicate, plays upon
these names. The story of Abraham has here in addition only
a single, characteristic, concluding narrative, peculiar to this
source. It relates how "God *proved* Abraham " by commanding the sacrifice of Isaac, who thus appears only in his boyhood and on his death-bed. Isaac's sons quarrel, but Jacob,
fleeing, receives a divine revelation at Bethel and vows service
to the God of this place, who *becomes his protector* in exile and
gives him children and wealth. On his return he founds the
shrines of Ramoth-Gilead, Mahanaim, Peniel and the ' pillar '
and altar by Shechem. At Shechem he places a parallel to P's
story of the Cave of Machpelah. For 100 *kesitahs* of silver
Jacob buys a parcel of ground at the hand of the children of
Hamor, the father of Shechem, but subsequently takes the city
" out of the hand of the Amorite, with his sword and with his
bow." His heathen wives "*put away their strange gods*" under
the oak at Shechem, and Jacob builds the altar at Bethel, con-
secrates the oak of Allon-bacuth, and erects the Pillar of
Rachel's grave.

The *career of Joseph* concludes the patriarchal epoch. "Joseph as a lad was feeding the flock with his brethren." His prophetic dreams excite the envy of his brethren, but when they have cast him in a pit and a kidnapping band of Midianites sell him a slave in Egypt this *prophetic power* exalts him to the highest place under Pharaoh. Joseph sends for his father and brethren to share his prosperity; the dying Jacob blesses Ephraim and Manasseh, and bestows Shechem as a special gift "above his brethren" upon Joseph; then after the patriarch's death Joseph forgives his brethren, explaining to them the providence of God. At great length and in most attractive colors the career of this "master of dreams" is depicted to the end. The story concludes with a repetition of the prophetic vision of Abraham:

"And Joseph said unto his brethren, I die: but God will surely visit you, and bring you up out of this land unto the land which he sware to Abraham, to Isaac and to Jacob. And Joseph took an oath of the children of Israel, saying, God will surely visit you, and ye shall carry up my bones from hence."

Again, as in P, it is conceivable that the author of this document did not live to see the fulfilment of the predicted events, but simply recorded what had been revealed to Abraham, Isaac, and Jacob as one miraculously guided to select just that which comes to subsequent fulfilment. But it is very surprising that a *subsequent historian* in relating the fulfilment of what E looks forward to, should employ the style, language and all other peculiarities of E, even where telling his own story, so that none could tell from the narrative, where one ends and his successor begins; whereas in giving us the sequel to the Priestly Lawbook of Genesis his style should be indistinguishable from that of this radically different document. It is conceivable that there was no sequel to the account of the promise to Abraham, the bequest of Jacob, or the oath of Joseph. But in point of fact, reading right on in the composite narrative of Exodus, we find an uninterrupted sequel to this story, characterized by the same style and expressions and the same peculiar use of "God" for Yahweh. From the *career of Joseph* it passes at once to the *career of Moses*. His birth and boyhood

are painted in the same sympathetic colors as the youth of
Isaac and Joseph, and serve to illustrate the depth of humiliation to which Israel had fallen in Egypt after the death of
Joseph. The youthful Moses performs an exploit of valor in
favor of his enslaved countrymen, but, repelled by them, flees
to Midian and marries there. God reveals himself to him from
" Horeb the mount of God." Then follows the explanation, so
closely paralleled in P, of the peculiar use of Elohim as the
divine name, a practice of E hitherto unexplained. As P in
Ex. vi. 2 makes clear the reason why previously in that
document, Elohim, or El Shaddai, is used to the exclusion
of Yahweh, but thereafter uniformly Yahweh, so in almost
identical terms in Ex. iii. we read the original, both of
P's story and his practise. Thereafter Moses and Aaron his
brother are sent to demand from Pharaoh release for Israel,
and Moses receives a *wonder-working rod*, whereby after inflict-
ing five plagues upon Egypt the Red Sea is divided and Israel
passes through, while Pharaoh and his host are overwhelmed.
E has thus far *no legislation*. Even the institution of the Passover is not so much as mentioned. But the *prophecy of Joseph*
is not forgotten. The Exodus is related in terms whose significance points both forward and backward :

"Now when Pharaoh had let the people go . . . God led the people about
by the way of the wilderness by the Red Sea . . . And Moses took the bones
of Joseph with him ; for he had straitly sworn the children of Israel, saying,
God will surely visit you ; and ye shall carry up my bones away hence with
you."

After " Miriam the prophetess " has sung their deliverance at
the Red Sea, the "*proving*" of Israel begins at Massah with the
gift of manna, and the gift of water brought from the rock by
Moses' rod at Meribah. Here at Horeb "God comes to
prove " them, pronouncing in voice of thunder the *moral law*
as summed up in *the Ten Commandments*. These he writes with
his own finger upon the tables of stone. *The career of Joshua*
begins here ; for now *as a youth* he serves Moses, as later Samuel does for Eli, and ascends with him to the presence of God.
Israel, *entrusted to the care of Aaron* falls into idolatry, but after

chastisement repents. Now, in place of the Covenant of the Ten Words, the record of which was shattered by Moses, a *ritual covenant* is enacted, and a portable sanctuary prepared. The youthful Joshua becomes its hierophant. Israel is dismissed under guidance of God's angel. At the instance of Jethro a *civil organization* is also effected, and, on Moses' petition, God takes of the *spirit of prophecy* which was upon him, and pours it upon 70 elders ; but Moses' prophetic preëminence is vindicated even against Aaron and Miriam, and later his civil supremacy against Dathan and Abiram. Arrived at Kadesh the people are discouraged at the report of twelve men sent to reconnoitre the land ; they murmur, and repent again, but incur disaster at Hormah through presumption. Forty years pass by in the steppes of Kadesh, where Miriam dies. They endeavor to reach the country east of Jordan, but are refused passage by Edom and Moab, make the circuit, fight with Sihon the Amorite, and occupy his land. Balaam, called to curse Israel, blesses. Reuben and Gad receive the land of Sihon. At Shittim by Jordan Moses gives his farewell admonitions to all Israel, delivers the *civil law* given him at Horeb to the elders, to be solemnly enacted by covenant at *Mount Ebal* and inscribed on great stones ; then, after receiving a charge for Joshua as his successor, he dies, and is buried in Moab. *No such prophet* has since appeared in Israel.

The career of Joshua is taken up without interruption (Jos. i. 1f. 10f.) and includes all the story of the conquest. A miraculous passage of the Jordan gives access to Jericho, whose walls fall before the invaders. The sin of Achan, the Judean, brings a reverse at Ai, but is expiated, and the capture of Ai and Bethel opens up the heart of the country. At Mount Ebal Joshua enacts the law of Moses as directed. The battle of Gibeon against a coalition of the south Amorite kings leads Joshua to the rapid conquest of all southern Palestine ; the defeat of a similar coalition under Jabin, king of Hazor, secures him all the north. The conquest complete, Joshua assembles all Israel "at Shechem," recapitulates the story of the divine dealings *as related in the document E* from the call of

Abraham down, pledges Israel to " put away the strange gods " and serve Yahweh only, prophesying prosperity in case of obedience and calamity otherwise, and erects a "great stone " under the oak in the sanctuary for a witness. The story then relates the death and burial of Joshua, adding that during the lifetime of Joshua and the men of that generation Israel was faithful to the pledge, and concludes with a passage whose terms and allusions we shall recognize :

" And the bones of Joseph which the children of Israel brought up out of Egypt, buried they *in Shechem, in the parcel of ground which Jacob bought* of the sons of Hamor the father of Shechem for 100 *kesitahs* of money : so they became the inheritance of the children of Joseph."

Once more, it is conceivable that not only Moses took pains to supply the sequel to all the unfinished data of a document employed by him for the patriarchal period, using the same style and vocabulary, but that Joshua, or some still later writer, continued the practise after Moses' death, and still another after Joshua's death. But can such an assumption stand for one moment before the probability that a narrative thus interconnected in its several parts at the same time that it often disagrees with the adjoining material, is a single unbroken work ?

But while the document P reaches an appropriate conclusion with the occupation of Canaan, it is far otherwise with E, the document we are now following. Not only is there as yet no completeness to the author's purpose, but the same signs which indicated in Genesis that more was to follow, are present here at the close of Joshua ; and as those were corroborated by unmistakable fragments of the same narrative in the books following, so the expectations raised by the farewell address of Joshua are met by an element of the story in Judges and the books of Samuel and Kings.

The story of the Judges in E is not, as in the parallel, which in many ways is identified as J, the account of how the tribes gradually enlarged and established their foothold against the native peoples, but how all Israel underwent a succession of reverses at the hands of *foreign* invaders, according as they successively fell away to the worship of "strange gods," then repented, and Yahweh "raised them up a deliverer." The last and greatest of these *prophet-deliverers* is Samuel, the *story of whose career* begins a new epoch.

In I and II Samuel E's story contrasts with that of J, first by making *Samuel the prophet* the most important figure, relating his career *from birth and childhood,* as in the case of Moses, instead of merely introducing him as J does in full maturity, when his part is to be played, and subordinating his role to that of Saul. On account of the *unfaithfulness of the priesthood* Israel is reduced to subjection by the Philistines. At the instance of Samuel the people repent and turn to Yahweh with all their heart, "putting away the strange gods." Samuel leads them to complete victory at Ebenezer, and rules the country in peace and justice. The origin of the monarchy is traced to the discontent and vanity of the people, who demand a king *in imitation of the neighboring peoples.* Samuel reveals to them their folly and sin in rejecting the *theocracy* they have hitherto enjoyed, but at Yahweh's command grants their request, selecting the king by lot at Mizpah. Moved by Samuel's speech of abdication the people repent and secure Samuel's promise of intercession and the promise of suspension of punishment during good conduct. Immediately thereupon Samuel, as representative of Yahweh's sovereignty, enjoins upon Saul, the newly-appointed king, a holy war against Amalek (cf. 1 Sam. xv. 1ff. with Ex. xvii. 8–14; Dt. xxv. 17–19). Saul at once proves his unfitness, and the story of the *shepherd-boy* David and his conflict with Goliath introduces the worthy successor. For their favor shown to David, whom Saul's jealousy has driven into hiding, Saul exterminates the house of Aaron (cf. Ex. xxxii. 33f.). A brief version of the romantic story of David, Jonathan and Saul ends in E with the account of David's sparing Saul's life (I Sam. xxvi.), whereupon Saul confesses his sin and is reconciled to his "son David." Afterward David hears of the death of Saul and Jonathan in the battle of Gilboa. His informant, an *Amalekite,* testifies to having killed Saul. David has him slain. David thereupon conducts the war against the Philistines to a successful issue, and when firmly established in Jerusalem consults with "Nathan the prophet" as to "building a house for Yahweh." Nathan responds at first with approval, but, receiving a message from Yahweh the same night, reports that *Yahweh will have none of the proposed house of cedar*, though for David's pious design *He* will "build *him* a house," *i. e.* establish his posterity upon the throne (cf. Ex. i. 21). There is no further report from E upon the reign of David and he appears to have proceeded at once to the accession of Solomon.

Solomon's reign imposed a "grievous yoke" upon Israel in the building of his temple and palaces, and at his death the people seek relief. At *Shechem* all Israel had gathered to make Rehoboam king. The folly of the young prince repels the ten (eleven?) tribes. Under the leadership of Jeroboam, who had previously been instructed by *the prophet Ahijah*, they rebel and set up the kingdom of Ephraim. "There was none that followed the house of David but the tribe of Judah only." Jeroboam sins by establishing bull-worship at Bethel (and Dan?"*) and is rejected by Yahweh at the mouth of Ahijah (I Kgs. xiv.).

E probably traced briefly the story of the kings of Israel as far as Ahab, and his work may have incorporated the great narrative of the prophets which begins abruptly with the story of Elijah in I Kgs. xvii.–xix., and continues in II Kings ii., iv.–viii. 15. Cornill thinks it probable that the source of II Kings xiv. 8–16 is E, and I would add in that case as extremely probable, vv. 23–29, in vs. 28 reading *we-jehudah*, "*and* Judah," for *le-jehudah*, "*to* Judah," of the text. It would seem therefore that in its present form the narrative of E came down very near, if not quite, to the fall of the northern kingdom, and in any case he must have brought his narrative down to date. The great catastrophe of 722 B. C. establishes a positive *terminus ad quem* for the Ephraimite history, not because literature

---

* Cf. Farrar's article: "Was there a golden calf at Dan?" *Expositor*, Dec., 1893.

ceased in Samaria after the loss of its independence, but because the hopeful and even triumphant patriotic feeling which pervades the bulk of this history is incompatible with the experience of utter national ruin. Again such a narrative would scarcely have grown up in independence of its Judean parallel after the coalescence of the two kingdoms. But perhaps the most conclusive argument for a limit within the eighth century B. C. is that in 701 the work seems to have been known to Isaiah the son of Amoz (cf. Is. x. 24–26). The brilliant reign of Jeroboam II. (circ. 800–759), marked by an at least attempted incorporation of Judah and restoration of the Davidic monarchy, fulfills the conditions under which such a document might naturally arise, and we are safe in concluding that its story reached to about the middle of the eighth century.

The argument for the continuity of the document J of Genesis throughout the preëxilic historical books very nearly, if not quite down to the revolution of Jehoiada, is exactly analogous to that presented in favor of P and E, but a mere perusal of the document should dissipate from any candid mind the notion that the materials the analysis sets aside from P and E in Genesis and the later Pentateuchal books are mere disconnected fragments, or even two or more separate though mutually supplementary narratives. The scope of J is far wider than that of either E or P, but a comprehensive purpose is intelligently pursued from its introductory chapters tracing the ethnological pedigree of Israel to " the Man " of Eden, down to the story of the great Yahwistic rebellion against the " house of Omri," which in Ephraim set Jehu, whom we might call the " flail of Elijah," upon the throne of Ahab, and in Judah, under the leadership of Jehoiada, overthrew the usurped throne of Athaliah, and set in her place the child Joash with the powerful chief-priest as regent.

Let the reader conceive, in the absence of adequate synopsis, what the history of Israel would be like, as written in the Pentateuch, Joshua, Judges, I and II Samuel and Kings, down to the epoch just defined, if the Deuteronomic and Priestly Codes, and the elements of P and E above reviewed were omitted. In Genesis the *origins of the Hebrew stock* are related in legends of idyllic beauty. Their affinity with all surrounding peoples is traced back to the creation of man. Primitive mythology is employed to account for the beginnings of moral and physical evil, with faint foreshadowing of an ultimate victory of humanity. The growth of art and invention accompanies the ramification of the race and the rise of corrupt civilizations. Presently the stock of Abram emerges as divinely chosen to inherit the land of Canaan. The folk-tales of Bethel, Hebron, Beersheba, the sacred wells, trees, altars, sanctuaries of the land are attached to the story of the patriarchs, and find their justification in it, while the splendid tribe-legend of Joseph leads over to the bondage of Egypt. That noble national lyric the Blessing of Jacob forms the subscript to the story of the primitive age.

In the rest of the Pentateuch the story continues with the account of the origin of the national institutions. The tradition of the plagues and deliverance from Egypt culminates in the story of the Passover *and its ritual legislation*, and affords a manifestly historical nucleus to the tradition of the battle at the Red Sea. At Sinai the same brief *ritual* law incorporated by E is given to Moses, who writes it on "tables of stones." Here also the primeval institutions of worship are supplemented by a *Levitical priesthood* and a portable sanctuary. Certain legends of the desert and the long "nomadic" period in the steppes of Kadesh, reveal a historical basis, as does the story of the conquest of the land of the Amorites (Gilead), which is subsequently allotted to Gad and Reuben. The period of the wilderness wandering concludes with the unsought Blessing of Balaam, the "diviner," foretelling the glory of the Davidic monarchy. A second magnificent national poem centering the national life in *the sanctuary at Jerusalem*, where Yahweh abides "on the mountain shoulders of Benjamin," and in a *faithful Levitical priesthood* preserving the rule of civil and religious order, is "the Blessing wherewith Moses the man of God blessed the children of Israel before his death."

The story of the conquest under Joshua is a comparatively

sober relation of the crossing of Jordan and taking of Jericho and Ai, whereupon follows the league with the Gibeonites and resultant battle and victory at Gibeon, Joshua and all Israel returning to Gilgal. The poetic excerpt from the "Book of Jashar" is well known. Central Palestine is now open, but "Joshua was old and well-stricken in years." The as yet unconquered territory is therefore allotted to the tribes, and from "the city of Palm-trees" (Jericho) the historian traces the gradual acquisition by the tribes first of a foothold, then a firm settlement, in their several territories.

In Judges J relates the varying fortunes of the tribes in their struggle against the unsubdued Canaanites. A great victory by a coalition of the northern tribes under Deborah and Barak against the Canaanite confederacy of Jabin secures control of northern Palestine and is celebrated in one more priceless national ode. The traditions of Dan and Benjamin lead over to the *story of Saul* and the war of deliverance from the Philistine yoke.

In the *story of the rise of the monarchy* we have our first introduction in J to *a prophet.* The heroic Benjaminite Saul in search of his father's asses turns aside to enquire of a soothsayer of local repute where he should look. A sixpence is the price of the augury, and a parenthetic note (probably a gloss) explains that he that is called in the narrative "a seer, is now called *a prophet.*" But a divine message is given to Saul by "Samuel the seer," and thus forewarned he rallies discouraged Israel to the relief of beleaguered Jabesh, leads against Ammon, and is crowned by the victors on the field. Now Saul and Jonathan move Israel to throw off the Philistine yoke and ultimately drive the oppressor from the country. Pathetically beautiful is the story of Saul and his still nobler son; but with the appearance of the Judean minstrel-warrior David, and the immortal friendship of Jonathan, a new interest takes its place. Saul's insane jealousy drives David into exile and culminates in the monstrous crime of attempted annihilation of *the priests of Yahweh.* With the escape to David of Ahimelech the sole survivor, carrying the supreme emblem of the divine presence, the sacred ephod, the national cause passes over to David, as doubtless did in large part the interest of the nation. Finally the fearful catastrophe of the battle of Gilboa and annihilation of Saul's dynasty is celebrated by our author in an authentic elegy written by the warrior poet David himself, and here excerpted from the "Book of Jashar."

II Samuel describes first the assumption of the crown by David at Hebron and crushing of the house of Saul, then the retrieving of the terrible defeat of Gilboa against the Philistines, the conquest of Jerusalem *and bringing up of the ark of Yahweh to a permanent abode in David's capital ;* then, after the firm establishment of national independence and sovereignty, the *acquisition of the floor of Araunah the Jebusite*, indicated by a theophany as the true site for the national sanctuary.* An unsparing review of the weakness of David's domestic administration and the calamities brought thereby upon Israel occupies the latter part of the book, but exhibits at once the righteous government of Yahweh, and the true greatness of David's character, for he comes out of the furnace of affliction humbled, submissive, grateful.

After the accession of Solomon and a description of his munificence, the narrative passes to the epoch-making event of *the building and dedication of the temple* drawing once more from its source the Book of Jashar an extract from the Dedicatory Prayer of Solomon. The subsequent calamitous history is related very briefly, but we find in I Kgs. xvi. 34 the sequel to J's story of the destruction of Jericho in Jos. vi. 26f. and in chh. xx.–xxii. a record of the reign of Ahab, including a version of his relation to Elijah the Tishbite, which contrasts with that of chh. xvii.–xix. almost as the Samuel of J does with the Samuel of E ; its sequel appears in II Kgs. (iii ?) viii. 16ff., where the fulfilment of Gen. xxvii. 40 (J ?) is related, and in a "photographic narrative" strongly recalling the style of the Books of Samuel (cf. Elisha in ch. ix. with Samuel in I Sam. ixf., and the gate scene, ix. 17–20, with II Sam. xiii. 34–36 ; xviii. 24–32), on account of the great revolution

---

* II Sam. xxiv. is displaced.

of Jehu in Ephraim, with its after-clap in the overthrow of Athaliah in Judah. The story apparently closes with the *repairing of the temple* under Jehoash during the years that " Jehoiada the priest instructed him."

The belief that the narrative of J extended down so late as II Kgs. xii. is as yet but a personal conviction, based on perhaps inadequate grounds ; but it is traceable with practical certainty to the dedication of the temple, and is traced by Cornill and others with great probability as far as I Kgs. xvi. 34. If now we look for such a great national movement as might naturally give birth to a masterpiece of the kind, there is no epoch comparable in appropriateness with that which ensued upon the great Yahwistic revolution, the seed whereof was sown by the great Ephraimite prophets of the school of Elijah, though in Judah it was carried through under the leadership of the head of the Jerusalem priesthood. On the other hand it is certain that the story of J¹ did not continue much beyond the year 800, for the work was, perhaps, already known to Amos (cf. ii. 10), and almost certainly to Hosea.

In fixing the contents of the two great preëxilic documents we have thus determined within tolerably close limits their probabl · dates, and found them to coincide with those determined on independent grounds before the completion of this analysis. The post-exilic origin of P was made sufficiently clear in the preceding volume. The questions we have now to ask, as to the character, purpose and authorship of the three, must needs have received already some degree of illumination from this review of their subject matter.

The comprehensive view thus afforded of each of the great historical documents of the Old Testament, when documentary analysis has completed its work, should serve a higher purpose than the mere enumeration of minor idiosyncrasies of the writers, favorite phrases, modes of expression, peculiarities of style and diction. In the standard critical works of Dillmann (Appendix to *Nu. Dt. Jos.* p. 592-690) or Wellhausen (*Comp. passim.*) the reader will find these criteria described at length. But the lists most convenient of access to the English reader

are those of Kuenen (*Hex.* p. 65–158) and of Driver ("Introd.
to O. T. Lit.", N. Y., 1891, p. 109–150).* In the present volume
it is expected that the references and the diacritical marks of
Part II. will enable the reader to judge for himself as to J's
partiality for the phrases 'find favor in the eyes of,' 'land flowing with milk and honey,' 'break forth,' 'ground,' 'Lord,'
(*adonai*) etc., his specification of the time of day, and similar
idiosyncrasies; E's form of address, use of 'Jethro' for
'Hobab,' 'Horeb' for 'Sinai,' 'Amorite' for 'Canaanite,'
'*amah*' ("maid"), for '*shiphchah*' ("maid"), 'mount of God,'
'rod of God,' 'angel of God,' 'rose up early in the morning,'
and the like ; and that above all he cannot fail to secure some
impression from the innumerable peculiarities and conventional
forms of P, however hasty his perusal. But these are not
results of criticism ; these are the mere tools of documentary
analysis. If a new definition of the higher criticism may be
permitted so late, we should call it *the study of the origin and
development of ideas.* The *ideas* of J, E and P are more important than their phrases, and to understand them and their
implications we must trace their history.

Even in J, whose work is far less dominated by theory even
than E,† and of course than P, we have not the work of a
mere annalist ; had it been so, the work would never have
become the substratum of a *Bible.* History is here made the
vehicle of an idea ; a very broad and simple one, but admirably

---

* The discussion of the documents does not look beyond the Hexateuch, and
is largely taken from Dillmann's Appendix referred to above.

† It is surprising that so careful and judicious a scholar as Driver should
write ("Introd." p. 111) : "It [the prophetical standpoint of E] is not brought so
prominently forward as in J, and in general the narrative is more "objective,"
less consciously tinged by ethical and theological reflection than that of J."
This complete reversal of the true relation would be unaccountable, were it
not that Driver's caution leads him to confine his view almost exclusively to
the inconclusive phenomena of Genesis, and to depend too much on Dillmann.
It should be remembered that pp. 629ff. of Dillmann's *Nu. Dt. Jos.* were written as a determined effort to support the now almost abandoned theory of the
priority of E and P and late date of J. Schrader is far more felicitous in calling E "the Theocratic Narrator."

carried out. That idea is : *Yahweh's righteous government of the world is manifested in the story of his chosen people.*

In E, and still more in P, the narrative of Israel is decidedly subordinated to a purpose of tracing the history of special institutions, but in J the nation itself, with all its institutions, and as a whole, is the object of supreme interest ; it may properly be called a HISTORY OF THE COVENANT PEOPLE OF YAH-WEH. For precisely the same reason that E takes delight in relating the birth and parentage, youth and development of his great prophetic characters ; whereas, once their rôle in the national history is about to begin, he subordinates the nation's career to the individual's, or even passes it over entirely, J follows a course exactly the opposite. Instead of beginning with the call of "the prophet Abraham," he begins with the remotest antecedents of the *Hebrew stock*, employs the cosmogonic myths to locate its true position in the world's history, and primitive ethnology in the form of discursive genealogies to determine its affinity with all surrounding peoples. Because J is supremely interested in the career of the *nation*, his great characters are introduced when their rôle affects the national destinies, and to this extent only. He brings in Moses, Joshua, Samuel, David, in every case in full maturity, without troubling himself about their birth and childhood or pious education ; their careers are only episodes in the great national drama. For the same reason archaeological data of even a purely secular character, if they have a bearing upon the history of Israel, are welcome to J. The origin of the arts and industries concerns him ; he is ready to take up aetiological folk-tales accounting for all sorts of practises, customs, localities and beliefs ; he does not refuse room even to the repulsive legend of Moab and Ammon, the superstitious association of the mandragora with the birth of Rachel's children, or the coarse clan-legends of the stocks of Judah. On the other hand he is not unnaturally led by the literary beauty of such idylls as the marriage of Isaac and Rebecca and the popular humor of Jacob's shepherd tricks to give them otherwise disproportionate space.

When we pass from the dim region of cosmogonic, ethnologic, and aetiologic myth to the dawn of quasi-historical tradition, it is clear that J seeks to tell the story as it was, not indeed purely for its own sake, but often satisfied to let it point its own moral. For him history has a value as such, and we doubtless owe it quite as much to this as to his greater antiquity and superior sources, that as a source for actual history his narrative must be almost the sole dependence of the judicious critic. More and more apparent does this fact become as we advance, till in the story of the rise of the monarchy through the personal exploits of Saul it is clear that we are treading on the firm ground of history; whereas in E the true course of events is obscured, or distorted out of all credibility, in the endeavor to magnify the importance of "the prophet Samuel" and to make clear the unpardonable folly and sin of the people in desiring a king, instead of continuing to prosper under a theocracy administered by "prophets and judges." The contrast is perhaps even more marked in the story of David. J's splendid *history of the nation* under Saul and David can be judged by the Book of II Samuel, almost entirely his. E contents himself with the story of the pious shepherd-boy and the giant, the romance of David's youth and a brief statement of his mounting the throne and ruling under the 'fear of God' and the tutelage of the 'prophet' Nathan. The same contrast will appear to every reader even in the Pentateuch, though here there is of course less to choose.

The broad and comprehensive patriotism of J is apparent in his treatment of all the tribes in Genesis, and particularly in Joshua and Judges. "The house of Joseph" is as dear to him as "the house of Judah." It comes most clearly to view in the grand national odes he attaches at salient points of the story, the Blessing of Jacob, Blessing of Balaam, Blessing of Moses and Song of Deborah. For him the ideal of national unity was realized when:

> "Yahweh was king in Jeshurun
> When the heads of the people were gathered
> All the tribes of Israel together."

But just as the devotion to history as such does not exclude a distinctly religious purpose, apparent in the narrative, so this fidelity to an impartial account of all the institutions of Israel does not exclude a decided tinge of personal predilection for the institutions of the *priesthood ;* and in the material at command, if not in his personal feeling, there appears an equally decided bent toward Judah. None but a *religious* historian would have given that faint glimpse toward a victory of humanity over the power of physical and moral evil in the world implied in the protevangelium ; nor would another have viewed in quite the same light the call of Abram, Gen. xii. 1ff., nor allowed the moral government of Yahweh to shine through so distinctly as in the unsparing record of David's crime and weakness, calamities and repentance. In the sense of being an ultimate outgrowth of the great Yahwistic reformation of Elijah, J's narrative may justly be called " prophetic," and it certainly follows the same motto : Israel the people of Yahweh. Otherwise it would seem anything but a " prophetic " document. Only *priestly* institutions are traced as far back as the age of Moses, and both Joseph and Moses are allied with great priestly families ; the function of interpreting the Mosaic law is given to " Aaron the Levite " (Ex. iv. 14 ; cf. Dt. xxxiii. 8–10) and both the Egyptian and Sinaitic legislation are solely concerned with ritual ordinances. Only Moses, Aaron, and the priests are admitted to the audience of Yahweh on Sinai, and, in striking contrast to E, the *fidelity of the Levites* in the mutiny is rewarded by a perpetual tribal prerogative of the priesthood. Prophetism does not appear at all among the early institutions of Israel. Samuel is only a local " soothsayer." Joseph and Balaam are " diviners." Not until Elijah the Tishbite confronts Ahab in the vineyard of Naboth does prophetism count for anything. On the contrary the profoundest interest is taken in the fate of the ark and its priesthood. The slaughter of Nob, and escape of Ahimelech with the ephod marks the transition point between Saul and David as bearer of the national destinies, and one of the most prominent elements of David's reign is always the ark, its abiding place and its guardians. Its solemn transfer to Jerusalem from Baalei-Judah, and the provision made for it by David by purchase of the threshing-floor of Araunah, lead up to the story of the *building and dedication of the temple* as the great event of Solomon's reign.

In agreement with this is the priestly conception of man's relation to God. Yahweh's anger is appeased by sacrifice (Gen. viii. 21), or by the mediation of the recipients of his personal favor ; and through these Yahweh makes known to the *ignobile vulgus* the ordinances and ritual by which it pleases him to be served. The sacred 'pillars' (*maççeboth*) so dear to E, however, were either obnoxious to J, or the mention of them has been obliterated by later hands (see, however, II Sam. xx. 8).

We should, in fact, expect nothing else than a priestly interest in a document whose material so clearly points to an origin in the southern kingdom. For with all the catholicity of J's patriotism the stories of Genesis tend to group about Hebron and Beersheba, much as those of E about Shechem and Bethel ; Judah and not Reuben is spokesman for the brethren in the Joseph-legend, and Judah's clans and Judah's birthright are kept in view in chh. xxxviii. and xlix. Later, Jerusalem becomes the real focus of attention. Now it would be scarcely possible, at the time and amid the circumstances from which this document thus seems to spring, that it should present any other view than the above of the relative importance of prophetism and the priesthood. Prophetism had never been the force in Judah which it had been in Ephraim. The far more influential *priests of the Jerusalem temple* here took the lead in Yahwistic reform. There is entire sympathy with the aims of the prophets, but as yet they count for but little in conservative Judah.

Politically, the contrast is the strongest possible between J and E. J looks upon the monarchy as the very salvation of Israel ; he is a thorough-going aristocrat and high-churchman. E, as we shall see, is intensely devoted to the opposite principles. But we are anticipating our discussion of this second document.

A first comprehensive glance at E's work would suggest as its proper title : The Story of the Prophets. If it pursues the course of the national history from the call of Abraham to the writer's day, it is not from a desire to give the story of divine providence for its own sake, but to vindicate the *theory of the theocracy*, by exhibiting the character of the leaders divinely raised up. To the careers of these men the history as such is entirely subordinate. In a single word the document E is a HISTORY OF THE THEOCRATIC SUCCESSION.

Doubtless the form assumed by this Ephraimite work was largely affected by the knowledge—perhaps only indirect, for there is no decisive evidence of actual use of J by E—of its great predecessor in Judah. It was inevitable that in the earlier portions it should bear a close resemblance to it. But it is well worthy of note that so far from showing the affinity of Israel with all surrounding peoples by tracing the stock back to "the Man," E sets out with the call of God to the 'prophet' Abraham to *come out from among the idolaters* of his fatherland, and upon his obedience gives the promise of the 'land of the Amorites' when their 'iniquity shall be full.' Except as to the 'proving' of Abraham, which incidentally reveals the boyhood of Isaac, the stories of Genesis do not differ largely from J's. However, E's more spiritual, less anthropomorphic views of God and decidedly more moral views of the patriarchs are brought out incidentally. Thus Isaac's falsehood to Abimelech in E's story becomes a mere *double-entendre* of Abraham, since Sarah "is indeed his sister." So instead of Reuben's mandrakes, as the efficient cause of fruitfulness in Rachel and Leah, we have in E prayer to God : and instead of Jacob's shepherd tricks, direct divine intervention in answer to the vow of Bethel. Special interest in Shechem and the northern sanctuaries has always been noted, and in view of this Ephraimite interest the tribe-legend of *Joseph* in E would naturally be based on sources even superior to J's. But here the method of E is again apparent. Joseph the shepherd-boy endowed with prophetic gifts, rising to the highest sovereignty, devoutly and piously interpreting the divine will, and on his death-bed pointing the future course of the people, is but the prototype of the shepherd-boy Moses, the shepherd-boy David, and, with slight variation, the youthful Joshua and the child Samuel, each rising to an ideal leadership in the theocracy.

With the possible exception of Joshua and David, these leaders of the theocracy are all 'prophets,' and the author gives free expression to his ideal in the story of the 70 elders upon whom Yahweh pours Moses' spirit of prophecy; Joshua's jealousy, says the noble-minded Moses, is uncalled for: "Would God that all Yahweh's people were prophets, that Yahweh would put his spirit upon them!"

With Samuel, second in greatness as a prophet only to Moses, the monarchical ideal comes into conflict with the theocratic. To fully appreciate the author's political idea this story of the people's foolish demand and Samuel's speech of abdication recapitulating the story of the past, should be read in 1 Sam. viii.; x. 17–24; xii.; xv. To E the monarchy is a concession to the weakness of humanity in the political world, just as ritual worship is an accommodation to human frailty in the moral sphere. When the covenant of the pure moral law bringing the people into direct relation with God was broken, the ritual Ten Words and priestly form of worship were instituted *as a measure of concession.* In like manner, though offended at the people's rejection of himself as their king, God consents to the monarchy and offers even a conditional blessing. Saul's first "proving" results in immediate rejection, but the seal of divine approval had been unmistakably stamped by the event upon the reign of David. David accordingly represents to E this modified ideal of the theocracy. Just enough is related of his career to bring out this ideal of monarchy.

This conception of a theocracy administered by 'prophets' springs from a mind imbued with religious and political convictions sharply contrasting with J's. E shares with the Ephraimite prophet Hosea a profound distrust both of kings and priests. The apostasy at Horeb was due to the *unfaithfulness of Aaron* when the people were left in his charge. In like manner the deep depression from which the people were rescued by Samuel was due to the *unfaithfulness of the priests* of Shiloh. He is the most radical of Puritans, a democrat profoundly sympathizing with the people, though impatient with their folly and weakness, an advocate of spirituality in religion and liberty in the state, jealous of foreign influence to the degree of narrowness and arrogance in his ideal of the kingdom of God, in all things a prophet of the prophets and a Hebrew of the Hebrews.

This Puritan morality and democratic jealousy of caste appear throughout. The covenant at Horeb is a voluntary compact. God pronounces the moral law "and all the people answered with one voice and said, All that Yahweh hath spoken we will do." Prosperity or adversity follow then in regular succession according as the people serve Yahweh only and keep his covenant, or forget his covenant and "worship strange gods." *Repentance* is invariably followed by rescue, but the writer takes extraordinary pains to guard against an abuse of the priestly idea of divine *favor*, 'smoothing the face of Yahweh' or appeasing his just indignation by anything short of deep 'mourning' and practical change. Any doctrine of forgiveness savoring of laxity in this respect is repeatedly and emphatically denied, the very language of J seeming sometimes to be criticised. In Num. xxiii. 19 we have :

> " God is not a man that he should lie
> Neither the son of man that he should repent."

In Ex. xxiii. 20 the 'angel of God' " will not forgive your transgression nor your sin, for my Name is in him." Jos. xxiv. 19 declares Yahweh himself implacable, and even Saul's prayer for forgiveness, 1 Sam. xv. 24f., is met by Samuel with

> " The Strength of Israel will not lie nor repent
> For he is not a man that he should repent."

Space forbids the further multiplication of instances: the hatred of idolatry (including teraphim and divination (?), tolerated by J ; but not including 'pillars') ; the living faith in a present God of righteousness ; but every student of the great Ephraimite prophets of the eighth century will recognize at once their characteristic features.

The prophetic type of religious thought of E, with all its spirituality and moral purity might easily tend without its priestly counterpoise to Pharisaism and legalistic morality. But as compared with J it marks an advance in the sphere of religious thought, and sheds new light upon that deep current of pure and spiritual ethical religion, the product of the prophetism of Ephraim, which was soon to flow side by side with the more priestly religious thought of Judah. The first outcome of their amalgamation was the Deuteronomic reformation; later the same prophetic "spirit and power" blaze out in the "greater Elijah"; ultimately the priestly and the prophetic type are blended in the doctrine of Jesus. In view of this advance in religious character we need scarcely regret the literary inferiority of E to J, nor the very limited use which can be made of its material in supplementation of the historical data of J. The author's *tendenz* so dominates the story that while material nearly as trustworthy and valuable as J's seems sometimes to have been at his command, his story can scarcely be called more than an adaptation of practically the same data in much less credible form to his theory of the theocracy. The stories of the boyhood of his prophetic heroes (Isaac), Joseph, Moses, (Joshua), Samuel, David are unique and characteristic, but what these add to the history of J has more of literary and religious, than of historical value.

We can afford to pass lightly over the character, purposes and doctrine of the Priestly Law-book, for the following reasons: 1. that its character is stamped upon its face, so that only wilful blindness can ignore it; 2. that it has been repeatedly characterized in practically the same terms by all competent critics from Nöldeke down; 3. that in "The Genesis of Genesis" we have already described it substantially as it now appears. Nevertheless the new type marks so wide a departure from either of its predecessors that we cannot refrain from a few words of description.

In P the practise of E of subordinating the history to a theory of the divine government is carried to a much greater extreme; here, however, the *hierocracy* takes the place of the *theocracy.* The high priest succeeds the theocratic 'judge,' or 'prophet,' and in the requirement of God, the general principles of morality are scarcely more than a matter of course, compared with the *written ordinances* of the priesthood and the *ceremonial law.* The work of P is a HISTORY OF THE RELIGIOUS INSTITUTIONS OF ISRAEL, THE PRIEST-NATION.

We are not here concerned with the ceremonial law, which together with the " inheritances in the land " is the matter of principal import to P, and hence need only compare the artificial skeleton of history he employs as a frame for his code, with its parallels in J and E. It is clear at the first glance that the process of reduction to theory, a theory moreover of divine rule by systematic miraculous intervention, has here reached its climax.

In the priestly narrative all natural relations and perspective of time and space are utterly lost from view. We are in the sphere of the purely marvellous. That this writer no longer has before his eyes a single remnant of historical realism and moves purely in an artificial, mechanical world of marvel, appears wherever the attempt is made to realize what his assertions imply. We need not repeat the familiar objections of Colenso, which almost invariably take effect against the representation of P only : the 200,000 *male* lambs of the first year required at every passover, as compared with the dearth of food and water, and the complaint of no flesh to eat ; the incredible wealth of material provided for the tabernacle ; the whole series of impossibilities involved in the enumerated millions of Israel ; above all the inconceivable war with Midian (Num. xxxi.). How little of a realistic conception the writer had before his mind appears when we ask ourselves such questions as the following : In P's account of the turning of water to blood, Ex. vii. 19 22, whence did the magicians obtain water, to " do in like manner with their enchantments " ? How could an altar of acacia wood, overlaid with brass, of the pattern of Ex. xxvii. 1 8 support the heat (supposing the fuel obtainable) of the whole burnt offerings enjoined ? The same astounding superiority to all the unities of historical narrative appear in P's story of the manna and quails in ch. xvi. compared with its relatively historical parallel in Num. xi., and in the ignoring of any opposition of the Canaanites to the appropriation of their land. This contrast between P and JE, especially J, it is important to draw for the sake of rescuing the historicity of the latter. It is fortunately not needful after what Kuenen has well designated "the pulverizing criticism" of Colenso, to perpetually reiterate the invidious task of exhibiting the unhistorical character of P; but it is needful to show by separation of the sources that we are not dependent upon this mere mechanical, late and artificial extract from JE, intended simply as a framework to the priestly law, for our knowledge of ancient Hebrew story.

It would be far from just to the post-exilic period to say that the religious ideals of P are those of that age. On the contrary there is much to show, that alongside of this rigid formalism of priestly legality and hierocracy something of the old Deuteronomic, and even the prophetic, type of thought continued to survive, at least among the hills of ancient Ephraim. But in the circles from which the Priestly Law-book comes to us the spirituality of ethical religion, and the idea of direct relations of man to God, seem to have died out. Still the appearance is in part deceptive. Israel has indeed become a priest-nation, and "the people of the book," but even if the spiritual, ethical monotheism of the prophets had died out among the people, the germ of its resurrection was safely enshrined in the literature so cherished. If we take the work of P, as we should, as throwing light upon the conditions of religious thought in Judea of the fifth century it should be borne in mind that this light is thrown only upon the outside, and that underneath this frozen surface is still moving the deep, still current of the religious consciousness of ancient Judah and Ephraim.

In passing now from our characterization of J, E and P to an enquiry into their history, we must of course begin with the sources, written and oral, employed in their make-up. But we need not delay with P, since the *narrative* parts of this document show no traces of any other source whatever than JE, though a possible trace of Babylonian influence may be indicated by its divergences from J's account of Creation and Flood. J is the real source for the critical historian, supplemented occasionally (as in Num. xxi., I Sam. iv.–vi., xv.) by E; but each of these appears to be based upon a primitive anthology, or collection of national ballad-lore, of its own; adding to this material folk-tales of various kinds, and at least two very ancient written codes.

Already in "The Genesis of Genesis" (p. 10–22, 61) it was pointed out that "the fountains of minstrelsy and ballad-lore yet flow copiously through the pages of J and E," though not of P; and some phenomena accompanying the transition of historical tradition from minstrelsy to prose were described. Have we now the means of forming a rational conjecture as to the character and content of these most primitive sources?

The only book cited by name in J is the Book of Jashar, from which we have extracts, in all cases songs of national interest, in Jos. x. 12f. (Battle of Gibeon), II Sam. i. 17–27 (David's elegy on Saul and Jonathan), and I Kgs. viii. 12 [53] LXX. (Solomon's Song of Dedication). Unfortunately the exact significance of the title *Jashar* ("the Upright"?) is unknown, but it is probable that it contains, as is so often the case, a play upon the name *Israel*, like the term *Jeshurun*. So far as it goes, therefore, this would confirm the indication of the extracts, that the book was a collection of *national* lyrics. This may seem a slender basis for conjecture, but it indicates that the collection was at least as late as the reign of Solomon— very likely of that reign; that it covered in extent at least the entire period from the conquest to the building of the temple, and contained one, and probably two, if not more, authentic poems of David (add the Elegy of Abner, II Sam. iii. 33f.), looking with favor on Solomon's temple. When we consider the broadly national character of J's great poems, Blessings of Noah, Isaac, Jacob, Balaam, Moses; Songs of Lamech, Moses, Joshua, Deborah and Barak, David, Solomon; and the fragments of similar lyrics which form the nucleus of a large proportion of his narratives, and compare with these the general spirit of the document, it does not seem an improbable supposition in view of the known structure of other Semitic histories, that these ancient national lyrics were all derived from the same anthology, in short that the *Book of Jashar-Israel* underlies the history of J throughout its whole extent, and that it suggested to its author the form of his history of Israel, J impressing upon it its *religious* character.

The only other written source quoted by J is a brief code, summing up in " Ten Words " the religious duties of the lay Israelite. J calls it " The Words of the Covenant," and declares them to have been written by Moses on " tables of stones " on Sinai. Curiously we have fragments of the same code in a somewhat later, but substantially identical form, in E ; here it is called " The Book of the Covenant " and is said to have been written by Moses at Horeb, though the material employed is not stated.* Neither writer professes to have personal knowledge of this autograph of Moses (or of God) and though their words would seem to indicate the existence of written copies of this primitive code, the very diversity of their versions proves that they did not have recourse to the same original.

E seems to have had at command a collection of national lyrics to some extent parallel to J's. In this case we learn more from the title, but much less from the single extract cited from the anthology by name. The *Book of the Wars of Yahweh* shows by its title that it possessed the same patriotic character we have attributed to the Book of Jashar, and was very likely the collection which in Ephraim had come to take the place of the former, as better agreeing with northern ideas. Its title also shows that the practice of E in the *elohistic* parts of Exodus and the later books in regard to the divine name,

---

* In my judgment these ritual Ten Words must have occupied in E¹—see below—the position now given by E² to the later ethical " Ten Words " of Ex. xx.; in other words Ex. xxiv. 12–14 applied originally to them, so that E¹ agreed with J as to the vexed question, What was written on the two tables of stone.

was not that of all his sources, if of any, and confirms our
view that it is more of a redactional than of a spontaneous
character. As to the contents of this work we have certain
knowledge regarding only the single extract Num. xxi. 14f.,
as to the border of Moab ; but the proximity of the ensuing
extract in vv. 27–30 has led nearly all critics to infer that the
song of the "taunting poets" over the ruin of Moab was
drawn from the same source, if not the same poem. This
further description in vs. 27 of the class of poems to which the
ensuing extract belongs is a further indication of at least one
group in the collection. It contained the songs of exultation
over fallen enemies, which the spirit of the times regarded as
worthy fruits of poetic genius. A magnificent example is the
ode of exultation over the fallen king of Babylon in Is. xiv.,
where the term "taunting poem" (*mashal*) is translated by the
Revisers "parable" (vs. 4). Another eminent example of this
class which could not be omitted from any collection, least of
all from a book of the Wars of Yahweh, is the Song of "Miriam the prophetess," Ex. xv. 20f. ; and here we doubtless have
not merely one of the poems contained in each anthology, but
probably the *first* selection of E's collection (cf. vs. 3 ?) ; at
least this was necessarily the first of the "wars of Yahweh."

It requires but a very reasonable supposition to include in this
collection the story of "Yahweh's war with Amalek" in the
poetic citation Ex. xvii. 16 ; for this also the present historian
found "written in a book," which it would be natural to
identify with the "Book of the Wars of Yahweh." Its sequel,
then, in I Sam. xv., where the same poetic structure is plainly
visible in vv. 22f., must also have formed part of the collection ;
nor will the reference to Agag in J's version of the Blessing of
Balaam Num. xxiv. 7 appear any longer strange, when we
reflect that E's parallel to this poem, which from its wide
divergence cannot possibly have been taken from J's anthology,
would naturally come from that same Book of the Wars of Yahweh from which he drew the extracts of the preceding chapter.
It may seem to us a little hard to bring Balaam's oracle under
the title "the Wars of Yahweh" ; but to E the episode belongs

in this category, for in Jos. xxiv. 9 he writes : "Then Balak the son of Zippor, king of Moab *arose and fought against* Israel ; and he sent and called Balaam," etc.

It is thus not impossible to obtain a reasonably trustworthy idea of the character and contents of each of the primitive anthologies. E's more limited, and perhaps later collection probably did not go much back of the Exodus, but must have been similar in character and content to the Book of Jashar, sometimes in verbal agreement (cf. Ex. xv. 1 with vs. 21). As with J, the anthology doubtless suggested much of the form and character of the prose history based upon it.

The most important prose source of the preëxilic writers is E's *Book of Judgments*, whose character has been widely discussed in special treatises by Rothstein, Baentzsch and others.* If, as we conjecture, it was incorporated by E in Moses' farewell discourse, and was the law of which he declares that Moses commanded the elders of Israel, after its formal promulgation and enactment *by the people* on mount Ebal, to inscribe it on stone stelae there, it corresponds to the traditional Roman Laws of the Twelve Tables, a charter of popular rights publicly recorded. Its inestimable value to the historian of ancient Israel is self-evident, though its character shows it to have grown up after Israel had become settled in a fixed agricultural civilization. The religious standpoint (xxii. 20) seems to presuppose the work of Elijah and Jehu. It does not require a great effort to imagine Jehu himself erecting the stelae in question.

The oral sources of J and E are folk-tales of various kinds, which might be classified as aetiologies, clan-stories (historical and ethnological) and historical tradition. We can indeed trace

* I regret exceedingly that the essay of Prof. Lewis B. Paton, of Hartford, Ct., in the "Journal of Bibl. Lit.," on The Original Form of the Book of the Covenant has reached me only in time for mention in this note. His conclusions are most interesting and his investigation worthy of study. But a separation of the Book of Judgments from the Book of the Covenant still seems to me necessary, if only to account for the extraordinary position of the civil "judgments" Ex. xxi.f. between the two halves of a religious code, Ex. xx. 23–26; and xxii. 27—xxiii. 19.

the presence, though we cannot extricate the material, of a written source in J's admirable history of the reigns of Saul and David. But even this, on close inspection, reveals the marks of the popular story-teller sitting in the city-gate. If written in the form transmitted to J, its earliest form was oral. The earlier narratives are of course to a large degree legendary, sometimes a fragment of ancient song, sometimes the suggestive name of a locality Massah, Meribah, Kibroth-hattaavah, Kadesh, Hormah, Lehi, giving rise, by fanciful etymologies, to fantastic developments in the story. Again the local traditions of a particular revered object, " pillar," sacred tree, altar, or well, the Nehushtan of Jerusalem (II Kings xviii. 4) the local sanctuaries of Palestine, have contributed their full share. The tribal and clan-stories include such material as the genealogies of J, the Joseph-legend of E, the story of the stocks of Judah in Gen. xxxviii. and the Calebite tradition in Num. xiiif., Jos. xiv. 6–15 ; xv. 13–19 ; Jud. i. 10–15. But certainly one of the most important classes of primitive, quasi-historical tradition is that connected with the sacred feasts. Here the recital of the traditional history was made a part of the ritual (Ex. xii. 26 ; xiii. 14 ; Dt. xxvi. 5ff.), and although the feasts are doubtless older than the historical events they are employed to commemorate, J even preserving a trace of this real relation in his story of the Exodus, where Israel demands release *in order to celebrate* the feast, still there can be no doubt that for ages the story of the Plagues of Egypt and the Deliverance from the House of Bondage has been told, and had been even in J's time, at the annual celebration of the Passover. Whether the story of the Law-giving at Sinai was likewise told at the Feast of Weeks it is not so easy to say. The Feast of Ingathering naturally retained its original agricultural character.

With such materials we may imagine a priest of Solomon's temple of about the period of Jehoiada, and doubtless of similar character and standing, compiling the Judean History of the Covenant people of Yahweh, under the impulse of the great Yahwistic revolution. In like manner in Ephraim the same plan was followed somewhat later, with very similar materials, by an intense devotee of that great school of prophets which had inaugurated the movement. A man of the type of Hosea gives to us the very embodiment of the prophetic ideals of that period in this Ephraimite History of the Theocratic Succession. Two such monuments of the great religious movement preceding the age of written prophecy could not fail to become the nucleus of an increasing aggregate of " Mosaic " thought. In fact critics are almost unanimous in tracing in both J and E the marks of repeated editings of the original works.

The presence of a J² in Genesis who has materially raised the moral tone of J¹ by his additions, was noted in the preceding volume. The most important addition is the grafting in from Assyro-Babylonian sources upon the ancient Hebrew stock of the great Flood-legend, with some accompanying geographic and ethnographic data of a learned character. In the intercession of Abram, Gen. xviii. 17-19, 23-33, its character appears as much more reverential toward Yahweh, and if Kuenen is right in attributing to it the story of Potiphar's wife, Gen. xxxix., its author would seem to have drawn, not only upon Assyrian, but also upon Egyptian literature for morally edifying material. The genealogy of the Horites, xxxvi. 10-39, is perhaps part of the same enrichment ; xxvi. 1, which refers to xii. 10-20 J², yet pays no attention to the much nearer and more striking parallel ch. xx., indicates that it preceded the union of J and E. The phenomena lead Budde to regard this as a quasi-official revision emanating from the highest quarter, perhaps about the time of Ahaz, a date for which there is some internal confirmation.

That this revision extended to the later books is not only an *a priori* probability, but seems to be indicated by the text itself. A revising hand has certainly retouched the Plague narratives quite independently of harmonistic or Deuteronomic requirement. Further, in the intercessory interviews of Moses and Joshua in J, Ex. iv. 10-13 ; xxxii. 7-14 ; xxxiii. 12—xxxiv. 9 ; Num. xiv. 11-24 ; Jos. vii. 7-9 ; we have not only a very remarkable coincidence of representation with Gen. xviii. 20-33, but a marked resemblance to J² in language (cf. *e. g.* Ex. xxxii. 12, 14 with Gen. vi. 6f. ; Ex. xxxiii. 13, with Gen. xviii. 19, and Ex. xxxiv. 9 with Gen. xviii. 30, 32.). Dt. xxxiii. 13*ab*-16 also impresses me as interpolated by J², and the legislative sections bear still clearer evidence of supplementation. Nevertheless, I have thought it wiser to refrain as yet from the attempt to systematically distinguish between J¹ and J², and even in E, where the discrimination is easier, the present volume makes but little use of the theoretic typographical distinction.

In the later books it is E which gives the clearest indications of having undergone revision and supplementation, as in Genesis we found it the case with J. In fact those portions of E which most strongly affect its present form and character, bear positive marks of the terrible period of depression after the fall of Samaria, whereas the great mass of the work has too much of the proud consciousness of national glory to be derived from that period of humiliation and gloom. Moreover, there is no explanation of E's use of the name *Elohim* in long, connected passages after Ex. iii, except from habit, independent of the *theoretical* grounds on which Elohim is made uniform up to Ex. iii., while Yahweh is generally used thereafter. The hand which follows the latter course cannot therefore be the same as that with which the use of Elohim is *habitual,* or rests on unknown grounds. The Book of the Wars of Yahweh did not follow this elohistic practise ; hence it cannot well be derived from any other than the *older element* of E, an element which in at least one instance lies plainly embedded in the later material, viz. 1 Sam. i-viii. where chh. iv.-vi. are required by, but do not themselves presuppose chh. i.-iii. viif. An admirable discussion of their relation may be found in Budde's *Richter und Samuel, Giessen,* 1890, p. 193-198. As to the evidence for a revision of E we cannot do better than to quote here the synopsis of one of the clearest, keenest and most judicious of analytical critics :—

"It is the merit of Kuenen to have first propounded this problem for the whole extent of E, and to have carried it into detail : he reaches the result,

Hex. § 13 n. 25 and 26, that in the 7th century an edition of E was prepared for Judaea (E²), because the substance of the work, E¹ could not permanently satisfy the requirements then existent there and gradually changing. It is not necessary to assume that this E² was prepared by a Judaean hand, since not all of Ephraim was deported in 722, and nothing compels us to assume the complete extinction of intellectual life among those left in the land: it would seem to me more natural to look for the origin of E² in these very circles. Kuenen claims first for E² the entire first Decalogue [Ex. xx.] with the kindred narrative parts belonging to it in Ex. xix.–xxiv. and the inseparable story of the golden calf Ex. xxxii. 1–xxxiii. 6. The latter offers the true point of departure. In this narrative there appears a palpable prophetic rejection of the cultus of Ephraim, ' the calves of Dan and Bethel,' given in the name of Moses himself. But this is insupposable at the hand of the same writer who takes such religious delight in relating the theophanies at these ancient sanctuaries, subsequently abhorred by the prophets, and who in particular connects the consecration of the sanctuary at Bethel with a glorious theophany, and manifestly regards Bethel as the proper central sanctuary of Jacob, at which all Israel should pay tithes of what Yahweh has given them. Above all if the words Ex. xxxii. 34b refer to the Assyrian Exile as a punishment for the calfworship of Samaria, this trait at least would necessarily form part of a revision later than 722. It is self-evident that the story of the golden calf stands in inseparable connection with the legislation of the first Decalogue, whence the latter also could not be from E¹. When now we observe that none of the older prophets who inveigh against idol-worship appeals to the Decalogue, and that the sole trace in the older literature of acquaintance with this Decalogue, in Hos. iv. 2, is robbed of significance by its diverse order and terminology for the sins, we must admit the force of Kuenen's reasoning. Other signs corroborate. The representation of the departure from Horeb to the promised land as a punishment, and the sanctuary of the ark a substitute, because Israel was not yet ripe for the pure religion of the Decalogue, cannot possibly have been the sense of the original tradition, to which the ark was the visible pledge of Yahweh's gracious aid [cf. I Sam. iv.–vi.] and their bringing in to Canaan a kindness of the mighty national Deity [cf. Ex. xiii. 17–19] . . . . Kuenen further attributes to E² Num. xi. 14, 16f. 24b–30, and ch. xii. in its present form. The story of Num. xi. 14ff. has no connection whatever with its present context, and is also difficult to reconcile with Ex. xviii., the more so, if, as would appear from Dt. i., Ex. xviii. originally stood after the breaking camp from Horeb [but cf. xviii. 5], therefore in almost the very spot of Num. xi. The 70 elders are derived from Ex. xxiv. 1f. 9–11 E¹, and the dependence on Ex. xviii. is also manifest; cf. Nu. xi. 14 with Ex. xviii. 18b, 22b. Accordingly we have in Nu. xi. 14ff. a specifically prophetic parallel to, or rather modification of Ex. xviii., E¹; and by this assumption all difficulties are removed. Nu. xii. also is not a uniform story. After Miriam and Aaron have found fault with Moses *because he had married a Cushite,* we do not expect a settlement of the question whether Moses alone is possessed of the prophetic spirit : vv. 2–8 accordingly must also be attributed to E², and in these and Nu. xi. 14ff. we have "two mutually related studies of prophetism." Kuenen further adduces Nu. xxi. 32–35, as an expansion of E¹, though perhaps not derived from E², a passage which Wellhausen, *Comp.* p.111, had recognized as a supplement : it developed from the idea that the whole country east of Jordan had been conquered by Moses, whereas in E¹ only the tribes of Reuben and Gad are concerned. I should myself attribute to E² the E form (*Z. A. W.* xi. 1–15) of the story Gen. xxxiv. It is hard to reconcile with Gen. xlviii. 21f. (certainly E¹) and on the other hand this very question of social and connubial relations between Israel-ites and heathen was of great practical significance to the north-Israelites left behind in a land flooded with foreign colonists. One is tempted, in spite of Jos. xxiv. 2, to attribute Gen. xxxv. 1–4 also to E²; since it scarcely agrees with the original character of the tradition, to conceive Jacob's wives, who even in E, ch. xxx., give names to their sons after the manner of genuine, devout moth-ers in Israel, as practical heathen : this is scholastic reflection, on the same plane with Laban's use of a foreign tongue xxxi. 47. It agrees with these results when Lagarde maintains, *Mittheilungen* III. 226–229, on the ground of the uniform employment of *Elohim*, and the Egyptian names occurring in Gen. xli., that E belongs "in the seventh century," and was a contemporary of Psammetichus I. 664–610 B.C. These portions of Genesis also would then be attributable to E². We reach therefore the result, that E¹ was written in the time of Jeroboam II. ca. 750, and about a century later was revised either by a Judean, or by one of the remaining north-Israelites, on the basis of that development of theological views effected by the great literary prophets (Corn-ill, *Einl.* p. 48ff.).

It seems to me probable that further investigation will reveal a more drastic revision on the part of E², particularly in the legislative sections ; and if we may attribute to it the *systematic* use of Elohim in Genesis and Yahweh after Ex. iii., it determined the present form of Ex. iii. 10–14. The character of this redaction, however, is clear. It *intensifies* the theocratic and prophetic *tenden*z of E¹.

The amalgamation of J with E soon after the unification of Ephraim with Judah under the Davidic kings in Jerusalem was most natural. The cause of prophet and priest was substan-tially the same, and Judah gained quite as much from the infu-sion of the prophetic spirit of Ephraim, as Ephraim from the more priestly religious feeling of Judah.

It is apparent from the use made of JE in both D and P

that the two primitive documents had already been interlaced
previous to 620 B. C. ; hence we are safe in attributing in general the passages whose sole object appears to be the adjustment of J and E to one another to this early redactor Rje.
When we come to set them side by side we gain a curious in-
sight into his method. The process of harmonization was of
the simplest and most transparent. J's work was of course
made the basis, both as fuller, and generally as more suited to
the Judean feeling of Rje; though in Gen. xxxiv., Ex. xix.-
xxxiv. E², whose work represents the thought of Rje's own
period, was naturally preferred. Examples of Rje's " harmo-
nistics " in Genesis are xxvi. 15 and 18, xxxix. 1ba, 20ag. Strikingly similar in simplicity of design are the clause " after he
had sent her away " Ex. xviii. 2, the curious verse xix. 23, and
the generally successful interlacing of the J and E versions of
the Balaam-story. But if we accept the very probable conclusions of Cornill (p. 81), by far the most radical part of Rje's
work affected the Sinai-Horeb chapters from Ex. xviii. to Num.
xii. It was the *omission* of J's version of the Covenant in Ex.
xxxiv. (save for the enrichment of E's version in xxiii. 15–19)
and the interweaving of J and E in Num. xi. with its consequences. In our Analysis 3 of § iv. we have endeavored to
follow the intricate processes of omission and combination, reincorporation and readjustment, which have involved these
chapters in such strange confusion.

The work of Rje does not affect Deuteronomy, but reappears
of course in the further course of the narratives J and E. This
indicates as the necessary date of the revision the period
between E² (650 ?) and the origin of Deuteronomy (620 B. C.).
Cornill and other critics generally, including Dillmann, maintain that the phenomena of Deuteronomy and its two envelopes,
Dh and Dp prove that these writers still possessed, *in addition*
to JE, the separate document E. We have, however, a different explanation of the E tinge in Deuteronomy, which does
not require the rather improbable assumption that the Deuter-
onomists took the pains to compare JE with one of its original
sources.

The appearance of Deuteronomy in 621 B. C. and the tremendous revolution it effected in the life of the nation through the reforms of Josiah and the prolonged influence of the Exile, marks an epoch but little, if at all, inferior in importance to the Yahwistic revolution of Elijah and his successors. By the time of the first return under Joshua and Zerubbabel in 555 the whole life of the nation had been transformed by it, the great exilic prophets having continuously labored from its standpoint. For still another entire century the Deuteronomic law continued to be the sacred canon of the Jews, and it was inevitable that this all-important legislation should ultimately attract to itself the preëxisting sacred history, precisely as the Priestly Code, once canonized, was soon amalgamated with JED. The history of the Deuteronomic Code from 621 to 444 B. C. would almost parallel in importance the history of the nation and of its great prophets during this, the critical period of its life. Here we can of course only present an outline of what appears from the present structure of Deuteronomy and from the so-called Deuteronomic redaction (Rd).

During the Exile the Deuteronomic Code seems to have circulated simultaneously in two different settings, each of which in its own way served to give it the necessary historical background, though they agreed in the representation of the whole as a farewell discourse of Moses to Israel on the plains of Shittim, communicating the oral law received on Horeb. That form of Deuteronomy which enclosed the code in a parænetic or *preaching* envelope, refers to it as an already written and published book. This introduction and appendix is designated Dp; the discussion of it is here inappropriate. Its rival makes the discourse of Moses a *recapitulation of the history*, strongly tinged by E's phraseology and ideas, though based upon JE *as combined* (cf. Dt. i. 23–26 with JE and E in Num. xiii.f.), and represents Moses as speaker throughout. Our own theory of the E tinge is that both Dp and Dh took the idea of a *farewell discourse of Moses* as the true setting for the Code, from the fact that JE's Story of the Exodus then concluded with a recapitulatory farewell discourse of Moses of the usual form of E (cf.

Jos. xxiv.) embodying the Book of Judgments; but Dh has followed the model much more closely than Dp. The latter, in fact, dwells purely in the field of present-day sermonic exhortation. When now Deuteronomy was at last attached to JE, the compiler, Rd, not only took up *both* envelopes of the code, combining them as best he could, but rescued the Book of Judgments by giving it a place in Ex. xxif., and, loath to lose any historical material in the process, attached the fragments of E's *Urdeuteronomium* where he could find a place for them (see Prolegomena to § vii.). This is not mere free-hand conjecture, for the method of Rd has been traced elsewhere, and in all cases, Exodus, Joshua, Judges, I and II Samuel it is marked by an apparent determination to rescue at almost any cost of incongruity in the resultant complex, the surviving fragments of the preëxilic literature. To Rd, or rather to one of the later hands of this long continued school, according to Budde and Cornill, we owe the *reincorporation* of much important material rejected by Rje, or earlier Deuteronomic hands. This seems to be the history of J's version of the Words of the Covenant, Ex. xxxiv.; of the E fragments in Dt. i. 1; x. 6f.; xxv. 17 –19; xxvii. 1–8, 11–13; xxxi. 14f, 23; of Jud. i. and the concluding chh. of the book; and of nearly one-fourth of the entire bulk of I and II Samuel. Although when first propounded by Budde in the case of the older elements of J in Gen. i. –xii. this theory of reincorporation was met almost with ridicule by so great a critic as Kuenen, who borrowed from Darwin the term "survival" to describe it, such a "theory of survivals" is really the reverse of improbable or unexampled A noted New Testament instance appears, in fact, in the story of the adulterous woman, John viii. 1ff. For when a redactor for any reason strikes out a passage in the copy of a work in his possession, there must remain of necessity a considerable number of copies of the same work, not in his possession, in which it still subsists. When now the new and (generally) enlarged edition begins to supersede the older and less popular, there is a very strong tendency for anything omitted, if not very palpably superfluous, or otherwise objectionable, to find its

way back ; the constant tendency of ancient writings being to
accumulate.

We can scarcely assign a limit to the Deuteronomic redaction ; for processes exhibiting its principles, standpoint and
style continued to affect the text down to a date even subsequent to the Greek translation.   It appears thus as partly con-
temporaneous with the priestly, and sometimes presupposes the
priestly elements, as in Num. xxxii. 9ff. ; * (Dt. iv. ?) Jos. xx. 4–
6 (wanting in LXX).

The most important work of Rd was the combination of the
Deuteronomic Code, inclosed in its double setting, with JE ;
and this of course necessitated thorough revision of the earlier
legislation (though Genesis could be left untouched save in
xxvi. 5); some adjustment of the preceding narrative (cf. *e. g.*
Num. xxi. 33–35 with Dt. iii. 1–3 and Num. xxxii. with Jos.
xxii.), and a drastic working over of the subsequent narrative,
as supposedly controlled by the Deuteronomic law.   The attachment of the Song of Moses Dt. xxxii. 1–43, while doubtless
preceding Rp, seems to have been subsequent to this work of
combination by Rd, for it is provided with an independent
introduction and subscript in xxxi. 16–22 ; xxxii. 44.   Its consideration belongs therefore with the history of Deuteronomy.

Ezra's "book of the law of his God" which he came authorized by the Persian government to introduce in the feeble col-
ony at Jerusalem, and which was ultimately solemnly enacted
there, was almost certainly a priestly code, pure and simple,
which was not amalgamated until later with the preëxisting
Deuteronomic *Torah* JED.   This final process of redaction was
of course not undertaken until Ezra's Law-book had itself
undergone the necessary and inevitable processes of supplementation and adjustment to practical requirement which any
complete system of law is sure to undergo.   The most important addition of Rp to P² was the preëxisting priestly Torah,
the Law of Holiness (P^h), the greater part of which now forms
the nucleus of Leviticus in chh. xvii.–xxvi.   Other and exten-

---

* Indicated in the text by the use of small italics.

sive *novellae* were doubtless attached to it before the work of R began, but these do not belong to our present subject.

The work of R, the final redactor of JEDP shows that to him P was preëminently the sacred code. Its views and phraseology are shared by him, and in cases of duplication he almost invariably sacrifices the older work to P, making the latter the "groundwork" of the entire structure. Under such conditions it is not difficult to distinguish and to characterize his work. It was thorough and comprehensive, but even towards JED manifests a scrupulous, not to say devout, regard for the material. It was unavoidable on this plan that JED's account of things which could not be told twice over, such as the construction of the ark, and deaths of the patriarchs, should be stricken out; but so far as possible the divergent traits of JED were preserved and inserted where room could be found, dislocating to some extent the earlier narrative, as in Num. xx. 1ff., but preserving the material to the verge of self-contradiction (cf. Num. xvi. 28-34, with vs. 35 and xxvi. 11). Examples of R's work in Genesis appear generally in slight touches of adjustment, but xxxvi. 1-5 is substantially his, and xlvi. 8-27 also, if not from P³. Similar light touches appear in the later books, where, as in Num. xvi.; xx. 1-13; Dt. i. 3; iv. 41-43, the narratives came into close contact. The difficulty is to distinguish R from P³, whose supplementations extended, as Popper has shown by a comparison of the LXX. text of Ex. xxxv.-xl. with the Massoretic, down to the third century B. C. But these latest occasional touches have scarcely affected the *narrative*, which received practically its final form at the hands of R, probably not far from the close of the fifth century B. C.

If there is one feature of the Documentary Theory which appears to be more offensive than another to the advocates of tradition it would seem to be the doctrine of repeated redactions of the text, which we have thus endeavored to set in outline before the reader. For some reason it appears to them incompatible with any view of *divine authorship* of the Bible. And yet it is to the very same principle of redaction that they have recourse when the improbability of Moses' writing the account of his own death is pointed out, or when appeal is made to the innumerable post-Mosaica alluded to in our preceding volume. These are explained as the work of later hands. In fact the phenomena of redaction become absolutely undeniable the moment we reach the epoch where comparison is possible with parallel versions and texts. But why should divine authorship be incompatible with an almost continuous process of human redaction? When through the extrication of J's inherently credible story of the passage of the Red Sea the divine element in the event—shall we say "*sinks*"? nay—*rises* to the level of *providential* instead of *miraculous* intervention, the story becomes not less, but more truly a manifestation of "God in history." In like manner, when deposits of the three great streams of religious thought of Ephraim, Judah and post-exilic Judaism gradually accumulate under providential control and guidance into the Bible of Jesus and the apostles, the resultant literary composite is more than ever entitled to be called the product of no mere human wisdom. It is seen to be a work and word of God, slowly-developed through many ages of his self-manifestation in Hebrew thought and literature.

TYPOGRAPHIC SIGNS AND ABBREVIATIONS.

J. **Judean prophetic writer, circ. 800 B. C., in this type.**

E.   Ephraimite prophetic writer, circ. 750 B. C., in this type.

P².   Priestly law-book, circ. 450 B. C., in this type.

J².   Editorial additions to J, 800–722 B. C., in this type.

E².   JE and Rd, additions to E, harmonistic adjustments of JE and Deuteronomic expansions, 722–200 B. C., in this type, or smaller.

P³.   Rp and R (sometimes Rd), additions to P or JEDP in the priestly style and sense, 450–200 B. C., in this type.

Ps.=Psalm ;   Dh=Historical Deuteronomist ;   Dp=Parenetic Deuteronomist.

Supplied material in [ ], displaced in —— —— ; characteristic expressions in Part II. in ' ', word-plays in " ". Corrupt text is indicated by *, omitted legislative sections by * * * *, words lost or unintelligible by . . . . Ch. chapter, chh. chapters ; vs.=verse, vv. verses ; f.=following verse, page or chapter ; ff. following verses, etc. ; cf.=compare, ct.=contrast. Sam. Samaritan text, LXX.=Septuagint, Vulg.=Vulgate. Arts. I. II. III. IV.=my discussions of § § I. II. III. IV., in "Journ. Bibl. Lit." ix. 2 xii. 1 (1890–1893). *Z. A. W. Zeitschrift für alttestamentliche Wissenschaft ; Comp.* Wellhausen's *Composition des Hexateuch's,* Berlin, 1889 ; *Ex. u. Lev.* and *Nu. Dt. Jos.=* Dillmann's commentaries on Ex. Jos., Leipzig, 1880 and 1886. *Hex.=*Kuenen's *Hexateuch, trans.* Wicksteed, London, 1886. Julicher's thesis, *Quellen von Ex. i. vii.,* Halle 1880, and his articles in *Jahrb. f. prot. Theol.* viii. are referred to as A and B. Other references explain themselves.

EXODUS.

A natural division of the story of Israel exists between the end of Genesis, the history of the primitive and patriarchal period, and the beginning of Exodus, the history of Israel's birth and development as a nation. This division would seem to be even more clearly marked in the earliest form of the story than at present, for critics discover in Exodus the same structure as in Genesis. The same principal sources, J, E and P, marked by the same characteristics, are here woven together in the same manner as there, and apparently by the same hands. Now in P, the priestly lawbook, commonly regarded by critics as the latest source, and in E, the Ephraimite document, which we regard as later than J, there is at least an attempt to bridge over the chasm between the story of Israel as a family of 70 individuals, and as a nation. In P the genealogies (i. 1–6; vi. 14–27) are continued in unbroken line, giving in the case of Miriam, Aaron and Moses the third, in other cases the fourth generation (Gen. xv. 16) as that of the Exodus. In E (Gen. l. 23) "the children of Machir the son of Manasseh were born upon Joseph's knees," and this same Machir is the one who in Num. xxxii. 39ff. is represented as receiving from Moses at the end of the 40 years' wandering the land of Gilead, and making conquest of it. Hence the date given by P in xii. 41, of 430 years, which nearly all interpreters agree is to be reckoned from the migration of Abraham (Gen. xv. 15f.) presents a period too long, if anything, for the genealogies of either P or E. But these genealogical data, while apparently adding to the continuity and historical value of the story, in reality obscure the fact, which in J seems to have been left plain, that a great gulf exists between the folk-

1

stories of Genesis, and the traditions of Exodus and the later
books. Three generations, or four or five—160 years, or 200,
or 430, are alike inadequate to account for the growth of a family
of 12, or of 70 persons, even under favorable, instead of the
extremely adverse circumstances of the Egyptian bondage, into
a nation of myriads if not millions, such as all forms of the story
of the Exodus represent. The reader need only be referred to
Colenso's *Pentateuch and Book of Joshua*, Part I. for a demonstration of the utter futility of the attempt to make this transition.
Nor is the difficulty met by the mere concession of possible textual inaccuracies in the numbers. Even were it possible to suppose that the many coincident footings of two complete censuses
were the result of accidental textual corruption, the entire
history in all its forms implies the transition from a family of
a few score to a great nation (cf. Dt. xxvi. 5) in the interval
between Joseph and the Exodus.*

The explanation of the discrepancy is simply that Israel's
meagre recollections of the time before the Exodus are
wrapped in the form universally employed for the earliest
traditions, the symbolism of the family, and the true method
of approximating a historically conceivable unity of the pre-
historic narrative with the semi-legendary traditions at the
beginning of national history, is the method of the earliest document, J, which leaves a chasm of indefinite extent between
the two periods, without any attempt, so far as now appears,
to bridge it over. The earliest dim recollections of the people,
of a time when, before the bondage of Egypt, a wave of Semitic migration had borne their ancestors upon its crest over
and past this land of Canaan, to leave them stranded on the
border of Egypt, were woven into narratives cast in the
form of family relations, and these traditions of Abraham and

---

* The comparison of the increase of the 70 persons of Jacob's family to a
nation of millions in four generations with the development of a nation of 65
millions from the " Mayflower" company (*Sic!*) in about the same length of time,
recently made by a noted Brooklyn preacher, based as it is on the ludicrous
assumption that the Pilgrims from Leyden were the actual progenitors of the
entire American people, well illustrates the fact that some modern minds have
not advanced beyond the mythopœic stage.

Isaac, Jacob and Esau, Joseph and Judah, attached themselves to the shrines and sacred wells and trees of Canaan, when the people at last found themselves definitely in possession of the land where their fathers had been unable to secure a permanent foothold. The very fact that from the beginning of Exodus the traditions largely lose the character of *family* life and make at least the attempt to relate *national* history, shows that we are crossing the line between legend-lore, and tradition having a larger basis of historical recollection.

How long the period of sojourn in Goshen may have been, is matter for the widest conjecture. The most that we can say is, it was not long enough to obliterate from the recollection of the nomads who settled there the remembrance of their migration, nor of the relationship which existed between themselves and the other peoples of the Arabian desert, of the Hebrew or Abrahamic stock ; not long enough under the circumstances to make a very great difference with their numbers. Still we find a real gain to our historical conception in falling back upon the simple, indefinite representation of the oldest narrative, that it was a long time, at the end of which Israel found itself a numerous people with cherished reminiscences of a long-lost liberty, restless under the heavy yoke of a Pharaoh, whose policy was to make them slaves instead of allies.

The story of the book of Exodus is the story of how Israel achieved independence and received a constitution. It corresponds to the story of the last quarter of the eighteenth century in our own history. The prophetic narrative JE rests here, as in Genesis, in both its parts, largely upon ancient poetic material, fragments of which are scattered throughout. Small bodies of primitive law (civil, criminal and religious of course undifferentiated) are also incorporated. The priestly lawbook P briefly sketches the history, to dwell at great length upon the ceremonial law, the mass of which is related as delivered at Sinai. Here the institution of the tabernacle, briefly mentioned in JE, is made the foundation of all the religious worship of the nation. The directions for its construction and furnishing, the inauguration of a priesthood and prescriptions for the ritual

service occupy nearly all of the last fifteen chapters of Exodus,
the whole of Leviticus (whose nucleus is an early body of
priestly law (P^1), the so-called *Heiligkeitsgesetz*, or Law of Holiness, incorporated by P^2), and the first ten chapters of Numbers ; besides scattered chapters of ceremonial law introduced
here and there in Numbers without historical connection.
This great mass of ceremonial law, forming the body of P's
work, is omitted from our present consideration as not
germane to the Triple Tradition of the Exodus. Its removal
shows that no such well-marked natural division exists in any
of the sources at the end of Exodus as has been shown to exist
at its beginning. The close of our present book of Exodus is
marked by the completion of the Tabernacle and its sanctification by the descent of the Cloud. But the narrative of P^2 goes
on uninterruptedly to the tenth chapter of Numbers with the
account of the directions for worship and inauguration of the
cultus. In general it may be said that the primitive book of
Exodus extended to the end of the stay at Sinai-Horeb, and the
primitive Numbers began with the breaking camp for the journey from Sinai-Horeb to Canaan. It would be more correct,
however, to consider Exodus i–xxiv, xxxii–xxxiv, and the
narrative parts of Numbers and Deuteronomy as forming
together the primitive Tradition of the Exodus. The Book of
the Exodus thus formed would be somewhat smaller than the
primitive Genesis, which we might call the Tradition of the
Patriarchal period; when followed by the Story of the Conquest in Joshua and part of Judges, where the three sources
are still found, the three together would form something like a
trilogy of the sacred history.

In the present volume the story of the Exodus, from the
bondage of Egypt to the death of Moses on the height of
Pisgah overlooking the Promised Land, is the field of inquiry.
The first subdivision of this story extends naturally to the end
of the stay at Horeb-Sinai and includes four principal sections:
§ I. The Bondage of Egypt; Ex. i–vi. § II. The Plagues; Ex.
vii–xii. § III. From Egypt to Sinai; Ex. xiii–xix. § IV. The
Covenant at Sinai; Ex. xx–Num. x. The second subdivision

includes the whole story of the wilderness period in three sections: § v. From Sinai to Kadesh; Num. xi–xx. § vi. From
Kadesh to the Jordan; Num. xxi–xxxvi. § vii. The Covenant
in the field of Moab; Dt. i–xxxiv.

§ 1. Ex. i–vi. The Bondage of Egypt.

In § i. we have the description of Israel's condition of bondage and of Moses' birth and call. The second group of six
chapters, § ii. relates the story of the contest of Moses and
Aaron on behalf of Israel with Pharaoh, until by the final
plague of the death of the firstborn the release of Israel is
extorted. In both sections the parallel sources stand in marked
contrast, exhibiting the characteristics found peculiar to each
already in the book of Genesis.

P gives first a list of "the names of the sons of Jacob
who came into Egypt"; then a statement of their increase,
the oppression suffered, their cry to God, who hears their groaning and "remembers his covenant"; thereupon a genealogy
of the house of Levi introducing Aaron and Moses. To the
latter God reveals himself as "Yahweh," commissioning him
to bring Israel forth. Aaron is commissioned to go with Moses
before Pharaoh because of the latter's "uncircumcised lips."

From JE comes all the detail and color of the picture. E
relates the secret attempt of the Egyptians to rid themselves of
the Hebrews, the story of the midwives and of the command to
cast the babes in the river. Then followed originally some
data now superseded by P, as to the family of Moses, his
older sister "Miriam, the prophetess" (Num. xii. 2), and his
older brother, Aaron, whom already God had chosen out of all
the tribes of Israel to be his priest, to go up to his altar (1 Sam.
ii. 27ff.). The stories of the babe in the ark of papyrus found
and adopted by Pharaoh's daughter, of the slaying of the
Egyptian, and of the flight to the wilderness are all from E. In
remarkable parallelism to the priestly source E relates how at
Horeb Moses received the revelation of the name "Yahweh"
and the commission to deliver Israel, together with a "rod of
God" endowed with miraculous powers, whereby the result is

to be achieved. He meets Aaron after taking leave of his
father-in-law Jethro, and the two together present their demand
to Pharaoh as divinely directed, but meet refusal.

J's narrative resembles E's. After Joseph's death Israel suffers oppression, but increases to great numbers . . . . Moses
for some act of rebellion is forced to flee, settles in Midian,
and marries there. When the king who sought his life is dead
he returns, meeting a strange encounter with Yahweh at the
"lodging-place," which leads to the rite of infant circumcision.
Thereafter Yahweh again appears to him and commissions him
to bring Israel forth out of their bondage to a "land flowing
with milk and honey." Moses objects his slowness of speech,
whereupon "Aaron the Levite," his brother, is made the
spokesman *to the people*. The people thankfully accept the
message (iv. 31 ; ct. vi. 9 P), and Moses and the elders appeal to Pharaoh for a limited concession ; but the first effect
is only to bring about a deplorable increase of the people's
burdens.

1. Chh. i, ii. BONDAGE OF ISRAEL. MOSES' BIRTH AND YOUTH.

ANALYSIS.

The sons of Israel multiply in Egypt (i. 1–7). In fear of their increasing strength, a new king of Egypt, unmindful of Joseph's services, vainly
endeavors to break their spirit and prevent their increase by forced and
servile labor (i. 8 14). The king of Egypt secretly endeavors to destroy
Israel by engaging the midwives to kill the male children. Unsuccessful
in this, he openly directs his people to cast them into the river. Under
these circumstances Moses is born of Levite parentage, and exposed in
an ark of papyrus upon the river. Discovered there by Pharaoh's
daughter he is adopted by her (ii. 1 10). When grown up Moses slays
an Egyptian who was abusing a Hebrew, and flees from Pharaoh's
wrath. He finds refuge in Midian in the house of the priest Reuel, marries the daughter of his protector, and has by her a son, whom he names
Gershom. The king of Egypt meantime dies. Israel's cry of bondage is
heard by God, who remembers his covenant with their fathers (ii. 11 25).

Portions of this story are easily seen to belong to the narrative heretofore extricated and designated P², for i. 5 refers back to Gen. xlvi. 27.
ii. 24 to Gen. xvii. and xxxv. 9ff. The genealogical list i. 1 5, 7, the

elaborately exact and mechanical style of i. 1-5, 7; ii. 23b-25 (notice in ii. 24f. the repetition of the subject and cf. Gen. ii. 1-3), and a large number of expressions found only in this document make it certain that in these verses, and a part at least of i. 13f. this source is present. By far the greater part of the two chapters, however, is of a totally different style, descriptive, natural and easy, with the characteristic features of JE. Moreover, it is not probable that the author of vi. 20 and Num. xxvi. 58f. (P²), if he had written the story of ii. 1ff. which stands connected with i. 15-22, would have *first* introduced in this anonymous style the characters Amram and Jochebed in ii. 1, the only place in the story where they have a part to play, and then *subsequently* inserted their names in a mere genealogy.

On the contrary, the very language of ii. 1ff. (see note *in loc.*) and its references to Moses' "sister," with subsequent allusions to Aaron and Miriam, before they are brought forward, as if for the first time, in ch. vi., prove that there was originally between chh. i. and ii. quite a family history of Moses. In a much later passage, ascribed by critics to the same document (E), we have an extended reference to a calling of the house of Eli's father (Aaronidae?) to the priesthood, in a manner totally irreconcilable with the priestly account of Ex. xxviii. and impossible to locate anywhere else than in these chapters : " I revealed myself unto the house of thy father *when they were in Egypt* in bondage to Pharaoh, and I chose him out of all the tribes of Israel to be my priest, to go up unto mine altar " etc., 1 Sam. ii. 27. All this, which originally appears to have preceded ii. 1, we can readily see would have to be stricken out by Rp. A further incongruity with P² appears in i. 11b, where *Raamses* (the word in the original Hebrew text is identically the same here and in xii. 37 as well as in Gen. xlvii. 11) is a *city* built by Israel, whereas in Gen. xlvii. 11 it is a *territory*, so called before their coming to Egypt, and parallel to "Goshen " of the source J. Further, the duplication of vs. 11 by vv. 13f, confirms the probability that the composite character of Genesis is exhibited also in this section.

If we inquire for the source of the material thus excluded from P², it will be found that this also (i. 6, 7 in part, 8-12, 14 in part, 15-22; ii. 1-23a) is not a uniform product of a single pen, as maintained by most critics, but presents the usual duplicate character of JE. In ch. i. the vv. 15-22 do not follow logically upon vv. 8-12, but are rather parallel to them, or even precede them in thought ; for the people whose requirements are met by *two* midwives cannot be the multitude who are too many and mighty even for the Egyptians. In vv. 8-12 we have a consistent representation of a single policy pursued by the Pharaonic ruler,

and still kept up in ch. v.   The effort is to break the spirit of a tributary or
subject nation (cf. xii. 37 ; 600,000 fighting men. J) by compelling them to
forge their own chains in constructing the fortresses which are to control
them.   The author contemplates a nation, not a mere clan ; and regards
them as having a geographical as well as political individuality (cf. ch.
v. where the brickmaking, "taskmasters" etc., reappear ; here Israel
have their own province, Goshen, whence they can be " scattered abroad,"
and their own " officers," besides the " elders " of iii. 16 ; the "taskmasters"
being apparently superior tribute-takers).   In point of fact, though not
apparently in J's conception, this province of Goshen extended even to
the southern boundary of Palestine ; cf. Jos. x. 41 ; xi. 16.   In i. 15ff.
(E) we are indeed brought back to the same point where we were in
i. 8 (J), or rather to a point anterior, since the secret and indirect assault
upon Israel must of necessity precede, and cannot follow, the openly hostile and forcible policy of repression of vv. 8ff. ; but the point of view in
15ff. is entirely different.   The Hebrews are isolated individuals in some
kind of domestic slavery, so that the Egyptians can interfere in their
family life (vs. 22).   They live in the royal city (ii. 5 ; ct. viii. 22 ; ix. 7, 26)
and are not so numerous but that *two* midwives suffice for their needs.
Vv. 15-22 lead up to the *family* history of Moses in ii. 1ff. and the author
throughout views Israel more as a group of families (cf. Gen. l. 23)
reserving the conception of nationality till later.   Coincident with these
contrasts in point of view we find in vv. 8-12 a number of expressions
peculiar to J (see refs. and Art. l.), and none of E, while in vv. 15-22 the
name *Elohim* (cf. iii. 11-14, and E *passim* in Genesis) and other peculiarities of E are present, whereas characteristics of J are here, in contrast
with vv. 8-12, with one exception (vs. 20b) wholly wanting.   Vs. 20b
interrupts in a most unaccountable way the obvious connection of 20a
with vs. 21.   The language of the intrusive clause, however, is identical
with 7a b, which again is pre-supposed by vs. 12 (J).   Here, then, and
in the middle clause of vs. 14, similarly distinguished, are probable fragments of J.   Vs. 6, which relates the death of Joseph, of which we have
an account *in extenso* in E in the preceding paragraph (Gen. l. 22-26),
and which contrasts in style with the regular formula of P², must also be
from J's pen.

In ch. ii. the phenomena are similar.   The story of Moses' childhood
we have no reason to expect in that narrative which introduces us
directly to the conditions which call for his life-work (J in i. 8-12) ; and,
in fact, there is no trustworthy trace in ii. 1-10 of either the thought or
the language of J.   On the contrary, the linguistic characteristics of E
are here so marked as to be absolutely decisive with all critics.   Vv.

11-14 (15a ?) again are inseparable from the preceding. They tell how "when Moses was grown up " he proved not to have been deprived by his education of sympathy with " his brethren." The slight linguistic evidences discoverable here incline also in favor of E. In vv. 15bff. however, we enter upon a somewhat different scene. With some critics the slightly different motive for Moses' flight (an actual attempt against his life by Pharaoh instead of anticipated peril) is of sufficient weight to determine a line of division after vs. 14; and it is indeed apparent from iv. 19, that J's narrative must have contained a similar datum. But the reference in xviii. 4 (E) seems to assure vs. 15 to E, except the last clause, where a real division exists ; for " *the* well " refers to something not given in the preceding context. A more important incongruity with E appears in the succeeding verses, where " the priest of Midian," Moses' father-in-law, appears as " *Reuel*," or (see note *in loc.*), is nameless ; whereas, in the section immediately following, which is most positively and indisputably from E, and in all subsequent E passages, he is called " *Jethro.*" Now, if ii. 16ff. and iii. 1ff. were by the same author we certainly should not have the name Reuel in ii. 18 and Jethro in iii. 1. It is, in fact, almost certain that if it had been at all the intention of the writer to name this character in this part of his story, he would have named him in ii. 16, where he is first introduced, and would not have brought in the name as if by afterthought in iii. 1. But even the *namelessness* of " the priest of Midian " here in contrast with iii. 1 ; iv. 18, and ch. xviii., is unfavorable to E as author of vv. 15ff.

A similar argument applies in the case of vs. 22a. On turning to ch. xviii. it unexpectedly appears that Moses had not one, but *two* sons by the daughter of Jethro, during the time covered by this chapter. If so, why should one be omitted ? This is not the work of R je, for the redaction pursues the opposite course, and makes a plural of " *sons* " in iv. 20 ; when iv. 25 proves that " *son* " was the original. Gen. xli. 50-52 shows that in a precisely analogous case E told of the two succeeding births together, and in connection with the marriage. The failure of any mention of more than one son as the fruit of Moses' union with Zipporah, in agreement with iv. 20, 25, must also weigh against E and in favor of J as author of vv. 15b, 23a.

It is worthy of note in connection with this passage that J certainly had a narrative of Moses' flight from certain men who sought his life, one of whom at least was Pharaoh, and of his taking refuge in Midian and marrying there ; for all this is referred to by J in iv. 19f. This alliance with a priestly family of Abrahamic stock (Gen. xxv. 2f), the author doubtless regards as an honor (cf. Gen. xli. 45 J). But in E. Num. xii. 1

(see note *in loc.*), this marriage of Moses with a " Cushite "—the assumption of an unknown second marriage is gratuitous—is treated as a *mésal-
liance.* " Cushite " is doubtless synonymous with Midianite (cf. Hab.
iii. 7), and it is certain from subsequent reference (*e. g.* xviii. 4) that E
and J here were almost exactly parallel. Yet a difference certainly suggests itself between ii. 15ff. and the view-point of E. With this result
agree (see references) the linguistic and stylistic marks of these verses,
with one exception. The word denoting " strange " in 22b seems to be
employed only by E, and the half-verse itself is identical with xviii. 3b
(E). As Rje would be obliged to bring the statement here into agreement with ch. xviii., or *vice versa*, it is probable that he has simply
adopted E's etymology in both instances, in preference to J's. The latter
may possibly have been led up to in some way by the story of vv. 16ff ;
in fact the Hebrew for " drove them away," vs. 17, is written identically with the name Gershom.

Vv. 23b-25 have been already characterized as displaying all the marks
of P², including an unmistakable reference to Gen. xvii. Vs. 25 breaks
off in the midst of a sentence. But the line of division between 23a and
23b can be drawn with a high degree of certainty. In the present form
of the verse the reader is at a loss to know who the king is who " died in the
course of those many days.' According to the unmistakeable reference
of vs. 23a to the preceding, it must be the oppressor whom Moses had
resisted, and from whom he has taken refuge in Midian. But if so, it is
extremely unnatural that the author should take the occasion of the
death of the oppressor to speak of Israel's complaint and cry to God.
The LXX. version unquestionably establishes here the true connection by
repeating ii. 23a before iv. 19. The death of the king is not, as would
appear from the text as we have it, the occasion of Israel's groaning, but
of Moses' return. The result of this is two-fold. First, there is no real
but only an artificial connection between 23a and 23b ; second, since the
occasion of Moses' return was according to iv. 19 (J) simply that " Yahweh said unto Moses in Midian, Go, return into Egypt, for all the men
are dead which sought thy life," and inasmuch as this motive excludes
the supposition of a previous direct, immediate and unqualified mission
to Pharaoh, such as iii. 10ff. (E), the story of Moses' commission to
deliver Israel, if it was given at all in this document, must have been
placed *subsequent* to his final departure from Midian. We shall find
that this really agrees much better with the incident, otherwise inexplicable, of iv. 24-26 (J).

Chh. i. and ii. appear accordingly to be composite, the strands identical with those already recognized as underlying the book of Genesis, and

not appreciably harder to disentangle. The presentation of the results of this documentary analysis in different fonts of type will show them to be unexpectedly illuminating to the well-known perplexities of the present text. For detailed discussion of evidence in the critical analysis the reader is referred to Art. 1. of the author's discussions.

(P) *¹Now these are the names of the sons of Israel, which* 1 *came into Egypt; every man and his household came with Jacob. Reuben, Simeon, Levi, and Judah, Issachar, Zebulun, and Ben-*2-3 *jamin, Dan and Naphtali, Gad and Asher. And all the souls* 4-5 *that came out of the loins of Jacob were seventy souls: and Joseph* (J) *was in Egypt already.* ²**And Joseph died, and all his** 6 (P) **brethren, and all that generation.** *And the children* 7 (J) *of Israel* ³*were fruitful, and increased abundantly,* **and [. . .]** (P) **multiplied, and** ⁴**waxed exceeding mighty;** *and the land was filled with them.*

(J) ⁵**Now there arose a new king over Egypt, which** 8 **knew not Joseph. And he said unto his people, Be-** 9 **hold the people of the children of Israel are more and mightier than we:** ⁶**come, let us deal wisely with** 10 **them: lest they multiply, and it come to pass, that, when there falleth out any war, they also join them-selves unto our enemies, and fight against us, and get them up out of the land. Therefore they did set over** 11 **them** ⁷**taskmasters to afflict them with their burdens. And they built for Pharaoh store cities, Pithom and Raamses. But the more they** ⁸**afflicted them, the more** 12 **they multiplied and the more they** ⁹**spread abroad. And they** ¹⁰**were grieved because of the children of Israel. [. . .]**

(P) ¹¹*And the Egyptians made the children of Israel to serve* 13 *with rigor: and they made their lives bitter with hard service,* 14 (J) **in** ¹²**mortar and in brick, and in all manner of ser-**

¹6 : 16. Gen. 36 : 10,40 : 46 : 8ff.   ²Jud. 2 : 10 ; Gen. 50 : 26.   ³Gen. 1 : 22,28.   ⁴Gen. 1? : 18, 26 : 16; Nu. 22 : 6 ; vv.9,20.   ⁵Nu 22 : 3-6.   ⁶Gen. 11 : 3,4,7 ; 38 : 16.   ⁷ : - : : Out ? ⁸Gen. 16 : 6; 31 : 50; 34 : 2 ; ch. 3 : 7.   ⁹Gen. 0 : 19; 10 : 18 ; 11 : 10,28; 14 :   . : . : t: ¹⁰Gen. 46 : 34; Nu. 22 . 3.   ¹¹Lev. 25 : 4ff.   ¹²Gen. 11 : 3.

(P) vice in the field, *all their service, wherein they made them serve with rigor.*

15 **(E)** [. . .] And the king of Egypt spake to the Hebrew midwives, of which the name of the one was Shiphrah, and
16 the name of the other Puah: and he said, When ye do the office of a midwife to the Hebrew women, and see them upon the birthstool; if it be a son, then ye shall kill him;
17 but if it be a daughter, then she shall live. But the midwives [13]feared God, and did not as the king of Egypt com-
18 manded them, but saved the men children alive. And the king of Egypt called for the midwives, and said unto them, Why have ye done this thing, and have saved the men chil-
19 dren alive? And the midwives said unto Pharaoh, Because the Hebrew women are not as the Egyptian women; for they are lively, and are delivered ere the midwife come unto them.
20 **(J)** And God dealt well with the midwives: [14]**and the people**
21 **(E) multiplied, and waxed very mighty** [. . .]. And it came to pass, because the midwives [15]feared God, that he
22 [16]made them houses. And Pharaoh charged all his people, saying, Every son that is born ye shall cast into the river, and every daughter ye shall save alive.

2   And there went a man of the house of Levi [.   .],* and
2 took to wife a [. . .] daughter of Levi [. .]. And the woman conceived, and bare a son: and when she saw him
3 that he was a goodly child, she hid him three months. And when she could not longer hide him, she took for him an ark of bulrushes, and daubed it with slime and with pitch; and she put the child therein, and laid it in the flags [17]by the riv-

---

[13]Gen. 40: 11; 42: 1. [14]Vv. 7,9. [15]Gen. 20: 11; 22: 12; 42: 18. [16]1 Sam. 2: 35. [17] 15.

---

* In vs. 1 we have literally "*the* daughter of Levi," which must grammatically refer to some person already mentioned, though the mention is now wanting. In vs. 4 "his sister" is introduced as if already known to the reader. Later both Miriam and Aaron appear in the story in the same way without introduction, though Miriam is styled "the prophetess," (xv. 20) as if we had already been informed as to her calling. The extreme brevity and generalizing character of vs. 1 may therefore be attributed to Rp., with whose material in ch. vi. the data of E conflicted. Cf. 1 Sam. ii. 27f. and see Analysis, p. 7 and Part II.

er's brink.   And his sister stood afar off, to know what would 4
be done to him.   And the daughter of Pharaoh came down 5
to bathe at the river; and her maidens walked along by the
river-side ; and she saw the ark among the flags, and sent
her ²handmaid to fetch it. And she opened it, and saw ³the child; * 6
and, behold, the babe wept   And she had compassion
on him, and said, This is one of the Hebrews' children.
Then said his sister to Pharaoh's daughter, Shall I go and 7
call thee a nurse of the Hebrew women, that she may nurse
the child for thee?   And Pharaoh's daughter said to her, Go. 8
And the maid went and called the child's mother.   And 9
Pharaoh's daughter said unto her, Take this child away, and
nurse it for me, and I will give thee thy wages. And the
woman took the child, and nursed it.   ⁴And the child grew, 10
and she brought him unto Pharaoh's daughter, and he became her son.   And she called his name Moses, and said,
Because I drew him out of the water.

And it came to pass in those days, when Moses was grown 11
up, that he ⁵went out unto his brethren, and looked on their
⁶burdens: and he saw an Egyptian smiting an Hebrew, one
of his brethren.   And he looked this way and that way, and 12
when he saw that there was no man, he smote the Egyptian,
and hid him in the sand.   And he went out the second day, 13
and behold, two men of the Hebrews strove together : and
he said to him that did the wrong, Wherefore smitest thou
thy fellow ?   And he said, Who made thee a prince and a 14
judge over us? thinkest thou to kill me, as thou killedst the
Egyptian ?   And Moses feared, and said, Surely the thing is
known.

Now when Pharaoh heard this thing, he ⁷sought to slay 15
Moses.   But Moses fled from the face of Pharaoh, and dwelt
(J) in the land of Midian [. . .]: **and he ⁸sat down by a**
well.   Now [. . .] the ⁹priest of Midian had seven 16
daughters: and they came and drew water, and filled

---

²Gen. 30 : 3, 12, 18, etc. ³Gen. 21 : 14-16, etc. 1 : 22. ⁴Gen. 21 : 8. ⁵Vs. 10. ⁶5 : 4. ⁷18:4.
⁸Gen. 24 : 11ff.; 29 : 3ff. ⁹Cf. Nu. 12 : 1.

---

* The clause is superfluous and appears to be a marginal gloss.

17 the ¹troughs to water their father's flock. And the
shepherds came and drove them away: but Moses
stood up and helped them, and watered their flock.
18 And when they came to ¹¹*Reuel** their father, he said,
19 ¹²How is it that ye are come so soon to-day? And they
said, An Egyptian delivered us out of the hand of the
shepherds, and moreover he drew water for us, and
20 watered the flock. And he said unto his daughters,
And where is he? why is it that ye have ¹⁵left the
21 man? call him, that he may eat bread. And Moses
was ¹⁴content to dwell with the man: and he gave
22 Moses Zipporah his daughter. And she bare him a
(E) son, and he called his name Gershom [. . .]: for he
said, I have been a sojourner in a strange land.

23　　(J) And it came to pass in the course of those many
(P) days, that the king of Egypt died: † *and the children
of Israel sighed by reason of the bondage, and they cried, and their*
24 *cry came up unto God by reason of the bondage. And God heard*
their groaning, and God ¹⁵remembered ¹⁶his covenant with Abraham,
25 *with Isaac, and with Jacob. And God saw the children of Israel,*
and God took knowledge [of them].

¹⁰Gen. 30 : 38. 41. ¹¹Cf. Nu. 10 : 29 ; Ex. 3 : 1, etc. ¹²Gen. 27 : 20. ¹³Gen. 2 : 24 ; 24 : 27 ;
28 : 15. etc. ¹⁴Gen. 18 : 27,31 ; Jos. 7 : 7. ¹⁵Gen. 8 : 1 ; 30 : 22. ¹⁶Gen. 17 : 7f.

* Throughout the J document Moses' father-in-law is always known as " Hobab the son of Reuel, the priest of Midian," cf. Num. x 29; Jud. iv. 11 ; in E
he is known equally without exception as Jethro (Ex. iv. 18, " Jether "), " Priest
of Midian " in E occurs only in Ex. xii. 1 and xviii. 1, passages recast by Rje, and
must therefore be considered doubtful. " Reuel " here is best explained as a
harmonistic insertion, *Chothen* (" father-in-law," *i. e.* wife's relation) when applied
to Hobab and Jethro being rendered " *brother*-in-law." This is still the Rabbinic explanation ; but the sense of the passage clearly is that " the priest of
Midian " who is here nameless (Rje, who supplies " priest of Midian " in iii. 1
must have struck out the name from vs. 16) has, not seven daughters *and two
sons*, but seven unprotected daughters. The theory of " Hobab son of " having
dropped out before " Reuel " is incredible. In the original " Reuel " and
" Raguel " (Num. x. 29) are written identically.

† The LXX. repeat vs. 23a in connection with iv.19. See Analysis, p. 130, and
note on iv. 19, 24 26.

Chh. III–IV.   The Call of Moses and Aaron.

ANALYSIS.

This story is related in duplicate by JE and P², the narrative of the latter in vi. 2–vii. 7 completely paralleling that of JE in chh iii. and iv.

God appears to Moses in " Horeb the mount of God " where he was keeping the flock of Jethro.   From a burning thorn thicket he reveals himself as the God of Moses' fathers, determined now to deliver Israel from their bondage.   Moses is commissioned to demand their release from Pharaoh, and receives the revelation of the sacred Name, and a token of the success of his mission : iii. 1–15.   He is sent to gather the elders of Israel and with them to ask of Pharaoh permission to go three days' journey into the wilderness and sacrifice.   Yahweh will compel release and enable the people to spoil the Egyptians.   Moses objects his lack of authority with the people, and receives power to exhibit three signs, his staff changing to a serpent, his hand to the hand of a leper, and water to blood ; iv. 1–9.   He objects his inability to speak well, and persists in refusal until Yahweh's anger is kindled.   Yahweh gives the office of spokesman to his brother " Aaron the Levite," and to Moses a wonder-working rod ; 10–17.   Moses returns to Jethro, takes leave of his father-in-law, and with wife and sons returns to Egypt.   On the way at the lodging-place Yahweh seeks to kill him, but is propitiated by Zipporah's circumcising the child ; 18–26.   Arrived at Horeb, Moses meets Aaron and the two announce Yahweh's message to the people, which is gratefully received ; 27–31.

No trace whatever of the style, language or thought of P occurs in chh. iii–v.   On the contrary we have seen that Rp has reserved the parallel account of P² for a distinct narrative in vi. 2–vii. 7, which repeats in briefer form all the essential points of chh. iiif. even to the reiteration of the revelation of the divine Name, of Moses' complaint of uncircumcision *of lip* (cf. iv. 10–16, and 24–26 with vi. 10–12, 28-vii. 2), and the appointment of Aaron as spokesman.   Ch. vi. 2 is found thus to join almost directly upon ii. 25.   But in spite of complete freedom from P, chh. iiiff. are anything but consistent and uniform.   We need only take iv. 17ff. as an example.   It becomes later manifest that vs. 17 refers to the wonders wrought by Moses " before Pharaoh " (vs. 21), one series of which (E) are wrought invariably by the rod.   But so far we know of no " signs" but those of iv. 1–9, only *one* of which can be performed with the rod ; and even these vs. 30 seems to attribute to *Aaron*.   Vs. 19 again is alternative to vs. 18, and cannot be the sequel to it (cf. Gen. xxxi,

2 and 3). But independently of this, its motive for Moses' return, as we have seen, excludes the possibility that he had previously received a divine commission to Pharaoh such as iii. 7-18 ; moreover it joins, as the LXX. text shows, upon ii. 23a. The name Jethro in vs. 18, agreeing with chh. iii. and xviii., is inconsistent with ii. 15ff. with which again vs. 19 ("in Midian") agrees. Vs. 20a, in agreement with 24-26, represents Moses taking his wife and *son* (see note *in loc.*) to Egypt with him. But in xviii. 1ff. Jethro comes to meet Moses *after* the exodus, at Horeb, and brings Moses' wife and her *two* sons with him. Of this the only explanation offered is the belated insertion in xviii. 3, "after he had sent her away" (see note *in loc.*). Vs. 20b would follow well upon vs. 17, but vs. 21 is not the sequel to vs. 20, nor is the anticipation of ch. xif. in vv. 21-23 appropriate to the present situation (see note *in loc.*). In ch. iii. the condition of the story is not materially better. The writer who relates the revelation of the Name Yahweh in vv. 10-15 cannot consistently employ it in vv. 2, 4, 7. In fact we discover immediately that there is a series of passages in which he does not. In these he consistently and invariably uses *Elohim*, as does the document E throughout Genesis ; and where these clauses with *Elohim* are simply taken out of the context and placed side by side, we discover that they make, in the order found, a continuous, independent and consistent narrative, nearly complete. At the same time the portions left behind make another equally independent, complete and consistent narrative, each of the two having its own point of view, and its own characteristics of language and style. In short the phenomena themselves of the text, not the *a priori* assumptions of criticism, compel a documentary analysis.

Vv. 1 and 6 obviously belong with vv. 10ff. (E), not merely because of "*Elohim*," but because vs. 13 refers to vs. 6, and in vs. 1 we have Jethro (so in E *passim*) instead of Hobab (J) as Moses' father-in-law, and "Horeb" (see references) instead of "Sinai" (so J *passim*). Vs. 4 is clearly composed partly of each. The means of determining each element are readily afforded by the references. Throughout E in Genesis we have a large number of theophanies in which the formula of address here employed is used with such regularity as to be thoroughly characteristic. Outside this document it does not appear. The fullest example is Gen. xlvi. 2, 3a, which shows an exact parallel to vs. 4b *when connected with 6a,* "And he said" etc. Again in E God never "appears" to men, as in J ; but either comes to them in a vision of the night" (Gen. xx. 3, etc.), or "calls to them out of heaven" (Gen. xxi. 17 ; xxii. 11, etc.) ; in Ex. xix. 3 he "calls to Moses" from the mount of God as here. Concrete and anthropomorphic representations are studiously avoided. The clause "out of the midst of the bush" which is identical with vs. 2a, is therefore probably not from E. If anything, this document would have had " out of the mountain " which Rje might have altered to agree with 2a. But with the clause, " And God called unto him, and said, Moses, Moses. And he said Here am I," we have all that we have any right to attribute to E in vv. 2-5. and this with vv. 1, 6, 9-14 makes the story of E practically complete. In like manner beginning with J, we might reverse the process. Vv. 7f. can be shown by reference to I : 11; Gen. xi. 5; xviii. 21 ; ch. xiii. 5, etc., to be characteristic of J, and are completely paralleled by vv. 9f. Vs. 2, inseparable from 3, 4a is referred to by Dt. xxxiii. 16 (J) and the theophany in fire is characteristic of J (Gen. xv. 17; Ex. xix. 18). Vs. 5 has but one counterpart in the Old-Testament, Jos. v. 15 (J). The scene however cannot be the " mount of God " (see above, p. 10) but the road-side, after Moses has left " the lodging-place " (iv. 24-26). The " holy ground," vs. 5, is therefore perhaps to be identified with the sanctuary of this well-known place (cf. Gen. xlii. 27). Moses " turns aside " *from the way.* The rod in his hand (iv. 2) is a wayfarer's staff.*

Vv. 9-15 are clearly uniform (see, however, note on vs. 15), vv. 9f. (=7f.) directing Moses to demand from Pharaoh the release of Israel ; and with this agree vv. 19, 20 (?), 21f. But in vv. 16-18 there is not only a second message to Israel and to Pharaoh of similar tenor with the first, but the point of view is different. If Israel at their leave-taking are to " spoil the Egyptians " (vv. 21f.) then all thought of return from the wilderness is excluded from the outset. True, the jewels and raiment are not demanded as a right. They are really " borrowed "; for it is not by fear, but by " favor " (vs. 21 ; cf. xi. 3 ; xii. 36) that they are obtained. Hence also *women ask* them. The Egyptians expect them to be returned; but the borrowers have no such expectation, for they regard them as " spoil." The standard of morality here may not be high, but doubtless in the writer's eyes the action is simple justice. But in combination with vs. 18 this story takes the aspect more of deliberate fraud than of open war, a fraud which cannot even be excused as the necessary resort of weakness. The sacrifice in the wilderness is a dishonest pretense, and quite unnecessary if *release* was the real demand, and miraculous compulsion the means of securing it. If, however, we separate vv. 16-18 from their environment and connect them with vv. 7f. to which they linguistically correspond (cf. " appeared "; " bring up "—vv. 10-12 " bring forth ";—" affliction "—vs. 9 " oppression ,"—" land flowing with milk

---

* In Art. I. the traces of J in iii. 2ff. are referred to Rje ; a more thorough study of the passage, however, leads me to the above result.

and honey ") there is no deception practiced. Yahweh indeed promises
to " bring them up," but does not say how. The first step is that Moses
and the elders shall go to Pharaoh and *in good faith* make the request
of vs. 18. What the result will be remains to be seen. The proof that
this is not the same as the demand of vv. 9-11 for *release*, is found in
ch. v. vv. 1f. 4, in contrast with vv. 3 and 5ff. Here vs. 3 carries out
verbatim the direction of iii. 18, and the antecedent of the pronominal
subject is accordingly Moses *and the elders*. The result (vv. 5ff.)
is increased " affliction " by the " taskmasters " (i. 11 ; iii. 7). Strictly
parallel to this in vv. 1f. 4 is another demand, probably for full release
(see note *in loc.*), by Moses *and Aaron*. It is abruptly terminated by
the expulsion of the petitioners (vs. 4). The linguistic marks of iii. 16-18
are quite sufficient, as we saw, to characterize this element as J's : but
independently it is possible to positively determine the E authorship of vv.
21f. Throughout J the people are always and consistently represented
as dwelling by themselves in the land of Goshen (cf. e. g. viii. 22 ;
ix. 26). In E on the contrary they live intermingled with the Egyptians
(x. 23). It is the latter condition which is very strikingly set forth in iii.
21f. and the connected passages. Under the conditions presupposed in
J the action they describe would in fact be impossible.

In ch. iv. I have modified the analysis presented in Art I. and must
therefore present somewhat more fully than would otherwise be necessary the grounds of the present analysis. Vv. 1-16 present. so far as I
can now see, no real break in the uniformity of thought save at vs. 14b
(see below p. 2). Only after the anger of Yahweh was kindled
against Moses " (vs. 14a) we do not expect the interview to close with
the honor conferred in vs. 16. We expect rather something like the
utterance repeatedly referred to in Deut., that " Yahweh sware in anger,
Thou shalt indeed bring up this people unto the land which I give them,
but thou thyself shalt not go in thither, only thou shalt see it with thine
eyes, but thou shalt not go in thither " (cf. Dt. xxxiv. 4 and i. 37 ; iv. 21 ;
xxxi. 3). The datum is wanting in what remains to us of JE, and there
is no more probable place for its insertion than after iv. 16. But the
uniformity of vv. 1 16 makes the inappropriateness of vs. 17 in its present connection only the more striking (see above p. 15).

Vv. 10-14a are so remarkably characteristic of J in language and style
(see references and cf. the use of " Levite," vs. 14a, as=priest with ii. 1)
as to leave no question of their relation to J ; but I formerly assigned
vv. 1-9 to E on grounds which indeed still appear to me to have some
weight, especially the reference in vii. 15 (Rje; see note *in loc.*); the
phrase in vs. 6b " leprous as snow " (cf. Nu. xii. 10. E) ; and the harsh-

ness of vs. 1. after iii. 18a. The clause in vs. 6b, however, is far from decisive, as the expression is such as might be found in both documents, and the relation of vs. 1 to iii. 18a is perhaps also inconclusive. If not, the clause iii 18a*a* may be assigned to E. At present therefore, it seems to me that the arguments in favor of iv. 1-9 as J's predominate. To this result I have been brought mainly by the following considerations. 1⁰ The principal objection to J as author disappears with the recognition that the scene need not be Horeb, *i. e.* anterior to vv. 19–26; nor need the rod, vs. 2, be the shepherd's crook; but the scene is at some place between "the lodging-place" and Goshen, whither Moses has turned aside (iii. 3) with his *wayfarer's* staff in hand, attracted by the unusual sight of the blazing thicket. 2⁰ On the positive side it should be considered that protracted arguments between Yahweh and Moses, are common in J, but are incongruous with E's religious conceptions. A more cogent argument is furnished by vs. 17, certainly E. Here "the signs" unquestionably mean the plagues of Egypt, wrought invariably in E by "the rod of God." But if vv. 1–9 had preceded vs. 17 as they now do, it would have been necessary for the author to distinguish in some way "the signs" of vs. 17 from "the signs" of vv. 1–9. As the latter passage now reads it certainly conveys the impression (Wellhausen, *Comp.* p. 72) that no other "signs" are entrusted to Moses than those to be worked before the people (in J Yahweh inflicts the plagues without Moses' intervention). On the contrary vs. 17 seems to know none but those shown before Pharaoh. It is really necessary therefore to assign vs. 17 and vv. 1–9 to different authors. Finally the duplication of the miracle of the water changed to blood is thus avoided (see text of vii. 14–25). I am glad thus to be able at length to coincide here with the unanimous verdict of criticism.

The assignment of vs. 18 to E, 19, 20a to J requires no further justification than the references and the grounds already noted. Vs. 20b follows of course upon vs. 18; cf. vs. 17. On vv. 21–23 see note *in loc.* Vv. 24–26 are most incongruous in their present position, but are easily seen to be from J (cf. Gen. xlii. 27), and when the theophany of iii. 2ff. is restored to its true position after them, much of their strangeness disappears. To the same narrative must belong vv. 29–31 (cf. iii. 16–18 and refs.). Only in iv. 27 is there a phrase undeniably indicative of E, and this verse again seems to be connected with vs. 14b. Moreover the motive given by Moses for his return in vs. 18 is more natural if he is in reality sent to meet his "brother" Aaron. Finally v. 1, 4, with its introduction of Aaron as Moses' coadjutor suggests that E also had some account of the association of Aaron with Moses in the call, and this is made positive by Jos. xxiv. 5 (E). Vs. 14b accordingly, whose connection with the context is at least loose, if not disturbing, 27, and 28, whose connection with 27 is closer than with 29, may be reckoned fragments of E's parallel to the main account in vv. 14ff.

A much easier analysis of iv. 13–17, 27–31 is that advocated by so excellent an authority as Cornill, who settles the whole difficulty by the sweeping declaration,* "iv. 13-16 and 27, 28 are manifestly interpolated, and 29, 30 worked over, by Rp." But we have strong prejudices against a wholesale process of this kind. Rp is admittedly not a composer but a compiler, extremely averse to composition on his own account, and not disposed to alter JE except where it comes in contact and conflict with P. There is no trace of P² in chh. iii-v and no motive for Rp to interpolate. Rje might have been tempted to insert something to introduce Aaron before ch. v; but Rp had this whole story in a much better form and better place for his purposes in vi. 10–12, 28ff. (P²). Moreover the motive of iv. 13–16 is not redactional. It is not a patch applied for the purpose of holding together more or less discrepant material nor has it a didactic motive. It manifests the religious archæological motive of J. Whence comes the idea that Moses is not a speaker, and hence must have an interpreter to the people?—"Manifestly" it serves to account for the interpretative function of the *priesthood.* "The priest's lips keep the Torah," they are the authorized custodians and interpreters of the law (cf. Dt. xxiv. 8; xxxiii. 10; Mal. ii. 7). The association of "Aaron the Levite" with Moses as his "spokesman to the people" is J's ætiology of this institution. The relation of vi. 10-12, 28ff. to iv. 13ff. is unmistakable. They cannot be independent. But assuredly iv. 13ff. is not derived from vi. 10ff.! P² did not originate an ætiological explanation of a priestly function, and of his own motive attribute "uncircumcision of lip" to Moses. Then he found it in JE (cf. vi. 12 vii. 2, where the datum of iv. 10 is taken without regard to its ætiological significance, as a mere historical fact). Rje again did not originate it, for he does not add *new* traits, but simply adjusts his material. E has a different account of the institution, committing the law to "judges." Only J remains, and J is just the one of whom, because of his semi-priestly interest (cf. xix. 22 J) and his ætiological method, we should expect it.

Finally iv. 10 is universally admitted to be positively J's. For what purpose then is the statement there made of Moses' incapacity for speech, unless the writer was intending to introduce the story of Aaron as

---

* *Einleitung,* Freiburg, 1892, p. 84.

"spokesman to the people?" Vv. 13ff. are therefore indispensable to 10ff.

The passage is an important one, as by its rejection it becomes possible to suggest as a probability * that the North Israelite character of Aaron is unknown to J. But we may expect the same fate for this suggestion as for the similar, but now rejected idea of Meyer and Stade in regard to the character of Joshua.

(E) Now Moses was keeping the flock of ¹Jethro his **3** father-in-law, the priest of Midian,† and he led the flock to the back of the wilderness, and came to the mountain of God, **(J)** unto ²Horeb. **And the angel of Yahweh appeared** 2 **unto him ³in a flame of fire out of the midst of a bush: and he looked, and, behold, the bush burned with fire, and the bush was not consumed. And Moses** 3 **said, 'I will turn aside now, and see this great sight, why the bush is not burnt. And when Yahweh saw** 4 **(E) that he turned aside to see, ⁵**God called unto him out of the midst of the bush† and said, Moses, Moses. And he said, **(J) Here am I. ⁶And he said, Draw not nigh hither:** 5

¹Ct 2 : 18 ; Nu. 10 : 29 ; Jud. 4 : 11. ²17 : 6 ; 33 : 6 ; 4 : 27 ; 18 : 5. ³Gen. 15 : 17 ; ch. 19 : 18 ; Dt. 33 : 16. ⁴Jud. 14 : 8. ⁵Gen. 22 : 1, 7, 11 ; 46 : 2 ; ch. 19 : 3. ⁶Jos. 5 : 15.

* Cornill, *Einleitung*, p. 51.

† For the discussion of the names given to Moses' father-in-law, see above (note on ii. 18). As the "priest of Midian" only appears twice in E, and in both cases in a context worked over by Rje, it seems more probable that it is a harmonistic interpolation of Rje than that Moses' father-in-law should have been "priest of Midian" in both J and E. In thus identifying Jethro with the priest of ii. 16ff. he would of course remove the discrepant name "Hobab" in ii. 16, though he let it stand in Num. x. 19 and Jud. iv. 11.

‡ The clause "out of the midst of the bush" might be a fragment of J, but is more likely to have been inserted by Rje to make vs. 4 correspond with vs. 2a. It is superfluous in either J or E. In this verse it should be observed that the Hebrew has, "*And* Yahweh saw . . . *and* God called"; not, "*when* Yahweh saw," etc. So in vs. 6 "moreover" is simply supplied by the translators to avoid the awkwardness of the two consecutive beginnings "And he said." Throughout the book allowance must be made for the looseness of Hebrew construction which readily lends itself to the style of compilation discovered by critics.

put off thy shoes from off thy feet, for the place whereon thou standest is holy ground.

6   (E)   Moreover he said. I [7]am the God of thy father, the God of Abraham, the God of Isaac, and the God of Jacob. And Moses hid his face ; for he was afraid to look upon God.

7 (J)[. .]**And Yahweh said, I have surely seen the [8]affliction of my people which are in Egypt, and I have heard their cry by reason of their taskmasters; for I**

8 **know their sorrows; and I am [9]come down to deliver them out of the hand of the Egyptians, and to bring them up out of that land unto a good land and a large, (Rd)unto a [10]land flowing with milk and honey;** unto the place of the Canaanite, and the Hittite, and the Amorite, and the Perizzite, and the Hivite, and the Jebusite.*

9   (E)   [11]And now, behold, the cry of the children of Israel is come unto me : moreover I have seen the oppression

10 wherewith the Egyptians oppress them. Come now therefore, and I will send thee unto Pharaoh, that thou mayest bring forth my people the children of Israel out of Egypt.

11 [12]And Moses said unto God, Who am I, that I should go unto Pharaoh, and that I should bring forth the children of

12 Israel out of Egypt ? And he said, Certainly I [13]will be with thee ; and this shall be the token unto thee, that I have sent thee : when thou hast brought forth the people out of Egypt,

13 [14]ye shall serve God upon this mountain. And Moses said unto God, Behold, when I come unto the children of Israel, and shall say unto them, [15]The God of your fathers hath sent me unto you ; and they shall say to me, What is his name ?

14 what shall I say unto them ? And God said unto Moses, I AM THAT I AM: and he said, Thus shalt thou say unto the chil-

---

[7]Vs. 13. [8]1 , 11f. vs. 17 ; 4 : 31 ; Gen. 16 : 11; 20 : 32. [9]Gen. 11 : 5 ; 18 : 21. [10]vs. 17 ; 13 : 5 ; 33 : 3 ; Num. 11 : 27; 14 : 8 ; 16 : 14; Jos. 5 : 6. [11]Cf. 6 : 2ff. [12]6 : 12. [13]Gen. 28 : 20 ; 46 : 4 [14]3 : 1 ; 24 : 5. [15]vs. 6.

---

* A common form of interpolation is the enlargement or introduction of the list of seven Canaanite peoples. It seems to be later than the union of J and E (cf. Gen. x. 16 ff ; xv. 19 ff ; Ex. xxiii. 23 and references above) and is probably from the hand of Rd. It is recognizable as an interpolation by its frequent interruption of the connection.

(Rd) dren of Israel, I AM hath sent me unto you.* And God 15
said moreover unto Moses, Thus shalt thou say unto the children of Israel,
Yahweh, the God of your fathers, the God of Abraham, the God of Isaac,
and the God of Jacob, hath sent me unto you: this is my name for ever,
and this is ¹⁶my memorial unto all generations.†

(J) **¹⁷Go, and gather the elders of Israel together,** 16
and say unto them, Yahweh the God of your fathers,
the God of Abraham, of Isaac, and of Jacob, hath ap-
peared unto me, saying, I have surely visited you,
and [seen] that which is done to you in Egypt: and I 17
have said, I will bring you up out of the affliction of
(Rd) **Egypt** unto the land of the Canaanite, and the Hittite, and the
(J) Amorite, and the Perizzite, and the Hivite, and the Jebusite,‡ **unto a**
land flowing with milk and honey. **¹⁸And they shall** 18
hearken to thy voice: **¹⁹and thou shalt come, thou and**
the elders of Israel, unto the king of Egypt, and ye
shall say unto him, **²⁰Yahweh, the God of the Hebrews,**
hath met with us: and now let us go, we pray thee,
three days' journey into the wilderness, that we may
sacrifice to Yahweh our God.

(E) ²¹And I know that the king of Egypt will not ²²give 19
you leave to go, ²³no, not by a mighty hand. ²⁴And I will put 20

¹⁴12 : 42 ; 13 : 9 . ¹⁷Vs. 7f ; 4 : 20ff. ¹⁻4 : 31 ; cf. 6 : 9. ¹⁸5 : 3. ²⁰5 : 3 ; 7 : 16 ; 9 : 1, 13 ; 10 : 3.
²¹9 : 30. ²²Gen. 20 : 6 ; 31 : 7 ; Nu. 20 : 21 : 22 : 13. ²³Cf. 6 : 1 ; 11 : 9. ²⁴11 : 1 ; Dt. 34 : 11f.

* From this point on the name Yahweh, which has of course hitherto been
avoided in the document E, is freely employed by the Ephraimite writer.
However, the criterion is by no means wholly lost; for in the most obviously
original and archaic parts of the document, and particularly in stereotyped expressions like "rod of God," "mount of God," "angel of God," the use of
Elohim and *ha-Elohim* is still continued. The facts can scarcely be accounted
for on any other supposition than that *Elohim* or *ha-Elohim* was the divine
name habitually employed in E's source, which E of course left as he found it
previous to Ex. iii. and *usually* left as he found it thereafter. But when writing
de suo, or freely reproducing his source, he employs Yahweh. In *these* portions
of the E document henceforth the divine name ceases to be a criterion. The
larger part, however, is still Elohistic in the strict sense.

† Vs. 15 is generally attributed to Rd. Its linguistic features ("generations"), its superfluous, reiterative character, and its solicitude for the instruction of posterity (cf. xii. 24, 26; xiii. 8f, etc.), support this view.

‡ See note on vs. 8.

forth my hand, and smite Egypt with all my wonders which
I will do in the midst thereof: and after that he will let you
21 go.*   23.And I will give this people favor in the sight of
the Egyptians: and it shall come to pass, that, when ye go,
22 ye shall not go empty: but every woman shall ask of her
neighbor, and of her that sojourneth in her house, jewels
of silver, and jewels of gold, and raiment: and ye shall put
them upon your sons, and upon your daughters; and ye
4 (J) shall spoil the Egyptians. **And Moses answered and
said, ¹But, ²behold, they will not believe me, nor
hearken unto my voice: for they will say, Yahweh
hath not appeared unto thee. And Yahweh said unto
2 him, What is that in thine hand? And he said, A
3 rod. And he said, Cast it on the ground. And he
cast it on the ground, and it became a ³serpent; and
Moses fled from before it. And Yahweh said unto
4 Moses, Put forth thine hand, and take it by the tail:
(and he put forth his hand, and laid hold of it, and it
became a rod in his hand:) that they may believe ⁴that
5 Yahweh the God of their fathers, the God of Abraham, the God of Isaac, and the God of Jacob, hath
6 ⁵appeared unto thee. And Yahweh said furthermore
unto him, Put now thine hand into thy bosom. And
he put his hand into his bosom: and when he took it
out, behold, his hand was ⁶leprous, as [white as]
7 snow. And he said, Put thine hand into thy bosom
again. (And he put his hand into his bosom again;
and when he took it out of his bosom, behold, it was
8 ⁷turned again as his [other] flesh.) And it shall come
to pass, if they will not believe thee, neither hearken
to the voice of the first sign, that they will believe
9 the voice of the latter sign. And it shall come to**

¹ ... d. ... cf. ... ... ² ... ³Cf. 7: 9ff. ⁴ ... 16. ⁵ ... . ⁶Num ... 10: 11.
Kgs ... : ... ⁷2 Kgs ... : 10: 14

* Vs. 19b contradicts vi. 1 and xii. 9 and is therefore treated as a gloss. We
may however (with Ewald) conjecture *im-lo* instead of *we-lo* (so LXX. and
Vulg.), "except" instead of "no, not," or even, with Jül. and others, reject vv.
19f *in tote*, as an anticipatory interpolation; cf. iv. 21-23.

pass, if they will not believe even these two signs,
neither hearken unto thy voice, that thou shalt take
of the water of the river, and pour it upon the dry
land: ⁸and the water which thou takest out of the
river shall become blood upon the dry land.

⁹And Moses said unto Yahweh, ¹⁰Oh Lord, I am not 10
eloquent, neither heretofore, nor ¹¹since thou hast
spoken unto thy servant: for I am slow of speech, and
of a slow tongue. And Yahweh said unto him, Who 11
hath made man's mouth? or who maketh [a man]
dumb, or deaf, or seeing, or blind? is it not I, Yahweh? 12
Now therefore go, and I will be with thy mouth, and 12
teach thee what thou shalt speak. And he said Oh 13
Lord, send, I pray thee, by the hand of him ¹²whom
thou wilt send. And the anger of Yahweh was 14
kindled against Moses, and he said, ¹³Is there not
Aaron thy brother the Levite? I know that he can
(E) speak well. [. . .]—And also, behold, he ¹⁴cometh
forth to meet thee : and when he seeth thee, he will be glad
(J) in his heart.*—And thou shalt speak unto him, 15
and put the words in his mouth : ¹⁵ and I will be with
thy mouth, and with his mouth, and will teach you
what ye shall do. ¹⁶And he shall be thy spokesman 16
unto the people : and it shall come to pass, that he
shall be to thee a mouth, and thou shalt be to him

---

*⁷: 20.   ⁹Cf. t: 10–12, 28 –7: 7.   ¹⁰Vs. 13 ; Gen. 43 : 20.   ¹¹3: 18, etc. 5: 23 ; 9: 24; Gen.
24 : 5.   ¹²33 : 14.   ¹³Gen. 13 : 9 : 37 : 13.   ¹⁴Vs 27.   ¹⁵Vs 12.   ¹⁶Cf. 7 : 11.

* Insert after iii. 14.

† "Yahweh" would be inappropriate here. The writer has in mind the
general relation of the *priest* ("Levite" here is not a tribal term; cf. Is. lxvi.
21.) to his authority (Dt. xvii. 9; xxiv. 8; Jer. xviii. 18, etc.), hence the
generic "Elohim," "as *his God* is to the priest." The special exaltation of
prophetism which Dillmann and others discover in this passage is not really
present. As the law-giver, Moses is to the priest "as God," and the "Levite,"
i. e. priest, accordingly, as interpreter of the law, is Moses' spokesman to the
people. As to *Elohim* in J cf. Gen. iii. 1ff.; vi. 1ff.; xxxii. 28 ; xliv. 16. As
to the omission of J material at this point, and transposition of that contained
in iii. 2–iv. 16 for combination with E, see Analysis, p. 10.

17 **(E) as God.†** [. . .] [17] And thou shalt take in thine hand
this rod, wherewith thou shalt do the signs.

18   And Moses went and returned to Jethro his father-in-law,
and said unto him, Let me go, I pray thee, and return unto
my [18] brethren which are in Egypt, and see whether they be yet

19 **(J)** alive. And Jethro said to Moses, Go in peace. —**And
Yahweh said unto Moses in Midian, Go, return
into Egypt: for [19] all the men are dead which sought**

20 **thy life. And Moses took his wife and his [20] sons ***
**and set them upon an ass, and he returned to the
(E) land of Egypt:** [21] and Moses took the rod of God in

21 his hand. [. . .] —And Yahweh said unto Moses, When
thou goest back into Egypt, see that thou do before Pharaoh all the [22] wonders which I have put in thine hand: but I
will [23] harden his heart, and he will not let the people go.—

22 **(Rd)** And thou shalt say unto Pharaoh, Thus saith Yahweh, [24] Israel is

23 my son, my firstborn: and I have said unto thee, Let my son go, that he
may serve me; and thou hast refused to let him go: behold, I will slay thy

24 **(J)** son, thy firstborn.†   **And it came to pass on the way
[25] at the lodging-place, that Yahweh met him, and**

25 **[26] sought to kill him. Then Zipporah took a [27] flint,
and cut off the foreskin of her son, and cast it at his
[28] feet; and she said, Surely a bridegroom of blood art**

26 **thou to me. So he let him alone. Then she said, A**

---

[17] Vv. 1-9, 20b. [18] Vs. 14b. [19] 2 : 15, 23a. [20] Vs. 25 ; 2 : 22 ; Ct. 18 : 3f. [21] Vs. 17. [22]
1.f. [23] 10 : 20, 27. [24] Dt. 1 : 31 ; 8 : 5. [25] Gen. 42 : 27 ; 43 : 21. [26] Gen. 32 : 24. [27] Jos. 5 : 2.
[28] Jud. 3 : 24 ; 1 Sam. 24 : 3 ; Is. 7 : 20.

* The plural termination seems from ii. 22 and vs. 25 to be a harmonistic
addition of Rje, necessitated by xviii. 3f.

† Vv. 21–23 are assigned by many critics as a whole to Deuteronomic interpolation, and the didactic or apologetic motive is indeed apparent in vv. 22f.
Moreover this command is never carried out, and is obviously a premature
anticipation of the result of Moses' mission. The whole passage rather disturbs
than helps the connection; but we are at a loss to account for a gratuitous
interpolation. More probably we should with Dillmann regard the substance
of vs. 21 as E's, removed from after iii. 22 (note " when thou goest back ").
Vv. 22f. were then added to afford a better connection.

bridegroom of blood [art thou] because of the circumcision—[. . .]*

(E) And Yahweh said to [29]Aaron, Go into the wilder- 27
ness to meet Moses. And he went, and met him in the
[31]mountain of God, and kissed him. And Moses told Aaron 28
all the words of Yahweh wherewith he had sent him, and [31]all
(J) the signs wherewith he had charged him. [32]**And Moses** 29
and Aaron went and gathered together all the elders
of the children of Israel: and Aaron† **spake all the** 30
words which Yahweh had spoken unto **Moses and** [33]**did**
the signs in the sight of the people. [34]**And the people** 31
believed: [35]**and when they heard that Yahweh had**
[36]**visited the children of Israel, and that he had seen**
their affliction, then they [37]**bowed their heads and wor-**
shipped.

[29]Jos. 24 : 5. [30]3 : 1 ; 18 : 5 etc. [31]Vv. 1-9. [32]3 : 16f. ; 4 : 16. [33]Vv. 1-9. [34]Vv. 1, 5, 3f. ;
ct. 6 : 9. [35]3 : 7f., 16f. [36]Gen. 21 : 1 ; (50 : 25). [37]Gen. 24 : 26, 48 ; Ex. 12 : 27.

  * The story of vv. 24-26, like the similar one of Gen. xxxii. 24-32 and that of
vv. 10-16, is ætiological. The rite of infant circumcision is here deduced from
the ancient Semitic practice of bridegroom circumcision; cf. Gen. xxxiv.
Hence the expression "bridegroom of blood." The act of Zipporah, vs. 25,
symbolizes substitution. Translate with margin, "made it touch his feet," i. e.
the corresponding part of Moses' person (see refs.). Moses is therefore uncircumcised (cf. vi. 12), though this was an Egyptian practice. In Jos. v. 2f. 8f.
(E's) we have the same representation of the uncircumcision of Israel in Egypt;
for "the reproach of Egypt" can have no other sense. The "flint knives"
confirm also the Egyptian origin of the rite.

  † In. vs. 30 Rje seems to have interposed slightly in behalf of a clearer division of labor between Moses and Aaron. The sense is not altered, though the
reader is left in doubt as to whether Moses or Aaron "did the signs." The
effort on the part of Rp to bring Aaron into greater prominence is very apparent in the succeeding chh.; but from J's usual practice it is probable that both
verbs of vs. 30 had the same construction as those of vs. 29. If the present
grammatical sense of vs. 30b is really intentional, it must be due to the
influence of vs. 28; but cf. vs. 17.

3. Chh. v. 1–vii. 7.　The Appeal to Pharaoh and (Second) Commission of Moses and Aaron.

ANALYSIS.

Moses and Aaron make their demand upon Pharaoh, but meet refusal. Additional burdens are laid upon the people. Compelled to make bricks without straw they protest in vain, and at length complain bitterly to Moses. The latter returns to Yahweh for further instructions and is reassured, v. 1–vi. 1. God reveals himself to Moses as Yahweh, a name by which hitherto he has not been known, and sends him to the oppressed children of Israel to announce deliverance, and that Yahweh will bring them to the land he covenanted to give to the patriarchs. In bitterness of spirit they refuse to believe the good news; vi. 2–9. Yahweh thereupon sends Moses to Pharaoh to demand Israel's release, but Moses objects his inability to speak; vv. 10–12. At this point is introduced a genealogical table, which at the beginning appears to be that of all the *beni-Israel*, but turns out to be that of Levi only, and is so described in vs. 25b. In vv. 26f. the author returns to the point of departure, in vv. 28–30 reiterating the statement interrupted by the genealogy; vv. 13–30. Yahweh appoints Aaron to be Moses' spokesman *to Pharaoh*, and promises that he will harden Pharaoh's heart, but compel submission by signs and wonders, bringing forth the " hosts " of Israel with great judgments. Moses and Aaron do as commanded. The age of Moses and Aaron; vii. 1–6.

The obliviousness of the writer of vi. 2–vii. 6 to all that has preceded in chh. iii.–v. is palpable. Not only is their narrative completely paralleled, but the author of ch. vi. seems totally unaware of the preceding account. The revelation of the divine Name not only ignores the previous revelation of iii. 10ff., but expressly presents the name Yahweh as hitherto unknown. No allusion is made to the previous promise, still unfulfilled, in the message given to Moses for Israel. In vv. 10–12 Moses is sent to Pharaoh to make the same demand already made and contemptuously refused in ch. v. Yet Moses makes no mention that Pharaoh has already refused, and even expelled him from his presence; but objects his own incapacity to speak, though this objection had already been doubly met by Yahweh in iv. 10–16, and though when previously urged it had excited the anger of Yahweh. Vv. 13ff. hereupon interrupt in extraordinary fashion the connection of the story, to make room for a genealogical table explaining who this Moses and Aaron are, whose history we have been following already for a period of more than 80 years according to the received chronology. At last the thread of the story is most laboriously and awkwardly resumed in vv. 26–30. Ch. vii. 1–7 brings us to the point where we were already in ch. v., where Pharaoh has refused, and the divine compulsion begins.

It is difficult to conceive how a passage of equal length could contain more, or more convincing proofs of being wholly out of joint with its context and in itself. Again, it is not theory but the state of the text which demands some classification of these chaotic elements, and once more it is the recognition of independent sources which furnishes the only adequate solution.

In ch. v we have already seen that vv. 1f. 4 form a duplicate account of the interview with Pharaoh related in vv. 3, 5ff. The latter belongs with iii. 16–18 (J) and is inseparable from the rest of the chapter (cf. vv. 8, 17, etc.) Brief as is this E element, nothing is wanting to its completeness, with the possible exception of vi. 1 (see note *in loc.*) The rest of ch. v. on the other hand shows all the characteristics of J's narrative, and might be assigned to that document on independent grounds. Thus we come here again upon the "taskmasters," i. 11 : iii. 7 : the policy of breaking the spirit of the people by forced labor, i. 10ff. ; Israel a people by themselves, vs. 12 ; brickmaking as their occupation, i. 11, 14. In E on the contrary, Israel's bondage is conceived as of a domestic character (iii. 21ff.) like that of Joseph. For linguistic and stylistic affinity, see refs.

A totally different style appears in vi. 2–vii. 7. Here we find not a trace of allusion to the preceding narrative of JE, or of resemblance to its style. On the contrary vi. 2ff. carries us back to ii. 23b–25, repeating its language in vs. 5, and ignoring all that intervenes. All the allusions (cf. *e. g.*, vv. 4 and 8 with Gen. xvii. 8 : xxviii. 4 ; xxxv. 11f.) are to passages of the priestly document, and the use of *El-Shaddai* and *Elohim*, which up to this point has been universal in P, is explained in vs. 3. From this point on moreover, these names are in the story to which they belong uniformly *superseded* by "Yahweh." There can accordingly be no reasonable doubt of the sense in which the statement of vi. 2 should be understood, nor of the document to which vi. 2–vii. 7 must be assigned. The disorder of the text in vv. 13–30 is the only point requiring elucidation.

In its present position the genealogy appears as an afterthought. The writer is about to say that Yahweh appointed Moses' brother Aaron to be his prophet (cf. vv. 28 ff. ; vii. 1.) when he is interrupted to explain who " *this* Moses and Aaron " are (vv. 26f.). For this purpose vv. 2–7 are briefly recapitulated in vs. 13 *and the name of Aaron is inserted.*

Vs. 13 is necessary to vv. 26f. Vv. 14f., which are singularly inappropriate in the pedigree of Moses and Aaron, are taken bodily from Gen. xlvi. 9f. and also depend upon vs. 13 ("*their* fathers"). But vs. 16 makes a new beginning and affords us a pedigree of Moses and Aaron according to the usual type of P title and all (see refs). Here, unlike vv. 14f., the ages are given, and the generations are brought down to the date of the Exodus (cf. vv. 14f. with Gen. xlvi. 9f.). Vs. 25b contains the colophon, and certifies that this is a genealogy of *Levi*, thus excluding vv. 14f. There is no reason whatever to question the genuineness of vv. 16-25. On the contrary they would be recognized as unmistakably from P² wherever found. Only their present position is impossible, and shown to be artificial by the elaborate patchwork of vv. 13-15, 26-30, which serve no other purpose than first to break the connection and then restore it again. On the other hand vv. 2ff., in accordance with all the previous structure of P², presuppose just such a genealogy of Levi as vv. 16-25; otherwise the elaborate system of dates from the creation down (cf. vii. 7; xii. 40f. and Gen. *passim*) is suddenly broken, and Moses and Aaron are ushered in unannounced. The conclusion is unavoidable that vv. 16-25 originally preceded vv. 2ff., probably following upon i. 7. The story of Moses' childhood and family relations in i. 15-ii. 23a is no doubt the occasion for the displacement.

---

5   **(E)** ¹And afterward ²Moses and Aaron came, and said
unto Pharaoh, Thus saith Yahweh, the God of Israel, Let my
   (Rje) people go, ³that they may hold a feast unto me in the wilder-
2 **(E)** ness.* And Pharaoh said, Who is Yahweh, that I should

* The last clause of vs. 1. is apparently harmonistic. Throughout E's narrative nothing is said of anything more or less between Pharaoh and Moses than the simple demand here made once for all: " Let my people go," which, when refused, is followed by stroke after stroke of the rod until granted. This is the demand Moses is commanded to make in iii. 10, 12. It is the demand Pharaoh actually accedes to. It is that which Israel undertakes to carry out from the outset. They are not unprepared to leave as in J, xii. 34f., 39, but on the contrary have supplied themselves with the portable " spoil " of the Egyptians and " the bones of Joseph." The latter are not supposed to be taken up for " a feast in the wilderness," but Canaan is the objective point from the beginning. We cannot suppose that Moses on his own responsibility changed the message to Pharaoh with which he was entrusted, and resorted to deceit; hence in the absence of anything to the contrary, we must assume that in E the demand made of Pharaoh was straightforward, as indicated by iii. 10f., 21f.

hearken unto his voice to let Israel go?   I know not Yahweh,
(J) and moreover, I will not let Israel go.[. . .]   **'And they*** 3
**said, The God of the Hebrews hath met with us: let
us go, we pray thee, three days' journey into the wilderness, and sacrifice unto Yahweh our God; lest he
⁵fall upon us with pestilence, or with the sword.**
(E) And the king of Egypt said unto them, Wherefore do ye, 4
⁶Moses and Aaron, loose the people from their works? get
(J) you unto your ⁷burdens. **And Pharaoh said, Behold,** 5
**⁸the people of the land are now many, and ye make
them rest from their burdens. And the same day** 6
Pharaoh commanded the ⁹taskmasters of the people,
and their officers,† **saying, Ye shall no móre give the peo-** 7
**ple straw to make ¹⁰brick, as heretofore: let them go
and gather straw for themselves. And the tale of the** 8
**bricks, which they did make heretofore, ye shall lay
upon them ; ye shall not diminish aught thereof: for
they be idle ; therefore they cry, saying, ¹¹Let us go
and sacrifice to our God. Let heavier work be laid** 9
**upon the men, that they may labour therein ; and let
them not regard ¹¹lying words. And the ⁹taskmasters** 10
of the people went out, and their officers, **and they spake to
the people, saying, Thus saith Pharaoh, I will not
give you straw. Go yourselves, get you straw where** 11
ye can find it: for naught of your work shall be di-

---

⁴3 : 18 ; 7 : 16 ; 8 : 27 ; 10 . 9. 25 ; 12 : 32 ; 15 : 22. ⁵4 : 24. ⁶Vs. 1. ⁷2 : 11. ⁸1 : 7ff. 20b.
⁹1 : 11 ; 3 : 7. ¹⁰1 : 14. ¹¹Vs. 3.

---

* *I. e.* Moses and the elders of Israel, cf. iii. 18. In vs. 20 the harmonistic
alteration here implied is made explicit by the insertion of " Aaron " to agree
with vv. 1 and 4. But if with most critics we reject " Aaron " in vv. 1 and 4
no adequate reason can be given for the alteration.

† The clause " and their officers " seems to be added for completeness' sake
in vv. 6 and 10. Hitherto in J we have heard only of " taskmasters " and it
is not explained until vs. 14 who these " officers " are. There they are introduced as Hebrews, and not. as in 6 and 10, apparently in alliance with the taskmasters, but beaten by them, and appealing to Pharaoh in vv. 15ff. as if they did
not realize that the command of vv. 6 and 10 had come from him. Previous to
vs. 14 therefore, the clause should probably be rejected.

12 minished. So the people were ¹²scattered abroad throughout all the land of Egypt to gather stubble
13 for straw. And the taskmasters were ¹³urgent, saying, Fulfil your works, [your] daily tasks, as when
14 there was straw. And the officers of the children of Israel, which Pharaoh's taskmasters had set over them, were beaten, and demanded, Wherefore have ye not fulfilled your task both yesterday, and to-day,
15 in making brick as heretofore? Then the officers of the children of Israel came and cried unto Pharaoh, saying, Wherefore dealest thou thus with thy ser-
16 vants? There is no straw given unto thy servants, and they say to us, Make brick: and, behold, thy servants are beaten; but the fault is in thine own
17 people. But he said, Ye are idle, ye are idle: ¹⁴there-
18 fore ye say, Let us go and sacrifice to Yahweh. Go therefore now, and work; for there shall no straw be given you, yet shall ye deliver the tale of bricks.
19 And the officers of the children of Israel did see that they were in evil case, when it was said, Ye shall not minish aught from your bricks, [your] daily tasks.
20 And they met Moses and Aaron*, who stood in the way,
21 as they came forth from Pharaoh: and they said unto them, ¹⁵Yahweh look upon you, and judge: because ye have made ¹⁶our savour to be abhorred in the eyes of Pharaoh, and in the eyes of his servants, to put
22 a sword in their hand to slay us. ¹⁷And Moses returned unto Yahweh, and said, Lord, wherefore hast thou evil entreated this people? why is it that thou
23 hast sent me? For since I came to Pharaoh to speak in thy name, he hath evil entreated this people; neither hast thou delivered thy people at all.

6   (E) ¹And Yahweh said unto Moses, Now shalt thou see what

¹²Gen. 11 : 8, 9 ; 40 : 7. ¹³Gen. 19 : 15 ; Jos. 10 : 13 ; 17 : 15. ¹⁴Vv. 3, 8. ¹⁵Gen. 16 : 5 ; 31 : ; 1 Sam. 24 : 12, 15. ¹⁶1 : 12 ; Gen. 34 : 30. ¹⁷Num. 11 ; 11f. 13 : 19f., 4 : 21.

* Cf. note on vs. 3.

I will do to Pharaoh : for [2]by a strong hand shall he let them go, and [2]by a strong hand shall he drive them out of his land.

(P) [3]*And God spake unto Moses, and said unto him, I am Yah-* 2
weh : and I appeared unto Abraham, unto Isaac, and unto Jacob, as 3
[4]*God Almighty, but by my name Yahweh I was not known to them.*
And I have also established my covenant with them, to give them the 4
land of Canaan, the land of their sojournings, wherein they so-
*journed.　*[5]*And moreover I have heard the groaning of the chil-* 5
dren of Israel, whom the Egyptians keep in bondage ; and I have
remembered my covenant.　Wherefore say unto the children of 6
Israel, I am Yahweh, and I will bring you out from under the
burdens of the Egyptians, and I will rid you out of their bondage,
and I will redeem you with a stretched out arm, and with great
judgments : and I will take you to me for a people, and I will be 7
to you a God : and ye shall know that I am Yahweh your God,
which bringeth you out from under the burdens of the Egyptians.
And I will bring you in unto the land, concerning which [6]*I lifted* 8
up my hand to give it to Abraham, to Isaac, and to Jacob ; and I
will give it you for an heritage : I am Yahweh.　And Moses 9
spake so unto the children of Israel : [7]*but they hearkened not unto*
Moses for anguish of spirit, and for cruel bondage.

[8]*And Yahweh spake unto Moses, saying, Go in, speak unto* 10-11
Pharaoh king of Egypt, that he let the children of Israel go out
of his land.　And Moses spake before Yahweh, saying, Behold, 12
the children of Israel have not hearkened unto me ; how then shall
(Rp) *Pharaoh hear me, who am of uncircumcised lips.　And Yah-* 13
weh spake unto Moses and unto Aaron, and gave them a charge unto the chil-
dren of Israel, and unto Pharaoh king of Egypt, to bring the children of
Israel out of the land of Egypt.

[9]*These are the heads of their fathers' houses : the sons of Reuben the first-* 14
born of Israel ; Hanoch, and Pallu, Hezron, and Carmi : these are the fam-
ilies of Reuben.　And the sons of Simeon : Jemuel, and Jamin, and Ohad, and 15
Jachin, and Zohar, and Shaul the son of a Canaanitish woman : these are
(P) *the families of Simeon.*＊—[10]*And†† these are the names of the* 16

[2]13 : 3, 9, 14 ; Num. 20 : 20.　[3]Cf. 3 : 1-6, 9-15.　[4]Gen. 17 : 1 ; 28 : 3 ; 35 : 11 ; 48 : 3.　[5]2 : 24.
[6]Gen. 17 : 8 ; 28 : 4 ; 35 : 11f. ; Nu. 14 : 30.　[7]Ct. 4 : 31.　[8]Cf. 4 : 10-16, and vv. 28-30.　[9]Cf.
Gen. 46 : 9f.　[10]Cf. 1 : 1 ; Gen. 10 : 1-7, 20, 31f. ; 36 : 9-30, 40-43 ; 6 : 8-27 etc.

＊ Supplementary redaction on basis of Gen. xlvi. 9f.　See Analysis.
†† Insert after 1. 5.　See Analysis, and Part II.

sons of Levi according to their generations ; Gershon, and Ko-
hath, and Merari : 11*and the years of the life of Levi were an*
17 *hundred thirty and seven years. The sons of Gershon ; Libni*
18 *and Shimei, according to their families. And the sons of Kohath ;*
Amram, and Izhar, and Hebron, and Uzziel : and the years of
19 *the life of Kohath were an hundred thirty and three years. And*
the sons of Merari ; Mahli and Mushi. These are the families of
20 *the Levites according to their generations. And Amram took him*
Jochebed his father's sister to wife ; and she bare him Aaron and
Moses : and the years of the life of Amram were an hundred and
21 *thirty and seven years. And the sons of Izhar; Korah, and Ne-*
22 *pheg, and Zichri. And the sons of Uzziel; Mishael, and Elza-*
23 *phan, and Sithri. And Aaron took him Elisheba, the daughter of*
Amminadab, the sister of Nahshon, to wife ; and she bare him
24 *Nadab and Abihu, Eleazar and Ithamar. And the sons of Ko-*
rah ; Assir, and Elkanah, and Abiasaph ; these are the families
25 *of the Korahites. And Eleazar Aaron's son took him one of the*
daughters of Putiel to wife ; and she bare him Phinehas. These
are the heads of the fathers' [houses] of the Levites according to
26 (Rp) *their families.—These are that Aaron and Moses, to whom Yahweh*
said, 12*Bring out the children of Israel from the land of Egypt according to*
27 *their hosts. These are they which spake to Pharaoh king of Egypt, to bring out*
the children of Israel from Egypt: these are that Moses and Aaron.
28   13*And it came to pass on the day when Yahweh spake unto Moses in the land*
29 *of Egypt, that Yahweh spake unto Moses, saying, I am Yahweh : speak thou*
30 *unto Pharaoh king of Egypt all that I speak unto thee. And Moses said before*
Yahweh, Behold, I am of uncircumcised lips, and how shall Pharaoh hearken
7 (P) *unto me?* * *And Yahweh said unto Moses, See,* 1*I have made*
thee a god to Pharaoh : and Aaron thy brother shall be thy prophet.
2   *Thou shalt speak all that I command thee : and Aaron thy*
brother shall speak unto Pharaoh, that he let the children of Israel
3   *go out of his land.* 2*And I will harden Pharaoh's heart, and*
4   *multiply my signs and my wonders in the land of Egypt. But*

11Cf. 7 : 7.   12Vs. 10.   13Cf. vv. 2 12.   1Cf. 4 : 16.   24 : 21 : 11 : 9f ; 14 : 4, 17 etc.

* A similar attempt to restore a broken connection by repetition of the
clauses preceding the point of rupture is observable in Gen. xiii. 3f., after the
thread of the narrative has been broken by the insertion of xii. 9-20. See
Genesis of Genesis, p. 121.

*Pharaoh will not hearken unto you, and I will lay my hand upon
Egypt, and bring forth my hosts, my people the children of Israel,
out of the land of Egypt by great judgments. And the Egyptians* 5
*shall know that I am Yahweh, when I stretch forth mine hand
upon Egypt, and bring out the children of Israel from among
them. And Moses and Aaron did so; as Yahweh commanded* 6
them, so did they. ⁸And Moses was fourscore years old, and 7
*Aaron fourscore and three years old, when they spake unto Pha-
raoh.*

———————◆———————

§ II.   Ex. vii. 8–xiii. 16.   The Plagues of Egypt.

Prolegomena.

The priestly writer relates the story in a series of five con-
tests of Moses and Aaron against the magicians of Pharaoh, in
which the advantage is more and more markedly on the side of
the former. No reason is given for this trial of strength
between Aaron and the sorcerers, except " that Yahweh's signs
and wonders may be multiplied, and the Egyptians may know
that he is Yahweh." To this end Yahweh hardens Pharaoh's
heart (vii. 3f.). It is simply assumed that Pharaoh will say,
" Shew a wonder for you " (vii. 8f.), and again tacitly assumed that
he did say so. Thereupon the series of " wonders " follows in
uninterrupted sequence. So mechanically uniform and laconic
is the series that there is nothing to show that the whole drama
extends over more than a single day, a single interview, or even
a single hour. The statement of Pharaoh's inflexibility after
one is followed immediately by the command to do the next.
In the first three the Egyptian sorcerers are able to parallel the
wonders of Aaron's rod. In the fourth they fail and acknowledge that " this is the finger of God." In the fifth they are
themselves attacked by the plague, and disappear in ignomin-
ious flight ; vii. 8–13, 19–22 in part ; viii. 5–7, 15–19 ; ix. 8–12 ;
ix. 9f. After the final discomfiture of the magicians Yahweh
himself interposes with directions to Moses to arrange for a

⁸6 : 16, 18, 20.

feast to be called the Passover, because Yahweh is now about to go through the land of Egypt smiting all the first-born, but will " pass over " the houses of the Hebrews. A sacred calendar is herewith begun, the year beginning with the time of this announcement. Directions are then given in minute detail for the observance of the Passover. The days of the month from the 10th to the 14th are to be occupied with preparations for the feast, which is to be eaten on the evening of the 14th in the manner prescribed ; xii. 1–14.—In addition a further period of seven days is to be observed from the 14th to the 21st of the month, in which no leaven shall be eaten, a " holy convocation " marking the first and seventh days. The 15th of the month, as the day on which Yahweh will bring " the hosts " of Israel out of Egypt, shall thus be commemorated forever and called the Feast of Unleavened Bread : xii. 15–20. Israel obeys, and Yahweh does according to his promise, and " brings out all the hosts of Yahweh " from the land of Egypt, at the end of 430 years, even the " self-same day " ; xii. 28, 40f. Afterward Yahweh gives to Moses and Aaron precise instructions as to who may participate in the Passover feast, and to Moses the law of consecration of the first-born.

In E also there is a series of five plagues, followed by the deliverance of Israel, except that here the death of the first-born is the fifth and final plague which breaks the obstinacy of Pharaoh, and not a separate divine intervention (xi. 1). Here too the rod plays even a more important part than in P, all the plagues (which here are really such, and not mere " wonders " as in P, vii. 9) being wrought by it, as directed in iv. 17. But the rod is by no means the rod of Aaron, as always in P, nor Moses' staff (iv. 1ff.), but " the rod of God," a special wonder-working rod given to Moses by God as the seal and power of his commission. It reappears later in the dividing of the Red Sea, smiting of the rock of Meribah, and defeat of Amalek. Again the narrative of E resembles that of P in its conciseness and the rapidity with which one stroke of the rod follows upon another until the climax. The necessary duration of the plague is the only time extension of the story. There is abso-

lutely no dialogue after Pharaoh's contemptuous refusal of the
demand of ch. v. All appeals to the eye alone. Stroke follows
stroke until Pharaoh yields, the greatest necessary interval of
time being implied in the fourth plague story, where "none rose
from his place for three days" (x. 23) ; vii. 15, 17 in part, 20 bc,
23 ; ix. 23-25 in part, 35 ; x. 12-15 in part, 20-23, 27. Before
the fifth and final plague, which will cause Pharaoh to "utterly
thrust them out" the people receive directions from Yahweh
through Moses to borrow from their neighbors gold, silver and
fine raiment. [The stroke falls], and Pharaoh calls for Moses
and Aaron and bids the people begone. In consequence of the
divine forewarning to ask jewels of silver and gold, and of
Yahweh's interposition to "give the people favor in the sight
of the Egyptians so that they let them have what they asked,"
Pharaoh's sudden edict of banishment finds the people laden
with the spoil of Egypt and ready to move in battle array ; xi.
1-3 ; xii. 3of. in part, 35f. There is no legislative material.

The main element of the narrative is J's. Here, however,
the representation bears a decided contrast to both P and E.
The series of plagues consists of six, culminating in the death
of the first-born as the seventh. But Aaron, who in P is the
prime agent in the execution of the " wonders," who in E drops
to the position of Moses' companion in the two interviews with
Pharaoh (v. 1f. and xii. 31), in J drops out of sight altogether.
(See note on " Aaron," viii. 8). Moses on the contrary, so far
from being a mere oracle to Aaron, as in P, or, as in E, a silent
wielder of the wonder-working rod, becomes here the ambassador plenipotentiary of Yahweh to Pharaoh. Nearly the whole
narrative consists of the long interviews of Moses with Pharaoh,
in which the vacillating monarch maintains first a stubborn
silence, then asks the intercession of Moses, resuming his
obstinacy when respite comes, then promises release and evades
his promise, then again repeats the same cycle of sullen silence,
temporary yielding, and evasion. Moses, divinely instructed,
goes to the royal audience chamber and announces in detail
what *Yahweh* will do if the demand of permission to sacrifice is
still refused. The infliction of the plague *by Yahweh* at the

time and in the manner predicted, and the immunity of Israel, is then fully described. Then follows the effect upon Pharaoh, of the three different kinds above mentioned, all coming, however, to the same result, that, " Pharaoh's heart was 'heavy' and he did not let the people go," whereupon Moses is again sent with heavier threats, until, after the king's second evasion (sixth refusal) and Moses' peremptory ultimatum, Pharaoh drives him out with the threat of death if he appears again. To this Moses replies " in hot anger," " Thou hast spoken well, I will see thy face no more," and proceeds to declare how Yahweh will now smite the first-born. Pharaoh's servants shall then come bowing down *to Moses* begging them to be gone, and after that they will go out ; vii. 14, 16f. in part, 21a, 24f.; viii. 1–3, 8–15a, 20–32 ; ix. 1–7, 13–21, 23b–35, in part ; x. 1–11, 13b, 14f. in part, 16–19, 24–26, 28f.; xi. 4–8. Moses then gives to Israel directions for the observance of a feast to be called the Passover (xii. 23, 26f.) with the same derivation as in P (xii. 13), the provisions also being similar ; xii. 21–27. Yahweh at midnight carries out the threat made by Moses. The Egyptians come entreating Israel to be gone, and urging them forth in such haste that " the people took their dough before it was leavened, their kneading-troughs being bound up in their clothes on their shoulders," and, with flocks and herds and a mixed multitude, go out. From the unleavened dough cakes are made, whence originated the feast of Unleavened Bread ; xii. 29, 30f. in part, 32–34, 37–39, 42. In addition to the feast of Passover, Moses accordingly enacts the observance of this feast and because of the smiting of the first-born of Egypt ordains a further law of consecration of the first-born to Yahweh ; xiii. 3–10, 11–16.

1. Chh. vii. 8–ix. 12. THE WONDERS WROUGHT BEFORE PHA-
RAOH AND THE EARLIER PLAGUES.

ANALYSIS.

Under divine direction Moses and Aaron appear before Pharaoh again.
Aaron casts his rod to the ground, whereupon it changes to a " reptile."
The " magicians of Egypt " do the same, but Aaron's rod swallows
theirs. Pharaoh's heart is hardened; vii. 8–13. The waters of Egypt
are next turned to blood, with a similar result ; vii. 14–25. A plague of
frogs is inflicted, which extorts from Pharaoh a petition for intercession ;
but he afterwards hardens his heart ; viii. 1–15. The " rod of Aaron "
brings lice, but " the magicians of Egypt " acknowledge their inability to
compete with this divine wonder. Pharaoh is still obstinate ; viii. 16–19.
A plague of flies is next inflicted, after which Pharaoh obtains intercession on the promise of concession, but afterward makes his heart
" heavy "; viii. 20–32. The plague of murrain is inflicted on the cattle
of Egypt to the destruction of all, while Israel's are spared. Pharaoh's
heart remains " heavy "; ix. 1–7. Moses and Aaron sprinkle ashes aloft,
which cause boils upon all the Egyptians. The magicians are stricken
and flee. Pharaoh's heart is still " hardened " ; ix. 8–12.

In justification of the description previously given of the contrasted
representations of J, E and P, it will be necessary to show that the present text involves incongruities and improbabilities for which the analysis
alone affords an adequate and probable solution. It will not be difficult
even in few words to make it apparent that such is the fact. Only, in
order not to weary the reader with a needless accumulation of evidence,
we will carry the analysis no further in detail than the end of ch. vii., referring those desirous of a complete array of the evidence to Art. II.

Vv. 8–13 are recognized as a unit in themselves, and as consistently
continuing the preceding narrative (cf. vs. 13 with vs. 3f, vs. 10 with vs.
6, etc.). The same characters (Moses, Aaron, Pharaoh, " the sorcerers ")
appear in the same *rôle*, with the same expressions and same representations, in a series of subsequent passages, which relate three other
" wonders " done by Moses and Aaron before Pharaoh with the same
result in vv. 19, 20a, 21c, 22 ; viii. 5–7, 15b–19 ; ix. 8 12. The type is so
exactly reproduced in each case that it is possible to give the regular
formula observed throughout, with only minor divergences : " And Yahweh said unto Moses, Say unto Aaron, take thy rod and . . . And they
did so : and the magicians did in like manner with their enchantments
. . . and Pharaoh's heart was hardened and he hearkened not unto them,

as Yahweh had spoken." There can be no question of the affinity of these passages. But it does not appear why, after *Moses* was commanded in iv. 17 to do the signs with his rod, or "the rod of God," *Aaron* should now be the agent, and *Aaron's* rod the means. Neither is it apparent why a totally different series of wonders, or plagues, should appear side by side with these whose purpose is different, (a punishment of the land) the actors in which, and phraseology of which are totally unlike, and in which Moses, so far from being in need of a spokesman to Pharaoh, conducts long negotiations without the assistance of Aaron. It does not appear why the rod which was changed to a " reptile " in vs. 9 should be spoken of as changed to " a serpent " in vs. 15 and iv. 3ff. nor why, in the stories of the contest of Aaron and the magicians, the invariable formula is " Pharaoh's heart was *hardened* as Yahweh had spoken " (cf. vii. 3) ; whereas in the series characterized by Moses alone as Yahweh's ambassador, we have invariably " Pharaoh's heart was heavy " (R. V. " stubborn ").

But passing now to vv. 14-25 we ask first, Who smote the river ? In vs. 19 Aaron is commanded to "stretch out his rod over the waters of Egypt," and it is naturally inferred that vs. 20 relates that *Aaron* (though not bidden) "smote the river with his rod." But in xvii. 5 Yahweh says to *Moses* "Take *thy* rod wherewith *thou* smotest the river." Still again vs. 25 explicitly states that " *Yahweh* smote the river," and vs. 17 makes confusion worse confounded by putting into the mouth of *Yahweh* the extraordinary utterance ; " Behold *I* will smite *with the rod that is in my hand* upon the waters of the river."

But now let it simply be recognized that there is a series of narratives in which every " sign " is worked by Moses with his rod, as iv. 17 requires, and as we actually find to be the case in the passages above assigned to E, just as in those characterized by the presence of the sorcerers they are worked by *Aaron* with his rod : and that there is still a third, in which neither Aaron nor Moses works the signs and no rod whatever appears, but Yahweh himself acts, as is explicitly required by vs. 25 and by every one of the announcements of Moses of what *Yahweh* will do, and this difficulty, together with a whole series of similar ones, vanishes. This supposition is again borne out by the series of passages already assigned to J. In both J and E we find in fact a regular type, almost as invariable as that of P. In E it is very brief, and appeals to the *eye* only : " And Yahweh said unto Moses, Stretch out thine hand (or " smite with the rod ") . . . and Moses stretched forth his hand (smote with the rod), and . . . But Yahweh *hardened* Pharaoh's heart and he would not let them go." In J it is more elaborate, and involves the cycle of changes in the effect on Pharaoh already described. It appeals almost exclusively to the *ear*, the scene being depicted almost wholly in *dialogue*: Yahweh says to Moses, " Go in unto Pharaoh and say unto him, Thus saith Yahweh, Let my people go that they may serve me. And if thou refuse, behold I will smite . . . (description of the plague then follows, with prediction of its unexampled severity and appointment of a specified time for its appearance). Where the immunity of Israel is not otherwise implied it is distinctly expressed, " And I will sever in that day the land of Goshen " or the like. Description of the occurrence of the plague follows, exactly as foretold, and the three different kinds of effects upon Pharaoh in regular rotation, as above described. The fullest form (four times) is that wherein Pharaoh calls for Moses and says, " Intreat for me, and Moses went out from Pharaoh and intreated Yahweh (or spread forth his hands to Yahweh) and the . . . ceased, and when Pharaoh saw . . . he made his heart *heavy* and did not let them go." Among the characteristic features not already mentioned is the emphasis which is laid upon the unique severity of the plague (" very grievous " " such as had never been ") ; its thoroughness, and its equally complete removal (" there remained not one," " not any green thing," " not one locust," etc.), in contrast with the complete immunity of the land of Goshen. In J moreover Yahweh is always the agent (not Moses as in E) and operates by natural causes, winds, etc. instead of the rod. The fixing of a time in advance for the plague and for its removal is also a natural characteristic of the narrative where Moses simply announces in advance what Yahweh will do. Pharaoh's audience chamber appears to be the scene of these negotiations, as the open air is the necessary scene of E's majestic pantomime with the rod. Other characteristics of style and language may readily be discovered from the references.

In the passage vii. 17-25 the observance of the references (*e. g.*, vs. 16 to v. 3, xvii. 5 to vs. 17) and of the consistent standpoint of each writer makes it easy to assign every clause of the confused whole, with practical certainty to its respective source (See Art. II, pp. 179ff.). One singular result is that whereas there appears to be not more than a single word or so lacking to any one, and even that single word capable of being supplied with certainty from the context, yet the miracle in J (who has already related the changing of water to blood, for a sign to the people), does not seem to have been a changing of water to blood at all, but only a destruction of life in the river (cf. xii. 12 P, the judgments executed against the gods of Egypt, and Is. l. 2). In viii. 1—ix. 12 there is no trace of E, and with the radically different types of J and

P in mind the reader will have no difficulty in personally verifying the analysis. Attention, however, should be given to the marginal notes of the R. V. ("heavy," and "strong") especially in vii. 9, 13f.; viii. 15, 32, and ix. 7, 12.

———

7-8 (P) ¹*And Yahweh spake unto Moses and unto Aaron, saying,*
9 *When Pharaoh shall speak unto you, saying, Shew a wonder for*
you: then thou shalt say unto Aaron, Take thy rod, and cast it
10 *down before Pharaoh, that it become a serpent. And Moses and*
Aaron went in unto Pharaoh, and they did so, as Yahweh had
commanded: and Aaron cast down his rod before Pharaoh and
11 *before his servants, and it became a serpent. Then Pharaoh also*
called for the wise men and the sorcerers: and they also, the magi-
12 *cians of Egypt, did in like manner with their enchantments. For*
they cast down every man his rod, and they became serpents:
13 *but Aaron's rod swallowed up their rods.* ⁵*And Pharaoh's heart*
was hardened, and he hearkened not unto them; as Yahweh had
spoken.

14 **(J) And Yahweh said unto Moses, Pharaoh's heart is ⁶stubborn, he refuseth to let the people go [. . .]**
15 **(E)** Get thee unto Pharaoh in the morning; lo, he goeth out unto the water; and thou shalt stand ⁷by the river's brink to meet him; and ⁸the rod which was turned to a serpent
16 **(J)** shalt thou take in thine hand.* **And thou shalt say unto him, Yahweh, the God of the Hebrews, hath ⁹sent me unto thee, saying, Let my people go, that they may serve me in the wilderness: and, behold,**
17 **hitherto thou hast not hearkened. Thus saith Yah-**

⁴Cf. 4 : 1-9 : vv. 10, 22 ; 8 : 5-7 ; 9-8-12, etc.   ⁵Cf. vs. 14 ; 8 : 15, 32 ; 9 : 7, 34 etc.   ⁶ : : 15, 32 : 9 : 7, 34 etc. ⁷2 : 3.   ⁸4 : 3, (17 LXX.); cf. vv. 9-12. ⁹3 : 18 ; 5 : 3, 5ff.

* In Art II. p. 179 the last clause of vs. 15 is not rejected. In view however of the preponderance of evidence for J in iv. 1ff. the general verdict of critics attributing the clause to Rje as preparatory to vs. 17b may be accepted; or we may consider that an original "and the rod which I gave thee," or the like, has been harmonistically altered to the present form. The assumption of such an addition or alteration is justified by the fact that the LXX. insert the same designation "which was turned to a serpent" in iv. 17, where it certainly is not genuine.

weh, In this thou shalt know that I am Yahweh
(E) behold, I will smite | . . . | [11]with the rod that is in
mine† hand upon the waters which are in the river, and [12]they
(J) shall be turned to blood. **And the fish that is in the** [18]
river shall die, and the river shall stink ; [13]**and the**
Egyptians shall loathe to drink water from the river.
(P) [14]*And Yahweh said unto Moses, Say unto Aaron, Take thy* [19]
rod, and stretch out thine hand over the waters of Egypt, over
their rivers, over their streams, and over their pools, and over all
their ponds of water, that they may become blood ; and there shall
be blood throughout all the land of Egypt, both in vessels of wood
and in vessels of stone. And Moses and Aaron did so, as Yahweh [20]
(E) *commanded ;* and he lifted up the rod, and smote the
waters that were in the river [15]in the sight of Pharaoh, and
in the sight of his servants ; and all the waters that were in
the river were turned to blood.

   (J) [16]**And the fish that was in the river died ; and the** [21]
river stank, and the Egyptians could not drink water
(P) from the river : *and the blood was throughout all the land*
of Egypt. [17]*And the magicians of Egypt did in like manner with* [22]
their enchantments ; and Pharaoh's heart was hardened, and he
(E) *hearkened not unto them ; as Yahweh had spoken.* And [23]
Pharaoh turned and [18]went into his house, neither did he lay
(J) even this to heart. **And all the Egyptians digged** [24]
round about the river for water to drink ; for they
could not drink of the water of the river. And seven [25]

[10]Vs. 25. [11]17 : 5. [12]Cf. 4 : 9. [13]Vs. 21. [14]Vs. 9 : 8 ; 5, 16 etc. [15]4 : 21, 30. [16]Vs. 1 ;
Is. 50 : 2. [17]Vs. 11 : 8 : 7, 18 etc. [18]Vs. 15.

  * After vs. 15 we are driven to supply, " And thou shalt smite " (one word in
Hebrew) which requires the reading " thine " instead of " mine " in vs. 17b.
The union of J in which Yahweh smites the river (vs. 25) with E in which
Moses smites it with his rod (xvii. 5) has compelled Rje to omit the word
above referred to, and make the necessary change of one letter in the posses-
sive pronoun. A comparison of vv. 17, and 20, vs. 25 and xvii. 5 shows that
the change has really taken place as thus assumed. The second clause of vs.
17 is possibly redactional, though the question is indifferent to the analysis
(See Art. II.)

days were fulfilled, after that [19]Yahweh had smitten
the river.

8 And Yahweh spake unto Moses, Go in unto Pharaoh, and say unto him, [1]Thus saith Yahweh, Let my
2 people go, that they may serve me. And if thou refuse
to let them go, behold, I will smite all thy borders
3 with frogs: and the river shall swarm with frogs,
which shall go up and come into thine house, and into
thy bedchamber, and upon thy bed, and into the house
of thy servants, and upon thy people, and into thine
4 ovens, and into thy [2]kneading-troughs: and the frogs
shall come up both upon thee, and upon thy people,
5 (P) and upon all thy servants. [. . .] [3]*And Yahweh
said unto Moses, Say unto Aaron, Stretch forth thine hand with
thy rod over the rivers, over the streams, and over the pools, and
6 cause frogs to come up upon the land of Egypt. And Aaron
stretched out his hand over the waters of Egypt: and the frogs
7 came up, and covered the land of Egypt. [4]And the magicians did
in like manner with their enchantments, and brought up frogs
upon the land of Egypt.*

8 (J) [. . .][5]Then Pharaoh called for Moses and Aaron,*
and said, Intreat Yahweh, that he take away the frogs
from me, and from my people; and I will let the
9 people go, that they may sacrifice unto Yahweh. And
Moses said unto Pharaoh, Have thou this glory over
me: against what time shall I intreat for thee, and
for thy servants, and for thy people, that the frogs be

[19]Vs. 17a. [1]7 : 16 ; vs. 20 ; 9 : 1, 13, etc. [2]12 : 34. [3]Cf. 7 : 19. [4]7 : 22 etc. [5]Vv. 20, 25 : 10 : 3 ff.

* The appearance of Aaron here and in vv. 12 and 25; ix. 27; and x. 3, 8, 16
is certainly due to harmonistic interpolation. It will be observed that in all
these cases Aaron is a pure figure-head, absolutely without a rôle. Though
Moses and Aaron are represented as entering together, in all cases save vs. 12
and. x 8ff., Moses goes out alone; and in all that is said by Pharaoh or Moses
the presence of Aaron is ignored ("Intreat thou," "shall I intreat," "he
said," etc.). So in x. 1 Moses alone is bidden by Yahweh to go in to Pharaoh,
and only Moses comes out, vs. 6, and Pharaoh's servants speak of the petitioners as "this man"; yet vs. 3a, connected with the certainly redactional vv. 1b,
2, has "Moses *and Aaron*." But in x. 24 Aaron is not even called.

destroyed from thee and thy houses, and remain in the
river only? And he said, Against to-morrow. And he 10
said, Be it according to thy word: "that thou mayest
know that there is none like unto Yahweh our God.*
And the frogs shall depart from thee, and from thy 11
houses, and from thy servants, and from thy people:
they shall remain in the river only. And Moses and 12
Aaron went out from Pharaoh: and Moses cried unto
Yahweh concerning the frogs [7]which he had brought
upon Pharaoh. And Yahweh did according to the 13
word of Moses; and the frogs died out of the houses,
out of the courts, and out of the fields. And they 14
gathered them together in heaps: and the land stank.
But when Pharaoh saw that there was respite, he 15
(P) [8]hardened his heart, [. . .] *and hearkened not unto
them: as Yahweh had spoken.†*

[9]*And Yahweh said unto Moses, Say unto Aaron, Stretch out 16
thy rod, and smite the dust of the earth, that it may become lice
throughout all the land of Egypt. And they did so; and Aaron 17
stretched out his hand with his rod, and smote the dust of the earth,
and there were lice upon man, and upon beast; all the dust of the
earth became lice throughout all the land of Egypt. And the 18
magicians did so with their enchantments to bring forth lice, but
they could not: and there were lice upon man, and upon beast.
Then the magicians said unto Pharaoh, This is the finger of God: 19
and Pharaoh's heart was hardened, and he hearkened not unto
them; as Yahweh had spoken.*

(J) And Yahweh said unto Moses, Rise up early in 20
the morning, and stand before Pharaoh; [10]lo, he cometh
forth to the water;‡ and say unto him, Thus saith Yahweh,

---

[8]7: 17; vs. 22.　[7]Vs. 9.　[8]Vs. 32; 7: 14; 9: 7, 34 etc.　[9]Cf. 7: 8ff. etc.　[10]7: 15.

* See note on vii. 17.

† In vs. 15 Rp has combined the concluding formulae of J and P as the language shows. See margin in R. V. (" made heavy ").

‡ The middle clause of vs. 20 is perhaps borrowed by Rje from vii. 15, because of failure to understand the location "before Pharaoh": cf. ix. 13, and
see Art. II. p. 180.

21 Let my people go, that they may serve me. Else, if thou wilt not let my people go, behold, I will send swarms of flies upon thee, and upon thy servants, and upon thy people, and into thy houses : and the houses of the Egyptians shall be full of swarms of flies, and
22 also the ground whereon they are. And I will sever in that day [11]the land of Goshen, in which my people dwell, that no swarms of flies shall be there ; to the end thou mayest know that I am Yahweh in the midst
23 of the earth.* And I will put a division between my people and thy people : by to-morrow shall this sign
24 be. And Yahweh did so ; and there came grievous swarms of flies into the house of Pharaoh, and into his servants' houses : and in all the land of Egypt the land was corrupted by reason of the swarms of flies.
25 And Pharaoh called for Moses and for Aaron, and said,
26 Go ye, sacrifice to your God in the land. And Moses said, It is not meet so to do ; for we shall sacrifice the abomination of the Egyptians to Yahweh our God : lo, shall we sacrifice the abomination of the Egyptians
27 before their eyes, and will they not stone us ? [12]We will go three days' journey into the wilderness, and sacrifice to Yahweh our God, as he shall command us.
28 And Pharaoh said, I will let you go, that ye may sacrifice to Yahweh your God in the wilderness : only
29 ye shall not go very far away : intreat for me. And Moses said, Behold, I go out from thee, and I will intreat Yahweh that the swarms of flies may depart from Pharaoh, from his servants, and from his people, to-morrow : only let not Pharaoh deal deceitfully any more in not letting the people go to sacrifice
30 to Yahweh. And Moses went out from Pharaoh, and
31 intreated Yahweh. And Yahweh did according to the word of Moses ; and he removed the swarms of flies from Pharaoh, from his servants, and from his

11 Gen. 46 : 28f., 34 ; 47 : 1, 4, 6. 27 ; Ex. 9 : 26. 12 3 : 18 ; 5 : 3 etc.

* See note on vii. 17.

people ; [19]there remained not one.   And Pharaoh hard- 32
ened his heart this time also, and he did not let the
people go.

[1]Then Yahweh said unto Moses, Go in unto Pharaoh, 9
and tell him, Thus saith Yahweh, the God of the
Hebrews, Let my people go, that they may serve me.
For if thou refuse to let them go, and wilt hold them 2
still, behold, the hand of Yahweh is upon thy cattle 3
which is in the field, upon the horses, upon the asses,
upon the camels, upon the herds, and upon the flocks :
[there shall be] a very grievous murrain. And Yahweh 4
shall sever between the cattle of Israel and the cattle
of Egypt : and there shall nothing die of all that belongeth to the children of Israel. And Yahweh ap- 5
pointed a set time, saying, To-morrow Yahweh shall
do this thing in the land. And Yahweh did that thing 6
[2]on the morrow, and all the cattle of Egypt died : but
of the cattle of the children of Israel died not one.
And Pharaoh sent, and, behold, there was not so much 7
as one of the cattle of the Israelites dead. But the
heart of Pharaoh was stubborn, and he did not let
the people go.

(P) [8]*And Yahweh said unto Moses and unto Aaron, Take to* 8
you handfuls of ashes of the furnace, and let Moses sprinkle it tow-
ard the heaven in the sight of Pharaoh.   And it shall become small 9
dust over all the land of Egypt, and shall be a boil breaking forth
with blains upon man and upon beast, throughout all the land of
Egypt.   And they took ashes of the furnace, and stood before 10
Pharaoh ; and Moses sprinkled it up toward heaven ; and it be-
came a boil breaking forth with blains upon man and upon beast.
And the magicians could not stand before Moses because of the boils ; 11
for the boils were upon the magicians, and upon all the Egyptians.
And Yahweh hardened the heart of Pharaoh, and he hearkened 12
not unto them : as Yahweh had spoken unto Moses.

[19]9 : 7 : 10 : 15, 19 ; 12 : 30 ; 14 : 28.   [1]8 : 1ff. 20ff. etc.   [2]8 : 9. 23 ; 10 : 13 ; 14 : 21, 24 ; Nu
11 : 18.   [3]7 : 8ff. 19f. etc.

2. Chh. ix. 13–xi. 10. THE FINAL PLAGUES.

ANALYSIS.

Moses is sent to Pharaoh to threaten, in case of further refusal, the plague of hail; ix. 13–21. He is bidden to stretch forth the rod toward heaven, whereupon comes hail and thunder killing man and beast and destroying the crops. Pharaoh begs Moses' intercession, but afterwards becomes again obstinate; ix. 22–35. Moses is again sent in to Pharaoh to demand the people's release under penalty of a plague of locusts. Pharaoh's servants intercede, but Pharaoh offers only to compromise; x. 1–11. Moses, at Yahweh's command, stretches out his rod toward heaven and the locusts appear. Pharaoh again begs Moses' intercession, but after removal of the plague is obdurate; x. 12–20. Moses' rod next brings three days' darkness. Thereafter Pharaoh summons Moses and proposes a final compromise; he refuses, and is driven out under threat of death; x. 21–29. In preparation for the final plague Yahweh bids Moses direct the people to obtain the portable riches of the Egyptians; xi. 1–3. Moses (again in Pharaoh's presence) foretells to him the vengeance of Yahweh, and goes out in hot anger; xi. 4–8. In a colophon to the series of plagues the author declares their lack of effect on Pharaoh to have been divinely intended for the multiplication of the wonders; xi. 9f.

In chh. ix. 13–xi. the only traces of P are the single clause, ix. 35b, "As Yahweh had spoken by Moses," and the colophon xi. 9f, which repeats at the conclusion of the plague section the preliminary explanation of vii. 3ff. (P). Both are probably due simply to supplementary redaction by Rp. (See Art. 11, and notes *in loc.*). Nevertheless we discover, as usual, that freedom from P by no means ensures unity of the text. If anything, the discordances and incongruities of chh. ix–xi. are greater than anywhere else.

Thus Moses, after having been expelled by Pharaoh in x. 28 with the threat of death upon his reappearance, and after having boldly answered, "Thou hast spoken well, I will see thy face no more," is found in xi. 1–3 directing the people how to spoil the Egyptians; but thereafter, without divine direction, without any apparent occasion, in xi. 4, *he reappears in Pharaoh's presence*, declaring how Israel will be brought out, and finally leaves the royal presence "in hot anger." We assume that his anger is because of the ill-treatment received on the former occasion, when he had gone away promising never to return; but how is it possible for anything to be more awkward than this return and belated indignation of Moses, as if he had subsequently recollected the anger he should have shown, and the threat he should have made before leaving the first time.

The supposition that xi. 1–3 was originally intended to interrupt the absolutely necessary connection of xi. 4–8 with x. 28f. involves absurdities greater than which it is almost impossible to conceive. Nothing in fact save the alternative absurdity of making Moses *first* denounce the final plague, as in xi. 4–8, and *afterward* receive notice of it from Yahweh, as in xi. 1, could have occasioned such an extraordinary combination by Rje. But omit the intrusive verses xi. 1–3 (E) and read xi. 4–8 after x. 28f. especially comparing xi. 8 with x. 29, and observe the magnificent climax of eloquence attained.

Scarcely less remarkable are the dissonances in chh. ixf. In ix. 19–21, 22, 25a the objects against which the hail is especially directed are the cattle, men and beasts in the field. But according to the preceding ix. 6 not one solitary beast of the Egyptians was left alive by the *murrain.* The only cattle left are the Hebrews' cattle ! In x. 3ff. Moses and Aaron go in and deliver to Pharaoh a long message purporting to be from Yahweh ; but have not yet received any, as at other times, to communicate ! In x. 13 after Moses has stretched out his rod for the locusts we expect them to come : but as the text stands, either Moses stood all night with outstretched hand waiting for them to appear, or else he stretched out his rod with the same dramatic effect as in previous instances, but this time nothing happened for twenty-four hours ! After this, duplications like ix. 23, where after sending hail, thunder and fire in response to the uplifted rod, Yahweh further rained more hail and more fire upon the land of Egypt, or like vs. 25a and b, or 34=35 or x. 15b =15c, scarcely surprise us. But we do ask why, after Moses in x. 4f. has fully foretold that on the morrow Yahweh will bring the locusts in such a way, and is driven out from Pharaoh's presence, it is still necessary for him to go out all alone and stretch out his rod over the land of Egypt, especially as nothing happens till the next day, and then it is not the rod, but the "east wind," that brings the locusts.

In place of these extraordinary discrepancies we have but to seek the elements in these chapters corresponding to the types respectively described as those of J and E, and every discrepancy vanishes. In place thereof appear two parallel narratives absolutely self-consistent, characteristic, and complete to the very last word, each a masterpiece of simplicity, force and realism. The hail is directed against the cattle *in E,* because this document knows no plague of murrain. The seemingly unauthorized address of Moses and Aaron to Pharaoh is explained when it appears that x. 1b, 2 is a Deuteronomic interpolation of a familiar type, whose insertion has compelled an alteration of vs. 3 from the imperative to the past indicative (See note *in loc.*). The apparently solitary pantomime of x. 12f. loses its absurdity when it is preceded by its original context, *i.e.* Moses in Pharaoh's presence, instead of the story of expulsion from the palace ; and when the story of Yahweh's bringing the locusts by a strong east wind blowing all night, is detached from that which makes the rod the agency, Moses is no longer obliged to wait all night for their appearance. The doublets are explained, the intolerable interruption of x. 28f.; xi. 4-8 by xi. 1-3 is also explained. Moreover each element thus extricated is found to reproduce the type already previously exemplified in the corresponding document.

For details of the analysis the reader's attention is called to the references, especially the close correspondence of prediction and fulfilment in J (cf. ix. 18 with vs. 24 ; x. 4f. with vs. 14, etc.) ; to the typical form of plague narrative in J and E ; and, for a complete presentation of the evidence, to Art. II. In the hail story of J it should be observed that "every herb of the field and every tree of the field" is the object of destruction ; hence the exception in ix. 31ff. of ungrown crops. In E where the hail is "upon man and upon beast" this exception has of course no place. Both however relate the entire consuming of vegetation (E, "herb of the *land*," J, "herb of the *field*") by the locusts. The plague of darkness (x. 21-23) is related by E alone ; for the passage displays its E origin by the part assigned to the "rod" and the presupposition that the "dwellings of Israel" are intermingled with the Egyptians' instead of in "the land of Goshen." At the same time there is no trace of a duplicate structure. Possibly the darkening of "the whole land" by the cloud of locusts (x. 15a. J) may to some extent be regarded as a parallel. Throughout this subsection the respective characteristics of J and E already spoken of will be found abundantly exemplified. In J the scene is depicted in the dialogue, in E related. J addresses the ear ; E the eye. In J Moses has only to deliver Yahweh's message and negotiate, while Yahweh, as agent, operates through natural causes ; in E Moses has only to act without speaking. Other characteristics are readily discoverable.

---

13   **(J)** **⁴And Yahweh said unto Moses, Rise up early in the morning, and stand before Pharaoh, and say**

48 : 1ff. etc.

unto him, Thus saith Yahweh, the God of the Hebrews, Let my people go, that they may serve me. For I will this time send all my plagues upon thine 14 heart, and upon thy servants, and upon thy people; that thou mayest know that there is none like me in all the earth. For now I had put forth my hand, and 15 smitten thee and thy people with pestilence, and thou hadst been cut off from the earth: but in very deed 16 for this cause have I made thee to stand, for to shew thee my power, and that my name may be declared throughout all the earth.* ⁵As yet exaltest thou 17 thyself against my people, that thou wilt not let them go? Behold, to-morrow about this time I will 18 cause it to rain a ⁶very grievous hail, such as hath not been in Egypt since the day it was founded even (Rd) until now. Now therefore send, hasten in thy cattle and all 19 that thou hast in the field; [for] every man and beast which shall be found in the field, and shall not be brought home, the hail shall come down upon them, and they shall die. He that feared the word of Yahweh among the 20 servants of Pharaoh made his servants and his cattle flee into the houses: and he that regarded not the word of Yahweh left his servants and his 21 cattle in the field.†

(E) And Yahweh said unto Moses, ⁷Stretch forth thine 22 hand toward heaven, that there may be hail in all the land of Egypt, upon man, and upon beast, ⁸and upon every herb of the field‡ throughout the land of Egypt. And Moses ⁹stretched forth 23 his rod toward heaven: and Yahweh sent thunder and hail, (J) and fire ran down unto the earth; and ¹⁰**Yahweh rained**

---

⁵7 : 16. ⁶Vv. 3, 24; 10 : 6, 14; 11 : 6. ⁷10 : 12f., 21f. ⁸Vs. 25 : cf. 10 : 12, 15. ⁹10 : 13, 22. ¹⁰Gen. 19 : 24.

*Probably, though not necessarily, vv. 13–16 are a didactic interpolation. See note on vii. 17 and Art. II.

†The didactic interest of vv. 19–21 is plain in the discrimination between " him that feared the word of Yahweh " and " him that regarded not the word of Yahweh among the servants of Pharaoh " and in the precautions against destruction of innocent life (Cf. Gen. xviii. 23–32); but cf. especially vs. 6 (J) and the observations above (Analysis, p. 49f.).

‡ The clause in small type is assigned on linguistic grounds to Rje; E has " herb *of the land* " in all cases; cf. x. 12, 15.

24 hail upon the land of Egypt. ¹¹So there was hail,—and fire mingled with the hail,—*very grievous, such as had not been in all the land of Egypt since it be-came a nation.

25 (E) And the hail smote throughout all the land of
(J) Egypt all that was in the field, both man and beast; and the hail smote every herb of the field, and brake
26 every tree of the field. ¹²Only in the land of Goshen, where the children of Israel were, was there no hail.
27 And Pharaoh sent, and called for Moses and Aaron, and said unto them, I have sinned this time: Yahweh is
28 righteous, and I and my people are wicked. Intreat Yahweh; for there hath been enough of [these] ¹³mighty thunderings and hail; and I will let you go,
29 and ye shall stay no longer. And Moses said unto him, As soon as I am gone out of the city, I will spread abroad my hands unto Yahweh; the thunders shall cease, neither shall there be any more hail; that thou mayest know that the earth is Yahweh's.
30 (Rp) *But as for thee and thy servants, I know that ye will not yet fear Yah-*
31 (J) *weh God.* And the flax and the barley were smitten: for the barley was in the ear, and the flax was bolled.
32 But the wheat and the spelt were not smitten; for
33 they were not grown up. And Moses went out of the city from Pharaoh, and spread abroad his hands unto Yahweh: and the ¹⁴thunders and hail ceased, and the
34 rain was not poured upon the earth. And when Pha-raoh saw that the rain and the hail and the thunders were ceased, he sinned yet more, and ¹⁵hardened his
35 (E) heart, he and his servants. And the heart of Pha-raoh was hardened, and he did not let the children of Israel go; ¹⁶*as Yahweh had spoken by Moses.*†

Vs. 18. ¹²8: 29 etc. ¹³Gen. 30: 8; 15: 5. ¹⁴Vs. 28. ¹⁵7: 14; 8: 15, 32 etc.; cf. Vs. 5. ¹⁶7: 13, 22; 8: 15, 17; 9: 12 etc.

* The first two clauses of vs. 24 should exchange places. Read " And Yah-weh rained hail upon the land of Egypt, and fire flashing continually amidst the hail. So there was a very grievous hail, such as " etc. Cf. vs. 18.

† For supplementary redaction in vv. 27, 29b see notes on viii. 8 and vii. 17

(J) ¹**And Yahweh said unto Moses, Go in unto Pha-** 10
(Rd) raoh : for I have hardened his heart, and the heart of his servants,
²that I might shew these my signs in the midst of them : ³and that thou 2
mayest tell in the ears of thy son, and of thy son's son, what things I have
wrought upon Egypt, and my signs which I have done among them, ⁴that ye
may know that I am Yahweh. And Moses and Aaron went in unto Pha- 3
(J) raoh* **and said unto him, Thus saith Yahweh, the**
God of the Hebrews, ⁵How long wilt thou refuse to
humble thyself before me? let my people go, that
they may serve me. Else, if thou refuse to let my 4
people go, ⁶behold, to-morrow will I bring locusts into
thy border: and they shall cover the face of the 5
earth, that one shall not be able to see the earth : and
they shall eat the residue of that which is escaped,
which remaineth unto you from the hail, and shall
eat every tree which groweth for you out of the field :
and thy houses shall be filled, and the houses of all 6
thy servants, and the houses of all the Egyptians ; ⁷as
neither thy fathers nor thy fathers' fathers have seen,
since the day that they were upon the earth unto this
day. And he turned, and went out from Pharaoh.
And Pharaoh's servants said unto him, How long shall 7
this man be a snare unto us? let the men go, that

¹8 : 1 ; 9 : 1 etc. ²11 : 9f. ³12 : 26f. ; 13 : 8, 14 etc. ⁴7 : 17 ; 8 : 10, 22 ; 9 : 14–16, 29.
⁵Vs. 7 ; 16 : 28 ; Nu. 14 : 11. ⁶Vs. 13f. ⁷Vs. 14 : 11 : 6.

respectively. Vs. 30 appears to be certainly late. It manifestly interrupts the
connection. The last clause of vs. 35 is a scribal attempt at assimilation to
ix. 12, (P). " Voices of God " (see margin, R.V., vs. 28) is a specific term for
thunder. It is in accordance with the usual practice of J to employ *Elohim* in
such cases. Cf. iv. 16 ; xxiv. 11 ; Gen. vi. 2ff., etc.

* It is the invariable practice of J in all the plague narratives (see type-form
in Analysis, p. 41) to give in full the instructions to Moses and leave to be understood the carrying out (cf. vs. 6). For "said" in vs. 3 we should therefore
in all probabilty read "say." The reason for the alteration appears in the
passage printed in smaller type, wherein every feature is characteristic of Rd.
We note *e. g.*, "hardened" for " heavy"; "that ye may know" etc.; the
didactic interest; solicitude for the instruction of posterity, etc. Moreover the
parenthetic character of 1b, 2 is apparent, and the interruption of the original
connection has the effect of making Moses deliver a message before he receives it.

they may serve Yahweh their God : knowest thou not
8 yet that Egypt is destroyed? And Moses and Aaron*
were brought again unto Pharaoh : and he said unto
them, Go, serve Yahweh your God : but who are they
9 that shall go? sAnd Moses said, We will go with our
young and with our old, with our sons and with our
daughters, with our flocks and with our herds will we
10 go : for we must hold a feast unto Yahweh. And he
said unto them, So be Yahweh with you, as I will let
you go, and your little ones : look to it ; for evil is
11 before you. Not so : go now ye that are men, and
serve Yahweh ; for that is what ye desire. And they
were driven out from Pharaoh's presence.

12   (E) ⁹And Yahweh said unto Moses, Stretch out thine
hand over the land of Egypt for the locusts, that they may
come up upon the land of Egypt, and eat every ¹⁰herb of the
13 land, even all that the hail hath left. And Moses stretched
(J) forth his rod over the land of Egypt, ¹¹and Yahweh
brought an east wind upon the land all that day, and
all the night ; and when it was morning, the east
14 (E) wind brought the locusts. And the locusts went up
(J) over all the land of Egypt, and rested in ¹²all the borders of Egypt ; ¹³very grievous were they ; before
them there were no such locusts as they, neither
15 after them shall be such. For they covered the face
of the whole earth, ¹⁴so that the land was darkened :
(E) ¹⁵and they did eat every herb of the land, and all† [. . .]
(J) the fruit of the trees which the hail had left ¹⁶and
there remained not any green thing, either tree or
¹herb of the field, through all the land of Egypt.

---

*1 : 18 ; 5 : 3 ; 6 : 25-28.   ⁸9 : 22f. vs. 21f.   ¹⁰Cf. 15a ; ct. 15b ; 9 : 22, 25.   ¹¹14 : 21 ; Nu.
11 . . 1.   ¹²8 : 2 ; vs. 4.   ¹³9 : 3, 18, 24 ; vs. 6.   ¹⁴Cf. vs. 21-23.   ¹⁵Vs. 12.   ¹⁶Vs. 19 ; 14 : 28.

* Read " the elders " or use singulars in vv. 8, 10f.

† Although not strictly necessary to the sense it is probable, from the close
resemblance in both J and E of the fulfillment of the plague to the prediction,
that J's story contained the substance of vs. 15b (cf. vs. 5 and vs. 12). The
clause in E and J must have been nearly identical.

Then Pharaoh called for Moses and Aaron in haste; and 16
he said, I have sinned against Yahweh your God, and
against you.   Now therefore forgive, I pray thee, my 17
sin only this once, and [17]intreat Yahweh your God,
that he may take away from me this death only.   And 18
he went out from Pharaoh, and intreated Yahweh.
[11]And Yahweh turned an exceeding strong west 19
wind, which took up the locusts, and drove them into
the Red Sea; there remained not one locust in all the
(E) border of Egypt.   But Yahweh [18]hardened Pharaoh's 20
heart, and he did not let the children of Israel go.

[19]And Yahweh said unto Moses, Stretch out thine hand 21
toward heaven, that there may be darkness over the land of
Egypt, even darkness which may be felt.   And Moses 22
stretched forth his hand toward heaven; and there was a
thick darkness in all the land of Egypt three days; they saw 23
not one another, neither rose any from his place for three
days : but all the children of Israel had light [21]in their dwell-
(J) ings.   [23]And Pharaoh called unto Moses, and said, 24
Go ye, serve Yahweh; only let your flocks and your
herds be stayed : let your little ones also go with you.
And Moses said, Thou must also give into our hand 25
sacrifices and burnt offerings, that we may sacrifice
unto Yahweh our God.   Our cattle also shall go with 26
us; there shall not an hoof be left behind; for
thereof must we take to serve Yahweh our God; and
we know not with what we must serve Yahweh, until
(E) we come thither.   [22]But Yahweh hardened Pharaoh's 27
(J) heart, and he would not let them go.   And Pharaoh 28
said unto him, Get thee from me, take heed to thyself, see my face no more; for [23]in the day thou seest
my face thou shalt die.   And Moses said, Thou hast 29
spoken well; [24]I will see thy face again no more.

(E)   [1]And Yahweh said unto Moses, Yet one plague more 11

[17]8 : 8f,; 28 ; 9 : 27 etc.   [18]9 : 35 ; vs. 27.   [19]9 : 22f.; vs. 12f ; cf. vs. 1sa.   [20]Cf. 3 : 22 ; ct.
8 : 22 ; 9 : 26.   [21]3 : 18 ; 5 : 3 : 8 : 25-28.   [22]9 : 35 ; vs. 20.   [23]Gen. 3 : 17.   [24]Ct. 11 : 1-3, 4ff.
[1]3 : 19-22 ; 12 : 35f.

will I bring upon Pharaoh, and upon Egypt; afterwards he
will let you go hence : when he shall let you go, he shall
2 surely thrust you out hence altogether. Speak now in the
ears of the people, and let them ask every man of his neighbour, and every woman of her neighbour, jewels of silver,
3 and jewels of gold.   And Yahweh gave the people favour in
the sight of the Egyptians.   Moreover ²the man Moses was
very great in the land of Egypt, in the sight of Pharaoh's
servants, and in the sight of the people. [. . .]

4   (J) ³And Moses said, Thus saith Yahweh, About
5 midnight will I go out into the midst of Egypt: and
all the firstborn in the land of Egypt shall die, from
the firstborn of Pharaoh that sitteth upon his throne,
even unto the firstborn of the maidservant that is
6 behind the mill ; and all the firstborn of cattle.* ⁴And there
shall be a great cry throughout all the land of Egypt,
such as there hath been none like it, nor shall be like
7 it any more.   But against any of the children of Israel
shall ⁵not a dog move his tongue, against man or
beast: that ye may know how that Yahweh doth put
8 a difference between the Egyptians and Israel.†   And
all these thy servants shall come down unto me, and
bow down themselves unto me, saying, Get thee out,
and all the people that follow thee: and after that I
will go out.   And he went out from Pharaoh in ⁶hot
anger.

9   (R) *And Yahweh said unto Moses, ⁷Pharaoh will not hearken unto you :*

²Nu. 12 : 3.   ³12 : 2 f.   ⁴7 : 15, 24 : 10 ; 6 etc.   ⁵Jos 10 : 21.   ⁶10 : 28.   ⁷3 : 20 ; 4 : 21.

* Supplementary redaction; cf. xiii. 15 and xiii. 12, where Rd bases the law
of sacrifice of the firstborn *beast* on the fact that " Yahweh slew all the firstborn of Egypt, both of man and *beast*."   But according to the original writer
(ix. 6; cf. ix. 25a, E) " all the cattle of Egypt " had been previously slain by
the murrain.   In his (J's) conception the firstborn of cattle are a *substitute* for
" the firstborn of man among thy sons " (xiii. 13) which were spared, when
the firstborn *sons* of Egypt were slain.   The above applies of course equally
to xii. 29b.

† Vs. 7b is of the same character as vii. 17 ; viii. 10, 22 ; ix. 14–16, 29b ; x. 2.
See note on vii. 17.

that my wonders may be multiplied in the land of Egypt. And Moses and 10
Aaron did all these wonders before Pharaoh: and Yahweh hardened Pha-
*raoh's heart, and he did not let the children of Israel go out of his land.**

---

3 Chh. xii. 1—xiii. 16. The Night of Deliverance. Institu-
tion of the Feasts of Passover and Unleavened
Bread. Consecration of the Firstborn.

ANALYSIS.

On the first day of the month Yahweh ordains the beginning of the
(ecclesiastical) year, and gives directions for celebration of the Passover
on the 14th, instituting the feast as a memorial of the deliverance he is
about to effect by smiting the firstborn of Egypt; xii. 1-13. In addition he directs the observance of a further feast of Unleavened Bread,
from the 14th, at evening, to the 21st at evening; xii. 14-20. Moses
summons the elders, and gives directions for the sacrifice of the passover
lamb, and the observance of the feast in memory of deliverance from
"the Destroyer." The people obey; xii. 21-28. At midnight Yahweh
destroys the firstborn of Egypt. Pharaoh and the Egyptians in terror
dismiss Israel in haste, and the latter enrich themselves with the
spoil of their oppressors; xii. 29-36. The people with cattle and a
mixed multitude journey from Ramses to Succoth, baking unleavened
cakes of their dough, which had not had time to be leavened. The
deliverance takes place exactly 430 years, to a day, after the beginning
of the sojourn in Egypt; xii. 37-42. Yahweh ordains through Moses
and Aaron the law for observance of the Passover; xii. 43-51. He
further enacts through Moses the sanctification of the firstborn to himself;
xiii. 1f. Moses ordains the feast of Unleavened Bread with its proper
ritual; xiii. 3-10, and the law of the first-born; xiii. 11-16.

In chh. xiif. we meet the same remarkable phenomena of duplication,
inconsistency, and contrast in style, representation and mode of conception, as in the preceding. In xii. 31 Pharaoh summons Moses and
Aaron before him and addresses them, in spite of x. 29; xi. 8, where
Moses has declared that instead of this, Pharaoh and his servants shall
come *to him*, humbly entreating him to go. In vs. 34 the people are
preparing to make their bread with leaven, in spite of the strict injunc-
tion of vv. 18ff.; and in vs. 39 it is explicitly related that the reason for

---

* The colophon to the plague narratives, xi. 9f., which repeats the substance
of vii. 3f., may be from P², but is at least superfluous, and is generally regarded
as a supplementary interpolation by Rp.

the making of unleavened cakes, instead of employing the leaven as usual, was simply because they had no time, being interrupted in the midst of ordinary household duties by the unexpected appearance of Pharaoh's messengers, who so urgently insist upon their going in haste. We are not only at a loss to understand how they can be thinking of using leaven after xii. 15ff., but still more to understand how they can be taken by surprise, when not only have they been instructed to supply themselves with gold, silver and raiment in readiness for flight, xi. 1–3 (E), but have been engaged since the tenth day of the month in preparing for nothing else ; xii. 1–12. Note especially vs. 11. True, we might attempt to account for the unreadiness by supposing the summons to go forth to have come between " midnight " (vs. 29) and morning, instead of after daybreak, as they certainly had a right to expect from vv. 10, 17, and 22. But turning to Num. xxxiii. 3f. we find it explicitly stated that " they journeyed from Rameses in the first month, on the *fifteenth* day of the first month ; *on the morrow after the passover* the children of Israel went out with an high hand in the sight of all the Egyptians, *while the Egyptians were burying all their firstborn.*" At least one Pentateuch writer therefore sees nothing unexpected about the going out, and does not believe that they were driven out at midnight unprepared.

In the present connection the jewels and raiment which the Israelites obtain from the Egyptians, vv. 35f., seem to be extorted by fear ; but this does not agree with the representation of the passage itself, with its kindred passages in iii. 21f. and xi. 1–3, wherein the credit of Moses, and a special inclining of the Egyptians' hearts by Yahweh is the means by which the jewels are obtained. In conformity to this idea it is not the *men*, who demand the gold and raiment as the equivalent of unrequited labor ; but the women, who " ask " it of their *women* friends and neighbors. But this again is inconsistent with Israel's dwelling apart in the land of Goshen (viii. 22 ; ix. 26) ; and if the " asking " be attributed to the night of the passover, when Israel had the power to extort, it is inconsistent with the representation that each Israelite family is then confined to its own abode, forbidden to stir outside the door, while the Egyptian families, just stricken by " the Destroyer," are certainly not in a mood of special " favor " toward Israel.

But in chh. xii. f. the duplications are perhaps more striking than the incompatibilities. By the present arrangement of the material the ordinance of the passover in vv. 21-27 is brought in after its parallel, vv. 1–13, as Moses' *reiteration* to the people of what Yahweh had spoken to him and Aaron. But in that case Moses ought at least to tell what he was told, and not something quite different. Yet he leaves out three-

fourths of what is directed in xii. 1ff., and quite alters the form of the
very simple direction he gives, vv. 21f., though usually where such
repetition occurs in legal passages the divine direction is repeated *verbatim*. He ought certainly to state that this is ordained by Yahweh ; but
he speaks in his own name, and ignores Aaron, who ought to be his
associate (cf. xii. 1), if not his spokesman. In short it is impossible to
call vv. 21-27 a sequel to vv. 1-13. They are a *parallel* passover law
strikingly simpler and more primitive, and the linguistic and stylistic
marks are as peculiarly " prophetic " in vv. 21-27, as they are " priestly "
in vv. 1-13, 28.*

The same relation is easily seen to subsist between the two passages
relating the institution of the feast of Unleavened Bread. Here xiii. 3-
10 is obviously the law of J, based upon the story of xii. 33ff. 37-39, and
characterized by the expressions peculiar to this author (cf. xiii. 5 with
iii. 8, 17 and see references). Instead of the day of the month being
specified as in xii. 14-20, and the month *numbered*, we have, " This day
ye go forth in the month *Abib* " (cf. xxxiv. 18 J,). As in xii. 21ff. where
Moses omits all the directions in regard to the lamb and the manner of
eating it prescribed in xii. 1ff., introducing, apparently on his own responsibility, a different ritual for the sprinkling of the blood (cf. xii. 22
with vs. 7), so here he omits all about the holy convocations with ab-
stinence from labor, which he was directed to prescribe (xii. 16), and
prescribes a ritual of his own. The same relation obtains again between
the ordinance of Yahweh to Moses as to consecration of the firstborn,
xiii. 1f., and the same ordinance as given by Moses to the people in vv.
11-16. Here, in fact, Moses permits himself to make large concessions
from the strict demand of vv. 1f. of " the firstborn of man *and* beast."
All the firstborn of man are to be redeemed by substitution, and for
the valuable ass a kid may be substituted. On any theory save that of
composite origin we must ask ourselves, Whence has Moses permission
to say to his lord's creditors, " Take thy bill and sit down quickly, and
write four-score, or write fifty ? " and why is the law *as given to the people* in these three cases of one character, and *as given to Moses* (or to
Moses and Aaron) of a totally different character, both as to matter and
form ?

---

* The stylistic peculiarities of P² in ch. xii are entirely too numerous for
even bare enumeration in the present work. A list of the more important will
be found in the article : *Die Gesetzgebung der mittleren Bücher*, by K. Budde,
Z. A. W., xi. 2 (1891) p. 196, together with an admirable comparison of the
parallels.

To the difficulties presented by the legislative material it is even less easy to find a solution without the analysis, than to those of the narrative portion. But the same key which unlocks all the mysteries of the one, solves all the problems of the other. The J narrative material which will not agree with either narrative material of E, nor the narrative or legislative of P, agrees perfectly with the legislative material of J (Ct. xii. 34, 39 with vv. 15ff. and cf. xiii. 3ff.; ct. xiii. 3ff with xii. 15ff.; but cf. iii. 8, 17 with xiii. 5) and *vice versa.* The priestly legislative material agrees with its own narrative (cf. xii. 8ff. with Num. xxxiii. 3f.) ; whereas it will agree with neither narrative nor legislation of J (ct. xii. 21-27, 33f., 37–39 etc.) nor narrative of E (xii. 31a, 35f). For the details of the process by which each clause of chh. xiif. is identified as from J, E or P, the reader is referred to Art. II. and the references. The analysis will be found easy and the inconsistencies of the text will disappear if it is borne in mind that in E the Hebrews have warning of their going forth, but not the Egyptians, who are not supposed to know of Moses' demand, or at least not of the impending result ; that in P both Hebrews and Egyptians are prepared ; " for the children of Israel went out with an high hand " (xiv. 8, P) ; but in J alone the people have no forewarning that the result of the long negotiations is suddenly achieved. The result in J fulfills of course the prediction of Moses in xi. 4–8 (cf. xii. 29f.; ct. 31a) ; the result in E, the anticipations of iii. 21f.; xi. 1–3 (cf. xii. 35f.; ct. vv. 32–34, 38f.), and that in P the promise of Yahweh in xii. 12, 17 (cf. xiv. 8 ; Num. xxxiii. 3f.).

---

12   **(P)**   *And Yahweh spake unto Moses and Aaron in the land of*
2   *Egypt, saying,* [1]*This month shall be unto you the beginning of*
3   *months: it shall be the first month of the year to you.* [2]*Speak ye unto all the congregation of Israel, saying, In the tenth* [day] *of this month they shall take to them every man a lamb, according to*
4   *their fathers' houses, a lamb for an household : and if the household be too little for a lamb, then shall he and his neighbour next unto his house take one according to the number of the souls ; according to every man's eating ye shall make your count for the lamb.*
5   *Your lamb shall be* [3]*without blemish, a male of the first year: ye*
6   *shall take it from the sheep, or from the goats : and ye shall keep it up until the fourteenth day of the same month : and the* [4]*whole as-*

[1] Ct. 23 : 16 ; 34 : 22.   [2] Cf. vv. 21 27.   [3] Lev. 3 : 1, 10 etc.; ct. Gen. 7 : 2f.   [4] 16 : 1 ; 17 ; 1etc.

sembly of the congregation of Israel shall kill it at even. [5]*And they* 7
shall take of the blood, and put it on the two side posts and on the
lintel, upon the houses wherein they shall eat it. And they shall 8
eat the flesh in that night, roast with fire, and unleavened bread;
with bitter herbs they shall eat it. Eat not of it raw, nor sodden 9
at all with water, but roast with fire; its head with its legs and
with the inwards thereof. [6]*And ye shall let nothing of it remain* 10
until the morning; but that which remaineth of it until the morn-
ing ye shall burn with fire. And thus shall ye eat it; with your 11
loins girded, your shoes on your feet, and your staff in your hand:
and ye shall eat it in haste: it is Yahweh's passover. For I will 12
go through the land of Egypt in that night, and will smite [7]*all the*
firstborn in the land of Egypt, both man and beast; and [8]*against*
all the gods of Egypt I will execute judgments: [9]*I am Yahweh.*
And the blood shall be to you for a token upon the houses where ye 13
are: and when I see the blood, I will [10]*pass over you, and there*
shall no plague be upon you to destroy you, * *when I smite the land*
of Egypt. [11]*And this day shall be unto you for a memorial, and* 14
ye shall keep it a feast to Yahweh: throughout your generations ye
shall keep it a feast by an ordinance for ever. [12]*Seven days shall* 15
ye eat unleavened bread; even the first day ye shall put away
leaven out of your houses: for whosoever eateth leavened bread
from the first day until the seventh day, that soul shall be cut off
from Israel. And in the first day there shall be to you an [13]*holy* 16
convocation, and in the seventh day an holy convocation; no manner
of work shall be done in them, save that which every man must
eat, that only may be done of you. And ye shall observe the [feast 17
of] unleavened bread; for in this selfsame day have I brought
your hosts out of the land of Egypt: therefore shall ye observe this
day throughout your generations by an ordinance for ever. In the 18
first [month] on the fourteenth day of the month at even, ye shall
eat unleavened bread, until the one and twentieth day of the month

[5]Cf. vs. 22. [6]Cf. 23 : 18; 34 : 25. [7]13 : 1f. [8]Nu. 33 : 4. [9]6 : 8; Lev. 17 : 1, 2, 4etc. [10]Cf.
vs. 23. [11]Vv. 24–27a. [12]Cf. 13 : 3–10. [13]Lev. 23 : 3–37 : ct. 13 : 6.

*Etymologies in P are rather suggested than propounded: ct. vs. 27, and cf.
Gen. xvii. 5, 17; Num. xx. 13. Personifications like that of vs. 23 he prefers
to tone down, as here (vs. 6.); cf. Gen. vi. 1ff. with 9ff.

19 *at even. Seven days shall there be no leaven found in your houses:
for whosoever eateth that which is leavened that "soul shall be cut
off from the congregation of Israel, whether he be a sojourner, or*
20 *one that is born in the land. Ye shall eat nothing leavened; in all
your habitations shall ye eat unleavened bread.*

21   **(J) Then Moses called for all the elders of Israel,
and said unto them, Draw out, and take you lambs**
22 according to your families, **and kill** the passover. **And ye shall
take a bunch of hyssop, and dip it in the blood that is
in the basin, and strike the lintel and the two side
posts with the blood that is in the basin; and none of
you shall go out of the door of his house** [15]until the morning.
23 **For Yahweh will pass through to smite the Egyptians; and when he seeth the blood upon the lintel,
and on the two side posts, Yahweh will pass over the
door, and will not suffer** [16]the destroyer **to come in**
24 **(Rd) unto your houses to smite you.*** [17]And ye shall observe
25 this thing for an ordinance to thee and to thy sons for ever. And it shall
come to pass, when ye be come to the land which Yahweh will give you,
26 according as he hath promised, that ye shall keep this service. And it
shall come to pass, when your children shall say unto you, What mean ye
27 by this service? that ye shall say, It is the sacrifice of Yahweh's passover,

[11]30 : 33, 38. Gen. 17 : 14. [15]Cf. vv. 31ff. [16]Cf. vv. 13. [17]13 : 3, 8-10, 14-16; Dt. 6 : 20f. etc.

* The legislative portions of J wherever met seem to be drastically worked
over and interpolated. It is principally due to this redactional modification
that in Art. II. this section was erroneously attributed to Rje on a basis of E.
It is easier to suppose that influenced by his strong archæological interest J
accounted for the ritual custom of sprinkling the doorpost with the blood of
"the sacrifice of the passover" instead of the altar or *maççebah* as in sacrifices
at the sanctuary, thus making it serve the purpose of "the difference (distinctive mark) which Yahweh put between the Egyptians and Israel" (xi. 7), although
usually no mark is required on account of the isolation of Goshen (viii. 22; ix.
26), than to suppose that E, who elsewhere ignores ritual interests, is the
author of even the basis of this bit of ritual archæology. Dr. Budde very
clearly points out how the priestly section is here throughout dependent on the
"prophetic," cf. e. g., vs. 13 with vs. 23.—The Deuteronomic style of vv. 24-27a
is striking, and characteristic of the didactic interpolator. The first clause of
vs. 27 may have been adopted from the original. See the article in *Z. A. W.*
above referred to (Analysis, p. 59).

who passed over the houses of the children of Israel in Egypt, when he smote the Egyptians, and delivered our houses. **And the people (P) bowed the head and worshipped.** [. . .] *And the* 28 *children of Israel went and did so; as Yahweh had commanded Moses and Aaron, so did they.*

(J) **And it came to pass at midnight, that Yahweh** 29 **smote all the firstborn in the land of Egypt, from the firstborn of Pharaoh that sat on his throne unto the firstborn of the captive that was in the dungeon;** and all the firstborn of cattle.—**And Pharaoh rose up in the** 30 **night, he, and all his servants, and all the Egyptians: —and there was a great cry in Egypt ; for there was (E) not a house where there was not one dead.*** **And** 31 he called for Moses and Aaron by night, and said, Rise up, get you forth from among my people, both ye and the chil- (J) dren of Israel [. . .]**and go, serve Yahweh as ye have said. Take both your flocks and your herds, as** 32 **ye have said, and be gone ; and bless me also. And** 33 **the Egyptians were urgent upon the people, to send them out of the land in haste; for they said, We be all dead men. And the people took their dough before** 34 **it was leavened, their kneading-troughs being bound (E) up in their clothes upon their shoulders.** **And the** 35 children of Israel did according to the word of Moses ; and they asked of the Egyptians jewels of silver, and jewels of gold, and raiment : and Yahweh gave the people favour in 36 the sight of the Egyptians, so that they let them have what they asked. And they spoiled the Egyptians.

(J) **And the children of Israel journeyed from Ram-** 37 **eses to Succoth, about six hundred thousand on foot that were men, beside children. And a mixed multi-** 38 **tude went up also with them ; and flocks, and herds,**

[18]4 : 31.   [19]11 : 4ff.   [20]11 : 8.   [21]11 : 6.   [22]Ct. 10 : 28f.   [23]3 : 18; 5 : 3 ; 8 : 25ff.; 10 : 24ff. etc. [24]8 : 3.   [25]3 : 21f.; 11 : 1-3.   [26]1 : 11.   [27]1 : 10, 20: Nu. 11 : 21.   [28]Nu. 11 : 4.

* Transpose in order 30a and 30bc. By the insertion of vs. 31 (E) in place of the real sequel to 30a (xi. 5, 6, 8, J) Rje found himself compelled to change the relation of 30a from consequent of 30bc and antecedent of " and came and bowed down " (cf. xi. 8) into an antecedent of 30bc.

39 **even very much cattle. And they baked unleavened cakes of the dough which they brought forth out of Egypt, for it was not leavened ; because they were thrust out of Egypt, and could not tarry, neither had**

40 **(P) they prepared for themselves any victual.** [29]*Now the sojourning of the children of Israel, which they sojourned*

41 *in Egypt, was four hundred and thirty years. And it came to pass at the end of four hundred and thirty years, even* [30]*the selfsame day it came to pass, that all the hosts of Yahweh went*

42 **(J)** *out from the land of Egypt.* *—**It is a night to be much observed unto Yahweh for bringing them (Rd) out from the land of Egypt:** this is that night of Yahweh to be much observed of all the children of Israel throughout their generations.†—

43   **(P)** [31]*And Yahweh said unto Moses and Aaron, This is the*

44 *ordinance of the passover : there shall no alien eat thereof : but every man's* [32]*servant that is bought for money, when thou hast cir-*

45 *cumcised him, then shall he eat thereof. A* [33]*sojourner and an*

46 *hired servant shall not eat thereof. In one house shall it be eaten ; thou shalt not carry forth aught of the flesh abroad out of the*

47 *house ; neither shall ye break a bone thereof. All the congregation*

48 *of Israel shall keep it. And when a stranger shall sojourn with thee, and will keep the passover to Yahweh,* [34]*let all his males be circumcised, and then let him come near and keep it ; and he shall be as one that is born in the land : but no uncircumcised per-*

49 *son shall eat thereof. One law shall be to him that is homeborn,*

50 [35]*and unto the stranger that sojourneth among you. Thus did all*

[29]Cf. Gen. 15 : 14, 16.   [30]Vv. 17 : 51; 19 : 1etc.   [31]Gen. 17 : 12, 27.   [32]Gen. 17 : 12, 13, 23, 27etc.   [33]Gen. 23 : 4etc.   [34]Gen. 17 : 10etc.   [35]Vs. 28, Gen. 6 : 22etc.

* Vv. 40, 41 have been removed from after xiii. 2 to combine with the "prophetic" story of the flight, or perhaps, better, xiii. 1f. from before vv. 40f. P's much less vivid narrative, the substance of which can be gathered from vs. 12 and from Nu. xxxiii. 4f, represented the Exodus as taking place "on the morrow after the passover," i. e. the morning of the 15th, ct. vv. 31–34. This account has been of necessity omitted by Rp. It probably stood between xii. 50 and xiii. 1, giving occasion to the enactment xiii. 1f.

† Vs. 42b seems to be due to the redactor (Rd) who takes such an interest in posterity ; it is introduced as a supplement to 42a. So Budde ; cf. Reuss, *La Bible, in loc.* Vs. 42a stood perhaps originally after vs. 27.

*the children of Israel ; as Yahweh commanded Moses and Aaron,
so did they. And it came to pass* [36]*the selfsame day, that Yahweh* 51
*did bring the children of Israel out of the land of Egypt by their
hosts.* [. . .]

[1]*And Yahweh spake unto Moses, saying, Sanctify unto me all* 13
*the firstborn, whatsoever openeth the womb among the children of
Israel, both of man and of beast : it is mine.*

(J) (Rd)   **And Moses said unto the people,** Remember this 3
day, in which ye came [2]out from Egypt, out of the house of bondage ; for [3]by
strength of hand Yahweh brought you out from this place : there shall no
(J) leavened bread be eaten. [4]**This day ye go forth in the 4
month Abib.** [5]**And it shall be when Yahweh shall 5
(Rd) bring thee into the land** of the Canaanite, and the Hittite,
and the Amorite, and the Hivite, and the Jebusite, **which he
sware unto thy fathers to give thee, a land flowing with
milk and honey, that thou shalt keep this service in
this month.** [6]**Seven days thou shalt eat unleavened 6
bread, and in the seventh day shall be a feast to Yahweh. Unleavened bread shall be eaten throughout the 7
seven days ; and there shall no leavened bread be seen
with thee, neither shall there be leaven seen with
(Rd) thee,** [7]**in all thy borders.** [8]And thou shalt tell thy son in 8
that day, saying, It is because of that which Yahweh did for me when I came
forth out of Egypt. And it shall be for a sign unto thee upon thine hand, 9
and for a memorial between thine eyes, that the law of Yahweh may be in
thy mouth : for with a strong hand hath Yahweh brought thee out of Egypt.
Thou shalt therefore keep this ordinance in its season from year to year. 10

(J)   **And it shall be when Yahweh shall bring thee 11
into the land of the Canaanite, as he** [9]**sware unto thee
and to thy fathers, and shall give it thee, that thou 12
shalt set apart unto Yahweh** [10]**all that openeth the
womb, and every firstling which thou hast that com-
eth of a beast ;** *the males* **shall be Yahweh's.** [11]**And every 13
firstling of an ass thou shalt redeem with a lamb ; and
if thou wilt not redeem it, then thou shalt break its**

---

[36]Vv. 17, 41 ; 16 : 1 ; 19 : 1. [1]28 : 41 ; etc cf. vv. 11ff. [2]Vs. 14 : 20 : 2 ; Dt. 5 : 6 : 6 ; 12 : 8 :
14 : 13 : 5, 10 etc. [3]Vv. 9, 16 ; 3 : 19f ; 6 : 1 etc. [4]34 : 18. [5]3 : 8 ; 33 : 2 etc. [6]Cf. 12 : 15f.
[7]8 : 2 ; 10 : 4, 14. [8]10 : 2 : 12 :24 ; Vs. 16 ; Dt. 6 : 4-9 ; 11 : 18-21 etc. [9]Gen. 15 : 18. [10]22 :
29f. ; 34 : 19 cf. vv. 1f. [11]34 : 20.

neck: and all the firstborn of man among thy sons
14 **(Rd) shalt thou redeem.** ¹²And it shall be when thy son asketh
thee in time to come, saying, What is this? that thou shalt say unto him,
¹³By strength of hand Yahweh brought us out from Egypt, from the house
15 of bondage: and it came to pass, when Pharaoh would ¹⁴hardly let us go,
that Yahweh slew all the firstborn in the land of Egypt, both the firstborn
of man, and the firstborn of beast: therefore I sacrifice to Yahweh all that
openeth the womb, being males; but all the firstborn of my sons I redeem.
16 ¹⁶And it shall be for a sign upon thine hand, and for frontlets between thine
eyes: for by strength of hand Yahweh brought us forth out of Egypt.

---

§ III.   EXODUS xiii. 17–xix. 25.   THE EXODUS: FROM EGYPT
TO SINAI.

PROLEGOMENA.

According to the priestly writer Israel went forth on the
morning of the fifteenth of the first month, in the sight of the
Egyptians engaged in the burial of their dead, and "with an
high hand" (Num. xxxiii. 3f.; xiv. 8). Taking their departure
from Succoth they reach Etham "in the edge of the wilderness"; xiii. 20. But Yahweh is not satisfied with so easy a
victory, purposing to make a signal exhibition of his power
upon Pharaoh and the Egyptians (cf. xiv. 4). Moses and the
people are therefore bidden to retrace their steps. Returning
again from the wilderness they place themselves in an apparent
cul-de-sac, south of the isthmus, where the road to the east is
cut off by the Gulf of Suez. Pharaoh's heart is hardened by
Yahweh, and he pursues after and overtakes his aggravating
foes "encamped beside Pihahiroth, before Baal-zephon." At
Yahweh's command Moses stretches out his hand over the sea,
which divides, and Israel passes over on dry land. Pharaoh's
army, divinely emboldened, follow after. Moses is again directed to stretch out his hand and the watery walls collapse,
engulfing the Egyptians; xiv. 1f.3 (?), 4., 8f., 15f., in part; 17f.,
21a, c, 22f., 26, 27a, 28a, 29. One month thereafter Israel
comes to the wilderness of Sin; xvi. 1. At this point is brought
in the story of Israel's murmuring for the flesh-pots of Egypt.

¹²Dt. 6: 20ff.   ¹³Vs. 4 etc.   ¹⁴9: 35; 10: 20, 27.   ¹⁶Dt. 6: 8f.; 11: 18.

Moses and Aaron summon the congregation before the tabernacle (*sic*), whereupon "the glory of Yahweh" appears in the
cloud (*sic*), and Yahweh rebukes the people, but promises flesh
and bread. In the evening quails cover the camp ; with the
morning dew appears a white edible flake, to which Israel gives
the name of "Manna." This becomes their food until they
come to Canaan. Aaron is bidden to lay up a pot thereof before
the "Testimony" (*sic*) to be kept ; ch. xvi., for the most part.
After a station at Rephidim (xvii. 1a) "the whole congregation"
comes to Sinai on the fifteenth of the third month ; xix. 2a, 1.

According to E Israel went forth in battle array, laden only
with the spoil of Egypt, gold and jewels, and the bones of
Joseph (with xiii. 19 cf. Gen. l. 25f.). God (*Elohim*) led them,
but not by the nearest road, on account of the hostility of the
Philistines ; a *détour* is made, which brings them to the Red
Sea ; xiii. 17-19 (cf. Jos. xxiv. 6). Here Pharaoh, pursuing
"with chariots and horsemen" (Jos. xxiv. 6), overtakes them.
Israel cries out to Yahweh, who puts darkness between them
and the Egyptians, the angel of God removing from before and
"going" behind the camp of Israel ; xiv. 3 (?), 7 in part, 10b,
19f. in part (cf. Jos. xxiv. 7). Moses stretches out his rod over
the sea [which opens a passage for Israel, (cf. Is. x. 24, 26 ; lxiii.
12)] while Yahweh brings the waters upon Pharaoh's pursuing
host and covers them ; xiv. 16a, 24c, 25a (?), 31a (?) ; (Jos. xxiv.
7). This victory is celebrated by Miriam and the women in
responsive song and dance ; xv. 20f. Hereafter Israel comes to
[Massah] where they are put to the "test" (*massah*) by Yahweh by a "statute and ordinance" preliminary to the covenant
at Horeb. This test consists in the giving of the food called
"manna," of which each is to take but a single day's supply.
Some endeavor to lay up for the morrow, and excite Moses'
wrath ; xv. 25b ; xvi. 4, 15, 16a, 20f., 35. Here (?) the people
suffer thirst, and rebel against Moses ; who at Yahweh's command goes before the people to [Meribah] and smites with the
rod upon "the rock in Horeb," whereupon water issues forth
for the people ; xvii. 3-6. At this point are inserted the story
of the battle with Amalek at Rephidim, in which Moses, by

means of the uplifted rod, obtains victory for Israel, and the story of Jethro's visit to Moses at the mount of God (*sic*) leading to the appointment of judges to assist Moses in administering justice, and in making the people know the statutes of God and his laws (*sic*): xvii. 8–16 ; ch. xviii. Arrived at Horeb Moses goes up to God and receives directions in preparation for a sublime theophany *to the people*, and a divine covenant ; xix. 3–10, 14–17, 19.

According to J Israel is led forth from Egypt by Yahweh in a pillar of fire and cloud. But when Pharaoh heard of their flight he changed his mind and pursued after them. Israel, seeing the pursuers and despairing of escape, murmurs against Moses, but is reassured by the promise of divine help ; xiii. 21f.; xiv. 5–7 mainly, 10a, 11–14. The pillar of fire and cloud removes from before the camp of Israel and "stands" behind them, intercepting the pursuers all night. Yahweh causes the sea to go back by a strong east wind all the night, exposing the shoals, over which Israel make their escape. In the morning watch the battle ensues, but Yahweh "looks forth from the pillar of fire and cloud," and puts the Egyptians to rout. They "flee against" the returning tide, Yahweh "shaking them off" in the midst of the sea, so that "not so much as one remained." The sight of the Egyptian dead upon the seashore, and the experience of Yahweh's salvation beget faith in the peoples' mind. Moses and Israel celebrate the triumph in song ; xiv. 19b, 20b, 21 in part, 24f. in part, 27f. in part, 30f. in part ; xv. 1. Moses leads Israel out into the wilderness, Yahweh directing him at Marah how to sweeten the bitter waters ; xv. 22–25a. They encamp at Elim, and later at a place called Massah, because the people there "tempted" Yahweh ; xv. 27 ; xvi. 1a ; xvii. 3, 2b, 7 in part. At *Sinai* Yahweh reveals himself in fire, directing Moses, *with the priests and elders*, to come up unto Yahweh, after precautions against intrusion by the people ; xix. 11–13, 18, 20–25.

In this entire section the superior worth of J over E as a historical source is peculiarly apparent, and this is most distinctly recognizable in the narratives where actual historic tra-

dition is undeniably present. There is no reasonable doubt
that the story of the crossing of the Red Sea, wherein, as Paul
well says, the nation was "baptized unto Moses," was *the* folk-
tale of Israel *par excellence*, related from time immemorial at
every Passover feast. It was the national independence-day,
birthday and christening-day in one : and the victory then
achieved over the host of Pharaoh was one which baptized the
nation unto Yahweh, the God in whose name Moses had summoned them to the liberty of the desert as the God of their
fathers, no less than "unto Moses." Its opportuneness and its
providential character both alike ensured a lasting remembrance
of it in the tradition of the nation then born, as the proof that
Yahweh is indeed the God of Israel, and Israel is his people.
Such a remembrance is certainly preserved in the essentially
plain and trustworthy account of J, wherein Moses leads Israel
off the high-road, to the south of the fortified isthmus, to where,
under favorable conditions and the guidance of one familiar
with the locality, a crossing could be effected over the shallows
of the "Sea of Reeds." Had not the providential "wind of
Yahweh," however, driven back the sea, the effort to cross,
with Pharaoh's troops unexpectedly attacking the rear, would
have been hopeless. The night-crossing, under the gloomy
thunder-clouds, the battle in the morning on the further shore,
when the breaking forth of the sun revealed the Egyptians entangled in the quicksands and drowned by the returning tide,
are not the work of imagination, but of grateful and undying
recollection, refreshed at every Passover feast.

All the greater appears the contrast in the parallel accounts.
The rigid, mechanical wonder-working of P^2 is indeed no more
than we have learned to expect from this writer ; but in E we
might expect something of the actual remembrance to survive.
Critics like Dillman and Kittel, who maintain the origin of
E to be earlier than of J, doubtless hold that if the E element
of ch. xiv. could be extricated we should find it to contain as
much, or more, of the historical character than J. Unfortunately this belief, if it exists, is here ill-founded. The passage
Is. x. 26, "As his rod was over the sea, so shall he lift it up

after the manner of Egypt," by an author who, on *any* theory, cannot possibly have known P², does not refer to J and may be seen when compared with vs. 24 to refer, beyond all reasonable doubt, to E. This, with the fragments remaining in Ex. xiv., and Jos. xxiv. 6f., is amply sufficient to prove that E's account was much nearer to P²'s than to J's.

The second great feature of this section, wherein the elements of actual history may be recognized, is the Visit to Sinai. Here beyond doubt we must recognize as most nearly related to the actual facts the representation which describes the law as received by Moses in solitary communion with Yahweh on Sinai, and engraved by his human hand upon stones, rather than that which describes a voice resounding from the mount in trumpet tones announcing to all the people the moral code in articulated words, and which afterward declares that God himself on Horeb wrote the Words with his finger upon the stone tables of his own making.

Nor is the relation essentially different in the narrative of the journey in the wilderness. In E Israel depends from the outset on miraculous provision for food and drink. The manna is "bread rained from heaven," xvi. 4 ; in J it is only referred to subsequently, in passing, as one of the meagre resources of the desert, the occasion of the peoples' complaint. The author speaks of it in just the same terms a modern manna gatherer of the same region might employ of the manna of to-day, the *mann es shema* or "gift of heaven" of the Arabs. In E water is miraculously supplied by "the rod of God." In J the people depend upon the wells along the route.

Let it not be considered that in drawing this contrast in *historical* value between E and J we are depreciating the former. On the contrary, the moral and religious standard of E is as much higher than J's as the historical accuracy is lower, and for the same reasons. Still less let it be imagined that critical estimates of this kind constitute an "attack" upon the Bible. The reverse is the case. If the historical value of the story of the Exodus depends upon the acceptation of the monstrosities of P, Colenso has given the Pentateuch its death-blow. If further the Bible is of no value unless a particular post-Reformation doctrine of inerrancy can make shift to lump all parts together as equally divine and equally accurate for all purposes, then the Bible is doomed. But the separation of earlier from later, historical from unhistorical, late and religiously developed from early and religiously primitive, will preserve all elements, and make each valuable for its appropriate function and teaching. The present attempt to extricate the primitive account of J, if successful, will go far to vindicate the Tradition of the Exodus as in its most essential features historical. It constitutes the true answer to Colenso's formidable indictment.

1. Chh. xiii. 17–xv. 21. THE CROSSING OF THE RED SEA.

ANALYSIS.

God leads the people to the Red Sea, where they encamp. Pharaoh pursues and overtakes them. Moses encourages the people ; the waters are divided, allowing Israel to pass through dry shod, but engulfing the pursuing Egyptians. Israel's song of triumph.

In this subsection the marks of compilation are as conspicuous as ever. We need not dwell upon such as merely repeat inconsistencies of view of the different sources already alluded to, such as the improbability of 600,000 fighting men (xii. 37) "armed " (xiii. 18) and defiant in the face of the Egyptians (xiv. 8) recoiling from an encounter with the Philistines (xiii. 17), in abject despair before a detachment of Pharaoh's army (xiv. 10ff.), and put to their utmost by the petty desert clan of Amalek (xvii. 8ff.) ; or such as the orderly preparation and mobilization which xiii. 18f. presuppose, in contrast with xii. 37–39, where not even victual could be prepared in advance. Apologetic ingenuity can perhaps discover also a reason why in xiii. 17–19 the story of the divine guidance should be told with the use (four times) of *Elohim* exclusively, but in vv. 21f. with the name Yahweh. It is more important to examine at once ch. xiv. as traditionally received, the story of the crossing of the Red Sea to which subsequent allusion is made in portions assigned to all the documents, and which, if the documentary theory is correct, should therefore probably exhibit traces of all three. Is ch. xiv. a unit ?

In vv. 15–22 we meet a difficulty analogous to that encountered in the story of the plague of locusts. If Moses' rod extended over the sea divides it, what use of the strong east wind blowing all night ? Did

Moses stretch out his hand with the rod over the sea on the evening before, and nothing happen for several hours? Or did the strong east wind drive back the sea, exposing the shallows, and afterward Moses extend his rod and divide what remained of it? What sort of "wind" had the writer in mind who describes the waters as cloven in twain, so as to leave a "wall" of waters on the right and left of the pursuers and pursued? and how could the Egyptians "flee against it" after "the sea returned to its wonted flow"? Again, we may ask the question, was it the writer's understanding that the crossing took place by daylight, or in the night? He seems to vacillate between the two. The dramatic gesture of Moses dividing the sea with the rod of God certainly seems to presuppose daylight, both for the beginning and end of the crossing. But according to vs. 24 when the morning watch appeared Israel is safe on the further shore, and the Egyptians have already engaged in conflict with them, and are embarrassed in the shoals and quicksands of the sea. Yet the former part of vs. 20 again seems to indicate that the barrier between the Egyptians and Israel was *darkness*, and this is confirmed by Jos. xxiv. 7 (E), " Ye cried out unto Yahweh, and he put darkness between you and the Egyptians, and brought the sea upon them and covered them." Then the event must have taken place in the *daytime* ; but cf. vs. 20b.

In ch. xv. there are no such decided contrasts in point of view. But neither is there the apparent relation between vv. 20f. and the preceding which the R. V. would establish. In vs. 21 we should translate simply " And Miriam *sang* (responsively) with them" (*i. e.* the women ; Vulg. *quibus praecinebat*) as in the exactly analogous passage 1 Sam. xviii. 7 (Budde J). Vv. 20f. then appear in their true light as a duplicate of vs. 1. Duplicates in xiii. 17–xiv. 31 are numerous. We need instance only the following : xiv. 5 7=vv. 8f. ; 19a–19b ; 27–28 ; 23, 28f.=xv. 19.

In this confusion we have only to apply the principles of analysis already found so successful, and the three independent narratives reappear, self consistent and characteristic as usual, though in the case of E less complete ; while all discrepancies and dissonances vanish.

The most easily identified is as usual P². " The passages assigned to P," says Prof. Driver (*Lit. of the O. T.*, p. 27), " will be found to be connected both with each other and with other parts of the Pentateuch belonging to the same source : thus ' harden (*harag*) the heart,' vs. 4, recurs vv. 8, 17, and is the same term that is used by P in the narrative of the plagues ; ' get me honor ' *ib.* recurs vv. 17, 18 ; Lev. x. 3 ; comp. also vv. 4, 18 ' and the Egyptians shall know,' etc., (cf. vi. 7 ; vii. 5 ; xvi. 12) ; vv. 9, 23, ' and the Egyptians pursued ' ; vv. 22, 29, ' the dry land '

and the ' wall '; vv. 16, 21, 'divide'; the *repetitions* (in the manner of P) in vv. 17f. as compared with vs. 4, in 28a as compared with 23, in 29 as compared with 22."

As xiv. 1–4, 8f. is thus unquestionably from P, vs. 20 of the preceding chapter must be from the same writer, since it is presupposed by vs. 2 (" turn back ").* The motive for this gratuitous return from the wilderness to Egyptian territory seems to be, as usual in P, purely *ad majorem Dei gloriam ;* cf. xiv. 4, 8, 17 with vii. 3–5 ; xi. 9f. It also appears from the above that the representation of the dividing of the sea by the stretching out of Moses' hand is P's, in contrast with the associated, but really incompatible, representation of a driving back of the sea by an east wind blowing all night (cf. x. 13, 19 and Num. xi. 31f.). This latter representation is very easily recognizable as J's from the references just given. It forms really a part of the cycle of plague narratives of this document, in which first the announcement is made of what Yahweh will do, thereafter Yahweh himself intervenes, not by the agency of Moses nor of the rod, but by natural means, and brings about the result. Here the announcement is made in vv. 10a, 11–14, where vs. 12 refers either to v. 21 (J) or else to something now wanting, and the style and language are characteristic of this document (see refs.), and the story of Yahweh's intervention during the night and on the following day (cf. x. 13b ; Num. xi. 31f.) ensues. In vs. 25b the fulfilment of the promise in vs. 14 is given *verbatim*, and vs. 30 is similarly connected with vs. 13. It thus appears with great positiveness that the narrative in which the crossing is effected during the *night* is J's ; for " in the morning watch," vs. 24, Yahweh looks forth from the pillar of fire and cloud upon the pursuing Egyptians. The mention of "the pillar of fire and cloud " proves that it is this same writer whose story we have in xiii. 21f. (cf. also " Yahweh " in contrast with " *Elohim* " in the parallel vv. 17–19) ; and it is a further necessary conclusion that xiv. 19b, 20b, from " yet gave it light " (*i. e.* lightnings?), where the " pillar of cloud " becomes a barrier of *fire* " all night," " *standing* " between the Egyptians and Israel, is from the same account ; whereas the parallel verses, 19a, 20a (to " darkness "), in which " the angel of God " (*Elohim*), is the guiding manifestation " which *went* before the camp of Israel " are necessarily from another source, since the barrier here is not light (or lightnings) but *darkness*. Hence it contemplates a passage by *day*. The further extrication of the J source

---

*This verse xiii. 20 is in a J context (vv. 21f.) and seems to connect with xii. 37 (J); but the form of expression in xii. 37 in the Hebrew is different from that of xiii. 20 and nowhere employed by P, while xiii. 20 belongs to a regular series of this writer identical in form (xvii. 1 ; xix. 1f. etc.).

after the establishment of this peculiarity is a matter so simple as to be readily left to the reader ; but further details of evidence for the analysis of the chapter will be found in Art. III.

Turning to the third source which has become apparent in vv. 19a, 20a it is quite obvious that we have here no mere fragment of P, although the writer seems to coincide with P's representation of a passage by day. On the contrary, to say nothing of the most remarkable characteristic, " the angel of God " (cf. Num. xx. 16 ; E), these clauses are inseparable from xiii. 17-19, a passage whose derivation from E is established beyond the possibility of doubt by its style and language, but particularly by the connection with Gen. v. 25 and Jos. xxiv. 32 (E). It is clear then that at least some fragments remain of that story of how " they came to the Red Sea, and the Egyptians pursued after your fathers with chariots and horsemen unto the Red Sea ; and when they cried out unto Yahweh, he put darkness between you and the Egyptians, and brought the sea upon them and covered them," which E himself thus subsequently refers to in the speech of Joshua, Jos. xxiv. 6f. Vs. 10b, first of all, is shown by this reference to be from the E narrative. Next vs. 16a is certainly from E, for no other document knows anything of such a use of *Moses'* rod ; but more particularly this is proved by Is. x. 26 (" His rod was over the sea "), and even E's agreement with P as to the *division* of the waters follows from the reference in Is. lxiii. 11f. which is older than P², and cannot refer to J. Finally, there is some reason (see Art. III.) for attributing also vs. 3 and a few other clauses, including vv. 25a and 31, to the same document.

In ch. xv. there is no trace of P², a document entirely devoid of poetic material. Only vs. 19 appears to be constructed on the basis of xiv. 23, 28f., and serves as a colophon to the psalm xv. 1–18, whose incorporation (in its present form) would accordingly be brought down to a late date. The inappropriateness of the poem itself to the circumstances, at least from vs. 11 onwards (cf. vs. 11 " praises," literally " psalms," 12 " earth " 13, the temple, 17, translating verbs in the past), is additional reason for thinking that the poem from vs. 2 onward is an independent incorporation. This view is strongly corroborated by the fact that the author of Is. xii. a postexilic writer, apparently refers to this song among others, speaking of it *as if it began with vs.* 2, and not with the preceding lines, which are identical with vs. 21. Had the poem been written, as assumed by many critics, as a development of vs. 21 the lines of this verse would not have been repeated, but simply vv. 2ff. attached to it. The independence of the poem 2–18 is further shown by the striking *in*appropriateness of its latter part to the situation ; while it is at the same time impossible to account for its incorporation here unless vv. 4ff. were also included in it to give it some color of appropriateness. Finally, as we have such strong reason to suppose its opening lines to have been those of vs. 2, the fact of its attachment here, instead of after vs. 21, is unaccountable, unless vs. 1 is an original fragment of J parallel to vv. 20f. (E). The verbal correspondence is not unexampled, but recurs in the " Words of the Covenant," Ex. xxiii. 14-19=xxxiv. 22-26, and parts of the Song of Balaam, Num. xxiiff.

——— ———

(E) And it came to pass, when Pharaoh had let the 17 people go, that God led them not by the way of the land of the Philistines, although that was near ; for God said, Lest peradventure the people repent when they see war, and they return to Egypt : but God led the people about, by the way 18 of the wilderness by the Red Sea : and the children of Israel went up armed out of the land of Egypt.   [19]And Moses took 19 the bones of Joseph with him : for he had straitly sworn the children of Israel, saying, God will surely visit you ; and ye shall carry up my bones away hence with you.*

(P) *And they took their journey from* [17]*Succoth, and encamped* 20 **(J)** *in Etham, in the edge of the wilderness.* [18]**And Yahweh** 21 **went before them by day in a pillar of cloud, to lead them the way ; and by night in a pillar of fire, to give them light ; that they might go by day and by night : the pillar of cloud by day, and the pillar of fire by** 22 **night, departed not from before the people.**

(P) *And Yahweh spake unto Moses, saying, Speak unto the* 2 **14** *children of Israel, that they turn back and encamp before Pi-hahiroth, between Migdol and the sea, before Baal-zephon : over*

[16]Gen. 50 : 24f. [17]12 : 37. [18]Nu. 10 : 34 ; 14 : 14 ; cf. 14 : 19. [1]13 : 20.

*The use of *Elohim* is no longer obligatory upon E, nor does he commonly employ it in his own composition ; rather he seems, like Rp and Rje, to favor personally " Yahweh." He seems, however, not to have taken the trouble to alter the name *Elohim* where employed in his source. Hence the use of *Elohim* without specific reason is still a criterion where it occurs. For similar retention of a source peculiarity cf. Dt. iv. 32 with Gen. 1. 27, and see Budde, *Bibl. Urgeschichte*, pp. 487ff., 497.

3 (E) *against it shall ye encamp by the sea.* And Pharaoh will
say* of the children of Israel, They are entangled in the land,
4 (P) the wilderness hath shut them in. *And I will harden
Pharaoh's heart, and he shall follow after them ; and I will get
me honor upon Pharaoh, and upon all his host ; and the Egyptians shall know that I am Yahweh. And they did so.*

5 **(J) And it was told the king of Egypt that the
people were ³fled : and the heart of Pharaoh and of his
servants was changed towards the people, and they
said, ⁴What is this we have done, that we have let
6 Israel go from ⁵serving us? And he made ready his**
7 **(E) chariot, and took his people with him :** and he took
six hundred chosen ⁶chariots, **and all the chariots of Egypt**
8 (P) [. . .] and captains over all of them. [. . .] *⁷And
Yahweh hardened the heart of Pharaoh king of Egypt, and he
pursued after the children of Israel : for the children of Israel
9 went out ⁸with an high hand. And the Egyptians pursued after
them, all the horses [and] chariots of Pharaoh, and his horsemen,
and his army, and overtook them ⁹encamping by the sea, beside Pi-
10 (J) hahiroth,* before *Baal-zephon.* **And when Pharaoh
¹drew nigh, the children of Israel lifted up their eyes,
and, behold, the Egyptians marched after them ; and
(E) they were sore afraid :** ¹⁰and the children of Israel
11 **(J) cried out unto Yahweh.** [. . .] **And they said unto
Moses, Because there were no graves in Egypt, hast
thou taken us away to die in the wilderness ?** ¹²**wherefore hast thou dealt thus with us, to bring us forth
12 out of Egypt? Is not this the word that we ¹³spake
unto thee in Egypt, saying, Let us alone, that we
may serve the Egyptians? For it were better for us
to serve the Egyptians, than that we should die in the
13 wilderness. And Moses said unto the people, Fear ye
not, stand still, and see the ¹⁴salvation of Yahweh,**

* It vs. 3 is assigned to E (see Art. III. *in loc.*) we must read " said."

**which he will work for you to-day : for the Egyptians
whom ye have seen to-day, ye shall see them again no
more forever.** [15]**Yahweh shall fight for you, and ye** 14
shall hold your peace.*

(P) (E) *And Yahweh said unto Moses,* Wherefore criest 15
(P) thou unto me ? *speak unto the children of Israel, that they*
(E) *go forward.* [16]And lift thou up thy rod, [. . .] *and* 16
[17]*stretch out thine hand over the sea, and divide it : and the children
of Israel shall go into the midst of the sea on dry ground.* [18]*And* 17
*I, behold, I will harden the hearts of the Egyptians, and they shall
go [in] after them : and I will get me honour upon Pharaoh, and
upon all his host, upon his chariots, and upon his horsemen.   And* 18
*the Egyptians shall know that I am Yahweh, when I have gotten
me honour upon Pharaoh upon his chariots, and upon his horse-*
(E) *men.*—And the [19]angel of God, which went before the 19
(J) camp of Israel, removed and went behind them ; **and
the pillar of cloud removed from before them, and**
(E) **stood behind them :** and it came between the camp of 20
Egypt and the camp of Israel ; and there was the cloud and
(J) the [20]darkness,†—**yet gave it light by night : and the**
(P) **one came not near the other all the night.** [21]*And* 21
(J) *Moses stretched out his hand over the sea :* [22]**and Yahweh
caused the sea to go [back] by a strong east wind all**
(P) **the night, and made the sea dry land,** *and the waters
were divided.   And the children of Israel went into the midst of* 22
the sea upon the dry ground : [23]*and the waters were a wall unto*

[15]Vs. 25.   [16]7 : 20; 9 : 22f.; 10 : 12f. 21f ; 17 : 5f. 9 : Is. 10 : 26.   [17]Vv. 21, 26f.   [18]Vs. 4.   [19]13:
17f ; cf. 13 : 21f, and vs. 19b.   [20]Jos. 24 : 7.   [21]Vs. 16.   [22]10 : 13, 19 ; Nu. 11 :31.   [23]Cf. 15 : 8.

* The motive for Israel's return from the wilderness to Egyptian territory in
P is more theological than historical ; but in E a reason is given why they were
brought to the sea. (cf. xiii. 17 and Jos. xxiv. 6).   In J, however, we are left to
infer that the people consent to leave the Isthmus and be led to the edge of the
sea, south of the usual road, because they know that in the absence of opposition the gulf is fordable, as at the present day.

† The displacement of vv. 19a, 20a is inferred from Josh. xxiv. 7, where the
putting of darkness between Israel and Egypt is the response to the people's
cry to Yahweh. The text of vs. 20b is probably corrupt, and the translation is
uncertain.

23 *them on their right hand, and on their left. And the Egyptians*
pursued, and went in after them into the midst of the sea, all Pha-

24 (J) *raoh's horses, his chariots, and his horsemen.* **And it came
to pass in the morning watch, that Yahweh** [24]**looked
forth upon the host of the Egyptians through the**
[25]**pillar of fire and of cloud, and discomfited the host**

25 (E) **of the Egyptians.** And he took off their chariot

(J) wheels, that they drave them heavily : **so that the
Egyptians said, Let us flee from the face of Israel ;**
[26]**for Yahweh fighteth for them against the Egyptians.**

26   (P) [27]*And Yahweh said unto Moses, Stretch out thine hand*
over the sea, that the waters may come again upon the Egyptians,

27 *upon their chariots, and upon their horsemen.* *And Moses*

(J) *stretched forth his hand over the sea,* **and the sea returned
to its strength when the morning appeared ; and the
Egyptians fled against it ; and Yahweh overthrew the**

28 (P) **Egyptians in the midst of the sea.** *And the waters*
returned, and covered the chariots, and the horsemen, even all the

(J) *host of Pharaoh that went in after them into the sea,* **there**

29 (P) **remained not so much as one of them.** *But the*
children of Israel walked upon dry land in the midst of the sea :
and the waters were a wall unto them on their right hand, and

30 (J) *on their left.* [29]**Thus Yahweh saved Israel that day
out of the hand of the Egyptians ; and Israel saw the**

31 (E) **Egyptians dead upon the sea shore.** And Israel
saw the [31]'great work which Yahweh did upon the Egyptians,
and the people [31]feared Yahweh ; and they believed in Yahweh, and in [32]his servant Moses.*

15   (J) [1]**Then sang Moses and the children of Israel
this song unto Yahweh, and spake, saying,**

[24]Gen. 18 : 16 ; 14 : 28 ; 26 : 8.   [25]Vs. 19.   [26]Vs. 14.   [27]Vv. 16, 21.   [28]8 : 31 ; 10 : 15, 19.
[29]Vs. 13.   [30]2 : 10 ; 6 : 1.   [31]Gen. 20 : 11 ; 42 : 18 ; Ex. 1. 17, 21 ; Jos. 24 : 14.   [32]Nu. 12 : 7f. ;
Dt. 34 : 5 ; Jos. 1 : 2.   [1]Cf. vs. 20f. ; Nu. 21 : 17 ; Jos. 10 : 12 ; Jud. 5 : 1.

---

* The separation of vs. 31 from the context is tentative rather than necessary.
There seems, however, to be some reduplication of thought as well as language ; cf. 30b. with 31a, and note the repetition of the subject. The references
indicate the linguistic reasons.

I will sing unto Yahweh, for he hath triumphed
   gloriously :
The horse and his rider hath he ²thrown into the
   sea.

(Ps) ³Yahweh is my strength and song,   2
And he is become my ⁴salvation :
This is my God, and I will praise him ;
My father's God, and I will exalt him.
Yahweh is a man of war :   3
Yahweh is his name.
Pharaoh's chariots and his host hath he ⁵cast into the sea :   4
And his chosen captains are sunk in the Red sea.
The deeps cover them :   5
They went down into the depths like a stone.
Thy right hand, O Yahweh, is glorious in power,   6
Thy right hand, O Yahweh, dasheth in pieces the enemy.
And in the greatness of thine excellency thou overthrowest them that rise   7
   up against thee :
Thou sendest forth thy wrath, it consumeth them as stubble.
⁶And with the blast of thy nostrils the waters were piled up,   8
⁷The floods stood upright as an heap ;
The deeps were congealed in the heart of the sea.
The enemy said,   9
I will pursue, I will overtake, I will divide the spoil :
My lust shall be satisfied upon them ;
I will draw my sword, my hand shall destroy them.
⁸Thou didst blow with thy wind, the sea covered them :   10
They sank as lead in the mighty waters.
Who is like unto thee, O Yahweh, among the gods ?   11
Who is like thee, glorious in holiness,
Fearful in praises, doing wonders ?
Thou stretchest out thy right hand,   12
⁹The earth swallowed them.
Thou in thy mercy hast led the people which thou hast redeemed :   13
Thou hast guided them in thy strength to thy holy habitation.
¹⁰The peoples have heard, they tremble :   14
Pangs have taken hold on the inhabitants of Philistia.
Then were the ¹¹dukes of Edom amazed ;   15
The mighty men of Moab, trembling taketh hold upon them :
All the inhabitants of Canaan are melted away.
Terror and dread falleth upon them ;   16

²Ct. vs. 4.   ³Is. 12 : 2.   ⁴14 : 13.   ⁵Ct. vs. 1.   ⁶14 : 21.   ⁷14 : 22.   ⁸14 : 27.   ⁹Nu. 16 : 32.
¹⁰Jos. 10 : 2.   ¹¹Gen. 36 : 21.

By the greatness of thine arm they are as still as a stone ;
Till thy people pass over, O Yahweh,
Till the people pass over which thou hast [12]purchased.
Thou shalt bring them in, and plant them in the mountain of thine in-

17   heritance,
The place, O Yahweh, which thou hast made for thee to dwell in,
The sanctuary, O Yahweh, which thy hands have established.

18   Yahweh shall reign for ever and ever.

19   (Rp)   *[13]For the horses of Pharaoh went in with his chariots and with his horsemen into the sea, and Yahweh brought again the waters of the sea upon them ; but the children of Israel walked on dry land in the midst of the sea.**

20 **(E)**   [14]And Miriam [15]the prophetess, the [16]sister of Aaron, took a timbrel in her hand ; and all the women went out

21 after her with timbrels and with dances. And Miriam answered them,†

     [17]Sing ye to Yahweh, for he hath triumphed gloriously :
     The horse and his rider hath he thrown into the sea.

———◆———

2. Chh. xv. 22—xvii. 7. THE DIVINE SUPPLY OF FOOD AND
WATER IN THE DESERT.

ANALYSIS.

Arrived at Marah the bitter waters are sweetened by a healing branch. A statute and ordinance is given. At Elim the people find a pleasant oasis ; xv. 22 27. In the wilderness of Sin manna and quails are provided in response to the murmurs of the people ; ch. xvi. They come to Rephidim, where the rod of Moses brings water from the rock. The place is called Massah and Meribah from the murmuring and " striving " of the people ; xvii. 1-7.

The present subsection affords the most difficult problems hitherto met in the analysis. Indications of the triplicity of sources are as positive as ever, and are accompanied by equally positive evidence of displacement of

[12]Is. 11 : 11.   [13]14 : 29.   [14]1 Sam. 18 : 6-8 ; Jud. 4 : 4.   [16]Nu. 12 : 2.   [15]2 : 4.   [17]vs. 1.

* Vs. 19 may be attributed to the redactor (probably Rp) who incorporated the psalm. It resembles in style xiv. 29, and may thus indicate the date of incorporation.

† *I. e.* sang responsively with the *women.* LXX. and Vulg. (*quibus praecinebat*) seem to have had here the feminine pronoun, to which R has given the masculine form for the sake of connecting with vv. 1ff.

material by Rp. But here the reconstruction of the sources is less easy, perhaps for the reason that so much displacement has occurred. Thus in
1 7 we appear to be at Rephidim, and such appears also to be the case xvii.
in vs. 8. But meanwhile, in 5f., Moses and the people have " passed on "
and come to *Horeb*. Here we indeed find them encamped in xviii. 5 ;
but this is in direct contradiction with xix. 1f., which relates their *subsequent* arrival there. Moreover, the incident of xvii. 1–7, which by vv. 1
and 8 is located at Rephidim and by vv. 5f. at Horeb, is unequivocally
stated in vs. 7 to have taken place at Massah-Meribah. We naturally
infer that at least Massah and Meribah are duplicate names for the same
locality ; but Dt. vi. 16 ; ix. 22 ; xxxiii. 8 (?) treat them as two different
localities, marked by different events. But, most remarkable of all, in
Num. xx. 1–13 we find another story of how Israel " strove with Moses "
in consequence of thirst for water, how Moses thereupon under divine
direction " smote the rock with his rod," and the waters gushed out, and
so *this place also* was called " Meribah " for the same reason as that of
Ex. xvii. The rabbinic legend, to which Paul alludes in 1 Cor. x. 1ff., of
" a spiritual following rock that followed them," and of which "they all
drank," may be accounted for as an attempt to explain this phenomenon of a smitten rock of Meribah, from which Israel drank at the begin-
ing of the desert wandering in Ex. xvii., followed by an identical
experience with the same rock at the end of the journey (Num. xx. 1–13).
But while the literary phenomenon may account for the legend, the legend does not account for the literary phenomenon. It only serves to
show that the rabbis were not blind to the extraordinary parallelism of
the narratives. As to the duplicate, xvii. 2=xvii. 3, Wellhausen re-
marks : (*Comp.* p. 81) : " It is in spite of myself that I recognize traces
of a double source in xvii. 2–7. For it were much to be desired if it were
possible to attribute this narrative to the one, and Num. xx. 2ff. to the
other source of the Jehovist." As the matter stands it cannot be maintained that the phenomena call for no explanation.

Ch. xv. 22–27 might be uniform in structure were it not for vv. 25b,
26, where a beginning is made of relating how Moses (?) enacted " a
statute and an ordinance " and put Israel to the test. We are apparently on the verge of hearing how this was done ; what the statute and
ordinance was ; what the manner, and what the result of the testing.
But vs. 26 leads us nowhere. The thread of narrative taken up in 25b
is ravelled out into a cluster of didactic generalities, and leaves us in
doubt even as to the subject of the verbs in 25b. Is it Moses ? or is it
Yahweh ?

But it is ch. xvi. which furnishes the most remarkable anomalies. In

vv. 6-8 Moses and Aaron deliver to the people a message from Yahweh.
Afterwards, vv. 11f., Moses *receives* the message he has just communicated, the terms being identical. Vv. 13f. relate how in response to the
murmuring of the people Yahweh sent manna *and quails*. We pass
over for the present the singularity of the fact that in this case also, as
in xvii. 1 7, we have a duplicate of the story in Num. xi. There again
we are informed of how Israel murmured for the flesh-pots of Egypt and
complained of the manna, which in a digression is minutely described as
if something hitherto unheard of, and of how Yahweh sent *quails*, which
proved a curse to the greedy and complaining people. Such duplication
we have found to be rather the rule than the exception in the Pentateuch.
But we are led to expect that the murmuring of the people here, to
which the manna and *the quails* are the divine response, will be visited
with punishment of some kind. But no. Vs. 13a relates, " And at even
the quails came up and covered the camp." That is absolutely all we
hear about them. No one pays any attention to them. It is not even
stated that any one discovered them, much less used them for food ; and,
instead of punishment for the murmurings, we hear nothing further save
a description of the wonderful gift of manna and what was done with it.

The question repeatedly suggests itself in the latter part of ch. xvi.
What was " the thing which Yahweh commanded " ? According to vs.
16 it is the manner in which the bread is to be gathered. According to
vv. 23ff. it is the Sabbath. According to vs. 32 " This is the thing which
Yahweh hath commanded, Let an omerful of it be kept," etc. Vv. 17f.
attempt apparently an explanation of the two conflicting statements of
vs. 16, *a*), " gather each according to his eating " *i. e., various* amounts ;
b), " an omer a head," *i. e.,* each *the same* amount. But the miraculous
readjustment of quantity does not remove the literary disagreement. According to vs. 21 the consistency of the manna is such that it melts like
hoar frost (cf. vs. 14) with the warmth of the sun. According to vs. 23
it is baked and boiled. An undeniable anachronism appears in vv. 9, 33
where the expression " before Yahweh " presupposes the place of Yahweh's presence or manifestation, *i. e.,* the sanctuary of the Tabernacle.
That the author presupposes the giving of the Tables of Stone and the
erection of the Tabernacle and its furnishings, which in our Pentateuch
are not related until chh. xxxv. ff., is made an absolute certainty by vs.
34, where, pursuant to the command of vs. 33, Aaron lays up a pot of
manna " *before the Testimony*." Vs. 10 contains besides the reference
to the " cloud " (anachronistic in P² before Sinai) a similar anachronism.*

---

* For the reading *mishkan* "tabernacle" instead of *midbar* " wilderness "
see note *in loc.* "The glory of Yahweh appearing in the cloud" is a charac-

Finally, vv. 22-30 certainly convey the impression that the people have already received the law of the Sabbath.

From these extraordinary phenomena three things are at once apparent with regard to ch. xvi. 1⁰. The story is composite. 2⁰. One of the elements is P, which alone contains any reference to "the Testimony." (See refs.) 3⁰. The priestly element is displaced, and belongs after the end of Exodus. We may conjecture with a very high degree of probability what the original position of P's narrative was, by comparing its description of the murmuring, vs. 3, of the manna, vv. 14, 31, and especially the unfinished introduction of the quails in conjunction with the manna, vv. 11-13, with the narrative of J in Num. xi. 4-9, 13, 18-23, 31-35 (cf. especially vs. 31 with Ex. x. 13. 19; xiv. 21). The dependence is here unmistakable. The narrative of Numbers certainly did not derive its story of the quails (the manna is here quite incidental) from that of Exodus; but that of Exodus does derive its account from Num. xi; the writer being so much occupied with the manna, as to leave the quails (which he even speaks of as "*the* quails") literally suspended in mid-air. As therefore the P narrative of Ex. xvi. cannot possibly have been related originally until after the erection of the Tabernacle it must almost certainly have come from the same connection as its model, Num. xi.

What then was Rp's motive for inserting it here? Not *a priori* considerations like the convenience of Israel's being supplied with food from the beginning of the wilderness journey, or not these alone; for Rp allows small weight to such; but the existence at this point of *another manna story*. We have in fact seen abundant reason for believing ch. xvi. composite; and, since the manna-quail story of Num. xi. is certainly J's, and (Wellhausen to the contrary notwithstanding) certainly in its original position, we should naturally incline to E. Kuenen, Jülicher and others, it is true, would attribute the dislocations, incongruities, etc. of Ex xvi. purely to P³ or Rp on a basis of P². But if the narrative was originally a uniform production of P², whose standpoint is doctrinally the same as that of P³ and Rp, why should the latter so unmercifully mutilate it? The arguments of Wellhausen (*Comp.* pp. 323ff.) for a JE element here, in reply to Kuenen, are unanswerable. But there is something still more decisive which Wellhausen has not observed. Dt. viii. 2f., 16 prove beyond a doubt that JE had a narrative of the manna which contained the etymology Ex. xvi. 15, and understood the intention of the divine gift to have been "to prove thee. . . . whether thou

teristic expression of P, *e. g.*, Num. xvi. 42; xx. 6; but of course subsequently to the occupation of the tabernacle by the cloud, Ex. xl. 34ff., which in P, first appears on Sinai.

wouldest keep his commandments or no." (Dt. viii. 2 ; see also vv. 3 and 16, and cf. with these Ex. xvi. 4, " that I may prove them, whether they will walk in my law or no " ; and xv. 25b, " There he made for them a statute and an ordinance, and there he proved them ").

We have now found at last the true sequel to the isolated verse xv. 25b. Eliminate the foreign element, xv. 26f. ; xvi. 1–3, and it follows in xvi. 4. The references show that this " proving of Israel " (as of Abraham in Gen. xxii.) is a characteristic trait in E, unknown elsewhere ; and the strong probability is that the place indicated by " there " in xv. 25b, was originally *Massah*, " the place of *proving*." The location had of course to be obliterated when the parallel account of J (Massah from Israel's " tempting," or " proving " *Yahweh*) was taken up in ch. xvii.

It follows from the disconnection of xv. 25b (E) with the preceding, that vv. 22–25a, which are of course totally foreign to the style and purpose of P², are from the other JE source, J. This corresponds in fact with the style, language and references of the Marah story where Moses (not Moses and Aaron, P², and not Elohim, E) leads Israel on into the desert. Here also " the three days' journey," so often spoken of to Pharaoh is accomplished, the ætiological interest is displayed, and the wonders of Yahweh are accomplished, not by the rod, but by natural means. Vs. 27 also, which separates vs. 25b from its true connection with xvi. 4, and which has the same interests, language and style as vv. 22–25a, must be from the same source, J. Vs. 26, as we have already seen, merely aims to patch up an ending for the truncated vs. 25b, and must be redactional (Rd). Vs. 1 of ch. xvi. is the regular formula of P², unmistakably genuine and in place. From the singular recurrence of " the Red Sea " as a station between Elim and " the wilderness of Sin " in Num. xxxiii. 10f. we may perhaps gather that P² once read here, " And they journeyed from *the Red Sea*," which Rp would of course alter to " Elim," to agree with the preceding. It is also probable that Marah and Elim had no place in E, for, *ceteris paribus*, this writer would naturally relate *first* after the beginning of the wilderness journey, how Israel was supplied with food and water in the desert (see below).

Ch. xvi., from vs. 2 on, has been hitherto one of the most perplexing battle-grounds of criticism. We can only hope to reach a satisfactory analysis by holding firmly to the clew afforded by the reference in Deut. viii. 3, 16.

From Deuteronomy, then, which knows nothing of P, we learn that in JE the manna was given to " prove " Israel *by humbling them* through hunger to a daily dependence upon a food which their fathers " knew not." We have seen that the reference of these statements is unmistakably to Ex. xvi. 4 and 15, which accordingly must be reckoned to JE ; and, since vs. 4 is connected with xv. 25b, and contains a play upon the name Massah, which in J (xvii. 7) is ætiologized quite differently, we may be certain that the JE basis of ch. xvi. is E's Massah story. But it is further abundantly apparent in Dt. viii. that in this original Massah-story, the 'testing' of Israel was not the external and formal one of obedience to a rule laid down, but a testing of Israel's *disposition* in view of certain commandments which are *afterwards* to be made known. Yahweh acted for the purpose of " knowing what was in their heart," to know whether they could be depended on to receive and keep a divinely given law with the right spirit of humility and trustful obedience ; and for this purpose he took away their usual supply of food and drink, and suffered them to hunger and thirst. Then he gave them manna, of which neither their fathers nor they had ever known, and " brought them forth water out of the rock of flint " (viii. 15), " that he might make thee know that man doth not live by bread only, but by everything which Yahweh ordains." Of course the moralising, parenetic spirit of D is plainly evident here ; but how comes he to say that *this* is the lesson and purpose of the Massah incident, if in the story as it lay before him a law of the Sabbath, or a sample ordinance explicitly laid down in regard to quantity of manna to be gathered, was the test? By the analogy of his treatment of JE elsewhere we are constrained to think that D does *not* misrepresent his source, but that this was the real sense of the original E story ; and that the external tests of various kinds, Sabbath law (Rp), or ordinance in regard to mode of gathering (P²), are the attempts of later hands unable to appreciate the " prophetic " idea of a moral test of disposition, without a positive commandment, to supply what they judged to be an omission. We must also acknowledge the accuracy of D in bringing together the story of the supply of food, and of water, as belonging in the same connection, and both preliminary to the giving of the law (viii. 15f.). The E elements of Ex. xv. 25-xvii. 7 are in fact not only connected by their subject matter, but the Massah and Meribah stories belong together geographically, and are certainly in place where they stand.

With this understanding of the meaning of E it becomes clear at once that the verses in which a humble dependence upon God is the spirit sought for in the " test," are original with E ; and these are easily iden-tified in xv. 25b: xvi. 4 (vs. 5, introducing the idea that the " ordinance " was the law of the Sabbath is Rj's), 15a, 16a (*not* a fixed amount, in contrast with 16b, and consequently not an amount which could be *doubled*, as in vs. 22, but enough only for the satisfaction of one day's re-

quirement), 19b (no provision for the morrow), 20f. (Israel show their in-
eradicable disposition toward self-sufficiency, refusing here already to
be taught the lesson of the sermon on the mount, but God compels them to
look to him for *daily* bread), 35a.   Then follows xxii. 1b, 2, 4-6, 7, in part,
(at Meribah the same lesson is taught in the supply of water. See below.)

Alongside of this story of E's runs the narrative of the sending of
manna *and quails* of P², built on the unvarying model of this writer, and
principally concerned with the miraculous power of Yahweh. The elements are taken from Num. xi. (J) and are easily recognizable from style
and language. The story of Israel's murmuring in vv. 2-12 is in the
unmistakable style of P² (see refs.) and has only suffered in consequence
of a transposition, perhaps accidental. No words are wasted in the dry
and laconic statement of the marvel, vv. 13f., nor in the directions for
gathering, which to this writer are indispensable and constitute "the ordinance"; these verses, 15b, 16b, 19a (?), are sharply distinguished from
"the ordinance" in E, in that (characteristically) the amount to be
gathered is defined as "an omer a head," requiring a harmonistic adjustment (vv. 17f.) by Rp. Vv. 31 and 35b are each duplicated by E
material, and are hence manifestly from P², completing the story.

The rest of the chapter takes a different view of "the ordinance," and
is devoted to an emphasizing of Rp's favorite theme, the *Sabbath*. In
its simultaneous dependence and independence of both the other accounts,
as well as in its explanatory, and harmonistic character, and its style,
combining the language of JE, D and P, it is clearly the work of this
redactor. For the evidence in detail see Art. III. There remains the
passage xvii. 1-7 whose confusion of localities, and duplication of Num.
xx. 1-13 has already been referred to. Here vs. 1a is simply the regular
formula of P. But the mention of Horeb, the use of the rod of Moses,
the reference to his smiting the river (cf. vs. 5 with vii. 17), all show that
vv. 4-6 are certainly from E, and undoubtedly in their original position,
since "Horeb" is the station immediately "before the people." But the
duplication of vs. 3 by 1b, 2 is undeniable (see above, p. 81), and in vv.
2b and 7 we have traces of a Massah-story quite different from E's.
Moreover the present narrative contains no allusion whatever to the
rebellious words the people are accused of uttering in vs. 7. The portions (vv. 2b, 7 in part) which have to do with the etymology of Massah
may therefore be assigned with confidence to J. Moreover, as only J
speaks of Israel's taking 'flocks and herds' with them from Egypt, and
is constantly mindful of them (cf. ix. 6; x. 9, 26; xii. 32, 38; xix; 13; xxxiv.
3) whereas E seems to conceive Israel as burdened with a quite different
species of wealth, xii. 35f.; xiii. 17-19, at least until their arrival in Kad-

esh, we may count vs. 3 ("our cattle") with J, especially as it strongly resembles xiv. 11 ; Num. xi. 5, 20 ; xvi. 13 ; xx. 5. Cf. also ch. xv. 24 and Nu.
xiv. 2. The duplicate of vs. 3, viz. 1b, 2a, critics have endeavored to derive
from J ; because, regarding vs. 7 as a unit, it seemed necessary to connect vs. 2 as a whole with it. In order to do this Cornill, in his acute
discussion of this chapter in *Z. A. IV.*, xi. 1, (1891), is obliged to suppose
a double recurrence of the Meribah story *in the same document*, so far
at least as concerns the key-clause, "and the people strove with Moses,"
once here and once again in Num. xx,. the repetition being supposed to
be accidental and due to transposition of material by Rp from Num. xx.
to this place. E had then *no* aetiology of Meribah, and J had *two* identical ones, one explained as a duplication by Rp. The explanation seems
no less far-fetched than the supposedly displaced material. But independently of this vs. 7 seems to me to indicate a composite character.
There is no trace elsewhere of a place Massah-Meribah. On the contrary, Deuteronomy always separates the two. In the nature of the
case it seems to me improbable that J should have represented Moses as
giving to a single place, on a single occasion, and because of a single
occurrence, two different names simultaneously. All things considered,
the probability seems immeasurably stronger that we have, as the "prophetic" element of Num. xx. J's Meribah-story, and in Ex. xvii. 1b-7
E's. To this latter have been added fragments of J's story of *Massah*,
vv. 3, 2b, 7 in part, which of course must have stood in proximity to E's
in ch. xvi. For details see refs. and Art. III. above cited.*

We have thus, as the order of journeying in E, first Massah, then, a
little beyond, Meribah (xvii. 5), which appears to be at the foot of Horeb
(xvii. 6; xxxii. 20: Cf. Dt. ix. 21, "the brook that descended out of
the mount "). In J they pass from Marah to Elim, and thence to (Rephidim?), where the well (discovered?) receives the name Massah, and
this correspondingly appears to be at the foot of Sinai, which may, or
may not, be the same as Horeb. At least the story of J in chh. xxxiif.
affords an appropriate answer to the rebellious demand of xvii. 7.

(J) **¹⁸And Moses led Israel onward from the Red Sea, 22
and they went out into the wilderness of Shur ; and**

¹⁸Cf. 13 : 17f.

* In Art. III. the analysis offered is somewhat closer than the above to
that of Cornill. Since the first effect of the arguments of this acute and scholarly critic I have felt constrained to return in some respects to my original
view.

they went ¹⁹three days in the wilderness, and found no
23 water. And when they came to Marah, they could
not drink of the waters of Marah, for they were bitter :
24 ²⁰therefore the name of it was called Marah. And the
people ²¹murmured against Moses, saying, What shall
25 we drink ? And he cried unto Yahweh, and Yahweh
shewed him a tree, and he cast it into the waters,
(E) and the waters were made sweet. [. . .] ²²There
he made for them a statute and an ordinance, and there he
26 (Rd) ²²proved them : [. . .] ²⁴and he said, If thou wilt diligently
hearken to the voice of Yahweh thy God, and wilt do that which is right in
his eyes, and wilt give ear to his commandments, and keep all his statutes, I
²⁵will put none of the diseases upon thee, which I have put upon the Egyptians : for I am Yahweh that healeth thee.*

27 (J) ²⁶And they came to Elim, where were twelve
²⁷springs of water, and threescore and ten palm trees :
16 (P) and they encamped there by the waters. [. . .] *And
they took their journey from Elim,† ¹and all the congregation of the
children of Israel came unto the wilderness of Sin, which is between
Elim and Sinai, on the fifteenth day of the second month after their
2 departing out of the land of Egypt.—²And the whole congregation
of the children of Israel murmured against Moses and against
3 Aaron in the wilderness : and the children of Israel said unto
them, Would that we had died by the hand of Yahweh in the land
of Egygt, ³when we sat by the flesh pots, when we did eat bread
to the full, for ye have brought us forth into this wilderness, to
4 (E) kill this whole assembly with hunger. Then said Yahweh
unto Moses, Behold, I will rain bread from heaven for you

¹⁹18 : 5 : : etc. ²⁰Gen. 11 : 8 ; 16 : 14 ; 19 : 22 etc. ²¹17 : : : Nu. 14 : 2a. ²²Jos. 24 : 25 ; 1
Sam. 30 : 25. ²³Gen. 22 : 1 ; Ex. 16 : 4 ; 20 : 22 ; Nu. 14 : 22etc. cf. 17 : 7 ; Dt. 33 : 8. ²⁴Dt.
28 : 1. ²⁵23 : 25. ²⁶Vs. 23. ²⁷Gen. 16 : 7. ¹17 : 1 ; 19 : 1etc. ²Nu. 14 : 2 ; 20 : 1ff. ³Cf.
Nu. 11 : 5.

* Vs. 26 is regarded by critics generally as from Rd. The motive would be
the separation of vs. 25b from its original context. It is possible that we have
here some original material, the last clause suggesting a possible ætiology of
the name Rephidim (*rapha* " heal "). The verse as a whole is certainly redactional. See Analysis, p. 81, and observe the confusion of subject.

† For " Elim " read " the Red Sea," and cf. Nu. xxxiii. 11, and Art. III. Rp
was of course obliged in xvi. 1 to bring the data of P into harmony with the
preceding.

and the people shall go out and gather a day's portion every
day, [4]that I may prove them, whether they will walk in my
(Rp) law, or no. *And it shall come to pass on the sixth day, that they* 5
shall prepare that which they bring in, and it shall be twice as much as they
(P) *gather daily.—And Moses and Aaron said unto all the children* 6
of Israel, [5]At even, then ye shall know that Yahweh hath brought
you out from the land of Egypt : and in the morning, then ye shall 7
see the glory of Yahweh ; for that he heareth your murmurings
against Yahweh : and what are we, that ye murmur against us ?—
(Rp) *And Moses said, This shall be when Yahweh shall give you in the* 8
evening flesh to eat, and in the morning bread to the full, [6]for that Yahweh
heareth your murmurings which ye murmur against him ; and what are we ?
(P) *your murmurings are not against us but against Yahweh.[*] And Moses* 9
said unto Aaron, Say unto all the congregation of the children of
Israel, Come near before Yahweh : for he hath heard your murmurings. And it came to pass, as Aaron spake unto the whole 10
congregation of the children of Israel, that [7]they looked toward
the wilderness,[†] and, behold, the glory of Yahweh appeared in the
cloud. [8]And Yahweh spake unto Moses, saying, I have heard the 11–12
murmurings of the children of Israel : speak unto them, saying, At
even ye shall eat flesh, and in the morning ye shall be filled with
bread ; and ye shall know that I am Yahweh your God. And it 13
came to pass at even, that the [11]quails came up, and covered the
camp : and [12]in the morning the dew lay round about the camp.
And when the dew that lay was gone up, behold, upon the face of 14
the wilderness a small round thing, small as the hoar frost on the
(E) ground. [. . .] And when the children of Israel saw it, 15

[4]Dt. 8 : 2, 16. [5]Vs. 12. [6]Nu. 16 : 11 ; vs. 7. [7]Nu. 16 : 42. [8]Cf. vs. 6f. [11]Nu. 11 : 31.
[12]Nu. 11 : 9.

[*] Vv. 6f. must obviously come after, not before, vv. 11f. Verse 8, which
repeats vv. 12 and 7, appears to be explanatory of vs. 7. Wellhausen (*Comp.*
p. 325) suggests that the displacement of vv. 6f. may have been caused by the
marginal gloss vs. 8 drawing 6f. into the margin with it.

[†] " Wilderness " (*midbar*) is an impossible reading, since Israel is encamped
in the midst of the wilderness. Repeated analogy (see refs.) suggests that the
original was *mishkan* " tabernacle," the regular place for the appearance of the
shekinah. This would of course strike Rp as an anachronism positively requiring alteration, though he has left others (vv. 9, 33f.), less conspicuous but no less
positive, as evidence of the displacement of the P element of this narrative.

[13]they said one to another, What is it? for they wist not what
(P) it was. And Moses said unto them, *It is the bread which*
16 (E) *Yahweh hath given you to eat.* This is the thing which
Yahweh hath [14]commanded, Gather ye of it every man accord-
(P) ing to his eating, [15]*an omer a head, according to the number*
of your persons, shall ye take it, every man for them which are in
17 (Rp) *his tent. And the children of Israel did so, and gathered some*
18 *more, some less. And when they did mete it with an omer, he that gathered*
much had nothing over, and he that gathered little had no lack ; they gathered
(P) *every man according to his eating.* *   —*And Moses said unto them*
19–20 (E)—† Let no man leave of it till the morning. Notwithstanding they hearkened not unto Moses ; but some of them
left of it until the morning, and it bred worms and stank :
21 and Moses was wroth with them. And they gathered it morning by morning, every man according to his eating : and
22 (Rp) [16]when the sun waxed hot, it melted. *And it came to pass,*
that on the sixth day they gathered twice as much bread, [17]*two omers for each*
23 *one : and all the* [18]*rulers of the congregation came and told Moses. And he*
said unto them, [19]*This is that which Yahweh hath spoken, To-morrow is a*
solemn rest, a holy sabbath unto Yahweh : [20]*bake that which ye will bake, and*
seethe that which ye will seethe : and all that remaineth over lay up for you to
24 *be kept until the morning. And they laid it up till the morning, as Moses*
25 *bade : and it did not stink, neither was there any worm therein. And Moses*
said, Eat that to-day : for to-day is a sabbath unto Yahweh : to-day ye shall
26 *not find it in the field.* [21]*Six days ye shall gather it ; but on the seventh day*
27 *is the sabbath, in it there shall be none. And it came to pass on the seventh*
day, that there went out some of the people for to gather, and they found
28 *none. And Yahweh said unto Moses,* [29]*How long refuse ye to keep my com-*
29 *mandments and my laws ? See, for that Yahweh hath given you the sabbath,*
therefore he giveth you on the sixth day the bread of two days ; abide ye every
30 *man in his place, let no man go out of his place on the seventh day. So the*
31 (P) *people rested on the seventh day.* [23]*And the house of Israel*
called the name thereof Manna : [24]*and it was like coriander*
seed, white ; and the taste of it was like wafers [*made*] *with*

---

[13]Dt. 8 : 3, 16 ; jcf. vs. 31.   [14]Vs. 4.   [15]18 : 36 ; Nu. 1 : 2, 18, 20 etc.   [16]Cf. vs. 23b.   [17]Vs.
16b. [18]Nu. 7 : 2, 3 etc   [19]Cf. vv. 16, 32.   [20]Nu. 11 : 8 ; cf. vs. 21.   [21]20 : 9f.   [22]10 : 3, 7 ;
Nu. 14 : 11, 26 ; Jos. 18 : 3.   [23]Vs. 15.   [24]Nu. 11 : 7.

* Harmonistic redaction. The miraculous adjustment of the amount explains how it could be true that " they gathered it every man according to his
eating " (E), and at the same time that they gathered " an omer a head " (P).

† Insert after vs. 14.

(Rp) *honey.   And Moses said,* ²⁵*This is the thing which Yahweh hath* 32 *commanded, Let an omerful of it be kept for your generations : that they may see the bread wherewith I fed you in the wilderness, when I brought you forth from the land of Egypt.   And Moses said unto Aaron, Take a pot,* 33 *and put an omerful of manna therein, and lay it up* ²⁶*before Yahweh, to be kept for your generations.   As Yahweh commanded Moses, so Aaron laid it* 34 *up* ²⁷*before the Testimony, to be kept.**

(E)   And the children of Israel did eat the manna forty 35
(P) years, until they came to a land inhabited ; ³⁶*they did eat* 36
the manna, until they came unto the borders of the land of Canaan.
(Rp) *Now an omer is the tenth part of an ephah.—*

(P)   ¹*And all the congregation of the children of Israel jour-* **17**
neyed from the wilderness of Sin, by their journeys, according to
(E) *the commandment of Yahweh, and pitched in Rephidim:* and
there was no water for the people to drink.   ²Wherefore the   2
people strove with Moses, and said, Give us water that we
may drink.   And Moses said unto them, Why strive ye with
(J) me ?—**wherefore do ye tempt Yahweh ?—And the** 3
people thirsted there for water ; ³and the people murmured against Moses, and said, ⁴Wherefore hast thou brought us up out of Egypt, to kill ⁵us and our chil
(E) dren and our cattle with thirst? [. . .] ⁶And Moses   4
cried unto Yahweh, saying, What shall I do unto this people ?
they be almost ready to stone me.   And Yahweh said   5
unto Moses, Pass on before the people, and take with thee
of the elders of Israel ; and thy rod, wherewith thou ⁶smotest
the river, take in thine hand, and go [. . .].   † Behold I will 6
stand before thee there upon the rock in ⁷Horeb ; and thou
shall ⁸smite the rock, and there shall come water out of it,

²⁵Vv. 16, 23.   ²⁶Vv. 9, 34 : Nu. 17 : cf. ²⁷27 : 21 ; 30 : 36etc. : Nu. 17 : 8, 10.   ^{2a}Jos. 5 : 12.
¹Nu. 10 : 12f. ; 33 : 2etc.   ²Nu. 20 : 3.   ³15 : 24 : Nu. 14 : 2.   ⁴14 : 11f. : Nu. 20 : 5.   ⁵10 :
9.   ⁶7 : 20.   ⁷3 : 1.   "Cf. Nu. 20 : 1–13.

* The authenticity of vv. 32–34 is doubtful. The occasion for their insertion appears to be the uncertainty of " the thing which Yahweh hath commanded ": cf. vv. 16 and 23. In spite of their peculiarly Deuteronomic interest in posterity there is no cogent reason for denying the verses to P² if the story be placed subsequently to the erection of the Tabernacle.

† The name, or description, of the place to which Moses is to " go " is missing; doubtless for harmonistic reasons, as in Gen. xxxi. 25.   The story of vv.

that the people may drink. And Moses did so [9]in the sight
7 of the elders of Israel. And he called the name of the place
[10]**Massah** and Meribah, because of the striving of the children
(J) of [11]Israel and **because they tempted Yahweh, saying
is Yahweh among us, or not?**

———◆———

3 Chh. xvii. 8–xix. 25.   ENCAMPMENT AT HOREB.   PRELIMINARIES
TO THE GIVING OF THE LAW.

ANALYSIS.

Under the above heading it is necessary to group together some of the
most remarkable products of R's compilatory necessities, the story of the
fight with Amalek and of Jethro's visit being obviously inserted where
they do not belong. Following, however, the text as we have it, we
learn first of Amalek's attack at Rephidim.   Joshua marshalls the forces
of Israel, while Moses, accompanied by Aaron and Hur, wields the rod
of God upon the hill-top.   The outstretched rod secures the victory to
Israel, and Moses commemorates it by the altar of Yahweh-nissi; xvii. 8–
16. Jethro visits Moses, bringing the wife and sons of the latter.
After salutations and a sacrifice "before God," Jethro, on the morrow,
sees Moses occupied with judgment and "making known the statutes of
God and his laws." He recommends the appointment of judges and
officers. This done, he departs to his own land; ch. xviii. Israel
arrives at Sinai.   Moses ascends the mount and receives a message for
the people, xix. 1–7. He returns again to the mount and is given
directions preliminary to a theophany, and these the people carry out ;

[9]7 : 20.   [10]Dt. 6 : 16 ; 9 : 22; 33 : 8.   [11]33 : 14 ; 34 : 9 ; Nu. 11 : 20.

1ff. opens without a specified locality, and the scene may perhaps originally
have been simply the wilderness route. But the place to which Moses betakes
himself is Meribah, so designated, however, as not to anticipate the etymology
in vs. 7.   This Meribah (identical with Meribah-Kadesh of Num. xx. ?) would
seem to have been at the foot of Horeb (vs. 6; cf. Dt. ix. 21).   Both Massah
and Meribah are names of sacred wells, which from their true etymology (Ka-
desh="sacred"; Meribah="waters of controversy"; Massah="place of
trial") must have been resorted to for divination and oracular decision of
questions, as at the sacred well of Daphne (see, W. Robertson Smith, "Religion of the Semites," pp. 156ff.).   So in Gen. xiv. 7 En Mishpat="fountain
of judgment."

vv. 8–15. On the third day the people are assembled at the foot of the mount, which burns and smokes as Yahweh descends upon it. The theophany begins; vv. 16–19. Yahweh descends upon Sinai, summons Moses, and reiterates in different form the instructions previously given. Moses protests that this is already done; but is again sent down to charge the people; vv. 20–25.

In xvii. 8–16 and ch. xviii. we have abundant evidence of the presence of E. The style and standpoint are unmistakable. The mention of the "rod of God" as Moses' divine equipment connects xvii. 8–16 with the previous series of E passages, in which the same agency invariably appears; that of "Aaron and Hur" as Moses' coadjutors, with Joshua as his lieutenant, connect the passage no less certainly with a subsequent series in which the same characters appear (cf. xxiv. 13f). Only it is highly improbable that Joshua should here be brought in for the first time, *unintroduced*, when in subsequent passages (xxiv. 13; xxxiii. 11) he is *introduced* to the reader as "Moses' minister," and as "a young man, the son of Nun, Moses' minister." Moreover we scarcely expect an attack from Amalek at this point in the story, where Israel is not seeking a settlement, but only visiting a sacred locality, even if the shrine were in Amalekite territory. But Amalek according to Num. xiii. 29; xiv. 25, 43, 45 is rather differently located, and from the same chapters it would appear that Israel came into collision with Amalek after turning northward from Horeb. Again "the top of the hill," vv. 9f., is a meaningless expression in the present connection. But cf. Num. xiv. 40. The *rôle* of Moses here is that of an old man, and that of Joshua of a mature and trusted warrior, to whom the burden of future wars is to be transmitted, vs. 14. Only "Rephidim," vs. 8, remains as the undoubted occasion for the insertion of the fragment at this point, and "Rephidim" in vs. 1, as we have already seen, is only from P, or at most originally from J, its connection with E's narrative at this point being purely redactional. Dt. xxv. 17–19 ("as ye came forth") is not in conflict with the idea of a displacement of Ex. xvii. 8–16; cf. Dt. xxiv. 9, and to this conclusion the facts impel us. The inference must be that in E Rephidim was a station reached *after removal* from Horeb, the story having been removed hither by Rp to make vs. 8 agree with vs. 1.*

It is quite needless to accumulate evidences of the E origin of ch. xviii.

---

* This passage xvii. 8–16 is one of several which tend strongly to show that our E of the Hexateuch is really an E², and this may well account for the displacement of xvii. 8–16, which might then be the work of E (E²) himself. Budde in fact thinks the battle presupposed by xviii. 8 ("all the travail"); but the first task must be the extrication of E (E²).

The habitual use of Elohim, "Jethro" as Moses' father-in-law, the position of Aaron, the "causes brought to God" (cf. xxii. 9; xxiv. 14) and interest in the administration of justice, (cf. chh. xxif.), are all characteristic of E, the whole story of the appointment of judges and officers being in a measure parallel to iv. 10–16 (J) where the priesthood (represented by Aaron) are entrusted with the functions of interpreters of the law. Only in vv. 1–4 are there manifest traces of Rje (see note *in loc.*) and in vv. 8–11 a certain redundancy, which may indicate the presence of a second source.

It is certain that J had also an account of the coming of "Hobab the son of Reuel, Moses' father-in-law" to meet him at Sinai; for in Num. x. 29-32 Moses is engaged in persuading this Hobab to accompany them " to the place of which Yahweh had said to Israel, I will give it you." It appears further from Jud. iv. 11, that contrary to Ex. xviii. 27 he actually did go. As we shall see, the true position of Ex. xviii. is practically the same as Num. x. 29. Under these circumstances it seems extremely probable that Rje may have preserved in ch. xviii. 1–12, some traces of J's parallel. The language of vs. 7 in fact shows affinity with J (see refs.), and one can hardly consider it natural that Jethro should be already talking with Moses, vs. 6, *before* Moses has gone out to meet him; vs. 7. Vv. 8–11 contain the real kernel of the story, which, as so often happens, proves to have a poetic nucleus, and here the recurrence of "Yahweh" in contrast with *Elohim* throughout the rest of the chapter, together with the manifest redundancy in vv. 9f. seems to indicate the presence of J. In the absence of decisive criteria it is impossible to do more than indicate by alteration of the type in vs. 7 and 10f. the occasion for an analysis for which, as yet, the final clew is wanting.

It appears distinctly in the latter part of ch. xviii. that the time is near the close of the stay at "the mount of God." In vs. 23 the departure is already in contemplation, and the natural inference from vs. 27 is that Jethro returns to his own land because the people are about breaking camp. Moreover vs. 12 ("before God" cf. xxi. 6; xxii. 9) indicates that a regular place of worship has been established; "the statutes of God and his laws," vs. 16, can hardly be any other than the "judgments" of ch. xxif., or at least those of xxiv. 12 (cf. vs. 20); finally we have an unmistakable reference to this whole story in Dt. i. 9-18, where it is expressly stated that this was *after* the command to depart from Horeb (Dt. i. 6–8; cf. Ex. xxxii. 34) and immediately before its execution (Dt. i. 19). The position thus determined for ch. xviii. as its original one is a matter of importance to the analysis, as indicating the relation into which

Israel has come with God subsequently to the apostacy of ch. xxxii., and previous to the departure from Horeb. (Cf. vs. 12 and note the position of Aaron.)

In ch. xix. we have beneath a surface appearance of unity the usual incongruities and contradictions. The most striking phenomenon is perhaps the addition of vv. 20ff., which carry us back to the first preliminaries in preparation for the theophany, when in the preceding verses the whole had not only been arranged for three days past already, but the theophany had actually begun. In this new arrangement Moses and Aaron are to " come up to the top of the mount " (previously, vv. 9, 17, 19 it had been arranged that Moses should stand below with the people, while God addressed him from the mount in their hearing,) the " priests " are to sanctify themselves (the whole people had already done so for three days), and most of all must elaborate precautions be taken against the curiosity of the people, which would impel them " to break through unto Yahweh to gaze." Yet previously not only had these precautions already been taken, as Moses indeed ventures to remind Yahweh (vs. 23 ; cf. 12f.), but, so far from the people's manifesting a desire to " break through to gaze," it had been necessary to overcome their terror and lead them out of the camp toward the foot of the mount (vv. 16f.). After all it does not appear that these second directions were carried out. Moses and Aaron do not go up, but the theophany proceeds in ch. xx. according to the former plan with Moses below, xx. 1ff., joining directly upon xix. 19, as if nothing whatever had intervened. Remarkable as is this interruption, it is by no means the only incongruity of ch. xix. The repetitions and inversions of order in vv. 1f., and the re-iteration of vs. 86 in 9b are a slight matter ; but the ascents and descents of the mountain which the present text requires of Moses—quite needlessly—are something prodigious. In vs. 3a Moses first ascends. But already in 3b he is below again ; for while a forced interpretation of Yahweh's " calling to him out of the mountain " might be made to show that Moses was himself on the mountain, vs. 7 " Moses *came* and told " (not came *down* as in vv. 14, 25 ; xxxii. 1. 15 etc.), shows that the sense in which we should naturally understand the expression is the true one. In vs. 8 Moses ascends again, or rather in 9ff., is again at the summit, descends in vs. 14, ascends in vs. 20, and again descends in vs. 25, *not* to ascend again, however, as directed in vs. 24. In vs. 8 the people promise to " do all that Yahweh hath spoken " but have not yet received commandment to do anything. Vs. 13b directs that " When the *yobel* soundeth loud, *these* (emphatic) shall come up to the mount." It is the last we hear of the *yobel* (the " trumpet " is quite a different matter) and who "these" may be we have no means whatever of knowing. After vs. 25 the connection is suddenly broken (see note *in loc.*).

Fortunately there is no lack of linguistic and stylistic peculiarities which accompany the contrasting representations, and suggest of themselves documentary analysis as the true explanation of the phenomena. Thus we observe that the series of passages in which the theophany is addressed to *the people*, Moses standing *at the foot* of the mount, and being there addressed by "a voice," has regularly *Elohim*. That on the contrary in which the people are repelled, Moses and Aaron invited to the top of the mount, and "the *priests* sanctified to come near," has invariably "Yahweh." But furthermore we observe that in this "Yahwistic" series the mount is invariably called "Sinai" (vv. 11, 18, 20), as subsequently appears to be the case in all J sections (cf. xxxiv. 2, 4), instead of "Horeb," as in E. The expressions "Yahweh came down" (Gen. xi. 5; xviii. 21; Ex. xxxiv. 5 etc.), "the smoke ascended as the smoke of a furnace" ((Gen. xv. 17 ; xix. 28) " break forth " (J *passim*) " the top of the mount " (Ex. xxxiv. 2) are all found exclusively in J. In this document alone have we "priests" (iv. 14 cf. xix. 22 etc., xxiv. 5) "cattle" (vs. 13; see above, p. 86, and cf. xxxiv. 3), the "*yobel*" (Jos. vi. 5) and theophanies in fire (Gen. xv. 17 ; Ex. iii. 2). All things considered we need have no hesitation in attributing vv. 11-13, 18, 20-25 to the J document. The difficulty of the chapter arises from the fact that there are passages connected with the "Elohistic" series which also have "Yahweh." It becomes necessary to decide according to mode of thought rather than by expression merely. The fundamental distinction between the two representations seems to be that in the Yahwistic series the curiosity of the people is guarded against, and they themselves are restricted to what appeals to the *eye* at a distance, only Moses, Aaron and "the priests" coming near ; whereas in the Elohistic the people are brought near in spite of their fears, and addressed by the "voice." In accordance with this is the direction to the *people* to wash their garments and sanctify themselves in vv. 10, 14f.; in contrast with vs. 22 where this becomes the duty of "the priests." That we are making no mistake in thus assigning vv. 10, 14f., to E in spite of a single "Yahweh" in vs. 10 appear at once from a comparison of their language with Gen. xxxv. 2 (E). But further, we have in vs. 9 the precise definition of this Elohistic representation. Yahweh will address Moses, and the people are to *hear* while he speaks (cf. vs. 19 and xx. 1ff.). Vv. 9f., 14 17, 19 appear thus to be a unit. We have but to connect these verses with their sequel xx. 1ff., and the Elohistic fragment, vs. 3a, to find E's narrative of the giving of the law complete, characteristic and unbroken, save for the accidental dittograph 9b=8b. Here we have the explanation of the exceptional " Yahweh " of vv. 9f. The first clause in each verse, " And Yahweh said unto Moses " is a redactional resumption (cf. vs. 24a) necessitated by the interruption of foreign material.

There remains the seemingly Yahwistic passage 3b (from " and Yahweh ")–8 which implies (vs. 7) that its true position was *after* the commandments of God had been uttered to Moses ; if, however, we turn to the LXX, we discover that in their text the passage was throughout *Elohistic*, " Yahweh " appearing first in vs. 9. The representation of a covenant made *viva voce* by the whole people belongs to E's mode of conception (cf. vs. 8 with xxiv. 3 and Jos. xxiv. 16ff.), and other expressions of E occur (see refs.). Yet vv. 4f. have a strongly Deuteronomic style and seem to show the work of Rd. To assume with critics generally under such conditions that vv. 3–8 are the pure composition of Rd is unjustifiable. The motive for addition is lacking. We shall see that an appropriate position for the substance of the passage is not lacking in the document with whose representation it is in affinity.

With the removal of this self-consistent, complete and characteristic story of E, in which not a single essential word is missing, we find the Yahwistic story which remains behind almost equally intact. A single displacement has occurred (see note on vv. 11–13) and the sequel does not yet appear (it has been incorporated in ch. xxiv.). But the narrative has neither incongruities nor inconsistencies ; it agrees perfectly in style, language, theological standpoint, and historical conception with J. Only in vv. 1f. (regular formula of itinerary) does the narrative of P come into conjunction with JE, occasioning some slight confusion (see note *in loc.*) ; and in vs. 23 the removal of vv. 11–13 from after 24a (to " priests ") has occasioned a curious redactional interpolation. With even a very slight acquaintance with the general style, language, theological prepossessions, and historical conceptions of J, E and P, and a moderately careful observance of the local difference in point of view, the reader can easily verify for himself the analysis of ch. xix.

———————

(E)—[12]Then came [13]Amalek, and fought with Israel in 8 Rephidim. And Moses said unto [14]Joshua, Choose us out 9 men, and go out, fight with Amalek : to-morrow I will stand on the [15]top of the hill with the [16]rod of God in mine hand.

[12]Dt. 25 : 17ff.   [13]Nu. 13 : 29 ; 14 : 40–44 ; 21 : 1–3.   [14]Ct. Nu. 13 : 8, 16.   [15]Nu. 14 : 40.
[16]4 : 17, 20 ; 7 : 20 etc.

10 So Joshua did as Moses had said to him, and fought with Amalek: and [17]Moses, Aaron, and Hur went up to the top
11 of the hill. And it came to pass, when Moses [18]held up his hand, that Israel prevailed: and when he let down his hand,
12 Amalek prevailed. But Moses' hands were heavy; and they took a stone, and put it under him, and he sat thereon; and Aaron and Hur stayed up his hands, the one on the one side, and the other on the other side; and his hands were steady
13 until the going down of the sun. And Joshua discomfited
14 Amalek and his people [19]with the edge of the sword. And Yahweh said unto Moses, Write this for a memorial in a book, and rehearse it in the ears of Joshua: that I will utterly blot out the remembrance of Amalek from under
15 heaven. [20]And Moses built an altar, and called the name of
16 it Yahweh-nissi: and he said, Yahweh hath sworn: Yahweh will have war with Amalek from generation to generation.—*

18   —Now† [1]Jethro, the priest of Midian, Moses' father-in-law, heard of all that God had done for Moses, and for Israel his
2-3 people, how that Yahweh had brought Israel out of Egypt. And Jethro, Moses' father-in-law, took Zipporah, Moses' wife, [2]after he had sent her away, and her two sons; of which—the name of the one was Gershom; [3]for he said, I have been a sojourner in a
4 strange land: and the name of the other was Eliezer; for *he said,*[4]The God of my father was my help and delivered me
5 from the sword of Pharaoh:—‡ and Jethro, Moses' father-in-law,

---

[17]24 : 14.   [18]9 : 22f.; 10 : 12f.   [19]Gen. 34 : 26; Nu. 21 : 24.   [20]Gen. 33 : 20; 35 : 7.   [1]3 : 1.
[2]Cf. 4 : 20ff.   [3]2 : 22.   [4]3 : 6.

* In vs. 16 translate with margin (R. V.) "There is a hand upon the standard (*nes*) of Yahweh." Vs. 15 gives the name of the shrine whose ætiology is here related, as *Yahweh-nissi* Yahweh my *standard.* Hence the true reading in vs. 16 must be *nes,* "standard" (cf. Num. xxi. 8), not *kes,* "throne" as in the text. N and K in Hebrew are often indistinguishable.

† For the original position of ch. xviii. see Analysis p. 94 and cf. Art. III.

‡ The harmonistic clauses, "the priest of Midian," and "after he had sent her away" require no further explanation than a reference to the notes on Ex. iii. 1 and iv. 20. The rest of vv. 1b-4 is probably composed of material from E's parallel to ii. 15ff. So far in J Moses has but one son and Zipporah accompanies him to Egypt. In introducing the section vv. 5ff., which represent

came with his sons and his wife unto Moses [5]into the wilderness where he was encamped, at the mount of God : and he said 6 unto Moses, I thy father-in-law Jethro am come unto thee, (J) and thy wife, and her two sons with her. [6]**And Moses 7 went out to meet his father-in-law, and did obeisance, and kissed him ; and they asked each other of their welfare ; and they came * into the tent. [. . .]** (E) And Moses told his father-in-law all that Yahweh had 8 done unto Pharaoh and to the Egyptians for Israel's sake, all the [7]travail that had come upon them by the way, and how Yahweh delivered them. And Jethro rejoiced for all the 9 goodness which Yahweh had done to Israel, in that he had (J) delivered them out of the hand of the Egyptians. **And 10 Jethro said, [8]Blessed be Yahweh, who hath delivered you out of the hand of the Egyptians, and out of the hand of Pharaoh ; who hath delivered the people from under the hand of the Egyptians. Now I know that 11 Yahweh is greater than all gods : yea, in the thing (E) wherein they [9]dealt proudly against them.** And 12 Jethro, Moses' father-in-law, took a burnt offering and sacrifices for God : and Aaron came, and all the elders of Israel, to [10]eat bread with Moses' father-in-law before God. [11]And 13 it came to pass on the morrow, that Moses sat to judge the people : and the people stood about Moses from the morning unto the evening. And when Moses' father-in-law saw 14 all that he did to the people, he said, What is this thing that thou doest to the people ? why sittest thou thyself alone, and all the people stand about thee from morning unto even ? And Moses said unto his father-in-law, Because the people 15 come unto me [12]to inquire of God : when they have a matter, 16

[5]Cf. 19 : 2.   [6]Gen. 18 : 2 ; 19 : 1 ; 43 : 27.   [7]Nu. 20 : 14.   [8]Gen. 24.   [9]21 : 14.   [10]Gen. 31 : 54.   [11]24 : 14.   [12]21 : 6 ; 22 : 8f ; vs. 19.

Jethro bringing Moses' wife to him with her *two* sons, Rje is obliged to add this supplementary and harmonistic material by way of explanation. The original story, vv. 5ff., indicates that the account of Moses' marriage and of the birth of his two sons had been given long since.

* Read with LXX. " And he brought them." Cf. Gen. xliii. 27.

they come unto me ; and I judge between a man and his
neighbor, and I make them know ¹³the statutes of God, and
17 his laws. And Moses' father-in-law said unto him, The
18 thing that thou doest is not good. ¹⁴Thou wilt surely wear
away, both thou, and this people that is with thee : for the
thing is too heavy for thee ; thou art not able to perform it
19 thyself alone. Hearken now unto my voice, I will give thee
counsel, and God be with thee : be thou for the people to
20 God-ward, and bring thou the causes unto God : and thou
(Rd) shalt teach ¹⁵them the statutes and the laws, and shalt
shew them the way wherein they must walk, and the work that they must
21 (E) do.* Moreover thou shalt provide out of all the people
able men, such as fear God, men of truth, hating unjust gain
and place such over them, to be ¹⁶rulers of thousands, rulers
22 of hundreds, rulers of fifties, and rulers of tens, and let them
judge the people at all seasons : and it shall be, that every
great matter they shall bring unto thee, but every small
matter they shall judge themselves : so shall it be easier for
23 thyself, and they shall bear [the burden] with thee. If thou
shalt do this thing, and God command thee so, then thou
shalt be able to endure, and all this people also shall ¹⁷go to
24 their place in peace. So Moses hearkened to the voice of
25 his father-in-law, and did all that he had said. And Moses
chose able men out of all Israel, and made them heads over
the people, rulers of thousands, rulers of hundreds, rulers of
26 fifties, and rulers of tens. And they judged the people at all
seasons : the hard causes they brought unto Moses, but
27 every small matter they judged themselves. ¹⁸And Moses
let his father-in-law depart ; and he went his way into his
own land.

19   (P) *In the third month after the children of Israel were gone
forth out of the land of Egypt, ¹the same day came they into the*

---

¹³Ch. 21. ¹⁴Dt. 1 : 12-18. ¹⁵Gen. 31 : 55 ; Ex. 20 : 25 ; Nu. 21 : 3. ¹⁶Dt. 1 : 15. ¹⁷32 :
4 ; 23 : 20ff. ¹⁸Ct. Nu. 10 : 29-32. ¹12 : 40f. 51 : 16 : 1.

---

* Vs. 20b. goes beyond the intention of the chapter to impute to Moses *moral*
instruction, clearly manifesting the Deuteronomic interest. Probably an interpolation of Rd.

wilderness of Sinai.—*And when they were departed from Rephi-* 2
dim, and were come to the wilderness of Sinai, they pitched in the
(J) *wilderness ;*—*and there Israel camped before the*
(E) mount. ²And Moses went up unto God,—and † Yah- 3
weh called unto him out of the mountain, saying, Thus shalt
thou say to the house of Jacob, and tell the children of Israel ;
(Rd) ³Ye have seen what I did unto the Egyptians, and how ⁴I bare you 4
on eagles' wings, and brought you unto myself. Now therefore, if ye will 5
⁵obey my voice indeed, and keep my covenant, then ye shall be a ⁶peculiar
treasure unto me from among all peoples : for all the earth is mine : and 6
(E) ye shall be unto me a kingdom of priests, and ⁷an holy nation. These
are the words which thou shalt speak unto the children of
Israel. And Moses came and called for the elders of the 7
people, and set before them all these words which Yahweh
commanded him. ⁸And all the people answered together, 8
and said, All that Yahweh hath spoken we will do. And
Moses reported the words of the people unto Yahweh.—And 9
Yahweh said unto Moses, Lo, I come unto thee in a thick
cloud, ⁹that the people may hear when I speak with thee,
(Rd) and may also ¹⁰believe thee for ever. And Moses told the
words of the people unto Yahweh. And Yahweh said unto Moses, ‡ 10

---

¹3 : 4. ³20 : 22 ; Jos. 24 : 7. ⁴Dt. 32 : 11. ⁵23 : 22. ⁶Dt. 7 : 6 ; 14 : 2 ; 26 : 18 ; 2 Sam
12 : 22. ⁷22 · 31. Dt. 26 : 19. ⁸24 : 3, 7 ; Jos. 24 : 16, etc. ⁹20 : 19-21. ¹⁰14 : 31.

* The order of xix 1., and 2a seems to have been inverted, perhaps (Jül). to
connect better with the material taken from J, or because of the presence of
material from this source in vs. 2a.

† The position which the passage 3b (from " and Yahweh ")—8 seems to demand for itself (see Analysis p. 97) is directly after xx. 21 ; cf. Dt. v. 28-31, where,
however, quite different language is attributed to Yahweh. Vs. 8 presents
Moses in the position required in xix. 17, 19 ; xx. 1-21 and presupposed nowhere
else ; for 8b is not to be understood as signifying an ascent of the mountain.
In removing the passage from its original position to the present, to form a sort
of preamble to the theophany, Rd has modified the language in vv. 4-6 ; cf.
xxiii. 22, where LXX. insert vv. 5f. between 22a and b.

‡ Vs. 9b. appears to be mere scribal error, a dittograph of 8b. The interruption compels R to supply : " And Yahweh said unto Moses " in repetition of
9a as in 9a the subject " Yahweh " (for simple " he " understood) had to be
supplied, after vv. 3b-8 were introduced separating 3a from vs. 9.

(E) Go unto the people, and [11]sanctify them to-day and to-
11 morrow, and let them wash their garments, and be ready
(J) against the third day:—**for the third day Yahweh will**
[12]**come down in the sight of all the people upon mount**
12 [13]**Sinai. [14]And thou shalt set bounds unto the people
round about, saying, Take heed to yourselves, that ye
go not up into the mount, or touch the border of it :
whosoever toucheth the mount shall be surely put to**
13 **death : no hand shall touch him, but he shall surely
be stoned, or shot through ; whether it be [15]beast or
man, it shall not live ; when the [16]trumpet soundeth**
14 **(E) long, they shall come up to the mount.**—* [17]And
Moses went down from the mount unto the people, and sanc-
15 tified the people ; and they washed their garments. And
he said unto the people, Be ready against the third day :
16 come not near a woman. And it came to pass on the third
day, when it was morning, that there were thunders and lightnings, and a [18]thick cloud upon the mount, and the voice of a
trumpet exceeding loud ; [19]and all the people that were in
17 the camp trembled. And Moses brought forth the people
out of the camp to meet God ; and they stood at the nether
18 **(J)** part of the mount. **And mount Sinai was altogether
on smoke, because Yahweh descended upon it in fire :**
[20]**and the smoke thereof ascended as the smoke of a**

---

[11]Vs. 14f.; Gen. 35:2.   [12]Gen. 11:5,7; Ex. 3:8 etc.   [13]Vv. 20; 34:2, 4; Dt. 33:2.   [14]Vv. 21-24; 24:2; 34:3.   [15]12:38; 17:3; 34:3.   [16]Cf. vv. 16, 19.   [17]Vs. 10.   [18]Vs. 9; 33:9f.   [19]20:18-21.   [20]Gen. 15:17; 19:28.

---

* Vs. 13 imperatively requires an antecedent for the emphatic *hemmah*
"*these*," who in contrast with the people, "shall come up." As the people are
to be kept away, the privileged individuals can be only those referred to in vv.
22, 24, "Moses and Aaron and the priests" (see note on vs. 24, and cf. xxiv. 1f.,
9-11). We find ourselves in fact in vv. 11-13 in the midst of the preliminary
interview of Moses with Yahweh (there is no need to suppose more than one
interview) in which Moses receives directions in preparation for the approaching theophany, which in J may have been on the morrow (cf. viii. 9, 23, etc.)
instead of "the third day," vs. 11. (E). Now this is precisely the condition of
affairs in vv. 20ff.; and here, *viz.* after 24a, "thou, and Aaron with thee, and
the priests," we discover the original position of vv. 11-13, whose removal has
made necessary the curious interpolation vs. 23.

furnace, and the whole mount quaked greatly.*
(E) And when the voice of the trumpet waxed louder and 19
louder, Moses spake, and God answered him by a voice.
(J) [21]And Yahweh came down upon mount Sinai, to the 20
top of the mount : and Yahweh called Moses to the top
of the mount ; and Moses went up. And Yahweh said 21
unto Moses, Go down, [22]charge the people, lest they
break through unto Yahweh to gaze, and many of
them perish. And let the [23]priests also, which come 22
near to Yahweh, sanctify themselves, lest Yahweh
(Rje) [24]break forth upon them. And Moses said unto Yah- 23
weh, The people cannot come up to mount Sinai: for thou [25]didst charge
us, saying, Set bounds about the mount, and sanctify it. And Yahweh 24
(J) said unto him, Go, get thee down ; † and thou shalt come up,
[2]thou, and Aaron with thee : but let not the priests‡
and the people break through to come up unto Yahweh, lest he break forth upon them. So Moses went 25
down unto the people, and told them. § [. . .]

[21]Vv. 11, 18 ; Gen. 11 : 5, etc. [22]Cf. vv. 16f. [23]4 : 14 ; 24 : 1 ; 32 : 30 ; Cf. vv. 6, 10, 17 ; 24 :
5. [24]1 : 12 ; Gen. 30 : 30, 43 ; 38, 9 ; 2Sam. 5 : 20 ; 6 : 8, etc. [25]Vv. 12f. [2a]24 : 1f. 9-11.

* The order 20a, 18, 20b is preferred by some critics.

† Vs. 23 in the present connection has almost the character of an imperti-
nence. No attention whatever is paid to it in what follows, save that the thread
of discourse in 24a is resumed where interrupted (cf. vs. 21). The obvious
occasion for the interpolation (see note on vv. 11–13) fully accounts for its
origin.

‡Insert at this point vv. 11–13, and translate with Kuenen (*Theol. Tijdschr.*
xv. p. 177) "thou, and Aaron with thee, and the priests ; but let not the
people," etc. This involves no change in the original text, but only in the
Massoretic accentuation. This sense is imperatively required by vs. 22, "the
priests *which come near* to Yahweh." Cf. also xxiv. 1f., 9f.

§ Literally " said unto them ". . . The sentence breaks off unfinished.

§ IV.   Ex. xx.—Num. x.   Israel at Sinai.

Prolegomena.

The great mass of this section is formed by the priestly
legislation, whose foundation is the sacred Tabernacle of the
Testimony, built at Sinai "according to the pattern shown in
the mount." It is manifest from xxv. 16, 21 ; xxxi. 18 a (P^2)
that the priestly law-book contained its own version of the
Ten Words, and of this a trace perhaps remains in xx. 11
which is either from the hand of P^2 or from Rp. But the
supreme interest of this document is the institution and construction of the Tabernacle ; for with its construction, the
preparation of its furniture, consecration of its priesthood, its
occupation by the *Shekinah*, and the lighting from heaven of its
fires of perpetual sacrifice the worship of Israel is supposed
to begin. Previously there is no trace of priest, or altar, or
ritual. Only in the narrative of JE do the patriarchs sacrifice or build altars. All this is reserved in P for elaborate
institution by divine fiat at Sinai. Now with what laborious
delight does the priestly author set himself to his task ! Every
detail of the Jerusalem temple and its elaborate ritual is reproduced on a scale adapted to the supposed requirements of the
wilderness. Even the great brazen altar which Ahaz had built
after the pattern he brought from Damascus (II Kings. xvi.
10-16) must have its counterpart before the Tabernacle of the
Congregation ; only, as adapting it for transportation, in Exodus
xxvii. 1ff., it is to be made of wood (!) and merely overlaid
with brass. The author carries his imitation of the Jerusalem
temple in the arrangements of its portable counterpart so far as
to speak of the north, south, east and west sides of the Tabernacle (xxvi. 18, 20, 22; xxvii. 9, 11ff., etc.) although no orienta-
tion of the sacred tent is anywhere prescribed, and the very
terms he employs ("seaward" for west, "desertward" for
south, etc.) prove that his point of view is Palestine. After
describing in almost incredibly elaborate detail all the minutiae
of specifications for construction in chh. xxv-xxxii., we are
treated to five more chapters (xxxv-xl.) for the most part

verbally identical with the preceding, only turning specifications into history by changing "Thou shalt make " to "and he
made." In justice to P² it should be added that the testimony
of the LXX. proves that this final straw of tediousness belongs to
some other, but kindred hand (P³) of the period but shortly
preceding the LXX. version (200 B. C.). After the erection of
the Tabernacle and its dedication, by the incoming of the cloud
and the "glory," (Ex. xl. 34–38), Moses receives elaborate
directions for the priestly ceremonial, including the various
kinds of sacrifice, consecration of the priests, Aaron and his
sons, the law of clean and unclean meats, of impurity, of lep-
rosy, atonement ; Lev. i–xvi. Hereafter comes a body of laws
semi-civil, semi-ecclesiastical, similar in character and style to
the legislation of Ezekiel, and partaking of the quasi-prophetic
character of Deuteronomy. This primitive code, Lev. xvii–
xxvi., forms the real nucleus of P²'s work. It is usually
designated H (*Heiligkeitsgesetz* "Law of Holiness") ; but with
Kuenen we employ the sign P¹. Lev. xxvii. gives the law of
things sanctified. Num. i–x. 10 contains the account of the
census preparatory to the consecration of the Levites, together
with the duties of the latter, the law of defilement, of trespass,
of the ordeal of the water of jealousy, of the Nazirite vow, and
Aaronic blessing, the offerings of the 12 princes of the congregation (a passage of 6 verses repeated 12 times over in
identical terms), dedication of the altar, candlestick, and Levites
(Aaron and his sons *wave* the 22,000 Levites before Yahweh,
Num. viii. 21), observance of the second passover, appearance
of the cloud upon the Tabernacle for journeying and encampment, and construction of the silver trumpets. All this
mass of priestly ordinances is of interest only to the spe-
cialist, and has no practical relation to the story. Here it is
accordingly omitted, although the older portion of it really constitutes the substance of P²'s work. A large part, however, is
from P³. We confine ourselves to the mere framework of P²'s
narrative, and to the earlier sources, from whose graphic story
this skeleton of history is derived. Of this narrative of J P²
there is in § IV. but the trace above mentioned in Ex. xx. 11 ;

the brief account of the appearance of the cloud and *Shekinah* on Sinai, and Moses' ascent, xxiv. 16-18a ; his descent, xxxi. 18 ; and a trace in xxxii. 15, added to by P² in xxxiv. 29-35. Of the story of the people's apostasy there is, as we should expect, no trace in P.

Much more copious is the narrative of E, although a large part of the material seems to be improperly placed at this point (chiefly The " Book of Judgments," chh. xxi. 1-xxiii. 9) ; and the rest has suffered alteration of the order. After the account of the utterance from the mount of the Ten Words, the divine Voice addressing the people, the latter withdraw in terror, entreating Moses to go near and hear what more God will say ; xx. 1-21. Moses approaches, and is directed to return to the people with the promise of God's special favor if they are obedient to the law. The people promise obedience, and Moses so reports to God ; xix. 3b-8. Yahweh bids him come up into the mount and remain there with him. God will give him the tables of stone on which he has written the Ten Words, and will teach him " laws and commandments." Moses and Joshua accordingly ascend the mount, leaving Aaron and Hur in charge of the people, and remain there 40 days ; xxiv. 12-15, 18b. In the meantime the people, impatient at the delay, prevail upon Aaron to make a golden calf " to go before them " as a representation of Yahweh, who " brought them up out of the land of Egypt." On the morrow they are engaged in festivities ; xxxii. 1-6. The same day God delivers to Moses the tables of stone, of divine workmanship, and Moses turns to descend the mount with Joshua. Approaching the foot, Joshua observes the clamor, which he interprets as war, but Moses discerns to be singing. Arrived in view of the proceedings in the camp, Moses in wrath dashes the tables in pieces, grinds the calf to powder, and makes the people drink water mixed with its dust. He reproaches Aaron, who makes a lame excuse ; xxxi. 18b ; xxxii. 15 in part, 16-24. On the morrow Moses goes up to make atonement, and pleads with Yahweh to forgive the people. Yahweh grants a suspension of punishment, but dismisses the people from his presence, granting angelic guidance, but predicting a day of visitation ; xxxii. 30–34. On hearing these evil tidings the people mourn, and strip themselves of their ornaments ; xxxiii. 4, 6. [Yahweh observes the repentance of the people, and provides a substitute for the covenant already broken before its ratification. Of the ornaments stripped off in penitence Moses shall prepare a Tent of Meeting for worship and intercourse with Yahweh, but " without the camp." For the ordering of this worship Yahweh furnishes a new code of ritual law followed by promises in case of obedience. These Words of the Covenant Moses is to write and deposit in an ark of shittim-wood in the Tent of Meeting.] The Words of the Covenant consist of (five ?) ritual laws concerning, I. Mode of worship : altars, sacrifices and the like ; II. Sabbaths ; weekly and yearly ; III. Feasts : of Unleavened bread, of Harvest, and of Ingathering ; IV. Sacred things to be presented in offering ; firstlings and first fruits ; V. Abominable things to be avoided. It is substantially the same code which in Ex. xxxiv. 10–27 (J) is called " The Words of the Covenant, the Ten Words ; " xx. 22 –26 ; xxiii. 10–19. This is followed by (five ?) promises : Yahweh is sending his angel before the people to bring them into the promised land. Obedience to his command will ensure : I. the help of Yahweh against all adversaries ; II. a blessing upon the bread and water of the people and continual health ; III. fruitfulness and long life ; IV. the hornet to go before Israel and gradually drive out the Amorite from the land ; V. possession of the land in its ideal extent ; xxiii. 20–33. (31b—33 = Rd). This (second) covenant between Yahweh and the people is immediately ratified with solemn ceremonies, in which Moses acts as hierophant, and " young men " as priests ; xxiv. 3–8. [Moses deposits the Book of the Covenant as directed in the ark of God in the Tent of Meeting.] At this juncture Jethro appears, bringing the wife and sons of Moses, and is hospitably received. On learning of the providence of God with the people he celebrates a sacrificial feast with Moses, Aaron,* and the elders of Israel " before God " ; xviii. 1–12 for the most part.

* The reappearance of Aaron here in a passage necessarily subsequent (cf. vs. 16 and 23) to the story of the golden calf, as if in the same favor as ever, is one of the things which give color to the theory of Kuenen, Cornill and others,

On the morrow Jethro observes the inability of Moses to administer the entire government of the people, and counsels him "If God direct him so" to appoint judges and officers, himself only acting in the ultimate appeal in bringing the causes to God. After adopting this advice Moses takes leave of his father-in-law, who departs to his own land ; xviii. 13–27.

As a preliminary to the narrative introducing another and kindred institution the author relates the practise of Moses in regard to the sacred Tent, which he pitched "without the camp" and called "the Tent of Meeting." When Moses entered it the people stood in reverence. Within, the pillar of cloud descended in the sight of the people, "stood at the door of the Tent and [God] spake with Moses." Joshua remained permanently in charge of the Tent ; xxxiii. 7–11. [In response to Moses' complaint of too great burdens?] Yahweh instructs Moses to gather 70 elders of the people to the Tent of Meeting, where he will equip them with the prophetic spirit. Moses does so, and the 70 men fall into the prophetic ecstasy when the spirit rests upon them. Two, however, who were of the 70 but had not gone out, "prophesy" in the camp. When this is reported to Moses in the Tent Joshua is jealous, and would forbid them ; but Moses nobly desires only that all Yahweh's people might have the gift ; Num. xi. 16f., 24–30. Hereupon follows originally the story of the murmuring of Miriam and Aaron against Moses' "Cushite" wife ; Num. xii ; and, after the departure from Horeb, the story of the conflict with Amalek ; Ex. xvii. 8–16. (See above Analysis 2 of § III.)

The narrative of J was interrupted in § III. at the point where preparation had just been made for Moses, Aaron and "the priests" to ascend Mount Sinai, every other living thing being barred away "lest Yahweh should break forth upon them." In xxiv. 1 we resume the thread almost exactly at the point where

that in Ex. xxxii. we have mainly an E², later than the deportation of Ephraim ; cf. xxxii. 34. Into this possible distinction of E² from E, we do not care to enter. Ch. xviii. in any case belongs to the oldest portions of E. This older portion might also include xxiv. 11, which we are perhaps overbold in assign-ing to J. In that case it doubtless followed after xx. 1–21.

broken off. Here, in addition to Aaron and "the priests" (Nadab and Abihu), 70 elders are permitted to come up with Moses and partake of a covenant meal with God ; xxiv. 1f., 9–11. Thereafter Yahweh gives special instructions to Moses. He must be ready by the morning with two stone tables [and an ark of shittim-wood to contain them] and come up entirely alone, all the former precautions being taken against the intrusion of any living thing. Moses ascends in the morning, carrying the tables he has hewn out. Yahweh appears in a theophany and offers to make a Covenant. The " Ten Words " of this covenant are the same, save for slight differences of form, with those of the *second* law of E. Moses remains 40 days on Mount Sinai, engaged in engraving them upon the stone tables ; xxxiv. 1–28, for the most part. Yahweh now bids Moses descend, because the people are in revolt. During his absence a mutiny has taken place in the camp ; xxxii. 7–14. Moses arrives at the gate of the camp, and, seeing the disorder, summons to his aid the tribe of Levi, who suppress the rebellion with the sword. For this act of loyalty to Yahweh they are rewarded with the priesthood, but " Yahweh smote the people ; " xxxii. 25–29, 35a. Yahweh bids Moses, " Depart, thou and the people which thou hast brought up " to the promised land ; but refuses to go among them because of their insubordination ; xxxiii. 1–3. Moses expostulates with Yahweh against his laying all the burden of the people upon his shoulders ; Num. xi. 10 in part, 11f., 14f. After long pleading Yahweh consents that his Presence shall precede the people and give them an abiding-place. As a signal token of his reconciliation he grants Moses the privilege of beholding his "glory." Moses is encouraged to ask the complete withdrawal of Yahweh's refusal to go " in the midst " of Israel [Yahweh agrees to dwell without the camp and directs the preparation of the sacred Tent] ; Ex. xxxiii. 12–23 ; xxxiv. 6–9. Hobab, Moses' father-in-law, visits the camp ; Ex. xviii. 7–11, (traces).

All this material of J, E, and P has undergone successive readjustment by Rje, Rd, (who seems to have removed the Book of Judgments from the present position of Deuteronomy

to the position it now occupies, and to have added a certain
characteristic interpolations) and Rp. The final recasting has
of course broken the lines of the original units and so adjusted
the material to new conceptions as to make it difficult, without
altering the order of passages to effect our usual subdivision.
Accommodating ourselves as far as possible to Rp's point of
view, we make the following classification of the material.

1. Chh. xx-xxiii.   THE FIRST COVENANT AT HOREB.

ANALYSIS.

In these four chapters, often designated, through a misapplication of
xxiv. 7, "the Book of the Covenant," we have no trace of more than a
single source, which, with only a single exception among critics of note,
is positively identified as E, * and it is the less needful to enter into any
extended proof that the material is in reality derived wholly from this
document in view of the thorough work of Budde on these chh., in *Z. A.
W.* xi. i. We need only refer here to the manifest traces of E, in the
language and style (see refs.) ; the exclusive use of *Elohim* throughout the
Ten Words (xx. 1-21) and Book of Judgments (xxi. 6, 13; xxii. 8, 9 *bis*,
11 (LXX.), 28) save in xxii. 20, where it was impossible ; the connection of
this code with ch. xviii. and xxiv. 12 ; the parallel in J's " Words of the
Covenant (xxxiv. 10-27) to the Book of the Covenant (xx. 22-26; xxiii
10-33) ; the connection of the latter at the beginning with Dt. xxvii. 4-6
(E ; cf. Ex. xx. 23ff.) and at the end with xxxii. 34, (E ; cf. xxiii. 20), and
xxiv. 3-8 ; its use of "the Amorite" (see note on xxiii. 28) generically
for the inhabitants of Canaan ; finally in xxiv. 3-8 the altar and *maççeboth*
(cf. Dt. xxvii. 1-8) ; disappearance of the "priests" of xix. 22, 24 (J) ; and
the part taken by the people in the covenant ; cf. xix. 7f ; ct. J, *passim*.†

---

* I am at a loss to understand the singular exception which must be made in
the case of so careful a scholar as Canon Driver ; yet in his Introd. to Lit. of
the O. Test. p. 29ff., he assigns xx. 22-xxiii. 33; xxiv. 3-8 to J (!). Is not this
an oversight due to dependence on Wellhausen (1876), and failure to observe
Wellhausen's retraction of the opinion as untenable (*Comp.* p. 327.—1889) in
his reply to the objections of Kuenen ? The same oversight appears in
Baentzsch *Bundesbuch*, p. 73.

† The important work of B. Baentzsch above referred to, *Das Bundesbuch*,
Halle 1892 has come to me too late to be adequately treated. For many points
of coincidence with my own analysis, such as the distinction between the *De-*

While there can really be but little doubt that the material of this sub-section is exclusively derived from E, it is equally certain that we have not here a single extract made at one time from this document. On the contrary the opinion of critics is unanimous that the present order and connection cannot possibly be original. Chh. xxi. f. constitute a thoroughly unique, and unquestionably ancient collection of case law. It is a series of precedents in supposititious cases for the administration of justice, and has an appropriate title of its own: " These are the judgments " (*mishpatim*), *i. e.*, legal precedents for the guidance of the judges (xviii. 21–26) in most cases. It is not only very strange that any original writer should think of connecting this body of case law with the solemn ethical and religious principles proclaimed to all the people in ch. xx., but it is quite impossible that they should be included in the conditions of Yahweh's covenant with the *people* (xxiv. 3–8) ; for how can the *people* promise to do the " judgments," *e. g.* those relating to injuries to property and person ? As a matter of fact, although in xxiv. 3a the words " and all the judgments " are inserted by Rd (see note *in loc.*), in vs. 3b they are wanting, and the people promise obedience only to "the words of Yahweh." But furthermore it is the object of Moses' 40 days' stay upon the mount (xxiv. 12–15, 18b) that he might receive " the law and the commandment," and Dt. v. 30–vi. 1 shows that in that writer's understanding " the commandments and the statutes and the *judgments*," which Moses was then instructed in, were not promulgated until at the end of Moses' life. In any case in xxiv. 12 they are still to come. The *mishpatim* accordingly really belong in a much later position. In fact if we look closely at Ex. xxiv. 12 we shall see that it has been altered to admit of the insertion of the " Book of Judgments " before it. What the original writer unquestionably intended to say was that God had written the *Ten Words* on the tables of stone which he would give to Moses (cf. xxxi. 18 ; xxxii. 15f.), and that he would give him *in addition* "laws and commandments that thou mayest teach them," cf. Dt. v. 31. These " statutes and laws of God " we find Moses actually engaged in teaching in xviii. 16, a passage which, as already pointed out, should come after ch.

barim and *Mishpatim :* the demonstration, p. 70f., that the *Mishpatim* cannot originally have stood between chh. xx. and xxiv. and are not adapted to form part of a covenant (xxiv. 3, " and all the judgments " being attributed to R); the recognition that the Ten Words must be younger than the Words of the Covenant because abstract and general (p. 96f.) and that ch. xxxiv=J, I am grateful. Unfortunately the main contentions of the book I am unable to admit, and with all the good will in the world I have found nothing to alter in my own manuscript after a thorough study of Baentzsch.

xxxiv. But xxiv. 12, *now* reads: "I will give thee the tables of stone, and the law and the commandment which I have written, that thou mayest teach them." It is obvious that the words "which I have written" ought to apply only to "the tables of stone," and hence should follow immediately thereupon. But when the transposition is effected we see a new light, a light incompatible with present arrangements. "The laws and commandments," instead of being already given are *still to come* and it is the object of Moses' 40 days' sojourn in the mount to be instructed in them. Therefore until this slight change of order in xxiv. 12 was made, there was no room for the Book of Judgments before it. We have already seen that the change was subsequent to the writing of Dt. v. 30ff. The inference must be that our Deuteronomy has crowded out the "Book of Judgments," which then had to obtain the best place it could in the Horeb legislation, Rd adjusting xxiv. 3 and 12 to admit it.

The Ten Words, xx. 1–17, like all the older legislative material, are drastically worked over and interpolated by Rd, but are of course in place, as they join directly upon xix. 19. The same is true in my opinion, critics to the contrary notwithstanding, of vv. 18–21 (see note *in loc.*); but the remainder of the "Book of the Covenant" together with the story of its ratification must find a place elsewhere. Ch. xxiv. 12ff. cannot be so long deferred from its true connection with xx. 1–21, (cf. Dt. v.); but the decisive indication of displacement appears in the fact that the intrusive material itself bears the mark of its original position. In xxiii. 20ff., "Behold I am sending," we stand immediately before Israel's departure. We are tempted to see the influence of the people's apostasy in vs. 21, (cf. xx. 23), and in the following verses the thought is fixed exclusively upon the journey about to be resumed and the conquest of Palestine. The next paragraph, xxiv. 3–8, with its story of the erection of the altar and twelve "pillars" is more naturally understood if the scene is now to be forsaken. This passage accordingly describes the final ratification of the covenant, without which Israel could not be supposed to proceed upon their journey. It distinctly marks the *conclusion* of the covenant transactions at Horeb. The "book" (*i. e.* writing) of the covenant therefore does not include the "Judgments," but is just what its name implies, the *reciprocal* promise of the people to worship Yahweh according to certain stipulated rites, and of Yahweh to bless the people in certain specified ways. The requirements which this Book of the Covenant makes of the people are substantially identical with those of the "Words of the Covenant," which in the parallel account of J (ch. xxxiv.) Moses wrote at the divine dictation on tables of stone. The significant difference in attitude toward this fundamental ritual law is that in E, it is based upon a voluntary compact by the people ; in J it is enacted by divine " favor."

Omitting the Book of Judgments, the residuum which constitutes the original Book of the Covenant consists of Ex. xx. 22-26 ; xxiii. 10-33. Like the Ten Words (where the LXX. shows the process of conformation to Dt. v. still going on in the third century B. C.), and like all the Jehovistic legislative material, it has suffered severely from interpolation as well as from its displacement. In xxiii. 14-19 especially, where it originally must have been substantially the same as Ex. xxxiv. 18-26, the resemblance has been heightened by introducing in the E version clauses and terms from its parallel. (See note *in loc.* and cf. the similar treatment of the Lord's Prayer in Matt. and Luke. For full treatment of the relation between the " Words of the Covenant " (J) and the " Book of the Covenant " see Art. iv.). It is worthy of note that from the story of the Apostasy on, the material of E becomes less exclusively Elohistic, the use of Elohim disappearing save in the most unmistakably antique fragments such as the Visit of Jethro, Battle with Amalek (" rod of Elohim " occurs once), Song of Balaam (in part) and Book of Judgments. Otherwise Elohim occurs only in a few isolated cases.

(**E**) ¹And God spake all these words, saying,   **20**
I ²am Yahweh thy God, ³which brought thee out of the land of Egypt, ⁴out of the house of bondage.

Thou shalt have none other Gods before me.   3

(**Rd**) Thou shalt not make unto thee a graven image, nor [the   4
likeness of] any form that is in heaven above, or that is in the earth beneath, or that is in the water under the earth : ⁵thou shalt not bow down thy-   5
self unto them, nor serve them : for I Yahweh thy God am ⁶a jealous God,
⁷visiting the iniquity of the fathers upon the children, upon the third and
upon the fourth generation of them that hate me ; and shewing mercy unto   6
thousands, of them that love me and keep my commandments. '

(**E**) Thou shalt not take the name of Yahweh thy God in   7
(**Rd**) vain ; for Yahweh will not hold him guiltless that taketh his name
in vain.

(**E**) Remember the sabbath day, to keep it holy.   8
(**Rd**) ⁸Six days shalt thou labor, and do all thy work ; but the   9-10

¹Cf. 34 : 10-27 ; Dt. 5 ; 1-21. ²3 : 13. ³32 : 4 ; Hos. 13 : 4. ⁴Jos. 24 : 17 (LXX). ⁵23 : 24 ;
Jos. 23 : 7. ⁶Jos. 24 : 10 ; cf. 34 : 14. ⁷Cf. 34 : 7 ; Num. 14 : 18, 33. ⁸23 : 12.

seventh day is a sabbath unto Yahweh thy God : [in it] thou shalt not do any work, thou, nor thy son, nor thy daughter, thy manservant, nor thy maidservant, nor thy cattle, nor [9]thy stranger that is within thy gates :

11 (P) [10]*for in six days Yahweh made heaven and earth, the sea, and all that in them is, and rested the seventh day : wherefore Yahweh blessed the sabbath day, and hallowed it.*

12 (E) (Rd) Honor thy father and thy mother : [11]that thy days may be long upon the land which Yahweh thy God giveth thee.

13 (E) Thou shalt do no murder.

14 Thou shalt not commit adultery.

15 Thou shalt not steal.

16 [12]Thou shalt not bear false witness against thy neighbor.

17 (Rd) Thou shalt not covet thy neighbor's [13]house, thou shalt not covet thy neighbor's wife, [14]nor his manservant, nor his maidservant, nor his ox, nor his ass, nor anything that is thy neighbor's.*

18 (E) [15]And all the people saw the thunderings, and the lightnings, and the voice of the trumpet, [16]and the mountain

19 smoking : and when the people saw it, they trembled, and stood afar off. And they said unto Moses, Speak thou with us, and we will hear : but let not God speak with us, lest we

20 die. And Moses said unto the people, Fear not : for God is come to [17]prove you, and that [18]his fear may be before you,

---

[9]Dt. 14 : 21,27-29 ; 31 : 12, etc.   [10]Gen. 2 : 1-3.   [11]Dt. 11 : 9 ; 25 : 15.   [12]23 : 1.   [13]Gen. 15 : 2.   [14]Vs. 10.   [15]19 : 16 ; Dt. 5 : 23-27.   [16]19 : 18.   [17]Gen. 22 : 1 ; 42 : 16 ; Ex. 15 : 25 ; 16 : 4.   [18]Gen. 20 : 11 ; 42 : 19 ; Ex. 2 : 17.

* Critics generally maintain that the original form of the " Ten Words " was such as their Hebrew name " Words " perhaps implies, viz., brief commands similar to vv. 13-16, the disproportionate length of the second, third, fourth, fifth and tenth being caused by redactional supplementation. This view is sustained by the looseness of connection of the expansions. Observe *e. g.* the ungrammatical attachment of 4b, to 4a. " House " in vs. 17a is comprehensive of all the enumerated objects in 17b (cf. Gen. xv. 2 ; Ex. 1. 21; Job. viii. 15). For an excellent discussion of the original form and the possible share of E in the elaboration of the " Words " see Driver, *Introd.* p. 30. Whether or not the original document intended a division into two "tables," one prescribing religious duties (*pietas*) the other duties to the community (*probitas*) is a question to be decided by comparison with contemporary literature. If, as seems probable, each " table " contained a pentad (so Philo, Josephus and others) the original length cannot have been so disproportionate as now.

that ye sin not.   And the people stood afar off, and Moses 21
drew near unto the [19]thick darkness where God was.*

(**E**)—[. . .] And † Yahweh said unto Moses, Thus thou 22
shalt say unto the children of Israel, [20]Ye yourselves have
seen that I have [21]talked with you from heaven.   [22]Ye shall 23
not make [other gods] with me ; [23]gods of silver, or gods
of gold, ye shall not make unto you.   An altar of [24]earth 24
thou shalt make unto me, [25]and shalt sacrifice thereon thy
burnt offerings, and thy peace offerings, thy sheep, and thine
oxen : [26]in every place where I record my name I will come
unto thee and I will bless thee.   [27]And if thou make me an 25
altar of stone, thou shalt not build it of hewn stones : for if
thou lift up thy tool upon it, thou hast polluted it.   [28]Neither 26

---

[19]19 : 9.   [20]Cf. 19 : 4.   [21]Gen. 21 : 17 ; 22 : 11.   [22]20 : 3 ; 34 : 14.   [23]20 : 4 ; 34 : 17.
[24]II Kings. 5 : 17 ; Ct. 27 : 1f.   [25]24 : 5 ; 31 : 6 ; Dt. 27 : 6f.   [26]Ct. Lev. 17 : 8f.; Dt. 12 : 6, 11,
etc. [27]Dt. 27 : 5f.; Jos. 8 : 31.   [28]Ct. 27 : 1 : Lev. 9 : 22.

---

* Vv. 18–21 are not necessarily displaced from after xix. 19 (Kuen. Jül.
Well. Bud.), and the evidence from Dt. v., so far from supporting this view,
goes to show that in the time of Dp these verses occupied their present position (cf. especially Dt. v. 23ff., and see Art. iv).   It is perhaps not claiming too
much to say with Prof. W. H. Greene (*Hebraica* viii. p. 45) that in vs. 19 the
people have no occasion to suppose God intends to speak to them, unless vv.
1–17 have preceded.   A stronger objection to the proposed transposition appears in the fact that the pains taken to impress the moral law as expressed
in the Ten Words upon the people by their actually hearing it pronounced by
God's voice as arranged in xix. 9, are then thrown away, since the people
remove out of hearing before the utterance takes place.   In vs. 18b read with
LXX., " And the people were afraid, and " in place of, " And when the people
saw it."   The mediatorial position assumed by Moses in vs. 21 seems to be
the indispensable antecedent to the scene of xix. 3–8 ; cf. Dt. v.   A touch of
Rje's hand appears in vs. 18a looking back to xix. 18.

† The various theories of a fourth source broached by Wellhausen, Kuenen
and Bruston (*Les deux Jehovistes, Rev. de Theol. et Phil.* 1882) are uncalled for.
The Book of the Covenant, which begins here (see Analysis), is the only *covenant*
at Horeb mentioned in E, unless the promise in xix. 8 be so regarded, in which
case the covenant here (vv. 22–26 : xxiii. 10–33) is a second, made after the
violation of the first.   In either case vv. 22–26 ; xxiii. 10–33 with their sequel
xxiv. 3–8 must come *after* xxxii. 30–34.   The introductory clauses in vs. 22
have perhaps been retouched by Rd.

shalt thou go up by steps unto mine altar ; ²⁶that thy nakedness be not discovered thereon.*

21 (E)—[. . .]¹Now these are the judgments † which
thou shalt set before them.

2   If thou buy an Hebrew servant, ²six years he shall serve :

²⁶₂8 : 42f.   ¹₂4 : 12 ;18 : 15-26; Dt. 5 : 31 ; 4 : 14 ; 6: 1.   ²₂3 : 10f.

---

* In the interest of the traditional theory it is sometimes denied that the
above provision for sacrifice by private individuals in various places is in conflict with the Deuteronomic restriction of sacrifice to Jerusalem only, and to the
Levitical priesthood ; or that it conflicts with the priestly centralization of the
whole ceremonial at the temple and limitation of sacrifice to the *Aaronic*
priesthood. The legislation must be interpreted by the history (see my
" Genesis of Genesis," pp. 50ff). Previous to the reformation of Josiah, 620 B.
C., the invariable representation of all the historical books, including the narratives of the patriarchs, is that altars of stone and earth were erected in honor
of Yahweh all over the land, " in every place where he caused his name to be
remembered," by those who were most anxious to please him ; and moreover
that Yahweh did " come unto them and bless them " at these sanctuaries (cf.
e. g. I Kgs. iii. 4ff). It is impossible to deny that vs. 25 contemplates *various* altars, as much as vs. 24 does *various* places, to which Yahweh will *come* to meet the
(lay) worshipper, not the *one* sanctuary of the tabernacle (and temple) where he
abides. Hence to Elijah(I Kgs. xix. 10) it is impious to overthrow these altars ;
but to the Deuteronomist the reverse (II Kgs. xxiii. 15, 19f). Thus although the
iconoclastic zeal of Josiah and his followers destroyed the old places of worship it
could not entirely obliterate from the literature the traces of the older practise
and older law. The treatment of the altar as an actual representative of Yahweh
in vv. 25f. agrees with the language of E in Gen. xxxiii. 20; xxxv. 7 ; Ex.
xxiv. 6. The object of vs. 26 is met in the priestly legislation by a different
provision. Cf. xxviii. 42 ; xxxix. 28 ; Lev. vi. 10 ; xvi. 4.

† The code of precedents in law here entitled " The judgments " (*mishpatim*)
has been incorporated by E, from unquestionably ancient material. Its original position in the E document would appear to have been after Dt. i.-iii.
and just before Dt. xxvii. 1-8 (cf Jos. viii. 30-35). See Kuenen's argument
(Hex. §13. n. 32) as to Ex. xx. 22-xxiv. 8. That Dt. xxvii. 1-8 in its original
form had to do with the original Book of Judgments, and was based upon the
actual existence of *stelæ* in Shechem in E's time, making public the general
principles of common law, would be perhaps too bold a conjecture ; but at
least it is far more easily conceivable of the brief Book of Judgments than of
the elaborate *Judean* expansion of Ex. xx.-xxiii. which constitutes our Deuteronomy. The code although very ancient presupposes an agricultural and settled
community (xxi. 6 ; xxii. 2, 5-7). It obviously rests upon a basis of consuetu-
dinary law.

and in the seventh he shall go out free for nothing. If he 3
come in by himself, he shall go out by himself : if he be
³married, then his wife shall go out with him. If his master 4
give him a wife, and she bear him sons or daughters ; the
wife and her children shall be her master's, and he shall go
out by himself.   But if the servant shall plainly say, I love 5
my master, my wife, and my children ; I will not go out
free : then his master shall ⁴bring him unto God, and shall 6
bring him to the door, or unto the door post ; and his master
shall bore his ear through with an awl ; and he shall serve
him forever.

(E) And if a man sell his daughter to be a ⁵maidservant, 7
she shall not go out as the menservants do. If she please 8
not her master, who hath espoused her to himself, * then
shall he let her be redeemed : to sell her unto a ⁶strange
people he shall have no power, seeing he hath dealt deceitfully with her. And if he espouse her unto his son, he shall 9
deal with her after the manner of daughters. If he take 10
him another [wife] her food, her raiment, and her duty of
marriage, shall he not diminish. And if he do not these 11
three unto her, then shall she go out for nothing, without
money.

He that smiteth a man, so that he die, shall surely be put 12
to death. And if a man lie not in wait, but God deliver 13
[him] into his hand ; then ⁷I will appoint thee a place whither he
shall flee.† And if a man come presumptuously upon his 14

---

³Vv. 22, 29, 30, 34, 36 ; 22 : 7, 10, 11, 13, 14 ; cf. Gen. 20 : 3 ; 37 : 19 ; ch. 24 : 14 ; Nu. 21 :
28 ; Jos. 24 : 11 ; ct. Gen. 3 : 6, 16, etc. ⁴18 : 19 ; 22 : 8f.   ⁵Vv. 20, 26f.; Gen. 21 : 10, 12, 13,
etc. ⁶Gen. 31 : 15 ; 35 : 2, 4 ; Ex. 2 : 22 ; 18 : 3 ; Jos. 24 : 20, 23.   ⁷Dt. 4 : 41-43 ; 19 : 1-13 ;
ct. vs. 14 : I Kgs. 2 : 28.

* The second clause of vs. 8 is perplexing. Budde, *Z. A. W.* xi. 1, proposes
a minute correction of the text giving "and he hath not known her"; *i. e.* the
three methods of repudiation below specified are allowable only on this condition.

† A very important and significant alteration.is that of vs. 13, originally, as
vs. 14 shows, "he shall flee to mine altar" (cf. I Kings. ii. 28). The right
of asylum was originally connected in Israel, as among other ancient peoples,
with the sanctuary and altar. When by the Deuteronomic legislation the local

neighbor, to slay him with guile ; thou shalt take him from mine altar, that he may die.

15 And he that smiteth his father, or his mother, shall be surely put to death.

16 And he that stealeth a man, and selleth him, or if he be found in his hand, he shall surely be put to death.

17 [8]And he that curseth his father, or his mother, shall surely be put to death.*

18 And if men contend, and one smiteth the other with a
19 stone, or with his fist, and he die not, but keep his bed : if he rise again, and walk abroad upon his staff, then shall he that smote him be quit : only he shall pay for the loss of his time, and shall cause him to be thoroughly healed.

20 —And if a man smite his servant, or his [9]maid, with a rod, and he die under his hand ; he shall surely be punished.
21 Notwithstanding, if he continue a day or two, he shall not be punished : for he is his money.—

22 [10]And if men strive together, and hurt a woman with child, so that her fruit depart, and yet no mischief follow : he shall be surely fined, according as the woman's [11]husband shall lay upon him ; and he shall pay as the judges determine.—†

23 But if any mischief follow, then thou shalt give life for life,
24 eye for eye, tooth for tooth, hand for hand, foot for foot,
25 burning for burning, wound for wound, stripe for stripe.—‡

[8]Lev. 20:19. [9]Vs. 7. [10]Vs. 18. [11]Cf. vs. 3 and refs.; ct. Gen. 3 : 6, 16, etc.

sanctuaries were abolished, it became necessary to create a substitute, in order not to destroy this humane institution. Hence the curious provision of the Deuteronomic legislation of " cities of refuge " Dt. iv. 41–43; xix. 1–13; cf. Num. xxxv. 6, 9–34 ; Jos. xxf. The provision, however, remained necessarily a dead letter. (Cf. Colenso. Pent. and Book of Josh. Pt. I. p. 193, and Well. Hist. of Israel. pp. 159ff.)

 * Vs. 17 should perhaps stand before xxii. 18. See note *in loc.*

 † For *hippelilim* (? R. V. " as the judges determine ") read with Budde, *Z. A. W.* xi. 1, *bannephalim* (" for the miscarriage "). The contradiction to the preceding clause, " as the woman's husband shall lay upon him " is thus avoided. Cf. also vv. 19 and 30.

 ‡ Vv. 23–25 must certainly have exchanged places with 20f. (See Budde's article above cited.) The injuries enumerated cannot possibly follow except

And if a man smite the eye of his servant, or the eye of 26
his [12]maid, and destroy it ; he shall let him go free for his
eye's sake.   And if he smite out his manservant's tooth, or 27
his [12]maidservant's tooth ; he shall let him go free for his
tooth's sake.

And if an ox gore a man or a woman, that they die, the ox 28
shall be surely stoned, and his flesh shall not be eaten ; but
the [13]owner of the ox shall be quit.   But if the ox were wont 29
to gore in time past, and it hath been testified to his [13]owner,
and he hath not kept him in, but that he hath killed a man
or a woman ; the ox shall be stoned, and his [13]owner also
shall be put to death.   If there be laid on him a ransom, then 30
he shall give for the redemption of his life whatsoever is laid
upon him.   Whether he have gored a son, or have gored a 31
daughter, according to this judgment shall it be done unto
him.   If the ox gore a manservant or a maidservant ; he 32
shall give unto their master thirty shekels of silver, and the
ox shall be stoned.

And if a man shall open a pit, or if a man shall dig a pit 33
and not cover it, and an ox or an ass fall therein, the owner 34
of the pit shall make it good ; he shall give money unto the
owner of them, and the dead [beast] shall be his.

And if one man's ox hurt another's, that he die ; then they 35
shall sell the live ox, and divide the price of it ; and the dead
also they shall divide.   Or if it be known that the ox was 36
wont to gore in time past, and his owner hath not kept him
in ; he shall surely pay ox for ox, and the dead [beast] shall
be his own.

If a man shall steal an ox, or a sheep, and kill it, or sell it ; **22**
he shall pay five oxen for an ox, and four sheep for a sheep.
—If the thief be found breaking in, and be smitten that he 2

---

[12]Vs. 7.   [13]V.v. 33f, 36 ; 22 : 8, 11f, 14f.; Gen. 14 : 13 ; 20 : 3 : 37 : 19 : (49 : 25) ; Nu. 21 : 29 ;
Jos. 24 : 11.

as results of the case supposed in vv. 18f. Vv. 20f. are equally out of place
except directly before 26f., which enumerate the less serious consequences of
injury to a slave in precise analogy to the order of 18f., 23–25, 22. The transposition appears to be due to a stupid attempt at readjustment from the seeming connection of 22a with 23a and other superficial resemblances.

3 die, there shall be no bloodguiltiness for him. If the sun be risen upon him, there shall be bloodguiltiness for him : he should make restitution ;*— if he have nothing, then he
4 shall be sold for his theft. If the theft be found in his hand alive, whether it be ox, or ass, or sheep ; he shall pay double.

5   If a man shall cause a [1]field or vineyard to be eaten, and shall let his beast loose, and it feed in another man's field ; of the best of his own field, and of the best of his own vineyard, shall he make restitution.

6   If fire break out, and catch in thorns, so that the shocks of corn, or the standing corn, or the field, be consumed ; he that kindled the fire shall surely make restitution.

7   If a man shall deliver unto his neighbor money or stuff to keep, and it be stolen out of the man's house ; if the thief be
8 found, he shall pay double. If the thief be not found, then the master of the house shall [2]come near unto God, [to see] whether he have not put his hand unto his neighbor's goods.

9 For every matter of trespass whether it be for ox, for ass, for sheep, for raiment, [or] for any manner of lost thing, whereof one saith, This is it, the cause of both parties shall come before God ; he whom God shall condemn shall pay double unto his neighbor.

10   If a man deliver unto his neighbor an ass, or an ox, or a sheep, or any beast, to keep ; and it die, or be hurt, or
11 driven away, no man seeing it : the oath of Yahweh† shall be

[1]Nu. 16:14 ; 20:17 : 21 :,22.   [2]18 : 15, 19 : 21 : 6.

*Vv. 2, 3a seem to be either a very ancient interpolation (Budde, *Z. A. W.* xi. 1. Baentzsch *B. Bb.* p. 42), or misplaced. Vs. 3b must necessarily connect with vs. 1, and cannot tolerate the interruption of 2, 3a. which suppose the thief to be dead. Vs. 4 presents the alternative to vs. 1. It is perhaps preferable to suppose that 2, 3a originally followed vs. 4, and were removed with the idea of carrying back the supposititious manslaughter to the point of time when the theft is being committed. The sense of 3a is as follows : "If the owner was not merely defending his property, but killed the thief in broad daylight, when he might have recognized him, and so, by bringing complaint, have obtained full redress, it must be reckoned malicious manslaughter. *The thief should have expiated the wrong by restitution, not by death.*

† Read "God" with LXX. "Yahweh" seemed to the editor more appropriate to the sense.

between them both, whether he hath not put his hand unto
his neighbor's goods ; and the [3]owner thereof shall accept it,
and he shall not make restitution. But if it be stolen from 12
him, he shall make restitution unto the owner thereof. If it 13
be torn in pieces, let him bring it for witness ; he shall not
make good that which was torn.

And if a man [4]borrow aught of his neighbor, and it be hurt, 14
or die, the [3]owner thereof not being with it, he shall surely
make restitution. If the owner thereof be with it, he shall 15
not make it good : if it be an hired thing, it came for its hire.

And if a man entice a virgin that is not betrothed, and lie 16
with her, he shall surely pay a dowry for her to be his wife.
If her father utterly refuse to give her unto him, he shall pay 17
money according to the dowry of virgins.

[5]Thou * shalt not suffer a sorceress to live.   18

[3]21 : 28 and refs.   [4]3 : 22 ; 11 : 2 ; 12 : 35.   [5]Lev. 20 : 27.

* A careful study of the *Mishpatim* seems to reveal an arrangement in three
divisions. Division A, ch. xxi., comprises cases involving the rights of the
person (*probitas*) : i. The Limit of Slavery, vv. 2-6 ; ii. of Concubinage, vv. 7-
11 ; iii. Murder, parricide, manstealing, vv. 12-17 ; iv. Injuries in quarrel, vv.
18f., 23-25, 22 ; v. Injuries to slaves, vv. 20f., 26f.; vi. Injuries to life from
unrestrained cattle, vv. 28-32. Division B, xxi. 33-36; xxii. 1-17 includes
cases involving the rights of property (*equitas*) : i. From criminal neglect, xxi.
33-36; ii. Theft, vv. 1, 3b, 4, 2, 3a.; iii. Trespass, vs. 5 ; iv. Arson, vs. 6 ; v.
Breach of trust, vv. 7-9 ; vi. Loss of cattle, vv. 10-13 ; vii. of borrowed Property, vv.14f.; viii. Seduction (=theft of dowry) vv. 16f. Division C includes
cases of trespass against the community (*pietas*) : i. Abominations (witchcraft,
defilement, cursing of parents (?)) vv. 18f.; xxi. 17 (?) ii. Worship of a strange
god (considered as treason to the commonwealth) vs. 20; iii. Wronging of the
widow and the *ger* (wards of the community) vs. 21; iv. Usury, vv. 25f.; v.
Disrespect to God and the magistrate, vs. 28 · vi. Just Judgment, xxiii. 1-3;
vii. Public Goodwill, vv. 4f. Vv. 6-8 make an appropriate conclusion to the
Code by commanding a just verdict from the Judges. These seem to be a conclusion to the code rather than a part of it and may have been added by E. Vs.
8 is palpably a proverb. It is natural that Division C, from its character should
exhibit the most traces of editorial working over, (cf. Ex. xx. 1-12 with 13ff.)
and these interpolations will be referred to later. It is noteworthy, however,
that Division C, in particular, shows many points of affinity with portions of the
so-called *Heiligkeitsgesetz* (P[1]) in Lev. xvii-xxvi, and as the enactment xxi. 17 is
found in Lev. xx. 9 among the obligations of *pietas*, it is possible it may have
originally stood before xxii. 18, having been attracted to its present place by
xxi. 15.

19 ⁶Whosoever lieth with a beast shall surely be put to death.

20 ⁷He that sacrificeth unto any god, save unto Yahweh only,

21 shall be utterly destroyed. ⁸And a stranger shalt thou not

   (Rd) wrong, neither shalt thou oppress him : ⁸for ye were strangers

22 in the land of Egypt. Ye shall not afflict any widow, or fatherless child.

23 ⁹If thou afflict them in any wise, and they cry at all unto me, I will

24 surely hear their cry ; and my wrath shall wax hot, and I will kill you with

   the sword ; and your wives shall be widows, and your children fatherless.*

25   **(E)** ¹⁰If thou lend money to any of my people with thee

   that is poor, thou shalt not be to him as a creditor ; neither

26 shall ye lay upon him usury. If thou at all take thy neigh-

   bor's garment to pledge, thou shalt restore it unto him by

27 **(Rd)** that the sun goeth down : for that is his only covering, it is

   his garment for his skin : wherein shall he sleep ? and it shall come to pass,

   when he crieth unto me, that I will hear ; for I am gracious.

28   **(E)** Thou shalt not revile God, nor curse a ruler of thy

29 people.—¹¹Thou shalt not delay to offer of the abundance of

   thy fruits, and of thy liquors. ¹²The firstborn of thy sons

30 shalt thou give unto me. Likewise shalt thou do with thine

   oxen, [and] with thy sheep : seven days it shall be with its

31 dam : on the eighth day thou shalt give it me. And ¹³ye shall

   be holy men unto me : therefore ye shall not eat any flesh

   that is torn of beasts in the field : ye shall cast it to the

   dogs.—†

⁶Lev. 18 : 23 ; 20 : 15. ⁷20 : 3 ; Lev. 25 : 22. ⁸23 : 9 ; Lev. 19 : 33f. ; 25 : 14 ; Dt. 10 : 19.
⁹Dt. 24 : 12, 21; 26 : 12f. ¹⁰Dt. 23 : 19f. ¹¹34 : 19f ; xxiii. 19. ¹²Cf. 13 : 12ff. ; 34 : 19. ¹³19 : 4;
Lev. 17 : 15 ; Dt. 14 : 2, 21.

  * Vv. 21b-24, 27 ; xxiii. 9b. strongly resemble the Deuteronomic style. The
main objection, however, to the originality of these verses, and perhaps to the
whole of vv. 21-27, and xxiii. 4f. as well, is that they are not *mishpatim*, (*jus*)
and do not belong in a code of rules for the decision of causes ; but are moral
precepts, (*fas*), to be supported by the divine favor or disfavor or by humane
sentiment, rather than by the authority of the courts. It is possible to say
with considerable confidence that they are not an original part of the Book of
Judgments, without being certain in all cases that they may not have been
taken up or added by E himself.

  † Vv. 29-31 are obviously not *mishpatim*, and the passage duplicates part of
" the Book of the Covenant " (firstfruits, xxiii. 19) while on the other hand the
law of the firstborn, which we should surely expect there, does not appear.
The explanation would seem to be that in the process of assimilation of the

(E) [1]Thou shalt not take up a false report : put not thine **23** hand with the wicked to be an unrighteous witness. Thou **2** shalt not follow a multitude to do evil ; neither shalt thou speak in a cause to turn aside after a multitude to wrest [judgment] : * neither shalt thou favor a poor man in his **3** cause.

If thou meet thine enemy's ox or his ass[2] going astray, **4** thou shalt surely bring it back to him again. If thou see **5** the ass of him that hateth thee lying under his burden, and wouldest forbear to help him, thou shalt surely help with him.

[3]Thou shalt not wrest the judgment of thy poor in his **6** cause. Keep thee far from a false matter ; and the innocent **7** and righteous slay thou not : for I will not justify † the wicked. [4]And thou shalt take no gift : for a gift blindeth **8** them that have sight, and perverteth the words of the **(Rd)** righteous. [5]And a stranger shalt thou not oppress for ye know **9** the heart of a stranger, seeing ye were strangers in the land of Egypt.—‡

[1] 20:16.   [2] Gen. 20:13 ; 21:14; 37:15.   [3] Dt. 16:19.   [4] I Sam. 12:3.   [5] 22:21 ; Dt. 16:12.
Book of the Covenant to the Words of the Covenant (xxxiv. 25f.) these verses (xxii. 29–31) were displaced by xxiii. 19a. The supposition finds curious confirmation in Dt. xiv. 21, where Ex. xxii. 31 is followed by xxiii. 19b (=xxxiv. 26b).—In vs. 31 "in the field " is a misreading of the words meaning " flesh torn of beasts " and should be omitted. See Budde *Z. A. W.* xi. i. p.113. and cf. LXX.

* The missing word "judgment " is to be supplied from LXX. But vs. 2 b requires further investigation for a satisfactory reading. In Art IV. an emendation is suggested giving, " neither shalt thou turn aside after a multitude to wrest judgment."

† Read with LXX. in 2d person sing., "Neither shalt thou justify."

‡ Vs. 9, a duplicate of xxii. 21, appended to the collection in the Deuteronomic interest, seems to mark the conclusion of the *Mishpatim* ; for in the verses which follow we have no longer instructions for the judges ("judgments ") but directions to the people for the popular worship. Indeed, the latter part of the code has certainly been interpolated, a process to which it lent itself both by character and position. Such humanitarian provisions as xxiii. 4f., for example, are characteristic of Rd, and these verses are exposed to further suspicion from the fact that they interrupt the connection of vv. 1–3 with 6–8, which otherwise would form an appropriate conclusion to the code. Vs. 8 seems to be referred to in I Sam. xii. 3. (E.)

10   **(E)** ⁶And six years thou shalt sow thy land, and shalt
11 gather in the increase thereof : but the seventh year thou
      (Rd) shalt let it rest and lie fallow ; ⁷that the poor of thy peo-
      (E) ple may eat: and what they leave the beast of the field shall eat. In
      like manner thou shalt deal with thy vineyard, [and] with
12 thy oliveyard. ⁸Six days thou shalt do thy work, and on the
      (Rd) seventh day thou shalt rest: ⁹that thine ox and thine ass may
      have rest, and the son of thy handmaid, and the stranger, may be refreshed.
13 **(E)** —And in all things that I have said unto you take ye
      heed : and make no mention of the name of ¹⁰other gods,
      neither let it be heard out of thy mouth.—*
14   ¹¹Three ¹²times thou shalt keep a feast unto me in the year.
15 **(Rd)** The feast of unleavened bread shalt thou keep : ¹³seven
      days thou shalt eat unleavened bread, as I commanded thee, at the time ap-
      pointed in the month Abib (for in it thou camest out from Egypt); and
91 **(E)** none shall appear before me empty: ¹⁴and the feast of harvest,
      the firstfruits of thy labors, which thou sowest in the field :
      and the feast of ingathering, at the end of the year, when
17 **(Rd)** thou gatherest in thy labors out of the field. ¹⁵Three
      ¹⁶times in the year all thy males shall appear before the Lord Yahweh.
18   **(E)** ¹⁷Thou shalt not offer the blood of my sacrifice with

* 21:2 ; Lev. 25: 1-7.   ⁷ Dt. 24:19ff.   ⁸ 20:8 ; 34:21.   ⁹ Dt. 5: 14f.   ¹⁰ 20:3, 23.   ¹¹34 : 18, 20c. 22f. ¹²Ct. vs. 17. ¹³34 : 18. ¹⁴Cf. 34 : 22. ¹⁵34 : 23 ; Dt. 16 : 16. ¹⁶Cf. 34 : 23 ; ct. vs. 14. ¹⁷ 34 : 25.

* The style and language of vs. 13 (see references) favor its genuineness; but its position, as if bringing the legislation to a close, is very strange. Jülicher (*Jahrb. Prot. Th.* viii. p. 300) is doubtless right in saying we must expect xxiii. 20ff. immediately after it. He is also right in finding traces of borrowing in vv. 14-19 from ch. xxxiv.

The theory of borrowing is confirmed by the singular fact that LXX. include after xxiii. 17 (= xxxiv. 23) the first half of xxxiv. 24 also, a palpable interpolation of post-Deuteronomic time. But a nucleus of genuine material similar to xxxiv. 10-27 must have been originally present to serve for a basis of assimilation. (Cf. Budde, *Z. A. W.* xi. pp. 230ff. and Art. IV. and see note following). Perhaps the simplest solution would be to suppose that the laws of E's second covenant, which followed vs. 12a, were nearly identical with xxxiv. 21-26, concluding with vs. 13. This E material Rd partly removed to a little earlier position (xxii. 29-31), partly (vv. 14-16) employed in combination with that which he took from J (xxxiv. 18, 23, 26) to make a new paragraph (vv. 14-19) which he simply added on after vs. 13. The same process of amplification by Rd is illustrated in ch. xx.

leavened bread ; neither shall the fat of my feast remain all
(**Rd**) night until the morning. ¹⁸The first of the firstfruits of thy 19
ground thou shalt bring into the house of Yahweh thy God. Thou shalt
not seethe a kid in its mother's milk.*

(**E**) ¹⁹Behold, I send an angel before thee, to keep thee 20
by the way, and to bring thee into the place which I have
prepared. Take ye heed of him, and hearken unto his voice ; 21
²⁰provoke him not : for he will not pardon your transgression ; for my name is in him. ²¹But if thou shalt indeed 22
hearken unto his voice, and do all that I speak ; then I will
be an enemy unto thine enemies, and an adversary unto thine
(**Rd**) adversaries. ²²For mine angel shall go before thee, and bring 23
thee in unto the Amorite, and the Hittite, and the Perizzite, and the Canaanite, the Hivite, and the Jebusite ²³and I will cut them off. ²⁴Thou shalt 24
not bow down to their gods, nor serve them, nor do after their works : but
thou shalt utterly overthrow them, and ²⁵break in pieces their pillars. And 25
(**E**) ye shall serve Yahweh your God, and he shall † bless thy
bread, and thy water ; and I will take sickness away from
the midst of thee. There shall none cast her young, nor be 26

---

¹⁸22 : 29 ; 34 : 26. ¹⁹32 : 34 ; Num. 20 : 16. ²⁰32 : 32-34 ; Jos. 24 : 19. ²¹19 : 5f. ²²33 : 2 ;
34 : 11-16. ²³Ct. vs. 30. ²⁴20 : 5. ²⁵34 : 13 ; Nu. 33 : 52 ; Dt. 12 : 3.

* Vv. 15bc, 17, 19a are certainly taken over here from ch. xxxiv. and not *vice
versa :* for 15b refers to xiii. 3ff.; (J), and 15c is here mistakenly separated
from the law of the firstborn. Both together interrupt the connection of 15a with
16.Vs. 17 repeats vs. 14, but in different language, which is not that of E., but of J
(cf. xxxiv. 23). Even in ch. xxxiv. vs. 23 (=vs. 17) seems to be in part("males")
or wholly, from Rd, and the lateness of the period to which the process of
assimilation here exemplified extended appears from the fact above spoken
of that LXX. take in also xxxiv. 24 ! Vs. 19a has also been taken from xxxiv. 26
displacing its E. equivalent to xxii. 29-31, which strikingly differs in language.
On the other hand the contrast in linguistic form of vs. 14 with 17, 16 with
xxxiv. 22, 18 with xxxiv. 25, and the occurrence in Dt. xiv. 21 of vs. 19b in the
connection of xxii. 31 shows how large a proportion of genuine E. material
here remains to explain the motive of assimilation. In verses 15 and 17, as
well as in xxxiv. 20, 23f. the expression "appear before" is derived by a,
change of vowel which has systematically been carried through the Old Test.
by the vocalizers (cf. Dt. xvi. 16; xxxi. 11; I Sam. i. 22; Ps. xlii. 3; Is. i. 12)
from an original "see the face of" which was open to dogmatic objections ; cf.
Gen. xxxiii. 10.

† Read "I will" with LXX. and Vulg., and cf. following clauses. For the
interpolation which has led to the change of person see note on vs. 33.

barren, in thy land: the number of thy days I will fulfil.

27 (Rd) ²⁶I will send my terror before thee, and will discomfit all the people to whom thou shalt come, and I will make all thine enemies turn their backs

28 (E) unto thee. And I will send the ²⁷hornet before thee, which (Rd) shall drive out the Hivite, the Canaanite, and the Hittite,

29 (E) from before thee. ²⁸I will not drive them out from before thee in one year ; lest the land become desolate, and

30 the beast of the field multiply against thee. By little and little I will drive them out from before thee, until thou be

31 increased, and inherit the land. And I will set thy border from the Red Sea even unto the sea of the Philistines, and (Rd) from the wilderness unto the River : for I will deliver the inhabitants of the land into your hand ; and thou shalt drive them out be-

32 fore thee. ²⁹Thou shalt make no covenant with them, nor with their gods.

33 ³⁰They shall not dwell in thy land, lest they make thee sin against me : for if thou serve their gods, it will surely be a snare unto thee.*

²⁶Dt. 2 : 25; cf. vs. 28. ²⁷Jos. 24 : 12. ²⁸Jud. 2 : 23-3 : 4 ; Ct. vv. 23, 31b-33. ²⁹34 : 12. ³⁰Cf. Jud. 2 : 1-3 ; ct. vv. 29-30 and Jud. 2 : 23 ; 31 : 1f.

*Vv. 20-33, as well as the earlier part of ch. xxiii., have been interpolated from ch. xxxiv. Thus vv. 23-25a𝑎 repeat vv. 20, 27 and 28 and are apparently derived from xxxiv. 11-13 ; for it is not to be supposed that the author (E). who hitherto has devoted himself to rebaptizing the ancient *maççeboth*, and so transforming them from symbols of the old heathen worship into memorials of "places where Yahweh has caused his name to be remembered," has suddenly adopted the new plan of decreeing their utter demolition. Again the enumeration of the six peoples is a suspicious trait (cf. xxxiii. 2 ; xxxiv. 11, and J, *passim*), especially as vs. 28 repeats the promise in a different form. Here "Amorite" should be supplied from LXX., and the other names stricken out as redactional. The following verses have "him" (not "them" as translated) and the pronoun in the singular can only refer to "the Amorite" (cf. Jos. xxiv. 15), by whom this author (E), designates the inhabitants of Canaan in general. Vv. 31-33 are also supplementary and derived, with the exception of vs. 31, which merely repeats the context, from xxxiv. 12. The LXX. carry this process of interpolation further than the Massoretic text (cf. vs. 17, LXX.) inserting after vs. 22a a repetition of xix. 5f. The (five ?) brief promises which remain after the removal of this supplementary material, form the counterpart to the brief ritual commands by which the people's service to Yahweh is to be regulated, and the two (tables ?) together constitute "the Book of the Covenant," whose solemn ratification is related in xxiv. 3-8.

2. Chh. xxiv.–xxxii. ISRAEL'S APOSTASY.

ANALYSIS.

The following seems to be the order of events intended by the final redactor :

Moses, the priests and elders are summoned to the top of the mount. Moses ratifies the covenant of God with the people by means of a sacrificial ceremony. He and the priests and elders ascend the mount, and are admitted to the presence of God, where a second covenant meal is celebrated ; xxiv. 1–11. Moses is summoned again to the top of the mount to receive instructions and the tables of stone. He ascends with Joshua, leaving Aaron and Hur in charge below. Appearance of the cloud and the "glory" on mount Sinai, into which Moses enters for 40 days; xxiv. 12–18. (Instructions as to the Tabernacle and its furniture and worship, chh. xxx.–xxxi. 17 ; omitted.) Moses receives the tables of stone ; xxxi. 18. The people, impatient at the non-appearance of Moses, induce Aaron to make a golden calf, to which they sacrifice ; xxxii. 1–6. Yahweh informs Moses of all that has taken place below. Moses entreats and secures forgiveness for the people ; vv. 7–14. Descending from the mount Moses and Joshua hear "the noise of the people," and question as to its meaning. Arrived in view of the camp, Moses sees the calf and the dancing, and dashes the tables of stone to pieces, rebuking and punishing the people ; vv. 15–24. Moses seeing the people "broken loose," stands in the gate of the camp and summons to his help the sons of Levi, who inflict a slaughter of 3000 ; vv. 25–29. On the morrow Moses ascends to God, entreats and obtains a suspension of punishment for the people, who, however, are dismissed from Horeb ; vv. 30–34. Yahweh smites the people ; vs. 35.

A careful, unprejudiced reading of chh. xxiv. and xxxii. which should fail to disclose manifold *prima facie* incongruities and contradictions would be an impossibility. It is not natural that in ch. xxiv. verses 3–8, the obvious sequel to ch. xxiii., should be inserted between vv. 1f. and 9–11, at once separating these necessarily connected verses from one another and divorcing the covenant from its ratification. But independently vv. 1f. are not in their natural position after ch. xxiii., in which Moses is still receiving the divine message ; for in the Hebrew we have : "And unto Moses he said," an order and form quite as suggestive in the Hebrew of a gap in the preceding context as in English, and entirely different from the usual formula : "And he (or Yahweh) said unto Moses." It is necessary accordingly to recognize that Yahweh has been

speaking to some other than Moses before xxiv. 1. Now if the significance of the names " Nadab and Abihu " be observed—they can be no
other than the sons of Aaron " the priests ; " cf. xxviii. 1, P— it will
readily be seen that we have in xxiv. 1f., 9-11 the real sequel, though
not quite immediate, to xix. 20-25, the fulfilment of xix. 24. The gap
accordingly need not have been large. It may have included no more
than the statement that (" on the morrow? ") Yahweh appeared on
mount Sinai before all the people and gave the appointed signal, (xix. 13)
of the long blast of the *yobel*, warning the people not to approach ; then :
" *but unto Moses he said*," etc.

The double breach of connection in this passage is so remarkable as
almost to convict the analysis of proving too much. It is not at first
apparent why Rje (if it were he) should have so mutilated his own
work. Why place vv. 1f. before vv. 3-8 ? Without anticipating the
results of our further inquiry into the history of the Book of the Covenant, we may point out now the restriction which vs. 11 would put upon
the editor who inserted the Book of the Covenant here—not Rje, as we
shall see, but Rd. This eating and drinking in the presence of God on
the holy mount, by representatives of the people, is no common meal.
It is a covenant meal, or sacrament, and typifies the same as the ratification of the covenant by sacrifice (which also included the covenant meal)
in vv. 3-8. Now Rd (or Rje) would be anxious to avoid the appearance
which would result from the order 3-8, 1f., 9-11, of relating two consecutive ratifications of covenant between Israel and Yahweh, at the
same time and under similar circumstances, especially in addition to xix.
3 8 ; hence the pains taken to associate vv. 1f., 9-11 so closely with vv.
3-8 as to make it apparent that both relate to the same, and not to two
consecutive ratifications.

We have already seen that vs. 12 originally preceded chh. xxi. f. Its natural position, and that in which it would appear to have stood when Dt. v.
22 was written, is immediately after xx. 1-21 and the E element of xix. 3-8.
The characters Joshua, Aaron and Hur (cf. xvii. 8-16), the " mount of
God " (iii. 1 ; xviii. 5, etc.), the judicial function of Moses, the expression for " hath a cause " (lit. " is owner of a cause " or " master of
words ; " cf. Gen. xxxvii. 19, and see refs.) and the connection with xxxii.
15ff. (in no other instances does Joshua appear as Moses' companion in
the mount) make it easy to assign vv. 12-14 with certainty to E. In its
present connection the passage seems to assert that Moses and Joshua
left the " nobles " engaged with their feast (presumably at a point below
the summit, though no such intimation appears in vv. 1 11) and went up
to God, leaving Aaron and Hur with the " elders." Now it might be

granted, if necessary, that Joshua and Hur happened to be among the 70, though not specifically mentioned ; but no explanation of the litigation (!) among the " elders " on the mount of God can be given, unless in some way " elders " is supposed really to mean " people." Let us then substitute " people." But in that case the verse will not agree with vv. 9–11, according to which it would not be true to say "*Aaron* and Hur are with you." The probability becomes very strong that an original " people," who were to bring their strifes to Aaron and Hur for adjustment in the absence of Moses and Joshua, has been altered by Rje to " elders," in order to avoid this plain contradiction (see note *in loc*).

Here, as in ch. xix., we find ourselves in a tangle when we try to conceive Moses' ascent and descent of the mountain. The only refuge from the dilemma of vv. 9–14 is to deny the apparent continuity of the verses, insert an assumed descent of the mountain after vs. 11, and deny that " elders " in vs. 14 has reference to the " elders " of vv. 1, 9 and 11 (?). In that case Moses goes down in vs. 11 with absolutely no other object than to ascend again in vs. 13, and this ascent is again related in vs. 15, and *yet again* in vs. 18. The last must be admitted to be an intentional reiteration. Dt. ix. 11 shows that we must connect vs. 18a*b* with JE and not P; hence it is a reiteration of vs. 13, not of vs. 15. Three ascents of the mount remain related, to add to the long list of ascents in ch. xix., without any statement of descents, though the latter if only for clearness' sake should have been mentioned. If, however, we analyze into documents we find all these three statements of ascent to be needful. They are simply the second ascent of J, the second of E and the first of P ; for vv. 15–18a are manifestly from this source. (See refs. for linguistic and other criteria). P's description of the appearance of the mount in the eyes of the children of Israel, and of the " cloud " and " glory " is naturally given thus fully (cf. ch. xix.) in connection with the *first* appearance.

To an unprejudiced mind the incompatibilities and incongruities of ch. xxxii. are as great, if not greater than those of ch. xxiv. In vs. 14 the divine forgiveness has been secured by Moses' intercession. "Yahweh repented of the evil which he said he would do unto his people." Yet severe punishment is meted out to them by Moses in vv. 19f., a still severer one by the sons of Levi in 25–28, and last of all, vs. 35, Yahweh himself " smote the people, because they made the calf which Aaron made." The last visitation moreover comes directly after a second intercession of Moses, in reply to which Yahweh, *for the second time*, has granted suspension of punishment. There is at least a *prima facie* difficulty here, which calls for explanation; and a similar one must be admitted to exist in the conversation of Moses and Joshua as they descend the mount, *after* the story of Yahweh's revelation to Moses of what has taken place in the camp, and *after* Moses' intercession. To the special pleader an interpretation of vs. 18 which assumes that Moses knows the facts, but conceals his knowledge from Joshua, will suffice. But candor will admit that this is not the *natural* sense of vv. 15-24, if taken by themselves. So, too, Moses' sudden anger at the sight of the calf and dancing, leading him to dash in pieces the tables of stone, which he has so far carried from the top of the mount, in contrast with the disposition manifested in vv. 11f., may be explained by saying that the mere *relation* of Israel's transgression in vv. 7ff. did not produce in Moses' mind a realizing sense of the facts, such as was first aroused by actual *sight* of the idol. The possibility may be granted, but the fact still remains that vv. 15-24 would be a great deal simpler and more intelligible if vv. 7-14 had *not* preceded. Again vv. 19-24 bring Moses first within sight of the camp, then *within* it, and the restoration of order and authority is already effected and Aaron apologizing, when, with vs. 25, we are suddenly carried back to the point where Moses is just discovering the insubordination *as he first enters the gate*, and summons to his aid his fellow-tribesmen. Vv. 25-29, in fact, when taken by themselves, treat, not apparently of religious crime, idolatry or the like, so much as rebellion, insubordination, mutiny, suppressed on Moses' appearance by the Levites. This corresponds well with the expression "broken loose" (vs. 25; cf. v. 5) and with that reiterated in the J sections as descriptive of Israel's sin, "stiff-neckedness" (cf. Gen. xxvii. 40; and vs. 9; xxxiii. 3; xxxiv. 9); but is incompatible with the entire submissiveness of the people in vv. 20ff. To make the Levites, moreover, the instruments of punishment for the sin of vv. 1-6, in which "Aaron, the Levite" was chief offender, is well-nigh as strange as to find him immediately after (in the priestly legislation) exalted to the highest possible priestly rank, and his offence apparently ignored, while the people are punished thrice over.

For all these inconsistencies the analysis furnishes the key and solution. J and E have each here a fairly complete story of apostasy by the people, Moses' return from the mount, infliction of chastisement (suppression of mutiny), his intercession with Yahweh, and obtaining of pardon. When separated, each is self-consistent, and the incongruities disappear. The process of analysis is comparatively simple. Vv. 15-18 (Moses and *Joshua* on the mount) we have already seen must be connected with xxiv. 12-14. 18a*b*b. Its E origin is independently shown by the use of *Elohim* and other phraseology, and by the reference to the stone tables (cf. xxiv. 12). In spite of Dillmann's fruitless attempt, it is impossible to separate vv. 15-18 from 19ff. Moses' words in vs. 18 anticipate precisely the discovery made in vs. 19. Were vv. 25ff. the sequel, Joshua would have been nearer right than Moses after all. But vs. 19, and especially vv. 23f., refer to almost every passage and clause in vv. 1-6, whose E origin might be independently determined by the language (see refs.), and the disfavor shown toward Aaron as priest, even if it were not here presupposed. Vv. 30-34 (see vs. 31) take the same view of the people's sin, and follow perfectly after vs. 24. Moreover vs. 34 is the necessary antecedent of xxiii. 20, as we saw above. The other elements of the chapter agree equally together. Vv. 7-14 have been interpolated and expanded by Rje (see note *in loc.*) but find themselves naturally in place before vv. 25-29 as soon as vv. 15-24 are removed. Only vs. 35 seems hard to reconcile with vs. 14 and has an awkwardness of structure that calls for explanation (see note *in loc.*). It is apparent, however, from the story itself that something must have gone before in J, as well as in E, to explain the prolonged absence of Moses upon the mount. The missing material we shall find has been utilized by Rje or Rd in ch. xxxiv, to form the content of the story of a *second* covenant and new " tables of stones," made in a *second* forty days' stay of Moses on " mount Sinai."

(J) [1]And he said unto Moses, Come up unto Yahweh, 24 thou, and [2]Aaron, Nadab, and Abihu, and seventy of the elders of Israel; and worship ye afar off: [3]and 2 Moses alone shall come near unto Yahweh; but they shall not come near; neither shall the people go up **(E) with him.*** [4]And Moses came and told the people all 3 **(Rd) (E)** the words of Yahweh, and all the [5]judgments : and [6]all the people answered with one voice, and said, All the words which Yahweh hath spoken will we do. [7]And Moses wrote 4 all the words of Yahweh, and [8]rose up early in the morning,

[1]10 : 13, 24 ; vv. 9-11. [2]Ct. vs. 5 ; cf. 19 : 22. [3]19 : 12, 21, 24 : 34 : 3. [4]20 : 22. [6]21 : 1 [5]10 : 8 ; vs. 7 ; Jos. 24 : 16. [7]Cf. 34 : 27. *Gen. 20 : 8 ; 21 : 14 ; 22 : 3 etc.

* Aaron, Nadab and Abihu can only be " the priests who come near before Yahweh " of xix. 22, in contrast with the " young men " of E, vs. 5. The institution of the Seventy Elders (prototype of the Sanhedrin ?) is related by E, in a different connection (Nu. xi. 16f., 24-29.)

and [9]builded an altar under the mount, and [10]twelve pillars,
5 according to the twelve tribes of Israel. And he sent
[11]young men of the children of Israel, [12]which offered burnt
offerings, and sacrificed peace offerings of oxen unto Yahweh.
6 And Moses took half of the blood, and put it in basons ; and
7 half of the blood he sprinkled on the altar. And he took
[13]the book of the covenant, and read in the audience of the
people : [14]and they said, All that Yahweh hath spoken will we
8 do, and be obedient. And Moses took the blood, and sprinkled it on the people, and said, Behold the blood of the covenant, which Yahweh hath made with you concerning all these
9 (J) words*— **[15]Then went up Moses, and Aaron, Nadab,**
10 **and Abihu, and seventy of the elders of Israel : and**
they saw the God of Israel ; and there was under his
feet as it were a paved work of sapphire stone, and as
11 **it were the very heaven for clearness. And upon the**
[16]nobles of the children of Israel he laid not his hand :
and they beheld God, † and [17]did eat and drink.
12 (E) And Yahweh said unto Moses, Come up to me into
the mount, and be there : and I will give thee the tables of
stone, and the law and the commandment,—which I have
13 written,—‡ that thou mayest teach them. And Moses rose

*Gen. 35 : 7 : Ex. 17 : 15. [10]Gen. 28 : 18 ; 31 : 45 ; 35 : 20; Jos. 4 : 9 ; 24 : 26 ; cf. 23 : 24.
[11]Cf. 19 : 22. [12]20 : 24 ; 32 : 6. [13]Vs. 3. [14]Vs. 3 and refs. [15]Vv. 1f.; 19 : 13, 22. [16]Jud.
20 : 2. [17]Gen. 31 : 54.

* In vs. 8 translate with margin " upon all these conditions." The clause in
small type in vs. 3 "and all the judgments" is of course an interpolation subsequent to the incorporation of the Book of Judgments (ch. xxi. f.) in its present position ; see Analysis above p. 111. Accordingly we find no mention of
" the judgments " in vv. 3b and 4.—With vs. 8 we reach the conclusion of the
two long displaced sections xx. 22–26 ; xxiii. 10–xxiv. 8, and xxi. 1—xxiii. 9,
and the next E passage, vv. 12–14, joins directly upon the account of the first
propounding of the Covenant, xx. 1–21 ; xix. 3–8.

† " God " (*ha-Elohim*) in vs. 11b is not an exception to the practise of J.
On the contrary, no writer of the Hexateuch is so sensitive to the appropriate-
ness of *Elohim* in passages where the sense requires it. Cf. Dill. *in loc.* and
Art. IV., and see refs.

‡ Insert the clause " which I have written " after " tables of stone " (see
Analysis p. 112); or transpose the whole latter part of vs. 12, reading : " that I

up, and [18]Joshua his minister : and Moses went up into the
[19]mount of God. And he said unto the [2]elders, *Tarry ye 14
here for us, until we come again unto you : and, behold,
[21]Aaron and Hur are with you : whosoever [22]hath a cause,
(P) let him come near unto them.   [23]*And Moses went up into* 15
the mount, and the cloud covered the mount.   And the [24]*glory of* 16
Yahweh abode upon mount Sinai, and the cloud covered it [25]*six*
days : and the seventh day he called unto Moses out of the midst
of the cloud. [26]*And the appearance of the glory of Yahweh was* 17
like devouring fire on the top of the mount [27]*in the eyes of the child-*
ren of Israel.   And Moses entered into the midst of the cloud, 18
(E) and went up into the mount : [28]and Moses was in the
mount forty days and forty nights.†   *   *   *   *
*   *   *   *   *   *   *   *   *   *

(P) *And he gave unto Moses, when he had made an end of* **31**
communing with him upon Mount Sinai, [1]*the two tables of the testi-*
(E) *mony,*—[. . .] [2]tables of stone, written with the finger
of God.—‡

And when the people saw that Moses [1]delayed to come **32**
down from the mount, the people gathered themselves together unto Aaron, and said unto him, Up, make us gods,
which shall go before us ; for as for this Moses, the man
that brought us up out of the land of Egypt, we know not

[18]33 : 11 ; Nu. 11 : 28. [19]3 : 1 ; 18 : 5. [20]Vv. 1, 9. [21]17 : 12. [22]18 : 15ff.: 21 : 3 and refs.
[23]16 : 10 ; 40 : 34. [24]40 : 34, 35. [25]29 : 35–37 ; Lev. 13. [26]Nu. 9 : 15. [27]Nu. 14 : 10 ; 16 : 19 ;
17 : 7. [28]Dt. 9 : 9, 11 ; cf. Ex. 34 : 28. [1]25 : 16, 21 ; 32 : 15. [2]24 : 12 ; 32 : 16 ; Dt. 9 : 10.
[1]24 : 18.

may give thee the tables of stone which I have written, and may teach thee the
law and the commandment."   The latter alternative requires a single minute
change in the Hebrew text.

* " Harmonistic change from " people " to agree with vv. 9–11.   See above
Analysis.

† Chapters xxv.—xxxi., which follow, and Ex. xxxiv. 29–Num. x. 10, both of
which we omit as immaterial, are paralleled by a few lines of the narrative of JE
which relate the construction of a wooden ark (Dt. x. 1, 3) for the tables of
stone and the arrangement of a " Tent of Meeting," Ex. xxxiii. 7ff., after the
people's sin, and preparatory to the departure for Canaan.

‡ Verse 18b would seem to have been taken from before xxxii. 15.   See Art.
IV.

2 what is become of him. And Aaron said unto them, Break
off the ²golden rings, which are in the ears of your wives, of
your sons, and of your daughters, and bring them unto me.

3 And all the people brake off the golden rings which were in

4 their ears, and brought them unto Aaron. And he received
it at their hand, and fashioned it with a graving tool, and
made it a molten calf : and they said, ³These be thy gods,*
O Israel, which brought thee up out of the land of Egypt.

5 And when Aaron saw [this,] he built an altar before it ; and
Aaron made proclamation, and said, ⁴To-morrow shall be a

6 feast to Yahweh. ⁵And they rose up early on the morrow,
and ⁶offered burnt offerings, and brought peace offerings ;
and the people sat down to eat and to drink, and rose up to
play. [. . .]

7 　　(J) ⁷**And Yahweh spake unto Moses, Go, get thee
down ; for thy people, which thou broughtest up out
of the land of Egypt, ⁸have corrupted themselves :**

8 (Rje) they have turned aside quickly out of the way which I commanded
them : ⁹they have made them a molten calf, and have worshipped it, and

²Gen. 35:4: Jud. 8:24-27; ch. 12:35. ³20:2; I Kgs. 12:28. ⁴I Kgs. 12:32. ⁵24:4 and
refs. ⁶24:5 and refs. ⁷9:24. ⁸Gen. 6:11f. [. . .] ⁹vs. 4 ; I Kgs. 12:28.

* In. vv. 1 and 4 render with margin in the singular "a god," "this is thy
God." Vs. 5 shows, however, that the god represented was intended for no
other than Yahweh. For "calf" v. 4ff. read "little bull." It is not the *age*
of the animal which occasions the change from the ordinary term for bull but
its diminutive *size*. For all to whom a Mosaic or very ancient date for this
writing is not an unalterable assumption, the story of the golden bull must
needs suggest the antipathy of Hosea (an Ephraimite) and the other prophets
to the "sin of Samaria" (Hos. viii. 4-6), the golden bulls of Jeroboam I. (Cf.
I Kings xii. 28). Yet these were unquestionably intended by their originator
to be an acceptable tribute to Yahweh, and gave no offense, so far as their
reported words and actions show, to Elijah, Elishah, or their successors among
the earlier prophets. Ephraim's " firstling bullock " is a matter of pride even
to the poet of Dt. xxxiii. 17. Hence the difficulty of carrying back the document E (at least in its present form) to a period earlier than the eighth century B. C. The author of this narrative seems to have as deep an antipathy to
the Aaronic priesthood as to " the sin of Samaria." Cf. the account of the
inauguration of the bull worship at Dan and Bethel, I Kings xii. 26-33, noting
especially the feast " at a time of his own devising," vs. 32 (Ex. xxxii. 5), and
comparing vs. 28, " behold thy God, O Israel, which brought thee up out of
the land of Egypt," with Ex. xxxii. 4.

have sacrificed unto it, and said, These be thy gods, O Israel, which brought thee up out of the land of Egypt. [. . .] And Yahweh said 9 **(J)** unto Moses, **I have seen this people, and, behold, it is a** [a]**stiffnecked people:** [b]**now therefore let me alone,** 10 **that my wrath may wax hot against them, and that I may consume them: and I will make of thee a great nation. And Moses besought Yahweh his God,** 11 **and said, Yahweh, why doth thy wrath wax hot against thy people, which thou hast brought forth out of the land of Egypt with great power and with a mighty hand? Wherefore should the Egyptians** 12 **speak, saying, For evil did he bring them forth, to slay them in the mountains, and to consume them from the face of the earth? Turn from thy fierce wrath, and** [c]**repent of this evil against thy people.** **(Rd)** [d]Remember Abraham, Isaac, and Israel, thy servants, to whom 13 thou [e]swarest by thine own self, and saidst unto them, I will multiply your seed as the stars of heaven, and all this land that I have spoken of will I **(J)** give unto your seed, and they shall inherit it forever. **And Yah-** 14 **weh** [f]**repented of the evil which he said he would do unto his people. [. . .]***

[a]33:3, 5; 34:9. [b]Nu. 14:11-24. [c]Vs. 14; Gen. 6:6f. [d]Gen. 8:1:1;9:15f; 19:29; 30:22; Ex. 2:24; 6:5. [e]Gen. 22:16.

* Vv. 7-14 constitute an interruption of the story of vv. 1-6, 15ff.; cf. vv. 17 ff. and Analysis. Moreover the atonement secured in vv. 12-14 is still to be obtained in vv. 30 ff.; and vs. 13 at least is from Rje or Rd, for it quotes Gen. xxii. 16, (Rje) and is late in style and language. Yet the substance of the passage is certainly primitive and not redactional, for it is impossible to attribute such resemblances as that of vv. 9-12 with Num. xiv. 11-25 (J) to imitation, and vv. 7 and 14 show the language of J (see refs.) Just how far the redaction has gone in vs. 8 (cf. vs. 4) cannot be determined. It is not impossible that the story of mutiny in the camp, presupposed by vv. 24-20 in J's narrative, may have included a golden bull story similar to E's, and this idea is favored by the fact that Rje combines it with E's. In that case it is highly improbable that the offense was attributed to Aaron, the representative head of the Jerusalem priesthood, who in J is charged with the priesthood even in Egypt (iv. 15), and whose office is treated with such respect (xix. 22). One might imagine something like the following as a possibility. Vs. 35 which has the style of J, but is scarcely compatible with vs. 14, and whose final clause is suspiciously awkward, may have read originally " And Yahweh smote *Nadab*

15 (P) *And Moses turned, and went down from the mount, with
the two tables of the testimony in his hand, ¹⁵tables that were written on both their sides; on the one side and on the other were they*
16 (E) *written.* ¹⁶And the tables were the work of God, and
the writing was the writing of God, graven upon the tables.
17 | . . .]   And when ¹⁷Joshua heard the noise of the people
as they shouted, he said unto Moses, There is a noise of
18 war in the camp. And he said, It is not the voice of them
that shout for mastery, neither is it the voice of them that
cry for being overcome: but the noise of them that ¹ˢsing do
19 I hear. And it came to pass, as soon as he came nigh unto
the camp, that he saw ¹ˢthe calf and the dancing: and Moses'
anger waxed hot, and he cast the tables out of his hands,
20 and brake them ¹⁹beneath the mount. And he took the calf
which they had made, and burnt it with fire, and ground it
to powder, and strewed it upon the ²⁰water, and made the
21 children of Israel drink of it. And Moses said unto Aaron,
What did this people unto thee, that thou hast ²¹brought a
22 great sin upon them? And Aaron said, Let not the anger
of my lord wax hot: thou knowest the people, that they are
23 [set] on evil. ²²For they said unto me, Make us gods, which
shall go before us: for as for this Moses, the man that
brought us up out of the land of Egypt, we know not what
24 is become of him. And I said unto them, Whosoever hath
any gold, let them break it off; so they gave it me: and I
cast it into the fire, and there came out this calf. | . . .]

¹⁶Cf. 34 : 20. ¹ˢ24 : 12. ¹⁷24 : 13. ¹ˢVv. 1-6. ¹ˢ24 : 4. ²⁰17 : 6. ²¹Gen. 20 : 9. ²²Vv. 1-6,
and Abihu because they (made the calf?)." These two sons of Aaron are
apparently introduced as priests in xxiv. 1, but disappear entirely from J from
this point on. J must have traced the line of Aaronic descent as E does (Dt.
x. 6; Jos. xxiv. 33) through Eleazar, or as P does, through Eleazar and Ithamar. Now P relates (Lev. x. 1ff.) a story of how Nadab and Abihu were smitten by Yahweh for offering with strange fire. It is practically certain that P
derived this story from JE, and as E seems to know but one son of Aaron,
Eleazar (Dt. x. 6; Jos. xxiv. 33), P took it from J. Now if J had a story corresponding in some degree to that of Ex. xxxii. 1-6, and of which xxxii. 35 is
the conclusion, the ill-starred "Nadab and Abihu" are the characters for it.
In vs. 35. however, Rp would be forced, in spite of vs. 14, to alter this to "people," on account of Lev. x. 1ff.

(J) And when Moses saw that the people were 25
(Rje) [23]broken loose ; for Aaron had let them loose for a derision
(J) among their enemies : * then Moses stood in the gate of 26
the camp, and said, [24]Whoso is on Yahweh's side, [let
him come] unto me. And all the sons of Levi gathered themselves together unto him. And he said 27
unto them, Thus saith Yahweh, the God of Israel,
[25]Put ye every man his sword upon his thigh, and go
to and fro from gate to gate throughout the camp,
and [26]slay every man his brother, and every man his
companion, and every man his neighbor. And the 28
sons of Levi did according to the word of Moses : and
there fell of the people that day about three thousand men. And Moses said, [27]Consecrate yourselves 29
to-day to Yahweh, yea, every man against his son,
and against his brother ; that he may [28]bestow upon
(E) you a blessing this day.† And it came to pass on 30

[23]5 : 4.   [24]Jud. 7 : 18 ; 9 : 44.   [25]Jud. 3 : 16 ; 1 Sam. 25 : 13.   [26]Nu. 25 : 5.   [27]Dt. 33 : 9 ; Jud. 17 : 10-12.   [28]Jud. 1 : 15.

* In vs. 25b Rje attempts to make the "breaking loose" of the people refer to the story of idolatry in vv. 1-6, but apparently, from Moses' procedure in vv. 26ff. and other allusions, it referred originally to something more of the nature of a rebellion. Probably the interpolator of vs. 25b took 25a in the sense understood by the A. V., translating "naked." It is difficult otherwise to understand the "whispering" or "derision" of Israel's enemies, which neither idolatry (practised by themselves), nor rebellion, could give occasion to.

† In vs. 29 appears the aetiological significance of the story. (See R. V. margin : "Heb. fill your hand.") The Hebrew idiom for "consecrate" is "fill the hand." From Jud. xvii. 10-12 we might infer that the expression referred originally to payment for services. Better, provide with offerings. In the story before us the "consecration" of the beni-Levi to the priesthood is explained aetiologically by their having "filled their hand" with the blood of their brethren. The "blessing" bestowed upon them was therefore the priest-hood, in association with Aaron (in place of Nadab and Abihu?) We may perhaps even trace, in this subsequent elevation of the Levites to equality with the original priests of iv. 14 ; xix. 22 ; xxiv. 1. the germ of that distinction between priest and Levite which acquired increasing importance in the later codes (See *Genesis of Genesis* pp. 54, 586). Dt. xxxiii. 8f. contains an appar-ent allusion to this narrative, and if, as we contend, this poem is from the pen of J. the authorship of vv. 25-29 would be established, and at the same time

the morrow, that Moses said unto the people, Ye have sinned a great sin : and now I will go up unto Yahweh ; perad-
31 venture I shall make atonement for your sin. And Moses
returned unto Yahweh, and said, ²⁹Oh, this people have sin-
32 ned a great sin, and have made them ³⁰gods of gold. Yet
now, if thou wilt forgive their sin—; and if not, blot me, I pray
33 thee, out of thy book which thou hast written. And Yahweh said unto Moses, Whosoever hath sinned against me,
34 him will I blot out of my book. ³¹And now go, lead the
people unto [the place] of which I have spoken unto thee :
³²behold, mine angel shall go before thee : ³³nevertheless in
the day when I visit, I will visit their sin upon them.*

35 (J) ³⁴And Yahweh smote the people because they made the calf, which Aaron made.†

²⁹Gen. 50 : 17. ³⁰20 : 23. ³¹Cf. 33 : 1–3. ³²23 : 20 ; Cf. 3⁹ : 2f. ³³Jos. 24 : 19f.; ch. 23 : 21 ; cf. 34·6f.; Nu. 14 : 19f. ³⁴12 : 29; Nu. 11 : 33.

light would be thrown upon the priestly interest of this document; for Dt.
xxxiii. may be assigned with considerable probability to one of the Jerusalem
(Aaronic) priesthood. Dt. x. 1–11 contains also an unmistakable reference,
including some material now missing, when the interpolated verses 6 and 7 are
removed and shows that this institution of a Levitical priesthood was preliminary to the account of the construction of the Tent, Ark, etc. Num. xxv. 6–13
affords a priestly parallel. There are, however, no decisive linguistic criteria
to place the authorship of Ex. xxxii. 25–29 beyond dispute. But it is clear,
that if this passage be assigned to E it would be almost necessary to attribute
vv. 19–24 and 30ff. to J, which is quite impossible; and moreover xxiv. 3–8
would have to retreat from its proper place at the conclusion of the Horeb
stories to a place before ch. xxxii.; since in xxiv. 5 there are still no priests.

 * The LXX. supply the missing word in vs. 34. " The place " is not specifically named in what remains to us of E, but xiii. 17ff. shows that Canaan is
distinctly in mind from the outset. Intercession with confession of sin are
characteristic features of E's narrative. Cf. Gen. xx. 7; l. 17; 1 Sam. ch. xii.,
etc., and see references. Of course the intercession of Moses and relenting of
Yahweh imply that the punishment has not been already inflicted, as related in
vv. 25–29, nor can it have been inflicted immediately after, as in vs. 35.

 † See note on vs. 14. Unless some other reading than " people " be adopted
the present verse will be difficult to harmonize with both vs. 14 and vv. 30ff.
An explanation without emendation may be found, by supposing vv. 9-14 to
have been displaced by Rje from *after* vs. 35. We should then miss only the
statement of Moses' ascent of Sinai to intercede. Something perhaps could be
made out from a careful study of Dt. ix. f.: but the problem of these two

3 Chh. xxxiii. f. RENEWAL OF THE COVENANT AND DEPARTURE
FROM SINAI.

ANALYSIS.

Moses receives command to depart without Yahweh, to the people's great distress ; xxxiii. 1–6. Practise of Moses in regard to " the Tent of Meeting ; " vv. 7–11. Moses expostulates with Yahweh against dismissal without the divine Presence, and obtains a mitigation of the sentence ; vv. 12–16. He obtains the further promise of a revelation of Yahweh's glory ; vv. 17–23. Yahweh directs Moses to prepare stone tables and again ascend the mount with the former precautions. Here he receives the promised revelation and entreats the forgiveness of Israel's sin ; xxxiv. 1–9. Yahweh proposes to make a covenant, giving Moses ten commandments for the people, which he is to write upon the tables of stone. Moses remains on Sinai 40 days without sustenance ; vv. 10–28.

The most singularly and obviously inappropriate element in chh. xxxiii. f. is xxxiii. 7–11, describing the practise of Moses and Joshua in regard to the " Tent of Meeting " (*ohel moed*). It is quite apparent that this was the place of worship, not only because : " Every one which sought Yahweh, went out unto the Tent of Meeting, which was without the camp," vs. 7, but because the Pillar of Cloud occupies it, and [God] " speaks with Moses " there. Yet this cannot be the Tabernacle of the Testimony (*mishkan ha-eduth*), though in P[2] this also bears the same name, primarily because we have yet to hear (chh. xxxv. ff.) of the erection of the Tabernacle and its occupation by the Cloud ; further because the access of all the people to Yahweh is here perfectly simple (vs. 7), and instead of the elaborate institutions and ritual of the priestly law, with its inner cordon of Aaronic priests and outer circle of Levites (Num. iii. 10, 38 ; xviii. 7), all is here simplicity itself. The *Ephraimite* Joshua appears as sole custodian of the shrine ; Aaron has disappeared ; Moses pitches the Tent alone, and enters it freely to speak with Yahweh, and the Tent is equally accessible to " everyone." Moreover the directions in regard to pitching the " Tabernacle " in the centre of the camp (Num. ii. 17 ; Ex. xxv. 8) are as explicit as the statement here that Moses was accustomed to pitch " the Tent " " without the camp." It has been maintained * that this " Tent of Meeting " was

chapters is extremely intricate. The latter part of vs. 35 is too awkward to be original. The redactional element may therefore include all of the verse except, " And Yahweh smote."

* So W. H. Green " The Pentateuchal Question," *Hebraica* viii. (Jan. 1892) p. 60. " The tense of the verbs in vv. 7–11 denotes habitual action ; but it

a more primitive shrine or place of worship employed by Moses, before the construction of the Tabernacle, and subsequently *superseded* by the latter. But in Num. x. 33 the sanctuary is still " without the camp ; " in Num. xi. 16, 24, 26, 27 ; xii. 4f. 10 ; Dt. xxxi. 15, it is still "the Tent of Meeting." " without the camp " which is in use ; Joshua and Moses are in charge ; the cloudy pillar stands at its door ; in all respects the simple provisions of Ex. xxxiii. 7–11 are assumed to obtain, without any more trace there than here of the elaborate ritual of the " Tabernacle " having superseded it. It is necessary to admit either that we have two mutually incompatible representations of the worship during the Exodus, or else that there were *simultaneously* two different sanctuaries, one within, one without the camp, contrasting with one another in comparative simplicity or elaborateness of ritual as above pointed out. But the fact that Moses gives to " the Tent," of whose construction or existence we have so far heard nothing, a name subsequently (see refs.) found applied to the sanctuary where the regulations of vv. 7–11 obtain, shows beyond question that the author here describes the origin of a *lasting* institution. That the story has been mutilated at its beginning is apparent ; but it is also apparent that Rp *could* not have left the story of the construction of this Tent, to stand side by side with that of the Tabernacle, chh. xxxv. ff.

Besides the story of the institution of the Tent of Meeting we have in chh. xxxiii f. the relation of two other incidents, with neither of which the story of the institution of the Tent of Meeting has any real connection ; one of which it flagrantly interrupts ; both of which are paralleled by similar narratives assigned already to E. These three elements of chh. xxxiii. f. we may discuss in the order in which they stand. The first is Moses' intercession for Yahweh's forgiveness of the people's sin and for his guiding presence. It is broken into three parts, first by the second element relating to the Tent of Meeting, second by a few verses of the third element, the story of the new Covenant, which separate xxxiv. 6–9, the true sequel of xxxiii. 12–23, from this passage.

Omitting those portions relating to other subjects than Moses' Intercession, and reading consecutively xxxiii. 1–3, 12–23 ; xxxiv. 6–9, we cannot fail to be impressed first of all with the wonderful power and beauty

cannot hence be inferred that this was the permanent sanctuary used throughout the journeyings in the desert. It simply describes the usage during the time of this provisional sanctuary, extending it may be to the erection of the Tabernacle proper." In order to avoid admitting the identity of this Tent of Meeting Ex. xxxiii. 7–11 with that of Num. xi. and xii. Prof. Green actually denies (*Hebraica* viii. p. 183) that the expressions of the latter chh. indicate a position outside the camp, though he admits that they do in Ex. xxxiii.

of this description of Moses' pleading with Yahweh. Its parallel in E, we found in xxxii. 30–34, a truly sublime passage ; but here the interces-sion is prolonged to an extent unexampled save in J ; moreover the peti-tioner advances from stage to stage as in the intercession of Abraham, Gen. xviii. 23–33, until, when the climax is reached in xxxiv. 6f., and Yah-weh has revealed his real nature of compassion, Moses falls on his face, confesses all the " stiff-neckedness " of the people (cf. xxxiii. 3), and entreats the complete withdrawal of the sentence of displeasure with which the interview began. The result though wanting can be anticipated. It is referred to, and the intercession itself quoted at considerable length, in the similar intercession of Moses, Num. xiv. 11–24, another character-istic J passage. But the element in hand itself refers to J passages (cf. xxxiii. 1 with Gen. xv. 7ff.; xxviii. 13ff. etc.). The phrases " land flowing with milk and honey," xxxiii. 3 ; " find grace in the eyes of," Num. xi. 11, 15 ; Ex. xxxiii. 12–23 *passim ;* xxxiv. 9 ; " rest," for the promised inherit-ance in Canaan xxxiii. 14 ; " upon the face of the *ground*" (for " earth "), xxxiii. 16 ; " stiff-necked," xxxiii. 3 ; xxxiv. 9 ; " mercy and truth," xxxiv. 6 (cf. xxxiii. 19) ; " Lord " (*Adonai*) to Yahweh, xxxiv. 9 ; are all peculiar to J. Moreover the allusions to Israel's sin are such as presuppose Ex. xxxii. 7–14 (cf. " stiff-necked," nowhere else in the Old Test. save in xxxii. 9 ; xxxiii. 3 (5) and here, though *quoted* in Dt. ix.) and the mutiny of xxxii. 25–29. There can be no question among critics as to the source of this element. It belongs to the bone and flesh of J. But what of the original connection? How account for the separation between xxxiii. 1–3 and 12ff., and the further isolation of xxxiv. 6–9?

As to the separation of vv. 12ff. from 1–3 it is simply intolerable. The interruption of an interjected descent to the people is insupposable in the original. In vs. 12 the Hebrew has, " See, *thou art saying* unto me," etc., repeating the language of vv. 1–3. This *cannot* be another interview. It must be the same one. But, still more strangely, we have in Num. xi. 10c, 11f. a similar reference quite as inseparable from Ex. xxxiii. 1–3 ; and containing the very same characteristic features and phrases : " And Moses was displeased, and Moses said unto Yahweh, Wherefore hast thou ' evil entreated' thy servant, and wherefore have I not ' found grace in thy sight,' that thou art laying the burden of all this people upon me ? Have I conceived all this people ? Have I brought them forth, that thou art saying unto me, Carry them in thy bosom, as a nursing father carrieth the sucking child, unto ' the land which thou swarest unto their fathers ? ' ' These words are just as inappropriate in Num. xi. as they would be appropriate after Ex. xxxiii. 1–3. In Num. xi. Yahweh not only has said nothing of the kind ; he has not even spoken

at all, when Moses breaks out in this vehement expostulation and there
is no other trace in the whole story of the quails that Moses felt over-
burdened with his responsibilities. This is what Moses *ought* to have
said after Ex. xxxiii. 1-3, but is not there. In Num. xi. it is, to say the
least, belated. But just as Num. xi. 11f. seems to be the reply to Ex.
xxxiii. 1-3, so does Yahweh's acknowledgment of *personal* favor toward
Moses in Ex. xxxiii. 12, 13, 16, 17ff.; xxxiv. 9 seem to be the answer to
some such discreet attempt of Moses to placate the anger of Yahweh
against the people by objecting the unmerited suffering which will thus
be brought upon himself, as that of Num. xi. 11f., 14f.

In presence of such undeniable and such complicated displacement as
has taken place within the limits covered by chh. xxxiii.f. it will be well
even at the cost of some digression and repetition, to form a clear idea
of what the original sequence of J and E must have been; and it is at
this point that the demonstration can most readily be made, since the
two narratives stand clearly side by side in the concluding verses of ch.
xxxii., and the opening paragraph of ch. xxxiii. Both have manifestly
related in common up to this point how after the bestowal of the Law
from Sinai-Horeb Moses left the people to go up into the mount and
abide with Yahweh for a time. If we have in our synopsis of the documents turned to ch. xxxiv. for J's narrative of this interview on Sinai this
is indeed only a provisional assumption; but some such account is presupposed in the J elements of ch. xxxii. where we find Moses returning
to the camp. In both Moses finds that the people have fallen into grievous sin during his absence, and after restoring order reascends the
mount to reëstablish the broken relation of the people with Yahweh. In
both the first result of his intercession is disappointing. Further punishment is remitted, but the people are dismissed in displeasure (xxxii. 34=
xxxiii. 1-3) the last words of Yahweh in both being a threat. What now
may we infer with certainty, from the subsequent narrative of both
sources, and from the possible hints in the ground already established,
was the sequel to this interview?

It is not only impossible *a priori* that either of the narrators of the
sacred history proceeded to relate that the people left the sacred mountain under divine displeasure, but *a posteriori* the subsequent narrative
with its allusion to Yahweh's renewed presence, its "ark of God" (of
Yahweh), its "Tent of Meeting," etc., establishes the certainty that *some
modus vivendi was* arranged, and some new relation, *including explicit
directions as to Yahweh's worship, and preparation of the paraphernalia thereof*, on the people's part, some relenting condescension on Yahweh's part to accompany them and be their God and king, of course

through Moses' mediation, was related *in both* as occurring before they left the mount.

In J this further account is not missing, or at least only a fragment has strayed. In the very next passage where the linguistic marks of J appear (xxxiii. 12-23) Moses is engaged in this very work of intercession, pleading every argument to induce Yahweh to relent and go with the people *in person*. After the manner of Gen. xix. 23-33, the intercessor advances from stage to stage. Material is missing (we have just seen that part of it at least is to be found in Num. xi. 10c-12, 13f.) from the beginning of this story, for vs. 12 refers to words of Yahweh which nowhere appear; and the end is also incomplete, even with the addition of vv. 6-9 of the succeeding chapter, for we are still uninformed as to the practical conditions on which Yahweh consents to recede from his original refusal to go with the people. One of these, as we know from the subsequent narrative of J, must have made provision for an " ark " and other accessories of worship. This, of course, even if Rje preserved it, Rp would be obliged to strike out, to make room for the much more elaborate account of P². But it must have stood in J, and in fact we are not entirely without a hint, even in the narrative of J as it remains to us, of what kind of stipulations Yahweh made. The story of the consecration of the Levites, in the preceding narrative (xxxii. 29, J) looks forward, as we can now readily see, to the sanctuary whose construction must have been prescribed after xxxiv. 9. Another hint appears in xxxiii. 3. The danger of the proximity of Yahweh's consuming presence (cf. Is. xxxiii. 14) to the unsanctified, is a characteristic trait in J (cf. xix. 21f., 24) and is made the ground in xxxiii. 3 of Yahweh's refusal to go with the people. This objection still remains to be overcome. It can scarcely be doubted that in connection with the instructions for his renewed relations with the people it was overcome, and that after xxxiv. 9, Yahweh prescribed to Moses a Tent of Meeting " *without* the camp," precisely as in xxxiii. 7 (E); though in the latter passage no other reason is given for this peculiar location than Moses' practice. As a matter of fact this trait seems to be one of J's aetiological data, as the usual position of the sanctuary of a town was *outside* the gate. (I Sam. ix. 14; II Kings xxii. 8, 10, 13.)

We have thus reached the point in J where the departure from Sinai *can* be related, and this in fact is found immediately after, in connection with the visit of Hobab, in Num. x. 29ff. The only portion of consequence which need be supposed missing is the story of Moses' 40 days in the mount with Yahweh presupposed by xxxii. 7-14. We shall see what reason there is to think this also preserved in the third element of this subsection.

Passing now to that element (the second) which relates to the Tent of Meeting, we discover in vv. 7-11 the unmistakable characteristics of E. Here the location of the Tent of Meeting and the whole religious *praxis* are of course absolutely incompatible with P, as we have seen. But J knows nothing of the *Ephraimite* Joshua as "Moses' minister." On the contrary this is one of the most marked peculiarities of E, where "Joshua, the young man, Moses' minister," even accompanies him to the mount of God, (xxiv. 12ff.; xxxii. 16ff.), and finally becomes his successor (Dt. xxxv. 14f.). Again the coming of Yahweh to the Tent-door in the pillar of cloud, and the method of divine converse with Moses are referred to in identical terms in Num. xii. 5ff., a passage which defines the whole theory of theophanies borne out by the entire work of E, and they are referred to again in Dt. xxxi. 14f.

Between Num. xii. and the present passage the only positive trace of E's hand is Num. xi. 16f., 24-30, relating the appointment of 70 elders to be Moses' assistants by the gift of *prophecy*. Here again we have identically the same circumstances and presuppositions ; "Joshua, Moses' minister from his youth;" the pillar of cloud descending at the door of the Tent, cf. xii. 5; Dt. xxxi. 14f. (E); Joshua not departing from it and hence aroused to jealousy by the report *brought from the camp* (vs. 28). Here the spirit of Moses is the spirit of *prophecy* (vs. 25; cf. Gen. xx. 7; Dt. xxxiv. 10 E); his character is that of unassuming meekness; cf. xii. 3 (E). The passage not only follows with perfect appropriateness after Ex. xxxiii. 7-11, but is essential to it ; otherwise we are at a loss to know the occasion *apropos* of which the *praxis* and location of the Tent are described in Ex. xxxiii. 7-11. It is almost needless to point out that this story of the appointment of the 70 elders (cf. Ex. xxiv. 1f., 9-11 J) is most loosely and artificially connected with the story of the quails and Kibroth-hattaawah (J) where it now stands, and has in fact much more relation to the J elements there which we believe transposed, viz. 11f., 14f. Let us then remove the manifestly unrelated intervening material, P and J, and allow this E passage to come together with the passage so clearly related to it.

But previous to vv. 7-11 we have in Ex. xxxiii., at least one unmistakable trace of E. "Horeb" in vs. 6 can come from no other hand, and vs. 6 by its allusion to the "ornaments" necessarily presupposes vs. 4. Vs. 5 on the contrary is not of the same connection. Here the spontaneous and natural act of the people is made the result of a command of Yahweh—a command based on different grounds, and belated, since it is not promulgated until the act is already complete. Moreover vs. 5 is simply made up by interlacing material taken from vv. 3 (J) and 4 (E) and adds no new fact whatever. It is certainly and solely redactional (Rp). In addition to its connection with vs. 6, vs. 3 has E features of its own (cf. Num. xiv. 39 and refs.).

We have now gathered all the material of E from the present subsection, and in fact down to Num. xii. But how shall we reëstablish the connection? Fortunately we have at least the analogy of J's narrative as summarized above.

It is a feature of E's history which becomes increasingly prominent in Judges and later, to point out the repeated apostasies of Israel, and how, when the people repented and " mourned greatly," turning back to Yahweh from " the false gods " or other sin, he forgave them and granted deliverance (cf. Num. xiv. 39ff.; 1 Sam. vii.). After xxxii. 34 therefore, in place of the further intercession of Moses after the pattern of Gen. xix. 23ff., in J, we are quite prepared in E to hear of *the people's repentance* as the motive of Yahweh's relenting, instead of Moses' *personal favor* with Yahweh. Such in fact is precisely the character of the next verses we come to, bearing the stamp of E, viz. xxxiii. 4, 6. The people hearing the evil tidings of Moses' ill-success in interceding for them (cf. xxxii. 30-34, ending " I will visit their sin upon them ") strip off their " ornaments," the spoil of Egypt. But there can scarcely be a doubt of what originally followed here. The people have sincerely " mourned " and shown contrition. From the religious belief of the writer as well as from the whole subsequent narrative it is positively certain that E did not stop here, but related next the relenting of Yahweh, and the perfecting of a new agreement between him and the people, in which the central feature would be the Sanctuary, the Ark, and certain prescriptions *as to worship*. From the elaborate description of the later and dependent P it is safe to assume that the use to which Yahweh directed the " ornaments " stripped off " from Horeb onward " should be put, was the construction of this Tent of Meeting, which in the subsequent E narratives we find everywhere in use.

Yet the passage which now follows xxxiii. 4-6, though certainly derived from the same document, E, is *not* the sequel we expect. To connect it with the dissevered parts of J, vv. 1-3, 12ff., which it interrupts, is quite out of the question. It will not join with J, and moreover it bears every mark of E, as we have seen. But neither is it possible to think of any other position that xxxiii. 7-11 could have occupied, than the present. The verses are E's and are in place. The only admissible explanation of the lack of connection with vs. 6, is therefore that we have here a *lacuna;* and such is the unanimous opinion of critics.

Between xxxiii. 6 and 7 then, there is missing the entire account of

how a new *modus vivendi* was offered by Yahweh and entered into by
the people, preparatory to their departure. This new covenant must
have been ritual in its character, since it accompanied the institution of
the Tent of Meeting and the subsequently employed elements of worship. The promises, which Yahweh would enter into on his part in it,
would most probably concern the journey in prospect, and the occupation of the land of the Amorite, which of course Israel cannot hope to
make conquest of without Yahweh; in short it must secure for Israel
what the intercession of Moses in xxxiii. 12ff. secures in J. To carry out
the apparently intended scheme of E in xixf., we should naturally expect
a formal ratification of this covenant to follow, in which the people's part
would probably be at least more conspicuous than Aaron's.

All this serves but to describe the section xx. 22-26; xxiii. 10-33;
xxiv. 3-8, which we have already seen must belong to E; must be out of
place where it stands, since it contemplates immediate departure (xxiii.
20), and constitutes a unit in itself, a Book of the Covenant as *finally*
ratified.

Besides this there must have followed before xxxiii. 7 an account of
the making of the Ark (in which the Book of the Covenant—the *Debarim*
—was deposited?) and of the Tent of Meeting. With this would be com-
prised all that we could infer *a priori* with certainty to have been included originally between xxxiii. 6 and 7. But it can be shown further
that *after* the account of the construction of the Tent came originally ch.
xviii., the story of Jethro's visit, in which Jethro bids Moses, Aaron and
the elders to a sacrificial feast "before God," *i. e. at the sanctuary.* We
have already seen, in fact, that the true position of ch. xviii. was necessarily *after* Moses' instruction in "the statutes of God and his laws" on
the mount (cf. xviii. 16 with xxiv. 12), and just *before* the departure from
Horeb (cf. vv. 23, 27 and Dt. i. 6-18) in precise analogy with J
("Hobab," in Num. x. 29ff.). Finally Ch. xviii. itself in turn (cf. especially vs. 23 "if God command thee só") looks forward to a further,
and final Horeb institution, the *administrative* organization of the people. But this does not come before xxxiii. 7. On the contrary xxxiii. 7
-11 is itself a preliminary to the expected narrative, which is now to be
found, as we have seen, in Num. xi. 16f., 24-30, and immediately after,
appropriately near the account of Jethro's visit bringing Moses' wife and
children, the story of how "Miriam and Aaron spake against Moses
because he had married a "Cushite" (Num. xii. 1-15).

We come now to that part of the subsection hitherto passed over, for
which, however, a vacancy has been for some time waiting. The third
element of Ex. xxxiii.f., the Covenant of Yahweh with Israel, presents

no trace whatever of E ;* but is more distinctly parallelled in ch. xxiii. (E) than any other passage in the Hexateuch, the coincidence in the commandments being to a great degree verbal. It is not, however, a difficult matter to demonstrate from style and language that ch. xxxiv. belongs with the J element. " Sinai " instead of " Horeb " as the place (vv. 2, 4 ; cf. xix. 11, 18, 20) ; " flocks and herds " forbidden to " feed before that mount " (vs. 3 ; cf. xix. 12f. and J's attention to the flocks and herds of Israel *passim*) ; Moses unattended by Joshua, and the people excluded from participation (vs. 3 ; cf. xix. 12, 21, 24 ; xxiv. 2) ; Yahweh " descending upon mount Sinai " (vs. 5 ; cf. xix. 18, 20) ; Moses " called to the top (*rosh*) of the mount " (vs. 2 ; cf. xix. 20) ; are all conceptions and phrases as entirely foreign to E as they are familiar to J. Finally we have in the legislation itself (vs. 18) a direct and positive reference to Ex. xiii. 4–7 (J), " as I commanded thee, at the time appointed in the month Abib." There can accordingly be no doubt whatever that xxxiv. 1–28 is from the J document as a whole. Nevertheless the chapter is by no means free from difficulties.

Vv. 6–9 we have already connected with xxxiii. 17–23 as promise and fulfilment, and indeed this connection needs no demonstration. The verses are inseparable. So much so in fact that it is surprising not to see xxxiv. 6–9 follow directly upon xxxiii. 23. Again vv. 1–4 refer to Moses' breaking certain former tables of stone, and in fact give to the whole chapter the character of a *renewal* of the broken covenant. Now the J document, so far as we have been able to trace it, has not hitherto alluded to any tables of stone, nor to Moses' breaking them. This story was found only in E. Still our analysis might be corrected perhaps in this respect, if this were all ; but in vv. 10ff. it turns out that the chapter itself does not support the character thus put upon it by vv. 1 and 4 of a *second* law. The covenant which Yahweh makes there, so far from being the renewal of one previously unkept, is brought in as wholly new, " Behold I make a covenant." It contains not the slightest allusion to a predecessor, nor to any unfaithfulness on the people's part. Again vs. 28 relates that Moses spent 40 days and nights on the mount without sustenance ; but pays no attention to the preceding datum of similar import in xxiv. 18 (E), nor to any previous sojourn in the mount whatever. It also appears in 27f. that the purpose of this prolonged stay is that *Moses* may write upon the tables (cf. vs. 27, " write thou ") the Ten Words, and even these, it appears, are not, as promised in 1b, the Ten Words of ch. xx., but " the Words of the Covenant " just uttered. In still another respect vs. 1b is found in irreconcilable contradiction with this, for in 1b

* See, however, the note on xxxiv. 4 a.

it is *Yahweh* who promises to "write upon the tables the words which were upon the first tables which thou brakest." The outcome of all this is very plain. Vv. 1b from "like unto the first," and 4a cannot possibly be genuine. The chapter itself rejects them. But if we strike them out the character of the chapter appears at the first glance. It is the missing parallel to E's story of the *original* giving of the tables of stone, and of Moses' stay upon the mount, presupposed in xxxii. 7–14 (J). The covenant is not a second, but the first; the tables of stone are not duplicates, but the original, and the final proof of it appears in the fact that they are called here tables of *stones*, whereas previously (in E) they have been known as "the tables of *stone*." Moses is here receiving "the Words of the Covenant" for which all the elaborate preparations of xix. 20ff., and the ceremonial covenant feast of xxiv. 1f., 9–11 have prepared the way. There is nothing to prevent xxxiv. 1ff. from forming an *immediate* connection with that passage, the descent of the party being of course understood. Similarly it precedes *immediately* the story of the descent xxxii. 7–14, and affords the occasion for the rebellion of the people in Moses' absence, xxxii. 25–29, thus filling practically the whole gap in J's narrative.

What then of vv. 6–9, which we have seen to be connected with xxxiii. 17–23? Here too a closer inspection affords only new confirmation. These verses have only an apparent connection with vs. 5. A comparison of similar passages in J. Gen. iv. 26; xii. 8; xiii. 4, etc., proves that the true sense of vs. 5 is that given by the R.V. in the margin, "He (Moses) stood with him (Yahweh) there and called upon the name of Yahweh." Hence the following verses 6–9, relating to forgiveness and Yahweh's guidance have no real connection whatever with the rest of the chapter. The association is purely artificial. The touches in vv. 1b and 4a are accordingly redactional, intended to make room for the chapter in the character of a *renewal* of the covenant, after the example set by E in his Book of the Covenant, xx. 22–26; xxiii. 10–33; xxiv. 3–8. Moreover it is clear from the ritual character of this code that it is a finality, since it prescribes the worship as actually practised subsequently. Moses' later intercession accordingly is only for a renewal of Yahweh's favor, *not* a renewal of the covenant. This code like all the "prophetic" codes has suffered much from the interpolation of Rd; but for this see notes *in loc.*

Our discussion of the Sinai-Horeb narratives will be incomplete if we fail to enquire the occasion of the great upheaval in ch. xxxiii. which led to the elimination of so large a part of the narrative of JE; a considerable portion at the end being forced to seek other points of attachment.

often incongruous ; another part, describing the institution of the Tent of Meeting being wholly obliterated ; and only the paragraphs relating the practise of Moses, and his intercession on behalf of the people, which *could* not take a different place, being allowed to remain. We are in some danger, however, of overestimating the extent of this displacement unless we remember that Num. xi. is really in almost immediate juxtaposition with Ex. xxxiii. ; for in Num. x. 29ff. we are no further advanced than in Ex. xviii., and all the great mass of priestly legislation in the last chh. of Exodus, the whole of Leviticus and first ten chh. of Numbers, is crowded into the very last moments of the stay at Horeb-Sinai, between the giving of the command to depart, Ex. xxxiii. 1, and the carrying of it into execution, Num. x. 29ff. In fact even Num. xii. seems still to belong to the Horeb-group, as one of the consequences of Jethro's visit, when Moses' wife was first brought into contact with Miriam and Aaron ; so that Num. xi. 11f., 14f. cannot be said to have strayed far.

It is by no means necessary to settle to a nicety the part played by any or all of the redactors Rje, Rd, and Rp in this rearrangement of the material at the close of the Horeb narrative. All that concerns us is to suggest an adequate motive for the transfer, so that the suggestion of displacement be not open to the accusation of arbitrariness, and this it is not really difficult to do.

If we take up the displaced and missing elements in the order of the events of the narrative it is perfectly easy to see why Rje, after adopting E.'s version of the 40 days in the mount, xxiv. 12-14, 18 b. ; xxxii. 1-6 ; xxxi. 18 b. should feel obliged to strike out from between xxiv. 11 and xxxii. 7, J's version of the same, viz. ch. xxxiv. The story of Moses' return to the camp, xxxii. 7-14 (J), and 16-24 (E), he found means to preserve for the most part in both versions, as well as that of Yahweh's anger at the people's sin, and their dismissal. The accounts of the peoples' repentance xxxiii. 4, 6 (E), and Moses' intercession, xxxiii. 12-23 ; xxxiv. 6-9 (J) he could retain from both, by putting the latter after the former, and striking out from it the duplicate account of the construction of the Tent, which from the traces in xxxiii. 4-11 he seems to have related in E's version. Next followed the renewal of the covenant xx. 22-26 ; xxiii. 10-33 ; xxiv. 3-8 (E) which there was no reason to interfere with, and Rje doubtless left it *in situ*. The story of Jethro's visit, which followed, he had no motive for removing, since he found it not incompatible with Num. x. 29ff. ; and Dt. i. 6-18 leads us to think it also remained for the present in this position, followed by the account of Moses' practise in regard to the Tent of Meeting, xxxiii. 7-11 (E).

Thereafter followed the account of the institution of the 70 endowed with the spirit of prophecy combined with the opening sentences of Moses' complaint of the burden of the people (cf. Dt. i. 6ff.) The story of the stay at Sinai-Horeb concluded with the noble intercession of Moses, finally prevailing upon Yahweh to go personally in their midst, xxxiii. 12-23; xxxiv. 6-9 (J). By this arrangement nothing of importance was omitted save " the Words of the Covenant," xxxiv. 1-5, 10-28 (J), and even of these a part was taken up, either at this time or later, into " the Book of the Covenant " xx. 22-26; xxiii. 10-33 (E), which in Rje's work described the renewal of the covenant, as the exigencies of the history required, before the departure from Horeb.

It seems to have been the work of Rd to reincorporate with JE the Words of the Covenant eliminated as duplicate by Rje. We find as the lower limit of time to which this process can be referred the passage, Dt. x. 1-11, in which, however, ch. xxxiv. has perhaps not yet obtained its final position (cf. Dt. x. 10f.) nor its present shape exactly (Dt. x. 1-5 has the *plus*, " And make thee an ark of wood " . . . " and put them in the ark " . . . " so I made an ark of acacia wood " . . . " and put the tables in the ark," all of which must, of course, have been stricken out by Rp as incompatible with P²'s account of the ark of gold). The Rd therefore to whom the reincorporation of Ex. xxxiv. is assigned must be earlier than Dt. x. Nevertheless the style and interest of the redactor whose hand appears in the ch. itself, and in the passages affected by its reincorporation, is so thoroughly Deuteronomic, that we have no choice but to refer the process to one of this school. It is clear, however, that in the time of Dt. x. 1-11, E's account of the *renewal* of the covenant had been superseded by J's story of the *giving* of the Words of the Covenant, the latter, in the present form of a *renewal*, being perhaps preferred on account of its presenting the tables of stone as still preserved (Dt. x. 5) whereas E's narrative left them shattered on the steeps of Horeb. This reincorporation was not effected without displacement, and while it would be foolhardy to attempt to state in detail what the process was, it is safe to maintain that it gave to Ex. xxxiii f., practically and as a whole, its present character of an intercession on Moses' part with Yahweh, resulting in the renewal of the covenant and rewriting (by Yahweh cf. Dt. x. 4) of the tables. But *two* accounts of the renewal of the covenant, E's (xx. 22-26; xxiii. 10-33; xxiv. 3-8) and J's (ch. xxxiv) could not stand side by side. If both were preserved one *must* retire to a position *before the apostasy* in order to avoid the glaring absurdity of two consecutive ratifications of the *same* covenant between Yahweh and Israel. In addition to E's Book of the Covenant, in order to bring ch. xxxiv. into the intended relation to ch. xxxii., Rd had to find a new place for other incidents of ch. xxxiii., including Jethro's visit, Ex. xviii. (E); the appointment of the 70 (with which went a seemingly connected verse or two of J), Num. xi. 10c–12, 14–17, 24–30 (JE); the rebellion of Miriam and Aaron, Num. xii. (E); most of which passages are more or less marked by Rd's hand. But the account of how the Tent of Meeting was constructed from the ornaments stripped off, Ex. xxxiii. 4, 6. . . (E) and of Moses' practise in regard to the Tent, had, of course, to remain, as the story of Moses' depositing there the " ark of wood " with the " tables of stones " came just after. Doubtless the process of readjustment was a slow one. It was not complete when Dt. i. 6ff. was written, and we cannot pretend to say how, or when, it finally brought these passages into their present position. Only, after ch. xxxiv. was taken up in its present character the disturbing element was present to exert a continuous pressure in this direction until the present order became fixed.

Rp's work is less difficult to define. He found the account of the construction of the Tent of Meeting after xxxiii. 6 in his way and struck it out, retaining, however, in a most commendably conservative spirit vv. 7–11, in spite of incongruities. To round off a little the broken edges of xxxii. 4, 6 he made a kind of ending out of the adjoining material in vs. 5. In ch. xxxiv. he was, of course obliged to strike out the parts relating to the *wooden* ark, perhaps adding vs. 4a. in place of the material referred to by Dt. x. 1–5. At the end of the Words of the Covenant he attached the *midrash* 29–34, leading over to P⁵'s account of the building of the Tabernacle, and resuming xxxii. 15 in such a way as to connect the P narrative, which of course had no story of apostasy, with that of the renewal of the covenant.

(J) And Yahweh spake unto Moses, Depart, ¹go up 33 hence, thou and the ²people which thou hast brought up out of the land of Egypt, unto the land of which ³I sware unto Abraham, to Isaac, and to Jacob, say- (Rd) ing, Unto thy seed will I give it: ⁴and I will send an   2 angel before thee; and I will drive out the Canaanite, the Amorite, and **(J)** the Hittite, and the Perizzite, the Hivite, and the Jebusite: **unto a**   3 **land flowing with milk and honey:** ⁵**for I will not go up in the midst of thee; for thou art a ⁶stiffnecked**

¹⁻⁻³⁴. ²32:7. ³Gen. 12:7; 26:3; 28:13. ⁴23:20; 23: 32,34. ⁵3:8. 17:13:5; Nu. 13:27: 16: 13f. ⁶34:9; vv. 14-16. ⁷32:10: 34:10.

4   **(E) people: lest I consume thee in the way.** And when the people heard these evil tidings, they mourned :

5   **(Rp)** and no man did put on him his [9]ornaments. *And Yahweh said unto Moses, Say unto the children of Israel, Ye are a stiffnecked people : if I go up into the midst of thee for one moment, I shall consume thee ; therefore now put off thy ornaments from thee, that I may know what to do*

6   **(E)** *unto thee*   And the children of Israel stripped themselves of their ornaments from [10]mount Horeb onward.*

7   [11]Now Moses used to take the tent and to pitch it without the camp, afar off from the camp ; and he called it, The tent of meeting. And it came to pass, that every one which [12]sought Yahweh went out unto the tent of meeting,

8   which was without the camp. And it came to pass, when Moses went out unto the Tent, that all the people rose up, and stood, [13]every man at his tent door, and looked after

9   Moses, until he was gone into the Tent. And it came to pass, when Moses entered into the Tent, [14]the pillar of cloud

10 descended, and stood at the door of the Tent : and [Yahweh] spake with Moses. And all the people saw the pillar of cloud stand at the door of the Tent : and all the people

11 rose up and worshipped, every man at his tent door. [15]And Yahweh spake unto Moses face to face, as a man speaketh unto his friend. And he turned again into the camp : [16]but his minister Joshua, the son of Nun, a young man, [17]departed not out of the Tent.†

[2]: 33f. ; Nu. 14 : 39.   [9]12 : 35f.   [10]3 : 1 ; 17 : 6.   [11]Nu. 11 : 16f., 24–30 ; cf. Ex. 25ff. ; Nu. 2 ff.   [12]18 : 15, 19 ; 22 : 9, etc.   [13]Vs. 10 ; Nu. 11 : 10.   [14]13 : 21f. ; 14 : 10f. ; Nu. 11 : 25 ; 12 : 5.   [15]Nu. 12 : 6–8.   [16]24 : 13 ; Nu. 11 : 28.   [17]13 : 22 ; Nu. 14 : 44.

* The interpolation of vs. 2 is of a stereotyped character and scarcely needs comment. It is apparent from vs. 12 that the "angel" comes also from the hand of the interpolator, who seems to have had xxiii. 23 and xxxiv. 11 before his eye. In vs. 5 the stripping off of the ornaments is not a spontaneous token of grief from the people but is done at the command of Yahweh. The verse merely repeats vs. 3b, and puts in the form of a divine command the statement of the context. Apparently it was a very late piece of redactional work ; for LXX. have, "See that I do not bring upon you another stroke and consume you ; now therefore put away the garments of your glory and your adornment and I will show thee what I will do to thee." For the connection after xxxiii. 6, see Analysis above.

† Vv. 7–11 were not originally written to stand above. The verbs of vv. 7–

(J) [. . .]* And Moses said unto Yahweh, See thou ¹²
¹⁸sayest unto me, Bring up this people: and thou hast
not let me know whom thou wilt send with me. Yet
thou ¹⁹hast said, I know thee by name, and thou hast
also ²⁰found grace in my sight. Now therefore, I ¹³
pray thee, if I have found grace in thy sight, shew
me now thy ways, that I may know thee, to the end
that I may find grace in thy sight: and consider that
this nation is thy people. ²¹And he said, My presence ¹⁴
shall go [with thee] and ²²I will give thee rest. And ¹⁵
he said unto him, If thy presence go not [with me,]
carry us not up hence. For wherein now shall it be ¹⁶
known that I have found grace in thy sight, I and
thy people? is it not in that thou goest with us, so
that we be separated, I and thy people, from all the
people that are upon the face of the earth? [. . .]
And Yahweh said unto Moses, I will do this thing ¹⁷
also that thou hast spoken: ²³for thou hast found
grace in my sight, and I know thee by name. And he ¹⁸
said, Shew me, I pray thee, thy glory. ²⁴And he said, ¹⁹
I will make all my goodness pass before thee, and
will proclaim the name of Yahweh before thee; and I
will be gracious to whom I will be gracious, and will

---

¹⁸Vv. 1–3 : Nu. 11 : 12. ¹⁹Vv. 17f. ²⁰Gen. 6 : 8 ; 10 : 19 ; 32 : 5 ; 33 : 8, 10, 15 ; 34 : 11
30 : 4 ; 47 : 25, 29 ; 50 : 4, etc. ²¹.4 : 9. ²²Nu. 11 : 11f. ²³Vs. 12 and refs. ²⁴34 : 6f.

II are indeed in the tense indicative of continued past action, but it must be
apropos of something that the space relations are thus depicted, and that we
are told of Moses' turning again into the camp, while Joshua remains behind.
What this missing occasion for the explanation is, appears clearly enough
when we connect after vs. 11 the next following E passage, Num. xi. 16f., 24–
30. (See Analysis, and Art. IV).

* It is apparent that some words of reassurance from Yahweh to Moses are
missing before vs. 12, for they are referred to in 12b. Vs. 14 as above translated
would be utterly premature, and indeed the whole passage, 12–23; xxxiv. 6–9,
in well-nigh hopeless disorder. To make sense of this confusion, it would be
needful with Dillmann to transpose vv. 14–16 after xxxiv. 9 and then after the
passage from Nu. xi. insert xxxiii. 17, 12f., 20–23, 18f. A far simpler cure for
the confusion is to assume, as above, a gap before vs. 12 and translate vs. 14
with Kautzsch as a question. (See Part II.)

20 shew mercy on whom I will shew mercy. And he
said, [25]thou canst not see my face: for man shall not
21 see me and live. And Yahweh said, Behold there is
a place by me, and thou shalt stand upon the rock:
22 and it shall come to pass, while [26]my glory passeth
by, that I will put thee in a cleft of the rock, and
will cover thee with my hand until I have passed by:
23 and I will take away mine hand, and thou shalt see
my back: but my face shall not be seen.

34—[1]And * Yahweh said unto Moses, Hew thee [2]two
(Rd) tables of stone like unto the first: and I will write upon the
2 (J) tables the words that were on the first tables, which thou brakest. And
be ready [3]by the morning, and come up in the morn-
ing unto mount [4]Sinai, and present thyself there to
3 me on the [5]top of the mount. [6]And no man shall
come up with thee, neither let any man be seen
throughout all the mount; neither let the [7]flocks
4 (Rp) nor herds feed before that mount. *And he hewed*
(J) *two tables of stone like unto the first:* † and Moses rose up

[25]Vs. 13; Gen. 32 : 31.　[26]34 : 6.　[1]Dt. 10 : 1-5.　[2]Ct. 34 : 1? : 31 : 18 ; 32 : 15f.　[3]Vs. 4.
[4]19 : 11, 18, 20, 23 ; vs. 4.　[5]10 : 20.　[6]19 : 12f., 21, 24 ; 24 : 2.　[7]12 : 36 ; 19 : 13.

* Insert xxxiv. 1–5, 10–28 after xxiv. 11 (See above, Analysis p. 148). The removal, it effected already by Rje, was doubtless for the sake of preserving this invaluable material, which could not stand alongside of ch. xx., but could be introduced as a *renewal* of the covenant, the proper renewal according to E (xx. 22
–26, xxiii. 10–33), being forced back to its present place. We adopt, however,
in our Analysis, the theory of Cornill (*Einleitung*, p. 82) that ch. xxxiv. is a
reincorporation by Rd

† The harmonistic touches in vv. 1 and 4 have already been discussed (see
Analysis, p. 148). The first clause of vs. 4 is, however, not included under the
evidence cited. On account of the absence of the article in 4b (" two tables of
stone "); of the phrase "rose up early in the morning " (frequent in E, but cf.
viii. 20 ; ix. 13, J), and of the repetition of the subject " Moses " in 4b, Budde
and others have claimed a trace of E in this verse. If the claim be admitted,
it goes to show that E had an account of renewal of the *tables*, as well as of the
covenant. But Dt. x. 1 shows that there has been omission here, so that in
any case 4a is only a synopsis of the original. As the clause itself is quite
superfluous and E has no monopoly of " rose up early in the morning " (cf. I
Sam. xxix. 10, J. Bud.) it seems much more probable that 4a is a substitute by
Rp for the missing J material than a fragment of E.

early in the morning, and went up unto mount 'Sinai
as Yahweh had commanded him, and took in his
hand two tables of [9]stone.   And Yahweh [10]descended   5
in the cloud, and stood with him there, and [11]pro-
claimed the name of Yahweh.*   And Yahweh [12]passed   6
by before him, and [13]proclaimed, Yahweh, Yahweh,
a [14]God full of compassion and gracious, slow to anger
and plenteous in mercy and truth ; keeping mercy   7
for thousands, forgiving iniquity and transgression
(Rd) and sin : [15]and that will by no means clear [the guilty ;] visiting
the iniquity of the fathers upon the children, and upon the children's child-
(J) ren, upon the third and upon the fourth generation.†   And Moses   8
made haste, and [16]bowed his head toward the earth
and worshipped.   And he said, If now I have found   9
grace in thy sight, [17]O Lord, let the Lord, I pray
thee, go in the midst of us ; for it is a [18]stiffnecked
people ; and [19]pardon our iniquity and our sin, and
take us for thine inheritance. ‡ [. . .]   And § he   10

*Vs. 2 and refs.   [9]Vs. 1 and refs.   [10]19 : 18, 20.   [11]Gen. 4 : 26, etc.   [12]13 : 22 ; cf. vs. 5.
[14]33 : 19.   [14]Nu. 14 : 18.   [15]23 : 21 ; 32 : 34 ; Jos. 24 : 10 ; cf. Ex. 20 : 5.   [16]4 : 31 ; 12 : 27.   [17]4 :
14, 13 ; Gen. 15 : 2.   [18]32 : 9 ; 33 : 3.   [19]Vs. 6f.

* In vs. 5 translate with margin, " And he stood with him there and called
upon the name of Yahweh." (See Analysis.)

† " Plenteous " (vs. 6, cf. Nu. xiv. 18) occurs only in post-exilic writings, but
6, 7a cannot be rejected save by rejecting also xxxiii. 19.   The portion above
assigned to Rd represents the minimum.   Cf. Part II.   Vs. 7bc seems to be
partly intended to harmonize vs. 6, 7a with E (cf. xxiii. 21 ; xxxii. 33 ; Jos. xxiv.
19, E), and is framed on the model of xx. 5.

‡ Vv. 6-9 belong after xxxiii. 23 (see Analysis).   Vs. 5 (misunderstood) furnished a point of attachment for this narrative of the Words of the Covenant,
whose earlier verses accordingly were inserted before vs. 6.   In vs. 9 Dillmann emends *nehitham*, " be our Guide," for *nehaltham*, " take us for thine
inheritance."

§ The code of Ex. xxxiv., like every other section throughout the Pentateuch devoted to ritual law, has undergone a drastic revision and interpolation;
and in this the hand of Rd is specially apparent.   The danger of corruption to
idolatry by "the inhabitants of the land " (vv. 11b, 12, 15f.) is the dominant
idea with the Deuteronomist and his followers.   " Jealousy for Yahweh " (vs.
14b Rje (?) ; cf. xx. 5 and Jos xxiv. 19) is the keynote of the great reformation of Elijah, which, when mature, swept both Ephraim and Judah with revo-

(Rd) said, Behold I make a covenant: before all thy peo-
ple I will do marvels, such as have not been [20]wrought in all the earth, nor
in any nation: and [21]all the people among which thou art shall see the work
11 of Yahweh, for it is a terrible thing that I do with thee. Observe thou
that which I command thee this day: [22]behold, I drive out before thee the
Amorite, and the Canaanite, and the Hittite, and the Perizzite, and the
12 Hivite, and the Jebusite. [23]Take heed to thyself, lest thou make a covenant with the inhabitants of the land whither thou goest, lest it be for a
13 snare in the midst of thee: [24]but ye shall break down their altars, and dash
14 in pieces their pillars, and ye shall cut down their Asherim: for

**(J) [25]thou shalt worship no other god: [26]for Yah-
weh, whose name is Jealous, is a jealous God:**
15 **(Rd)** [27]lest thou make a covenant with the inhabitants of the land, and
they go a whoring after their gods, and do sacrifice unto their gods, and
16 one call thee and thou eat of his sacrifice; and thou take of their daughters unto thy sons, and their daughters go a whoring after their gods, and
17 **(J)** make thy sons go a whoring after their gods. [28]**Thou shalt**
18 **make thee no molten gods.—[29]The feast of unleav-
ened bread, shall thou keep. Seven days thou**

[20]Nu. 16 : 30 ; cf. Gen. 1 : 1.   [21]Jos. 2 : 10f ; 5 : 1 ; 9 : 24, etc.   [22]23 : 23f. 31b-33 : 33 : 2.
[23]23 : 32f ; Nu. 33 : 55 ; Jud. 2 : 1-18.   [24]23 : 24 ; Nu. 33 : 52.   [25]20 : 3, 23.   [26]20 : 5 ; Jos. 24 :
10.   [27]Vs. 12 ; Jud. 2 : 17.   [28]20 : 4, 23.   [29]23 : 15.

lution, (I Kgs. xix. 10, 14-18; II Kgs. xf.). But the abolition of the local
altars, *bamoth, asherim,* and *maççeboth* ("pillars"), (vs. 13) belongs to the
iconoclastic revolution of Josiah and the Deuteronomic requirement. The
Mosaism of J and E simply *rebaptizes* these objects of the popular worship
into "memorials" of the patriarchs (cf. Genesis *passim*), though J seems
already to avoid mention of the maççeboth, and lifts a protest against the
"molten," or "graven" image, while E rejects both these and the *teraphim.*
Apart from the interruption which vv. 11b, 12f., 15f., 24 occasion in the series
of "Ten Words" (vs. 28), it would be an anachronism, in defiance of the
whole attitude of J and E toward the ancient shrines and sacred objects, not to
recognize that these verses belong to the later Deuteronomic period of reform
in which iconoclasm took the place of toleration or accommodation. In vs. 10
the lateness of the interpolation is evidenced by the language (*bara,* "create").
It reflects also the Deuteronomic conceptions. In vs. 18, "as I commanded
thee," we have a manifest comment of J himself upon the code he incorporates,
and very possibly in vs. 14b also. Vs. 20, with its provisions of redemption in
modification of the law of firstlings, may well be from his hand, or at least
from some very early interpolator. For this reason no change is made in the
type, though clearly the unusual length of the law of firstlings and of the feast
of unleavened bread is against the original standing of 18b and 20 in the Code.
The interpolations of vs. 23f. require special consideration. (See note *in loc.*)

shalt eat unleavened bread, [30]as I commanded
thee, at the time appointed in the month
Abib: for in the month Abib thou cam-
est out from Egypt.* — [31]All that openeth the 19
(Rd) (J) womb is mine; and all thy cattle that is male, † the
firstlings of ox and sheep. And the firstling of an 20
ass thou shalt redeem with a lamb: and if thou wilt
not redeem it, then thou shalt break its neck. All
the first-born of thy sons thou shalt redeem. [32]And
none shall appear before me empty. [33]Six days thou 21
shalt work, but on the seventh day thou shalt rest:
in plowing time and in harvest thou shalt rest.
[34]And thou shalt observe the feast of weeks, [even] of 22
the first fruits of wheat harvest, and the feast of
(Rd) ingathering at the year's end.   [35]Three times in the 23
year shall all thy males appear before the Lord Yahweh, the God of Israel. 24
For I will cast out nations before thee, and enlarge thy borders : neither shall
any man desire thy land, when thou goest up to appear before Yahweh
(J) thy God three times in the year.‡ [36]Thou shalt not offer the 25

[30]13:4 7.   [31]13:12f. : 22:29f.   [32]23:15.   [33]:0 :8f ; 23:10-12.   [34]23:16.   [35]23:14. 17.
[36]23:18f.

* Vs. 18 belongs of course between vv. 21 and 22 (cf. xxiii. 15f.). The
removal may have been made for the sake of attaching the law of firstlings (vs.
19f.), which were offered at the feast of unleavened bread, with the law for the
observance of the feast.

† Vs. 19b*a* misunderstands 19a which has no reference to first-born *sons* (cf.
Jer. xix. 5) and the language ("male") is post-exilic. The special cases,
first-born sons and first-born of asses are provided for (by J ?) in vs. 20. The
last clause of the verse should be preceded only by a comma. The Hebrew
has simply, "nor let them (*i. e.* the first-born) appear empty (unredeemed)
before me (*i. e.* in the sanctuary)." LXX. and Vulg. have, "appear thou."

‡Vv. 23 and 24 are probably not from the same hand. Vs. 23 is of course
merely supplementary, but of comparatively late origin, perhaps imported from
xxiii. 14, whither (xxiii. 17) it has itself in return been at a still later time
exported back. Vs. 24, however, has a curious motive. "Going up to appear
before Yahweh" was of course in the early legislation and practise a very simple matter (I Sam. 1. 3), since the local sanctuary was easily accessible, within
a mile or two of every peasant. But with the abolition of the local *bamoth* the
requirement, "Three times in the year shall all thy males go up to appear
before Yahweh" acquired a new and extraordinary sense. Previous to the

blood of my sacrifice with leavened bread; neither
shall the sacrifice of the feast of the passover be left
26 unto the morning. The first of the firstfruits of thy
ground thou shalt bring unto the house of Yahweh
thy God. Thou shalt not seethe a kid in its mother's
27 milk. [37]And Yahweh said unto Moses, Write thou
these words: for [38]after the tenor of these words [39]I
have made a covenant with thee and with Israel.
28 [40]And he was there with Yahweh forty days and forty
nights; and he did neither eat bread, nor drink
water. And [41]he wrote upon the tables [42] the words of
the covenant, the ten commandments.*—

[37]Ct. vs. 1; cf. 24:4. [38]Gen. 43:7. [39]Vs. 10. [40]24:18. [41]Vs. 27; ct. vs. 1. [42]24:4.

deportation of the ten tribes it would have been in fact a palpable impossibility. Even in the little kingdom of Josiah and of the Restoration a journey of
all the male inhabitants three times a year *to Jerusalem* was a formidable
requirement, as its enforcement would leave the land helpless before invaders.
In face of this difficulty, as in several similar cases, the Deuteronomic
reformers fell back upon religious faith. God would take away from the
hearts of their enemies the desire to take advantage of their obedience to his
prescription. No man should desire their land when they went up three times
in the year. The same unpractical but sublime faith moved the Jews of the
Maccabaean period to offer no resistance to invaders on the Sabbath.

　* Translate with margin "the Ten Words," perhaps a gloss. The version
of the Ten Words here given is probably older than that of ch. xx., where the
laws of the second table are ethical. It differs from its closer parallel, xx. 22–
26; xxiii. 10–33, principally in the omission (perhaps intentional) of the altar
prescriptions, xx. 24ff., and in the lack of any reciprocal promise on Yahweh's
part corresponding to xxiii. 20ff. It seems to be the understanding of J.
however, that Yahweh's goodwill is manifested from the outset in xxiv. 1f. 9–11,
and the prescriptions are given as the means of maintaining that goodwill.
Hence after the people's sin no renewal of the covenant is needed, but only the
pacification of Yahweh's anger, which is effected by Moses' intercession.

NUMBERS.

PROLEGOMENA.

What we may call the primitive "Numbers" comprises the narratives of JE relating to Israel's 40 years' wandering in the wilderness, of which period, however, all but a few months at the beginning and end are understood to be spent at the oasis of Kadesh (Meribath-Kadesh in J, Kadesh-barnea in D, Kadesh-Meribah in P). The Hebrew title for it, *Bammidbar*, "In the wilderness" is therefore really a more appropriate one than our own, derived from the versions. This part of the primitive tradition might well be called The Book of the Wilderness Wandering.

As to the events of this period Israel's traditions were few; and generally they attach to suggestive names of the desert region in the neighborhood of Kadesh, and of the cities in the extreme south of Palestine which were the scenes of Israel's first, unsuccessful attempt to invade the country.

The flights of quails, which are a phenomenon of the desert that might well persist in the recollection of a half-starved, nomad people as a special divine interposition, appear connected in this early narrative with a suggestive name, *Kibroth-hattaawah*, which the author interprets as "graves of lust." The manna, which is to this day employed by the Arabs of the peninsula to stay the pangs of hunger, and whose Arab name, *mann es shema* "gift of heaven," shows the still persisting devout conception of its origin, is another of the phenomena of the desert which might well survive even the dark ages which followed the Conquest, transfigured and idealized in the popular recollection. We surely do not think amiss in seeing here the traces of actual national recollection. The story of the fiery serpents had a tangible point of attachment in the brazen idol Nehushtan, of whose destruction by the reforming zeal of Hezekiah we read in II Kings xviii. 4. Here, as so often, the accommodator (if we may invent a term for the rebaptizers of the pagan symbols into "memorials" of Yahweh worship) had preceded the iconoclast;

for the event narrated doubtless originates ætiologically from the material object, and not *vice versa*.

Ancient songs, of which one collection is actually cited by title in Num. xxi. 14, contributed their full share to the scanty recollections of this period, strange fabrics being often woven out of passages whose poetic allusions had lost their original application in the lapse of time. That cited from the " Book of the Wars of Yahweh " celebrates the conquest of the city of Beer in Moab, (Jud. ix. 21 ; cf. Beer-elim, Is. xv. 8), with punning play upon the name (*Beer*=" Well " ; *Beer-elim*, " Well of the Princes "). " That is the well," says the historian, " of which Yahweh said, Gather the people together and I will give them water." The poet doubtless gave account of the mustering of the people by the princes with their rods of office (Gen. xlix. 10) to the attack and conquest of the city, and, after the triumph, the exulting song of the victors.

> " Spring up, O Well ; spring up and flow
> The Well, which the princes digged,
> Which the nobles of the people delved,
> With the rod [and] with their staves."

It is not impossible that the story of the cleft rock at Meribah which has found a place in all the narratives, (though in J no trace of the rod appears) received its form (in E) through the influence of this punning song. " The satiric poets " (cf. Is. xiv. 4 for an example of the " proverb "—R. V. " parable "—of exultation over a defeated foe) are again drawn upon to corroborate and embellish the historian's report of the conquest of the territory of Reuben, Israel's first permanent foothold, and of certain geographical relations involved. Again the poem appears to have referred originally to later events, and is so employed in Jer. xlviii. 45f. Doubtless, however, the story it is connected with is by no means devoid of historical foundation. A much larger contribution from poetic sources is the Oracle of Balaam, the splendid lyric which forms the real nucleus of the Story of the Wandering. Although the poem itself manifestly contemplates the bloom of national life under the reign of David, and must emanate originally from that period, the historical setting which the poet adopts consists of the tradition (which should be fairly reliable) of Israel's relations with Moab immediately before the crossing of Jordan to the Conquest.

We are thus brought to that which constitutes the essentially valuable material in this ancient collection of traditions of the 40 years' wandering, the later reminiscences of Israel's relation with the kindred peoples and of the attacks upon Canaanite territory. There can be no doubt that we are treading here upon comparatively firm ground of actual historical recollection. The story of the unsuccessful attempt from Kadesh toward the north was not invented ; nor is the connection of Hebron with the expedition of Caleb which attaches to it (cf. Num. xiv. 11ff., with Jos. xiv. 6–15) valueless. The story of repulse and defeat by "the Amalekite," or "the king of Arad," though attaching to a name (Hormah) which may have long preceded the event, is not likely to be the fruit of imagination only. We may feel sure, further, that the national recollection is not at fault when, after this first repulse on the south, it represents an indefinite period (40 years) of nomadic life in the desert with headquarters in the rich oasis of Kadesh and the neighboring wells. Even tradition has nothing to tell of this long period of depression, approaching no doubt even dissolution ; but we may again be sure it is right in representing the next attack to have been made from the east, after a prolonged march around the southern extremity of the Dead Sea. This flank movement moreover must have been effected peacefully, by consent, if not solicitation of Edom and Moab. There is no good reason to doubt that an Amorite occupation of the territory between Moab and Ammon had really taken place, according to the story of E, xxi. 26, and it may well be that this was the occasion which led Israel to break up for good and all their connections with Kadesh, and strike one blow for their kindred of Edom and Moab, and two for themselves, against the Amorite beyond Jordan. E takes great pains to exhibit the careful respect shown by Israel on this march for the territory of Edom, Moab and Ammon. We must, however, at least question whether this respect was carried to such an extent as to lead them off the regular route of travel through the midst of Edom and Moab, clear out into the desert of Kedemoth as E represents. But it is far from improbable that after the victory over the Amorite and establishment of Israel in the territory of Reuben (the first-born of Israel, *i. e.* first to come to settled life) Moab (and " Midian in the field of Moab?") began to exhibit feelings of jealousy and hostility towards a poor relation whose welcome was already worn out when his services were no longer needed. The setting of the poem of Balaam's oracle may therefore be derived from genuine tradition. The settlement of Reuben (and Gad? cf. Dt. xxxiii. 20f.) may also well belong to the national recollection, though we cannot of course accept the idea presented by Num. xxxii. in its present form, that Moses assumed to distribute the territory tribe by tribe, and that only the women and children of the transjordanic tribes remained in the newly conquered country, until the conquest of Palestine proper was accomplished. Reuben secured a foothold here, no doubt, as first comer. The merit of loyalty with which the national tradition credits the two tribes, Gad and Reuben (cf. Dt. xxxiii. 20f.) was amply deserved, if, after having secured a " restingplace " for themselves, they did not lose interest in the fortunes of the brother tribes, but, when occasion led these across the Jordan, made common cause with them, as indeed was necessary in order that Israel's meagre force (Dt. vii. 7) might make any impression against the formidable fortresses of central Palestine.

An unbiassed critical judgment will scarcely be able to reject the narratives of this primitive Story of the Wilderness Wandering, legendary in form though they be, as historically worthless. On the contrary, the further the process of disentanglement of the earlier sources proceeds, the more certain does it become that we have here at bottom the material out of which trustworthy history is made.

As to the priestly element in Numbers it is so exclusively occupied with interests concerning the Levitical ritual that it scarcely calls for our further attention. Aside from its pre-

scriptions in regard to various sacrifices and ceremonies it uti-
lizes the history only as a basis for its ideal classification of the
tribes and their inheritances, and sketches in summary outline,
and from an artificial and ideal standpoint, a brief parallel to
the cardinal events of the story of JE. One event, however,
only lightly touched by JE, the rebellion of Dathan and Abiram
(E) combined by Rje with a somewhat similar narrative of J
concerning the priestly ambitions of a certain Korah, P has
developed at great length in order to set forth in historical
form his conception of the true dignity of the Aaronic priest.
What was the original location, or ætiological occasion, if any,
of the story as given in JE does not appear. J's version may
perhaps have had something to do with priestly prerogative.
Upon the basis of a brief story in JE as to Israel's idolatrous
conduct at Shittim, P also develops quite a story, whose outcome is the establishment of the priestly succession in the
house of Phinehas. What the historical, or other, basis for the
story in JE may have been, it is not possible to say ; but both
J and E seem to have had a part in it.

With Num. xxvii. 12–23, which, however, belongs after, not
before, the story of the allotment of an inheritance to Gad and
Reuben, P²'s story of the Exodus obviously draws to a close.
The census preparatory to the distribution of inheritances has
been taken. All the directions are given for this distribution
beyond Jordan and whatever else could fall to the part of
Moses to arrange for. These directions themselves are intermingled with various *novellae*, laws pertaining to the ritual, and
a repulsive *midrash* on an expedition by Joshua against Midian,
ch. xxxi. In xxvii. 12ff. Moses is at his last hour ; he has received
the command to "go up into this mountain of Abarim," and,
when he has viewed the land, to die there as Aaron had died
on mount Hor. To his request for leave to appoint a successor Yahweh accedes, and Moses gives Joshua a charge in
the presence of all the congregation. The final hour has come ;
but, like the patriarchs of Genesis whose abnormally long lease
of life, according to P², would not suffer them to die for years,
or even centuries, after the narrative of JE has them stretched

upon their deathbeds *in articulo mortis*, Moses remains, so far as P² is concerned, in a condition of suspended animation until the entire legislation of Deuteronomy has been introduced. Then at last, in Dt. xxxii. 48ff., the direction of Num. xxvii. 12ff. is resumed, and, after the Blessing of Dt. xxxiii., in Dt. xxxiv. 5, 7–9 he actually breathes his last.

The long period of silence covering Israel's stay at Kadesh affords a natural separation of the Story of the Wilderness Wandering, and the book of Numbers thus easily divides itself into two sections, § V. including chh. x. 11–xx. 13, relating the events From Sinai to Kadesh; § VI. including chh. xx. 14–xxxvi. 13 describing the journey, From Kadesh to the Jordan.

§ V. Num. x. 11.—xx. 13. From Sinai to Kadesh.

In § V., as before, we confine ourselves to the Tradition of the Exodus, excluding the irrelevant legislative sections principally derived from P^a, chh. xv. and xviii. 8–32 ; xix.

According to P² Israel journeyed in the prescribed order from Sinai and pitched in the wilderness of Paran ; x. 11f. Here Moses appoints twelve spies who explore in 40 days the entire land of Palestine up to Hamath, the extreme limit of the Solomonic domain ; but return with an evil report of the land ; xiii. 1–16, 17 a, 21, 25, 26 a, 32. The people are rebellious ; but Joshua and Caleb protest that the land is good ; the people, however, are mutinous, until the appearance of the *Shekinah ;* xiv. 1f., 5–7, 10. Yahweh then pronounces the sentence of 40 years' wandering, till all the congregation save Joshua and Caleb shall have died ; vv. 26–30, 34–38. (Certain laws follow in ch. xv. quite disconnected from the narrative). Korah and 250 followers aspire to the priesthood but are swallowed up alive by the earth ; xvi. 2–7, 15a and parts of 16–18, 19–24, 27a, and traces in vv. 31ff. On the morrow the people murmur against Moses and Aaron, and are smitten with a plague, which destroys 14,700 ; vv. 41–50. The rods of the princes are laid up before the Testimony, and Aaron's rod buds ; ch. xvii. Institution of the Levites as assistants of the priests :

xviii. 1–7. (In chh. xviii. 8–32 ; xix., miscellaneous Levitical laws disconnected with the history are given). At Kadesh-Meribah the people murmur for water, Moses and Aaron rebel against Yahweh's word and are punished ; but the rock is smitten with the rod and gives forth water for the people ; xx. 1–13, except traces of J in vv. 1, 3, 5.

The narrative of E in Numbers is very closely interwoven with J. Passing over in the present review, the Institution of the Seventy, (xi. 16f., 24–30) and the insubordination of Aaron and Miriam (ch. xii.), as not properly belonging to this section, (see § IV. Analysis) ; E probably gave after xii. 15 an itinerary of the journey from Horeb to Kadesh, of which fragments may perhaps be discerned in Dt. x. 6f. and i. 1f. ; cf. Num. xxxiii. 16–36. To this belonged doubtless the story of Taberah, a station which received its name from the "burning" sent by Yahweh in punishment of murmuring ; xi. 1–3. At Kadesh E gives a version of the story of the spies, and of the complaint and rebellion excited by their report ; xiii. 17–33 in part, and traces in xiv. 1ff. Yahweh commands a return to the wilderness by the way to the Red Sea. Repentant, the people presumptuously undertake to invade the country but meet disaster at Hormah ; xiv. 25, 39–45. The story of the rebellion of Dathan and Abiram and how the earth swallowed them up is combined with the story of the rebellion of Korah and On, xvi. 12–15 in part, 23–34 in part. We should infer from the analogy of J (cf. xiv. 22) that this was related of the time before the arrival in Kadesh.

According to J, Moses prevails upon his father-in-law Hobab to accompany Israel from Sinai as guide. They set forward, the ark and cloud in advance ; x. 29–36. Arrived at Kibroth-hattaawah the people weep for the flesh-pots of Egypt. Yahweh in anger sends a wind bringing great flights of quails which the people devour, and are in consequence smitten with a plague. Hence the name "Graves of lust." Incidentally the manna is described as a desert food, and the method of its preparation ; xi. 4–9, 10 in part, 13, 18–23, 31–35. (Vv. 10c–12, 14f. belong to §IV.; see above, p. 141). Leaving Kibroth-hattaawah, they come, after a stay at Hazeroth, to Kadesh ; whence Moses sends spies into Canaan to explore the land and its defences. The spies come to Hebron, where they find the three sons of Anak ; returning, they report the richness of the country and the great strength of the people ; xiii. 17–33, in part. Israel is discouraged, and breaks out in mutiny. Yahweh in anger proposes to destroy them, but is again appeased by Moses, who intercedes on their behalf. They are doomed, however, to wander for a generation in the desert, until all who came out of Egypt are consumed. Caleb alone, who had been of the number of the spies, but encouraged the people to go up, is excepted from this fate and receives the promise of the land trodden by his feet, (Hebron) ; xiv. 1ff., in part, 8f., 11–24, 31–33. At some time not specified, but probably previous to the arrival at Kadesh, another mutiny took place, in which Korah (?) a Calebite (?) and On a Philistine (?) were principal actors. The rebellion was directed against the prerogative of (Aaron and ?) the Levites, and was quelled by the mutineers being swallowed up by the opening of the ground ; xvi. 1f. in part, 12–15 in part, 25–33 in part. At Kadesh also (again previous to the sending of the spies) the people murmur for water, and "strive with Moses." The water is miraculously supplied from the rock, the place, Meribah-Kadesh, taking its name from the incident ; xx. 1b, 3a, 5.

The usual contrasts in historical standpoint, doctrinal presuppositions, purpose, style and language between J, E and P', already familiar to the reader are the same in §V. as before, and quite as noticeable. A comparison of P²'s Story of the Spies with the "prophetic" account of the same is specially instructive as to the development away from primitive tradition toward history (?) as conceived in the age of Ezra. In J the traces of the clan-story of the Calebite stock in Hebron are still distinct and if not history, we have here at least the *material* for history. Had only the story of P² remained, the attempt to discover the facts of the fourteenth century B. C would have been almost hopeless. There is nothing left but the dry bones of the preexilic tradition "restored" into a "history" whose single guiding principle was the requirement of a crude systematic theology. The story became what the theodicy and the doctrinal preconceptions of the writer required it to be. This may be unfortunate for the reader if the reader is principally in search of a critical and scientific knowledge of the facts of Israel's external relations in the fourteenth century B. C.; but it is well to remember that for the purpose of conveying a trustworthy idea of the religious conceptions and internal relations of Israel in the *fifth* century B. C., which is far more important to the Bible student than an infallibly accurate critical history of the Exodus and Conquest, P is indispensable ; while the most important to all classes of readers and students of the Pentateuch is to frame a true idea of the *development* in religious conceptions and internal relations which went on in Israel *between* the fourteenth century B. C. and the fifth ; for herein was the teaching of God. For this purpose it is most helpful to leave J and E and P to compare with one another.

---

1 Chh. x–xii. Through the Desert of Paran.

ANALYSIS.

The latter part of Num. x. is devoted to a description of the departure of Israel from Sinai ; but is by no means the uniform product of a single pen. Vv. 11f. in fact carry us on to the point where we stand at the end of ch. xii. But detailed and explicit as is the statement in vv. 11f., it is much too cursory for the writer of vv. 13-28, who has before his eyes the elaborate provisions for breaking camp in ch. ii. Accordingly he makes room for a second and more detailed statement of the departure by means of the otherwise utterly meaningless verse 13 (see note *in loc.*) But not even yet are we permitted to think the departure actually made. Vv. 29ff. carry us back again to a time considerably previous, in which Moses is negotiating with his father-in-law, Hobab the son of Reuel, who is all at once and unexpectedly with them again at "the mount of the Lord" (ct. Ex. xviii. 27), to serve as their guide. "And he said, Leave us not, I pray thee ; for as much as thou knowest how we are to encamp in the wilderness, and thou shalt be to us instead of eyes." It transpires in the subsequent history (Jud. i. 16 ; iv. 11 ; I Sam. xv. 5f.; xxvii. 10 ;

xxx. 29) that Hobab consented, and went with Israel; but what then of the divine guidance by means of the pillar of fire and cloud so elaborately described in ix. 15-23? Either one guide or the other was superfluous.

Finally the departure is once more stated to have taken place in vv. 33f. But here is an equally great disagreement with the story of vv. 11-28. There, in accordance with the positive requirement of the priestly law, the tabernacle is guarded on each side, in front and behind, by three tribes, always maintaining the *central* position. Here it certainly is stated that the ark went in *advance* of the people, and, it even seems to say, three days' journey in advance (see note *in loc.*).

It is not difficult to discover from the highly characteristic language (see refs.), from the presence of Hobab (not "Jethro") and from subsequent references (Jud. i. 16; iv.; 11 J; ch. xiv. 14) that vv. 29-36 are J's; while the priestly origin of vv. 11-28 needs no demonstration.

In ch. xi. the principal difficulty is caused by the inappropriateness of the verses which we have already seen must belong elsewhere (§IV. Analysis 3). Moses' vehement expostulation with Yahweh, and reference to words which Yahweh has not here used at all, constitutes a singular interruption to the story of the quails, which from vs. 10b should proceed to vs. 13 and vv. 18-23. The story is only mutilated by the introduction of an entirely different subject, viz. the lightening of Moses' responsibilities; and this is even more true of the account, vv. 16f., 24-30, in which the sequel to Moses' complaint is the appointment of the Seventy, than of that whose sequel we have seen to be Yahweh's promise himself personally to go with Moses and relieve him of the burden, Ex. xxxiii. 12-23; xxxiv. 6-9. The intercalated portions have much more affinity with one another than with the story whose connection they so rudely break into. As they are derived partly from J, partly from E the probability is that the displaced elements (vv. 11f., 14f., J) were brought hither in connection with 16f., 24-30 (E) by Rd, after they had previously been amalgamated by Rje in Ex. xxxiii. After the removal of this intrusive element ch. xi. from vs. 4 on is a perfectly uniform, consistent and characteristic narrative of J (cf. vv. 4 and 21, with Ex. xii. 37f.; and vs. 31 with Ex. x. 13, 19; xiv. 21 and see refs.), the obvious parallel to EP in Ex. xvi. and source of P's description of the manna; cf. vv. 7-9 with Ex. xvi. 31, 14; vv. 4-6 with Ex. xvi. 3, and "the quails," Ex. xvi. 13. The apparent inconsistency between vv. 19f. and 33 is removed by proper translation (See note *in loc.*) Vv. 7-9 are not displaced (Wellhausen), but the description of the manna is introduced in this casual, incidental way, as of something employed since the beginning, but only now mentioned, for the reason that J regards it only as one of the normal products of the desert, un-

familiar indeed to his readers, and to be considered in a special sense
" the gift of heaven " (but not exceptional in the desert). In common
with the modern manna gatherer he doubtless believed it to drop from
heaven (there are indications of a similar belief as to the origin of honey ;
cf. I Sam. xiv. 26) ; but did not regard it as limited to the Exodus period,
or specially given for Israel's benefit ; hence he defers the description of
it until the story of Israel's murmuring for flesh furnishes special occasion. The combination of the manna story with that of the quails in P²,
on the contrary, Ex. xvi. 13, is purely artificial, and can only be explained
by the dependence of P² on Num. xi.

As between J and E it is impossible to determine with certainty the
derivation of vv. 1-3. Vv. 4ff. (J) could perfectly well connect with x.
34 and we should understand the failure to give the name of the station
reached in x. 34 as due to the intention to narrate its origin. So ch.
xxxiii. in fact makes Kibroth-hattaawah the first station after Sinai. But
unless we make the violent supposition that Taberah and Kibroth were
the same place there is no room for vv. 1-3 between. The intercession
of Moses is also a strong evidence of E. (See refs.). The passage
should of course come *after* ch. xii.

Ch. xii. is universally recognized as E's. " Prophecy " as the mark of
greatness, vs. 6 ; the attitude towards Aaron ; the representation of the
Tent of Meeting without the camp, and the pillar of cloud standing at
its door ; the interest in Miriam, are all of great significance ; but the
most important characteristic is found in the poetic citation, vv. 6-8, in
which we have outlined the precise conception of divine communications
which underlies the entire history of E, viz. " by visions and dreams,"
(see refs.) with the sole exception of Moses (cf. Ex. xxxiii. 11). The
true position of Num. xii. we have already seen to be after Ex. xviii. It
is attached to the itinerary of P (cf. x. 12) by means of the clause vs.
16a, taken from J (see refs.).

——— - --

(**P²**) *And it came to pass ¹in the second year, in the second* 11
*month, on the twentieth day of the month, that ²the cloud was taken
up from over the tabernacle of the testimony. ³And the children of* 12
*Israel set forward according to their journeys out of the wilder-
ness of Sinai ; and the cloud abode in the wilderness of*
(**P³**) *Paran. ⁴And they first took their journey according to the com-* 13

¹9 : 5 ; Ex. 12 : 1, 4ff, 16 : 1 ; 19 : 1. ²Ex. 40 : 34-38. ³Ex. 17 : 1 ; 19 : 1 ; cf. vv. 28, 33.
⁴2 : 3-9.

14 *mandment of the Lord by the hand of Moses. And in the first [place] the*
   standard of the camp of the children of Judah set forward according to their
15 *hosts: and over his host was Nahshon the son of Amminadab. And over the*
   host of the tribe of the children of Issachar was Nethanel the son of Zuar.
16 *And over the host of the tribe of the children of Zebulun was Eliab the son of*
17 *Helon. ⁵And the tabernacle was taken down; and the sons of Gershon and*
18 *the sons of Merari, who bare the tabernacle, set forward. And the standard of*
   the camp of Reuben set forward according to their hosts: and over his host was
19 *Elizur the son of Shedeur. And over the host of the tribe of the children of*
20 *Simeon was Shelumiel the son of Zurishaddai. And over the host of the tribe*
21 *of the children of Gad was Eliasaph the son of Deuel. And the Kohathites*
   set forward, bearing the sanctuary: and [the other] did set up the tabernacle
22 *against they came. And the standard of the camp of the children of Ephraim*
   set forward according to their hosts: and over his host was Elishama the son of
23 *Ammihud. And over the host of the tribe of the children of Manasseh was*
24 *Gamaliel the son of Pedahzur. And over the host of the tribe of the children*
25 *of Benjamin was Abidan the son of Gideoni. And the standard of the camp*
   of the children of Dan, which was the rearward of all the camps, set forward
   according to their hosts: and over his host was Ahiezer the son of Ammishaddai.
26 *And over the host of the tribe of the children of Asher was Pagiel the son of*
27 *Ochran. And over the host of the tribe of the children of Naphtali was Ahira*
28 *the son of Enan. ⁶Thus were the journeyings of the children of Israel accord-*
   *ing to their hosts; ⁷and they set forward.**

29 **(J) [. . .] And Moses said unto ⁸Hobab, the son
   of Reuel the Midianite, Moses' father in law, We are
   journeying unto ⁹the place of which Yahweh said, I
   will give it you: come thou with us, and we will ¹⁰do
   thee good: for Yahweh hath spoken good concerning**
30 **Israel. And he said unto him, I will not go; but I
   will depart to ¹¹mine own land, and to my kindred.**
31 **And he said, Leave us not, I pray thee; ¹²forasmuch**

⁵2 : 10-16. ⁶Ex. 12 : 51. ⁷Vv. 12, 34. ⁸Ex. 2 : 18; Jud. 1 : 16; 4 : 11. ⁹Ex. 3 : 8, 17, etc.
¹⁰Gen. 12 : 16; 42 : 10, 13; vs. 32. ¹¹Gen. 12 : 1; 24 : 4, 7; 32 : 10; 31 : 3. ¹²Gen. 18 : 5, etc.

* Vv. 13-28, which simply repeat the imperatives of ii. 3-9, 10-16 in the past
indicative, belong to the later supplementation of the priestly law (P³), and
seem to have originated, like Ex. xxxv.-xl. after xxvff., or Num. vii, in pure
delight in the endless elaboration of tedious detail characteristic of this extra-

as thou knowest how we are to encamp in the wilderness, and thou shalt be to us instead of eyes. And it 32 shall be, if thou go with us, yea, it shall be, that what [14]good soever Yahweh shall do unto us, the same will we do unto thee. [...]

(J) And they set forward from the mount of Yahweh, 33 three days' journey; [14]and the ark of *the covenant of* (J) (Rp) Yahweh went before them *three days' journey to* (Rp) (J) *seek out* a resting place *for them*. [15]And the cloud 34 of Yahweh was over them by day, when they set forward from the camp.

And it came to pass, when the ark set forward, 35 that Moses said, Rise up, O Yahweh, and let thine enemies be scattered; and let them that hate thee flee before thee. And when it rested, he said, Return, O Yahweh, unto the ten thousands of the thousands of Israel.*

(E)—And the people were as [1]murmurers, [speaking] evil 11

[13]Ex. 34 : 10. [14]Dt. 1 : 33; Ct. 2 : 17 ; 10 : 21. [15]14 : 14 ; Ex. 13 : 21f. [1]Ct. Ex. 1 . : 24 ; 17 : 3.

ordinary school. (Cf. Ezra. 1f., Neh. 11. i ; f., etc.) Vv. 13 and 28 are the characteristically repetitious seams by means of which the insertion is patched in ; cf. Gen. xii. 8f.; xiii. 3f. and Ex. vi. 10–13, 28–30.

* Vv. 29–32 are only a fragment of J's parallel to the story of Jethro's visit, Ex. xviii (E). Both the account of how Hobab came to the camp at Sinai (except for the possible fragments incorporated in Ex. xviii), and of his answer to the prayer of Moses that he would be their guide to the camping-places in the desert, are omitted ; the former, because it duplicated E ; the latter because it contradicted P (1x. 17ff).—Vs. 33 is manifestly corrupt in text, the language (see Couard, *Z. A. W.* xii. 1, p. 62) indicating the hand of Rp. But Rp. could not of course have spoken of the ark going *before* the host (cf. ch. ii.) of his own motion. The inconsistency with vs. 31 and awkwardness of the repetition "three days' journey" indicate an interference with the original, which may have declared the fulfilment of the promise Ex. xxxiii. 14. No sufficient reason appears to suspect traces of E, (Dillmann) here or in 35f., though the latter have no intrinsically decisive characteristics. To reject the whole of 33b, 34 as from R (Couard), is quite out of the question; cf. Dt. 1. 33; Ex. xiii 21f., but especially Nu. xiv. 14, from which, and from vs. 35, we can see what the original form must have been. The poetic fragment vs. 35f., is of course very ancient, derived no doubt from the actual early practise, as well as from J's anthology.

in the ears of Yahweh : and when Yahweh heard it his anger
was kindled ; and the [2]fire of Yahweh burnt among them,
2 and devoured in [3]the uttermost part of the camp. And the
people cried unto Moses ; and Moses [4]prayed unto Yahweh,
3 and the fire abated. And the name of that place was called
Taberah : because [5]the fire of Yahweh burnt among them.—
4 (J) **And the [6]mixed multitude that was among
them fell a lusting : and the children of Israel also
wept again, and said, [7]Who shall give us flesh to eat ?
5 We remember the fish, which we did eat in Egypt for
nought ; the cucumbers, and the melons, and the
6 leeks, and the onions, and the garlic : but now our
soul is dried away ; there is nothing at all : we have
7 nought save this manna to look to. [8]And the manna
was like coriander seed and the appearance thereof
8 as the appearance of [9]bdellium. The people went
about, and gathered it, and ground it in mills, or
beat it in mortars, and [10]seethed it in pots, and made
cakes of it : and the taste of it was as the taste of
9 fresh oil. And when the dew fell upon the camp in
10 the night, the manna fell upon it. And Moses heard
the people [11]weeping throughout their families,
[12]every man at the door of his tent : and the anger of
Yahweh was kindled greatly.*—[. . .] and †Moses
11 was displeased. And Moses said unto Yahweh,
Wherefore hast thou evil [13]entreated thy servant ?
and wherefore have I not [14]found favor in thy sight,
that [15]thou layest the burden of all this people upon
12 me ? Have I conceived all this people ? have I brought
them forth, that thou shouldst [16]say unto me, Carry**

[2] [illegible]. [3] 20 : 16 ; 22 : 36, 41. [4] Gen. 20 : 7, 17 ; ch. 21 : 7. [5] Dt. 9 : 22. [6] Ex. 12 : 38. [7] Cf. Ex. 16 : 3. [8] Cf. Ex. 16 : 31, 14. [9] Gen. 2 : 12. [10] Ex. 16 : 23 ; cf. vs. 21. [11] Vs. 4. [12] (Ex. 33 : 8, 10). [13] 16 : 29 and refs. [14] Ex. 33 : 12 and refs. [15] Ex. 33 : 1-3.

* The second clause of vs. 10a might suggest its belonging in the E connection (see ref.) ; vs. 10b*a* is too awkwardly placed to have stood originally thus. Insert before it the displaced vs. 13.

† Insert Vv. 10c—17 and 24-30 after Ex. xxxiii. 3 (see above p. 141ff ; and cf. Dt. i. 8ff.). Vs. 17c is possibly from the hand of Rje, but see refs.

them in thy bosom, as a nursing-father carrieth the
sucking child, unto the [16]land which thou swarest
unto their fathers?—Whence should I have flesh to [13]
give unto all this people? for [17]they weep unto me,
saying, give us flesh, that we may eat.—[18]I am not [14]
able to bear all this people alone, because it is too
heavy for me. And if thou deal thus with me, kill [15]
me, I pray thee, out of hand, if I have found favor
in thy sight; and let me not see my wretchedness.

(E)   [19]And Yahweh said unto Moses, Gather unto me [16]
seventy men of the elders of Israel, whom thou knowest to
be the elders of the people and officers over them; and
bring them unto the tent of meeting, that they may stand
there with thee. And I will come down and talk with thee [17]
there: and I will take of the spirit which is upon thee, and
will put it upon them; [20]and they shall bear the burden of
the people with thee, that thou bear it not thyself alone.—

(J) [. . .] And say thou unto the people, [21]Sanc- [18]
tify yourselves [22]against to-morrow, and ye shall eat
flesh: [23]for ye have wept in the ears of Yahweh, saying, Who shall give us flesh to eat? for it was well
with us in Egypt: therefore Yahweh will give you
flesh, and ye shall eat. [24]Ye shall not eat one day, [19]
nor two days, nor five days, neither ten days, nor
twenty days; but a whole month, until it come out [20]
at your nostrils, and it be loathsome unto you: because that ye have [25]rejected Yahweh which is among
you, and have wept before him, saying, Why came
we forth out of Egypt? And Moses said, The people, [21]
among whom I am, [26]are six hundred thousand footmen; and thou hast said, I will give them flesh,
that they may eat a whole month. Shall flocks and [22]
herds be slain for them, to suffice them? or shall
all the fish of the sea be gathered together for them,
to suffice them?

---

[16]Ex. 33:1 and refs. [17]Vs. 4. [18]Vs. 11f. and refs. [19]Ex. 12:18ff; 33:7–11; cf. Ex 24:
1f., 9; Dt. 1:8ff. [20]Ex. 8:18, 22; cf. vv. 11, 14. [21]Ex. 19:22; Jos. 3:5. [22]Ex. 8:20, 23.
[23]Vv. 4f. [24]Vv. 31f. [25]14:11, 31. [26]Ex. 12:37.

23 **And Yahweh said unto Moses, Is Yahweh's hand waxed short? now shalt thou see whether my word**
24 **(E) shall come to pass unto thee or not**—And Moses went out, and told the people the words of Yahweh : and he gathered seventy men of the elders of the people, and set
25 them round about the Tent. [27]And Yahweh came down in the cloud, and spake unto him, and took of the spirit that was upon him, and put it upon the seventy elders : and it came to pass, that, when the spirit rested upon them, they
26 prophesied, but they did so no more. But there remained two men in the camp, the name of the one was Eldad, and the name of the other Medad : and [28]the spirit rested upon them ; and they were of them that were written, but had not gone out unto the Tent : and they prophesied in the
27 camp. And there ran a young man, and told Moses, and
28 said Eldad and Medad do prophesy in the camp. And [29]Joshua the son of Nun, the minister of Moses, one of his chosen men,* answered and said, My lord Moses, forbid
29 them. And Moses said unto him, Art thou jealous for my sake? would God that all Yahweh's people were prophets, that Yahweh would put his spirit upon them! And Moses
30 gat him into [3']the camp, he and the elders of Israel.—
31 **(J) And there went forth a [31]wind from Yahweh and brought quails from the sea, and let them fall by the camp, about a day's journey on this side, and a day's journey on the other side, round about the camp, and**
32 **about two cubits above the face of the earth.†** And **the people rose up all that day, and all the night, and all the next day, and gathered the quails : he that gathered least gathered ten [32]homers : and they spread them all abroad for themselves round about**

[27]Ex. 33:9; Nu. 12:5; Dt. 31:15. [28]Vs. 17. [29]Ex. 24:13; 32:17; 33:11. [30]Nu. 12: 14f. [31]Ex. 10:13, 19:14:21. [32]Ex. 16:18.

* Translate with R. V. margin, "from his youth;" cf. Ex. xxxiii. 10. This characterization of Joshua, as against the introduction in Ex. xvii. 8ff. shows this passage to have originally stood first.

† *I. e.* flying so low as to be within easy reach.

the camp. **While the flesh was yet between their** 33
teeth,* ere **it was chewed, ³³the anger of Yahweh**
was kindled against the people, ³⁴and Yahweh smote
the people with a very great plague. And the name 34
of that place was called Kibroth-hattaavah: because
there they buried the people that lusted. ³⁵From Ki- 35
broth-hattaavah the people journeyed unto Haze-
roth; and they abode at Hazeroth.

(E) And Miriam and Aaron ¹spake against Moses be- 12
(Rp) cause of ³the Cushite woman whom he had married : *for*
(E) *he had married a Cushite woman.* * And they said, Hath Yah- 2
weh indeed spoken only with Moses? ³hath he not spoken
also with us? And Yahweh heard it. Now ⁴the man 3
Moses was very meek, above all the men which were upon
the face of the earth. And Yahweh spake suddenly unto 4
Moses, and unto Aaron, and unto Miriam, ⁵Come out ye
three unto the tent of meeting. And they three came out.
⁶And Yahweh came down in a pillar of cloud, and stood at 5
the door of the Tent, and called Aaron and Miriam: and
they both came forth. And he said, Hear now my words: 6
if there be a ⁷prophet among you, I Yahweh will make

---

³³Vv. 1, 10. ³⁴Ex. 32 : 35. ³⁵Ex. 12 : 37; ch. 12 : 16. ¹21 : 5, 7; vs. 8. ²Ex. 18 : 5.
³I Sam. 2 : 27-30. ⁴Ex. 11 : 3. ⁵Ex. 33 : 7ff. ⁶Ex. 33 : 7-11 ; ch. 11. 16ff., 24ff. ⁷Gen. 20 :
7; Ex. 15 : 20 ; ch. 11 : 17, 26-29; Dt. 34 : 10.

* Not in contradiction with vv. 19f. In the preceding verse the preparation
of quantities of the flesh by drying and curing in the sun is described. The
plague came " while the flesh was yet between their teeth, ere it was consumed," *i. e.* before the stock was exhausted.

† The explanatory clause vs. 1b is omitted by Vulg. and is obviously only a
fruitless redactional attempt to supply lost information. According to J Zipporah is a Midianite. If the harmonistic interpolations of Rje in Ex. iii. 1 ;
xviii. 1. be removed (see notes *in loc.*) there is nothing in E to prevent the supposition that the daughter of Jethro (nameless in E) is here referred to. The
fact that the story of Jethro's visit, bringing Moses' wife and sons (Ex. xviii.),
must in the original order have almost immediately preceded Nu. xii., corroborates this idea, and there is absolutely no ground for supposing an otherwise
unheard-of marriage of Moses. The reference in vs. 2 is perhaps to the material missing before Ex. ii. 1.; see note *in loc.*

myself known unto him in a *vision, I will speak with him in
7 a dream. My servant Moses is not so; he is faithful in all
8 mine house: with him will I speak °mouth to mouth, even
manifestly, and not in dark speeches; and the form of Yahweh shall he behold: wherefore then were ye not afraid to
9 ¹⁰speak against my servant, against Moses?¹¹ And the anger
of Yahweh was kindled against them; and he departed.
10 And the cloud removed from over the Tent; and, behold
Miriam was ¹²leprous, as [white as] snow: and Aaron looked
11 upon Miriam, and behold, she was leprous. And Aaron said
unto Moses, Oh ¹³my lord, lay not, I pray thee, ¹⁴sin upon
us, for that we have done foolishly, and for that we have
12 sinned. Let her not, I pray, be as one dead, of whom the
flesh is half consumed when he cometh out of his mother's
13 womb. And Moses cried unto Yahweh, saying, Heal her, O
14 God, *I beseech thee. And Yahweh said unto Moses, If her
father had but spit in her face, should she not be ashamed
seven days? let her be shut up ¹⁵without the camp seven
15 days, and after that she shall be brought in again. And
Miriam was shut up without the camp seven days: and the
people journeyed not till Miriam was brought in again.†

16 **(J) And afterward the people journeyed from Haze-
(Rp) roth, and ¹⁶pitched in** *the wilderness of Paran.*‡

*Gen. 15:1; 46:2. °Ex. 33:11; Dt. 34:10. ¹⁰Vs. 1 and refs. ¹¹11:1, 10. ¹²Dt. 24:
9; cf..Ex. 4:6. ¹³Ex. 32:22. ¹⁴Gen. 20:9; Ex. 32:21, 31; ch. 14:40, etc.; cf. 22:34.
¹⁵Ex. 33:7. ¹⁶Ct. 10:11.

* Probably we should read *al-na* "not so," for *El-na*, " O God."

† Vv. 6–8 are poetic in form, but contain the doctrinal axiom which seems to
lie at the basis of all accounts of theophanies in E. Vv. 3 and 10 contain
each a single expression characteristic of J, and Dillmann concludes that there
must therefore be an admixture in the story of some J material. But there is
no sign of duplication, and the section as a whole can be assigned to none but
E.

‡ Kadesh, and not " the wilderness of Paran " is the scene of the following
event in JE (xiii. 26). But P locates it as here; cf. x. 12; xiii. 3, 26. The
phrases here may be from P after x. 12, or a harmonistic alteration from
" Kadesh " by R.

2. Chh. xiii–xiv. THE STORY OF THE SPIES.

ANALYSIS.

Moses sends one representative of each tribe to explore the land of Canaan and its defences, including Joshua and Caleb; xiii. 1–20. They bring back a discouraging report; xiii. 21–33. The people rebel, exciting Yahweh's anger; xiv. 1–10. Moses intercedes and secures for them a mitigation of punishment; vv. 11–25. Yahweh addresses Moses and Aaron with reproaches against the people, and condemns all save Caleb and Joshua to die in the wilderness. The ten other spies are smitten at once; vv. 26–38. The people are penitent, and resolve to invade the land, but meet disaster at Hormah; vv. 39–45.

In chh. xiii., xiv. we find the usual conglomeration, the composite character of the material being perhaps somewhat more apparent than usual. Thus, as to geographical conception, in the element agreeing with Nu. x. 12; xii. 16 (P²), which appears in vs. 3 and part of 26a, the point of departure and of return is " the wilderness of Paran." The twelve spies in this story experience no more opposition, difficulty or danger in exploring the land than if they were transported invisibly through the air, without susceptibility to the needs and limitations of ordinary men. Accordingly they inspect the entire country from its extreme southern to its extreme northern boundary " from the wilderness of Zin unto Rehob, to the entering in of Hamath," in a tour of 40 days' duration. Consistently the question of what the present inhabitants may have to say as to the occupation of their land by Israel does not seem so much as to present itself to the author's mind. The ten unworthy spies report on their return that the land costs more to cultivate than it is worth (vs. 32a; cf. Lev. xxvi. 38; Ez. xxxvi. 13); only Joshua and Caleb indignantly protest before the people " saying, The land, which we passed through to spy it out, is an exceeding good land." The ten men are slain, " because they made the congregation to murmur, by bringing up an evil report against the land," xiv. 36f.

On the other hand we have a second element which represents that the spies went up but a little way into the Negeb ("the South," vs. 22) and came to Hebron. The point of departure and return is " Kadesh " (vs. 26 cf. Nu. xxxii. 8; Dt. i. 19; Jos. xiv. 6). The object of investigation is partly the quality of the land, but largely, if not principally, the character of the inhabitants and the strength of their defences. The report of the spies is not in the least unfavorable to the land. Quite the contrary. They acknowledge that, " It floweth with milk and honey;"

they bring with them a great cluster of grapes to witness to its extraordinary fertility. The discouragement of the people is caused simply by their report of the great strength of the inhabitants and their defences. With this representation Dt. i. 19–46 agrees to the extent of flat contradiction of the other; cf. Dt. i. 25 with Num. xiii. 32. A still more remarkable contrast in the representation of these same elements appears in the *personnel* of the expedition. In that whose scene is Kadesh and the region of Eshcol and Hebron (southern Judah) Joshua does not appear as one of the spies. To quote from Prof. Driver's analysis (*Introd. to O. T.* p. 58) " *Caleb alone* stills the people and is exempted in consequence from the sentence of exclusion from Palestine (xiii. 30 ; xiv. 24) ; in P [the ' Zin to Rehob ' element] Joshua as well as Caleb is among the spies; *both* are named as pacifying the people, and are exempted accordingly from the sentence of exclusion (xiv. 6, 30, 38 ; cf. xxvi. 65, P). This last difference is remarkable, and will meet us again ; had the whole narrative been by a single writer, who thought of Joshua as acting in concert with Caleb, it is difficult not to think that Joshua would have been mentioned beside Caleb—not, possibly, in xiii. 30, but—in xiv. 24, when *the exemption from the sentence of exclusion from Palestine is first promised.*" In the subsequent narrative of J (Jos. xiv. 6–15 ; xv. 14–19=Jud. i. 20, 10–15) Hebron becomes the portion of Caleb, because his brethren that went up with him when Moses sent them to spy out the land discouraged the people, but he wholly followed Yahweh. Caleb in fact had received at the time (cf. Jos. xiv. 9 with Num. xiv. 24) the promise that " the land whereon his foot had trodden," Hebron and " the cities great and fenced," " where were the Anakim, Ahiman, Sheshai and Talmai," should be his. The passage in Joshua has been worked over by Rd, but the original sense unmistakably corroborates the representation of that element in Num. xiii. f. where Caleb *alone* opposes the report of the men that went up with him.

The combination of these divergent representations has been effected with skill; but it was unavoidable that traces should remain of incongruity, disagreement and duplication. Thus it is plain that xiii. 22 is parallel to vs. 21, vs. 32 to vv. 27–31, and xiv. 26–34 in general to xiv. 11 22 25, not to mention smaller redundancies and parallels. No amount of redactional skill could preserve vv. 8 and 16b and avoid their appearing most incomprehensibly strange after we have heard of " Joshua the son of Nun, Moses' minister " repeatedly, and never of Hoshea ; (but cf. Dt. xxxii. 44 (Rd). The explanation is very simple when we realize that this is in reality the *first* appearance of Joshua in P. The description of the country, vv. 27 29 corresponds naturally with the directions given in vv. 17b-19, but when the exploration is made to extend to a distance of 400 miles, it is strange that the report should relate exclusively to what could be discovered in the first 40. Moreover in vs. 25f. the journey of the spies is certainly described from south northwards. The combined text therefore makes it appear that the spies came to Eshcol, in the south of Judah, cut down there, according to directions, vs. 20, an immense cluster of grapes which they bore on a staff between two, besides other fruit, and then carried all this with them a journey of some 800 miles through a hostile country !

The redaction has left a further little awkwardness in that Caleb " stills the people before Moses " already in xiii. 30, whereas the people have not given, so far as the present text shows, the first sign of discontent or made any objection whatever until xiv. 1ff.

We scarcely need point out further evidence of the need of analysis ; it remains to indicate how by disentanglement of the interwoven strands all these difficulties may be removed.

All critics are practically agreed, 1st in general as to the portions assignable to P, and 2nd as to the presence of both J and E in the element remaining after removal of P. The phraseology and view-point of the latter are easily recognizable, in the list of names, including both Caleb and Joshua (cf. xxvi. 65); the change of Joshua's name ; "the wilderness of Paran" as the starting point (x. 12 ; xii. 16b); " Moses and Aaron " and " the whole congregation of the children of Israel " as the actors ; " the glory of Yahweh appearing in the Tent of Meeting ; " and a great number of characteristic expressions, of which only one need be mentioned, *tur* for " spy out," occurring eleven times, and used only by P (and Rp in x. 33). These make it easy to extricate the narrative of P which appears complete in xiii. 1–17a, 21, 25, (cf. xiv. 34), 26a (except " Kadesh ") 32a ; xiv. 1a, 2b, 5–7, 10, 26–30 (Dill. vs. 30=J, but cf. Ex. vi. 8) 34–38.

The separation of E from J is far more difficult. From Dt. i. 19–46 we are able to reconstruct the narrative of JE (no trace of P's narrative appears in Deuteronomy) and to supply certain features now missing. Thus it appears that instead of the list of names, JE contained a statement similar to Jos iii. 12 ; iv. 2, 4 (E), that Moses took a man from each tribe, and that the suggestion of a reconnaissance emanated from the people. The writer of Deut. i. 19ff. seems also to have had mainly before him an account of a reconnaissance to Eshcol, in which the produce of the country was a main consideration. In curious contradiction with the element of P, Dt. i. 25 not only imputes no blame whatever to the spies (no specific reason appears in the whole chapter for the special

favor shown in vv. 36-38 to Caleb and Joshua) but simply says they
declared the land to be "a good land" (ct. xiii. 32). From Dt. i. alone
we should not guess that the spies had done anything but their duty.
This agrees very well with a part of the JE element of ch. xiii. especially
vv. 20, 23f., 26b, 32b, 33; but it scarcely harmonizes with vv. 30f.,
although this series of passages in which Caleb is set in sharp contrast
with the other spies is obviously employed by him. This slight indication of a double point of view in the Deuteronomist is fully corroborated
when we look at his source. The duplications of vv. 17b-20 are unmistakable, and it also appears that vv. 22 and 23 are not consecutive, but
parallel. Taking up the strand in which Caleb is contrasted with the
other spies, we find that in xiv. 24 Caleb receives the promise of the land
on which his foot had trodden. This of course does not mean "the
land from the wilderness of Zin unto Rehob at the entering in of Hamath" (vs. 21, P); but neither does it include Eshcol and its vicintiy.
Jos. xiv. 12-14 gives us an unimpeachable interpretation of its meaning:
"Now therefore give me *this mountain* whereof Yahweh spake in that
day (*i. e.* Num. xiv. 24); for thou heardest in that day how the Anakim were there and cities great and fenced (Debir is mentioned in the
story of Caleb's conquest); . . . . *Therefore Hebron became the inheritance of Caleb the son of Jephunneh the Kenizzite, unto this day ; because
that he wholly followed Yahweh* the God of Israel" (cf. Num. xiv. 24).
The sequel to this allotment of Hebron to Caleb appears in Jos. xv. 14-
19 (= Jud. i. 10-15) and the whole together is the sequel to J's story of
the spies, which now appears almost in the light of a story of Caleb and
the conquest of *Hebron* from the three sons of Anak, Sheshai, Ahiman,
and Tolmai (cf. Jud. i. 10). It includes in ch. xiii. at least vv. 22, 28,
30f.

To E accordingly must be assigned that element of the story whose
scene is Eshcol, and in which "the fruit of the land" figures so prominently. This is in agreement with the version of Deuteronomy, which,
for reasons to be hereafter explained, admittedly favors the version of E.
Vv. 20b, 23f. and parts of vv. 26 and 27 of ch. xiii. are thus assignable
to E; and to this the linguistic marks will be found to agree (see refs.).
The separation of the double strand of vv. 17b-20 is facilitated by a comparison of Dt. i. 24f., and a scrutiny of the subsequent relation of how
the orders here given were carried out (see refs.). The narrative of J
seems to reach a full stop with vv. 30f., and accordingly the resumption
of the report of the spies in vv. 32f. is belated. From this it appears
that the description of the giants in 32b, 33 is not really a continuation
of vv. 22, 28, but rather parallel; and the identification of the *Nephilim*

with the *beni-Anak* is not original with the source, but belongs to the harmonistic redaction (see note *in loc.*). The manifestly legendary tone of vs. 33 is also less surprising in E than in J; moreover in the sequel of J (Jos. xiv. 6–15; xv. 13–19; Jud. i. 10–15) it does not appear that the *Anakim* were giants, not is there any mention of *Nephilim.* Vv. 32b, 33 may accordingly be added with confidence to the E element of ch. xiii. Only vs. 29 remains doubtful. Here, in spite of the urgent reasoning of Meyer, Budde and others, the indications of E seem predominant. The argument on this intricate and important question is too involved and technical for these pages and the reader is referred to the authorities mentioned. For answer to Meyer and Budde cf. Dillmann, *Nu, Dt. and Jos.* p. 73, to whose linguistic argument I would add a comparison of the last clause of the verse with Ex. ii. 5. Further considerations are the agreement of vs. 29ac with xiv. 25, 43, 45 (E according to both Budde and Meyer; cf. Jos. v. 1; xi. 3, and discussion of these passages in Bud. *Urg.* pp. 345ff.), and the fact that the spies' report in J seems, here and in the sequel, exclusively occupied with Hebron and the *beni Anak*, reaching a conclusion in vs. 28; whereas that of E takes in a wider reach, vv. 32b, 33 presupposing the mention of other peoples besides the Nephilim. After vs. 28 we expect to hear of the murmuring of the people. It is much more appropriate after vs. 28 than after vs. 29, which contains purely general information not at all terrifying, and Caleb's stilling the people, vs. 30, shows that originally it must have stood at this point. Of course, however, when the 2d and 3d version of the spies' report (vv. 32a, 32b, 33) were inserted, the description of the people's murmuring had to be postponed. This account of the murmuring is easily discoverable by means of the references in xiv. 31 and Dt. i. 39 (but cf. LXX.) combined with both P and E in xiv. 1ff. The J element here is 2aα (cf. Ex. xv. 24), 3b (vs. 31), 4 (?). Vs. 1b must be from E, unless we suppose *two* rebellions in J; for according to J (xiii. 30) the murmuring takes place while Caleb and his companions and the people are still in the presence of Moses, not during the night. The linguistic features of vv. 8f. and the effort to overcome the people's fear of the Anakim instead of to counteract the evil report of the other spies, as in vs. 7, mark these verses also as J's. In Dt. i. 29 Moses claims to have made this speech himself. If the words are Moses' we must insert them and the fragments in vv. 2–4 before xiii. 30. If Caleb's (P, vs. 6) they belong between xiii. 30 and 31. Vs. 3a must be assigned to E (cf. vs. 43), vs. 4 is from E or J, as a parallel of 3c, probably the former; the rest of xiv. 1–10 is unmistakably from P. (With vs. 2 cf. vs. 28 and xx. 3, and see refs.). We have thus the story of J of the spies and their report practically complete ; and the insertion of the fragments in xiv. 1ff. in their necessary position gives one more indication that we are right in assigning vs. 29 to E, since no room is left in it in J.

In xiv. 11–38 after the removal of the priestly element (see above, p. 179) we have nothing save a complete and consistent narrative of Moses' intercession for the people, which, in its characteristic argumentation with Yahweh ; its phraseology (see refs.) ; its explicit and remarkable reference to, and quotation of, Ex. xxxiv. 6f. (J) and of Num. x. 33f. (in vs. 14) ; from the subsequent reference made to it in Jos. xiv. 14 ; and from the view-point evinced by the author (Caleb alone resists the discouraging report of the other spies) can only be J's. To this statement only one exception is to be made. Vs. 25 is certainly from E. The detour around Edom and Moab is a conception peculiar to this source, and the expressions, " by the way to the Red Sea " etc., are no less unmistakable (see refs.) ; moreover this " command " is referred to in vs. 41 (E). It should be observed that Yahweh's utterance to Moses in vv. 20–24 is not complete ; for if we stop with vs. 24 the impression conveyed is that Israel is *entirely* disinherited in favor of Caleb ; which cannot be the author's intention. He must have gone on to say that the subsequent generation should inherit the land after the present has expiated its unbelief in the wilderness. We know in fact from Am. ii. 10 ; v. 25, that the 40 years' wandering was an integral element of the oldest tradition. In other words vv. 31–33 which largely duplicate their context (cf. vs. 32 with vs. 29) are not to be classed with vv. 26–38 as a late passage in imitation of the style of both J and P (so Well. Kuen.) ; but form properly the immediate sequel to vs. 24, their context being from P, who here as in Ex. xvi. is dependent on J, to some extent even verbally. By adding vv. 31–33 to vs. 24 we obtain still further confirmation of our judgment of vs. 25, which finds no room in J.

We are again in agreement with critics generally in attributing vv. 39–45 to E. In xxi. 1–3 and Jud. i. 17, one of which is from J, if not both, we have a subsequent story of the naming of this place " Hormah " from the fact of its " destruction " by Israel ; the former name having been Zephath. But besides this incompatibility with J, we have in 39b, 40a and b, 41, 43 and 44 phrases characteristic of E (see refs.). In vv. 43 and 45 it is easy to see the connection with vs. 25 and xiii. 29.

On the whole, chh. xiiif. yield with tolerable ease and certainty to analysis, and the results are of subsequent importance. We find, however, that the JE element here has been removed from a later position to accommodate it to P. In xiii. 26a*b* (J or E ; cf. Jos. xiv. 6, J) the people are already settled at Kadesh, though the narrative in xx. 1–13 necessarily pertains to the first arrival there. If the transfer of chh. xiii f. be made, we find the E element connecting directly with · xx. 14ff., where the command of xiv. 25 is carried out (cf. also xxi. 4, E) and E's story of Hormah, xiv. 39-45, brought into the same relative position as J's, xxi. 1-3, while in J the disaster of xxi., 1ff. follows suitably after Yahweh's language in ch. xiv. Finally the hyperbole in xiv. 22 is more natural and less exaggerated if the " provocations " of chh. xvi. and xx. 1-13 have preceded, than when they come after.

(P) *¹And Yahweh spake unto Moses, saying, ²Send thou* **13—2** *men, that they may ³spy out the land of Canaan, which I give unto the children of Israel : ⁴of every tribe of their fathers shall ye send a man, every one a ⁵prince among them. ⁶And Moses sent them* **3** *from the wilderness of Paran according to the commandment of Yahweh : all of them men who were heads of the children of Israel. And these were their names : of the ⁷tribe of Reuben,* **4** *Shammua the son of Zaccur. Of the tribe of Simeon, Shaphat* **5** *the son of Hori. Of the tribe of Judah, Caleb the son of Jephun-* **6** *neh. Of the tribe of Issachar, Igal the son of Joseph. Of the* **7–8** *tribe of Ephraim, Hoshea the son of Nun. Of the tribe of Ben-* **9** *jamin, Palti the son of Raphu. Of the tribe of Zebulun, Gaddiel* **10** *the son of Sodi. Of the tribe of Joseph,* [namely,] *of the tribe of* **11** *Manasseh, Gaddi the son of Susi. Of the tribe of Dan, Ammiel* **12** *the son of Gemalli. Of the tribe of Asher, Sethur the son of* **13** *Michael. Of the tribe of Naphtali, Nahbi the son of Vophsi.* **14** *Of the tribe of Gad, Geuel the son of Machi. These are the* **15–16** *names of the men which Moses sent to spy out the land. ⁹And Moses called Hoshea the son of Nun Joshua. And Moses sent* **17** **(J)** *them to spy out the land of Canaan,—*[. . .]***and said**

[1]Cf. Dt. 1 : 19-46; Jos. 14 : 6-15. [2]Ct. Dt. 1 : 21. [3]Vv. 16, 17, 22, 25, 32. etc.; cf. 21 : 32 ; Dt. 1 : 24 ; Jos. 2 : 1, 22, 25 ; Jud. 18 : 2, 14, 17, etc. [4]1 : 16, 47 ; 26 : 55 ; 33 : 54 etc. [5]3 : 24, 30, 35 ; 16 : 2. [6]10 : 12 ; 4 : 37. [7]Vs. 2 and refs. vv. 4-15. [8]Ct. Jos. 14 : 6, 14 ; Jud. 1 : 13 ; Gen. 15 : 19 ; 36 : 11 ; cf. 34 : 19 ; 32 : 11 ; 1 Chron. 2 : 9-55. [9]Cf. Ex. 17 : 9ff ; 24 : 13, etc.

* The personnel of the expedition according to J can be determined only by the sequel. The only exception to the disheartening report of vs. 31 is of a hitherto unknown " Caleb," vs. 30 ; it is probable accordingly that we should supply before vs. 17b some brief account of Moses' appointing Caleb and (eleven ?) others to reconnoitre. Caleb's companions may have been named ;

18 **unto them, Get you up this way** [10]**by the South, and**

⌐ **(E)** go up [11]into the mountains : and see the land, what it is ;

(J) and the people that dwelleth therein, [. . .] **whether**

(E) they be [12]**strong or weak,** whether they be [13]few or

19 **(J) many; and what the land is that they dwell in, whe-**
ther it be good or bad ; and what [14]**cities they b that**
they dwell in, whether in camps, or in strong holds ;

20 **(E)** and what the land is, whether it be fat or lean, whether
there be wood therein, or not. And be ye of good courage,
and bring of the [15]fruit of the land. Now the time was the

21 **(P)** time of the firstripe grapes. *So they went up, and* [16]*spied*
out the land from the wilderness of Zin unto Rehob, to the entering

22 **(J)** *in of Hamath.* **And they went up by the South, and**
came unto Hebron ; and [17]**Ahiman, Sheshai, and Tal-**
mai, the children of Anak, were there. (Now Hebron

23 **(E) was built seven years before Zoan in Egypt.)** And
they came unto the valley of Eshcol, and cut down from
thence a branch with one [18]cluster of grapes, and they bare
it upon a staff between two : [they brought] also of the

24 pomegranates, and of the figs. [19]That place was called the
valley of Eshcol, because of the cluster which the children of

25 **(P)** Israel cut down from thence. *And they returned from spy-*

26 *ing out the land at the end of* [20]*forty days. And they went and*
came to Moses, and to Aaron, and to all the congregation of the

(E) *children of Israel, unto the wilderness of Paran* [. .] *to*

(Rp) Kadesh : and brought back word unto them, *and unto*

27 **(J)** *the congregation,* and shewed them the fruit of the land. **And**
they told him, and said, [21]**We came unto the land**
whither thou sentest us, and surely it [22]**floweth with**

(E) milk and honey ; [. . .] and this is the fruit of it.

28 **(J)** [23]**Howbeit the people that dwell in the land are**
strong, and the cities are fenced, [and] very great :

[10]Cf. vs. 22 ; cf. 20. [11]Vs. 2 ; 14 : 40, 45. Dt. 1 : 24. [12]Vv. 28, 31. [13]Vs. 20. [14]Vv. 20,
28 ; Dt. 1 : 28 ; Jos. 14, 12. [15]Vv. 23f, 26. [16]Vs. 2 and refs. [17]Jud. 1 : 10. [18]Gen. 40 : 10.
[19]Cf. Gen. 14 : 13, 24. [20]14 : 34. [21]Vs. 10. [22]Ex. 3 : 8 and refs. [23]Vs. 18 ; Dt. 1 : 28 ; Jos. 14 : 1 .

more probably were not. Joshua of course could not have been of their number. For the displacement of JE in chh. xiiif., see above (Analysis p. 182).

and moreover we saw the children of Anak there.
(E) [. . .] Amalek dwelleth in [24]the land of the South : and 29
the H:ttite, and the Jebusite, and the Amórite, dwell [25]in the
mountains : and the Canaanite dwelleth by the sea, and
(J) [26]along by the side of Jordan. [. . .] **And** [27]**Caleb** 30
stilled the people before Moses, and said, Let us go
up at once, and possess it; for we are well able to
overcome it. But the men that went up with him 31
said, We be not able to go up against the people; for
(P) they are stronger than we. [28]*And they brought up an* 32
evil report of the land which they had spied out unto the children of
Israel, saying, The land, through which we have gone to spy it out,
(E) *is a* [29]*land that eateth up the inhabitants thereof ;* and all the
people that we saw in it are men of great stature. And 33
(Rd) there we saw the [31]Nephilim, the sons of Anak, which come
(E) of the Nephilim: * and we were in our own sight as grass-
hoppers, and so we were in their sight.

　　(P) (J) *And* [1]*all the congregation* **lifted up their voice,** 14
(E) (J)and cried : and the people wept that night— **And** 2
(P) all the children of Israel— *murmured against Moses*
and against Aaron : and the whole congregation said unto them,
[2]*Would God that we had died in the land of Egypt! or would*
(E) *God we had died in this wilderness!* And [. . .] where- 3
fore doth Yahweh bring us unto this land, [3]to fall by the sword?
(J) [4]**Our wives and our little ones shall be a prey:**
were it not better for us to return into Egypt?
(E) And they said one to another, Let us make a captain, 4
(P) and let us return into Egypt. *Then Moses and Aaron* 5

---

[24]Gen. 20 : 1 ; ct. vs. 17.　[25]Vs. 17 and refs.　[26]Ex. 2 : 5 ; Jud. 11 : 26.　[27]14 : 23f.　[28]14 : 36;
ct. Dt. 1 : 24.　[29]Lev. 26 : 38 ; Ez. 36 : 13.　[30]Gen. 6 : 4.　[1]Vs. 5, 26 etc.　[2]20 : 3.　[3]V. 43.
[4]Vs. 31 ; Dt. 1 : 39.

---

* Vs. 33*a b* is a harmonistic gloss not found in LXX, intended to identify the
Nephilim, or giants, of E with the "children of Anak" of J, vv. 22, 28, though
here a different expression (*beni*-Anak) is used. The latter are also taken by
D to be giants, perhaps from this identification. Cf. the gloss in Gen. vi. 4,
where (in spite of the intervening Flood) the same *Nephilim* are identified with
the *Gibborim*.

*fell on their faces before *all the assembly of the congregation of
6 the children of Israel. And *Joshua the son of Nun and Caleb
the son of Jephunneh, which were of them that spied out the land,
7 rent their clothes: and they spake unto all the congregation of the
children of Israel, saying, The land, which we passed through to
8 (J) spy it out, is an exceeding good land. **If Yahweh
delight in us, then he will bring us into this land,
and give it unto us; a land which *floweth with
9 milk and honey. Only rebel not against Yahweh,
neither fear ye the people of the land; for they
are bread for us: their defence is removed from
over them, and Yahweh is with us: fear them not.—***

10 (P) *But all the congregation bade stone them with stones. *And
the glory of Yahweh appeared in the tent of meeting unto all the
children of Israel.*

11   **(J) And Yahweh said unto Moses, **How long will
this people **despise me? and how long will they not
**believe in me, for all the signs which I have
12 wrought among them? I will smite them with the
pestilence, and disinherit them, and **will make
of thee a nation greater and mightier than they.
13 And Moses said unto Yahweh, **Then the Egyptians
shall hear it; for thou broughtest up this people in
14 thy might from among them; and they will tell it to
**the inhabitants of this land: they have heard that
thou Yahweh **art in the midst of this people; for
thou Yahweh art seen **face to face, and thy cloud
standeth over them, and thou **goest before them, in
a pillar of cloud by day, and in a pillar of fire by**

*Ch. 4, 22 : 17 : 16 : 20 : 1. *Ex. 12 : 6. *Vv. 30, 38 ; cf. 23f. *13 : 27 and refs. *Ex. 13 :
12 and refs. *Ex. 16 : 3 ; cf. vs. 20, *11 : 30. *Ex. 14 : 31. *Ex. 32 : 10. *Ex. 32 : 11.
*Gen. 50 : 11. *Ex. 34 : 6. *Cf. 12 : 8 ; Ex. 33 : 11. *Ex. 13 : 21f ; ch. 10 : 34.

* Vv. 2a, 3b and 8f. should be inserted before xiii. 30 (see Analysis), where
it is pointed out that in Dt. i. 29f. vv. 8f. are attributed to *Moses.* The reverse
process (Wellh. *Comp.* p. 104) is impracticable, because according to xiii. 30f.
the revolt must have taken place while Caleb and his companions were still
standing in presence of Moses and the people ; whereas the events of xiv. 10.
belong to the next day ; cf. xiv. 1b (E.).

night. Now if thou shalt kill this people as one man, 15
then the nations which have heard the fame of thee
will speak, saying, Because Yahweh was not able to 16
bring this people into the land which he sware unto
them, therefore he hath slain them in the wilder-
ness. And now, I pray thee, let the power of [19]**the** 17
(Rd) Lord be great, according as [20]thou hast spoken, saying, 18
Yahweh is slow to anger, and plenteous in mercy, forgiving iniquity and
transgression, and that will by no means clear [the guilty] ; visiting the iniquity of the fathers upon the children, upon the third and upon the fourth
generation.* **Pardon, I pray thee, the iniquity of this** 19
people according unto the greatness of thy mercy,
and according as thou hast forgiven this people,
from Egypt even until now. And Yahweh said, I 20
[21]**have pardoned according to thy word: but in very** 21
deed, as I live, and as all the earth shall be filled
with the glory of Yahweh; because all those men 22
which have seen my glory, and my signs, which
I wrought in Egypt and in the wilderness, yet
[22]**have tempted me these ten times, and have not**
harkened to my voice; surely they shall not see the 23
land which I sware unto their fathers,† neither shall
any of them that [23]**despised me see it :** [24]**but my ser-** 24

---

[19]Ex. 4 : 10 and refs.   [20]Ex. 34 : 6f.   [21]Ex. 32 : 14   [22]Ex. 17 : 2, 7.   [23]Vs. 11 and refs.
[24]Jos. 14 : 6-15.

* The accounts in J of Moses' intercessions (Ex. xxxii. 7–14 ; xxxiii. 12–
xxxiv. 7 etc.) have generally undergone revision by Rd. as in the present instance. The quotation of Ex. xxxiv. 6f. establishes the lateness of vv. 17b, 18,
and the same hand has doubtless been busy in the rest of the paragraph (cf.
LXX,), making the translation uncertain and construction confused. In vs.
17 read with LXX., "let thy power be magnified, O Lord." The idea of the
original writer is precisely as in Jos. vii. 8f. (J); the appeal is not, as in 17b,
18, to Yahweh's promise of mercy, but to his jealousy of his reputation for
"power." Thus 17b, 18 (Rd) give a wrong turn to 17a and anticipate vs. 19.

† The LXX. insert here, " But as for their children who are here with me, as
many as have not known good or evil (cf. Gen. iii. 5 : Is. vii. 15 : vs. 29 and
xxxii. 11—LXX.) to them I will give the land." In Dt. i. 39 the same language appears as part of the divine utterance here, and LXX. may have taken it
thence. The fact shows at least a recognition by LXX. that the passage above is

vant Caleb, because he had another spirit with him, and hath followed me fully, him will I bring into the land whereinto he went ; and his seed shall possess

25 **(E) it.** [. . .] Now the [25]Amalekite and the Canaanite dwell in the valley : to-morrow turn ye, and get you into the wilderness [26]by the way to the Red Sea.

26   (P) *And Yahweh spake unto Moses and unto Aaron, saying,*
27 *[27]How long [shall I bear] with this evil congregation, which murmur against me ? I have heard the murmurings of the chil-*
28 *dren of Israel, which they murmur against me. Say unto them, As I live, saith Yahweh, surely as [28]ye have spoken in mine ears,*
29 *so will I do to you : your carcases shall fall in this wilderness ; and all that [29]were numbered of you, according to your whole number, from twenty years old and upward, which have mur-*
30 *mured against me, surely ye shall not come into the land, concerning which I [30]lifted up my hand that I would make you dwell therein, save Caleb the son of Jephunneh, and Joshua the son of Nun.*

31 **(J) But your little ones, which [31]ye said should be a prey, them will I bring in, and they shall know the**
32 **land which ye have [32]rejected. But as for you, your**
33 **carcases shall fall in this wilderness. And your children shall be [33]wanderers in the wilderness forty years, and shall bear your [34]whoredoms, until your**
34 **(P) carcases be consumed in the wilderness.** *[35]After the number of the days in which ye spied out the land, even forty*

[25]13 : 20 ; vv. 43, 45. [26]Ex. 13 : 18 ; ch. 21 : 4. [27]17 : 10 etc ; cf. vs. 11. [28]Vs. 2 ; cf. vs. 22.
[29]Chh. 1-3. [30]Ex. 6 : 8. [31]Vs. 3 ; Dt. 1 : 39. [32]11 : 20. [33]Gen. 4 : 12 ; 46 : 34. [34]Ex. 34 :
16. [35]13 : 27.

incomplete without the substance of vv. 31–33. But Dt. i. 20–46 which keeps very close to JE in Num. xiii. f., presents a further statement in vv. 37f. of Yahweh's anger with Moses for Israel's sake, and denying to him admission to the land of promise (reiterated in iv. 21 ; xxxi : 3) which contradicts P (xx. 1–13), and was certainly part of the older tradition. The story of Yahweh's anger with Moses may not originally have belonged here (see above p. 18), or may have been from the hand of E or Rje, but the concurrent witness of LXX., Deuteronomy and P in vv. 26–30, 34f. who here reproduces, to some extent even verbally, the story of vv. 11–24 (cf. vv. 11 with 27 ; 21, 32 with 28 ; 33 with 34f. ; and the *plus* of LXX. in vs. 23 with 29b) seems to indicate the former existence of somewhat more of JE in and after vs. 24. From this connection, as appears from Dt. i. 38–40, vv. 31–33 have been removed.

days, for every day a year, shall ye [36]*bear your iniquities, even forty years, and ye shall know my* [37]*alienation. I, Yahweh, have* 35 *spoken, surely this will I do unto all this evil congregation, that are gathered together against me : in this wilderness they shall be consumed, and there they shall die. And the men, which Moses* 36 *sent to spy out the land, who returned, and* [38]*made all the congregation to murmur against him, by bringing up an evil report against the land, even those men that did bring up an evil report* 37 *of the land, died by the plague before Yahweh. But* [39]*Joshua* 38 *the son of Nun, and Caleb the son of Jephunneh, remained alive* **(E)** *of those men that went to spy out the land.* And Moses 39 told these words unto all the children of Israel : [40]and the people mourned greatly. [41]And they rose up early in the 40 morning, and gat them up to the top [42]of the mountain, saying, Lo, we be here, and will go up unto the place which Yahweh hath promised : [43]for we have sinned. And Moses 41 said, Wherefore now do ye transgress the commandment of Yahweh, seeing it shall not prosper ? Go not up, for Yah- 42 weh is not among you ; that ye be not smitten down before your enemies. For there the [44]Amalekite and the Canaanite 43 are before you, and [45]ye shall fall by the sword : because ye are turned back from following Yahweh, therefore Yahweh will not be with you. But they presumed to go up to the 44 **(Rd)** top of the mountain : nevertheless the ark of the cove- **(E)** nant of * Yahweh, and Moses, [46]departed not out of the camp. Then the Amalekite came down, and the Canaanite 45 which dwelt in that mountain, and smote them and beat them down, even unto [47]Hormah.

*   *   *   *   *   *   *   *   *   *

[36]18 : 1, 23.   [37]Ex. 6 : 6-8.   [38]13 : 32.   [39]Ct. vs. 24. Dt. 1 : 36.   [40]Ex. 33 : 4.   [41]Gen. 20 : 8; 21 : 14 etc.   [42]Vs. 44 : 13 : 17, 29.   [43]Ex. 32 : 31 ; ch. 12 : 11 ; 21 : 7 ; (22 : 34) ; Jos. 7 : 20 etc. [44]13 : 29 ; vv. 25, 45.   [45]Vs. 3.   [46](Ex. 13 : 22) ; 33 : 11.   [47]Cf. xxi. 1-3 ; Jud. 1 : 17.

* There is no other passage in JE where the name " ark of the covenant of Yahweh " is found in a context of unquestionable genuineness. On the other hand there are several passages where an original " ark of Yahweh " has been altered by the insertion of *berith* (" covenant of "). The probability is accordingly against the genuineness of the word here.—After vs. 45 LXX. add, " So they returned to the camp."

3. Chh. xv.—xx. 13. ISRAEL AT KADESH.

ANALYSIS.

Ch. xv. is a section of various fragments of priestly law, and, having no connection whatever with the story, is accordingly omitted. In ch. xvi. the mutiny of Korâh, Dathan and Abiram is related. Certain prominent individuals aspire to the priesthood, and raise a rebellion against Moses. Moses protests, and appeals to Yahweh ; vv. 1-19. Yahweh intervenes ; Korah and his followers are swallowed up by the earth, (consumed by fire from the sanctuary) ; vv. 20-35. An altar-covering is made from the censers of the burnt ; vv. 36-40. The people, sympathizing with the punished rebels, are visited by a plague ; vv. 41-50. Aaron's rod buds, as a token of the preëminence of Levi ; xvii. 1-11. Israel's complaint of the danger of approaching the Tabernacle is met by the appointment of the Levites for its service ; xvii. 12—xviii. 7. (Chh. xviii. 8-xix. contain only Levitical laws unconnected with the narrative, and are accordingly omitted). Arrived at Kadesh in the wilderness of Zin, the people murmur for water, and are supplied by Moses' smiting the rock with the rod ; xx. 1-13.

It is difficult even to frame a synopsis of these chapters without exhibiting the patent self-contradictions which they embody. In the story of Korah's mutiny, for example, it is impossible to conceive how after " the earth opened her mouth and swallowed them up (the mutineers), and their households, and all the men that appertained unto Korah, and all their goods," so that " they, and all that appertained to them, went down alive into the pit, and the earth closed upon them " (xvi. 32f.), it could still be possible not only for " fire to come forth from Yahweh and devour the 250 men that offered the incense," but for Eleazar to take up the censers out of the burning and scatter the fire (vv. 35ff.). But after we have adjusted our minds by some harmonistic process to a double destruction of Korah and his followers, and all that appertained to them, and their households ; one is really staggered to read in Num. xxvi. 11., " Notwithstanding the sons of Korah died not."* Moreover in xvi. 3 the complaint of the mutineers is that Moses and Aaron have arrogated to themselves *as Levites* a special priestly right which properly belongs to " all the assembly." In accordance with this both Reubenites and 250 princes of the congregation, presumably from all the tribes, are mentioned as of the company of Korah. In xxvii. 3 it is unequivocally

---

* An interpolation intended to account for the Levitical guild of temple-singers " the sons of Korah :" see titles of Pss. and cf. Num. xxvi. 58.

implied that this company was not exclusively of Levites. Yet the representation of vv. 8–11 is positive that the mutiny was a revolt of *Levites* against the exclusive privileges of the *Aaronic* priesthood. It would appear, however, from xxvii. 3 that this representation comes from a later hand than P², and this conclusion is established with certainty by the story of xvii. and xviii, 1–7, according to which Aaron's rod which buds is "the rod of *Levi*" as against the other eleven tribes, xvii. 1–3, and the Levites are first endowed with their peculiar office in consequence of the event of ch. xvi. and xvii. 12—xviii. 7. The story of the revolt of Korah and others of the *laity* (P²) is therefore to be distinguished from a later element (P³) observable in vv. 8ff. where the mutineers are *Levites*.

But a much more remarkable phenomenon appears when we look at the references of Deuteronomy, supposed by the Grafian critics to depend on JE, but regarded as older than P². Deuteronomy not only ignores any distinction between priests and Levites, treating the words as synonyms, but in xi. 6 makes explicit reference to this story as the story of what Yahweh "did unto Dathan and Abiram the sons of Eliab the son of Reuben, how the earth opened her mouth and swallowed them up, and their households and their tents and every living thing that followed them, in the midst of all Israel." Either the Deuteronomist practised "higher criticism," or else the story of Num. xvi. to him was not a mutiny of *Korah* at all; but of "*Dathan and Abiram* the sons of Eliab, the son of Reuben." Curiously enough there are portions of Nu. xvi. also, where Dathan and Abiram appear alone, as sole leaders of the mutiny; and others where Korah appears alone in a like capacity (cf. vv. 12, 25, 27b.; with 5, 8, 16, 19, 32, 40, 49). The latter appears as the representation of P² in subsequent passages (Vs. 49; xxvii. 3). It is also remarkable that according to Dt. xi. 6 the fate of the mutineers was to be swallowed up alive by the earth, and this again in Nu. xvi. 27b—32a is certainly the fate of Dathan and Abiram, and apparently of Korah's companions (32b), though "the 250 men who offered the incense" met a very different fate, and what became of Korah can only be inferred. Again it is to be observed that where Moses is speaking with Dathan and Abiram (vv. 12–15, 25, 27b–32) the subject of priestly or Levitical rights does not enter into the controversy at all. Dathan and Abiram accuse Moses of wanting to make himself a *prince* over them, of having been untrue to his promise to lead them to "a land flowing with milk and honey," of wishing to "bore out the eyes of these (?) men." Moses on his part prays that their offering (?) may not be respected (cf. Gen. iv. 4f.), and denies having injured a single individual. But nothing whatever is said of priestly rights. It is needless to refer in addition to minor difficulties, such as vs. 1. where the verb "took" has no object ; vs. 24, 27a. where Korah, Dathan and Abiram appear to have one tent in common, and that not a tent at all, but a sacred "tabernacle" (*mishkan*) for *mishkan* is never used in prose of anything but the sanctuary of Yahweh ; and vs. 7b, which so singularly and inappropriately repeats a part of 3a. From what has already been said minds in any degree susceptible to critical evidence cannot fail to recognize the probably composite character of ch. xvi, and that the story told in Dt. xi. 6 represents at least one element of JE, while even P is here composite also.

The priestly element as a whole is easily separated. The two characteristic features, that Korah alone is leader of the revolt, and that the subject of controversy is the priestly prerogative, are amply sufficient for the extrication of vv. 1–11 (exc. traces in vv. 1-3), 16-24a, 26, 27a, 32b. and from vs. 35 to xviii. 7 as the element of P^2 and P^3. The phraseology and point of view are alike unmistakable. Only in the portion where a close combination of JE and P has been attempted, viz. vv. 24-32, is there any difficulty in the separation ; and here the linguistic criteria are decisive. The association of the words " tabernacle (*mishkan*) of Korah, Dathan and Abiram " in vv. 24 and 27a has been already spoken of as an impossible one. To make assurance doubly sure it is only necessary to observe that "all the congregation," according to vs. 19, have already been assembled by Korah "at the door of the Tent of Meeting," and hence cannot possibly be in the vicinity of " the tabernacle of Korah, Dathan and Abiram," supposing such a place to be conceivable. There is only one *Mishkan*; hence we have no trouble in replacing the impossible "Korah, Dathan and Abiram " of Rp by the original " Yahweh." The harmonistic purpose of Rp in making the change is very obvious, as he is intent upon weaving together the story of Korah (P) and that of Dathan and Abiram (JE). It should be obvious, although apparently overlooked by critics, that vs. 26, built upon the model of vs. 23f., and priestly in tone and language, is purely the work of Rp, a kind of solder whose material is derived from the verses 23-27 which it is intended to unite, but which melts and separates without the application of a great amount of analytical heat. The same is true of vs. 32b, where Rp betrays himself further by the use of the late priestly word *rekush*, "goods" (Gen. xiv. 11f.; xv. 14; xvi. 21) ; it may be true also of the last clause of vs. 33.

Nor is the separation of the element P^3 from P^2 a difficult matter. Vv. 36-40 are shown in vs. 40 to take the view of P^3, that the controversy concerns the prerogative of Aaron and his sons over the other Levites, as in vv. 8-11. Vv. 16f. simply illustrate the usual practise of Rp and the late priestly interpolators, of leading back to the point of interruption by repeating the preceding context (cf. vv. 16f. with 5-7; and both with Ex. vi. 10-12 and 28-30). The result of this awkwardness is that Moses makes three consecutive addresses to Korah of nearly the same import, viz., vv. 4-7; 8-11; 16ff.

A far more difficult matter is the separation of JE into its elements; for we must agree with critics generally, in view of the patent duplications of vv. 28-34 (see text below), and the incongruities of vv. 12-15, that the JE strand is also duplicate. To begin with, it is a very singular thing that Rp should have attempted a combination of two such widely different narratives as (a) a story of the mutiny of Dathan and Abiram, (JE), and (b) the aspiration of Korah and others to the priesthood (P), if in JE there was no allusion at all to the priestly prerogative, and no resemblance in the names (in a and b). What then of the names in vs. 1, and the *minchah*, (" sacrificial offering "; impossible to identify with incense-burning) which the leaders of the revolt ("*their* offering ") are preparing to make in vs. 15?

Vs. 1 is in fact an extraordinary complex. We may take as the most reliable portion the words " Dathan and Abiram the sons of Eliab, the son [so LXX. and Dt. xi. 6] of Reuben." In all subsequent JE references these, and these alone, appear as the leaders of the revolt. We may safely say that this was the representation of E; for in vs. 27b, where they thus appear, the language is E's (see refs.), and the reference in Deuteronomy is also an indication. Whence then is " On the son of Peleth," who is just as unknown to P as to E? And whence has P, who nowhere gives the slightest indication of independent sources, the name " Korah," which he certainly did not get from E? There is none but J to whom they can be attributed. But the argument is not merely negative, for there is one more item in the *dramatis personae* of vv. 1f. reappearing neither in P nor E, viz. the "men of renown," vs. 2. The only other instance of this phrase in the Old Testament is Gen. vi. 4 (J). The remaining portion of vs. 1 gives the pedigree of Korah; but this pedigree agrees neither with P², according to whom " Korah and his company," are not Levites (ch. xvii.; xx. 3; xxvii. 3); nor could it with J, if, as there seems reason to suppose, the subject of controversy here also was the priestly prerogative (Ex. xxxii. 25-29). It comes then from P³, and P² agreed with J in making Korah a non-Levite. On independent grounds Wellhausen has conjectured that the Korah of the original narrative was of the tribe of Judah (*Comp.* p. 108). Strictly the pedigree of I Chron. ii. 43 makes him a descendant of Caleb, *i. e.* a *Kenizzite*, and not an Israelite at all. As to the other individual who we have reason to suppose, figured in J, but whom P² does not take over, we need only point out for the present that Peleth is a name significant of nothing else than the royal bodyguard established by David, whose popular designation ("Pelethites") seems to have been formed by paronomasia with the "Cherethites," or Cretans, always named with them, from the regular word for "Philistine," and with reference to their alien origin. If, then, by process of exclusion from all the other sources we may take as J's the objectless verb "took" of vs. 1, we may conjecture for the original J element of this verse, "Now Korah the son of Kenaz, and On the son of Peleth, men of renown, took " . . .

We have next to enquire whence P² derived the idea of an assault by Korah and others upon the priestly prerogative of Moses and Aaron, vv. 2f., and how Rp came to combine his narrative with that of JE. If we look first at Moses' petition in vs. 15a we see at once that it has no connection with the story of Dathan and Abiram's revolt in the midst of which it stands. Dathan and Abiram have no apparent notion of offering sacrifice, and if they had, E's legislation offers no objection, but rather commends the idea (Ex. xx. 24; xxiv. 5). In vs. 15 on the other hand, the complaint of the mutineers is at least accompanied by a proposal to sacrifice, if this be not indeed the principal *casus belli*. Moreover Moses' intercourse with Yahweh in vs. 15 is much freer than in E, and the two verses preceding are full of characteristic J phrases (see refs. ; "fields and vineyards" with which Dillmann would compare xx. 17 ; xxi. 22 is no exception, cf. 1 Sam. xxii. 7, J), vs. 14a refers verbally to Moses' promise Ex. iii. 17. Vv. 13-15 accordingly are J's fuller companion piece to 12b (E). Here the offering (*minchah*) of certain men opposed to Moses is the subject of dispute. Looking back now to the fragments of J in vs. 1 it would not be unnatural to supply as the missing object of "took" " an offering (*minchah*) for Yahweh," and if Dillm. is right in claiming for J the clause "and Yahweh is among them," in vs. 3 (cf. Ex. xvii. 7; xxxiii. 16; Num. xi. 20) his story may well have contained also the equivalent of vs. 3, together with the stray clause 7b, which *must* belong after this verse. Vv. 12, 25, 27b (Dathan and Abiram) must of course be attributed to E. But in E Moses is no talker. Preliminary announcements of the miracle Yahweh is going to perform, as we saw in the plague stories, belong to J. Vv. 28-30 should therefore be J's, and this judgment is confirmed by the language (see refs). One of the most striking instances to be found anywhere is in fact the persistent contrast between J's habitual use of "ground" (*adamah*) and E's "earth" (*eretz*), which is finely exemplified here in the palpable duplicates, 31, 33a (cf. 30a), J=32a, 33b, 34, E. Here the interweaving is as close as in the plague narratives, and in particular the verbal correspondence of fulfilment with prediction in J repeats one of the most remarkable of the phenomena there.

We are able thus to extricate the strands of J and E and to adduce some evidence that J's story, combined by Rje with E's narrative of the revolt of Dathan and Abiram perhaps because of their similar conclusion, related how Korah, a Kenizzite, and On, a Pelethite (Philistine), presumptuously brought an offering to Yahweh, claiming the right of sacrifice for all the people (3a *b*, 7b ?), and accusing Moses of arbitrarily assuming the prerogative (vs. 13). We have already found J vindicating the preëminent right of the Levites to the priesthood of the ark (Ex. xxxii. 25–29), and recognizing an even prior right in the family of Aaron (Ex. iv. 14; xix. 22 ; xxiv. 1f. 9–11). We shall find him subsequently emphasizing the prerogative of the Jerusalem priesthood (Dt. xxxiii. 8–10) and providing finally a third grade of temple functionaries in the *nethinim*, or *hierodouloi*, whom Joshua institutes from the Gibeonites (Jos. ix. 22–27—J). All these distinctions of priestly rank are pre-Deuteronomic ; for the pre-exilic "*chief*-priest " is a very different personage from the exclusively post-exilic " *high*-priest ; "and, although they carry back the *germs* of P's hierarchical system to a period by several centuries earlier, they are by no means improbable representations to be made by a priest of the Solomonic temple, circ. 800 B. C., such as we suppose J to have been. Nor do they conflict with J's representations of the priestly functions of the Ephraimite Samuel *at the high place* of Zuph, 1 Sam. ix., which is a different matter from the priesthood before the ark of 1 Sam. xxii. (J). But one element of the evidence for this theory of J in Num. xvi. is still to be mentioned. We know from Zeph. 1. 9 and Ez. xliv. 6ff. that the presence of certain "foreigners " as functionaries in the Jerusalem temple was extremely obnoxious to the stricter Mosaists of the Deuteronomic period. One class of these are known to have occupied this position since the time of David. (W. Robertson Smith, O. T. in Jew. Ch. first ed. pp. 249ff, 359). They were the *Pelethites*, or Philistines of the royal body-guard. Whether this fact may have any connection with the story of " On the son of Peleth " is for critics to decide. As to the original position of the JE portion of Num. xvi. it can only be said that it probably preceded the reference in xiv. 22. No location whatever is given.

The story of Kadesh-Meribah, xx. 1–13 must also of course precede that of the spies, chh. xvi f. since the lack of water would be felt immediately, if at all; moreover vs. 1 indicates a first arrival. P's location of the story of the spies in " the wilderness of Paran " necessitated the transfer. But the story of Meribah, the strife of the people with Moses and the smitten rock, has already been related in Ex. xvii. 1-7. According to the results there obtained we need expect in the Meribah story of Num. xx. no trace of E ; but vs. 3a which is incongruous with vs. 13 (the people strive with *Yahweh*), and is identical with Ex. xvii. 2, is almost certainly from J ; as well as vs. 5, which duplicates vs. 4, and is throughout characteristic of J in style and language (cf. Ex. xiv. 11f; xvii. 3 ; Nu. xi. 5, 20 ; xvi. 13). We also know from Dt. xxxiii. 2 (emended reading) that J connected Meribath-Kadesh as in the etymology of vs. 13 (P^2). Besides 3a, 5, 13 (?) there is nothing in xx. 1-13 traceable *prima facie* to J or E, save vs. 1bc, which should probably be assigned to E (cf. Ex. xv. 20f ; ii. 4ff ; Num. xii. and Dt. x. 6). The datum is referred to by Dt. i. 46 and quoted verbally by Jud. xi. 17. These references also point to an E origin. The clause cannot be from P, whose elaborate date it interrupts (see note *in loc.*).

No evidence is required to demonstrate that the principal narrative in Num. xx. 1-13 is from P. The date, vs. 1a ; the reference to xvi. 35 in 3b ; the subsequent allusions in xxvii. 14 ; Dt. xxxii. 15 to "the strife of the congregation at the waters of Meribah of Kadesh in the wilderness of Zin ;" the characteristic phraseology and style (cf. vs. 6 with xvi. 18-22, 42-45 and see refs.) leave no possibility of doubt. A moment's attention however to the subsequent references to the "rebellion" of Moses and Aaron will show that the hand of Rp or P^3, has been here at work, completely obliterating all trace of the real sin of Moses and Aaron. For the treatment of this phenomenon in detail the reader is referred to the notes *in loc.* and to the careful discussion of Cornill. *Z. A. W.* xi. 1. The question must arise, however, whether in this working over of P's story of the rebellion of Moses and Aaron Rp has not been to some extent influenced by the story of J. Now in vs. 8a *b* there is an element quite incongruous with the story of P^2, as appears both from the direction as given in 8a, and as carried out in vs. 11. If Moses is bidden to "take the rod " in vs. 8 it is because Yahweh means him to use it, as he actually does in vs. 11. But the directions proceed in vs. 8, " And *speak* ye unto the rock before their eyes that it give forth its water, and thou shalt bring forth to them water out of the rock." Thus, in the present form of the command the use of the rod is entirely ignored ; moreover 8c is superfluous after 8b. The substitution of a blow of the rod, or of two blows (vs. 11) for a verbal appeal, is certainly not the sin of " rebellion " of which Moses and Aaron were guilty. At most they could be blamed for presumptuous over-confidence, but certainly it could not be said that they " believed not in Yahweh to sanctify him " (vs. 12). And if they were not to smite with the rod why were they bidden to

take it? Why at least are they not blamed for the fault of smiting in
place of speaking, instead of for a different fault? In 8a*b* we have
clearly an independent representation, differing from both E and P in
that no wonder-working rod appears. As there is nothing in the clause
incompatible with J authorship, it seems at least probable that this different representation is J's and not a mere modification of P², by Rp. That
in J's story of " Meribath-Kadesh " the rod-feature should be absent is
not at all surprising, in view of the fact above referred to, that this author
had a totally different conception of the story how " Yahweh said unto
Moses, Gather the people together and I will give them water " and of
the " Well " " digged by the rod of the law-giver, and the princes' staves "
(xxi. 16–20 f.)

(P) (Rp) *Now* [1] *Korah the son of Izhar, the son of Kohath, the* **16**
(E) *son of Levi.* [. . .] with [2]Dathan and Abiram, the sons
(J) (E) of Eliab, [. . .] **and On, the son of Peleth,** sons
(J) (E) of Reuben, **took [men]** * and they rose up 2
(P) before Moses, with certain of the children of Israel
[. . .] *two hundred and fifty* [3]*princes of the congregation,*
(J) (P) *called to the assembly,* [4] **men of renown :** *and* 3
[5] *they assembled themselves together against Moses and
against Aaron, and said unto them,* [6] *Ye take too much upon you,*
(J) *seeing* [7]*all the congregation are holy, every one of them,* **and**
(P) [8]**Yahweh is among them:** [. . .] *wherefore then
lift ye up yourselves above the assembly of Yahweh ? And when* 4
Moses heard it, he [9]*fell upon his face : and he spake unto Korah* 5
*and unto all his company, saying, In the morning Yahweh will
shew who are his, and who is holy, and* [10]*will cause him to come
near unto him : even him whom he shall choose will he cause to*

---

[1] Chron. 2 : 43.　[2] Dt. 11 : 6 ; ct. 26 : 8ff.　[3] Ch. 7.　[4] Gen. 6 : 4.　[5] Vs. 42 ; 20 : 2 ; 27 : 3.
[6] 7b.　[7] 17 : 1ff.　[8] Ex. 33 : 16 ; Num. 11 : 20.　[9] Vv. 22, 45, etc.　[10] 17 : 5, 13 ; 18 : 2.

*In vs. 1 the text is corrupt. Dillmann conjectures in place of " took " (no
object) a dittograph of the following " rose up." The emendation of Köhler,
endorsed by Graf, Nöld., Col., Kuen., and Dillm., to make 1b agree with the
genealogies (xxvi. 8ff) by reading " Eliab, the son of Pallu, the son of Reuben,"
is too easy, not explaining the corruption, and makes shipwreck on Dt. xi. 6.

6 *come near unto him.   This do* ; [11] *take you censers, Korah, and*

7 *all his company ; and put fire therein, and put incense upon them*
  before Yahweh to-morrow : and it shall be that the man whom
  Yahweh doth choose, he [*shall be*] *holy:—ye take too much upon you,*

8 **(Rp)** *ye sons of Levi.—†And Moses said unto Korah, Hear now,* [12]*ye sons*

9 *of Levi:* [*seemeth it but*] [13]*a small thing unto you, that the God of Israel*
  [14]*hath separated you from the congregation of Israel, to bring you near to him-*
  self ; to do the service of the tabernacle of Yahweh, and to stand before the

10 *congregation to minister unto them : and that he hath brought thee near, and*
   all thy brethren the sons of Levi with thee ?   and seek ye the priesthood also ?

11 *Therefore* [15] *thou and all thy company are gathered together against Yahweh :*

12 **(E)** [16]*and Aaron, what is he that ye murmur against him ?*   And Moses
   [17]sent to call Dathan and Abiram, the sons of Eliab: and they

13 **(J)** said, We will not come up [. . .] **is it a small thing
   that thou hast brought us up out of a** [18]**land flowing
   with milk and honey,** [19]**to kill us in the wilderness.
   but thou must needs make thyself also a prince over**

14 **us ?   Moreover thou hast not brought us into a land
   flowing with milk and honey, nor** [20]**given us inheritance of fields and vineyards: wilt thou** [21]**put out the**

15 **eyes of these men ? we will not come up.   And Moses
   was very wroth, and said unto Yahweh,** [22]**Respect
   not thou their offering: I have not taken one ass
   from them, neither have I hurt one of them.**

16 **(Rp)** [23]*And Moses said unto Korah, Be thou and all thy congregation before*

17 *Yahweh, thou, and they, and Aaron, to-morrow : and take ye every man his*
   censer, and put incense upon them, and bring ye before Yahweh every man his
   censer, two hundred and fifty censers ; thou also, and Aaron, each his censer.

18 **(P)** *And they took every man his censer, and put fire in them, and*
   laid incense thereon, and stood at the door of the tent of meeting

19 *with Moses and Aaron.   And Korah assembled all the congrega-*

---

[11]Vs. 18. [12]Vv. 3, 7 ; ct. vs. 1. [13]Vs. 13. [14]Ct. 18 : 1ff. [15]27 : 3. [16]Ex. 16 : 7f. [17]vv. :
5, 20. [18]Ex. 4 : 8 and refs. [19]Ex. 14 : 11 ; 17 : 3 ; Ch. 14 : 3cf ; ch. 20 : 5. [20]1 Sam.   7.
[21]Jud. 16 : 21. [22]Gen. 4 : 4, 5. [23]Vv. 5-7.

† It is scarcely needful to point out that the proper place for vs. 7c is after vs.
3. " Korah and his company," vs. 5, are not " sons of Levi."   At most Korah
himself is one ; but according to vs. 2, his followers are simply " of the children of Israel," princes of the congregation.   The clause is either displaced, or,
possibly, a fragment of J.

tion against them unto the door of the tent of meeting : [24]*and the glory of Yahweh appeared unto all the congregation.*

[25] *And Yahweh spake unto Moses and unto Aaron, saying,* 20 *Separate yourselves from among this congregation, that I may con-* 21 *sume them in a moment. And they fell upon their faces, and said,* 22 *O God,* [26]*the God of the spirits of all flesh, shall one man sin, and wilt thou be wroth with all the congregation? And Yahweh* 23 *spake unto Moses, saying, Speak unto the congregation, saying,* [27]*Get* 24 **(Rp)** *you up from about the tabernacle of Korah, Dathan, and Abiram.*
(E) And Moses rose up and went unto Dathan and Abiram; 25
(Rp) [28]and the elders of Israel followed him. [29]*And he spake* 26 *unto the congregation, saying, Depart, I pray you, from the tents of these wicked men, and touch nothing of theirs, lest ye be consumed in all their sins.*

(P) (Rp) *So they gat them up from the tabernacle of Korah,* 27 (**E**) *Dathan, and Abiram,* *on every side :* and Dathan and Abiram came out, and stood at the door of their tents [. . .]
(J) and their wives, and their sons, and their little ones. And Moses said, [30]**Hereby ye shall know that** 28 **Yahweh hath sent me to do all these works;** [31]**for [I have] not [done them] of mine own mind. If these** 29 **men die the common death of all men, or if they be visited after the visitation of all men ; then Yahweh hath not sent me. But if Yahweh** [32] **make a new** 30 **thing, and the** [33]**ground** [34]**open her mouth, and swallow them up, with all that appertain unto them, and they** [35]**go down alive into the pit; then ye shall understand that these men have** [36]**despised Yahweh.**

---

[24]Ex. 16: 10; ch. 14 : 5, 10 ; vs. 42. [25]Vv. 44f. [26]27 : 16. [27]9 : 17, 21f ; 10 : 11, etc. [28]11 : 30. [29]Vs. 24. [30]Gen. 24 : 14 ; (42 : 33) ; Ex. 7 : 16, 17. [31]24 : 13. [32]Ex. 34 : 10 ; cf. Gen. 1 : 1. [33]Ex. 33 : 16 and refs. [34]Gen. 4 : 11. [35]Gen. 37 : 35 ; 42 : 38 ; 44 : 31. [36]11 : 20 ; 14 : 11, 23.

---

* Harmonistic redaction; see Analysis. Vs. 26 in its present form, is dependent on the alteration of the original " Yahweh " to " Korah, Dathan and Abiram " and on 23f. This attempted fusion of Korah with Dathan and Abiram is certainly very late, as in Ps. cvi. 17 they are still kept apart, and LXX. have a different text.—The latter part of the verse (Moses' words) may be from E.

I

31 **And it came to pass, as he made an end of speaking all
these words, that the ground clave asunder that**
32 **(E) was under them :** and the [37]earth opened her mouth,
(Rp) and swallowed them up, and their households, *and all the*
33 **(J)** *men that appertained unto Korah, and all their goods.** **So they,
and all that appertained to them, went down alive
(E) into the pit:** and the earth closed upon them, and they
34 perished from among [38]the assembly. And all Israel that
were round about them fled at the cry of them : for they
35 **(P)** said,[39] Lest the earth swallow us up. [40]*And fire came
forth from Yahweh, and devoured the two hundred and fifty men
that offered the incense.*

37   **(Rp)** [41]*And Yahweh spake unto Moses, saying, Speak unto Eleazar the
son of Aaron the priest, that he take up the censers out of the burning,*
38 *and scatter thou the fire yonder : for they are holy : even the censers of these
sinners against their own lives, and let them be made beaten plates for a covering of the altar : for they offered them before Yahweh, therefore they are holy :*
39 *and they shall be a sign unto the children of Israel. And Eleazar the priest
took the brasen censers, which they that were burnt had offered : and they beat*
40 *them out for a covering of the altar : to be a memorial unto the children of
Israel, to the end that no [42]stranger, which is not of the seed of Aaron, come
near to burn incense before Yahweh : that he be not as Korah, and as his
company : as Yahweh spake unto him by the hand of Moses.*

41   **(P)** *But on the morrow all the congregation of the children of
Israel murmured against Moses and against Aaron, saying.* [43]*Ye*
42 *have killed the people of Yahweh. And it came to pass, when the
[44]congregation was assembled against Moses and against Aaron,
that they [45]looked toward the tent of meeting : and, behold, the*
43 *cloud covered it, and the glory of Yahweh appeared. And Moses*
44 *and Aaron came to the front of the tent of meeting.* [46]*And Yah-*
45 *weh spake unto Moses, saying, Get you up from among this con-*

[37]Vs. 33f ; ct. 30f. [38]2 : 4. [39]Vs. 34. [40]17 : 13 ; 20 : 3. [41]Ct. Ex. 27 : 2 ; 38 : 2 ; cf. Ex.
38 : 3b. [42]Vv. 8-11. [43]Vs. 4. [44]Vv. 3, 19. [45]Ex. 16 : 10 and ref. [46]Vv. 20-24.

* Harmonistic redaction ; see Analysis. The idea of Rp seems to be that
Korah is involved in the fate of Dathan and Abiram while engaged in assem-
bling the congregation to the door of the Tent of Meeting (vs. 19), the 250 men
remaining there.

gregation, that I may consume them in a moment. And they fell upon their faces. And Moses said unto Aaron, Take thy censer, 46 and put fire therein from off the altar, and lay incense thereon, and carry it quickly unto the congregation, and make atonement for them: for there is wrath gone out from Yahweh; the [47]plague is begun. And Aaron took as Moses spake, and ran into the midst 47 of the assembly; and, behold, the plague was begun among the people: and he put on the incense, and [48]made atonement for the people. And he stood between the dead and the living; and the 48 plague was stayed. Now they that died by the plague were four- 49 teen thousand and seven hundred, besides them that died about the matter of Korah. And Aaron returned unto Moses unto the door 50 of the tent of meeting: and the plague was stayed.

And Yahweh spake unto Moses, saying, [1]Speak unto the chil- **17** dren of Israel, and take of them rods, one for each father's house, 2 of all their princes according to their fathers' houses, twelve rods: write thou every man's name upon his rod. And thou shalt 3 write Aaron's name upon the rod of Levi: for there shall be one rod for each head of their fathers' houses. And thou shalt lay 4 them up in the tent of meeting [2]before the testimony, where I meet with you. And it shall come to pass, that the man whom I shall 5 choose, his rod shall bud: and I will make to cease from me the murmurings of the children of Israel, which they murmur against you. And Moses spake unto the children of Israel, and all their 6 princes gave him rods, for each prince one, according to their fathers' houses, even twelve rods: and the rod of Aaron was among their rods. And Moses laid up the rods before Yahweh in 7 the tent of the testimony. And it came to pass on the morrow, that 8 Moses went into the tent of the testimony; and, behold, the rod of Aaron for the house of Levi was budded, and put forth buds, and bloomed blossoms, and bare ripe almonds. And Moses brought 9 out all the rods from before Yahweh unto all the children of Israel: and they looked, and took every man his rod. And Yah- 10 weh said unto Moses, [3]Put back the rod of Aaron before the testimony, to be kept for a token against the children of rebellion; that thou mayest make an end of their murmurings against me, that

---

[47]S : 10.   [48]Cf. Ex. 32 : 30.   [1]Cf. 21 : 8.   [2]Vs ~; Ex. 16 : 33f.   [3]20 : 9; cf. vs. 10.

11 *they die not. Thus did Moses: as Yahweh commanded him, so
did he.*

12   *And the children of Israel spake unto Moses, saying, Behold,*
13 *we perish, we are undone, we are all undone. Every one that
cometh near, that cometh near unto the tabernacle of Yahweh,
dieth: shall we perish all of us?*

18   *And Yahweh said unto Aaron, Thou and thy sons and thy
father's house with thee shall* [1]*bear the iniquity of the sanctuary:
and thou and thy sons with thee shall bear the iniquity of your*
2 *priesthood.* [2]*And thy brethren also, the tribe of Levi, the tribe of
thy father, bring thou near with thee, that they may be* [3]*joined
unto thee, and minister unto thee: but thou and thy sons with thee*
3 *shall be before the tent of the testimony. And they shall keep thy
charge, and the charge of all the Tent: only they shall not come
nigh unto the vessels of the sanctuary and unto the altar, that they*
4 *die not, neither they, nor ye. And they shall be joined unto thee,
and keep the charge of the tent of meeting, for all the service of the*
5 *Tent: and a stranger shall not come nigh unto you. And ye
shall keep the charge of the sanctuary, and the charge of the altar:*
6 [4]*that there be wrath no more upon the children of Israel. And I,
behold, I have taken your brethren the Levites from among the
children of Israel: to you they are a gift,* [5]*given unto Yahweh,*
7 *to do the service of the tent of meeting. And thou and thy sons
with thee shall keep your priesthood for every thing of the altar,
and for that within the veil; and ye shall serve: I give you the
priesthood as a service of gift: and the stranger that cometh nigh
shall be put to death.*

    *   *   *   *   *   *   *

20   [1]*And the children of Israel, even the whole congregation, came*
(E) *into the wilderness of* [2]*Zin in the first month:* [. . .] * *and*

[1]Cf. Ez. 44 : 10.   [2]Cf. chh. 3f.   [3]Gen. 29 : 34.   [4]16 : 35.   [5]Cf. 3 : 41.   [1]Ex. 16 : 1 and refs.
[2]13 : 21.

* The year is omitted for harmonistic reasons. In vv. 22ff., however, compared with xxxiii. 38f., it is apparent that this was the last year of the desert
wandering, *i. e.* the 40th. But according to JE (xiii. 26) they come to Kadesh
before the beginning of the 38 years' wandering (cf. Dt. 1f.); hence the omission. From the play in vs. 12 upon the name Kadesh ("sanctified") and from

the people abode in Kadesh ; [3]and Miriam died there, and
(P) was buried there. *And there was no water for the congre-* 2
gation : [4]and they assembled themselves together against Moses and
(J) *against Aaron.* [5]**And the people strove with** 3
(P) **Moses,** [. . .] *and spake, saying, [6]Would God that we*
had died [7]when our brethren died before Yahweh! And why 4
have ye brought the assembly of Yahweh into this wilderness,
(Rp) (J) *that we should die there, we and our cattle.** [8]**And** 5
wherefore have ye made us to come up out of Egypt,
to bring us in unto this evil place? it is no place of
seed, or of figs, or of vines, or of pomegranates ;
(P) **neither is there any water to drink.** [. . .]—[9]*And* 6
Moses and Aaron went from the presence of the assembly unto the
door of the tent of meeting, and fell upon their faces : and the
glory of Yahweh appeared unto them. And Yahweh spake unto 7
Moses, saying, Take the [10]rod, and assemble the congregation, 8
(J) *thou, and Aaron thy brother,* and [11]**speak ye unto the**
rock before their eyes, that it give forth its water ;
and thou shalt bring forth to them water out of the
(P) **rock :** *so thou shalt give the congregation and their cattle drink.*
[. . .] [12]*And Moses took the rod from before Yahweh, as he* 9
commanded him. And Moses and Aaron gathered the assembly 10
together before the rock,—and he said unto them, Hear now, [13]ye

[3]Dt. 10 : 6. [4]16 : 3 and refs. [5]Cf. Ex. 17 : 2. [6]14 : 2. [7]16 : 35. [8]Ex. 14 : 11 ; 17 : 3, etc.
[9]17 : 42f. and refs. [10]17 : 10 ; Ex. 7 : 9 etc. [11]Cf. 21 : 16ff. ; Ex. 17 : 2-7. [12]Cf. Ex. 17 : 2-7.
[13]Vs. 24 ; 27 : 14.

vv. 22 and 24 it is clear that the scene in P was Meribah Kadesh as in J. The
latter element is displaced ; see Analysis.

* The introduction of the " cattle " in vv. 4, 8, 11 has been shown by Cornill (*Z. A. W.* xi. 1) to be the work of Rp. The same writer confirms the conjecture of Nöldeke and Kayser that vs. 10b was originally addressed by
Yahweh to Moses and Aaron, " Hear now ye rebels (in P[2] Moses and Aaron
are the " rebels " ; cf. vs. 24 and xxvii. 14), [sc. who say] shall we bring forth
water out of this rock ? " and formed part of the material eliminated after vs.
8, which related the obnoxious story of Moses' sin. This view is supported by
the LXX., which has " Hear *me* " in vs. 10. In Cornill's more radical conclusions as to the original form of P[2] and J we are not prepared wholly to con-
cur, regarding the analysis above given as a simpler explanation.

11 *rebels ; shall we bring you forth water out of this rock?—*And Moses lifted up his hand, and smote the rock with his rod twice: and water came forth abundantly, and the congregation drank, and*
12 *their cattle. And Yahweh said unto Moses and Aaron, Because ye believed not in me, to sanctify me in the eyes of the children of Israel, [14]therefore ye shall not bring this assembly into the land*
13 *which I have given them. These are the [15]waters of Meribah :* [. . .] because the children of Israel [16]strove with Yahweh, and he was sanctified in them.*

---

§ VI. Nu. xx. 14—xxv.; xxvii. 12–23 ; xxxii. 1—xxxiii. 49. From Kadesh to the Jordan.

Prolegomena.

All the sources pass over in silence the 39 years of wandering : so much so that it is not at first apparent where these years are supposed to come in. The difficulty comes from the fact that in J and E, Kadesh is reached before the episode of the spies, from which depends the sentence of wandering, and is, in fact, their point of departure ; whereas according to P Kadesh is not reached until the 40th year (see note on xx. i.). Num. xx. 14–22a ; xxi. 4ab–9 (E) takes up the story after xiv.

[14]Ct. Dt. 1 : 37. [15]Vs. 24 ; 27 : 14. [16]Ct. vs. 3 ;Ex. 17 : 2-7.

* For the displacement of vs. 10b see note preceding. In vv. 8b and 11 the hand of Rp is demonstrably present, and it may fairly be presumed that he altered the verbs of vv. 5 and 8 from the singular addressed to Moses alone to the plural. For "*the* rod " in place of "*his* rod " we have the authority of LXX. and of vv. 8f. " Twice," vs. 11 may be genuine, but looks like an attempt to explain the sin of Moses, as an exceeding of his commission.

† Insert "of Kadesh" as in xxvii. 14. The etymology " strove," "was sanctified," demands both elements of the name. J also employs the term " the waters of Meribah," Dt. xxxiii. 8, and Meribath-Kadesh, Dt. xxxii. 2, but the verse cannot be assigned to JE (Kautzsch notwithstanding), partly because in both J and E the name Meribah is connected with a strife of the people against *Moses*, not Yahweh; partly because it is only in P that the name Kadesh is played upon. (Cf. vs. 12 and 24, and xxvii. 14). Plays upon words are comparatively rare in P[2], but not unknown ; cf. Gen. xvii. 5, 17 ; Num. xviii. 2.

25, 39–45 (command to make the circuit of Edom, and disaster at Hormah, E) and continues it without any apparent break; but it is probable from Num. xx. 1b, 16. Jos. xxiv. 7, and Dt. i. 46, (note also the + of LXX. in xiv. 45) that E in like manner with J (xiv. 33) supposes the principal part of the 40 years to be spent in Kadesh and its neighboring oases (cf. xx. 1 and 16). In Num. xx. our principal source is E, but both P² and J have a part, the former being as usual easier to disentangle, but in this section remarkably dislocated and confused in process of redaction.

P² relates the coming of the " congregation " from Kadesh-Meribah to mount Hor, where Aaron dies, and is succeeded by Eleazar. A 30 days' mourning is observed by the people; xx. 22b–29. Thence by regular stages Israel journeys to the plains of Moab; xxi. 11f.; xxii. 1. Here a disaster befalls them, brought about by the machinations of Balaam the son of Beor, who had counselled the Midianites to entice Israel to sin through their women (supplied from xxxi. 16). On account of Israel's intermarriage with the Midianite women a plague is sent upon the camp and stayed only by the summary act of Phinehas; xxv. 6–15. Yahweh commands a war of extermination against Midian, [whose land is taken from them, xxxii. 4]; xxv. 16–18, possible traces in ch. xxxi. (P²ᵃ). The rest of the book of Numbers from ch. xxv. on contains nothing belonging to the narrative, save the direction to Moses to ascend mount Abarim and die there, after installing Joshua, and the priestly element in the story of the inheritance of Gad and Reuben. The latter should probably precede the preliminaries to Moses' death xxvii. 12–23. Upon the request of Gad and Reuben that the territory taken from Midian may be reserved for their inheritance, Moses directs Eleazar the priest *and Joshua* (hence the displacement of xxvii. 12–23) to bestow the trans-Jordanic territory on the two tribes, on condition of their participation in the conquest; xxxii. 1a, 2b, 4, 18f., 28–33. Thereafter Moses is commanded, after installing Joshua, to ascend mount Abarim, view the land and die there; xxvii. 12–23. Chh. xxvi.–xxvii. 11 belong to the priestly legislative material giving the census

preparatory to distribution of the inheritances, and directions
for the inheritance of daughters. Chh. xxviii.-xxx., various
Levitical offerings, (no connection). Ch. xxxi., a late *midrash*,
expanding and supplanting P²'s story of the war against Midian.
Chh. xxxiv.-xxxvi., *novellae* to the priestly law relating to the
distribution of the land. These latter are omitted as immaterial to the narrative.

The narrative of E is as follows : From Kadesh Moses sends
messengers to the king of Edom, asking leave to pass through
his territory, but meets peremptory and armed refusal. Israel
therefore turns "to compass the land of Edom ; " xx. 14-21.
The people are discouraged, and complain against the manna ;
fiery serpents are sent as a punishment, and on Moses' intercession the serpent of brass is erected and heals the bitten ;
xxi 4-9. Skirting the eastern border of Edom and Moab,
Israel reaches and crosses the upper Arnon, the border
between Moab and the Amorites ; vv. 12-15. Moses thereupon
sends to Sihon, king of the Amorites, repeating the request
made to Edom, and is again refused. Sihon comes out into
the wilderness to attack Israel at Jahaz, but meets overwhelming defeat. Israel occupies his land ; vv. 21-24. Balak, king
of Moab, alarmed at the fate of Sihon, sends to Aram-Naha-
raim for the prophet Balaam to curse Israel ; Balaam at first
refuses, but at the second request, by divine instruction, goes
with Balak's messengers ; xxii. 4-21 in part. Arrived in Ar on
the border of Moab he is met by Balak, and after sacrifices,
pronounces not a curse but a blessing upon Israel. When
Balak protests he reiterates it , xxii. 36-41 in part, ch. xxiii.
Israel is led into idolatry by the daughters of Moab ; xxv. 1f.
4. Gad and Reuben receive Gilead as their portion, upon
promise to assist the other tribes in the conquest of the land
beyond Jordan ; xxxii. 1b, 2a, 16f., 24, 34-38.

According to xiv. 33 we must suppose in J a period of 40
years of nomadic life in the desert with Kadesh as headquarters. This period, however, is doubtless to be put, as in E,
after the disaster at Hormah (xxi. 1-3) since the order of
events in the two documents is the same. After the incident

of the report of the spies the Canaanite king of Arad fights against Israel and inflicts a defeat upon them, which Israel avenges in the neighborhood of the city of Zephath, afterwards called Hormah; xxi. 1–3. Thence Israel journeys by stages *through* the territory of Edom and Moab, and encamps at the peak of Pisgah in the field of Moab; vv. 16–20. Israel makes conquest of Amorite territory east of Jordan; vv. 24b, 25, 31f. In fear and envy of Israel's greatness, Balak, son of Zippor, king of Moab, sends to the children of Ammon to hire the prophet Balaam to come and curse Israel; xxii. 2–21 in part. On the way Balaam encounters the angel of Yahweh, who is recognized by the prophet's ass, "the dumb ass speaking with man's voice and staying the madness of the prophet;" vv. 22–35. Arrived at Kirjath-huzzoth in Moab, Balaam, confronting Israel, pronounces a blessing instead of a curse, and after Balak's protest, a second blessing; xxii. 39, traces in xxiii. 27ff., ch. xxiv. Israel makes a league with Baal-peor and is punished; xxv. 3, 5. Reuben and Gad obtain permission from Moses to occupy the Amorite cities east of Jordan; Machir takes Gilead, and Jair and Nobah perform similar exploits—perhaps at a later time: xxxii. 3, 5f., 20–23, 25–27. Vv. 39, 41f. have probably been displaced from after Jos. xvii. 18.

1. Chh. xx. 14–xxii. 1. THE CIRCUIT OF EDOM AND MOAB, AND CONQUEST OF GILEAD.

ANALYSIS.

In this part of §vi. the priestly element is very easily distinguished. The marked and peculiar phraseology of xx. 22b–29 is enough of itself to determine. But we have in vs. 24 an explicit reference to the "rebellion" of Moses and Aaron related by P² only (vv. 1–13; cf. xxvii. 12–14) and the whole paragraph follows faithfully the model of the death of Moses, as related by the same writer in xxvii. 12–14; Dt. xxxii. 48–52; xxxiv. 1ff, where the story of Aaron's death as here told is again referred to (cf. Dt. xxxii. 50 with vv. 23f). We have on the other hand a wholly different and contradictory account of the death of Aaron in Dt. x. 6, an isolated bowlder of ancient material, broken off in some unaccountable manner from the itinerary of E preceding Num. xx. 1 (cf. Num. xxi. 12ff), and introduced in most extraordinary fashion into the midst of a discourse of Moses. This context it interrupts in so flagrant a manner that the imagination is at a loss to conceive an explanation of its insertion. But we need only compare this singular fragment Dt. x. 6f. (vv. 8f. are in place) with Jos. xxiv. 33, to see that it forms the middle link between this and the account of Aaron's calling as priest, in the data, now missing, which originally preceded Ex. ii. There is good reason therefore to consider it a fragment of E's itinerary. Now the formula employed in this itinerary corresponds exactly to that of Num. xxi. 12ff, but differs from that invariably employed by P, in that the verb is not put first. This latter formula (P²) appears only in vv. 1of. of ch. xxi. and in xxii. 1, verses which are disconnected from, and sometimes interrupt (xxii. 1) the context, but agree with one another and with the rest of P². No other trace of the priestly writer appears elsewhere in this subsection, but everywhere material demonstrably connected with JE.

In considering the "prophetic" element we have first to observe that xxi. 1-3 is a passage which in any event interrupts the connection, and no less so after the removal of xx. 22b-29 than before. In xxi. 4 we have the immediate sequel of xx. 21, which does not tolerate separation from it, and the fulfilment of xiv. 25. "From mount Hor" in xxi. 4 is of course harmonistic; otherwise the verse connects directly with xx. 21. Now xiv. 25 was assigned to E. But we have strong independent ground for assigning xx. 14-21, 22a; xxi. 4ab ff. to E. Beginning with xx. 14ff. we find a number of characteristics peculiar to this writer such as the term, "travail," unexampled save in Ex. xviii. 8; "the angel of God" who brought them out of Egypt (cf. Ex. xiv. 19; xxiii. 20; xxxii. 34) and others indicated by the references. But, as we saw, xx. 14ff. is inseparable from xxi. 4ff. Here the references again favor E as unmistakably as before, and include the very important item that *Elohim* is used in vs. 5, where in either P or J we should certainly have "Yahweh," and probably "murmured" instead of "spake against" (cf. xii. 1; ct. Ex. xv. 24). But again, whichever source xx. 14 ff. and xxi. 4ff. are assigned to, xx. 1-3, which interrupts their sequence, must be from the other. Hence if marks of E were found in xxi. 1-3 it would throw doubt upon the case. But we have already attributed one story of the disaster at Hormah (xiv. 39-45) to E, and should be impelled independently to assign xxi. 1-3 to J on account of the language (see refs.). But we have still further to go, and shall find corroborations of our analysis as we advance. Vv. 21-24a have a structure identical with xx. 14ff. and must unavoidably be attributed to the same author. The geographical situation here is unique and important. Israel is "out in the wilderness" at Jahaz (vs. 23), *i. e.* beyond the eastern outskirts of Edom, Moab and the Amorite, who, in the order named, extend from the Gulf of Akaba to the Jabbok, along the east shore of the Dead Sea and Jordan. In other words they have made the circuit of Edom, and of Moab as well, respecting the territory of these kindred peoples. Now this not only agrees with xiv. 25 ; xx. 14-21 ; xxi. 4-9, but is exactly the representation of vv. 12-15, the geographical situation in vs. 13 being identical with vs. 23. But this itinerary was found to show affinity with Dt. x. 6f., a passage which in its turn showed evidence of derivation from E ; and thus the chain of connection with E is completed in still another direction.

These geographical data are significant from their perfect self-consistency, but much more so from the fact that in Deuteronomy we have the traces of a wholly different and contradictory itinerary, and that this latter is also represented in Num. xxi. The author of Num. xx. 14-21 ; xxi. 4-9, 12-15, 21-24 (E) takes great pains to make clear and positive the statement that Israel did not pass *through* the territory of Edom and Moab, but when their request for permission to pass through under guarantee of peaceful behavior was refused, turned quietly away, respecting the rights of these kindred peoples, and addressed themselves to the laborious journey entirely around Edom and Moab, " by the way of the Red Sea " ; *i. e.* southward from Kadesh to the northernmost point of the Gulf of Akaba, and so eastward and northward across the upper courses of the Zered and Arnon, keeping outside of the settled country for the entire distance. True, this may be, as critics claim, historically insupposable, the passage between Edom and the Gulf of Akaba being impossible to achieve peacefully without the consent of Edom, in fact requiring the crossing of Edomite territory ; but such is E's representation, made in most positive and unambiguous terms ; and in support of it he cites a few lines from an ancient collection of ballads called " the Book of the Wars of Yahweh " apparently with the sole object of showing the border of Moab to have been formed at the time by the lower course of the Arnon. Israel has crossed the *upper* course of Arnon " which cometh out of the border of the Amorites," but is " in the wilderness" ; hence, if a trespasser at all, a trespasser against the Amorite only, and according to vv. 21ff. not really in the territory even of the Amorite. This representation is only partly followed by D. As far as Dt. ii. 1 he agrees with E, but in ii. 3 we read the divine command, " Ye have compassed this mountain long enough : turn you northward, and command thou the people, saying, Ye are to pass through the border of your

brethren the children of Esau, which dwell in Seir." In vs. 29 it is positively asserted that both Edom and Moab did actually thus permit Israel
to pass through. On the contrary, in another part of Dt. (xxiii. 3-8)
which follows E's form of the Balaam-story (vs. 4) it is asserted with
equal positiveness that Moab refused them bread and water in the way ;
and in Jud. xi. 17 this is expressly stated of both Edom and Moab.
Deuteronomy does not state that Edom showed a fraternal spirit ; but
this may be inferred from the fact that in Dt. xxiii. 7, in contrast to the
Moabite, the Edomite is not to be abhorred ; "for he is thy brother."
It is certain that these conflicting statements of Dt. and Judges are not
from the same hand. It is not yet certain, though probable, that they
go back to conflicting data in the historical sources of Dt., *viz.* J and E.
But this probability becomes a certainty, when we turn again to Num.
xxi. and observe the contrast of vv. 16-20 with the preceding. Vv. 12-
15 bring us to the point of junction of the borders of Moab and the
Amorite. The poetic citation undertakes to show how Israel has con-
scientiously respected the territory of both. In vs. 13, as later in vs. 23,
Israel is "in the wilderness," and when, in vv. 14f., they are brought to
the actual line, there is no room for any further relation of their journeyings, especially not inside the territory of Moab or the Amorite. The
author *must* go on to tell us how they either got permission to cross the
border or fought. The envoys of vs. 21 start from the geographical
point of vv. 12-15 ; in other words vv. 21ff. *must* be the immediate
sequel of vv. 12-15, and this context will not tolerate the interruption of
vv. 16-20 which relate how Israel continues from stage to stage *in
Moabite territory*, and actually represents them as passing "from
Bamoth (of Moab ; cf. vs. 28 R. V. margin) *to the valley that is in the
field of Moab*, to the top of Pisgah which looketh down upon the desert" ; yet in vs. 23 they are still "out in the wilderness at Jahaz." Not
only vs. 20b, as claimed by Meyer and others, must be separated
from E ; but the whole of vv. 16-20 must be assigned to J (see refs.),
and forms a kind of parallel in this source to the story of the smitten
rock. (See above p. 160). Whether the Beer here referred to be the Beer of
Jud. ix. 21, or Beer-elim of Is. xv. 8, it is a *Moabite* city like Bamoth.
In fact the whole list of vv. 16-20 is a list of *Moabite* localities, representing a totally different tradition from that of vv. 12-15 and Dt. xxiii.
4 ; but apparently the same as that of Dt. ii. 29.

The rest of ch. xxi. is commonly taken as a unit, with the exception
that vv. 32-35 are assigned to a later hand. Vv. 21-24 are indeed inseparable from xx. 14ff. and are vouched for by Jos. xxiv. 8. There can be
no doubt that they come from E. But in vv. 24b-32 the structure is by

no means uniform. In 24a we have a description of the territory of
Sihon *by its two boundaries*, Arnon and Jabbok. What follows in the
rest of the verse and in vs. 25 is part of a description of the territory *by
its cities*. Vs. 24b, " for Jazer was the border-town toward the children of Ammon " (see note *in loc.*) refers to this city as if we had already
heard of its conquest. Vs. 25 is still more unexpected ; for there we
learn that " Israel took all these cities." But no city has been mentioned
save Jahaz, which it does not appear that Israel took, and Jazer; but
both together will not make " all these cities," moreover it appears from
the rest of the verse that the principal one meant was Heshbon. Now
we do indeed hear of the capture of Jazer in vs. 32, but this story
does not seem as if it could be part of the preceding narrative of how
Israel took all the country of Sihon, king of the Amorites, from Arnon
even unto Jabbok, for that certainly reaches a full stop in vs. 31, " Thus
Israel dwelt in the land of the Amorites." Yet Jazer according to vs. 32
is an Amorite town. Again it appears from xxxii. 3, 5, that this territory was taken, and it is there also described by its cities. But this part
of ch. xxxii. is positively J's. It appears then that J had an account of
the conquest of this territory, specifically of Heshbon and Jazer, and
from xxxii. 39 it appears that J did call the inhabitants of some of these
Gileadite cities *Amorites*, using in fact in that verse exactly the same
expression as in xxi. 32 ; cf. Jud. i. 34f. We must accordingly attribute
xxi. 24 from " even unto the children of Ammon." 25 and 32, to J. Vv.
27-31 on the other hand are certainly E's, both from the connection
(Sihon) and the language (see 28b, refs.). The poem is doubtless taken
from the same source as vv. 14f. whose scheme is nearly the same. It
certainly might well belong from its subject in the Book of the Wars of
Yahweh. Vv. 24b, 25 have been taken from after vs. 32 to bring the
mention of Heshbon into connection with the reference in the poem.
Vs. 26 is redactional; see note *in loc.* So Meyer on independent
grounds, *Z. A. IV.* 1881. The striking duplication of vs. 25b (J) by vs.
31 (E) is thus explained.

Vv. 33-35 may possibly contain a trace of primitive material ; for the
defeat of Og, king of Bashan, at Edrei, is not an editorial invention.
But the primitive portions of ch. xxxii. do not show the conquest to have
extended north of Jabbok. The passage here simply rounds out the
story of the conquest of Gilead and, whatever its original source, appears
here to be taken *verbatim* from Dt. iii. 1ff. The language of vs. 33 is
that of D and not of E. (cf. vs. 23 with Dt. ii. 32), that of vs. 35 has a similar character, while vs. 34 contains nothing but Deuteronomistic ideas
and phrases. Nevertheless the *data* may well be supposed to have

come originally from a primitive source, perhaps E. But the entire absence of Og from subsequent references in E passages where Sihon is spoken of is significant (cf. xxii. 2 ; Jos. xxiv. 8 ; Jud. xi. 22).

The remarkable fragment from " the satirists " (27a, R. V. " they that speak in proverbs ; " cf. Is. xiv. 4off. where the " proverb " (R. V. " parable ") seems to be a poem of exultation over a defeated foe) has been shown by Meyer, Z. A. W. 1881, to the satisfaction of the majority of critics, to be a song of triumph over one of the victories of Israel over Moab, in the wars of the 9th century (2 Kings iii. 4ff.) of which the stone of Mesha remains a precious memorial. Sihon, according to Meyer, was a Moabite, not an Amorite king ; hence the author of vv. 21, 26 and 29bb (see note *in loc.*) misunderstands the application of the poem. As with other ancient fragments of song the text is exceedingly corrupt, though much has been done by Meyer and others to improve it through comparison of the versions, but especially of the singularly fortunate citation in Jer. xlviii. 45f. For these emendations and comments in detail the reader is referred to the notes *in loc.* The representation of J seems to have been practically the same as E's, and may have served as its model. Both take pains to show that Moab's treachery (chh. xxii.ff.) preceded any act of hostility on Israel's part.

14　　(E) [17] And Moses sent messengers from Kadesh unto the [18]king of Edom, Thus saith [19] thy brother Israel, Thou know-
15　est all the [20] travail that hath befallen us : how our fathers went down into Egypt, and [21] we dwelt in Egypt a long time :
16　and the Egyptians evil entreated us, and our fathers : and when we cried unto Yahweh, he heard our voice, and [22]sent an angel, and brought us forth out of Egypt : and, behold,
17　we are in Kadesh, a city in the uttermost of thy border : let us pass, I pray thee, through thy land : we will not pass through [23] field or through vineyard, neither will we drink of the water of the wells : we will go along the king's [high] way, we will not turn aside to the right hand nor to the left, until
18　we have passed thy border. And Edom said unto him, Thou shalt not pass through me, lest I come out with the
19　sword against thee. And the children of Israel said unto

[17] ... ; Jud. 11 : 17 : cf. Dt. . : . . . [18]Gen. 36 : 1ff. [19]Dt. 2 : 8 ; 2 : 4. [20]Ex. 18 : [21]Jos. 24 : 7. [22]Ex. 23 : 20 : . : 24. [23]v. : 14 ; 21 : 22. [24]Dt. 2 :

him, We will go up by the high way : and if we drink of thy
water, I and my cattle,* then will I give the ²⁴ price thereof :
let me only, without [doing] any thing [else] pass through
on my feet. And he said, Thou shalt not pass through. 20
And Edom came out against him with much people, and
²⁵ with a strong hand. Thus Edom ²⁶ refused to give Israel 21
passage through his border : wherefore Israel turned away
from him.

(P) ²⁷ *And they journeyed from Kadesh :* † *and the children of* 22
Israel, even the whole congregation, came unto mount Hor.
² *And Yahweh spake unto Moses and Aaron in mount Hor, by* 23
the border of the land of Edom, saying, Aaron shall be gathered 24
unto his people : for he shall not enter into the land which I have
given unto the children of Israel, because ²⁹ *ye rebelled against my*
word at the waters of Meribah. Take Aaron and Eleazar his 25
son, and bring them up unto mount Hor : and strip Aaron of his 26
garments, and put them upon Eleazar his son : and Aaron shall
be gathered [unto his people] and shall die there. And Moses did 27
as Yahweh commanded : and they went up into mount Hor in the
sight of all the congregation. And Moses stripped Aaron of his 28
garments, and put them upon Eleazar his son ; and ³⁰ *Aaron died*
there in the top of the mount : and Moses and Eleazar came down
from the mount. And when all the congregation saw that 29
Aaron was dead, they ³¹ *wept for Aaron thirty days, even all the*
house of Israel.

(J) **¹And the Canaanite, the king of Arad, which 21
dwelt in the South, heard tell that Israel came by the
way of Atharim ; and he fought against Israel, and
took some of them captive. And Israel vowed a vow** 2

²⁴Dt. 2 : 6. ²⁵Ex. 3 : 19 and refs. ²⁶Gen. 20 : 6 ; ch. 22 : 13. ²⁷21 : 11 ; Ex. 16 : 1 and
refs. ²⁸Dt. 32 : 50. ²⁹Vs. 10 ; 27 : 14. ³⁰Ct. Dt. 10 : 6. ³¹Dt. 34 : 8. ¹Cf. 14 : 40ff.

* After the 40 years' nomadic life in Kadesh it is no marvel if Israel appears
even in E supplied with flocks and herds ; cf. xxxii. 16 (E).

† "Kadesh," in the opinion of most critics, is R's adaptation of the verse to
the preceding context (cf. vv. 14, 16) ; but P² might perhaps have written
Kadesh, or at least Meribath-Kadesh (Dt. xxxii. 51), instead of Wilderness of
Zin after vs. 13.

unto Yahweh, and said, If thou wilt indeed deliver
this people into my hand, then I will utterly destroy
3 their cities.   And Yahweh harkened to the voice of
Israel, and delivered up the ²Canaanites; and they
utterly destroyed them and their cities: and the
name of the place was called ³Hormah.*

4   (P) (E) *And they journeyed from mount Hor* [. . .] ⁴by
the way to the Red Sea, to compass the land of Edom: and
the soul of the people was much discouraged because of
5 the way.   And the people ⁵spake against God, and against
Moses, Wherefore have ye brought us up out of Egypt to
die in the wilderness? for there is no bread, and there is no
6 water; and our soul loatheth ⁶this light bread.   And Yahweh sent fiery serpents among the people, and they bit the
7 people; and much people of Israel died.   And the people
came to Moses, and said, ⁷We have sinned, because we have
spoken against Yahweh, and against thee; pray unto Yahweh, that he take away the serpents from us.   And Moses
8 prayed for the people.   And Yahweh said unto Moses, Make
thee a fiery serpent, and set it upon a ⁸standard: and it
shall come to pass, that every one that is bitten, when he
9 seeth it, shall live.   And Moses made a ⁹serpent of brass,
and set it upon the standard: and it came to pass, that if a
serpent had bitten any man, when he looked unto the ser-
10 (P) pent of brass, he lived [. . .]† ¹⁰*And the children of*
11 *Israel journeyed, and pitched in Oboth.   And they journeyed*

---

²Ex. 3:8 and refs.   ³Jud. 1:16;   ⁴14:25; 20:21.   ⁵12:1.   ⁶Ex. 16:4ff; cf. ch. 11:
4ff.   ⁷14:40 and refs   ⁸Ex. 17:16.   ⁹II Kgs. 18:4.   ¹⁰22:1.

* The name of Hormah (= "Fortress") is derived here by an imaginative
etymology from *herem* to "ban" or "devote" (see Lev. xxvii. 28f).   The
word should not be translated "utterly destroy," but "devote."   Here in fact
the cities are not even captured until Jud. i. 16f (J).   Israel suffers a reverse
from the king of Arad, as related by E in xiv. 40ff., *devotes* their cities to Yahweh, and is enabled to win a victory.   "The place" is called Hormah, and
when afterward (Jud. i. 16f.) the cities are taken and burnt, Zephath receives
this name; because the *herem* or vow of destruction is then carried out.

† Insert here the data of Dt. ii. 8f., 17-19 referred to in Dt. ii. 29 and add
Dt. x. 6f. and the traces in Dt. i. 1.

(E) *from Oboth, and pitched at Iye-abarim,* in the wilderness
which is before Moab, toward the sunrising. [11]From thence 12
they journeyed, and pitched in the valley of Zered. From 13
thence they journeyed, and pitched on the other side of Arnon,
which is [12]in the wilderness, that cometh out of the border
of the Amorites : for Arnon is the border of Moab, between
Moab and the Amorites. Wherefore it is said in the book 14
of the Wars of Yahweh,

> Vaheb in Suphah,*   15
> And the valleys of Arnon,
> And the slope of the valleys
> That inclineth toward the dwelling of Ar,
> And leaneth upon the border of Moab.

(J) And from thence [they journeyed] to [13]Beer : that 16
is the well [14]whereof Yahweh said unto Moses [15]Gather
the people together, and I will give them water.
Then sang [16]Israel this song :   17

> **Spring up, O well ; sing ye unto it :**   18
> **The well, which the princes [17]digged,**
> **Which the nobles of the people [18]delved,**
> **With the [19]sceptre, [and] with their staves.**

And from the wilderness [they journeyed] to Matta- 19
nah ; ʼand from Mattanah to Nahaliel : and from
Nahaliel to Bamoth : and from Bamoth to the val- 20
ley that is in the field of Moab, [20]to the top of Pisgah,
which looketh down upon the desert.†

---

[11]Dt. 10:6. [12]Vs. 23. [13]Jud. 9:26 ; Is. 15:8. [14]10:29. [15]Cf. 20:7f ; Ex. 17:sf.
[16]Ex. 15:1 ; Jos. 10:12 ; Jud. 5:1. [17]Gen. 21:30 ; 26:15ff ; Ex. 7:24. [18]Gen. 26:25.
[19]Gen. 49:10. [20]23:28.

* The LXX. seems to have had Zahab, which seems also to have been the
reading known by the Jewish Midrash. Both Vaheb, or Zahab, and Suphah
are doubtless proper names, whose collocation recalls the Suph of Dt. i. 1 connected there with a certain Di-zahab.—After vs. 12 Sam. insert Dt. ii. 18f.

† For the probable significance of the fragment in vv. 17f. to which LXX give
the title " Song of the Well," see above p. 160. Similar instances of word plays
giving rise to stories of miracles are cited in my " Gen. of Gen." pp. 13–18. cf.
Ex. xv. 8 with P in Ex. xiv ; Jud. xv: 16 with 15 ; Dt. xxxiii. 25 (Heb.) with
xxix. 5 etc. In vs. 18 read, with LXX. " from Beer " (*umibeer* instead of

21   **(E)** [21]And Israel sent messengers unto Sihon king of the
22   Amorites, saying, Let me pass through thy land : we will not
turn aside into field, or into vineyard ; we will not drink of
the water of the wells : we will go by the king's [high] way,
23 until we have passed thy border. And Sihon would not suffer Israel to pass through his border : but Sihon gathered
all his people together, and went out against Israel into the
wilderness, and came to Jahaz : and he fought against Israel.
24 And Israel smote him with the edge of the sword, and [22]pos-
(J) sessed his land from Arnon unto Jabbok,—[. . .] **even
unto the children of Ammon : for the border of the**
25 **children of Ammon was strong.* And Israel took all
these cities : and Israel dwelt in all the cities of the
Amorites, in Heshbon, and in all the** [23] **towns thereof.**
26 **(Rje)**—For Heshbon was the city of Sihon the king of the Amorites,
who had fought against the former king of Moab, and taken all his land out
27 **(E)** of his hand, even unto Arnon.†   Wherefore they that speak
in proverbs say,

[21]20 : 14ff and refs.   [22]Jos. 24 : 8.   [23]Vs. 32 : 32 : 42 ; Jos. 16 : 11ff ; Jud. 1 : 27.

umimidbar) ; cf. vs. 16. The Mass. reading is very likely connected with the
foolish *haggadah* about the "well of Miriam." In vs. 20 the Hebrew has only
" the top of Pisgah," without the preposition. The LXX. translates ," border-
ing on," which may be better than to supply "to." If " top " (literally "head")
here means peak, " the top of Pisgah " would be an extraordinary place for
Israel to encamp, moreover the preceding clause expressly states that they
were " in the valley " and in xxiii. 14f. 28 we find this very spot occupied by
Balak and Balaam who are looking down upon the camp of Israel. Possibly
Pisgah may be used of the entire plateau ; but the situation in vs. 19f. is the same
as that already reached in vv. 13ff. and also that of xxiii. 28 ; xxiv. 1 ; certainly
not that of E, vs. 23.

    The reading of LXX " Jazer " for *az* " strong," is to be preferred. The
strength of Ammon's border would scarcely be given as a reason for
Israel's halting there. Jazer is here one of the cities taken, cf. xxxii. 3. Vv.
24b, 25 come after vs. 32 ; see Analysis.

    † Vs. 26 seems to be of an explanatory character and aims to connect vs. 25
with 27ff. See Meyer *Z. A. W.* '81 for the evidence against its genuineness.
E cannot have written " the former (?) king of Moab " ; ct. xxii. 2, 4.—Instead
of " out of his hand," for which LXX have " from Aroer," we should doubtless
read " from Jabbok " ; cf. vs. 24a.

Come ye to Heshbon,
Let the city of Sihon be built and established :
For a fire is gone out of Heshbon,   28
A flame from the city of Sihon :
It hath devoured Ar of Moab,
The [24]lords of the high places of Arnon.
Woe to thee, Moab !   29
Thou art undone, O people of Chemosh :
He hath given his sons as fugitives,
And his daughters into captivity,

(Rje) Unto Sihon king of the Amorites.*

(E) We have shot at them ; Heshbon is perished even unto 30
     Dibon,
And we have laid waste even unto Nophah,
Which [reacheth] unto Medeba.†

(J) Thus [25]Israel dwelt in the land of the Amorites. [26]**And 31–32
Moses sent to spy out Jazer, and they took the
[27]towns thereof, and [28]drove out the Amorites that
(Rd) were there.** [29]And they turned and went up by the way of Ba- 33
shan : and Og the king of Bashan went out against them, he and all his
people, to battle at Edrei. And Yahweh said unto Moses, Fear him not : 34
for I have delivered him into thy hand, and all his people, and his land ;
and thou shalt do to him as thou didst unto Sihon king of the Amorites,
which dwelt at Heshbon.‡ So they smote him, and his sons, and all his 35
people, until there was none left him remaining : and they possessed his
(P) land. [1]*And the children of Israel journeyed, and pitched in* **22**
the plains of Moab beyond the Jordan at Jericho.

[24]Ex. 21 : 3 and refs. [25]Jos. 24 : 15. [26]Jud. 1 : 23. [27]Vs. 25 and refs. [28]32 : 39. [29]Dt.
3 : 1-4. [1]21 : 10f.

* An explanatory gloss unsupported by the metre and parallelism.

† The text of vs. 30b is certainly corrupt. Meyer emends and translates :
"Their seed is perished from Heshbon unto Dibon. Their women have set
fire unto Medeba." So substantially the LXX. Dillmann translates "And we
have laid waste till the fire hath kindled unto Medeba."

‡ Vv. 33-35 seem to be added by way of supplementation from Dt. iii. 1-3.
The addition may, however, have been first made to E.

2. Chh. xxii–xxiv. The Oracle of Balaam.

ANALYSIS.

Moab, jealous of Israel's greatness, sends to Pethor on the Euphrates for Balaam the seer, to come and curse the people. Balaam by divine instruction refuses to go. Balak, king of Moab, sends a second, more honorable embassy. Balaam again waits for divine instruction, and is bidden to go, taking care to give none but the message God shall give him; xxii. 2-21. On the way he is met by the angel of Yahweh, who is angry because he went and would have slain him but for the intelligence of the soothsayer's ass. Balaam offers to return, but is bidden by the angel to continue his journey, taking care to speak only the word that Yahweh shall speak unto him; 22-35. Arrived in Moab he declares to Balak the condition imposed upon him; 36-40. In the sequel he acts accordingly. Three times Balak attempts, after suitable preparations, to obtain an effectual curse from Balaam against Israel. First on the height of Bamoth-baal, from whence the extremity of Israel can be seen, then from the more northerly peak of Pisgah, whence a part of the camp is visible, finally on the peak of Peor, whence Israel is seen encamped according to its tribes. Each attempt brings only increasing blessing instead of curse, till Balak in rage dismisses the seer; xxiii. 1-xxiv. 10. Balaam reminds Balak of the conditions imposed, adds a further, unsolicited prophecy, and returns home; 11-25.

With the exception of certain difficulties in ch. xxii., this story of the Oracle of Balaam seems fairly self-consistent and agrees well with the representation of the preceding chapter. Israel is seen occupying the territory won by Sihon from Moab, and subsequently reconquered by Moses, but carefully respecting the territorial rights of its kindred, Edom, Moab and Ammon. Moab thereupon secretly conspires against the unwelcome intruders by witchcraft (xxiii. 23); but God turns the curse into a blessing. That this was the representation of E is placed beyond question by the reference to it in Jos. xxiv. 9f., confirmed by Dt. xxiii. 5f.; Jud. xi. 25; Mic. vi. 5ff.

But another representation coexists with this, which no harmonist can bring into anything more than the semblance of agreement with it. According to the story of xxv. 6-18; xxxi. 8-16, confirmed by Jos. xiii. 21f., Balaam was not a prophet of Yahweh from Pethor on the Euphrates, who came at Balak's solicitation to curse Israel, received commandment to bless, and, when he had obeyed it, "*rose up, and went and returned to his place*" (xxiv. 25); but was a *Midianite*, who with the

five princes of Midian *conspired against Israel to corrupt them* by their
women and *was slain* together with these princes, in the war of extermination which Israel undertook against Midian. There is no difficulty
or possibility of doubt in assigning this latter representation to the
priestly document. It stands quite apart from JE, and shows in every
line its thoroughly priestly character, so that argument is superfluous.
The only question must be whence this radically different tradition of
Balaam was derived by P². This writer could not indeed tolerate in his
rigidly exclusive, hierocratic system such a character as Balaam in
genuine intercourse with Yahweh, sacrificing, and receiving in return true
oracles ; but in previous cases where his sources presented obnoxious
material his method has been simply to omit. *Elaboration* of material
germane to his subject is the delight of the priestly writer ; but we have
no reason to suspect him anywhere of the *creation* of such material. As
in many previous instances we must look for the traces of this original
material developed by P² and P³ in the traces of J, which are not wanting
even in the splendid legend of chh. xxii–xxiv., the main source of which
we have seen reason to regard as E.

The independent indications of a double source in these chh. are in
fact conclusive. In xxii. 2–4, vs. 2 = vs. 4b, and 3a and 3b are also
doublets. Moreover there is a difference in the use of the divine names
which cannot be explained on grounds of sense. True we have everywhere save in xxii. 38 " Yahweh " in the mouth of Balaam (with some
variation in the versions *e. g.* LXX. in vs. 13) ; but it is probable (see note
on xxiii. 5) that this is an intentional alteration of R, to indicate that the
oracle comes in reality from Yahweh and no other. Balak also of course
conforms to this in conversation with Balaam. But that the author himself should use *Elohim*, xxii. 8–22a is inexplicable save as a source
peculiarity, marked throughout the Hexateuch ; accordingly vv. 9f., 12,
20, 22a; xxiii. 4, which use invariably " *Elohim*," in contrast with xxii.
22b–35 ; xxiii. 5—xxiv. 14 (exc. xxiv. 2) where " Yahweh " is uniformly
employed, must, with their connected context, be attributed to E. The
references will show that this principal linguistic difference is accompanied by the use of other expressions characteristic respectively of the
two writers.

We have already referred to certain sense-incompatibilities in chh.
xxii. It is of prime importance to observe whether the discrimination
according to sense coincides with that indicated by linguistic peculiarities.
In vv. 7b–21 we have *in the author's own words* " *Elohim*." In 22b–
35 " *Yahweh*." In the latter passage not only is no notice taken of the
former, but it is contradicted in a manner past all reasonable reconcilia-

tion. In the former Balaam appears above reproach as the inflexible servant of God, following the divine command to the letter. In vs. 21 he departs "*with the princes of Moab*" because expressly *commanded of "God"* to do so. In the latter passage, it appears that he has incurred the *anger of "Yahweh"* by going, "Yahweh's" angel standing in the way to slay him. Moreover he is not accompanied by "the princes of Moab" but by "*two servants.*" It is further well worthy of notice that the circumstances of the journey are quite different from what they would be if Balaam were coming from Pethor on the Euphrates. (vs. 5; xxiii. 7). Such a journey is not made in the East on ass's back with two servants. It is a caravan or *camel*-journey (cf. Gen. xxiv.), and moreover one does not ride "between the vineyards, a fence being on this side, and a fence on that side," unless at the very end of the journey. The author of this passage has different conceptions before his mind from those of the preceding and following context. Finally the conclusion, vs. 35. simply resumes vs. 20f. at the point of interruption. The singular story of the speaking ass has but one parallel in Hebrew literature viz.: Gen. iii. 1ff. (J); and on the other hand the coming of "God" to the prophet at night vv. 8ff., is a striking characteristic of E (see refs.). Hence we cannot go astray in assigning in general the former passage to E and the latter to J.

In the oracles which follow in chh. xxiiif. we have at the beginning a decisive correspondence with E's point of view: "From *Aram* hath Balak brought me; the king of Moab from the mountains of the East." On the other hand ch. xxiv. can hardly be derived from the same source. Balaam's introduction of himself by name would come necessarily at the beginning in a uniform narrative, and not after two oracles have already been pronounced, as a preface to the third and fourth only. Moreover the third oracle repeats *verbatim* a part of the second (cf. xxiv. 8 with xxiii. 22); Balak has got through with Balaam already in xxiii. 25, and will have him utter neither curse nor blessing, yet in vs. 27 already he has changed his mind. There are also unmistakable indications in xxiii. 27ff. (see note *in loc.*) of alteration by Rje looking to the appending of ch. xxiv.

But it is not enough to have established the main lines of division between J and E. Indications of duplication were observed in xxii. 2-4. and we have now to notice further the curious introduction of "the elders of Midian" in vv. 4 and 7, only to disappear entirely in the sequel. Again it is almost certain that in vs. 5, in place of the tautological "to the land of the children of his people" (*ammo*), we should read, with LXX. Sam. Syr. Vulg. and some Hebrew MSS., "to the land of the children of *Ammon.*" It is easy to see how, to avoid the contradiction with the preceding clause, Ammon should be changed to *ammo ;* but the reverse process would be inexplicable. Now if Ammon was the home of Balaam according to 5*ab*, this agrees with J in vv. 22ff., and if in this account "the elders of Midian" conspired with Balak, and Balaam went from among "the children of Ammon" with evil intent (vs. 32) against Israel, we may perhaps have a clew to that problematic source of the *priestly* Balaam-story. Two passages remain from which some further light can be drawn. The first, in Gen. xxxvi. 35 (J), merely informs us that this author knew of a branch of Midianite stock anciently established "*in the field of Moab ;*" cf. xxi. 20. The second, in Jos. xiii. 16-22, forms part of a chapter of singular complexity, but which certainly includes traces of J. In vv. 15ff. reference is made to "Sihon king of the Amorites, which reigned in Heshbon, whom Moses smote with the chiefs of Midian, Evi and Rekem and Zur and Hur and Reba, the princes of Sihon (!) that dwelt in the land. Balaam also the son of Beor, the soothsayer did the children of Israel slay with the sword among the rest of their slain." This singular mixture of data from JE and P seems hardly explicable if the stories of the war with Sihon and that with Midian were no more confused than in Nu. xxi. and xxxi. as we know them. It seems to point to some basis in J for P's story of Balaam and the war with Midian, connected perhaps with xxv. 1-5. More we can hardly suggest with caution.

We have now the necessary data for attempting a disentanglement in detail of the two sources in ch. xxii. J, like E, represents Israel as in peaceful relations with Moab, encamped in Moabite and Midianite territory, but having made conquest of Amorite territory between Moab and Ammon. Resident among the latter people is Balaam the son of Beor (cf. Gen. xxxvi. 32 "Bela the son of Beor") perhaps a Midianite, in any case a prophet (or soothsayer) of Yahweh (cf. vs. 18, "Yahweh my God ").[*] He becomes through avarice party to the conspiracy of Balak with the elders of Midian, but on the way to curse Israel is met by the angel of Yahweh who comes intending to slay Balaam, but suffers him to proceed on condition of uttering none but the message given him. It is apparent, however, from xxiv. 13 (J, as above indicated ; see also refs.)

---

[*] It is noteworthy in this connection that Moses according to this oldest document brings the elements of the great Yahwistic revival to Egypt with him "from the land of Midian" and from the household of "the priest of Midian, the same tribe who here, in conspiracy with Moab call a prophet of *Yahweh* to curse Israel. In E also Jethro becomes a convert to Yahwism, Ex. xviii. 11. Was Yahweh worshipped in Midian also ?

that Balaam, while consenting to go for money, had even at the beginning answered Balak's "messengers," "if Balak would give me his
house full of silver and gold I cannot go beyond the word of Yahweh."
The passage xxiv. 11–14 thus not only presupposes in J an account of
Balak's sending for Balaam, as in xxii. 2ff., but specifically requires us by
its back-references to assign xxii. 17f., which verbally correspond to it,
to J. In addition vv. 3b (see refs.), 4a, which introduce the "elders of
Midian" and give a somewhat different motive for Moab's hostility, 4b
(= vs. 2), parts of vv. 5 and 6 (?), (see refs., and note *in loc.*) 7ab, and vs.
39, which changes the geographical location after the most favorable
position, from E's point of view, has already been reached in vs. 36, may
all be assigned to J.

With the extrication of these fragments there remains a consistent
and uniform narrative of E. Balaam, an incorruptible and obedient
prophet of Yahweh, from Pethor on the Euphrates, who goes to Balak
by express divine command, stands with him on the extreme northern
boundary of Moab (vs. 36) whence they ascend to a peak overlooking
part of Israel's camp; there Balaam, after sacrifice, pronounces two blessings.

The minor touches of the redaction will be discussed in the notes.

————————

2   (E) And Balak the son of Zippor * saw all that Israel
3   had ²done to the Amorites. And Moab was sore afraid of
      (J) the people, because they were many : **and Moab ³was**
4   **distressed because of the children of Israel. And
      Moab said unto the elders of Midian, Now shall this
      multitude lick up all that is round about us, as the ox
      licketh up the grass of the field. And Balak, the son
      of Zippor was king of Moab at that time. [. . . .]**
5   (E) And he sent messengers unto Balaam, the son of Beor,
      (J) to ⁴Pethor, which is by the River, **to the land of the**
      (E) **children of his people,** [. . .] † to call him, saying,
      Behold, there is a people come out from Egypt : behold,

²xx. 24ff.   ³Ex. 1 : 12.   ⁴23 : 7.

* Unless Balak had been previously mentioned as king of Moab, which is
quite probable (cf. Dt. ii. 9, 29 and Jud. xi. 17), we should supply here "king
of Moab" as in vs. 10.

† Read " children of Ammon." See Analysis.

⁵they cover the face of the earth, and ⁶they abide over
against me : come now therefore, I pray thee, curse me this 6
people ; for they are too mighty for me : peradventure I
shall prevail, that we may smite them, and that I may drive
them out of the land : for I know that he whom thou bless-
(J) est is blessed, and he whom thou cursest is cursed. * **And 7
the elders of Moab and the elders of Midian departed 7
with the rewards of ⁷divination in their hand : [. . .]**
(E) and they came unto Balaam, and spake unto him the
words of Balak.   And he said unto them, Lodge here this 8
night, and I will bring you word again, as Yahweh shall
speak unto me : and the princes of Moab abode with Balaam.
And ⁸God came unto Balaam, and said, What men are these 9
with thee ?   And Balaam said unto God, ⁹Balak the son of 10
Zippor, king of Moab, hath sent unto me, [saying,] Behold, 11
the people that is come out of Egypt, it covereth the face of
the earth : now, come curse me them ; peradventure I shall
be able to fight against them, and shall drive them out.
And God said unto Balaam, Thou shalt not go with them ; 12
thou shalt not curse the people : for they are blessed.   And 13
Balaam rose up in the morning, and said unto the princes of
Balak, Get you into your land : for Yahweh ¹⁰refuseth to
give me leave to go with you.   And the princes of Moab 14
rose up, and they went unto Balak, and said, Balaam refuseth
to come with us.   And Balak sent yet again princes, more, 15
and more honorable than they.   And they came to Balaam, 16
and said to him, Thus saith Balak the son of Zippor, Let
nothing, I pray thee, hinder thee from coming unto me
**(J) [. . .] for ¹¹I will promote thee unto very great 17
honor, and whatsoever thou sayest unto me I will
do : come therefore, I pray thee, curse me this people.   And Balaam answered and said unto the ser-** 18

⁵Ex. 10 : 5, 15.   ⁶Gen. 25 : 18.   ⁷Gen. 44 : 5.   ⁸Gen. 20 : 3 : 31 : 24.   ⁹Vv. 2, 5f.   ¹⁰Ex. 3 : 19 : Nu. 20 : 21 : 21 : 23.   ¹¹(Vs. 37) : 24 : 11.

* The message of Balak in vv. 5f. is perhaps expanded by means of material taken from J (see refs.) ; the style seems redundant and in vs. 11 the report is simpler.

vants of Balak, If Balak would give me his house full
of silver and gold, I cannot ¹²go beyond the word of
19 (E) Yahweh my God, to do less or more. Now therefore, I pray you, tarry ye also here this night, that I may
20 know what Yahweh will speak unto me more. ¹³And God
came unto Balaam at night, and said unto him, If the men
be come to call thee, rise up, ¹⁴go with them ; but only the
21 word which I speak unto thee, that shalt thou do. And
Balaam rose up in the morning, ¹⁵and saddled his ass,
22 (J) and went with the princes of Moab. And God's *anger
was kindled because he went : and ¹⁶the angel of Yahweh placed himself in the way for an adversary
against him. Now he was riding upon his ass, and
23 his two servants were with him. And the ass saw
the angel of Yahweh standing in the way, ¹⁷with his
sword drawn in his hand : and the ass turned aside
out of the way, and went into the field : and Balaam
24 smote the ass, to turn her into the way. Then the
angel of Yahweh stood in a hollow way between the
vineyards, a fence being on this side, and a fence on
25 that side. And the ass saw the angel of Yahweh, and
she thrust herself unto the wall, and crushed Balaam's foot against the wall : and he smote her again.
26 And the angel of Yahweh went further, and stood in
a narrow place, where was no way to turn either to
27 the right hand or to the left. And the ass saw the
angel of Yahweh, and she lay down under Balaam :
and Balaam's anger was kindled, and he smote the
28 ass with his staff. And Yahweh opened the mouth
of the ass, and ¹⁸she said unto Balaam, What have I
done unto thee, that thou hast smitten me these
29 three times? And Balaam said unto the ass, Because thou hast mocked me. I would there were a
30 sword in my hand, for now I had killed thee. And

the ass said unto Balaam, Am not I thine ass, upon which thou hast ridden all thy life long unto this day? was I ever wont to do so unto thee? And he said, Nay. Then Yahweh [19]opened the eyes of Ba- [31] laam, and he saw the angel of Yahweh standing in the way, with his sword drawn in his hand: and [20]he bowed his head and fell upon his face. And the [32] angel of Yahweh said unto him, Wherefore hast thou smitten thine ass these three times? behold, I am come forth for an adversary, because thy way is perverse before me; and the [21]ass saw me, and turned [33] aside before me these three times: [22]unless she had turned aside from me, surely now I had even slain thee, and saved her alive. And Balaam said unto the [34] angel of Yahweh, I have sinned; for I knew not that thou stoodest in the way against me: now therefore, if it [23]displease thee, I will get me back again. And the angel of Yahweh said unto Balaam, Go [35] (Rje) (J) with the men: but only the word that I shall speak unto thee, that thou shalt speak. So Balaam (E) went with the princes of Balak.* And when Balak [36] heard that Balaam was come, he went out to meet him, [24]unto the City of Moab, which is on the border of Arnon, which is in the utmost part of the border. And Balak said [37] unto Balaam, Did I not earnestly send unto thee to call thee? wherefore camest thou not unto me? [25]am I not (E) able indeed to promote thee to honor? † And Balaam said [38] unto Balak, Lo, I am come unto thee: have I now any power at all to speak anything? [26]the word that God putteth

---

* [19]Gen. 3:7 (cf. 21a); ch. 24:3. [20]Gen. 24:26, 48; 43:28; Ex. 4:31 etc. [21]Ex. 3; Gen. 16:13; 50:32. [22]Gen. 12:4; 41:13; 14:40. [23]11:10. [24]22:36; 21:13. [25]22:10; 24:11. [26]23:5, 12. [27]22:40.

* Vs. 35 resumes vv. 20f. and seems to have been worked over in the clauses indicated, since "the men" and "the princes of Balak" have no place in the preceding context; but Wellhausen's conjecture of a return of Balaam to his own country is improbable.

† The clause 37c must either be from Rje or else indicates the presence of J material in this connection; see refs.

39 (J) in my mouth, that shall I speak. [. . .] **And Balaam went with Balak, and they came unto Kiriath-hu-**
40 (E) **zoth.** And Balak sacrificed oxen and sheep, and sent
41 to Balaam, and to the princes that were with him. And it came to pass in the morning, that Balak took Balaam, and brought him up into the high places of Baal, and he saw
23 from thence the utmost part of the people. And Balaam said unto Balak, Build me here seven altars, and prepare me
2 here seven bullocks and seven rams. And Balak did as
(**E**) Balaam had spoken : and Balak and Balaam offered
3 on every altar a bullock and a ram. And Balaam said unto Balak, Stand by thy burnt offering, and I will go : perad-venture Yahweh will come to meet me : and whatsoever he sheweth me I will tell thee. And he went to a bare height.
4 [1]And God met Balaam—and he said unto him, I have pre-pared the seven altars, and I have offered up a bullock and
5 (**E**) a ram on every altar.—* And Yahweh [2]put a word in Balaam's mouth, and said, Return unto Balak, and thus
6 thou shalt speak. And he returned unto him, and, lo, he stood by his burnt offering, he, and all the princes of Moab
7 And he took up his parable, and said,

>From [3]Aram hath Balak brought me,
The king of Moab from the mountains of the **East** :
Come, curse me Jacob,
And come, defy Israel.

8 How shall I curse, whom God hath not cursed ?
And how shall I defy, whom Yahweh hath not defied ?

9 For [4]from the top of the rocks I see him,

[1]Vs. 16. [2]22 : 38. [3]22 : 5.

* The displacement of vs. 4 is very obvious. Where it now stands it is in the highest degree unsuitable. It is hard to see on the other hand how it could have been removed from after vs. 2, where it really belongs. Its resto-ration shows " Balak and Balaam " in vs. 2b to be an incorrect supplying of the subject of the verb, which is simply " he." The same phenomenon of a subject wrongly supplied is revealed in vs. 5a, where we have simply to strike out " Yahweh " in .the same way as " Balak and Balaam " in vs. 2. The use of the divine names will then be found to correspond to the practise described above. (Analysis, p. 219).

And from the hills I behold him :
Lo, it is a people that dwell alone,
And shall not be reckoned among the nations.
Who can count the dust of Jacob,   10
Or number the fourth part of Israel ?
Let me die the death of the righteous,
And let my last end be like his !

And Balak said unto Balaam, What hast thou done unto 11
me ? I took thee to curse mine enemies, and, behold, thou
hast blessed them altogether. [5]And he answered and said, 12
Must I not take heed to speak that which Yahweh putteth
in my mouth ? And Balak said unto him, Come, I pray 13
thee, with me unto another place, from which thou mayest
(Rje) see them : thou shalt see but the utmost part of them, and shalt
not see them all : * and curse me them from thence. And he 14
took him into the field of Zophim, to [6]the top of Pisgah, and
built seven altars, and offered up a bullock and a ram on
every altar. And he said unto Balak, Stand here by thy 15
burnt offering, while I meet [Yahweh] yonder. [7]And 16
(E) Yahweh † met Balaam, and put a word in his

---

[5]22 : 38 ; cf. 24 : 12f. [6]Cf. vs. 28 and 21 : 20. [7]Vs. 5.

---

* The middle clause of vs. 13 is clearly due to Rje, as it is in irreconcilable
contradiction with the context. Balak's first thought is (xxii. 41) that if
Balaam sees only "the utmost part of Israel" his task will be lighter. It is
because this proves unsuccessful that he leads him, in vs. 13, to a more commanding position, "the field of the watchers (*Zophim*) on the top of Pisgah,"
vs. 14, "a place from whence he might see them all." So the original. But
Rje wishes to incorporate also the two Balaam oracles of J, the scene of
which (xxiii. 28 ; xxiv. 1 ; cf. xxi. 20) is "the top of Pisgah that looketh down
upon Jeshimon" (the desert north-east shore of the Dead Sea), and as a
change of place is necessary, after the example of vs. 13, in vs. 28 also, two
alterations become necessary : *a*, Pisgah in vs. 28 must be altered (cf. xxi. 20)
to Peor, a name not elsewhere employed of the peak, in order not to conflict
with vs. 14, which really represents identically the same spot as vs. 28 ; *b*, the
sight of the whole camp of Israel must be reserved for the third and final
point of outlook. Hence the contradictory addition in vs. 13.

† The LXX have "God" ; (cf. vs. 4) but the variations of the versions and
texts seem to be largely affected in chh. xxiiff. by an uncertainty as to whether

mouth, and said, Return unto Balak, and thus shalt thou
17 speak. And he came to him, and lo, he stood by his burnt
offering, and the princes of Moab with him. And Balak
18 said unto him, What hath Yahweh spoken? And he took
up his parable, and said,

Rise up, Balak, and hear ;
Harken unto me, thou son of Zippor :
19 God is not a man, that he should lie ;
*Neither the son of man, that he should repent :
Hath he said, and shall he not do it ?
Or hath he spoken, and shall he not make it good ?
20 Behold, I have received [commandment] to bless :
And he * hath blessed, and I cannot reverse it.
21 He hath not beheld iniquity in Jacob,
Neither hath he seen perverseness in Israel :
Yahweh his God is with him,
⁹And the shout of a king is among them.
22 **(J)—God bringeth them forth out of Egypt ;**
He hath as it were the strength of the wild-ox.
23 **Surely there is no enchantment with Jacob.**
Neither is there any ¹⁰divination with Israel :
Now shall it be said of Jacob and of Israel,
What hath God wrought !—†

*Cf. Gen. 6:6f.; Ex. 22:14.   ⁸24:8; Dt. 23:17.   ¹⁰22:7; Gen. 30:27; 44:5.

Yahweh in the mouth of Balak and Balaam was suitable or not. Hence great
reliance cannot be placed upon this criterion.

* Sam. and LXX have first person, and in 21a, "is not seen."

† Vs. 23 is rejected by Dillmann and others on account of its interruption of
the connection. It would seem better to regard both 22 and 23 as derived
from xxiv. 8 (J), removed perhaps on account of xxiv. 1 in its present form.
Certainly there is no allusion whatever to enchantment or divination in ch.
xxiii. In E the representation of Balaam throughout is of a sincere and true
prophet of Yahweh, who refuses to trifle with the divine word, but obeys
implicitly. The contrasted representation of a mercenary sorcerer compelled
(xxii. 35) against his will to bless, is confined to J. The use of *Elohim* on the
other hand is inconclusive, as the *poem* employs Yahweh and Elohim inter-
changeably. Vs. 22 is duplicated in xxiv. 8, but seems to be in more original
form there (cf. "them," vs. 22, with vs. 21, and with "him," xxiv. 8, and "he,"

(**E**) Behold, the people riseth up as a lioness,   24
And as a lion doth he lift himself up :
He shall not lie down until he eat of the prey,
And drink the blood of the slain.

And Balak said unto Balaam, Neither curse them at all, nor 25
bless them at all.   But Balaam answered and said unto 26
Balak, **"Told not I thee, saying, All that Yahweh speaketh,**
(**Rje**) that I must do? [. . .]   And Balak said unto Balaam, 27
Come now, I will take thee unto another place; peradventure it will please
(**J**) God that thou mayest curse me them from thence. **And Balak** 28
took Balaam unto ¹²the top of Peor, **that looketh**
(**Rje**) **down upon the desert.**   ¹³And Balaam said unto Balak, 29
Build me here seven altars, and prepare me here seven bullocks and seven
rams.   And Balak did as Balaam had said, and offered up a bullock and a
(**J**) ram on every altar.   **And when Balaam saw that it 24**
(**Rje**) **pleased Yahweh to bless Israel, he went not,** as
(**J**) at the other times, * **to meet with ¹enchantments, but he**
set his face toward the ²wilderness. And Balaam 2
lifted up his eyes, and he saw Israel dwelling accord-
ing to their tribes; and the spirit of God † came
upon him. And he took up his parable, and said, 3
   ³Balaam the son of Beor saith,
And the man whose eye was closed saith :

¹¹22 : 38.   ¹²Ct. vs. 14; Cf. 21 : 20.   ¹³Vv. 1f.   ¹22 : 27 ; 23 : 23.   ²21 : 20 : 23 :   ³Vs.
15 : ct. 23 : 7.

line succeeding).   The duplication may have been effected in process of transfer, or *may* be original with J and E.

   * **The hand of Rje** comes out very distinctly in the somewhat uneven joint
between chh. xxiii. and xxiv.   A consideration of xxiii. 27ff. will show the process of connection.   Vs. 27 repeats vs. 13 with touches from xxii. 6, but uses
"God," whereas Balak in vs. 17 says "Yahweh."   "Peor" for Pisgah is an
alteration referred to in the note on vs. 13.   Vv. 29f. repeat *verbatim* vv. 1f.
(cf. note on the original form of vs. 2) whereas E himself, when relating the
sacrifice the second time, vs. 14, abbreviates notably.   Finally the clause "as
at the other times," xxiv. 1, assumes a statement which does not exist in ch.
xxiii, and betrays itself thus as harmonistic, if indeed all xxiv. 1a be not from
Rje (Dillmann).

   † So consistently in J; but the expression Spirit of Yahweh is rare.   Even
P has "Spirit of God" (Ex. xxxi. 3; xxxv. 31).

4   He saith, which heareth the words of God, * [. . .]
      Which seeth the vision of the Almighty,
      Falling down, and having his eyes open:

5   How goodly are thy tents, O Jacob,
      Thy tabernacles, O Israel!

6   As † valleys are they spread forth,
      As gardens by the river side,
      As lign-aloes ⁵which Yahweh hath planted,
      As cedar trees beside the waters.

7   ⁵Water shall flow from his buckets,
      And his seed shall be in many waters,
      And his king shall be higher than ⁶Agag,
      And his kingdom shall be exalted.

8   ⁷God bringeth him forth out of Egypt;
      He hath as it were the strength of the wild-ox:
      He shall eat up the nations his adversaries,
      And shall break their bones in pieces,
      And smite [them] through with his arrows. ‡

9   ⁸He crouched, he lay down as a lion,
      And as a lioness; who shall rouse him up?
      ⁹Blessed be every one that blesseth thee,
      And cursed be every one that curseth thee.

10 And Balak's anger was kindled against Balaam,
and he smote his hands together: and Balak said
unto Balaam, I called thee to curse mine enemies, and,
(Rje) behold, thou hast altogether blessed them these
11 (J) three times. Therefore now flee thou to thy place:
¹⁰I thought to promote thee unto great honor; but,
12 lo, Yahweh § hath kept thee back from honor. And

---

⁴Gen. 2 : 8f.   ⁵Gen. 49 : 25.   ⁶I Sam. 15 : 8ff.   ⁷23 : 22   ⁸Gen. 49 : 9.   ⁹Gen. 27 : 29.   ¹⁰22 : 17, 37.

   * Supply from vs. 16 " And knoweth the knowledge of the Most High."
As in other J poems the divine appellations are multiplied.

   † In this and the succeeding line read *be*, " in," for *ke*, " as."

   ‡ Read with Dillmann *welochatzain yimchatz*, " and his oppressors will he
crush," or else translate " and shall trample upon his (their) arrows."

   § After xxii. 18 " Yahweh " in Balak's mouth is appropriate.

Balaam said unto Balak, [11]Spake I not also to thy
messengers which thou sentest unto me, saying, If 13
Balak would give me his house full of silver and gold,
I cannot go beyond the word of Yahweh, to do either
good or bad [12]of mine own mind; what Yahweh speak-
eth, that will I speak? And now, behold, I go unto 14
my people: come, [and] I will advertise thee what
this people shall do to thy people [13]in the latter days.
[14]And he took up his parable, and said, 15
　　Balaam the son of Beor saith,
　　And the man whose eye was closed saith:
　　He saith, which heareth the words of God, 16
　　And knoweth the knowledge of the Most High,
　　Which seeth the vision of the Almighty,
　　Falling down, and having his eyes open:
　　I see him, but not now: 17
　　I behold him, but not nigh:
　　There shall come forth a star out of Jacob,
　　And a [15]sceptre shall rise out of Israel,
　　[16]And shall smite through the corners of Moab,
　　And break down * all the sons of tumult.
　　And Edom shall be a possession, 18
　　Seir also shall be a possession, [which were] his ene-
　　　mies;
　　While Israel doeth valiantly.
　　And out of Jacob shall one have dominion, 19
　　And shall destroy the remnant from the city.

(Rd) And he looked on Amalek, and took up his parable, and said, 20
Amalek was the first of the nations;
But his latter end shall come to destruction.

And he looked on the [17]Kenite, and took up his parable, and said, 21
[18] Strong is thy dwelling place,

[11]22:17f. [12]16:28. [13]Gen. 4):1. [14]Vv. 3f. [15]Gen. 49: 10; ch. 21:18. [16]Jer. 48:45.
[17]Jud. 1:16; 4:11. [18]Gen. 49:24.

* Read with Sam. and Jer. xlviii. 45, by a minute change of text, "the skull
of," parallel to corners (*sc.* of the head, *i. e.* "temples") of preceding line (so
Dillmann, Ewald *et. al.*).

And thy nest is set in the rock.

22   Nevertheless Kain shall be wasted,

Until [19]Asshur shall carry thee away captive.

23   And he took up his parable, and said,

Alas, who shall live when God doeth this ?

24   But ships [shall come] from the coast of Kittim,

And they shall afflict Asshur, and shall afflict Eber,

And he also shall come to destruction.

25   (J) [20]And Balaam rose up, and went and returned to his place: and Balak also went his way.*

⊸ — ·

3. Chh. xxv. ; xxvii. ; xxxiif. THE INHERITANCE OF THE TRIBES BEYOND JORDAN.

ANALYSIS.

At Shittim, on the east shore of Jordan, Israel falls into idolatry and is punished, xxv. 1–5. Phinehas, son of Eleazar, receives the covenant of the priesthood because of his zeal in slaying one who had taken to wife a Midianite woman; 6–15. Moses receives commandment to ascend mount Abarim and die there. Upon his entreaty Yahweh directs the appointment of Joshua as his successor ; 12–23. War is declared against Midian because they had beguiled Israel into uncleanness. Under Joshua's command a force of 12,000 Israelites exterminate Midian without the loss of a man, and return to Moses with enormous booty ; ch. xxxi. The tribes of Gad and Reuben appeal to Moses for permission to settle in the conquered lands beyond Jordan. Permission

---

[19]II Kings. 15:29. [20]Ct. 31:8; Jos. 13:22.

---

* From vs. 19 on the poem has been supplemented by one or more later hands. Vv. 23f., which differ from the other oracles in having no special object (LXX supply " he looked on Og "), have been added subsequently to the union of J and E, to make the group of *seven* oracles complete. Vv. (19) 20–22 may be older, but contemplate a later period than that of brilliant triumph represented in 17f. (certainly the Davidic) ; a period in which the heavy hand of Assyria has been felt. Even Greek interference from Cyprus is anticipated in vs. 24. Vv. (19) 20ff. go beyond the intention of the original writer, which confined itself, vs. 14, to what Israel should do to Moab and Edom.

is given them on condition of their participating first with the other tribes in the conquest of Canaan. To this they consent, and receive Gilead, in whose cities their wives, children and possessions are bestowed until their return. List of cities and towns occupied in Gilead, ch. xxxii. An itinerary of Israel's wanderings in the desert, xxxiii. 1-49.

The last chapters of Numbers are in unmistakable disorder. The death of Moses, which already at the close of ch. xxvii. is immediately impending, the appointment of Joshua as his successor being expressly related as the final act of Moses preliminary to his death, is obviously entirely out of place ; since the war with Midian, the distribution of the inheritances in Gilead, the appointment of the trans-Jordanic cities of refuge, not to mention the entire Deuteronomic legislation, besides several other important transactions, are inserted before Dt. xxxiv., where Moses obeys the command of xxvii. 12ff. and his death actually takes place. . The command, and the charge to Joshua have of course to be related over again after so long an interval, and the paragraph is accordingly repeated in Dt. xxxii. 48ff. The elements of P² found in chh. xxxiiff. prove that the displacement of ch. xxvii. is not merely due to the insertion of material foreign to this document, but the ch. has been taken from a position after xxxiv., to which its opening paragraph, relating to the inheritance of the daughters of Zelophehad, forms the natural sequel, and has been inserted at this earlier point, perhaps for the sake of bringing in Joshua's installation as leader (cf. vv. 18-23) before the story of the war with Midian (P³), in which he acts as chief, and into closer connection with the directions for distributing the inheritances, which he is to carry out (cf. xxxii. 28).

Again, the two parts of ch. xxv. arbitrarily cemented together at vv. 5-6 are manifestly mismated. The story of Israel's idolatry at the *Moabite* shrine of Beth-peor has not the slightest real connection with the story of miscegenation with *Midianite* women ; (cf. Ex. xxxiv. 16) ; neither can the " plague," which according to vs. 8f. has been raging in Israel on account of the people's wrong-doing, be identified by any stretch of imagination with the punishment inflicted in vv. 4f. On the contrary, xxxi. 16 points to a story of P², now obliterated, in which the connection with Midianitish women at Beth-peor and consequent plague was ascribed to the counsel of Balaam. Accordingly it is Midian and not Moab on whom the Israelites are directed to avenge themselves in vv. 16-18a. Vs. 18b is the work of the interpolator of ch. xxxi. (see note *in loc.*) ; but it is apparent from the reference of P² in xxxii. 4, that this extravagant *midrash* only takes the place of an original account by P² of the conquest of the trans-Jordanic territory from *Midian*. On account of this connection with chh. xxxii., and which Rp seems to follow, our third subdivision is made to include ch. xxv., though the JE elements of the chapter have very likely nothing to do with the inheritance of the tribes beyond Jordan. J's may even possibly be connected with the Balaam episode. This brief paragraph, which the subject, style and language as well as the reference in Dt. iv. 3 prove to belong in JE, seems to be duplicate (see note on vs. 4) but is difficult to analyze. From the location (cf. Jos. ii. 1; iii. 1, E; ct. xxi. 20, J) vs. 1a would seem to be from E; but E's conception of the relation of Moab to Israel is one of non-intercourse, and Dt. xxiii. 5ff. and Jos. xxiv. 9 make no allusion to such plots. His idea of the danger to Israel appears in Jud. and Sam. especially as temptation to idolatry pure and simple. In J, "whoredom," vs. 1b; Ex. xxxiv. 15, is part of the danger. Now vs. 3 manifestly stands connected with vs. 5, which with any translation is hard to reconcile with vs. 4, and the "judges" of Israel (vs. 5) are one of the great features of E (cf. Ex. xviii.; Num. xi. 16ff. and Jud. *passim*). The most probable conclusion is that we have here fragments of both J and E, the former possibly connected with the curious reference to "elders of Midian" in J's Balaam story, and the remarkable difference in the priestly representation of the character of Balaam.

The character of ch. xxxi. is self-evident, and we may therefore spare ourselves the disagreeable task of analyzing it in detail. The chapter depends throughout on P², but is of considerably later origin, as appears from the style and language, the elaborate specification of the numbers and amount of spoil, cf. Ex. xxxviii. 24ff (P³), and the independent appearance of the high priest, vv. 21ff., as developer and expounder of Mosaic law. Driver appropriately reiterates the characterization of Dillmann: "Though cast into narrative form, the ch. has really a legislative object, *viz.* to prescribe a principle for the distribution of booty taken in war [cf. 1 Sam. xxx. 18-25]. Of the place, circumstances, and other details of the war we learn nothing; we are told only the issue, how, *viz.*, 12,000 Israelite warriors, without losing a man (vs. 49), slew all the males and married women of Midian, took captive 32,000 virgins, and brought back 800,000 head of cattle, besides other booty. In the high figures, and absence of specific details, the narrative resembles the descriptions of wars in the Chronicles or in Jud. xx." The hand of Rp is discernible in vs. 2b and 16.

Ch. xxxii. is made extremely difficult of analysis by the incoming of Rd, who seems to have rewritten vv. 8-15 and perhaps made other alterations in this chapter. It is in fact intimately connected with Jos. xxii., a narrative derived in its present form almost wholly from the hand of Rd. Yet it is apparent from the discrepancies and incongruities of ch. xxxii. that more than one writer is here represented. The verses 39, 41f., which relate the conquest of parts of Gilead by Machir, Jair and Nobah (Manassites), are in the first place, quite obviously incompatible with the rest of the chapter, in which the territory is already conquered and has just been bestowed upon Gad and Reuben. The matter is not mended by the belated authorization by Moses introduced in vs. 40, which is in contradiction with both P and JE, and is purely harmonistic (see note *in loc*). Similarly the unexpected introduction of " the half-tribe of Manasseh " in vs. 33 as co-recipients of the inheritance with Gad and Reuben, is, to be sure, the persistent representation of P elsewhere, but agrees neither with the earlier part of the ch., nor with vv. 39ff., since Machir, according to the priestly genealogies is the *only* son of Manasseh, and thus the whole tribe and not one half, would be trans-Jordanic. Again vv. 34ff. in giving the list of cities of the territory in question come just near enough to the list of vs. 3 to show that the same are meant, but use such differences in the names as to show that the two lists cannot possibly be by the same hand. Again, after Moses and the Gadites and Reubenites have already been discussing for some time the question of the inheritance, we are told in vs. 16 that they approached Moses, preferring the same request which had been the subject of debate from the beginning. Vv. 24-27 thereupon repeat also the answer of Moses which had already been given in vv. 20-23. Still a third version of the same request and conditional permission is given in 18f., 28-32. There is here undeniable redundancy and duplication, with a considerable amount of contrast in the representation and the geographical and historical data. The materials however have been so closely interwoven and retouched as to make a definite and positive analysis impossible. Great assistance, however, is rendered in determining the form of the earlier sources by the subsequent references in JE, and especially by the detailed recapitulation in Dt. iii. 12-22. Dt. xxxiii. 20f. (J) contains a reference to the loyalty of Gad in going over Jordan with the other tribes after having " received for himself the portion of a first born son," and vs. 5 presents unmistakable linguistic marks of J. It is therefore certain that the substance of vv. 1-33 was related here by J. From xxxiv. 14f.; Jos. xiii. 15ff. it is also demonstrable with still greater positiveness that P² had here a similar narrative. The presence of this element in the text as well as that of J is made manifest by the frequent duplications, 1b = 3, 1 = 4, 2 = 16, 25-27 = 31f., and the presence of the characteristic style and prepossessions of the priestly writer (cf. *e.g.* vv. 2b, 4, 28).

Far more difficult is it to decide whether E has any share in this chapter. It is indeed certain that he related the conquest and possession of the country east of Jordan (cf. Jos. xxiv. 8 with the narrative of the conquest *and occupation* by Israel in Num. xxi.) ; but whether he anywhere gave full account of the distribution of the land among the individual tribes is doubtful (yet cf. Jos. xix. 49f.). Still the representation which he gives of the conquest of Canaan by the united action of all Israel seems to presuppose some mention of how Gad and Reuben "executed the justice of Yahweh" when they "came with the heads of the people" ; and hence also a relation of the disposition made meanwhile of their already conquered inheritance. This probability of mention by E is borne out by the phenomena of ch. xxxii., which point to a double source even after the removal of P. Thus the phrase employed to denote "non-combatants" in vv. 16f. and 24 is that elsewhere employed by E (see refs.). On the contrary we find the fuller expression in vs. 26 "our little ones, *our wives*, our flocks," etc. This peculiarity of language coincides with the remarkable new beginning in vs. 16, and with the fact that the verses in question can be separated from the context without affecting it, and when so separated present a parallel account with a somewhat altered point of view. Here in fact Gad and Reuben appear as proposing *from the outset* to accompany Israel, upon which Moses readily accedes to their request ; whereas in vs. 5, which most unmistakably possesses the linguistic marks of J, the request is made in express terms to be allowed to remain behind. "Bring us not over Jordan," and is met by Moses with severe rebuke. The most striking characteristic which vv. 16f. and 24 possess in common is the proposal to "build cities and sheep-folds," and this proposal is carried out in vv. 33*-38 (cf. vs. 36). Nowhere else is this expression "cities and sheep-folds" employed ; hence there can be no doubt that vv. 33*-38 should be connected with 16f. and 24. Moreover vs. 33, (which, however, is for the most part, if not wholly, redactional) makes express reference to E's narrative of the conquest of this territory "from Sihon king of the Amorites" in ch. xxi. Herewith then we have the element of E practically complete. We miss only the occasion for the tribes' preferment of their request, which from the allusion in vs. 16 to the purpose of the "sheep-folds" must have been that related in vv. 1 and 4. It is perhaps worth noting in this connection that the same verse which uses a different expression from that of vv. 16f. and 24 for "non-combatants," uses also a different geographical description of the territory in question from vs. 1b (and 33). In the latter it is "the land of Gilead and the land of Jazer" (vs. 33, "the kingdom of Sihon king of the Amorites ") ; in the former it is the district containing "the cities of Gilead," referring doubtless to those

enumerated in vs. 3, where Jazer appears simply as one. It appears to
be in fact the usage of J (cf. Bud. *Urg.* p. 344) to speak of the trans-
Jordanic region in general as Gilead, and the cis-Jordanic as Canaan,
and we have already observed the incompatibility of the list in vs. 3 with
vv. 34ff. Accordingly we have manifold reasons for connecting vs. 3
with 25ff., and for assigning its parallel, 1b, 2a, to E.

Another peculiarity of diction used by some in determining the
priestly element of ch. xxxii. is, the order of age, "children of Reuben
and children of Gad," in vs. 1, for which we have in the rest of the ch.
the order of importance, Gad, Reuben.   The Sam., however, has
throughout Reuben, Gad, and LXX. varies.   Still it is easy by means of
the well-known stylistic peculiarities of P² to extricate the story of this
author in vv. 1a, 3b, 18f., 28–30.

The remainder has already been in part demonstrated to be J's and
constitutes the principal narrative; vv. 39-42, however, belong at a later
point in this document (see note *in loc.*); the story has also been redac-
tionally expanded and embellished in vv. 8-15, 20-23, and 31f. (see note
in loc.)

Ch. xxxiii. is a late itinerary made up of material from all the sources,
and apparently aims to produce a total of 40 stations, corresponding to
the 40 years of wandering.   It follows the style and phraseology of P to
some extent but displays its redactional character by such meaningless
collocation of borrowed material as vv. 39ff. (cf. xx. 22; xxi. 11.)

(E) (J) And Israel abode in ¹Shittim, **and the people 25
began to commit ²whoredom with the daughters of
Moab: for they called the people unto the sacrifices** 2
**of their gods; and the people did eat, and bowed
(E) down to their gods.** ²And Israel joined himself unto 3
Baal-peor: and the anger of Yahweh was kindled against
(J) Israel. **And Yahweh said unto Moses, Take all** 4
the chiefs of the people, and hang them up * unto

¹Jos. 2:1; 3:1; Ex. 34:15. ²Dt. 4:3; Hos. 9:10.

* If the translation "hang them up" is retained, we must with Dillmann
regard vs. 4 as a doublet of 5, and 3a as parallel to vs. 1.   But the translation
is uncertain.   Kautzsch renders doubtfully "set them [*i. e.* the guilty ones]

Yahweh before the sun that the fierce anger of Yah-
5 **(E) weh may turn away from Israel. [. . .]** And
Moses said unto the judges of Israel, [4]Slay ye every one his
men that have joined themselves unto Baal-peor. [. . .]

6 **(P)** *And, behold, one of the children of Israel came and brought*
unto his brethren a Midianitish woman in the sight of Moses, and
in the sight of [5]*all the congregation of the children of Israel,*
7 *while they were weeping at the door of the tent of meeting. And*
when [6]*Phinehas, the son of Eleazar, the son of Aaron the priest,*
saw it, he rose up from the midst of the congregation, and took a
8 *spear in his hand ; and he went after the man of Israel into the*
pavilion, and thrust both of them through, the man of Israel, and
the woman through her belly. [7]*So the plague was stayed from the*
9 *children of Israel. And those that died by the plague were*
twenty and four thousand.

10–11　*And Yahweh spake unto Moses, saying, Phinehas, the son of*
Eleazar, the son of Aaron the priest, hath turned my wrath away
from the children of Israel, in that he was jealous with my jeal-
ousy among them, so that I consumed not the children of Israel in
12 *my jealousy. Wherefore say,* [8]*Behold, I give unto him my cove-*
13 *nant of peace : and it shall be unto him, and to his seed after him,*
the covenant of an everlasting priesthood ; because he was jealous
for his God, and made an atonement for the children of Israel.
14 *Now the name of the man of Israel that was slain, who was*
slain with the Midianitish woman, was Zimri, the son of Salu, a
15 [9]*prince of a fathers' house among the Simeonites. And the name*
of the Midianitish woman that was slain was Cozbi, the daughter
of Zur ; he was head of the people of a fathers' house in Midian.
16　*And Yahweh spake unto Moses, saying, Vex the Midianites,*
17 *and smite them : for they vex you with their wiles, wherewith*
18 **(Rp)** *they have beguiled you in the matter of Peor, and in the matter of*

---

[1]Ex. 32 : 29.　[5]Ex. 16 : 1 and refs.　[6]Jos. 22 : 14ff.　[7]16 : 46-48.　[8]Gen. 9 : 8ff. ; 17 : 1ff.
[9]1 : 16 etc.

forth unto Yahweh before the sun." This would be compatible with unity of
the narrative ; nevertheless the duplication seems to be too great to permit us
to regard vv. 1–5 as a unit.

Cozbi, the daughter of the prince of Midian, their sister, which was slain on the day of the plague in the matter of Peor.*

*   *   *   *   *   *   *   *   *   *

(P)—[1]*And Yahweh said unto Moses, Get thee up into this* **27**—12 *mountain of Abarim, and behold the land which I have given unto the children of Israel. And when thou hast seen it, thou also shalt* 13 *be gathered unto thy people,* [2]*as Aaron thy brother was gathered: because* [3]*ye rebelled against my word in the wilderness of Zin,* 14 *in the strife of the congregation, to sanctify me at the waters before their eyes. (These are the waters of Meribah of Kadesh in the wilderness of Zin.)* [4]*And Moses spake unto Yahweh, saying,* 15 *Let Yahweh,* [5]*the God of the spirits of all flesh, appoint a man* 16 *over the congregation, which may go out before them, and which* 17 *may come in before them, and which may lead them out, and which may bring them in ; that the congregation of Yahweh be not as sheep which have no shepherd. And Yahweh said unto Moses,* 18 **Take thee Joshua the son of Nun, a man in whom is the spirit, and lay thine hand upon him ;** *and set him before Eleazar the priest,* 19 *and before all the congregation ; and* [6]*give him a charge in their sight. And thou shalt put of thine honor upon him, that all the* 20 *congregation of the children of Israel may obey. And he shall* 21 *stand before Eleazar the priest, who shall inquire for him by the judgment of the Urim before Yahweh : at his word shall they go out, and at his word they shall come in, both he, and all the children of Israel with him, even all the congregation. And Moses* 22 *did as Yahweh commanded him : and he took Joshua, and set him before Eleazar the priest, and before all the congregation : and he* 23 *laid his hands upon him, and gave him a charge, as Yahweh spake by the hand of Moses.*——†

*   *   *   *   *   *   *

[1]Dt. 32 : 48ff. [2]20 : 22-29. [3]20 : 12f. [4]Cf. Dt. 31 : 1-8, 14ff. [5]16 : 22. [6]Cf. Dt. 31 : 14, 23.

* The latter part of vs. 18 is a clumsy addition, intended to make room for ch. xxxi.; cf. xxxi. 16. The redactional character of the addition appears plainly in the attempt to connect " the matter of Peor, and the matter of Cozbi," which really have no connection. (see Analysis.)

† The duplication of vv. 12-14 in Dt. xxxii. 48ff. is a remarkable phenome-

32 **(P)** *Now the children of Reuben and the children of Gad had*
(E) *a very great* [. . .] multitude* *of cattle:* and when
they saw the land of [1]Jazer, and the land of Gilead, that, be-
2 hold, the place was a place for cattle; the children of Gad
(P) and the children of Reuben *[2]came and spake unto Moses,*
and to Eleazar the priest, and unto the princes of the congregation,
3 **(J)** *saying,* [. . .]**Ataroth, and Dibon, and Jazer, and**
Nimrah, and [3]Heshbon, and Elealeh, and Sebam, and
4 **(P) Nebo, and Beon,** *the land which Yahweh [4]smote before*
the congregation of Israel, is a land for cattle, and thy servants
5 **(J)** *have cattle.* **[5]And they said, [6]If we have found grace**
in thy sight, let this land be given unto thy servants
6 **for a possession; [6]bring us not over Jordan. And**
Moses said unto the children of Gad and to the chil-
7 **dren of Reuben, Shall your brethren go to the war,**

---

[1]21 : 24, 32. [2]27 : 2 etc. [3]Cf. vv. 34ff. [4]Ch. 31. [5]Ex. 33 : 12ff. and refs [6]Dt. 3, : 21.

non which cannot be accounted for on the supposition of intentional repetition
by I[2]. In one passage or the other we have the work of Rp, and on some
accounts (see Dillmann's criticism of the language, *Num., in loc.*) Dt. xxxii.
48ff. appears more original. From the immense discrepancy in time between the
giving of the command, vv. 12ff., and its fulfilment, Dt. xxxiv., it is obvious
that the passage here is quite premature; so much so that it is incredible that
a redactor having the elements of our Pentateuch before him should have *carried back* this command from its proper position immediately before Dt. xxxiv.
to the present. On the contrary the insertion of the book of Deuteronomy
necessitated the *repetition* of this passage after so long an interval; thus Dt.
xxxii. 48–52 finds itself most naturally and easily in the category of Dt. i. 3–5;
iv. 41–43, which are also priestly in style and references, but have been inserted
by Rp for the purpose of adjusting Deuteronomy to a place in the Pentateuch
story. In fact xxxii. 48ff. is accommodated to Deuteronomy, so that an impartial
examination will by no means show the linguistic argument conclusive in its
favor. On the other hand Nu. xxvii. has indeed been brought to an earlier
than its true position, doubtless in order that Joshua's installation may precede
his conduct of the war with Midian (P[s]) and the directions for distribution of
inheritances, but this might take place at any time after the insertion of Dt.
xxxii. 48–52.

* Literally, " And much cattle belonged to the children of Reuben and to the
children of Gad, very numerous "; the redundancy probably arises from duplication of source.

(Rd) and shall ye sit here? *And wherefore discourage ye the heart of the children of Israel from going over into the land which Yahweh hath given them? Thus did your fathers, when I sent them from* Kadesh- 8 *barnea to see the land. For when they went up unto the valley of Eshcol, and* 9 *saw the land, they discouraged the heart of the children of Israel, that they should not go into the land which Yahweh had given them.* And Yahweh's 10 *anger was kindled in that day, and he sware, saying, Surely none of the men* 11 *that came up out of Egypt, from twenty years old and upward, shall see the land which I sware unto Abraham, unto Isaac, and unto Jacob; because they have not wholly followed me: save Caleb the son of Jephunneh the Kenizzite,* 12 *and Joshua the son of Nun: because they have wholly followed Yahweh.* And Yahweh's anger was kindled against Israel, and he made them wan- 13 *der to and fro in the wilderness forty years, until all the generation, that had done evil in the sight of Yahweh, was consumed. And, behold, ye are risen* 14 *up in your fathers' stead, an increase of sinful men, to augment yet the fierce anger of Yahweh toward Israel.* For if ye turn away from after him, he 15 *will yet again leave them in the wilderness; and ye shall destroy all this peo-*

(E) *ple.** And they came near unto him, and said, We 16 will build sheepfolds here for our cattle, and cities for our 17 little ones: but we ourselves will be ready armed to go be- fore the children of Israel, until we have brought them unto their place; and our little ones shall dwell in the fenced cities because of the inhabitants of the land. [. . .]

(P) *We will not return unto our houses, until the children of* 18 *Israel have inherited every man his inheritance. For we will not* 19 *inherit with them on the other side Jordan, and forward; because*

---

[7]Dt. 1:22-28. [8]14:4; Dt. 1:2, 19:2:14:0:23. [9]Dt. 1:34ff.; ch. 14:28-30. [10]Dt. 1: 63 [11]14: 34. [12]Dt. 30:17. [13]Vv. 24, 36. [14]Vs. 24; Gen. 47:12; 50:21; cf. v. 26. [15]Ex. 23: 20.

* The interpolation vv. 7–15 belongs to the latest period of redaction, pre-supposing P²'s conception of the narrative of the spies (cf. vs. 11 with xiv. 29) but the tone and character are not priestly but Deuteronomic. (cf. Kadesh-barnea with Dt. *passim*. From this point on, in fact, the analysis of the sources is embarrassed by the copious interpolations of this Rd, the book of Joshua especially being tinged by it throughout. Cf. Dt. i.–iii. and Jos. xxii. where the theme is the same as here. In Jos. xx. and elsewhere the evidence of LXX. proves this *Deuteronomic* redaction to have continued to a very late period. The motive here is clearly didactic.

our inheritance is fallen to us on this side Jordan eastward.

20 (J) And Moses said unto them, If ye will do this thing: if ye will arm yourselves to go before Yah-
21 weh to the war, and [16]every armed man of you will pass over Jordan before Yahweh, until he hath
22 driven out his enemies from before him, and the land be subdued before Yahweh: then afterward ye shall return, and be guiltless towards Yahweh, and towards Israel: and this land shall be unto you for a posses-
23 sion before Yahweh. But if ye will not do so, behold, ye have sinned against Yahweh: and be sure
24 (E) your sin will find you out. Build you cities for your [17]little ones, and folds for your sheep; and do that
25 (J) which hath proceeded out of your mouth. And the children of Gad and the children of Reuben spake unto Moses, saying, Thy servants will do as my lord
26 commandeth. [18]Our little ones, our wives, our flocks, and all our cattle, shall be there in the cities of Gil-
27 ead: but thy servants will pass over, [19]every man that is armed for war, before Yahweh to battle, as my lord saith.*

28 (P) *So Moses gave charge concerning them [20] to Eleazar the priest, and to Joshua the son of Nun, and to the heads of the*
29 *fathers' [houses] of the tribes of the children of Israel. And Moses said unto them, If the children of Gad and the children of Reuben will pass with you over Jordan, every man that is armed to battle, before Yahweh, and the land shall be subdued before you:*
30 *then ye shall give them the land of Gilead for a possession: but if*

---

[16]Cf. vs. 29 and Jos. 18:1. [17]Vs. 16 and refs. [18]Ch. 16:24; Gen. 34:29; 43:8; 50:8; cf. vs. 6 and refs. [19]Vs. 29. [20]34:16; Jos. 14:1; 10:51.

---

* The resemblances in expression between vv. 20ff. 27 (J) and 28ff. (P²) are too close to allow of any theory of complete independence, and are commonly held among critics to show the retouching of the chapter by Rd. It is worth noting, however, that in previous instances (Ex. xvi. compared with Num. xi. and Num. xiv. 26ff.) we have found similar resemblances where the relation was certainly one of direct dependence of P² upon J. The phrases employed in common are not such as are elsewhere distinctive of either document.

they will not pass over with you armed, they shall have possession among you in the land of Canaan. *And the children of Gad and* 31 *the children of Reuben answered, saying, As Yahweh hath said unto thy servants, so will we do.* *We will pass over armed before* 32 *Yahweh into the land of Canaan, and the possession of our inheritance [shall remain] with us beyond Jordan.*[21] *And Moses gave* 33 (Rd) *unto them, even to the children of Gad, and to the children of Reuben, and unto the half tribe of Manasseh the son of Joseph* [22] *the kingdom of Sihon* (P) *king of the Amorites, and the kingdom of Og king of Bashan, the land* [. . .]* *according to the cities thereof with [their] borders, even* (E) *the cities of the land round about.* And the children of Gad 34 built[23]Dibon, and Ataroth, and Aroer, and Atroth-shophan, and 35 Jazer, and Jogbehah ; and Beth-nimrah, and Beth-haran : fen- 36 ced cities, and folds for sheep. And the children of Reuben 37 built Heshbon, and Elealeh, and Kiriathaim ; and Nebo, and 38 Baalmeon, (*their names being changed*) and Sibmah : and gave (J) other names unto the cities which they builded. —**And** 39 **the children of Machir the son of Manasseh went to**

[21]34 : 14f. Dt. 3 : 12-17 ; 29 ' 8 ; Jos. 12 : 6 ; 13 : 8 ; 22 : 4. [22]21 : 24ff. [23]Ct. vs. 3.

*The introduction of the half-tribe of Manasseh here is plainly an afterthought, but the insertion is not due to the amalgamation of P with JE, for throughout the subsequent representations of JE and Rd it is always " Reuben, Gad and half-Manasseh " who play this part (cf. Dt. iii. 12ff ; Jos. i. 12ff.) precisely as in P (xxxiv. 14f.) But in Nu. xxxii neither in the P element, so far as preserved to us, nor in the E element, in the original form, does there seem to have been any mention of any besides Reuben and Gad, (cf. also Jos. xxii. 34. E) A possible solution of the puzzle is as follows : Rje amalgamated in Num. xxxii. according to his usual practise the data of J and E as to the occupation of the country east of Jordan by Gad and Reuben. To this, for completeness' sake, he added (from a subsequent part of J's narrative ; see note following) the story of the occupation of the rest of the East-Jordan territory, Gilead, Havvoth Jair and Nobah, by three Manassite clans, inserting vs. 40. In later writers accordingly Moses' gift to the transjordanic tribes includes " half Manasseh," *i. e.* Machir. Thus the easy comprehensiveness of the (unhistorical) conception found in JE, Rd, P[2], and Rp is reached, all the territory east of Jordan subdued by Moses at one time and given to Reuben, Gad and half-Manasseh, who afterwards accompany all Israel under Joshua. P[2]'s account is therefore strictly dependent upon JE. Insert in vs. b " of Gilead," cf. vs. 29.

Gilead, and took it, and [24]dispossessed the [25]Amorites*
40 (Rje) which were therein. [26]And Moses gave Gilead unto Machir
41 the son of Manasseh; and he dwelt therein. And Jair the son of
Manasseh went and took the towns thereof, and called
42 them Havvoth-jair. And Nobah went and took Kenath,
and the villages thereof, and called it Nobah, after his
own name.—†

33   (Rp) [1]*These are the journeys of the children of Israel, when they went*
forth out of the land of Egypt by their hosts under the hand of Moses and
2   *Aaron. And Moses wrote their goings out according to their journeys by the*
commandment of Yahweh: and these are their journeys according to their go-
ings out. And they journeyed from Rameses [2]in the first month, on the fif-
teenth day of the first month: on the morrow after the passover the children of
4   *Israel went out [3]with an high hand in the sight of all the Egyptians, while*
the Egyptians were burying all their firstborn, which Yahweh had smitten
5   *among them: [4]upon their gods also Yahweh executed judgments. [5]And the*
6   *children of Israel journeyed from Rameses, and pitched in Succoth. And they*
journeyed from Succoth, and pitched in Etham, which is in the edge of the
7   *wilderness. [6]And they journeyed from Etham, and turned back unto Pi-ha-*

---

[24]21 : 32 ; Jud. 1 : 19ff. [25]13 : 29 ; 21 : 32 ; Jud. 1 : 34f. [26]Dt. 3 : 15. [1]Ex. 12 : 51 ; 17 : 1
and refs. [2]Ex. 12 · 2 ; 13 : 4. [3]Ex. 14 : 8. [4]Ex. 12 : 12. [5]Ex. 12 : 37. [6]Ex. 14 : 2, 9.

* " Amorite " *as a generic term* for the inhabitants of Canaan is certainly a
distinctive mark of E. J speaks of them preferably as "Canaanites," or by
enumeration of the various tribes. It by no means follows that J knows no
Amorites. On the contrary Jud. i. 34f. shows that he knew of them, and Jud.
x 8 shows that to Rd at least Gilead was "the land of the Amorites" *par*
excellence. "Amorite" here and in Num. xxi. 32 is therefore no argument
against derivation from J.

†Vv. 39, 41f., contain an invaluable fragment of the ancient account in J of
how the individual tribes and clans made conquest of the territory allotted to
them. A full example is shown in Jud. 1, particularly in the account of Judah
and his minor satellites, Calebite and Kenite. The present fragment bears the
same relation to the story of " the house of Joseph," Jos. xvii. 14–18 as Jud. i.
10–16 to that of Judah, and has almost certainly been taken from after Jos.
xvii. 18 (see Bud. *Richt. u. Sam.* p. 38f, 59f.). The incident related belongs
both historically and in its original literary connection to post-Mosaic times.
Vs. 40 thus appears as a purely redactional and harmonistic addition (see note
preceding), its very language (" Machir " for " *beni*-Machir " of vs. 39) in fact
betrays it, as well as its belated position. It is not, however, from P[2] (Dill-

hiroth, which is before Baal-zephon: and they pitched before Migdol. And 8
they journeyed from before Hahiroth, and passed through the midst of the sea
into the wilderness: and they went three days' journey in the wilderness of
Etham, and pitched in Marah. [7]*And they journeyed from Marah, and came* 9
unto Elim : and in Elim were twelve springs of water, and threescore and ten
palm trees ; and they pitched there. And they journeyed from Elim, and 10
pitched by the Red Sea. And they journeyed from the Red Sea, [8]*and pitched* 11
in the wilderness of Sin. And they journeyed from the wilderness of Sin, and 12
pitched in Dophkah. And they journeyed from Dophkah, and pitched in 13
Alush. [9]*And they journeyed from Alush, and pitched in Rephidim, where* 14
was no water for the people to drink. [10]*And they journeyed from Rephidim,* 15
and pitched in the wilderness of Sinai. [11]*And they journeyed from the wild-* 16
erness of Sinai, and pitched in Kibroth-hattaavah. And they journeyed from 17
Kibroth-hattaavah, and pitched in Hazeroth. [12]*And they journeyed from* 18
Hazeroth, and pitched in Rithmah. And they journeyed from Rithmah, and 19
pitched in Rimmon-perez. And they journeyed from Rimmon-perez, and pitch- 20
ed in [13]*Libnah. And they journeyed from Libnah, and pitched in Rissah.* 21
And they journeyed from Rissah, and pitched in Kehelathah. And they 22—23
journeyed from Kehelathah, and pitched in mount Shepher. And they journ- 24
eyed from mount Shepher, and pitched in Haradah. And they journeyed from 25
Haradah, and pitched in Makheloth. And they journeyed from Makheloth, 26
and pitched in Tahath. And they journeyed from Tahath, and pitched in 27
Terah. And they journeyed from Terah, and pitched in Mithkah. And 28—29
they journeyed from Mithkah, and pitched in Hashmonah. And they jour- 30
neyed from Hashmonah, and pitched in [14]*Moseroth. And they journeyed from* 31
Moseroth, and pitched in [14]*Bene-jaakan. And they journeyed from Bene-jaa-* 32
kan, and pitched in [15]*Hor-haggidgad. And they journeyed from Hor-haggid-* 33
gad, and pitched in [15]*Jotbathah. And they journeyed from Jotbathah, and* 34
pitched in Abronah. And they journeyed from Abronah, and pitched in Ezion- 35

[7]Ex. 15 : 27. [8]Ex. 16 : 1. [9]Ex. 17 : 1. [10]Ex. 19 : 1. [11]11 : 34f. [12]12 : 16 ; Dt. 1 : 1. [13]Dt.
1 : 1. [14]Dt. 10 : 6. [15]Dt. 10 : 7.

mann) nor even in the interest of P[2]; for P[2] represents Machir as the only son
of Manasseh, and the daughters of Zelophehad, a great-grandson of Machir, as
contemporaries of Moses (cf. Gen. l. 23, E)—The parenthetic clause in vs. 38 is
probably a mere marginal direction to the synagogue reader to avoid pronouncing the offensive names of heathen deities, Nebo and Baal, which occur in the
names of the Reubenite cities. The patronymic of Nobah (vs. 42) has also,
apparently, been omitted or lost.

36 *geber* ¹⁶*And they journeyed from Ezion-geber, and pitched in the wilderness*
37 *of Zin (the same is Kadesh). And they journeyed from Kadesh, and pitched*
38 *in mount Hor, in the edge of the land of Edom.* ¹⁷*And Aaron the priest went*
   up into mount Hor at the commandment of Yahweh, and died there, in the
   fortieth year after the children of Israel were come out of the land of Egypt,
39 *in the fifth month, on the first day of the month. And Aaron was an hundred*
40 *and twenty and three years old when he died in mount Hor.* ¹⁸*And the Can-*
   aanite, the king of Arad, which dwelt in the South in the land of Canaan,
41 *heard of the coming of the children of Israel. And they journeyed from mount*
42 *Hor, and pitched in Zalmonah. And they journeyed from Zalmonah, and*
43 *pitched in Punon.* ¹⁹*And they journeyed from Punon, and pitched in Oboth.*
44 *And they journeyed from Oboth, and pitched in Iyeabarim, in the border of*
45–46 *Moab. And they journeyed from Iyim, and pitched in* ²⁰*Dibon-gad. And*
47 *they journeyed from Dibon-gad, and pitched in Almon-diblathaim. And they*
   journeyed from Almon-diblathaim, and ²¹*pitched in the mountains of Abarim,*
48 *before Nebo. And they journeyed from the mountains of Abarim,* ²²*and*
49 *pitched in the plains of Moab by the Jordan at Jericho. And they pitched by*
   *Jordan, from Bethjeshimoth even unto Abel-*²³*shittim in the plains of Moab.**

*   *   *   *   *   *   *   *   *   *

¹⁶20 . 1. ¹⁷20 : 22ff ; Dt. 32 : 50 ; cf. Dt. 10 : 6. ¹⁸21 : 1-3. ¹⁹21 : 1off. ²⁰32 : 34. ²¹21 : 20,
Dt. 32 : 49. ²²22 : 1. ²³25 : 1; Jos. 2 : 1.

* Num. xxxiii. 1–49 is a late redactional colophon which may at some period
of the text have served as a conclusion to the story of the wandering. Unfortunately its principal historical value, the supplying of gaps in the sources, as
e. g. P in Ex. xii., supplied from vv. 3-5, is materially reduced by its artificial
numerical scheme (40 stations for 40 years ; see Analysis);for the list of authentic names has almost certainly been supplemented. Nevertheless it may reasonably be inferred from vs. 2 that an actual list of JE, attributed by the writer
to Moses, underlies this chapter, and of this we have, no doubt, fragments in
xxi. 12-20, Dt. x. 6f. (Dt. i 1 ?) and Num. xxi. 12-20.

DEUTERONOMY.

PROLEGOMENA.

It is not within the scope of our present undertaking to speak of the Deuteronomic *Code* further than merely to point out that by this term we mean Dt. xii–xxvi, a revised and enlarged edition of the Mosaic institutions, adapted to the circumstances of the last quarter of the seventh century, B. C. It presents itself as "the Words of the Covenant which Yahweh commanded Moses to make with the children of Israel in the land of Moab, besides the covenant which he made with them in Horeb" (xxix. 1 ; Heb. xxviii. 69), and it is a gratuitous aspersion to assert that this "covenant in the land of Moab, besides that of Horeb" is a pure fiction of the Deuteronomist. On the contrary we have every reason to believe that there was such a law, of immemorial antiquity in D's time (620, B.C.) embodied mainly in the Book of Judgments of JE, whose adoption, *by covenant*, was attributed to the last days of Moses in the land of Moab. In addition to this, which forms the principal stock of Deuteronomy, there were the Words of the Covenant, Ex. xxxiv. ; the Book of the Covenant, Ex. xx. 22–26, xxiii. 10–33 ; the Ordinances of Ex. xii. 21–27 ; xiii. 3–16, and whatever tradition had transmitted as part of the Mosaic institutions under the comprehensive head of the "teaching (*torah*) and commandment" (*mitzwah*) which according to Ex. xxiv. 12, Moses had received in the mount for oral transmission (" that thou mayest "teach them "). The need for a recodification of the Mosaic institutions after the reactionary reign of Manasseh was imperative. The conflicting claims as to what was, and what was not, Mosaic (cf. Jer. vii. *passim*, especially vv. 21–23, and 31b), with the growing mass of *torah* among the priestly guilds, was urgent enough in itself, but before all else was the necessity for the rescue of pure Yahwism from the increasing corruption of rural sanctuaries, where Canaanitish practises rivalled with Egyptian and Assyrian idol-worship in degrading the high standard of old Yahwistic monolatry, the "jealousy for

Yahweh " of Elijah. The war of the " true " prophets and the better class of the priesthood against Canaanitism, begun in the days of Hezekiah had gone heavily against them during the 57 years of Manasseh, and Amon. With the revolution which put the child Josiah upon the throne and the chief priest Hilkiah in the regency, the opportunity and the duty of the prophetic party and the supporters of unadulterated Mosaism was equally clear. A recodification of the Mosaic institutions took place at the hands of those properly and legitimately entrusted with this common inheritance of the nation, the prophets and priests ; and the noble work which they produced was the Deuteronomic Code. Whether by accident or design, it came into the hands of Hilkiah in the course of the repairs undertaken upon the temple, and after consultation with " Huldah the prophetess " and the king's confidential advisers, it was made by royal decree the official standard and platform of the government. From the year 621 B. C. until the canonization of the Priestly Code under Ezra and Nehemiah *circa* 444 B. C., the Deuteronomic Code was *par excellence the* Book of the Torah, and it is not improbable that for a century or more it circulated as an independent work, before being attached to JE. At least it is difficult to conceive for what purpose it received the double framework of introductions and appendices which now encloses it, unless to fit it for independent circulation.

The code itself should be discussed in connection with the legislative elements of the Pentateuch. The *inner* framework which encloses it, consisting of an introduction, chh. iv. 44—xi. 32 for the most part ; and an appendix, xxvii. 9f ; xxviii–xxx ; and xxxi. 9-13 (so Cornill), forms a sermonic exhortation in true preaching (parenetic) style, assumes Moses to have *written* the code, and clearly dates from the Exile. With this also we have little to do, as it contains no trace of anything derived, except indirectly, from JE. But in addition to this framework of *sermonic* exhortation, which Cornill designates Dp (parenetic Deuteronomist), there is another, also in the form of a discourse, in which, however, the *historical* interest predominates. This framework also, so far from being adapted to connect the

book with JE, seems to be intended to take the place of the
prophetic narrative, and thus supply the book with a historical setting. This outer framework consists, like Dp, of an
introductory discourse x. 1–11 ; i. 6–iii. 29 (iv. 1–40) (xi.
26–32 ?), and an appendix containing according to Cornill
xxxii. 45–47 and xxvii. 1–8. In Dh iv. 9–40 ; xxvi. 16–19 are
later growths. One might prefer on some accounts to regard
xxix. 2–xxx. 20 ; xxxi. 16–22 ; xxxii. 1–47 as constituting Dh's
appendix, and iv. 1–40 instead of iv. 9–40 as the later growth,
with which xxxi. 24–30 might then be connected. But the
question of the history and relation of Dh and Dp does not
concern us save in a single point, and as to this we may en-
dorse the conclusions of Cornill with confidence. *Dh is a
framework for the Deuteronomic Code, wholly independent of Dp,
and equally independent of any other Hexateuchal document.* It has
been taken up and combined with the Deuteronomy enclosed
by Dp, perhaps by the author of xxxi. 24–30, (Rd) who supplies
a new introduction to the Song (ch. xxxii.) after vs. 23 has separated its original introduction, vv. 16–22 from it. Part of it is
missing before i. 6, part appears displaced in x. 1–9 where it
makes good the failure of Dp to mention the second tables. It
has, therefore, met rough treatment. Dh also, as well as Dp,
is free from any material which in its present form can be assigned to J or E. *But where Dh has been connected with the Deuteronomy of Dp we find fragments of E.* The curious feature of
the case is that these fragments are not part of Dh, and cannot
possibly have been taken up by him ; for in some instances they
are as completely foreign to the context in which they stand as
if clipped at random out of some other book, and inserted where
they happened to fall ; in every instance the context of Dh is
only injured by their insertion. They have no relation to
Deuteronomy, to Dp nor to Dh, except in some cases an artificial and mechanical one to the last mentioned ; and where this
relation subsists, as in xxvii. 1–8, 11ff. (introduced by xxvi.
16–19 and drastically retouched) and xxxi. 14f. 23 (connection
of vs. 22 with ch. xxxii. reëstablished by means of vv. 24–30) it
seems to be by a later hand than that of Dh. The most prob-

able conclusion is that these E fragments were put in where they now stand at the time when Deuteronomy with its double framework, or envelope, of Dp and Dh was united to JE, the "prophetic" sacred history ; or, to put it still more simply and intelligibly, that when room was made in the closing chh. of JE for the incorporation of D + Dp + Dh, these fragments of the sacred history were regarded by the incorporator (Rd) as too valuable to be lost, and accordingly were attached as best they might be to Dh. It is perhaps significant that the most erratic fragment of all, is found embedded in that paragraph of Dh, which has been removed from the beginning of the historical discourse and interpolated after ch. ix., apparently on account of Ex. xxxiv., which we have already seen reason to regard as one of the reincorporations of Rd.

What theory can we frame to account for these curious fragments ? We must look at the fragments themselves to determine, after the satisfactory establishment of their origin, what their original connection and setting may have been. Afterwards the limits derivable from the admittedly dependent writings may shed some additional light.

The fragments in i. 1b (2 ?) and x. 6f. give little information. It is clear that they are taken from an itinerary of the journey from Horeb to Kadesh, and, as we shall see, from the source E ; i. 2 informs us, perhaps on the same authority, that it was "eleven days' journey." The names in x. 6f. are parallel to Num. xxxiii. 31–33, where they appear *before* Kadesh. From the structure of the names it is probable that the region is that of mount Seir. From Num. xx. 1, which relates in an E frag ment the death of Miriam on the people's arrival in Kadesh, it is natural to think that in this document that of Aaron was related somewhat later. We found no traces of the itinerary of E before Num. xx., where we should have expected its original position to have been. Had it been removed to the end of the Story of the Wilderness Wandering for such a purpose as Num. xxxiii. now subserves ? And is this late itinerary of Rp rewritten on the basis of the E original ? The itinerary Num. xxxiii. had a documentary source, else vs. 2 would not read as it does. But there is now unfortunately little room for anything more than fancy in answer to the question, what this source may have been.

The fragments xxv. 17–19, xxvii. 1–8, 11ff. and xxxi. 14f., 23 give more satisfactory indications. They probably stand, relatively to the story, in about the same positions they have always occupied. The charge to destroy Amalek and to enact a covenant in ratification of the law, erecting the *stelae* and the altar on Ebal, are the appropriate legacy of Moses in his last hours to the people, and are amply supported in E by the analogy of Ex. xvii. 14–16; 1 Sam. xv.; Ex. xxiv. 3–8 and Josh. xxiv. The fragment xxxi. 14f., 23 is presupposed by the whole subsequent narrative of E, and needs no vindication of its right to the place it now occupies. How much then, is presupposed between the end of the narrative of E, where we could last identify it with certainty and Dt. xxvii. 1–8 ? It is true that Dt. xxvii. 1–8 has been thoroughly recast by Rd, but if it had not been adapted to his purpose he would have either passed it over or written something to the purpose himself. It is safe to say that its *essential* character of directions for the ratification of a *torah* of Moses by sacrifice on mount Ebal has not been altered. Traces of the same conception appear also in vv. 11–26, though in a different sense (cf. xi. 29–32), and a much altered account of the fulfilment of the requirement here made appears in Jos. viii. 30–35. In all these passages, at least as they now read, the reference is to Deuteronomy. But in xxvii. 1–8 we have material, in fact the whole basis of the paragraph, which goes back of Deuteronomy to E. It is impossible to avoid the conclusion that *in E also* before the charge to Joshua there was a *torah* of Moses given to the *people* in the plains of Moab ; there was a pre-Deuteronomic Deuteronomy.

This result does not follow merely from the presuppositions of Dt. xxvii. 1–8, but is an inevitable consequence of Ex. xxiv. 12–14, where the intention certainly is not merely to describe the source of Moses' judicial wisdom in his own day, but the source of the Mosaic *torah* of the *writer's* day, as of divine authority. If Moses did not, on the plains of Shittim, before the installation of Joshua, communicate to "the elders of Israel" (Dt. xxvii. 1) the statutes and judgments given him of God "that he might teach them" (Ex. xxiv. 12), then this invaluable divine *torah* died with him. For it is not communicated at Horeb. The author of Dt. v. 31–vi. 3 would have the Deuteronomic Code pass for this law ; xxix. 1 positively affirms that there was such a "Covenant in the Land of Moab, besides the Covenant made in Horeb." If E did not relate it, then in his series of great characters Joseph, Moses, Joshua, Samuel, Moses alone, Moses the lawgiver, prophet and teacher *par excellence*, is the only one who passes off the stage without a final address to the people adjuring them to be faithful to the divine institutions. Such a supposition is incredible. Deuteronomy itself presupposes its predecessor. Its two introductory discourses were suggested by the model of E's farewell discourses in the mouths of his heroes, most of all by that which he undoubtedly put in the mouth of Moses himself in these very circumstances. Most of all must Dh have followed the model of this primitive Deuteronomy of E, to the extent of giving to his work, especially in the first paragraphs, so pronounced an E coloration as to make it seem necessary to many critics to assume that in addition to JE combined he had also before him the document E in the separate form !

How much then can we recover of this primitive Deuteronomy of E ? Traces of the narrative which preceded and followed the code itself are found *in situ*. Rd preserved them at the cost of a good deal of inconvenience. Did he then entirely reject the primitive Mosaic code ? On the contrary, when superseded by the revised and enlarged edition, the primitive Deuteronomy went to take its place in the midst of the Horeb legislation, as a part of "the first covenant which Yahweh made with the people at Horeb." There we found it somewhat incongruously embedded in the Book of the Covenant, and obviously out of place with its separate title, "Now these are the judgments which thou shalt set before them" ; but in order to preserve its character of a *covenant* law it had to be inserted in the Book of the Covenant room or no room.

The Deuteronomic Code with its double envelope Dp and Dh could now take the place of The Book of Judgments with some adjustments (by Rd) to the remaining fragments of E, and a retouching of the whole work JED, especially in the legislative parts of Exodus. Then finally, when P² was added, a date in Dt. i. 3ff., a harmonistic touch in iv. 41–43, possibly some modifications of xxvii. 14–26 and a resumption of Num. xxvii. 12ff. in xxxii. 48–52 were all that Rp needed to add before inserting P's notice of Moses' death, xxxiv. 7–9 in the JE narrative of xxxiii. f.

In the above sketch of the history of the Deuteronomic Code and its two Introductions and Appendices the attempt has been made to convey a clear idea of the theory on which we proceed in extricating the fragments of the narrative from their present connection with the purely legislative work of Deuteronomy. It is not our present purpose to defend this theory of Deuteronomy, nor to demonstrate the existence of a Dp and a Dh. All this belongs to the history of the legal element of the Pentateuch. After the above description of the book and its history, as we understand it, we have only to turn to the passages above laid claim to as parts of the narrative JEP and demonstrate their independence of the context in which they now stand, in contrast with their real and organic connection with the Triple Tradition of the Exodus.

§ VII. (Narrative parts of Deuteronomy). THE COVENANT IN THE PLAINS OF MOAB.

The mere concluding sentences of the story of Moses' life in P² are found in Deuteronomy, detached from their necessary connection with Num. xxvii. 12–23, and appended to Deuteronomy by a few lines of date and connection, mainly a repetition of Num. xxvii. 12–23, supplied by R. The genuine elements derived from P² simply relate the death of Moses and the 30 days' mourning, as in Aaron's case (Num. xx. 28f.) ; xxxiv. 1a ; 5b ; also how Joshua his successor, according to the promise Num. xxvii. 15–23, is filled with the Spirit of Wisdom ; vv. 7–9.

E seems to have had an itinerary similar to Num. xxxiii. which may, however, have been displaced from between Num. xii. 15 and xx. 1. If it stood originally, or by transfer of Rje, where Num. xxxiii. now stands, *i. e.*, at the conclusion of the Story of the Wilderness Wandering, the presence of fragments in the early part of Dh may be understood from the preceding comments on the book of Deuteronomy (see above, p. 250). Either here, or before Num. xx. 1, E synopsized the journey from Horeb to Kadesh in eleven stages, at one of which, Moserah, Aaron died and was buried, Eleazar his son succeeding to the priestly office ; Dt. i. 1b, 2 ; x. 6f. [In the plains of Shittim Moses assembles the elders of Israel (xxvii. 1) and all the people for a parting address, in the nature of Jos. xxiv. He recapitulates the Story of the Wilderness Wandering, emphasizing particularly the facts relating to the appointment of judges and officers, and the disobedience of the people at Kadesh which had excluded them 40 years from the land of promise and commands vengeance on Amalek (Dt. i. 6–iii. 29 ; xxv. 17–19). He is now about to deliver to them the *torah* and commandment he received at Horeb (Ex. xxiv. 12–14)]. At this point followed the little code of Mishpatim under the title, "These are the Judgments which thou shalt set before them," communicated by Moses to elders, judges, officers and people as the principles received at Horeb for the permanent administration of social order ; Ex. xxi. 1–xxiii. 9. The address was then concluded by directions to the "elders" to erect on mount Ebal, after conquest of the land, an altar according to the prescription of Ex. xx. 24, and (twelve ?) *stelae*, on which this primitive "law of the twelve tables" is to be inscribed. The ratification of this new covenant is to be celebrated by a sacrificial feast ; and a covenant by the people on Ebal and Gerizim. Dt. xxvii. 1–8 * ; 11–13. Thereafter Yahweh summons Moses and Joshua to the Tent of Meeting and bestows upon the latter a charge as Moses' successor ; xxxi. 14f. 23. Moses dies in the land of Moab, but his sepulchre is unknown. No prophet like him has since appeared ; xxxiv. 5a, 6b, 10.

According to the J element of Deuteronomy, when Moses

had given inheritance to the tribes of Reuben and Gad (Num.
xxxii.) he gathered together the princes and tribes of Israel
(Dt. xxxiii. 5) and pronounced upon the people tribe by tribe
such a blessing as that which in the mouth of Jacob (Gen. xlix.)
concludes the first epoch of the sacred history, the patriarchal
period, and that other which in the mouth of Deborah (Jud. v.)
seems to mark the close of the Conquest of Canaan ; Dt. xxxiii.
This " Blessing of Moses" shows a similar structure to the " Blessing of Jacob," Gen. xlix., and even an unmistakable dependence
upon it ; perhaps also upon the Song of Balaam, Num. xxiv.
Ascending to the top of Pisgah Moses beholds the land he is
forbidden to enter, dies there and is buried " in the valley in the
land of Moab, over against Beth-peor " ; Dt. xxxiv. 1 a*b*, 4, 6a.

1. Dt. 1. 1ff ; x. 6f. ch. xxvii. THE ITINERARY, AND THE SECOND
LAW.

ANALYSIS.

The opening sentence of Deuteronomy is in such confusion as to be
unintelligible. Vs. 3 is intended to connect the book with the scheme of
dates of P², though it not only has no connection with the Priestly Law-
book but is constantly found in irreconcilable contradiction with it. In
addition it is entirely excluded by Num. xxvii. 12 23, which leaves no
room for a further legislation between it and the story of Moses' death.
We may therefore strike out vs. 3 as inserted by Rp. Vv. 4 and 5 again
bear a precisely analogous relation to JE. The words are doubly superfluous between vs. 3 and iv. 44-49, looking past both introductions, chh.
i.-iv., and v. xi., to Deuteronomy as a whole. Preceded by vs. 1a they
form the link by which Rd unites Deuteronomy to the ' prophetic " history JE. The address which follows in vv. 6ff. (Dh) begins, however,
much too abruptly to have come from the same hand, and, from its
character cannot have been intended to *follow*, but only to *replace*, the
narrative of JE. The opening words of vs. 1 as far as " beyond Jordan
in the wilderness " are appropriate enough, and connect well enough
with vs. 4 ; but what can be made of 1b and 2 ? " Suph " is not probably the Red Sea, as some of the versions make it. May we perhaps
identify it with " Suphah," mentioned in the song quoted by E in Num.
xxi. 14 ? But what of " Paran " at the northern extremity of the Gulf of
Akaba or somewhat further west, the place from which the wilderness of

that ilk is named ? • What of " Tophel," some five miles north of Bozrah in Edom, southeast of the Dead Sea ? What is it of which the scene is laid " between Paran and Tophel " ? These words would well describe the extent of the isthmus between the Gulf of Akaba and the Dead Sea; but what have they to do with the " plains of Moab " opposite Jericho, the scene of Deuteronomy? What, if anything, can be located " be- tween Paran and Tophel *and* Laban (Num. xxxiii. 20, " Libnah ") *and* Hazeroth (Num. xi. 35) *and* Di-zahab " ? If the latter places mentioned define the locality, is it not superfluous to mention the former, as if one should say, between Jerusalem and Damascus, and Capernaum and Bethsaida and Chorazin ? But what, above all, is the pertinence of vs. 2, giving the number of days' journey from Horeb to Kadesh ? What connection has this with the location of Moses' address opposite Jericho ? It is 40 years since Israel went from Horeb to Kadesh, and since the journey was made thither they have come by an almost opposite course to *Shittim*, as far from Kadesh by the route they have come as Damas- cus itself. The only answer that can be given to the question is simply, there is no connection. The latter part of Dt. i. 1, and vs. 2 is an erratic fragment. The phenomenon, however, has a parallel in x. 6f. That the relation, or lack of relation, to Dh in which the latter is given may be clearly seen, we will present the context.

10   "At that time Yahweh said unto me, Hew thee two tables of stone like unto the first, and come up unto me into the mount, and

2   make thee an ark of wood. And I will write on the tables the words that were on the first tables which thou brakest, and thou shalt put

3   them in the ark. So I made an ark of acacia wood, and hewed two tables of stone like unto the first, and went up into the mount, having

4   the two tables in mine hand. And he wrote on the tables, according to the first writing, the ten commandments, which Yahweh spake unto you in the mount out of the midst of the fire in the day of the assembly :

5   and Yahweh gave them unto me. And I turned and came down from the mount, and put the tables in the ark which I had made ; and there

6   they be, as Yahweh commanded me.—And the children of Israel journeyed from Beeroth Benejaakan to Moserah : there Aaron died, and there he was buried ; and Eleazar his

7   son ministered in the priest's office in his stead. From thence they journeyed unto Gudgodah ; and from Gudgodah to Jot-

8   bathah, a land of brooks of water.—At that time Yahweh separated the tribe of Levi, to bear the ark of the covenant of Yahweh,

to stand before Yahweh to minister unto him, and to bless in his
name, unto this day. Wherefore Levi hath no portion nor inheritance   9
with his brethren; Yahweh is his inheritance, according as Yahweh
thy God spake unto him. And I stayed in the mount, as at the first   10
time, forty days and forty nights: and Yahweh hearkened unto me
that time also; Yahweh would not destroy thee. And Yahweh said   11
unto me, Arise, take thy journey before the people; and they shall go
in and possess the land, which I sware unto their fathers to give unto
them."

We are familiar with the story to which vv. 1-5, 8-11 refer in Ex.
xxxii. and xxxiv.; for the separation of the tribe of Levi here referred to
is that of Ex. xxxii. 25 29, referred to again in Dt. xxxiii. 8f.; the situation in vs. 10 shows this very clearly, even if we had not the second
person (" thy God ") in vs. 9, and the characteristic " at that time " of Dh
(*eleven* times in chh. i.-iv.) in vv. 1 and 8, to show that the parenthesis
must be closed after vs. 7, and not where the R. V. closes it after vs. 9.
Into the connection of Moses' discourse, where he is reminding Israel of
what occurred "at that time," when they were in Horeb, breaks in, without any warning or occasion whatever, a section speaking of the children
of Israel in the third person, which describes a part of the journey in the
wilderness and the death of Aaron and investiture of his son Eleazar at
Moserah! If there is any connection at all, it is the mere fact that vv.
6f. and 8f. both have something to do with the priests' office. One must
be credulous indeed to suppose that the writer of the surrounding context (Dh) himself put it here, making nonsense of his own work.
Whence then, is it and what? It does not come from Dp, nor from the
hand of P, nor is it likely to have been inserted after Deuteronomy came
into union with P; for nothing could be more flatly in contradiction with
the plain statement of the priestly writer as to when and where and how
the death of Aaron took place (cf. Num. xx. 22-29), and the usual harmonistic expedient of a double occurrence of the same event this time
will not apply. Moreover the names of the stations, though similar to
the corresponding list of Num. xxxiii. 30 33, which we know to be dependent upon P, are at the same time so different that it cannot possibly
originate from the priestly element. But knowing as we do that E
afforded an itinerary (cf. Num. xxi. 12ff.) drawn up in this form, a different form from P's; finding, as we do in Jos. xxiv. 33, that the death and
burial of " Eleazar the priest, the son of Aaron," is subsequently related
by E, who consequently must have related Aaron's death and the succession of Eleazar to " the priest's office," and probably defined the place of

Aaron's burial (cf. Dt. xxxiv. 6b ; Jos. xxiv. 30, 32, 33), the probability is very strong that Dt. x. 6f. is a fragment of this itinerary of E ; and, since in i. 1b, 2 a similar erratic block has been already found, and moreover there is good reason to think that x. 1–11 (Dh) belongs as a whole before i. 6ff. (Dh) it is further in the highest degree probable that the erratic fragment in i. 1b, 2, containing only a list of names and the statement of the number of stations from Horeb to Kadesh is part of the same itinerary.

How could these erratic blocks of E get here at the beginning of Deuteronomy ? I can suggest but one way, viz : that they always were here ; or at least were here before the present Deuteronomy with its envelopes was taken up into JED. If the primitive Deuteronomy of E was preceded, like our present Deuteronomy, by an itinerary recapitulating the wilderness wandering similar to Num. xxxiii., whether removed by Rje from after Num. xii., or originally in this position, the fragment in i. 1b, 2 might well be a remnant of it, describing the road from Horeb to Kadesh as passing "between Paran and Tophel," and leading to the stations Laban, Hazeroth and Di-zahab, Beeroth-bene-jaakan, Moserah, Gudgodah and Jotbatha. As Dt. i. 2 seems to conclude the account of the journey, we may perhaps assume that x. 6f. originally preceded it. Another fragment preserved by Rd. is xxv. 17–19, which as to content has no relation to Deuteronomy, but a close one with E. It even shows his language (see refs.), though like xxvii. 1 8 expanded by Rd. It would seem to be a remnant of Moses' discourse.

It is not necessary after what has been said already in connection with the Book of Judgments, Ex. xxi. f., and in the general discussion of Deuteronomy as a whole, to point out that this book with its two introductions forms an independent work with a style eminently peculiar to itself, and having had a long and interesting history of its own (II Kings xxi. ff.) before its incorporation with JE. It is mainly for the following reasons that we conclude that originally the place now occupied by Deuteronomy was filled by a recapitulatory discourse of Moses similar to Jos. xxiv., which introduced as the Second Law, the Book of Judgments, Ex. xxi. f. :

1⁰. Deuteronomy itself presupposes the existence of such a tradition. It claims to present the commandments and teachings which Moses communicated to the people in the plains of Moab "besides the covenant which Yahweh made with them at Horeb"; in fact the nucleus of this second law is the Book of Judgments, practically all of which is taken up by D in a revised form. 2⁰. E itself looks forward to a deliverance of this kind in the "*torah* and commandment" received by Moses, Ex. xxiv. 12 14, "that thou mayest teach them " to the people. 3⁰. The Book of Judgments is egregiously out of place where it now stands, interrupting the connection of the Book of the Covenant ; whereas its whole character as a law for settled agricultural life, a life of fields and vineyards, houses and lands, sanctuaries and altars, is such as to make it appropriate only when the people are about to enter, if not already entered, upon the possession of the land. 4°. At the close of Joshua's career, and that of Samuel in E, and, in less degree, of Joseph's, the occasion is used for such a recapitulation as this of Yahweh's providential guidance, and an adjuration of the people to fidelity to him. We should expect the most important address of the kind to come at the farewell of Moses. 5°. We find fragments of the narrative of E at the beginning and end of Deuteronomy, which have no connection with the book itself. We have now to add : 6°. Dt. xxvii. is one of these fragments of E, unconnected with the work of D ; and this chapter presupposes that Moses has just been communicating a *torah* which could be inscribed on great stones as a national inheritance.

In this instance we find the E material retouched and in a measure adapted to the context. But the position of the chapter is a very singular one. In chh. xxviii. ff. we have an inculcation of obedience to the law just given, because Yahweh will bless obedience, but visit a disobedient nation with fearful curses. In fact the first 14 verses of ch. xxviii. alone comprise the blessing, whereas the 54 verses following scarcely suffice to describe the terrors of the curse ; and even so we do not reach the end, for in two more chapters, xxixf., the theme is resumed, and here it is even taken for granted that the curse and not the blessing will be Israel's portion, and a promise of return from exile is given on condition of repentance. In all this the *preacher* (Dp) is in his element. But ch. xxvii., which describes two different ceremonies for the ratification of the law, takes a different course, one which connects it with the *history* JE. What follows it is even rendered less effective by being separated from the matter to which it applies. In xxviii. 58, 61 ; xxix. 20f. ; xxx. 10 the law referred to is one written in a book. In ch. xxvii. it has just been communicated orally, and *is to be* written on stones at Shechem. Ch. xxvii. is therefore not preliminary to xxxi. 9-13 ; for if it were we should at least find it in the same connection, not before, but after the blessing and curse, which are the penalty clause of the law. It is a *parallel* to xxxi. 9-13 ; and its sequel in Jos. viii. 30-35 is parallel to xxxi. 24-30, where, moreover, (vs. 28), the elders and officers are not already before Moses, as in xxvii. 1, but have yet to be assembled. Finally xxvii. 1-8 belongs clearly to the *history*, more than to the law in itself considered, being connected on the one side with Ex. xx. 24 (cf. Dt. xxvii. 5f.) and on the other with Jos. viii. 30-35.

In like manner the blessing and cursing of xxvii. 11-26 is obviously a parallel, and not a preliminary, to the blessing and curse of chh. xxixff. Here too the scene is *Shechem*, as in vv. 1-8; moreover in vs. 12 Levi, as in the most ancient part of the Pentateuch (Gen. xxxiv. 30, xlix. 5), is placed on a footing of equality with the secular tribes, which is contrary to the whole attitude of Deuteronomy, and even more so toward that of the later writings. True, vv. 14-26 are conceived in the spirit of the priestly post-exilic period, and presuppose the legislation of P[1] and D, if not P[2]. We must assign them to Rd if not to Rp. But vv. 14-26 are a foreign attachment to vv. 11-13, or rather a late expansion thereof. Levi in vs. 12 has not this independent, priestly part to play, and the whole conception of how six *tribes* are to bless the *people* and six to curse them in vv. 11-13 is different from that of vv. 14-26, where this part is taken away from the tribes and given to the Levites. Finally even vv. 11-13 though clearly referring to the same event as xi. 29f. (Dp) are not in harmony with them. It is quite clear that the nucleus of ch. xxvii. is ancient material from the "prophetic" narrative, worked over by a very late hand (Rd) and attached to Deuteronomy in spite of the fact that it is more than superfluous there. Whence then is this material derived? There is but one writer of the Hexateuch for whom Shechem is the religious centre, or who would even dream of locating there the formal adoption of the national Mosaic institutions, and that is E (cf. *e.g.* Jos. xxiv.). There is but one writer, if any, who treats Levi after Ex. xxxii. as a secular tribe; and that is E. There is but one to whom the directions for the altar and sacrificial feast *in mount Ebal* (?) can be assigned; and that is the author of Ex. xx. 24f., already shown to be E. In short, no course is open to the critic save to recognize that the primitive material of ch. xxvii. belongs to E, and if so this furnishes further confirmation of our decision in regard to the fragments preceding.

As to the manner in which this material has been adjusted to the surrounding Deuteronomic context, we need only point out that the passage has clearly been retouched to fit it for the present context, (see note *in loc.*), doubtless by the same hand as xxvi. 16-19, where (vs. 19) the late verse, Ex. xix. 6, is referred to, and the writer (Rd) leads over from the Deuteronomic context to the idea of the covenant in xxvii. 1-8. On the other hand xxvii. 9f., which are missed before xxviii. 1, may well be original with Dp. The Deuteronomic character of these verses is so plain from the style and language as to be unmistakable even in translation and to the tyro. Vv. 9f., accordingly, we may here pass over. On the other hand we have all the material derived from E in xxvii. 1-8, 11-26, and in xxvi. 16-19 we have the link connecting it with Deuteronomy. That which is clear, finally, from the moment that the basis of ch. xxvii. is admitted to be E's, is that our Deuteronomy has taken the place of a Second Law of Moses in the plains of Shittim, a law to be written on great stones in Ebal, and there to be ratified *by the people*, in solemn sacrificial feast and covenant ; for this is the significance not only of the sacrificial meal of vs. 7, but also, no doubt, of the ceremony on Ebal and Gerizim (cf. Jer. xxxiv. 18f. and Gen. xv. 10, 17). This book of the law of this second covenant we infer to have been that given to Moses at Horeb during his 40 days' sojourn in the mount, and preserved to us, for the most part if not entire, under the title " These are the Judgments " in Ex. xxi.-xxiii. 9. In one more respect then the writer of Hilkiah's law-book with its terrible curses (2 Kings xxii.) was true to tradition , and Jeremiah also, in reminding the people how they themselves and all their princes and nobles had ratified the covenant of Yahweh's law by passing between the severed parts of the sacrificial calf, referred to no recent or doubtful claim, but to the immemorial belief and tradition of his day.

———

(**Rd**) These be the words which Moses spake unto all Israel beyond **1** Jordan in the wilderness, in the Arabah over against Suph, [. . .] (**E**) between Paran, and Tophel, and ¹Laban, and ²Hazeroth, and Di-zahab. It is eleven days' [journey] from Horeb ³by **2** the way of ⁴mount Seir unto Kadesh-barnea.* [. . .] (**Rp**) *⁵And it came to pass in the fortieth year, in the eleventh month, on the* **3** *first day of the month, that Moses spake unto the children of Israel, according unto all that Yahweh had given him in commandment unto them,* (**Rd**) ⁶after he had smitten Sihon, the king of the Amorites, which dwelt in **4** Heshbon, and Og the king of Bashan, which dwelt in Ashtaroth, at Edrei beyond Jordan, in the land of Moab, began Moses to declare this law, saying,† **5**

*   *   *   *   *   *   *   *

¹Nu. 33:20. ²Nu. 11:35. ³Ex. 13:17; Nu. 14:25; 21:4. ⁴Jos. 24:4. ⁵Nu. 10:11; 14·34: 20:1. ⁶4:46; 31:4.

* Kadesh-barnea is the form usually employed by D (but cf. vs. 46) and we do not find it outside of Deuteronomic passages. E, however, may have used it when speaking of Kadesh in such a connection as the present, though elsewhere he employs simply " Kadesh," or Rd may have added " barnea " here. Still the assignment of vs. 2 to E must be admitted to be very doubtful, and depends mainly on the fact that the passage has no other intelligible connection than with the itinerary from Horeb to Kadesh.

† Vv. 4f. appear to connect with 1a, and afford a curious parallel to iv. 44ff.

10—6 (E)—[1]And the children of Israel journeyed from Beeroth
Benejaakan to Moserah: [2]there Aaron died, and there he was
buried ; and [3]Eleazar his son ministered in the priest's office
7   in his stead.   From thence they journeyed unto [4]Gudgodah ;
and from Gudgodah to Jotbathah, a land of brooks of
water.—*

*   *   *   *   *   *   *   *

25—17 (E) [. . .] [1]Remember what Amalek did unto
18 thee by the way as ye come forth out of Egypt ; how he
met thee by the way, and smote the hindmost of thee,
(Rd) all that were feeble behind thee, when thou wast faint and weary;
19 and he [2]feared not God.   Therefore it shall be, when Yahweh
thy God hath [3]given thee rest from all thine enemies round
about, in the land which Yahweh thy God giveth thee for an inheritance
to possess it, that [4]thou shalt blot out the remembrance of Amalek from under heaven ; thou shalt not forget.†

*   *   *   *   *   *   *   *

26—16 (Rd) [1]This day Yahweh thy God commandeth thee to do these
statutes and judgments : thou shalt therefore keep and do them with all
17 thine heart, and with all thy soul.   Thou hast avouched Yahweh this day
to be thy God, and that thou shouldest walk in his ways, and keep his stat-

---

[1]Nu. 26 : 12f ; 33 : 30-33.   [2]Ct. Nu. 20 : 22ff.   [3]Jos. 24 : 33.   [4]Nu. 33 : 32f.   [1]1 Sam. 15 :
...   [2]Ex. 1 : 17 and refs.   [3]1 Sam. 12 : 11.   [4]Ex. 17 : 14 ; 1 Sam. ch. 15.   [1]11 : 32.

In order to connect the recapitulatory address of Dh, which formed the outer
envelope of Deuteronomy, with JE, it was necessary to introduce some such
date.   In removing x. 1–11 from this connection to its present position Rd was
no doubt influenced by its relation to ch. ix. (Dp) as well as by a desire to
supply the sequel to the story of the Apostasy.

* From the name Jotbathah, taken to mean " excellent in water." For the
connection, or rather complete lack of connection of this fragment see above,
Analysis p. 256.   The reinstatement of Aaron to the priestly office presupposed
here and in Jos. xxiv. 33 must be understood to have taken place after Ex.
xxxii. 33, as Dt. ix. 20 in fact declares it did, referring to something not preserved in the narrative.   In Ex. xviii. 12 also, a passage certainly to be placed
later in than Ex. xxxii., Aaron appears in good favor.   All these passages confirm the idea of Kuenen, Cornill *et al.*, attributing Ex. xxxii. 1–6, 16–24, 30–34
to an E[2].

† Ch.   xxv. 17-19 has been taken up by Rd from the discourse of Moses.

utes, and his commandments, and his judgments, and harken unto his
voice: and Yahweh *hath avouched thee this day to be a peculiar people 18
unto himself, as he *hath promised thee, and that thou shouldest keep all
his commandments; and to make thee *high above all nations which he 19
hath made, in praise, and in name, and in honor; and that thou mayest be
an holy people unto Yahweh thy God, *as he hath spoken.*

(E) [. . .] ¹And Moses and the elders of Israel com- 27
(Rd) manded the people, saying, ²Keep all the commandment
which I command you this day. And it shall be on the day when ye shall 2
pass over Jordan unto the land which Yahweh thy God giveth thee, that
thou shalt set thee up great stones, and plaister them with plaister: and thou 3
shalt write upon them all the words of this law, when thou art passed over;
³that thou mayest go in unto the land which Yahweh thy God giveth thee,
a land flowing with milk and honey, as Yahweh, the God of thy fathers,
(E) hath promised thee. And ⁴it shall be when ye are passed 4
over Jordan, that ye shall ⁵set up these stones, which I command you this day, in ⁶mount Ebal, and thou shalt plaister them
with plaister. ⁷And there shalt thou build an altar unto 5
Yahweh thy God, an altar of stones: thou shalt lift up no
[tool iron] upon them. Thou shalt build the altar of Yahweh 6
thy God of unhewn stones: and thou shalt offer burnt offerings thereon unto Yahweh thy God: and thou shalt sacrifice 7
peace offerings, and shall eat there: and thou shalt rejoice before
Yahweh thy God. And thou shalt write upon the stones all the 8
words of this law very ⁸plainly.†

---

²7 : 6 ; 14 : 2 : 28 : 9. ³Ex. 19 : 5f. ⁴4 : 7f. ; 28 : 1. ⁵Ex. 19 : 6. ¹Jos. 24 : 1. ²26 : 16f.
etc. ³5 : 16 : 10 : 9. ⁴Jos. 8 : 30-35. ⁵Jos. 24 : 26. ⁶Ct. 11 : 29. ⁷Ex. 20 : 24 : 24 : 5 ;
32 : 6. ⁸1 : 5.

* Vv. 16-19 introduce the directions for the covenant in ch. xxvii. Their
position, character, language (see refs.) and purpose all show them to be Rd's,
and the references in vv. 18f. to Ex. xix. 5f. show their origin to have been
even later than the latter.

† The passage providing for the solemn ratification of a covenant at Shechem similar to that at Horeb (Ex. xxiv. 3-8), which Rd has here adopted as a
suitable conclusion to the Deuteronomic law, has naturally been very thoroughly retouched by him, like the story of its fulfillment in Jos. viii. 30-35.
Still the additions of Rd, recognizable both from their redundancy (cf. 2f. with
4) and from the style and language, scarcely affect the substance of the para-

11   And Moses charged the people the same day, saying,
12 [9]These shall stand upon mount Gerizim to bless the people,
    when ye are passed over Jordan ; Simeon and Levi, and
13 Judah, and Issachar, and Joseph, and Benjamin : and these
    shall stand upon mount Ebal for the curse ; Reuben, Gad,
14 **(Rd)** and Asher, and Zebulun, Dan, and Naphtali. And the
    Levites shall answer, and say unto all the men of Israel with a loud voice,

15   Cursed be the man that maketh a [10]graven or molten image, an abomina-
    tion unto Yahweh, the [11]work of the hands of the craftsman, and setteth it
    up in secret. And all the people shall answer and say, Amen.

16   [12]Cursed be he that setteth light by his father or his mother. And all
    the people shall say, Amen.

17   [13]Cursed be he that removeth his neighbor's landmark. And all the
    people shall say, Amen.

18   [14]Cursed be he that maketh the blind to wander out of the way. And all
    the people shall say, Amen.

19   [15]Cursed be he that wresteth the judgment of the stranger, fatherless, and
    widow. And all the people shall say, Amen.

20   [16]Cursed be he that lieth with his father's wife ; because he hath uncov-
    ered his father's skirt. And all the people shall say, Amen.

21   [17]Cursed be he that lieth with any manner of beast. And all the people
    shall say, Amen.

22   [18]Cursed be he that lieth with his sister, the daughter of his father, or the
    daughter of his mother. And all the people shall say, Amen.

23   [19]Cursed be he that lieth with his mother in law. And all the people
    shall say, Amen.

24   [20]Cursed be he that smiteth his neighbor in secret. And all the people
    shall say, Amen.

25   [21]Cursed be he that taketh reward to slay an innocent person. And all
    the people shall say, Amen.

[9]Jer. 34 : 18f.   [10]Ex. 20 : 4, 21 ; Lev. 19 : 4.   [11]Is. 40 : 19ff.   [12]Ex. 21 : 15, 17.   [13]19 : 14. [14]Lev. 19 : 14.   [15]Ex. 22 : 21f.   [16]Lev. 18 : 8 ; 20 : 11.   [17]Ex. 22 : 19 ; Lev. 18 : 23 ; 20 : 15. [18]Lev. 18 : 9 ; 20 : 17.   [19]Lev. 18 : 17 ; 20 : 14.   [20]Ex. 21 : 12, 14 ; Lev. 24 : 17.   [21]Ex. 23 : 7f.

graph. In vs. 1 we should read with Dillmann : " And Moses commanded the
elders of Israel " ; LXX. omit " the people " ; cf. vs. 11, Moses' charge to *the
people.*

[22]Cursed be he that confirmeth not the words of this law to do them. 26 And all the people shall say, Amen.*

---

2. Dt. xxx. 1f. THE CHARGE TO JOSHUA.

ANALYSIS.

In Dt. xxx. 1f., after the hortatory appendix to the Code, we begin to find traces of the resumption of the narrative. These however are intermingled with elements clearly belonging to the Code, or rather to its envelope Dh, which it is not our purpose to touch, since the legislation is here more than ever independent of the narrative. To Dh, and to his successor, the author of ch. iv., belongs the " Song of Moses," xxxii. 1–44 ; its *double* introduction, xxxi. 16-22 and 24-30; and the verses, xxxii. 45-47, which bring the Law-book of Dh to a close. The passage Dt. xxxi. 9-13 has the same function and must accordingly be from another hand (Dp) ; but it is also purely related to the law-book. All this material therefore must be treated in a different connection. The remaining portions of the concluding chapters of Deuteronomy belong more or less strictly to the Tradition of the Exodus. In xxx. 1-8, we have, beyond dispute, the link which attaches Deuteronomy at its latter part to the Story of the Conquest, as i. 1a, 4f. at its beginning attached it to the Story of the Wilderness Wandering. Moses announces to the people his own impending death, and presents to them Joshua as his successor, giving him a charge, and assuring him of Yahweh's presence and irresistible aid in the conquest. The passage is unmistakably by the same hand as that which has given to Joshua i. its present form ; the agreement is in fact to a great extent verbal. The relation to the editor who attaches Deuteronomy to JE in i. 1a, 4f. is also clear from the style. There will be no difference of opinion among critics in ascribing the passage to Rd.

Connected in a way with this charge to Joshua are the remarkable

[22]Jer. 11 : 3.

* It is very obvious from the references that the writer of vv. 14-26 is acquainted with all the older codes of the Pentateuch, the *Mishpatim* (E), Law of Holiness (P¹) and Deuteronomy. Reasons have already been given above (Analysis p. 260.) for regarding vv. 14-26 as much later than 11-13. But it is not impossible that they are written on the basis of the original sequel to vv. 11-13.

verses xxxi. 14f., 23; for in spite of some striking differences in the conception both passages are adapted to lead over to the Story of the Conquest by relating the Charge to Joshua. That vv. 14f., 23 have no original connection with 1–8 is very clear. Their separation by vv. 9–13 might indeed be accidental; but in vv. 1–8 the charge is given by *Moses*, in vv. 14f., 23 by *Yahweh*. In vv. 1–8 Moses has already presented Joshua to the people as his successor; whereas in 14f., 23 Moses has yet to call him and be informed by Yahweh that Joshua has been chosen to take his place. Vv. 14f., 23 again have no connection with the context in which they stand (Dh), nor with the preceding passage (Dp). They appear very much in the same relation, or rather want of relation, as the erratic blocks in chh. i. x., xxv. and xxvii. Vv. 9–13 bring the book of Deuteronomy to a full stop with directions for its perpetual preservation and inculcation to the everlasting benefit of Israel. Vs. 14 abruptly introduces the charge to Joshua. Still worse is it with vv. 16–22. Right in the midst of this charge to Joshua comes the first introduction to the Song of Moses. In vs. 15 Yahweh has descended in the cloud at the door of the Tent of Meeting, announcing that he is about to give a charge to Joshua. The latter now stands beside Moses prepared to receive it. Instead, Yahweh addresses *Moses* on the subject of a certain Song he is to teach the people, and the new incident concludes without Joshua's being addressed at all. When Yahweh has concluded his directions to Moses about the Song, we are told " So Moses wrote *this* Song the same day and taught it the children of Israel." Thereafter we naturally expect the Song to follow. But no; in the next verse Yahweh is giving Joshua the charge for the purpose of which he had descended in the cloud in vs. 15. and not until a new introduction has again paved the way for it does the Song finally appear. When, in addition, we contrast the brevity and simplicity of the style in vv. 14f., 23 with the hortatory and high-flown rhetoric of vv. 16–21, 24–30, it becomes very clear that here again we have one of the fragments of JE preserved by Rd.

This time also the source from which it is derived admits of no question. The position filled by Joshua (cf. Jos. xxiv.), above all the unmistakable relation of the passage to Ex. xxxiii. 7–11; Nu. xi. 16f.; xii. 5, shows us that here once more is a genuine fragment of E associated by Rd with Dh, but forming no part of the latter's material. The passage indeed is indispensable in the narrative whose conclusion is found in Jos. xxiv.

This fragmentary account in E of the charge to Joshua is not without its close parallel in P². We have in fact already discussed (see note on Num. xxvii. 12ff.) the double story of the command to Moses to ascend "this mountain of Abarim and die there"; which, in P² as in E (Dt. xxxi. 14), is naturally connected with the charge to Joshua. In the discovery of P²'s source, (Dt. xxxi. 14f., 23) where the announcement to Moses that the time has come for him to die is directly associated with the command " Call Joshua and present yourselves in the tent of meeting that I may give him a charge," we have an additional reason for the conclusion arrived at in connection with Nu. xxvii. 12ff. that this passage, whose principal theme is the charge to Joshua, and not Dt. xxxii. 48-52, which makes no reference to Joshua, is the original P². The latter passage must then be due simply to Rp, resuming the thread of Num. xxvii. 12-23 after the prolonged interruption. It would seem almost superfluous to point out the priestly character of xxxii. 48-53, its incongruous position, relation to the P narratives of the death of Aaron (Num. xx. 22ff. P²) and trespass at Meribath Kadesh (Num. xxi. 13 P²)

(**Rd**) And Moses went and spake these words unto all Israel. **31**—1 And he said unto them, I am an hundred and twenty years old this day; I can 2 no more go out and come in : and ¹Yahweh hath said unto me, Thou shalt not go over this Jordan. Yahweh thy God, he will go over before thee ; he will 3 destroy these nations from before thee, and thou shalt possess them : [and] Joshua, he shall go over before thee, as Yahweh hath spoken. ²And Yah- 4 weh shall do unto them as he did to Sihon and to Og, the kings of the Amorites, and unto their land; whom he destroyed. And Yahweh shall 5 deliver them up before you, and ye shall do unto them according unto all ³the commandment which I have commanded you. ⁴Be strong and of good 6 courage, fear not, nor be affrighted at them : for Yahweh thy God, he it is that doth go with thee; he will not fail thee, nor forsake thee. And Moses 7 called unto Joshua, and said unto him in the sight of all Israel, ⁵Be strong and of good courage : for thou shalt go with this people into the land which Yahweh hath sworn unto their fathers to give them ; and thou shalt cause them to inherit it. And Yahweh, he it is that doth go before thee ; 8 he will be with thee, he will not fail thee, neither, forsake thee : fear not, neither be dismayed.*

¹1 : 37 : 4 : 21.   ²1 : 4f. ; 4 : 46f.   ³7 : 16ff.   ⁴Jos. 1 : 5f.   ⁵Vs. 23 ; Jos. 1 : 9.

* Vv. 1-8 serve to connect Deuteronomy with Jos. i. (see refs. and Analysis). As in Dt. i. 1, 4f. Rd seems here also to have woven in the E fragments left *in situ.* The passage seems to have vv. 14f. in view, although it really antici-

· 14　(E) [. . .] ⁶And Yahweh said unto Moses, Behold, thy
days approach that thou must die : call Joshua, and ⁷present
yourselves in the tent of meeting, that I may give him a
charge.　⁸And Moses and Joshua went, and presented them-

15 selves in the tent of meeting.　And Yahweh appeared in
the Tent in a pillar of cloud : and the pillar of cloud stood
over the door of the Tent.

*　　　*　　　*　　　*　　　*　　　*　　　*　　　*

23　And ⁹he gave Joshua the son of Nun a charge, and said,
Be strong and of a good courage : for thou shalt bring the
children of Israel into the land which I sware unto them :
¹⁰and I will be with thee.

*　　　*　　　*　　　*　　　*　　　*　　　*　　　*

32—48　(Rp) *¹And Yahweh spake unto Moses that selfsame day, saying,*
49 *Get thee up into this mountain of Abarim, unto mount Nebo, which is in the*
land of Moab, ²that is over against Jericho ; and behold the land of Canaan,
50 *which I give unto the children of Israel for a possession : and die in the mount*
whither thou goest up, and be gathered unto thy people ; as ³Aaron thy
51 *brother died in mount Hor, and was gathered unto his people ; because ⁴ye*
trespassed against me in the midst of the children of Israel at the waters of
Meribah of Kadesh, in the wilderness of Zin ; because ye sanctified me not in
52 *the midst of the children of Israel. ⁵For thou shalt see the land before thee :*
but thou shalt not go thither into the land which I give the children of
Israel.*

⁶Cf. Nu. 27 : 12—23 ; vv. 1–8.　⁷Jos. 24 : 1.　⁸Ex. 33 : 7–11 ; Nu. 11 : 16f. ; 12 : 5.　⁹Ct. vs.
7.　¹⁰Gen. 46 : 3f.　²Nu. 27 : 12 23.　³34 : 1.　²Nu. 20 : 22ff.　⁴Nu. 20 : 13 ; cf. Dt. 1. 37.　⁵Cf.
31 : 2.

pates them so far as to make them well-nigh superfluous.　Cf. vs. 7 *before* vs.
14, and vv. 7f. with vs. 23.

　* The passage xxxii. 48–52 resumes the story of P² from Num. xxvii. 12–23,
but is here separated from its connection with the charge to Joshua, which
must have been original (cf. xxxiv. 7–9, and xxxi. 1–8), and assimilated to J in
xxxiv. 1f. (cf. " that is over against Jericho," vs. 49, with xxxiv. 1).　Otherwise
the verses are a close, but somewhat expanded copy of Num. xxvii. 12–14.　It
is worthy of note that " rebelled against my word," Num. xxvii. 14, is here
altered to the more indefinite " trespassed against me," which agrees better
with the present modified form of P² in Num. xx. 1–13.

3. Chh. xxxiii-f. THE BLESSING AND DEATH OF MOSES.

ANALYSIS.

In a poem of unmistakable antiquity Moses surveys the tribes of Israel in order, first the four older sons of Leah, from eldest to youngest ; then the sons of Rachel, proceeding from south to north ; then the two late-born sons of Leah, Zebulun and Issachar ; and lastly the sons of Bilhah and Zilpah, Gad, Dan, Naphtali, Asher, apparently in the order of importance. Upon each he pronounces a blessing, concluding in the style of the exordium, vv. 1-5, with the felicitation of Israel as a whole, vv. 26-29. Immediately after the conclusion of this " blessing " Moses ascends mount Nebo (Pisgah), surveys the Promised Land, dies, and is buried " in the valley of the land of Moab, over against Beth-peor." After reference to the mourning for Moses, and an anticipatory allusion to the qualification of Joshua to be his successor, the author concludes his account of the life and work of Moses with a characterization of his hero as *the* prophet *par excellence.*

In attributing ch. xxxiii. to J the present writer is consciously opposing the all but unanimous consent of critics, which since the time of Graf has not only fixed its date, with what must be admitted to be a high degree of probability, in the prosperous period of Jeroboam II. (786-746 B. C.), when a reunited Israel felt itself victorious and secure in the possession of its fertile land ; but has confidently declared the authorship Ephraimitic, in short that it formed part of the document of E.

The grounds for the current belief are briefly set forth by Addis in his recent work presenting the results of Hexateuch analysis as follows : " Judah (vs. 7) is to ' come ' to the people, not the people to him. The poet says little of Judah, nothing of Simeon. It is of the north tribes, and particularly of Joseph, 'the prince among his brethren,' that he speaks at length and with enthusiasm." *

Dillmann, moreover, finds an affinity of language to the Aramaean and traces of influence by Nu. xxiii. To this might be added the reference in vs. 16 to Ex. iii. 2f., (J's, but attributed by critics generally to E), and the use of ' Elohim ' in vs. 26, were it not that the reading " the God of Jeshurun " is almost certainly to be preferred. Cornill (*Einl.* p. 72), with others, is influenced also by the reference in vs. 9 to Ex. xxxii. 25-29. (J), of which, however, he will go no further than to say " it appears in an E connection." Of the reference in vs. 21 to Num. xxxii. we can only say that either J or E might be referred to, though it is the former who lays

---

* Addis, *Documents of the Hexateuch.* N. Y. 1893, Vol. I., p; 194.

stress upon Gad's having " executed the justice of Yahweh and his judgments with Israel " by " coming with the heads of the people." The reference in vs. 8 to Yahweh's " proving " Levi (or Moses?) and striving
with (or for) him cannot, perhaps, be identified with J's story of Massah
in Ex. xvii. 7 ; but neither can it with E's in xv. 25b ; xvi. 4 and xvii. 2,
so that vs. 8 appears at most neutral ; rather, since, with Cornill, we may
regard the treatment of Levi as a *secular* tribe in xxvii. 12 as from E, vs.
8 is really inconsistent with E authorship. Now we may lay no stress
upon the sympathy with J in vs. 21 ; but it is significant that on wholly
independent grounds our analysis has led to the assignment of the two
passages unmistakably alluded to in vv. 16 and 26 to J and not to E. As
for the other arguments for E, Dillmann's three words explicable from
the Aramaean are very inconclusive evidence for an Ephramite origin, and
of the three possible traces of influence by Nu. xxiii. (see refs.) two are
found also in the J version of that poem, if not exclusively there. See
note on Nu. xxiv. 8. They might all be accounted for by an acquaintance with the poem independent of E. *Per contra* the reminiscences of
Gen. xlix. (J) are indisputable, and these affect the whole structure of our
poem. The same in less degree may be said of Jud. v. (J). The argument that the supreme interest of the poet centres in Joseph is an over-
statement. The proportionate interest in Joseph is no greater than the
relative importance of Ephraim and Manasseh demanded in the time of
the writer ; no greater than appears in J's treatment of the tribal origins
in the narratives of Genesis , no greater than in Gen. xlix., from whence
the greater part of the blessing of Joseph here has been taken bodily.
Graf, who regarded this poem as the work of a priest of the Solomonic
temple, had a truer perception of the author's patriotic feeling. The
survey is comprehensive, but the supreme interest is in " Jeshurun," or
Israel as a whole ; cf. vv. 2-5, 26-29. The centre of unity here is neither
Joseph nor Judah, but Jerusalem ; specifically the temple. So far as a
preference appears for any tribe it is rather the tribe of Levi, (here distinctly a priest-tribe, vs. 10) who are " the people of Yahweh's conse-
crated one " (Moses); or Benjamin, who is " the favorite of Yahweh "
by virtue of the fact that Yahweh's dwelling-place (the temple) is on his
|mountain| shoulders ; vv. 8-10, 12. It is certainly difficult to believe
that an Ephraimite writer, before the time of Josiah, preëminently
*un*priestly in his proclivities, a prophet of the prophets, could have
written, or even incorporated, a poem so incongruous with his own point
of view.

But the crucial objection to Judean or Levitical authorship is sought
in vs. 7, with its apparently curt treatment of Judah, and above all the

clause "bring him in unto his people," which is interpreted as a prayer
that Judah may become reunited to the main stock of Israel, from which
he, and not the ten tribes, had separated himself. Admitting the possibility of this interpretation, and the apparent omission of reference to
Simeon, it is not surprising that vs. 7 should have seemed to the critics
conclusive evidence of authorship by E. Yet it is certainly surprising
after an exordium in which the attention has just been fastened upon " all
the tribes of Israel together," even if the blessing was not originally put
in the mouth of Moses, that the author should at the very outset omit
the oldest but one of all the tribes, and count only *eleven*. It is strange,
therefore, that Dillmann, who recognizes the singularity of this omission,
should reject with the curt verdict of " too violent," the brilliant conjecture of Heilprin (*Histor. poetry of the ancient Hebrews*, 1889, 1. p.
113ff.; following Gratz and Kohler), which places 7b after vs. 10 and
reads in 7a : " And of *Simeon* he said : Hear, Yahweh, the voice of
Simeon, and bring him in unto his people."

It is to be observed in the first place that the true place for the blessing of Judah cannot be after Reuben, with which it is neither geographically contiguous nor historically associated ; but after Simeon and Levi,
as in Gen. xlix. the true model of the present poem. Secondly, the blessing of Levi manifestly reaches its climax and conclusion in vs. 10.
What follows in vs. 11 is impossible to connect with Levi, which as a
priestly guild cannot have enemies on the field of battle, such as are
referred to in vs. 11. Thirdly, the present poem partakes of the character of Gen. xlix. and of ancient poems of this class in general, in the fact
that its tribal oracles attach to the name of the tribe in question with
repeated plays upon its sense (cf. vs. 24 with Gen. xlix. *passim*). Of
this punning character are both parts of vs. 7. The " Hear, (*shem'a*)
Yahweh " is nothing else than a play upon the name Simeon (*shime'on*)
who is represented as praying to be reunited to the principal stock of
Israel, a prayer which, though he might offer it himself, an Ephraimite
could hardly imagine *Judah* as offering ; Simeon, however, in immediate danger at this time of entire extinction by absorption into the neighboring Edomite and Amalekite stocks, might well be supposed to offer
it. There is here, in fact, no reference to the division between the northern and southern kingdoms ; this on the contrary is ignored by the poet,
who dwells upon the national unity. Our conclusion is corroborated by
the second part of the verse, which has the same play upon the name
Judah (*yehudah*) as Gen. xlix. 8, connecting it with the stem *yad*,
" hand." Nor is this all. The same warlike " hands " of Judah are
those which reappear in vs. 11, and the same " adversaries " against

whom Yahweh's help is implored in vs. 7b are those of vs. 11 whose loins Yahweh is entreated to smite through. What possible connection on the other hand can 7b have with 7a? And what better connection can it possibly have than with vs. 11? Finally it is worth while to point out that the running title 7aa, " And this is of Judah: and he said," differing as it does from all the others in vv. 8, 12, 13, 18, 20, 22, 23, 24 which uniformly have " And of——he said " seems to bear the mark of the confusion which has here existed, as if the application of the lines to Judah had been disputed. When to all this we add the fact that some LXX. Mss. have here "Simeon," the conjecture seems anything but "violent." The running titles are in fact no integral part of the poem, which does not even afford justification of the expression " he (*i. e.* Moses) said," though this of course agrees with the introductory formula. It is probable that the blessing of Simeon, like the preceding blessing of Reuben, had no separate title, as it was unnecessary. If then in any way the name Simeon became illegible, it would be most natural for the scribe at once to infer, and to set down on the margin, " This is [the blessing] of Judah," for the double reason that on account of the insignificance, or disappearance, of Simeon, Judah, in his mind, would be the name to follow after Reuben in the order of inheritances, and secondly because the generally geographical order of the poem from south to north would to him suggest Judah at this point. However the dislocation of Judah's blessing be accounted for, the conjecture of Heilprin cannot fairly be dismissed as improbable. On the contrary, apart from all questions of authorship the preponderance of evidence suggests that Simeon *was* mentioned, Yahweh being entreated to " hear " his prayer to be brought in unto his own people ; and Judah was *not* lightly passed over ; but on the contrary receives such attention as could proceed only from one in heartiest sympathy with Judah's side in at least his present battles. *Judaean* authorship, in the strict sense, would be too much to claim for the poem, even with this emendation ; but the supposition of Graf, that it was composed by a priest of the Jerusalem temple acquires well-nigh convincing force. If this be its origin we must certainly look to J rather than E as the document in which it was incorporated, and we shall then find it no small corroboration of the analysis which regards J as the author of the passages, Ex. iv. 10–16 ; xix. 22 ; xxiv. 1f., 9–11 ; xxxii. 25–29 where a semi-priestly interest is displayed. It is in fact a priestly interest, though of the pre-exilic kind which gives the ritual version of the Ten Words, Ex. xxxiv. 10–27, and affords the J nucleus, whatever that be, to which Rp attaches J²'s story of the mutiny of Korah. Such a truly broad and comprehensive patriot-

ism as appears in the selection of narratives of the patriarchal period as
well as in the three great poems of Gen. xlix. ; Dt. xxxiii., and Jud. v. is
what we might expect of a priest of the Solomonic temple in the time of
Jeroboam II.

As positive evidence of connection with the J document we have not
only the references already spoken of ; the manifest interest in the Jerusalem temple and priesthood as centre of the national life ; the remarkable dependence upon Gen. xlix., and relation to the poems of this document ; and the vigorous hatred of Judah's enemies ; but also important
linguistic criteria. The use of " Sinai," vs. 2, is unexampled in either E
or D, which have uniformly " Horeb," but invariable in J ; " Meribath-
Kadesh," in the same verse (see note *in loc.*), like " Sinai," is known
only to J and P. Finally vs. 17, besides a doubtful reminiscence of Nu.
x. 36 (J), can scarcely be interpreted with fairness in a manner compatible with the hatred of Joseph's " firstling bullock " exhibited in Ex. xxxii.,
and the counting of Joseph as one tribe instead of two agrees with J,
whatever may have been E's practice (cf. Gen. xlviii. 20-22 with xlix. 22;
Jos. xvii. 14, 17 ; Jud. i. 22).

Chapter xxxiv. is certainly of a very composite character. Vv. 6, 9
and 12 contain three separate conclusions by as many different hands.
Vv. 7-9 are certainly the sequel to Num. xxvii. 12-23 (P²), vs. 7a being
in the exact form of Num. xxxiii. 39 (P³) and Ex. vii. 7 (P²), and 8f. corresponding to Num. xx. 29 ; xxvii. 18ff. Vv. 10-12 are not due purely to
Rd ; for, as an addition to the work already fully completed and rounded
out they would be the reverse of helpful to his purpose. The Deuteronomic phraseology simply marks the addition in vv. 11f. to an original
datum of E, author of Ex. xxxiii. 11 ; Num. xi. 25 ; xii. 8, and other passages where Moses is presented as the ideal prophet. The geographical
data in 5f. recall Nu. xxi. 20 ; xxv. 3 (J), though the linguistic usage
shows the final clause of vs. 5 to be from P². Vs. 4a repeats Ex. xxxiii.
1 (J) and follows his linguistic usage (Dt. says, " sware *to* give,") and the
latter part of vs. 1, which names a different peak from P and D, is from
the same writer ; though the beginning of the verse continues the
account of P², Num. xxvii. 12ff. (=Dt. xxxii. 48-52). The geographical
amplification between 1b and 4b is redactional (see note *in loc.*), and
probably of late date, but contains the only explanation of the name
" City of Palm-trees," for Jericho, employed by J in Jud. i. 16.

(J) And this is the blessing, wherewith Moses the 33

man of God blessed the children of Israel [2]before his
2 death. And he said,

[2]Yahweh came from Sinai,
And rose from Seir unto them;
He shined forth from mount Paran,
And he came from the ten thousands of holy ones:
At his right hand was a fiery law unto them.

3   Yea, he loveth the peoples;
All his saints are in thy hand:
And they sat down at thy feet; *
[Every one] shall receive of thy words. [. . .]

4   (Rd) Moses commanded us a law,
An inheritance for the assembly of Jacob.

5   And he was 'king in [5]Jeshurun,
When the [6]heads of the people were gathered,
All the tribes of Israel together.

6   Let Reuben live, and not die;
Yet let his men be few.

7   —And this is [the blessing] of Judah—: and [. . .]
     he said,
Hear, Yahweh, the voice of Judah,
And bring him in unto his people:
—With his [7]hands he contended for himself:
And thou shalt be an help against his adversaries.—†

[1]Gen. 27:7; (50:16). [2]Jud. 5:4f. [3]Ex. 19:11, 18, 20 etc. [4]Num. 23:21. [5]32:12.
[6]Vs. 21. [7]Gen. 49:8.

* Vv. 2b, 3 are very corrupt in text. In 2b we should certainly translate
K D S H with LXX. "Kadesh," and the preceding M R B B T H should probably
be M M R B T H or M' R B T H i. e. "from Meribath-(Kadesh):" or "from the
fields of (Kadesh)." What in the last line of vs. 2 was the original of "from
Yahweh's right hand" can only be conjectured, though as between the two
marginal readings of R. V. "streams" is preferable to "fire." Vs. 3 appears
hopeless.

† Vs. 4a interprets the "inheritance" (certainly the land of Canaan) in the
sense of Rd as the Torah. Both sense and language show it to be a late gloss,
perhaps intended to throw light upon the puzzle of vs. 3. It also alters the
sense of vs. 5, which should refer to Yahweh (cf. Num. xxiii. 21).—The blessing of Judah is displaced (see Analysis). Insert 7a*b* after vs. 10, and read, in,
7a *b*, "the voice of Simeon." In 7b read perhaps, "With thy hand contend

And of Levi he said,   8
Thy Thummim and thy Urim are with thy godly
    one,
Whom thou didst ⁷prove at Massah,
With whom thou didst ⁹strive at the waters of
    Meribah;
¹⁰Who said of his father, and of his mother, I have   9
    not ¹¹seen him;
Neither did he acknowledge his brethren,
Nor knew he his own children:
For they have observed thy word,
And keep thy ¹²covenant.
¹³They shall teach Jacob thy judgments,   10
And Israel thy law:
They shall put incense before thee,
And whole burnt offering upon thine altar.
Bless, Yahweh, his substance,   11
And accept the work of his hands:
¹⁴Smite through the loins of them that rise up
    against him,
And of them that hate him, that they rise not
    again.

Of Benjamin he said,   12
The beloved of Yahweh shall dwell in safety by
    him;
He covereth him all the day long,
And he dwelleth between his shoulders.

And of Joseph he said,   13
¹⁵Blessed of Yahweh be his land;
For the precious things of heaven, for the dew,
And for the deep that coucheth beneath,
And for the precious things of the fruits of the   14
    sun,

---

⁸(Ex. 17 : 7). ⁹(Nu. 20 : 3). ¹⁰Ex. 32 : 29. ¹¹Gen. 29 ; 32. ¹²Ex. 34 : 10-27. ¹³Ex 4 : 10 16.
¹⁴Nu. 24 : 8 9. ¹⁵Gen. 41 : 51.

for him." Part II. must be consulted throughout this chapter, as the changes
in text and translation are very numerous.

And for the precious things of the growth of the
     moons,

15 And for the chief things of the ancient mountains,
And for the precious things of the everlasting
     hills,

16 And for the precious things of the earth and the
     fulness thereof,
And the good will of him [16] that dwelt in the bush:
Let [the blessing] come upon the head of Joseph,
And upon the crown of the head of him that was
     separate from his brethren.*

17 The firstling of his bullock, majesty is his:
And his horns are the horns of the[17] wild-ox:
With them he shall push the peoples all of them,
     [even] the ends of the earth:
And they are the [18]ten thousands of Ephraim,
And they are the thousands of Manasseh.

18   And of Zebulun he said,
Rejoice, Zebulun, in thy [19]going out:
And, Issachar, in thy tents.

19 They shall call the peoples unto the mountain:
There shall they offer sacrifices of righteousness:
For they shall suck the abundance of the seas,
And the hidden treasures of the sand.

20   And of Gad he said,
Blessed be he that enlargeth Gad:
He dwelleth as a lioness,
And teareth the arm, yea, the crown of the head.

21 [21]And he provided the first part for himself,
For there was the lawgiver's portion reserved:

---

[16]Ex. 3:22ff.   [17]Nu. 23:22   [18]Nu. 10:36.   [19]Jos. 17:16.   [20]Nu. 32:2ff.

* Vv. 13–16 are peculiar in the fact that they reproduce so closely the blessing of Joseph by Jacob in Gen. xlix. 25f. We might, moreover, simply omit these verses and still have a perfect connection and a blessing of Joseph (vs. 17) corresponding in structure to that of Asher, vv. 24f. In fact the thought seems to approach a climax and conclusion in vs. 16. and vs. 17 to make a new beginning. Still there is no cogent reason for making a separation.

²¹And he came [with] the heads of the people,
He executed the justice of Yahweh,
And his judgments with Israel.

And of Dan he said,   22
Dan is a lion's whelp,
That leapeth forth from Bashan.

And of Naphtali he said,   23
O Naphtali, satisfied with favour,
And full with the blessing of Yahweh:
Possess thou the west and the south.

And of Asher he said,   24
Blessed be Asher with children;
Let him be acceptable unto his brethren,
And let him dip his foot in oil.
Thy ²²bars shall be iron and brass;   25
And as thy days, so shall thy strength be.

There is none like unto God, *O Jeshurun,   26
Who ²³rideth upon the heaven for thy help,
And in his excellency on the skies.
The eternal God is [thy] dwelling place,   27
And underneath are the everlasting ²⁴arms:
And he thrust out the enemy from before thee,
And said, Destroy.
And Israel dwelleth in safety,   28
The fountain of Jacob ²⁵alone,
In a ²⁶land of corn and wine:
Yea, his heavens drop down dew.
Happy art thou, O Israel: 29
Who is like unto thee, a people saved by Yahweh,
The ²⁷shield of thy help,
And that is the sword of thy excellency!
And thine enemies shall submit themselves unto
    thee;
And thou shalt tread upon their high places.

---

²¹Nu. 32 : 26f. ²²Cf. 29 : 5. ²³Jud. 5 : 4. ²⁴Gen. 49 : 24. ²⁵Num. 23 : 9. ²⁶Gen. 27 : 28.
²⁷(Gen. 15 : 1.)

*A better translation of the text (not of the vowel-points) is that of Dillmann

34 (P) [1]*And Moses went up from the plains of Moab unto mount*
(J) *Nebo,* [2]**to the top of Pisgah, that is over against
Jericho.   And Yahweh shewed him all the land**
2 (Rj) **of Gilead, unto Dan; and all Naphtali, and the land of
Ephraim and Manasseh, and all the land of Judah, unto the**
3 **hinder sea; and the South, and the Plain of the valley of Jericho**
4 (J) **the** [3]**city of palm trees, unto Zoar.*   'And Yahweh said
unto him, This is the land which I sware unto Abra-
ham, unto Isaac, and unto Jacob, saying, I will give
it unto thy seed: I have caused thee to see it with
thine eyes, but thou shalt not go over thither.**
5 (E) So Moses the [5]servant of Yahweh died there in the land
6 (P) (J) of Moab, *according to the word of Yahweh.* [. . .] **And
he buried him in the valley in the land of Moab over**
(E) **against Beth-peor:** but no man knoweth of his sepul-
7 (P) chre unto this day.† *And Moses was an hundred and
twenty years old when he died: his eye was not dim, nor his natu-*
8 *ral force abated.* [6]*And the children of Israel wept for Moses in
the plains of Moab thirty days: so the days of weeping in the*
9 *mourning for Moses were ended.* [7]*And Joshua the son of Nun
was full of the spirit of wisdom; for Moses had laid his hands
upon him: and the children of Israel hearkened unto him, and did*
10 (E) *as Yahweh commanded Moses.* [8]And there hath not
arisen a prophet since in Israel like unto Moses, whom Yah-
11 (Rd) weh [9]knew face to face, [10]in all the signs and the wonders,
which Yahweh sent him to do in the land of Egypt, to Pharaoh, and to all
12 his servants, and to all his land; and in all the mighty hand, and in all the
great terror, which Moses wrought in the sight of all Israel.

[1]32:49. [2]Nu. 21:20 and refs. [3]Jud. 1:16. [4]Ex. 33:1ff. [5]Ex. 14:31; Nu. 12:7f.
[6]Nu.20:29. [7]Nu. 27:18ff. [8]Nu. 11.25; cf. ch. 18:15. [9]Ex. 33:11. Nu. 12:8. [10]Ex. 3:
19f.; 4:29, etc.

and of the A. V. "the God of Jeshurun" (cf. Ps. lxviii. 36; cxlvi. 5). Here
and in vs. 27 Elohim is of course necessary and affords no evidence against J.

* The geographical explanation in vv. 2f. is not found in Sam. and is, therefore, probably a redactional expansion of late date, perhaps a " survival."

† In vs. 6 translate with margin R. V. " was buried."

PART II.

The separate documents J, E and P conjectur-
ally restored in a revised translation, with textual
emendations of good authority.

PART II.

THE JUDÆAN PROPHETIC NARRATIVE, CIRC. 800 B. C,

(THE) EXODUS.

STORY OF ISRAEL'S SERVITUDE IN EGYPT. MOSES' DEED OF VIOLENCE, AND FLIGHT TO MIDIAN ; HIS MARRIAGE THERE AND THE BIRTH OF HIS SON.

And Joseph died, and all his brethren, and all that 1—6
generation. But [the children of Israel] multiplied and 7
waxed exceeding mighty. Therefore they did set over them 11
'taskmasters' to 'afflict' them with their burdens. And they
built for Pharaoh store cities, Pithom and Raamses. But the 12
more they 'afflicted' them, the more they multiplied and the
more they 'spread abroad' ; so that they 'stood in dread of'
the children of Israel. [And they imposed forced labor on 13
them], in mortar and in brick, and in all manner of service in
the field ; but the people multiplied, and waxed very mighty. 20b

[. . . And one of the house of Levi named Moses, a son
of Amram, rose up against an Egyptian and slew him. And
Pharaoh sent men to take him, but Moses fled, and escaped
to the land of Midian. And he saw a well in the field and
flocks] ; so he sat down by the well.   2—15b

Now [Hobab] the priest of Midian had seven daughters : 16
and they came to draw water, and fill the 'troughs' to water
their father's flock ; but the 'shepherds' came and drove 17
them away : and Moses stood up and helped them, and watered their flock. And when they came to their father, he 18
said, How is it that ye are come so soon to-day ? And they 19
said, An Egyptian delivered us out of the hand of the 'shepherds,' and moreover he drew water for us, and watered the
flock. And he said unto his daughters, And where is he ? 20

why is it that ye have deserted the man? call him, that he
21 may eat bread. And Moses 'decided' to dwell with the
22 man : and he gave Moses Zipporah his daughter. And she
bare a son, and he called his name Gershom :

DEATH OF THE TYRANT, AND RETURN OF MOSES TO EGYPT. HE ENCOUNTERS YAHWEH AT THE LODGING-PLACE, AND ZIPPORAH CIRCUMCISES HER CHILD AS A SUBSTITUTE FOR BRIDEGROOM CIRCUMCISION.

2—23 And it came to pass in the course of those many days,
4—19 that the king of Egypt died : And 'Yahweh' said unto
Moses in Midian, Go, return into Egypt : for all the men are
20 dead which sought thy life. So Moses took his wife and his
son, and set them upon an ass, and he set out to return to
24 the land of Egypt : And it came to pass on the way at the
'lodging-place,' that 'Yahweh' 'fell upon' him, and sought
25 to kill him. Then Zipporah took a flint and touched his
person with it, saying, Surely a " blood-bridegroom " art
26 thou to me. So he let him alone. Then it was that she
gave rise to the saying, "a bridegroom of blood " with reference to circumcision.

YAHWEH'S APPEARANCE TO MOSES IN THE BURNING BUSH AND COMMISSION TO HIM TO DELIVER ISRAEL.

[And on the morrow Moses set forward from the lodging-
3—2 place]. And the angel of 'Yahweh' 'appeared' unto him
in a flame of fire out of the midst of the thorn thicket. And
when he looked 'behold' the whole thicket was burning with
3 fire, but the thicket was not consumed. And Moses said to
himself, I will turn aside now and see this great sight, why
4 the thicket is not consumed. And when ' Yahweh 'perceived
5 that he turned aside to see, he said, Draw not nigh hither,
' put off thy sandals from off thy feet ; for the place where-
7 on thou standest is holy ground.' And ' Yahweh ' said, I have
surely seen the 'affliction' of my people which are in Egypt,
and have heard their cry by reason of their 'taskmasters ';
8 for I know their sorrows ; and I am 'come down' to deliver

them out of the hand of the Egyptians, and to bring them
up out of that land unto a good land and a large, unto a
'land flowing with milk and honey.' Go, and gather the 16
elders of Israel together, and say unto them, Yahweh, the
God of your fathers, the God of Abraham, of Isaac, and of
Jacob, hath 'appeared' unto me, saying, I have surely
visited you, and seen that which is done to you in Egypt :
and I have said, I will bring you up out of the 'affliction' of 17
Egypt unto a 'land flowing with milk and honey.' And they 18
shall hearken to thy voice : and thou shalt come, thou and
the elders of Israel, unto the king of Egypt, and ye shall say
unto him, Yahweh, the God of the Hebrews, hath 'met' with
us : and now let us go, we pray thee, 'three days' journey into
the wilderness,' that we may sacrifice to Yahweh our God.
And Moses answered and said, But, what if they will not 4
believe me, nor hearken unto my voice, but say, Yahweh
hath not 'appeared' unto thee? And Yahweh said unto him, 2
What is that in thine hand? And he said, A rod. And he 3
said, Cast it on the 'ground.' And he cast it on the 'ground,
and it became a 'serpent'; and Moses fled from before it.
And Yahweh said unto Moses, Put forth thine hand, and 4
take it by the tail : (so he put forth his hand, and laid hold
of it, and it became a rod in his hand :) that they may be- 5
lieve that Yahweh, the God of their fathers, the God of
Abraham, the God of Isaac, and the God of Jacob, hath
'appeared' unto thee. And Yahweh said furthermore unto 6
him, Put now thine hand into thy bosom. So he put his hand
into his bosom : and when he took it out, behold, his hand
was leprous, as [white as] snow. And he said, Put thine 7
hand into thy bosom again. (Then, when he had put his
hand into his bosom again, and had taken it out of his bosom,
behold, it was turned again as his [other] flesh.) And it shall 8
come to pass, if they will not believe thee, neither hearken
to the voice of the first sign, that they will believe the voice
of the latter sign. And it shall come to pass, if they will not 9
believe even these two signs, neither hearken unto thy voice,
that thou shalt take of the water of the Nile, and pour it

upon the dry land : and the water which thou takest out of
the Nile shall become blood upon the dry land.

THE PRIESTHOOD THE AUTHORIZED EXPOUNDERS OF THE LAW. AARON IS MADE MOSES' SPOKESMAN TO THE PEOPLE.

10 And Moses said unto Yahweh, 'I pray thee, Lord, have
me excused,' I am no speaker neither 'heretofore,' nor since
thou hast spoken unto thy servant : for I am slow of speech,
11 and of a slow tongue. And Yahweh said unto him, Who
hath made man's mouth ? or who maketh [a man] dumb, or
12 deaf, or seeing, or blind ? is it not I Yahweh ? Now therefore go, and I will be with thy mouth, and teach thee what
13 thou shalt speak. But he said, 'I pray thee, Lord, have me
excused,' send I pray thee rather by the hand of whomsoever
14 thou wilt. And the anger of Yahweh was kindled against
Moses, and he said, Is there not Aaron thy brother, the
15 'Levite'? I know that he can speak well [. . .] And
thou shalt speak unto him, and put the words in his mouth :
and I will be with thy mouth, and with his mouth, and will
16 teach you what ye shall do. And he shall be thy spokesman
unto the people : and it shall come to pass, that he shall be
to thee a mouth, and thou shalt be to him as God [to the
29 priest] So Moses and Aaron went and gathered together all
30 the elders of the children of Israel : and he [Moses] spake
all the words which Yahweh had spoken, and did the signs in
31 the sight of the people. And the people believed when they
heard that Yahweh had visited the children of Israel, and
that he had seen their 'affliction,' and they 'bowed their
heads and worshipped.'

THE APPEAL TO PHARAOH. MOSES AND THE ELDERS MEET REBUFF, AND THE PEOPLE'S BURDENS ARE INCREASED.

[Then Moses and the elders of Israel came unto Pharaoh]
5—3 and said, The God of the Hebrews hath 'met' with us :
let us go, we pray thee, 'three days' journey into the wilderness,' and sacrifice unto Yahweh our God ; lest he 'fall
upon' us with pestilence, or with the sword.

And Pharaoh said, Behold, the people of the land are now 5
many, and would ye make them rest from their burdens?
And the same day Pharaoh commanded the 'taskmasters' 6
of the people, saying, Ye shall no more give the people 7
straw to make brick, as heretofore : let them go and gather
straw for themselves. And the stint of bricks, which they 8
did make heretofore, ye shall lay upon them ; ye shall not
diminish aught thereof : for they be idle ; therefore they
cry, saying, Let us go and sacrifice to our God. Let heav- .9
ier work be laid upon the men, that they may labor therein,
and they will not regard lying words. And the 'task- 10
masters' of the people went out, and spake to the people,
saying, Thus saith Pharaoh, I will not give you straw. Go 11
yourselves, get you straw where ye can find it : for naught
of your work shall be diminished. So the people were 12
'scattered abroad' throughout all the land of Egypt to
gather stubble for straw. And the 'taskmasters' were 13
urgent, saying, Fulfil your works, [your] daily stint, as
when there was straw. And the officers of the children of 14
Israel, which Pharaoh's 'taskmasters' had set over them,
were beaten, and demanded, Wherefore have ye not fulfilled
your stint both yesterday and to-day, in making brick as
heretofore? Then the officers of the children of Israel 15
came and cried unto Pharaoh, saying, Wherefore dealest thou
thus with thy servants? There is no straw given unto thy 16
servants, and they say to us, Make brick : and, behold, thy
servants are beaten; but . . . .* But he said, Ye are idle, ye 17
are idle: therefore ye say, Let us go and sacrifice to Yahweh.
Go therefore now, and work ; for there shall no straw be 18
given you, yet shall ye deliver the stint of bricks. And the 19
officers of the children of Israel did see that they were in
evil case, when it was said, Ye shall not minish aught from
your bricks, [your] daily stint. And they met Moses and 20
the elders, who were awaiting them, as they came forth from
Pharaoh : and they said unto them, 'Yahweh look upon you, 21

---

* Unintelligible: LXX. translate (from a different text) " thou wrongest thy
people."

and judge'; because ye have made us 'odious' in the eyes
of Pharaoh, and in the eyes of his servants, to put a sword
22 in their hand to slay us. And Moses returned unto Yahweh,
and said, 'Lord,' wherefore hast thou 'evil entreated' this
23 people? why is it that thou hast sent me? For since I
came to Pharaoh to speak in thy name, he hath 'evil entreated' this people; neither hast thou delivered thy people
at all.

THE WONDERS OF EGYPT. FIRST PLAGUE: YAHWEH SMITES THE NILE AND DESTROYS ITS FISH.

7--14   And Yahweh said unto Moses, Pharaoh's heart is 'sullen,' he refuseth to let the people go. [Go in unto Pharaoh]
16 and say unto him, Yahweh, the God of the Hebrews, hath
sent me unto thee, saying, Let my people go, that they may
'worship' me in the wilderness: and, behold, hitherto thou
17 hast not hearkened. Thus saith Yahweh, behold, I will
18 smite [the Nile]. And the fish that is in the Nile shall die,
. and the Nile shall 'stink'; and the Egyptians shall loathe
19 to drink water from the Nile. [So on the morrow Yahweh
21 smote the Nile.] And the fish that was in the Nile
died; and the Nile 'stank,' and the Egyptians could not
24 drink water from the Nile. And all the Egyptians digged
round about the Nile for water to drink; for they could not
drink of the water of the Nile.

THE SECOND PLAGUE: FROGS.

7--25 And when seven days were fulfilled after that Yahweh
8--1 had smitten the Nile, Yahweh said unto Moses:
Go in unto Pharaoh, and say unto him, Thus saith Yahweh,
2 Let my people go, that they may 'worship' me. And if
thou refuse to let them go, behold, I will smite all thy bor-
3 ders with frogs: and the Nile shall swarm with frogs, which
shall go up and come into thine house, and into thy bedchamber, and upon thy bed, and into the house of thy servants, and upon thy people, and into thine ovens, and into
4 thy 'kneading-troughs'": and the frogs shall come up both

upon thee, and upon thy people, and upon all thy servants.
[And Yahweh did so on the morrow, and the frogs covered
the land.] Then Pharaoh called for Moses and said, 'In- 8
treat' Yahweh, that he take away the frogs from me, and
from my people ; and I will let the people go, that they may
sacrifice unto Yahweh. And Moses said unto Pharaoh, Only 9
command me : for what time shall I 'intreat' for thee, and
for thy servants, and for thy people, that the frogs be destroyed from thee and thy houses, and remain in the Nile
only ? And he said, For to-morrow. And he said, It shall be 10
according to thy word. And the frogs shall depart from 11
thee, and from thy houses, and from thy servants, and from
thy people ; they shall remain in the Nile only. And Moses 12
went out from Pharaoh : and Moses cried unto Yahweh concerning the frogs which he had brought upon Pharaoh.
And Yahweh did according to the word of Moses ; and the 13
frogs died out of the houses, out of the courts, and out of the
fields. And they gathered them together in heaps : and 14
the land 'stank.' But when Pharaoh saw that there was 15
respite, he made his heart 'sullen' [and did not let the people go].

THE THIRD PLAGUE: GAD-FLIES.

And Yahweh said unto Moses, Rise up early in the morn- 20
ing, and stand before Pharaoh ; and say unto him, Thus
saith Yahweh, Let my people go, that they may 'worship'
me. Else, if thou wilt not let my people go, behold, I will 21
send gad-flies upon thee, and upon thy servants, and upon
thy people, and into thy houses : and the houses of the
Egyptians shall be full of gad-flies, and even the 'ground'
whereon they are. But I will sever in that day 'the land of 22
Goshen,' in which my people dwell, that no gad-fly shall be
there. And I will put . . . * between my people and thy 23
people : by to-morrow shall this sign be. And Yahweh did 24
so ; and there came 'grievous' gad-flies into the house of
Pharaoh, and into his servants' houses : and in all the land

---

* The untranslated word elsewhere means " redemption."

of Egypt the land was ruined by reason of the gad-flies.
25 And Pharaoh called for Moses and said, Go, sacrifice to
26 your God in the land. And Moses said, It is not meet so to
do ; for we shall sacrifice that which the Egyptians abhor to
Yahweh our God. What then if we sacrifice a thing abhor-
rent to the Egyptians before their eyes? Will they not stone
27 us? We will go 'three days' journey into the wilderness,'
and sacrifice to Yahweh our God, as he hath commanded us.
28 And Pharaoh said, I will let you go, that ye may sacrifice to
Yahweh your God in the wilderness ; only ye shall not go very
29 far away : 'intreat' for me. And Moses said, Behold, I go out
from thee, and I will 'intreat' Yahweh that the gad-flies
may depart from Pharaoh, from his servants, and from his
people, to-morrow : only let not Pharaoh deal deceitfully
any more in not letting the people go to sacrifice to Yah-
30 weh. So Moses went out from Pharaoh, and 'intreated'
31 Yahweh. And Yahweh did according to the word of Moses ;
and he removed the gad-flies from Pharaoh, from his ser-
32 vants, and from his people ; 'there remained not one.' And
Pharaoh made his heart 'sullen' this time also, and he did
not let the people go.

The Fourth Plague: Murrain.

9   Then Yahweh said unto Moses, Go in unto Pharaoh, and
2 tell him, Thus saith Yahweh, the God of the Hebrews, Let
3 my people go, that they may 'worship' me. For if thou
refuse to let them go, and wilt hold them still, behold, the
hand of Yahweh shall be upon thy cattle which is in the
field, upon the horses, upon the asses, upon the camels, upon
the herds, and upon the flocks in a 'very grievous' murrain.
4 And Yahweh shall sever between the 'cattle of Israel' and the
cattle of Egypt : and there shall nothing die of all that
5 belongeth to the children of Israel. And Yahweh appointed
a set time, saying, To-morrow Yahweh shall do this thing in
6 the land. And Yahweh did that thing on the morrow, and
all the cattle of Egypt died : but of the 'cattle of the chil-

dren of Israel' 'died not one.' And Pharaoh sent, and, be- 7
hold, there was 'not so much as one' of the 'cattle of the
Israelites' dead. But the heart of Pharaoh was 'sullen,' and
he did not let the people go.

THE FIFTH PLAGUE: HAIL.

And Yahweh said unto Moses, Rise up early in the morn- 13
ing, and stand before Pharaoh, and say unto him, 'Thus
saith Yahweh, the God of the Hebrews,' Let my people go,
that they may worship me. Standest thou still out against 17
my people, that thou wilt not let them go? Behold, ' to- 18
morrow about this time ' I will cause it to rain a 'very grievous' hail, such as hath not been in Egypt since the day it
was founded even until now. Then Yahweh rained hail upon 23b
the land of Egypt, and an incessant fire flashing amidst the
hail. So there was a 'very grievous' hail such as had not 24
been in all the land of Egypt since it belonged to a nation,
and the hail smote every 'herb of the field,' and brake every
'tree of the field.' Only in ' the land of Goshen,' where 26
the children of Israel were, was there no hail. And Pharaoh 27
sent, and called for Moses, and said, I have sinned this time :
Yahweh is right and I and my people are wrong. ' Intreat ' 28
Yahweh ; for there hath been enough of thunderings and
hail ; and I will let you go, and ye shall stay no longer.
And Moses said unto him, As soon as I am gone out of the 29
city, I will spread abroad my hands unto Yahweh [in prayer];
the thunders shall cease, neither shall there be any more
hail. (Now the flax and the barley were smitten : for the 31
barley was in the ear, and the flax in bloom. But the wheat 32
and the spelt were not smitten : for they were not grown
up.) So Moses went out of the city from Pharaoh, and 33
spread abroad his hands unto Yahweh : and the thunders
and hail ceased, and the rain was not poured upon the earth.
And when Pharaoh saw that the rain and the hail and the 34
thunders were ceased, he sinned yet more, and made his
heart 'sullen,' he and his servants.

The Sixth Plague: Locusts.

10—36 And Yahweh said unto Moses, Go in unto Pharaoh, and
say unto him, Thus saith Yahweh, the God of the Hebrews,
How long wilt thou refuse to humble thyself before me?
4 let my people go, that they may 'serve' me. Else, if thou
refuse to let my people go, behold, to-morrow will I bring
5 locusts into thy 'border :' and they shall cover the face of
the earth, that one shall not be able to see the earth : and
they shall eat the residue of that which is escaped, which
remaineth unto you from the hail, and shall eat every tree
6 which groweth for you out of the field : and thy houses
shall be filled, and the houses of all thy servants, and the
houses of all the Egyptians ; 'as neither thy fathers nor thy
fathers' fathers have seen, since the day that they
were upon the 'ground unto this day.' And he turned, and
7 went out from Pharaoh. And Pharaoh's servants said unto
him, How long shall this man be a snare unto us ? let the
men go, that they may 'worship' Yahweh their God : know-
8 est thou not yet that Egypt is destroyed ? And Moses and
the elders were brought again unto Pharaoh : and he said
unto them, Go, 'worship' Yahweh your God : but who are
9 they that shall go ? And Moses said, We will go with our
young and with our old, with our sons and with our daughters, with our 'flocks and with our herds' will we go ; for
10 we must hold a feast unto Yahweh. And he said unto
them, So be Yahweh with you, as I will let you go, and your
11 little ones : look to it ; for ye mean mischief. Not so : go
now ye that are men, and 'worship' Yahweh ; since that is
what ye desire. And they were driven out from Pharaoh's
13b presence. Then Yahweh brought an 'east wind' upon the
land all that day, and all the night : and when it was morning, the 'east wind' brought the locusts, and they rested in
14 all the 'borders' of Egypt ; 'very grievous' were they, 'before them there were no such locusts as they, neither after
15 them shall be such.' For they covered the face of the
whole earth, so that the land was darkened ; and 'there

remained not any ' green thing, either tree or ' herb of the field,' through all the land of Egypt. Then Pharaoh called 16 for Moses in haste ; and he said, I have sinned against Yahweh your God, and against you. Now therefore forgive 17 I pray thee, my sin only this once, and ' intreat ' Yahweh your God, that he may take away from me this deathly [plague] only. And he went out from Pharaoh, and ' in- 18 treated ' Yahweh. And Yahweh turned an exceeding strong 19 ' west wind,' which took up the locusts, and drove them into the Red Sea ; there ' remained not one ' locust in all the ' border ' of Egypt. And Pharaoh called Moses, and said, 24 Go ye, worship Yahweh ; only let your ' flocks and your herds ' be stayed : let your little ones also go with you. And Moses said, Thou must also give into our hands sacri- 25 fices and burnt offerings, that we may sacrifice unto Yahweh our God. Our ' cattle ' also shall go with us ; there shall 26 ' not a hoof ' be left behind ; for thereof must we take to worship Yahweh our God ; and we know not with what we must worship Yahweh, until we come thither. And Pharaoh 28 said unto him, Get thee from me, take heed to thyself, see my face no more ; for ' in the day thou seest my face thou shalt die.' And Moses said, Thou hast spoken well ; I will 29 see thy face again no more.

And he said, Thus saith Yahweh, About midnight will **11—**4 I go out into the midst of Egypt : and all the firstborn in 5 the land of Egypt shall die, from the firstborn of Pharaoh that sitteth upon his throne, even unto the firstborn of the ' maidservant ' that sitteth at the hand mill. And there 6 shall be a great cry throughout all the land of Egypt, ' such as there hath been none like it, nor shall be like it any more.' But against any of the children of Israel shall ' not 7 a dog wag his tongue,' against man or ' beast.' And all 8 these thy servants shall come down unto me, and bow down themselves unto me, saying, Get thee out, and all the people that follow thee : and after that I will go out. So he went out from Pharaoh in hot anger.

THE SEVENTH PLAGUE: YAHWEH SMITES THE FIRSTBORN OF
EGYPT AND DELIVERS ISRAEL. THE PASSOVER.

12—21 Then Moses called for all the elders of Israel, and
said unto them, Go forth, and take you lambs and kill them.
22 And ye shall take a bunch of hyssop, and dip it in the blood
that is in the bason, and strike the lintel and the two side
posts with the blood that is in the bason ; and none of you
23 shall go out of the door of his house. For Yahweh will pass
through to smite the Egyptians ; and when he seeth the
blood upon the lintel, and on the two side posts, Yahweh
will " pass over " the door, and will not suffer ' the destroyer '
27b to come in unto your houses to smite you. And the people
27a ' bowed the head and worshipped.' [Therefore do the
children of Israel keep this feast unto Yahweh ; for that he
" passed over " the houses of the children of Israel in Egypt
when he smote the Egyptians and delivered their houses.]
42a It is a night of watching unto Yahweh for that he brought
them forth out of the land of Egypt.
29 And it came to pass at midnight, that Yahweh smote all
the firstborn in the land of Egypt, 'from the firstborn of
Pharaoh that sat upon his throne unto the firstborn of the
30b captive' that was in the dungeon ; and there was a great
cry in Egypt ; for there was 'not a house' where there
30a was not one dead.' And Pharaoh rose up in the night,
(11—8) he, and all his servants, and all the Egyptians, [and
came and bowed themselves down unto Moses, saying,
Thus saith Pharaoh, Get thee out, both thou and all the
31b people that follow thee] and go, ' worship ' Yahweh, as ye
32 have said. Take both your ' flocks and your herds,' as ye
33 have said, and be gone : and bless me also. And the
Egyptians ' were urgent ' upon the people, to send them
out of the land in haste ; for they said, We be all dead men.
34 And the people took their dough before it was leavened,
their ' kneading troughs ' being bound up in their clothes
upon their shoulders.

THE EXODUS. ORIGIN OF THE FEAST OF UNLEAVENED CAKES, AND LAW OF FIRSTLINGS.

And the children of Israel journeyed from Rameses 'to 37
Succoth,' about six hundred thousand on foot that were
men, besides children. And a mixed multitude went up also 38
with them; and 'flocks, and herds,' even very much 'cattle.'.
And they baked "unleavened cakes" of the dough which 39
they brought forth out of Egypt, for it was not leavened;
because they were thrust out of Egypt, and could not tarry,
neither had they prepared for themselves any victual.
And Moses said unto the people, This day ye are 13—3a-4
going forth in the month 'Abib.' And it shall be when 5
Yahweh shall bring thee into the land which he sware unto
thy fathers to give thee, a 'land flowing with milk and honey,'
that thou shalt keep this service in this month. Seven days 6
thou shalt eat unleavened cakes, and in the seventh day shall
be a feast to Yahweh. Unleavened cakes shall be eaten 7
throughout the seven days; and there shall no leavened
bread be seen with thee, neither shall there be leaven seen
with thee, in all thy 'borders.'

And it shall be when Yahweh shall bring thee into 11
the 'land of the Canaanite,' as he sware unto thee
and to thy fathers, and shall give it thee, that thou 12
shalt cause to pass over unto Yahweh all that 'openeth
the womb,' and every firstling which thou hast that cometh of a beast; they shall be Yahweh's. And every 13
firstling of an ass thou shalt redeem with a lamb; and if
thou wilt not redeem it, then thou shalt break its neck: and
all the firstborn of man among thy sons shalt thou redeem.

And *Yahweh went before them by day in a 'pillar of 21
cloud,' to lead them the way; and by night in a 'pillar
of fire,' to give them light; that they might go by day
and by night: 'the pillar of cloud' by day, and the 'pillar 22
of fire' by night, departed not from the people.

---

* Vv. 21f. would seem more appropriately placed after xii. 38, but in the
uncertainty as to whether parts of J are not missing, we do not venture to
transpose.

THE PASSAGE OF THE RED SEA.

14—5   And it was told the king of Egypt that the people
were fled ; and the heart of Pharaoh and of his servants was
'changed' towards the people, and they said, What is this
we have done, that we have let Israel go from serving us?
6 And he made ready his chariot, and took his people with
7 him, and all the chariots of Egypt, [and pursued after
10 them]. And when Pharaoh drew nigh, the children of Israel
lifted up their eyes, and, behold, the Egyptians marched
11 after them ; and they were sore afraid. And they said unto
Moses, Because there were no graves in Egypt, hast thou
taken us away to die in the wilderness? wherefore hast thou
12 'dealt' thus with us, to bring us forth out of Egypt? Is
not this the word that we spake unto thee in Egypt, saying,
Let us alone, that we may serve the Egyptians? For it
were better for us to serve the Egyptians, than that we
13 should die in the wilderness. And Moses said unto the
people, Fear ye not, stand still, and see the salvation of Yahweh, which he will work for you to-day : for such as ye have
seen the Egyptians to-day, thus shall ye see them again no
14 more forever. Yahweh shall fight for you, and ye shall
19 hold your peace. Then the 'pillar of cloud' removed from
before them, and stood behind them : and it gave forth
lightnings through the night, so that the one came not near
21 the other all the night. And Yahweh caused the sea to go
[back] by a 'strong east wind' all the night, and made the
24 sea dry land. And it came to pass 'in the watch before
the dawn,' that Yahweh 'looked forth' upon the host of the
Egyptians through the 'pillar of fire and of cloud,' and
25 threw the Egyptian host into confusion ; so that the Egyptians said, Let us flee from the face of Israel ; for Yahweh
27 fighteth for them against the Egyptians. And the sea returned to its wonted flow 'when the morning appeared,'
while the Egyptians were fleeing against it : and Yahweh
28 shook off the Egyptians in the midst of the sea; 'there re-
30 mained not so much as one of them.' Thus Yahweh saved

Israel that day out of the hand of the Egyptians; and Israel saw the Egyptians dead upon the seashore.

Then 'sang Moses and the children of Israel this song' **15** unto Yahweh, and spake, saying,

> I will sing unto Yahweh, for he is highly exalted.
> The horse and his rider hath he hurled into the sea.

MARAH, ELIM, AND MASSAH.

And Moses led Israel onward from the Red Sea, and they **22** went out into the wilderness of Shur; and they went 'three days in the wilderness,' and found no water. And they **23** came to Marah, but they could not drink of the waters of Marah, for they were "bitter": therefore the name of it was called Marah (*i. e.* "Bitterness"). And the people 'mur- **24** mured' against Moses, saying, What shall we drink? And **25** he cried unto Yahweh; and Yahweh shewed him a tree, and he cast it into the waters, and the waters were made sweet. And they came to Elim, where were twelve springs **27** of water, and threescore and ten palm trees: and they encamped there by the waters. [And on the third day they came to Massah.] And the people thirsted there for **17—3** water; and the people 'murmured' against Moses, and said, Wherefore hast thou brought us up out of Egypt, to kill us and our children and our 'cattle' with thirst? [If Yahweh **(7)** be among us let him give us water that we may drink. And Moses rebuked the people and said], Wherefore do ye put **2b** Yahweh to the "proof"? [If Yahweh delight in us he will give us water even here in the desert. And Yah- **(Dt. 33—8)** weh said unto Moses, By this I have "proved" thee that thou art faithful. . . . So he gave them water for themselves and their cattle. And the name of the place was called] Massah (*i. e.* "Proving") because they put Yahweh **7** to the "proof," saying, 'Is Yahweh among us' or not?

THE THEOPHANY AT SINAI. YAHWEH PREPARES MOSES, AARON AND THE PRIESTS TO RECEIVE A LAW.

[And when they were departed from Massah they

19—2b came to Sinai]. And Israel encamped there before
18 the mount. And mount 'Sinai' was altogether on smoke,
because Yahweh had 'come down' upon it in fire : and the
smoke thereof 'ascended as the smoke of a furnace,' and
20 the whole mount quaked greatly. So Yahweh 'came down'
upon mount 'Sinai,' to the 'top of the mount' : and Yahweh called Moses to the 'top of the mount"; and Moses
21 went up. And Yahweh said unto Moses, Go down, charge
the people, lest they 'break through' unto Yahweh to 'gaze,'
22 and great numbers of them fall dead. And let the 'priests'
also, which come near to Yahweh, sanctify themselves, lest
24 Yahweh 'break forth' upon them. And thou shalt come up,
thou, and Aaron with thee, and the 'priests' : but let not 'the
people break through' to come up unto Yahweh, lest he
11 'break forth' upon them. For to-morrow Yahweh will come
down in the sight of all the people upon mount 'Sinai ;'
12 and thou shalt set bounds unto the people round about,
saying, Take heed to yourselves, that ye go not up into the
mount, or touch the 'border' of it : whosoever toucheth the
13 mount shall be surely put to death : no hand shall touch
him, but he shall surely be stoned, or shot through ; whether
it be 'beast' or man, it shall not live : when the 'ram's
25 horn' soundeth long, these shall come up to the mount. So
Moses went down unto the people, and said unto them [. . .]

YAHWEH'S COVENANT-MEAL WITH MOSES AND THE ELDERS.

[And on the morrow there were lightnings and thunders
on the mount with fire and smoke. And when the rams-
horn was heard sounding long Yahweh spake, saying. . . .]
24—1 But unto Moses he said, Come up unto Yahweh, thou, and
Aaron, Nadab, and Abihu, and seventy of the elders of Israel ;
2 and worship ye afar off : and Moses alone shall come
near unto Yahweh : but they shall not come near ; neither
9 shall the people go up with him. Then went up Moses,
and Aaron, Nadab, and Abihu, and seventy of the elders of
10 Israel : and they saw the God of Israel ; and there was
under his feet as it were a paved work of sapphire stone,

and as it were the very heaven for clearness. And upon 11
the nobles of the children of Israel he laid not his hand : and
they beheld God, and did eat and drink [a covenant meal].

THE COVENANT AT SINAI. THE TEN WORDS WRITTEN ON THE TABLES OF STONE.

And Yahweh said unto Moses, Hew thee two tables of 34
'stones.' And be ready by the morning, and come up in 2
the morning unto mount 'Sinai,' and present thyself there
to me on the 'top of the mount.' And no man shall come 3
up with thee, neither let any man be seen throughout all
the mount ; neither let the 'flocks nor herds' feed before
that mount. So Moses rose up early in the morning, and 4
went up unto mount 'Sinai,' as Yahweh had commanded
him, and took in his hand two tables of 'stones.' And 5
Yahweh 'descended' in the cloud, and he [Moses] stood
with him there and 'called upon the name of Yahweh.' And 10
he said, Behold, I make a covenant in the presence of all
thy people.

Thou shalt worship no other god : for Yahweh, whose 14
name is Jealous, is a jealous God :

Thou shalt make thee no molten gods. 17

All that 'openeth the womb' is mine ; the firstlings of ox 19
and sheep. And the firstling of an ass thou shalt redeem 20
with a lamb : and if thou wilt not redeem it, then thou shalt
break its neck.

All the firstborn of thy sons thou shalt redeem nor let
them see my face empty handed.

Six days thou mayest work, but on the seventh day thou 21
shalt rest : in plowing time and in harvest thou shalt rest.

The feast of unleavened cakes shalt thou keep. Seven 18
days thou shalt eat unleavened cakes as I commanded thee,
at the time appointed in the month 'Abib' : for in the
month Abib thou camest out from Egypt. 22

And thou shalt observe the feast of weeks, [even] of the
first fruits of wheat harvest, and the feast of ingathering at
the year's end.

Thou shalt not offer the blood of my sacrifice with leav- 25 ened bread ; and the sacrifice of the feast of the passover shall not be left unto the morning.

26   The first of the firstfruits of thy 'ground' thou shalt bring unto the house of Yahweh thy God.

Thou shalt not seethe a kid in its mother's milk.

27   And Yahweh said unto Moses, Write thou these words : for after the tenor of these words I have made a covenant with thee and with Israel.

28   And he was there with Yahweh forty days and forty nights ; he did neither eat bread, nor drink water. And he wrote upon the tables the words of the covenant, the Ten Commandments.

THE PEOPLE'S SIN. CONSECRATION OF LEVI.

32—7 [And it came to pass after the forty days] that Yahweh spake unto Moses, Go, get thee down ; for thy people, which thou broughtest up out of the land of Egypt, have 'corrupted' themselves : . . . I have seen this people, and,

10 behold, it is a 'stiffnecked' people : now therefore leave me that my wrath may wax hot against them, and that I may 'consume' them : and 'I will make of thee a great nation.'

11 And Moses sought to appease Yahweh his God, and said, Yahweh, why doth thy wrath wax hot against thy people, which thou hast brought forth out of the land of Egypt

12 with great power and with a mighty hand ? 'Wherefore should the Egyptians speak, saying, For evil did he bring them forth, to slay them in the mountains, and to 'consume ' them from the face of the earth ?' Turn from thy fierce

14 wrath, and 'repent' of this evil against thy people. So Yahweh 'repented' of the evil which he said he would do unto his people. [And Moses turned and went down from

25 the mount, and came into the gate of the camp.] And

26 when Moses saw that the people were broken loose ; then Moses stood in the gate of the camp, and said, Hither to me, whosoever is on Yahweh's side ! And all the sons of Levi

27 gathered themselves together unto him. And he said unto them, Thus saith Yahweh, the God of Israel, Put ye every

man his sword upon his thigh, and go to and fro from gate
to gate throughout the camp, and slay every man his
brother, and every man his companion, and every man his
neighbor. And the sons of Levi did according to the word 28
of Moses : and there fell of the people that day three thousand men. And Moses said, " Fill your hand " [with an offer- 29
ing of consecration to the priesthood] to-day unto Yahweh ;
for every man hath been against his son, and against his
brother ; and he shall bestow upon you a blessing this day.
And Yahweh smote . . . . because they. . . .   35

DISMISSAL OF THE PEOPLE FROM SINAI. MOSES' INTERCESSION.

And Yahweh spake unto Moses, Depart, go up hence, **33**
thou and the people which thou hast brought up out of the
land of Egypt, unto ' the land of which I sware ' unto Abraham, to Isaac, and to Jacob, saying, Unto thy seed will I
give it : ' unto a land flowing with milk and honey ': for 3
I will not go up in the midst of thee ; for thou art a
' stiffnecked ' people : lest I ' consume ' thee in the way.
And Moses was displeased : and Moses said **Nu. 11.** 10b–11
unto Yahweh, Wherefore hast thou ' evil entreated ' thy servant ? and wherefore have I not ' found favor in thy sight,'
that thou layest the burden of all this people upon me ? Have 12
I conceived all this people ? have I brought them forth,
that thou shouldest say unto me, Carry them in thy bosom,
as a nursing-father carrieth the sucking child, unto ' the
land which thou swarest unto their fathers ' ? I am not able 14
to bear all this people alone, because it is too heavy for me.
And if thou deal thus with me, kill me, I pray thee, out of 15
hand, ' if I have found favor in thy sight ' ; and let me not
see my wretchedness. [And Yahweh said, Thou shalt not
bear the people alone, for thou hast found favor in my sight
and I know thee by name, therefore I will give thee aid.]
But Moses said unto Yahweh, See, thou art say- **Ex. 33.** 12
ing unto me, Bring up this people : and thou hast not let me
know whom thou wilt send with me. Yet thou hast said, I
know thee by name, and thou hast also ' found favor in my

13 sight.' Now therefore, I pray thee, if I have 'found favor
in thy sight,' shew me now thy purposes, that I may know
thee, to the end that I may 'find favor in thy sight': and
14 consider that this nation is thy people. And he said, What
if I go with thee in person and give thee an 'abiding-place'?
15 And he said unto him, If thou go not in person with me,
16 carry us not up hence. For wherein else shall it be known
that I have 'found favor in thy sight,' I and thy people? is
it not in that thou goest with us, so that we be separated, I
and thy people, from all the people that are upon the face
of the 'ground'?

17 And Yahweh said unto Moses, I will do this thing also
18 that thou hast spoken : for thou hast 'found favor in my
19a sight,' and I know thee by name. And he said, Shew me, I
21 pray thee, thy glory. And Yahweh said, Behold, there is a
22 place by me, and thou shalt stand upon the rock : and it
shall come to pass, while my glory passeth by, that I will
put thee in a cleft of the rock, and will cover thee with my
23 hand until I have passed by : and I will take away mine
hand, and thou shalt see my back : but my face shall not be
34 —6-8 seen. So Yahweh passed by before him, and Moses
made haste, and 'bowed his head toward the earth, and wor-
9 shipped.' And he said, If now I have 'found grace in thy
sight,' 'O Lord,' let 'the Lord,' I pray thee, go in the midst
of us : for it is a 'stiffnecked' people ; and pardon our iniquity and our sin, and take us for thine inheritance.
(Dt. 10. 1) And Yahweh commanded Moses saying : [Make
thee an ark of wood for the tables of stone which thou hast
written, and a tent for the ark, and I will go before you unto
the land which I sware to give you ; for I will not go up in the
midst of you lest I consume you. And the Levites who
were faithful to me when the people sinned against me, they
shall be my priests to bear the ark and to do all the service
of the Tent.]

THE COMING OF HOBAB.

[Now Hobab the son of Reuel, Moses' father in law, heard

that Moses and the children of Israel were come out of Egypt,
and he came to meet Moses at mount Sinai.] And 7—18
Moses went out to meet his father in law, and did obeisance,
and kissed him ; and they 'asked each other of their welfare' ; and he brought them into the tent. [And Moses
told his father in law of all that had befallen them, and how
Yahweh delivered them at the Red Sea.] And he said,   10

'Blessed be Yahweh,' who delivered you out of the hand
   of the Egyptians,
And out of the hand of Pharaoh ;
Who delivered the people from under the hand of the
   Egyptians.
Now I know that Yahweh is greater than all gods :   11
For in that wherein they exalted themselves against them.

.   .   . *

———————◆———————

NUMBERS. (HEB. "IN THE WILDERNESS.")
DEPARTURE FROM SINAI.   HOBAB ISRAEL'S GUIDE.

And Moses said unto ' Hobab, the son of Reuel ' the 29—10
Midianite, Moses' father in law, We are journeying unto the
place of which Yahweh said, I will give it you : come thou
with us, and we will 'do thee good': for Yahweh hath
spoken good concerning Israel. And he said unto him, I 30
will not go ; but I will depart to ' mine own land,' and to my
kindred. And he said, Leave us not, I pray thee ; 'foras- 31
much' as thou knowest how we are to encamp in the wilderness, and thou shalt be to us instead of eyes. And it shall 32
be, if thou go with us, yea, it shall be, that what good soever
Yahweh shall do unto us, the same will we do unto thee.

And they set forward from the ' mount of Yahweh ' three 33
days' journey ; and the ark of Yahweh went before them

*The text is manifestly corrupt and the sense incomplete. Dillmann sup-
plies, " In that very thing Yahweh showed himself stronger than they." The
resumption of 10a in 10b might suggest that 10b is the missing line which
has been accidentally transposed from after vs. 11. There is, however, no adequate support for conjecture.

34 [to bring them unto] their abiding-place.* And the cloud
of Yahweh was over them by day, when they set forward
from the camp.

35   And it came to pass, when the ark set forward, that
Moses said,
>   Rise up, O Yahweh, that thine enemies may be scattered;
>   And let them that hate thee flee before thee.

36   And when it rested, he said,
>   Return, O Yahweh, unto the ten thousands of the thou-
>   sands of Israel.

KIBROTH-HATTAAWAH.   MURMURS AT THE MANNA :   YAHWEH
SENDS A FLIGHT OF QUAILS.

11—4   And ' the mixed multitude ' that was among them fell a
lusting : and the children of Israel also wept again, and
5 said, Who shall give us flesh to eat ? We remember the
fish, which we did eat in Egypt for nought ; the cucumbers,
6 and the melons, and the leeks, and the onions, and the gar-
lick : but now our soul is dried away ; there is nothing at
7 all : we have nought save this manna to look to.—Now the
manna was like coriander seed, and the appearance thereof
8 as the appearance of 'bdellium.' The people went about,
and gathered it, and ground it in mills, or beat it in mortars,
and seethed it in pots, and made cakes of it : and the taste
9 of it was as the taste of cakes baked with oil. And when the
dew fell upon the camp in the night, the manna fell with
10 it.—And Moses heard the people weeping throughout their
families, every man at the door of his tent : [and he cried
13 unto Yahweh saying] Whence should I have flesh to give
unto all this people ? for they are weeping unto me, saying,
10b Give us flesh that we may eat. Then the anger of Yahweh

---

* Both subject matter and language forbid us to suppose that we have the
original form of vs. 33b. But it is not improbable that originally it declared
the fulfilment of Yahweh's promise (Ex. xxxiii. 14) personally to accompany
the journey until he should have brought the people to " their abiding-place "
i. e. Canaan. If original, the " resting-place " can not of course mean " camp-
ing-place," for Hobab selects these; but a permanent home as in Gen. xlix.
15; Ex. xxxiii. 14; Dt. xxxiii. 25.

was kindled greatly : and [he said unto Moses] say thou 18
unto the people, Sanctify yourselves 'against to-morrow,'
and ye shall eat flesh : for ye have wept in the ears of Yahweh, saying, Who shall give us flesh to eat? for it was well
with us in Egypt : therefore Yahweh will give you flesh, and
ye shall eat. Ye shall not eat one day, nor two days, nor 19
five days, neither ten days, nor twenty days ; but a whole 20
month, until the odor of it revolteth you, and it be loathsome
unto you : because that ye have 'despised Yahweh' which
is 'among you,' and have wept before him, saying, Why came
we forth out of Egypt? And Moses said, The people, 21
among whom I am, are six hundred thousand footmen ;
and thou hast said, I will give them flesh, that they may eat
a whole month. Shall 'flocks and herds' be slain for them, 22
to suffice them? or shall all the fish of the sea be gathered
together for them, to suffice them?

And Yahweh said unto Moses, Is Yahweh's hand waxed 23
short? now shalt thou see whether my word shall come to
pass unto thee or not. So Moses went out and told the people 24
the words of Yahweh. And there went forth a 'wind' from 31
Yahweh, and brought quails from the sea, and directed their
flight over the camp, about a day's journey on this side, and a
day's journey on the other side, round about the camp, and
[flying] about two cubits above the face of the earth. And 32
the people rose up all that day, and all the night, and all the
next day, and gathered the quails : he that gathered least
gathered ten 'homers': and they spread them all abroad
for themselves round about the camp [to dry]. While they 33
were still eating the flesh, ere it was consumed, the anger
of Yahweh was kindled against the people, and 'Yahweh
smote the people' with a very great plague. And the name 34
of that place was called Kibroth-hattaavah ("Graves of
lust") : because there they buried the people that lusted.
From Kibroth-hattaavah the people journeyed unto Haze- 35
roth ; and they abode at Hazeroth.

And afterward the people journeyed from Hazeroth 16a—**12**
[and pitched in Meribath-Kadesh].

THE MUTINY OF KORAH.

16—1 [Now Korah the son of Kenaz] and On the son of
Peleth, 'men of renown' took [an offering for Yahweh, and
assembled the people together against Moses and the Levites,
saying, Wherefore exalt ye yourselves above the people to
3b offer sacrifice for them? are not all the people holy?] and is
13 not 'Yahweh among them'? Is it a small thing that thou
hast brought us up out of 'a land flowing with milk and
honey,' to kill us in the wilderness, but thou must needs
14 make thyself also a prince over us? Moreover thou hast
not brought us into a 'land flowing with milk and honey,'
nor 'given us inheritance of fields and vineyards.' [To get
thyself a name hast thou brought forth all this people to die
in the wilderness, neither hath Yahweh sent thee at all].
15 And Moses was very wroth, and said unto Yahweh, 'Respect'
not thou their offering: I have not taken one 'ass' from
them, neither have I hurt one of them. [And Korah and
the men that were with him assembled themselves together over against Moses before all the people to sacrifice
27bb unto Yahweh] and their 'wives and their sons and their
28 little ones.' And Moses said, 'Hereby ye shall know that
Yahweh hath sent me to do all these works'; for [I have]
29 not [done them] 'of mine own mind.' If these men die the
common death of all men, or if they be 'visited' after the
30 visitation of all men; then Yahweh hath not sent me. But
if Yahweh 'make a new thing,' and the 'ground' open her
mouth, and swallow them up, with all that appertain unto
them, and they 'go down alive into the pit'; then ye shall
31 understand that these men have 'despised Yahweh.' And it
came to pass, as he made an end of speaking all these words,
33 that the 'ground' clave asunder that was under them: and
they, and all that appertained to them, 'went down alive
into the pit'

MERIBATH-KADESH. WATER FROM THE ROCK.

20—3 And the people "strove" with Moses, and [cried out

again] wherefore hast thou made us to come up out of Egypt, 5
to bring us in unto this evil place ? it is no place of seed, or
of figs, or of vines, or of pomegranates ; neither is there any
water to drink. [And Yahweh said unto Moses, I have
heard the words of this people, which strive with (**Dt. 33.** 8)
thee. Behold I will " strive " for thee, and will shew myself
" holy " against them. Speak now unto the rock that is
before their eyes that it give forth its water. And Moses
did so, and there came forth water abundantly. And the
people drank and their cattle. Therefore was the name of
the place called Meribath-Kadesh, because Yahweh " strove "
(*rib*) for him there and shewed himself " holy " (*Kadesh*) in
the eyes of the people.]

CALEB SENT TO HEBRON TO RECONNOITRE. THE PEOPLE REBEL AT HIS REPORT.

[And from Kadesh Moses sent out Caleb the (**Jos. 14.** 6ff.)
son of Jephunneh the Kenizzite and others with him to
search out the land]. And he said unto them, Get you 17b
up this way into the Negeb (wilderness south of Judah)
[and see what people dwell there] whether they be strong 19
or weak ; and what the land is that they dwell in, whether
it be good or bad ; and what cities they be that they dwell
in, whether in camps, or in 'strong holds.' So they went 22
up into the Negeb, and came unto ' Hebron ' ; and ' Ahiman,
Sheshai, and Talmai,' the children of Anak, were there. (Now
' Hebron ' was built seven years before Zoan in Egypt.)
[And when they had seen the land and the strength of the
cities they returned unto Moses]. And they told him, and 27
said, We came unto the land whither thou sentest us, and
surely ' it floweth with milk and honey.' Howbeit the peo- 28
ple that dwell in the land are strong, and the cities are
fenced, [and] very great: and moreover we saw the children
of Anak there.

And all the children of Israel lifted up their voice **14—**1
and cried [saying] : 'Our wives and our little ones' shall 3b
be a prey: were it not better for us to return into Egypt ?

8 [But Moses said] : If Yahweh delight in us, (**Dt. 1.** 29f.)
then he will bring us into this land, and give it unto us : a
9 'land which floweth with milk and honey.' Only rebel not
against Yahweh, neither fear ye the people of the land ; for
they are bread for us : their defence is removed from over
13—30 them, whereas Yahweh is with us : fear them not.   And
Caleb stilled the [murmurs of] the people before Moses,
and said, Let us go up at once, and possess it ; for we
31 are well able to overcome it.   But the men that went up
with him said, We be not able to go up against the people ;
for they are stronger than we.

YAHWEH'S REJECTION OF THE PEOPLE. MOSES INTERCEDES FOR THEM.

14—11 And Yahweh said unto Moses, How long will this
people 'despise me'? and how long will they not believe in
12 me, for all the signs which I have wrought among them ?   I
will 'smite them with the pestilence,' and disinherit them,
and 'will make of thee a nation greater and mightier than
13 they.'   And Moses said unto Yahweh, 'Then the Egyptians
shall hear it ; for thou broughtest up this people in thy might
14 from among them; and they will tell it to the inhabitants
of this land' : they have heard that thou Yahweh art 'in the
midst of this people' ; for thou Yahweh art seen 'face to
face,' and thy cloud standeth over them, and thou 'goest
before them, in a pillar of cloud by day, and in a pillar of
15 fire by night.'   Now if thou shalt kill this people as one
man, then the nations which have heard the fame of thee
16 will speak, saying, Because Yahweh was not able to bring
this people into ' the land which he sware unto them,' there-
17 fore he hath slain them in the wilderness.   And now, I
19 pray thee, let thy power be magnified,* 'O Lord.'   Pardon,
I pray thee, the iniquity of this people according unto
the greatness of thy mercy, and according as thou hast for-
20 given this people, from Egypt even until now.   And Yahweh
21 said, I have pardoned as thou sayest : but in very deed, as I

* So LXX.

live, and as all the earth shall be filled with the glory of Yah- 22
weh ; because all those men which have seen my glory, and
my signs, which I wrought in Egypt and in the wilderness, yet
have tempted me these ten times, and have not hearkened to
my voice ; surely they shall not see 'the land which I sware 23
unto their fathers,' neither shall any of them that 'despised
me' see it : but my servant Caleb, because he had another 24
spirit with him, and hath followed me fully, him will I bring
into the land whereinto he went ; and his seed shall possess
it. [Go, say unto the people, Turn you, and get you into
the wilderness of Seir, by the way of Atharim ; for I will
not bring you into the land]. But your little ones, which ye 31
said should 'be a prey,' them will I bring in, and they shall
know the land which ye have 'rejected.' But as for you, 32
your carcases shall fall in this wilderness. And your chil- 33
dren shall be 'nomads' in the wilderness forty years, and
shall bear your 'whoredoms,' until your carcases be consumed in the wilderness.

THE DISASTER AT HORMAH, ISRAEL INFLICTS A BLOW UPON THE CANAANITES OF THE NEGEB.

And the 'Canaanite,' the king of Arad, which dwelt in **21**
'the South,' heard tell that Israel was coming by the way
of Atharim ; and he fought against Israel, and took some of
them captive. And Israel vowed a vow unto Yahweh, and 2
said, If thou wilt indeed deliver this people into my hand,
then I will "devote" their cities. And Yahweh hearkened 3
to the voice of Israel, and delivered up the 'Canaanites';
so they "devoted" them and their cities : and the name of
the place was called Hormah. (*i. e.* "Fortress," but here in-
correctly derived from the stem meaning to "devote," *i. e.*
place under the ban, vow to destruction.)

THE WILDERNESS STATIONS. THE STORY OF BEER- [ELIM], THE WELL OF THE PRINCES.

[And when they had dwelt in mount Seir many (**Dt. 2.** 1ff.)
days Yahweh said unto Moses, Turn you northward and pass

over the brook Zered into the border of Moab, and I will give
you the cities of the Amorites which dwell beyond Jordan,
but of the land of Seir and of the land of Moab I will not
give you, for I have given it unto the children of Edom and
the children of Lot. So Israel passed through the border of
Edom and Moab and they journeyed from . . . . to . . . .
16 and from thence to . . . .] 'And from thence' to Beer :
that is the " well " (*beer*) whereof Yahweh said unto Moses,
Gather the people together, and I will give them water.

17   ' Then sang Israel this song : '
        Spring up, O " well " ; spring up and flow ;
18   The " well," which the princes digged,
        Which the nobles of the people delved,
        With the 'sceptre,' [and] with their staves.
19   ' And from Beer to ' Mattanah : 'and from Mattanah to '
20 Nahaliel : 'and from Nahaliel to ' Bamoth : 'and from
    Bamoth to ' the valley that is in the field of Moab, by 'the
    peak of Pisgah, which looketh down upon Jeshimon ' (*i. e.* the
    eastward slope of the mountains of Judah by the Dead Sea).

CONQUEST OF TRANS-JORDANIC TERRITORY.

(32—3) [And Moses sent to search out the cities of the Amor-
    ites, Ataroth, Dibon, Jazer, Nimrah, Heshbon, Elealeh, Sebam,
21—24b Nebo and Beon] even unto the children of Ammon: for
25 Jazer was the border of the children of Ammon. And Israel
    took all these cities : and Israel dwelt in all the cities of the
32 Amorites, in Heshbon, and in all the towns thereof. And
    Moses sent to 'search out' Jazer, and they took [it together
    with] the towns thereof, and ' drove out ' the Amorites that
    were there.

THE ORACLE OF BALAAM. BALAK, KING OF MOAB. SEEKS TO PROCURE A CURSE UPON ISRAEL. THE PROPHET STAYED BY THE SPEAKING ASS.

22—3   Now Moab ' held the children of Israel in dread.'
4 And Moab said unto the elders of Midian, Now shall this
    multitude lick up all that is round about us, as the ox lick-

eth up the grass of the field. And Balak the son of Zippor
was king of Moab at that time. [And he took counsel with
them to send unto Balaam the son of Beor the diviner] to
the land of the children of Ammon [saying, Come curse me
Israel]. And the elders of Moab and the elders of Midian de- 7
parted with the rewards of ' divination ' in their hand. [And
they came unto Balaam and said, Thus saith Balak the son
of Zippor, Delay not, I pray thee, to come unto me], for I 17
will promote thee unto very great honor, and whatsoever
thou sayest unto me I will do : come therefore, I pray thee,
curse me this people. And Balaam answered and said unto 18
the servants of Balak, If Balak would give me his house full of
silver and gold, I cannot go beyond the word of Yahweh my
God, to do less or more. So he saddled his ass [and went 21b
with them]. And Yahweh's anger was kindled because he 22
went : and the 'angel of Yahweh' placed himself in the way
to oppose him. Now he was riding upon his ass, and his
two servants were with him. And the ass saw the 'angel 23
of Yahweh' standing in the way, ' with his sword drawn in
his hand :' and the ass turned aside out of the way, and
went into the field : and Balaam smote the ass, to turn her
into the way. Then the ' angel of Yahweh ' stood in a hollow 24
way between the vineyards, a fence being on this side, and a
fence on that side. And the ass saw 'the angel of Yahweh,' 25
and she thrust herself unto the wall, and crushed Balaam's
foot against the wall : and he smote her again. And ' the 26
angel of Yahweh ' went further, and stood in a narrow place,
where was no way to turn either to the right hand or to the
left And the ass saw ' the angel of Yahweh,' and she lay 27
down under Balaam : and Balaam's anger was kindled, and
he smote the ass with his staff. And ' Yahweh opened the 28
mouth ' of the ass, and she said unto Balaam, What have I
done unto thee, that thou hast smitten me these three times ?
And Balaam said unto the ass, Because thou hast mocked 29
me : I would there were a sword in mine hand, for now I
had killed thee. And the ass said unto Balaam, Am not I 30
thine ass, upon which thou hast ridden all thy life long unto

this day ? was I ever wont to do so unto thee ? And he
31 said, Nay.   Then ' Yahweh opened the eyes ' of Balaam, and
he saw 'the angel of Yahweh standing in the way, with his
sword drawn in his hand : ' and he 'bowed his head, and fell
32 on his face.' And 'the angel of Yahweh' said unto him,
Wherefore hast thou smitten thine ass these three times ?
behold, I am come forth to oppose thee, because the way is
33 . . . . * and the ass saw me, and turned aside before me
these three times : unless she had turned aside from me,
34 surely now I had even slain thee, and saved her alive. And
Balaam said unto ' the angel of Yahweh,' I have sinned ; for
I knew not that thou wert standing in the way against me.
Now, therefore, if it displease thee, I will get me back again.
35 And 'the angel of Yahweh' said unto Balaam, Go thy way :
but only the word that I shall speak unto thee, that thou
shalt speak. [So Balaam went his way and came unto Balak
in Ar of Moab. And Balak made him a feast ; and on the
39 morrow he brought him to the border of Israel]. So Balaam went with Balak and they came unto Kirjath-huzzoth (?)

THE ORACLE OF BALAAM.

23—28   And Balak took Balaam unto 'the top of Pisgah that
24 looketh down upon Jeshimon.' And when Balaam saw that
it pleased Yahweh to bless Israel, he went not to meet [him]
with enchantments, but he set his face toward the wilder-
2 ness. And Balaam lifted up his eyes, and he saw Israel
3 dwelling according to their tribes ; and the spirit of God
came upon him. And he took up his oracle, and said,
    Balaam the son of Beor saith,
    And the man whose eye . . . . † saith :
4   He saith, which heareth the words of El,
    And knoweth the knowledge of Elyon

---

* Corrupt text. Usually translated " thy way is perverse before me."

† Translation doubtful. Either " is closed " (*i. e.* to the outward world) or
" is opened " (*i. e.* clairvoyantly).

Which seeth visions of Shaddai
Falling down, and having his eyes open :
How goodly are thy tents, O Jacob,   5
Thy dwellings, O Israel !
In the valleys are they spread forth,   6
In gardens by the river side,
As lign-aloes which Yahweh hath planted,
As cedar trees beside the waters.
Water floweth from his buckets,   7
And his seed hath abundance of water,
And his king shall be higher than Agag,
And his kingdom shall be exalted.
God, that bringeth them forth out of Egypt   23—22
Is to them as it were the horns (?) of the wild-ox.
Surely there is no enchantment with Jacob,   23
Neither is there any ' divination ' with Israel :
Even now may one tell [the fate] of Jacob
And of Israel what God hath wrought.
He shall eat up the nations his adversaries,   24—8b
And shall crunch their bones,
And his oppressors will he crush.
He coucheth, he lieth down as a lion,   9
And as a lioness ; who shall rouse him up ?
' Blessed be every one that blesseth thee,
And cursed be every one that curseth thee.'

And Balak's anger was kindled against Balaam, and he 10
smote his hands together : and Balak said unto Balaam, I
called thee to curse mine enemies, and, behold, thou hast
altogether blessed them.   Therefore now flee thou to thy 11
place : I thought to ' promote thee unto great honor ' ; but,
lo, Yahweh hath kept thee back from honor.   And Balaam 12
said unto Balak, Spake I not also to thy messengers which
thou sentest unto me, saying, ' If Balak would give me his 13
house full of silver and gold, I cannot go beyond the word
of Yahweh, to do either good or bad ' of mine own mind ' ;
what Yahweh speaketh, that will I speak ? '   And now, be- 14
hold, I go unto my people : come, [and] I will foretell thee

what this people shall do to thy people in the latter days.
15 And he took up his oracle, and said,

    Balaam the son of Beor saith,
    And the man whose eye is . . . saith :

16   He saith, which heareth the words of El,
    And knoweth the knowledge of Elyon
    Which seeth the vision of Shaddai,
    Falling down, and having his eyes open :

17   I see him, but not now :
    I behold him, but not nigh :
    There cometh forth a star out of Jacob,
    And a 'sceptre' riseth out of Israel,
    And smiteth through the temples of Moab,
    Even the skull of all the sons of "tumult"   (*Seth*).

18   And Edom shall be a possession,
    Seir also shall be a possession, [which are] his enemies ;
    While Israel doeth valiantly.

19   And out of Jacob shall one have dominion,
    And shall destroy the fugitives from the city.

25   Then Balaam rose up, and went and returned to his place :
    and Balak also went his way.

ISRAEL CORRUPTED BY THE WOMEN OF MOAB.

Now the people began to commit 'whoredom' with the **25**
daughters of Moab : for they called the people unto the 2
sacrifices of their gods ; and the people did eat, and bowed
down to their gods. And Yahweh said unto Moses, Take 4
all the chiefs of the people, and hang them up unto Yahweh
before the sun, that the 'fierce anger of Yahweh may turn
away' from Israel.   .   .   .   .   .

THE INHERITANCE OF GAD AND REUBEN. MOSES PLEDGES THE TWO TRIBES TO HELP IN THE CONQUEST OF CANAAN.

[Now the children of Gad and the children of Reuben saw
32—3 the land which Yahweh had smitten before Israel].
Ataroth, and Dibon, and Jazer, and Nimrah, and Heshbon,

and Elealeh, and Sebam, and Nebo, and Beon. [And they
desired the land because it was a good land for cattle. So
they came near unto Moses] and said, 'If we have found 5
favor in thy sight,' let this land be given unto thy servants
for a possession ; bring us not over Jordan. And Moses 6
said unto the children of Gad and to the children of Reuben,
Shall your brethren go to the war, and shall ye sit here ?
And Moses said unto them, If ye will do this thing ; if ye 20
will arm yourselves to go before Yahweh to the war, and 21
every armed man of you will pass over Jordan before Yahweh, until he hath 'driven out' his enemies from before him, 22
and the land be subdued before Yahweh : then afterward
ye shall return, and be guiltless towards Yahweh, and
towards Israel ; and this land shall be unto you for a possession before Yahweh. But if ye will not do so, behold, ye 23
have sinned against Yahweh : and be sure your sin will find
you out. And the children of Gad and the children of 25
Reuben spake unto Moses, saying, Thy servants will do as
my lord commandeth. 'Our little ones, our wives, our 26
flocks, and all our cattle,' shall be there in 'the cities' of
Gilead : but thy servants will pass over, every man that is 27
armed for war, before Yahweh to battle, as my lord saith.

DEUTERONOMY.   (Heb. "Words of Moses.")

[Last Words of Moses. Joshua his Successor.]

[And Yahweh said unto Moses, The time is come that
thou must die, for thou mayest not pass over this Jordan,
[because thou believedst not when I called thee to lead my
people forth out of Egypt (?)]. Call now Joshua the son of
Nun, the Ephraimite, and make him leader over this people ;
for he shall bring them into the land which I sware unto
their fathers, saying, I will give it you. And when thou hast
given him this charge, then go up into mount Pisgah, which
is before thee, and when thou hast seen the land thou shalt

die there in the mount. So Moses called Joshua and gave
him commandment as Yahweh had said. And he blessed
him and all the tribes of Israel, each one according to his
blessing].

THE BLESSING OF MOSES.

33   Now this is the blessing, wherewith Moses the man of God
2 blessed the children of Israel before his death.   And he said,
    Yahweh came from ' Sinai,'
    And rose from Seir unto them ;
    He shined forth from mount Paran,
    And he came from ' Meribath-Kadesh.'
    In his right hand . . . .
3   With love he cherished his people.
    All his holy ones were in thy hand
    And they . . . .

    . . . .
4b An inheritance for the assembly of Jacob.
5 A king arose for Jeshurun,
    When the heads of the people were gathered,
    All the tribes of Israel together.

    Let Reuben live and not die ;
    And let not his men be few.

7b   And of Simeon he said,
    " Hear" (*shem'a*), Yahweh, the voice of Simeon
    And bring him in to his own people.

8   And of Levi he said,
    Thy Thummim and thy Urim are with the men of thy con-
       secrated one,
    Whom thou didst " prove " at Massah,
    For whom thou didst " strive " at the waters of Meribah ;
9 [With him] who said of father, and of mother, I have not
       seen them ;
    Who neither acknowledged his brethren,
    Nor knew his own children :

For they gave themselves to thy word,
And kept thy covenant [law].
They shall teach Jacob thy judgments,   10
And Israel thy law :
They shall put incense in thy nostrils,
And whole burnt offering upon thine altar.

   And of Judah he said,   7a
Bless, Yahweh, his substance,   11
And accept the work of his hands :
" With thy hands " contend for him ;
And be thou an help against his adversaries.
Smite through the loins of them that rise up against him,
And of them that hate him, that they rise not again.

   Of Benjamin he said,   12
Yahweh's favorite is he ;
He dwelleth in safety by him
He covereth him all the day long,
And hath taken up his abode between his [mountain] shoul-
    ders.

   And of Joseph he said,   13
' Blessed of Yahweh ' be his land ;
'With the precious things of heaven, with the dew,
And with the ' deep ' that coucheth beneath,
And with the precious things which the sun doth ripen   14
And with the precious things that the moon bringeth forth,
And with the chief things of the ancient mountains,   15
And with the precious things of the everlasting hills,
And with the precious things of the earth and its fulness,' 16
And the good will of him that dwelt in the bush :
Let [it] come upon the head of Joseph,
'And upon the crown of the head of the crowned one
    among his brethren.'

Majesty surrounds his firstling bullock ;   17
And his horns are like the horns of the wild-ox :

With them he shall gore the nations all of them, [even] the
    ends of the earth :
These are the ten thousands of Ephraim,
And these are the thousands of Manasseh.

18   And of Zebulun he said,
Rejoice thou, Zebulun, in thy voyages ;
And thou, Issachar, in thy tents.
19   They invite the peoples unto the mountain ;
They offer there sacrifices of righteousness :
For they suck the abundance of the seas,
And the hidden treasures of the sand.

20   And of Gad he said,
' Blessed be He that enlargeth ' Gad :
He ' hath couched as a lioness,'
And teareth the arm, yea, the crown of the head.
21   He sought out for himself the lot of a firstborn **son**,
For there a ruler's portion lay ready ;
Yet he came [with] the heads of the people,
He executed the justice of Yahweh,
And his judgments with Israel.

22   And of Dan he said,
Dan is a lion's whelp,
That leapeth forth from Bashan.

23   And of Naphtali he said,
O Naphtali, satisfied with [gifts of divine] 'favor,'
And full with the ' blessing of Yahweh ' :
Possess thou the sea [of Galilee] and southward.

24   And of Asher he said,
Blessed be Asher above [the other] sons ;
Let him be the favorite of his brethren,
And let him dip his foot in oil.
25   Thy bars shall be iron and brass ;
And thy strength endure all thy days.

There is none like the God of Jeshurun,   26
Who rideth on the heaven for thy help,
And in his majesty on the skies.
The eternal God is a refuge,   27
And everlasting arms are [stretched out] beneath,
He thrust out the enemy from before thee,
And commanded [thee], Destroy.
So Israel dwelt in safety,   28
The fountain of Jacob by itself,
In a 'land of corn and wine';
Yea, his heavens drop down dew.
Hail to thee, Israel ! Who is like thee,   29
A people victorious by Yahweh?
He is the 'shield' of thy help,
And the sword that maketh thee glorious.
Thy foes shall feign thee friendship ;
And thou shalt tread [victorious] on their high places.

MOSES' DEATH AND BURIAL.

[So Moses went up] to 'the top of Pisgah' that is **34**—1b.
over against Jericho [the City of Palm-trees]. And Yahweh
shewed him all the land. And Yahweh said unto him, This 4
is the 'land which I sware' unto Abraham, unto Isaac, and
unto Jacob, saying, I will give it unto thy seed : I have
caused thee to see it with thine own eyes, but thou shalt not
go over thither. [So Moses died there] and he was buried 6
in the valley in the land of Moab over against Beth-peor.

THE EPHRAIMITE PROPHETIC DOCUMENT E,
CIRC. 750 B. C.

(THE) EXODUS.

STORY OF THE OPPRESSION IN EGYPT. PHARAOH'S CRUEL COMMANDS FRUSTRATED.

Now there arose a new king over Egypt, which had not 1—8
known Joseph. And he said unto his people, Behold, the peo- 9
ple of the children of Israel is becoming 'too many and too
mighty' for us: come, let us deal wisely with them; lest they 10
multiply, and it come to pass, that, when we are entangled
in some* war, they also join themselves unto our enemies,
and fight against us, and get them up out of the land.

So the king of Egypt spake to the Hebrew midwives, of 15
which the name of the one was Shiphrah, and the name of
the other Puah: and he said, When ye do the office of a 16
midwife to the Hebrew women, look [while they are still]
upon the birthstool (?); if it be a son, then ye shall kill him;
but if it be a daughter, then she may live. But the midwives 17
'feared God,' and did not as the king of Egypt commanded
them, but saved the men children alive. And the king of 18
Egypt sent for the midwives, and said unto them, Why
have ye done this thing, and have saved the men children
alive? And the midwives said unto Pharaoh, Because the 19
Hebrew women are not as the Egyptian women; for they
are vigorous, and are delivered ere the midwife come unto
them. And 'God' dealt well with the midwives. And it 20–21
came to pass, because the midwives 'feared' 'God,' that he
established clans for them. Then Pharaoh charged all his 22
people, saying, Every son that is born to the Hebrews† ye
shall cast into the Nile, and every daughter ye shall save
alive.

* Text of Sam. and all versions.

† Sam., LXX., Jer. Targum.

Parentage and Birth of Miriam, Aaron and Moses.

2—1   And there went a man of the stock of Levi [named (Amram?)] and took to wife [(Jochebed?)] the daughter of Levi. [And she bare unto him a daughter and called her name Miriam. And again she bare a son and called his name Aaron. And God came unto Amram (?) in a dream and said, I have chosen thy house that from thee there should come deliverance for my people. For thy daughter shall be a prophetess unto me, and the son that is born to thee shall be my priest, to go up unto mine altar, to burn incense, to wear an ephod before me, and unto his house and the house of thy father will I give all the offerings of the children of Israel made by fire (1. Sam. iii. 27ff). And I will give thee a second son who shall be the deliverer of my people.

And it came to pass after these things, when Pharaoh had commanded his people, saying, Ye shall cast the men-children of the Hebrews into the Nile, that Amram visited his

2   wife]. And the woman conceived, and bare a son : and when she saw him that he was a 'child' of goodly form, she

3   hid him three months. And when she could not longer hide him, she took for him an ark of papyrus, and daubed it with bitumen, and with pitch ; and she put the 'child' therein, and

4   laid it in the flags by the 'brink' of the Nile. And his sister stood afar off, to know what would be done to him.

5   And the daughter of Pharaoh came down to the Nile to bathe ; and her maidens walked along by the 'side' of the Nile ; and she saw the ark among the flags, and sent her

6   'maidservant' to fetch it. And she opened it, and, behold, a babe weeping. And she had compassion on him, saying

7   to herself, This is one of the Hebrews' 'children.' Then said his sister to Pharaoh's daughter, Shall I go and call thee a nurse of the Hebrew women, that she may nurse

8   the child for thee? And Pharoah's daughter said to her,

9   Go. So the girl went and called the child's mother. And Pharaoh's daughter said unto her, Take this 'child' away,

and nurse it for me, and I will give thee thy wages. And
the woman took the 'child,' and nursed it. And the 'child' 10
grew up and she brought him unto Pharaoh's daughter, and
he became her son. And she called his name Moses, (as if
from Hebrew *mashah*, to "draw out") and said, Because I
"drew him out" of the water.

MOSES' FRUITLESS ATTEMPT TO DELIVER HIS PEOPLE. HIS FLIGHT TO MIDIAN AND MARRIAGE THERE.

And it came to pass in those days, when Moses was grown 11
up, that he went out unto his brethren, and looked on their
burdens : and he saw an Egyptian smiting an Hebrew, one
of his brethren. And he looked this way and that way, and 12
when he saw that there was no man [in sight], he smote the
Egyptian, and hid him in the sand. And he went out the 13
second day, and, behold, two men of the Hebrews were
striving together : and he said to him that did the wrong,
Wherefore smitest thou thy fellow? And he said, Who 14
made thee a prince and a judge over us? thinkest thou to
kill me, as thou killedst the Egyptian? And Moses was
taken with fear, saying to himself, Of a truth then the thing
is known. And Pharaoh also heard of this thing, and he 15
sought to slay Moses. But Moses fled from the face of
Pharaoh, and dwelt in the land of Midian. [And Moses
took refuge in the house of a Midianite named Jethro, and
Jethro gave him his daughter to wife. And she bare unto
Moses two sons in Midian]. The name of the one was 18—3
Gershom ; for he said, I became a "stranger" (*ger*) 2—22b
in a 'strange' land ; and the name of the other was 18—4
Eliezer, for [he said], The "God" (*el*) of my father was
my "help" (*ezer*) and delivered me from the sword of
Pharaoh.

THE DIVINE CALL OF MOSES AT HOREB. GOD REVEALS HIS NAME YAHWEH.

Now Moses was keeping the flock of 'Jethro' his father 3
in law, and having once led the flock to the further side of

the wilderness, he came to 'the mountain of God,' unto
4 'Horeb.' And 'God' called unto him [out of the mountain]
6 and said, 'Moses, Moses. And he said, Here am I.' 'And
he said, I am the God of thy father,' the God of Abraham,
the God of Isaac, and the God of Jacob. And Moses hid his
face ; for he was afraid to look upon 'God.' [And God
said unto Moses, Fear not ; for I have called thee that thou
9 mayest deliver my people Israel.] And now, behold, the
cry of the children of Israel is come unto me : and I have
seen the 'oppression' wherewith the Egyptians 'oppress'
10 them. Come now therefore, and I will send thee unto
Pharaoh, that thou mayest bring forth my people the chil-
11 dren of Israel out of Egypt. And Moses said unto 'God,'
Who am I, that I should go unto Pharaoh, and that I should
12 bring forth the children of Israel out of Egypt? And he
said, Certainly I will be with thee ; and this shall be the
token unto thee, that I have sent thee : when thou hast
brought forth the people out of Egypt, ye shall serve 'God'
13 with sacrifice upon this mountain. And Moses said unto
'God,' Behold, when I come unto the children of Israel, and
shall say unto them, The God of your fathers hath sent me
unto you ; and they shall say to me, What is his name ?
14 what shall I say unto them ? And 'God' said unto Moses,
I AM WHAT I AM : and he said, Thus shalt thou say unto the
children of Israel, I AM hath sent me unto you. [And thou
4—14 shalt go unto Pharaoh, thou and Aaron thy brother], behold he cometh forth to meet thee ; and when he seeth thee
(5—1) he will be glad in his heart. [And ye shall say unto Pharaoh, Thus saith Yahweh the God of Israel, Let my people
3—19 go]. And I know that the king of Egypt will not give you
20 leave to go, save by [compulsion of] a 'mighty hand.' And
I will put forth my hand, and smite Egypt with all my
'wonders' which I will do in the midst thereof : and after
21 that he will let you go. And I will give this people favor
in the sight of the Egyptians : so it shall come to pass, that,
22 when ye go, ye shall not go empty : but 'every woman shall
ask of her neighbor, and of her that sojourneth in her

house, jewels of silver, and jewels of gold, and raiment : and
ye shall put them upon your sons, and upon your daughters ;
and ye shall spoil the Egyptians.' . . . And Yahweh said 4—21
unto Moses, When thou goest back into Egypt, see that thou
do before Pharaoh all the 'wonders' which I have put in thine
hand : but I will 'harden' his heart, and he will not let the
people go. And thou shalt take in thine hand this rod, 17
wherewith thou shalt do the signs.

Moses' Return to Egypt. He and Aaron Deliver Yahweh's Message to Pharaoh.

And Moses went and returned to 'Jether' his father in 18
law, and said unto him, Let me go, I pray thee, and return
unto my brethren which are in Egypt, and see whether they
be yet alive. And 'Jethro' said to Moses, Go in peace, and
Moses took the 'rod of God' in his hand [and departed].

And Yahweh said to Aaron, Go into the wilderness to 27
meet Moses. And he went, and met him in the 'mountain
of God,' and kissed him. And Moses told Aaron all the 28
words of Yahweh wherewith he had sent him, and all the
signs wherewith he had charged him. And afterward Moses 5
and Aaron came, and said unto Pharaoh, Thus saith Yahweh,
the God of Israel, Let my people go. And Pharaoh said, 2
Who is Yahweh, that I should hearken unto his voice to let
Israel go? I know not Yahweh, and moreover I will not let
Israel go. And the king of Egypt said unto them, Where- 4
fore do ye, Moses and Aaron, loose the people from their
works? get you unto your burdens.

The Plagues of Egypt. First Plague: The Nile Turned to Blood.

And Yahweh said unto Moses, Now shalt thou see what 6
I will do to Pharaoh : for by [compulsion of] a 'strong hand'
shall he let them go, and by a 'strong hand' shall he drive
them out of his land. Get thee unto Pharaoh in the 15
morning ; lo, he goeth out unto the water : and thou shalt
stand 'by the river's brink' to meet him ; and 'the rod

which [I gave thee] shalt thou take in thine hand.'   [And
'thou shalt smite] with the rod that is in thine hand'
upon the waters which are in the river, and they shall be
turned to blood. [So Moses went unto Pharaoh in the
morning] 'and he lifted up the rod, and smote' the waters
that were in the river, 'in the sight of Pharaoh, and in the
sight of his servants'; and all the waters that were in the
23 river were turned to blood. But Pharaoh turned and went
into his house, neither did he lay even this to heart.

SECOND PLAGUE: THE HAIL.

22   And Yahweh said unto Moses, 'Stretch forth thine hand'
toward heaven, that there may be hail in all the land of
Egypt, 'upon man, and upon beast,' throughout the land of
23 Egypt. And 'Moses stretched forth his rod' toward
heaven : and Yahweh sent thunder and hail, and fire ran
25 down unto the earth. And the hail smote throughout all
the land of Egypt all that was in the field, 'both man and
35 beast.' But the heart of Pharaoh was 'strong,' and he did
not let the children of Israel go.

THIRD PLAGUE: THE LOCUSTS.

12   'And Yahweh said unto Moses, Stretch out thine and '
over the land of Egypt for the locusts, that they may come
up upon the land of Egypt, and eat every 'herb of the land,'
13 even all that the hail hath left. 'And Moses stretched forth
14 his rod' over the land of Egypt, and the locusts came up
over all the land of Egypt ; and they did eat every 'herb
20 of the land,' even all that the hail had left. 'But Yahweh
made Pharaoh's heart strong and he did not let the children
of Israel go.'

FOURTH PLAGUE: THE DARKNESS.

21   'And Yahweh said unto Moses, Stretch out thine hand
toward heaven,' that there may be darkness over the land
22 of Egypt, even darkness which may be felt. 'And Moses
stretched forth his hand toward heaven'; and there was a

'thick darkness' in all the land of Egypt 'three days'; 23 they saw not one another, neither rose any from his place for 'three days': but all the children of Israel had light in their dwellings. 'But Yahweh made Pharaoh's heart strong, 27 and he would not let them go.'

Fifth Plague. Death of the Firstborn. The Exodus.

And Yahweh said unto Moses, Yet one plague more will I 11 bring upon Pharaoh, and upon Egypt; afterwards he will let you go hence :. . . .* yea, he shall even thrust you out by force. Speak now in the ears of the people, and let them 2 'ask every man of his neighbor, and every woman of her neighbor, jewels of silver, and jewels of gold. And Yahweh 3 gave the people favor in the sight of the Egyptians.' Moreover 'the man Moses' was very great in the land of Egypt in the sight of Pharaoh's servants, and in the sight of the people. [And it came to pass that night that the angel of God passed through all the land of Egypt and smote all the firstborn of Egypt]. And [Pharaoh] called for Moses 31 and Aaron by night, and said, Rise up, get you forth from among my people, both ye and the children of Israel. [So Moses and all the people rose up and went forth from the land of Egypt, and the angel of God went be- (Nu. 20. 16) fore them]. And the children of Israel did according to 12—35 the word of Moses; and 'they asked of the Egyptians jewels of silver, and jewels of gold, and raiment: and Yahweh 36 gave the people favor in the sight of the Egyptians, so that they let them have what they asked. So they spoiled the Egyptians.'

The Journey out of Egypt. Passage of the Red Sea and Song of Miriam.

And it came to pass, when Pharaoh had let the people 13—17 go, that 'God' led them not by the way of the land of the Philistines, although that was near: for 'God' said to himself, Lest peradventure the people repent when they see war,

---

* The text is corrupt. Literally, "when he shall wholly let you go."

18 and they return to Egypt : but 'God' led the people about,
'by the way of the wilderness towards' the Red Sea : and
the children of Israel went up in battle array out of the
19 land of Egypt. And Moses took the bones of Joseph with
him : for he had straitly sworn the children of Israel, saying, 'God will surely visit you ; and ye shall carry up my
bones away hence with you.' [But when Pharaoh saw that
14—3 the people went toward the Red Sea] he said to himself
as to the children of Israel, They are entangled in the land,
5 the wilderness hath shut them in. So he took six hundred
(Jos. 24—6) chosen chariots and captains over all of them [and
pursued after Israel. And they came to the sea]. And
10b–19 the children of Israel 'cried out unto Yahweh.' And
'the angel of God' which was going before the camp of
Israel removed and went behind them ; and it came to pass
[. . .] the cloud and the darkness.* [And Moses cried
15 out unto Yahweh. And Yahweh said], Wherefore 'criest
16 thou unto me'? 'Lift thou up thy rod' [over the sea, and
the waters shall withdraw themselves, and the children
(Is. 10—26) of Israel shall go forward. So Moses lifted up
(15—8) his rod over the sea, and the waters receded and stood
upright, so that Israel went forward into the midst of the sea.
And the Egyptians pursued after them, for Yahweh had
25a brought a thick darkness upon them]. And he bound their
chariot wheels so that they drave them heavily. [And when
(Jos. 24—7) Israel was clean passed over, Yahweh brought
31 back the sea upon the Egyptians and covered them]. And
Israel saw the great miracle which Yahweh had wrought
against the Egyptians, and the people 'feared Yahweh';
and they 'believed in' Yahweh, and in 'Moses his servant.'

---

* Literally, "And it came to pass the cloud and the darkness." The versions give no help. The words belong to E, for it is in E's version that the
crossing takes place by day, when "darkness" would be a protection ; whereas
in J it takes place by night. Moreover Jos. xxiv. 7 (E) expressly refers to the
fact that Yahweh "brought thick darkness between you and the Egyptians."
The sense may perhaps have been that the "angel" (i. e. manifestation) of
God assumed the form of cloud and darkness ; or more probably something
parallel to xiii. 21f. (J) has been stricken out.

'And Miriam the prophetess,' the 'sister of Aaron,' 15—20
took a timbrel in her hand ; and all 'the women went out
after her with timbrels and with dances.' And Miriam 21
'sang in reponse with them.'

Sing ye to Yahweh, for he is highty exalted,
The horse and his rider hath he hurled into the sea.

MASSAH. YAHWEH "PROVES" ISRAEL WITH HUNGER, AND GIVES THEM MANNA TO EAT.

[And Yahweh led Israel onward into the wilderness, and
they came to Massah ("Place of Proving")]. There he 25b
'made for them a statute and an ordinance,' and there 'he
"proved" them.' [For the people hungered, and they cried
unto Moses saying, Give us bread to eat]. Then said 16—4
Yahweh unto Moses, Behold, I will rain bread from heaven
for you ; and the people shall go out and gather a day's
portion every day, that I may "prove" them, whether they
will walk in my law, or no. [And they rose up early in the
morning and, behold, there lay upon the face of the wilderness round about the camp a small flake]. And when the 15
children of Israel saw it, they said one to another, "*man hu*"
("what is it"?), for they wist not what it was. And Moses said 16
unto them, This is the thing which Yahweh hath ordained.
Gather ye of it every man according to his eating ; let no 19b
man leave of it till the morning. Notwithstanding they 20
hearkened not unto Moses ; but some of them left of it until
the morning, and it bred worms, and stank : and Moses was
wroth with them. So they gathered it morning by morning, 21
every man according to his eating : and when the sun waxed
hot, it melted. [And they called the name thereof *manna*].
So the children of Israel did eat the manna forty years, until 35a
they came to a land inhabited.

MERIBAH : WATER FROM THE SMITTEN ROCK.

And there was no water for the people to drink. 17—1b
Wherefore the people "strove" with Moses, and said, Give 2
us water that we may drink. And Moses said unto them,

4 Why "strive" ye with me? And 'Moses cried unto Yahweh' saying, What shall I do unto this people? they be
5 almost ready to stone me. And Yahweh said unto Moses, Pass on before the people, and 'take with thee of the elders of Israel'; and 'thy rod, wherewith thou smotest the river, take in thine hand,' and go [unto the place where I called
6 thee at the first]. Behold, I will stand before thee there upon the rock in Horeb; and thou shalt smite the rock, and there shall come water out of it, that the people may drink. And Moses did so 'in the sight of the elders of Israel.'
7 And he called the name of the place Meribah, because of the "striving" of the children of Israel.

THE THEOPHANY AT HOREB TO ALL THE PEOPLE.

19—3a And Moses went up unto 'God.' And he said unto Moses, Lo, I am about to come unto thee in a 'thick
9 cloud,' so that the people may hear when I speak with thee, and may also 'believe thee' forever. Go unto the
10 people and 'sanctify them to-day and to-morrow,' and let
11 them 'wash their garments' and be ready against 'the
14 third day.' So Moses went down from the mount unto the people, and 'sanctified the people'; and they 'washed
15 their garments.' And he said unto the people, Be ready
16 'against the third day:' come not near a woman. And it came to pass on the 'third day,' when it was morning, that there were thunders and lightnings, and a 'thick cloud' upon the mount, and the voice of a 'trumpet' exceeding loud; and all the people that were in the camp trembled.
17 And Moses brought forth the people out of the camp 'to meet God;' and they stood at the nether part of the mount.
19 And when the voice of the 'trumpet' waxed louder and louder, Moses spake, and 'God' answered him by a voice.
20—1   And 'God' spake all these words, saying,
2   I am Yahweh thy God, which brought thee out of the land of Egypt.
3   Thou shalt have none other Gods beside me.
4   Thou shalt not make unto thee a *pesel* (cut or hewn idol).

Thou shalt not invoke the name of Yahweh thy God upon 7
a falsehood.

Remember the Sabbath day to sanctify it. 8

Honor thy father and thy mother. 12

Thou shalt do no murder. 13

Thou shalt not commit adultery. 14

Thou shalt not steal. 15

Thou shalt not bear false witness against thy neighbor. 16

Thou shalt not covet thy neighbor's goods. 17

And when all the people saw the thunderings, and the 18
lightnings, and the voice of the trumpet, the people were
afraid and trembled, and stood afar off. And they said unto 19
Moses, Speak thou with us, and we will hear : but let not
'God' speak with us, lest we die. And Moses said unto the 20
people, Fear not : for 'God' is come 'to prove you,' and
that 'his fear' may be before you, that ye sin not. So the 21
people stood afar off, and Moses drew near unto the 'thick
darkness' where 'God' was.

And Yahweh 'called unto him out of the mountain,' 19—3b
saying, Thus shalt thou say to the house of Jacob, and
tell the children of Israel ; [I have heard the words (**Dt. 5**—28)
which ye have spoken. Now therefore if ye will obey my
voice indeed and keep these my commandments, I will be
your God and ye shall be my people, and I will bring you in
and establish you in the land which I sware unto your **19**—6b
fathers]. These are the words which thou shalt speak unto
the children of Israel. And Moses came and called for 'the 7
elders of the people,' and set before them all these words
which Yahweh commanded him. And 'all the people 8
answered together, and said,' All that Yahweh hath spoken
we will do. And Moses reported the words of the people
unto Yahweh.

MOSES AND JOSHUA ON THE MOUNT. THE TABLES OF STONE AND THE LAW.

And Yahweh said unto Moses, Come up to me into the 12
mount, and abide there : and I will give thee the tables of

stone, which I have written, and the judgment and the law,
13 that thou mayst teach them. So Moses rose up, and
'Joshua his minister': and Moses went up into 'the mount
14 of God.' And he said unto the people, Tarry ye here for us,
until we come again unto you: and, behold, 'Aaron and
Hur' are with you: whosoever 'hath a cause' to plead let
18b him come near unto them. So he went up into the mount:
and Moses was in the mount forty days and forty nights.

The People's Apostasy. Story of the Golden Bull.

32   And when the people saw that Moses delayed to come
down from the mount, the people gathered themselves together unto Aaron, and said unto him, Up, make us a god,
which shall go before us; for as for this Moses, the man
that brought us up out of the land of Egypt, we know not
2 what is become of him. And Aaron said unto them, Break
off the golden 'rings,' which are in the ears of your wives,
of your sons, and of your daughters, and bring them unto
3 me. And all the people brake off the golden 'rings' which
4 were in their ears, and brought them unto Aaron. And he
received it at their hand, and fashioned it with a graving
tool, and made it a little molten bull: and they said, 'This is
thy god, O Israel, which brought thee up out of the land of
5 Egypt.' And when Aaron saw it, he built an altar before
it; and Aaron made proclamation, and said, To-morrow shall
6 be a feast to Yahweh. So 'they rose up early on the morrow,' and 'offered burnt offerings, and brought peace offerings'; and the people sat down to eat and to drink, and rose
up to play.

    [Now when Yahweh had given Moses the law and com-
mandment to teach the people, and had made an end of speak-
31 —18 ing with him, he gave unto him] two tables of stone, 'writ-
32—16 ten with the finger of God.' And the tables were the
work of 'God,' and the writing was the writing of 'God,' graven
upon the tables. [So Moses turned, with Joshua his minister,
17 and they came down from the mount.] And when Joshua
heard the noise of the people as they shouted, he said unto

Moses, There is a noise of war in the camp. And he said, It 18
is not the sound of voices that shout in victory, neither is it
the (answering) cry of them that are overcome : but the sound
of them that sing do I hear. And it came to pass, as soon 19
as he came nigh unto the camp, that he saw the little bull
and the dancing : and Moses' anger waxed hot, and he cast
the tables out of his hands, and brake them beneath the mount.
And he took the little bull which they had made, and burnt 20
it with fire, and ground it to powder, and strewed it upon
the water, and made the children of Israel drink of it. And 21
Moses said unto Aaron, What did this people unto thee, that
thou hast brought a great sin upon them ? And Aaron said, 22
Let not the anger of my lord wax hot : thou knowest the
people, that they are [set] on evil. For they said unto me, 23
'Make us a god, which shall go before us : for as for this
Moses, the man that brought us up out of the land of Egypt,
we know not what is become of him.' And I said unto
them, 'Whosoever hath any gold, let them break it off '; so 24
they gave it me : and I cast it into the fire, and there came
out this little bull.

MOSES' INTERCESSION FOR THE PEOPLE. THEY PUT OFF THEIR ORNAMENTS IN PENITENCE.

And it came to pass on the morrow, that Moses said unto 30
the people, ' Ye have sinned a great sin ' : and now I will go
up unto Yahweh ; peradventure I shall make atonement for
your sin. So Moses returned unto Yahweh, and said, ' Oh, 31
this people have sinned a great sin,' and have made them a
god of gold. Yet now, if thou wilt forgive their sin—; and 32
if not, blot me, I pray thee, out of thy book which thou hast
written. And Yahweh said unto Moses, Whosoever hath 33
sinned against me, him will I blot out of my book. And 34
now go, lead the people unto the place of which I have
spoken unto thee : behold, ' mine angel ' shall go before thee :
nevertheless in the day when I requite, I will requite their
sin upon them. And when the people heard these evil **33—4**
tidings, they ' mourned ' : and no man did put on him his

6 'ornaments.' So the children of Israel stripped themselves of their 'ornaments' from mount 'Horeb' onward.

THE RENEWAL OF THE COVENANT. CONSTRUCTION OF THE ARK AND TENT OF MEETING.

[And Yahweh said unto Moses, I have heard the mourning of the people. Go thou unto them and say, If with all your heart ye will turn unto me I will yet make my covenant with you, and be your God ; and of these ornaments which ye have put off shall ye make a tent where I will meet with you,

24—4 and I will teach you how ye shall worship me. And thou shalt write the words of the covenant and put the book of this covenant in an ark of wood, and it shall be kept there in the Tent. So Moses went unto the people and told them. And he prepared the Ark of God and the Tent.]

THE BOOK OF THE COVENANT. A SECOND TEN WORDS.

20—22 And Yahweh said unto Moses, Thus thou shalt say unto the children of Israel, Ye yourselves have seen that I have talked with you from heaven.

23 Ye shall not make [other gods] with me ; 'gods of sil-

24 ver' or 'gods of gold' ye shall not make unto you. An altar of earth thou shalt make unto me, and shalt 'sacrifice thereon thy burnt offerings, and thy peace offerings,' thy sheep, and thine oxen : in every place where I establish a memorial of myself I will come unto thee and I will bless

25 thee. And if thou make me an altar of stone, thou shalt 'not build it of hewn stones' : for if thou lift up thy tool

26 upon it, thou hast polluted it. Neither shalt thou go up by steps unto mine altar, that thy nakedness be not uncovered towards it.

23 —10 And six years thou shalt sow thy land, and shalt

11 gather in the increase thereof : but the seventh year thou shalt let it rest and lie fallow. In like manner thou shalt

12 deal with thy vineyard, [and] with thy oliveyard. Six days thou shalt do thy work, and on the seventh day thou shalt keep sabbath.

Three times thou shalt 'keep a feast' unto me in the 14 year. The 'feast of unleavened bread' shalt thou keep : 15 and 'the feast of harvest,' the firstfruits of thy labors, 16 which thou sowest in the field : and 'the feast of ingathering,' at the end of the year, when thou gatherest in thy labors out of the field.

Thou shalt not withhold of thine abundance, nor of 22—29 the fruits of thy wine-press. 'The firstborn of thy sons' shalt thou give unto me. Likewise shalt thou do with thine 30 oxen, with thy sheep and with thy beast of burden ;* seven days it shall be with its dam ; on the eighth day thou shalt give it me. And ye shall be holy men unto me : therefore 31 ye shall not eat any flesh that is 'torn of beasts' in the field ; ye shall cast it to the dogs.

Thou shalt not offer the blood of my sacrifice with 23—18 leavened bread ; neither shall the fat of my feast remain all night until the morning. Thou shalt not seethe a kid in its 19b mother's milk. And in all things that I have said unto you 13 take ye heed : and make no mention of the name of 'other gods,' neither let it be heard out of thy mouth.

THE PROMISE.

Behold, I am 'sending an angel before thee,' to keep thee 20 by the way, and to bring thee into the place which I have prepared. Take ye heed of him, and hearken unto his 21 voice ; be not rebellious against him : for he will 'not pardon your transgression' ; for my name is in him. But if thou 22 shalt indeed hearken unto his voice, and do all that I speak ; then :

I will be an enemy unto thine enemies, and an adversary unto thine adversaries.

I will bless thy bread, and thy water ; and I will take 25 sickness away from the midst of thee. There shall none 26 cast her young, nor be barren, in thy land.

The number of thy days I will fulfil.

And I will send 'the hornet' before thee, which shall 28

* " And with thy beast of burden," supplied from LXX.

29 drive out the 'Amorite' from before thee. I will not drive
him out from before thee in one year ; lest the land become
desolate, and the beast of the field multiply against thee.

30 By little and little I will drive him out from before thee,
until thou be increased and inherit the land.

31 And I will set thy border from the Red Sea even unto
the Sea of the Philistines,and from the wilderness unto the
Euphrates.

THE COVENANT RATIFIED.

24—3 And Moses came and told the people all the words of
Yahweh : and 'all the people answered with one voice, and
said,' All the words which Yahweh hath spoken will we do.

4 And Moses wrote all the words of Yahweh, and 'rose up
early in the morning,' and 'builded an altar' under the
mount, and 'twelve pillars, according to the twelve tribes

5 of Israel.' And he sent 'young men' of the children of Israel, which 'offered burnt offerings, and sacrificed peace

6 offerings' of oxen unto Yahweh. And Moses took half of
the blood, and put it in basons ; and half of the blood he

7 sprinkled on the altar. And he took the 'writing of the
covenant,' and read in the audience of the people : and
'they said, All that Yahweh hath spoken will we do,' and be

8 obedient. And Moses took the blood, and sprinkled it on
the people, and said, Behold the blood of the covenant,
which Yahweh hath made with you on [the basis of] all these
commandments. [And Moses placed the book of the Covenant in the ark and set it in the Tent.]

JETHRO'S VISIT. HE BRINGS THE FAMILY OF MOSES.

18 Now when Jethro, 'Moses' father in law,' heard of all that

2 'God' had done for Moses, and for Israel his people, 'Jeth-

3 ro, Moses' father in law,' took Zipporah, Moses' wife, and

5 her two sons, and came with his sons and his wife unto
Moses into the wilderness where he was encamped, 'at the

6 mount of God' : and he said unto Moses, I thy 'father in law

Jethro' am come unto thee, and thy wife, and her two sons with her. And Moses told his father in law all that Yahweh 8 had done unto Pharaoh and to the Egyptians for Israel's sake, all the 'travail' that had come upon them by the way, and how Yahweh delivered them. And 'Jethro' rejoiced 9 for all the goodness which Yahweh had done to Israel, in that he had delivered them out of the hand of the Egyptians. And 'Jethro, Moses' father in law,' took [cattle for] 12 a burnt offering and a sacrificial feast at the shrine of 'God': and Aaron came, and 'all the elders of Israel,' to feast with Moses' father in law at the sanctuary of 'God.'

JETHRO'S COUNSEL. APPOINTMENT OF JUDGES.

And it came to pass on the morrow, that Moses sat to 13 'judge the people': and the people stood about Moses from the morning unto the evening. And when Moses' 14 father in law saw all that he did for the people, he said, What is this thing that thou doest for the people? why sittest thou thyself alone, and all the people stand about thee from morning unto even! And Moses said unto his father 15 in law, Because the people come unto me 'to obtain an oracle of God': when 'they have a suit to plead' they come unto me; and I judge between a man and his neighbor, and 16 I make them know the 'judgments of God,' and his laws. And Moses' father in law said unto him, The thing that 17 thou doest is not good. Thou wilt surely wear out both 18 thyself and this people that is with thee: for the thing is too heavy for thee; thou art not able to perform it thyself alone. Hearken now unto my voice; I will give thee coun- 19 sel, and 'God' shall be with thee: be thou at the people's service toward 'God,' and 'bring thou the causes unto God': and thou shalt teach them the 'judgments and the 20 laws.' And for the rest thou shalt provide out of all the 21 people able men, such as 'fear God,' men of truth, hating unjust gain, and place such over them, to be 'rulers of thousands, rulers of hundreds, rulers of fifties, and rulers of tens'; and let them 'judge the people' at all seasons: and 22 it shall be, that every great matter they shall bring unto thee, but every small matter they shall judge themselves : so shall it be easier for thyself, and they shall bear [the 23 burden] with thee. If thou shalt do this thing, and 'God' command thee so, then thou shalt be able to endure, and all 24 this people also shall go to their place in peace. So Moses hearkened to the voice of his father in law, and did all 25 that he had said. And Moses chose able men out of all Israel, and made them heads over the people, 'rulers of thousands, rulers of hundreds, rulers of fifties, and rulers of 26 tens.' And they 'judged the people' at all seasons : the hard 'causes' they brought unto Moses, but every small 27 matter they judged themselves. And Moses let his father in law depart ; and he went his way into his own land.

MOSES' INTERCOURSE WITH YAHWEH AT THE TENT. APPOINT-MENT OF SEVENTY ELDERS

33—7 Now Moses used to take the Tent and to pitch it without the camp, afar off from the camp ; and he called it, The Tent of meeting. And it came to pass, that every one which 'sought an oracle from Yahweh,' would go out unto 8 the Tent of meeting, which was 'without the camp.' And it came to pass, when ever Moses went out unto the Tent, that all the people rose up, and stood, every man at his tent door, and looked after Moses, until he was gone into 9 the Tent. And it came to pass, as often as Moses entered into the Tent, 'the pillar of cloud would descend, and stand at the door of the Tent': and he would speak with Moses. 10 And when all the people saw the pillar of cloud stand at the door of the Tent, all the people would rise up and 11 worship, every man at his tent door. And Yahweh spake unto Moses 'face to face,' as a man speaketh unto his friend. And he would return again into the camp : but 'his minister Joshua, the son of Nun, a young man,' never departed out of the Tent.

Num. 11—16 And Yahweh said unto Moses, 'Gather unto me seventy men of the elders of Israel,' whom thou knowest to be

the elders of the people, and ' officers ' over them ; and bring
them unto the Tent of meeting, that they may stand there
with thee.   And I will come down and talk with thee there : 17
and I will take of ' the spirit ' which is upon thee, and will
put it upon them ; and they shall ' bear the burden of the
people ' with thee, that thou bear it not thyself alone.   So he 24
' gathered seventy men of the elders ' of the people, and set
them round about the Tent.   And Yahweh came down in 25
the cloud, and talked with him, and took of ' the spirit ' that
was upon him, and put it upon the seventy elders : and it
came to pass, that, when ' the spirit ' rested upon them, they
' fell into prophetic ecstasy ' but they did so no more.   But 26
there remained two men in the camp, the name of the one
was Eldad, and the name of the other Medad   and ' the
spirit ' rested upon them ; for they were of them that were
written, but had not gone out unto the Tent : so they ' were
in the ecstasy ' in the camp.   And there ran a young man, 27
and told Moses, and said, Eldad and Medad ' are in
ecstasy ' in the camp.   And ' Joshua the son of Nun, the 28
minister of   Moses from his youth,' answered and said,
My lord Moses, forbid them.   And Moses said unto him, 29
Art thou jealous for my sake ? would God that all Yahweh's
people were ' prophets,' that Yahweh would put ' his spirit '
upon them !   And Moses gat him into the camp, he and 30
' the elders of Israel.'

MIRIAM AND AARON MURMUR AT MOSES' MARRIAGE.

And ' Miriam and Aaron spake against Moses ' because 12—1
of the Cushite woman whom he had married.   And they 2
said, Hath Yahweh indeed spoken only by Moses? hath he
not spoken also by us ?   And Yahweh heard it.   Now ' the 3
man Moses ' was very meek, above all the men which were
upon the face of the ' earth.'   And Yahweh spake suddenly 4
unto Moses, and unto Aaron, and unto ' Miriam,' Come out
ye three unto the Tent of meeting.   And they three came
out.   And Yahweh ' came down in a pillar of cloud, and stood 5

at the door of the Tent,' and called Aaron and 'Miriam':
and they both came forth. And he said,

6   Hear now my words:
If there be a 'prophet' among you
I Yahweh will make myself known unto him in a 'vision.'
I will speak with him in a 'dream.'

7   'My servant Moses' is not so;
He is entrusted with all my affairs:

8   With him will I speak 'mouth to mouth,'
Even manifestly, and not in dark speeches;
And the form of Yahweh shall he behold:
Wherefore then were ye not afraid to 'speak against'
'my servant,' against Moses?

9   And the anger of Yahweh was kindled against them; and

10 he departed, and the cloud removed from over the Tent.
But, behold, 'Miriam' was leprous, as [white as] snow: and
Aaron looked upon 'Miriam,' and, behold, she was leprous.

11 And Aaron said unto Moses, Oh my lord, blame us not, I
pray thee, for that we have done foolishly, and for that we

12 have sinned. Let her not, I pray, be as one still-born, of
whom the flesh is half consumed when he cometh out of his

13 mother's womb. And 'Moses cried unto Yahweh,' saying,
Not so, I beseech thee. Heal her, Yahweh, I beseech thee.

14 And Yahweh said unto Moses, If her father had but spit in
her face, should she not be put to shame seven days? let her
be shut up 'without the camp' seven days, and after that

15 she shall be brought in again. And Miriam was shut up
'without the camp' seven days: and the people journeyed
not till Miriam was brought in again.

[DEPARTURE FROM HOREB]. REPHIDIM AND THE BATTLE WITH
AMALEK.

[And afterward the people set forward from the mount of
God and the angel of God went before them. And they
came unto Rephidim].

Ex. 17—8 Then came forth Amalek, to fight with Israel in Rep-

hidim. And Moses said unto ' Joshua,' Choose us out men, and 9
go out, fight with Amalek to-morrow : but I will stand on the
top of the hill ' with the rod of God in mine hand.' So Joshua 10
did as Moses had said to him, and went to fight with Amalek :
and Moses, ' Aaron, and Hur ' went up to the top of the hill.
And it came to pass, when Moses held up his hand, that 11
Israel prevailed : and when he let down his hand, Amalek
prevailed. But Moses' hands were heavy ; and they took a 12
stone, and put it under him, and he sat thereon ; and ' Aaron
and Hur ' stayed up his hands, the one on the one side, and
the other on the other side ; and his hands were steady until
the going down of the sun. And Joshua discomfited Amalek 13
and his people with the edge of the sword. And Yahweh 14
said unto Moses, Write [the account of] this for a memorial
in a book, and rehearse [the song] in the ears of Joshua : for
I will utterly blot out the remembrance of Amalek from
under heaven. And Moses ' built an altar,' and called the 15
name of it Yahweh-nissi : " Yahweh my standard " and he 16
said,

A hand upon the " standard of Yah."
Yahweh hath war with Amalek from generation to gen-·
eration.*

———————◆———————

NUMBERS. (HEB. " IN THE WILDERNESS.")
MURMURS AT TABERAH.

And the people were as men who bewail their misfortunes 11
in the ears of Yahweh : and when Yahweh heard it, his anger
was kindled ; and ' the fire of Yahweh ' burnt among them,
and devoured in the uttermost part of the camp. And the 2
people cried unto Moses ; ' and Moses prayed unto Yahweh,'
and the fire abated. And the name of that place was called 3

* As in the case of ch. xv. vv. 1 and 21 and elsewhere, only a line or two,
probably the opening lines, of the poem are given. The original must of course
have been longer and doubtless served the author as source. Cf. 1 Sam. xv.
especially the lines of vv. 22f.

Taberah (*i. e.* " Burning ") because 'the fire of Yahweh' "burnt" among them.

THE REBELLION OF DATEAN AND ABIRAM.

18—1 Now Dathan and Abiram the sons of Eliab, sons of
2 Reuben, rose up against Moses, with certain of the children
12 of Israel. And Moses sent to call Dathan and Abiram, the
sons of Eliab : and they said, We will not come up. [And
Dathan and Abiram gathered the people together in the
camp and sent word unto Moses, saying, Come down unto
14b us if thou have aught to say unto us . . .] : wilt thou put
25 out the eyes of these men ? we will not come up. So Moses
rose up and went unto Dathan and Abiram ; and 'the elders
28b of Israel' followed him. And Dathan and Abiram came out,
32 and stood at the door of, their tents, [. . .] and the
'earth' opened her mouth, and swallowed them up, and
their 'households.' And the 'earth' closed upon them, and
34 they perished from among the assembly. And all Israel
that were round about them fled at the cry of them : for
they said to themselves, Lest the 'earth' swallow us up.

THE STORY OF THE SPIES. THE GRAPES OF ESHCOL,

20—1 And the people abode in Kadesh, and 'Miriam' died
there 'and was buried' there.   .
(Dt. 1—20ff.)   [And Moses said unto the people, Ye are come
unto the land which Yahweh hath given you, Go up therefore and take it in possession, and he will be with you. And
they came near unto him and said, Let us send men that
they may spy out the land, and bring us word again how we
must go up and what cities are in it. So Moses hearkened
unto them, and he chose twelve men, out of every tribe a
13—17b man, and said unto them], Go up into the hill-country
18 and see the land what it is, and the people that dwelleth
20 therein, whether they be few or many, and what the land is,
whether it be fat or lean, whether there be wood therein,
or not. And be ye of good courage, and bring of the fruit
of the land. Now the time was the time of the firstripe

grapes. [So they went up] and came unto the valley of 23
Eshcol, and cut down from thence a branch with one cluster
of grapes, and they bare it upon a staff between two ; [they
brought] also of the pomegranates, and of the figs. That 24
place was called the valley of Eshcol, (*i.e.* "Grape-cluster ")
because of the "cluster" which the children of Israel cut
down from thence. [And they returned to Moses and all 26b
the people] to Kadesh ; and brought back word to them and
shewed them the fruit of the land. [And they said unto
Moses, The land whither we went up to search it out is an
exceeding good land] and this is the fruit of it [but the people that dwell in it are many and strong]. Amalek dwelleth 29
in the 'land of the South' : and the Canaanite dwelleth by
the sea, and 'along by the side of' Jordan, and all the people that we saw in it are men of great stature. And there 33
we saw the Nephilim, and we were in our own sight [as
compared with them] as grasshoppers, and so we were in
their sight.

REBELLION AT THE REPORT OF THE SPIES.

And the people wept that night, and [said], ' Where- 14—1b–3
fore doth Yahweh bring us unto this land' 'to fall by
the sword'? And they said one to another, Let us make a 4
captain, and let us return into Egypt.

[And the anger of Yahweh was kindled, and he said unto
Moses, Surely not one of these that have rebelled against
me shall see the land which I promised to their fathers. Go
not up hence ; for I will not be with you, and ye shall be
beaten down before your enemies ; for the Amorite dwelleth
on the table-land] and 'the Amalekite and the Canaanite' 25
dwell in the low country : to-morrow turn ye, and get you
into the wilderness 'by the way to the Red Sea.'

THE DISASTER AT HORMAH. ISRAEL GOES UP PRESUMPTUOUSLY.

And Moses told these words unto all the children of 39
Israel : 'and the people mourned greatly.' 'And they rose 40

up early in the morning,' and gat them up to the top of the
mountain, saying, Lo, we be here, and will go up unto the
place which Yahweh hath promised : 'for we have sinned.'
41 And Moses said, Wherefore now do ye 'transgress the com-
42 mandment' of Yahweh, seeing it shall not prosper ? Go
not up, for Yahweh is not among you ; that ye be not smit-
43 ten down before your enemies. For there 'the Amalekite
and the Canaanite ' are before you, and 'ye shall fall by the
sword' : because ye are turned back from following Yah-
44 weh, therefore Yahweh will not be with you. But they presumed to go up to the top of the mountain : nevertheless
the ark of Yahweh and Moses, 'departed not' out of the
45 camp. Then the 'Amalekite came down, and the Canaanite' which dwelt in that mountain, and smote them and beat
them down, even unto Hormah. (LXX) So they returned
to the camp [and Israel abode many days in Kadesh.]

THE EMBASSY TO THE KING OF EDOM. ISRAEL JOURNEYS AROUND EDOM AND MOAB.

20—14 And Moses sent messengers from Kadesh unto the
king of Edom, Thus saith thy brother Israel, Thou knowest all the 'travail' that hath befallen us : how our fathers
15 went down into Egypt, and we dwelt in Egypt a long time ;
16 and the Egyptians evil entreated us, and our fathers : and
when we 'cried unto Yahweh,' he heard our voice, and
'sent an angel,' and brought us forth out of Egypt : and, behold, we are in Kadesh, a city 'in the uttermost of thy
17 border' : let us pass, I pray thee, through thy land : we will
not pass through field or through vineyard; neither will we
drink of the water of the wells : we will go along the
king's [high] way, we will not turn aside to the right hand
18 nor to the left, until we have passed thy border. And
Edom said unto him, Thou shalt not pass through me, lest
19 I come out with the sword against thee. And the children
of Israel said unto him, We will go up by the high way :
and if we drink of thy water, I and my cattle, then will I
give the price thereof : let me only, without [doing] any

thing [else], pass through on my feet. And he said, Thou 20
shalt not pass through. And Edom came out against him
with much people, and 'with a strong hand.' Thus Edom 21
refused to give Israel passage through his border; wherefore Israel turned away from him, 'by the way to the 21—4
Red Sea,' to compass the land of Edom.

THE SERPENT OF BRASS. MURMURS AT THE MANNA ARE VISITED WITH FIERY SERPENTS.

Now the people became disheartened because of the 21—4b
[long] journey. And the people 'spake against' 'God,' 5
and 'against Moses,' 'Wherefore have ye brought us up out
of Egypt to die in the wilderness'? for there is no bread,
and there is no water; and our soul loatheth this miserable
food. And Yahweh sent the fiery serpents among the peo- 6
ple, and they bit the people; and much people of Israel
died. And the people came to Moses, and said, 'We have 7
sinned,' because we have 'spoken against Yahweh, and
against thee'; 'pray unto Yahweh,' that he take away the
serpents from us. And 'Moses prayed for the people.'
And Yahweh said unto Moses, Make thee a fiery serpent, 8
and set it upon a 'standard': and it shall come to pass, that
every one that is bitten, when he seeth it, shall live. So 9
Moses made a serpent of brass, and set it upon the 'standard':
and it came to pass, that if a serpent had bitten any man,
when he looked unto the serpent of brass, he lived.

THE DESERT JOURNEY. DEATH OF AARON AND APPOINTMENT OF ELEAZAR TO THE PRIESTHOOD.

[And the people journeyed many days in the wilderness,
and they encamped at . . .] and Laban and Hazeroth **Dt. 1**—1
and Dizahab. [. . .] And the children of Israel journeyed 10—6
from Beeroth Benejaakan ("Wells of the Jaakanites" [in
mount Seir]) to Moserah: there Aaron died, and 'there he
was buried'; and Eleazar his son ministered in the priest's
office in his stead. From thence they journeyed unto Gud- 7
godah (Num. xxxiii. 32f, " Hor-haggidgad "); and from Gud-

godah to Jotbathah, a land of "brooks of water" [. . .]
Num. 21—11b. in the wilderness which is eastward of Moab
12 toward the sunrising. 'From thence they journeyed, and
13 pitched' in the valley of Zered. 'From thence they journeyed, and pitched' on the further side of Arnon, which is
in (*i. e.* where it flows through?) the wilderness, [the stream]
that cometh out of the border of the 'Amorites': for
Arnon is the border of Moab, between Moab and the 'Amor-
14 ites.' Wherefore it is said in the book of the Wars of Yahweh,

> Vaheb in Suphah,
> And the valleys thereof;
15   Arnon, and the slope of the valleys
> That incline toward the dwelling of Ar,
> And lean on the border of Moab.

THE WAR WITH SIHON KING OF THE AMORITES. CONQUEST OF THE TERRITORY OF GAD AND REUBEN.

21   And Israel sent messengers unto Sihon king of the 'Amor-
22 ites,' saying, 'Let me pass through thy land : we will not
turn aside into field, or into vineyard ; we will not drink of
the water of the wells : 'we will go by the king's [high] way,
23 until we have passed thy border.' And Sihon would not
suffer Israel to pass through his border : but Sihon gathered
all his people together, and went out against Israel into the
wilderness, and came to Jahaz : and he fought against
24 Israel. And Israel smote him with the edge of the sword,
27 and possessed his land from Arnon unto Jabbok. Wherefore the taunting poets say,

> Come ye to Heshbon,
> Let the city of Sihon be built and established :
28   For a fire went forth out of Heshbon,
> A flame from the city of Sihon :
> It devoured Ar of Moab,
> The lords of the high places of Arnon.
29   Woe to thee, Moab !
> Thou art undone, O people of Chemosh :
> He (Chemosh) gave his sons as fugitives,

And his daughters into captivity.
We shot at them ; Heshbon perished even unto Dibon, 30
And we laid it waste,
Until fire was kindled (?) unt Medeba.
Thus Israel dwelt in the land of the 'Amorites.'   31

THE PROPHECY OF BALAAM. BALAK'S MESSENGERS COME TO BRING YAHWEH'S PROPHET FROM ARAM NAHARAIM.

And Balak the son of Zippor [king of Moab] saw all **22**—2
that Israel had done to the 'Amorites.' And Moab was 3
sore afraid of the people, because they were many. And he 5
sent messengers unto Balaam the son of Beor, to Pethor,
which is by the 'Euphrates' to call him, saying, Behold,
there is a people come out from Egypt : behold, they cover
the face of the earth, and they abide over against me : come 6
now therefore, I pray thee, curse me this people ; for 'they
are too mighty for me'; peradventure I shall prevail, that
we may smite them, and that I may drive them out of the land:
for I know that he whom thou blessest is blessed, and he
whom thou cursest is cursed. And they came unto Balaam, 7
and spake unto him the words of Balak. And he said unto 8
them, Lodge here this night, and I will bring you word
again, as Yahweh shall speak unto me : and the princes of
Moab abode with Balaam. And ' God came unto ' Balaam, 9
and said, What men are these with thee ? And Balaam said 10
unto ' God,' Balak the son of Zippor, king of Moab, hath
sent unto me, [saying], Behold, the people that is come out 11
of Egypt, it covereth the face of the earth : now come, curse
me them ; peradventure I shall be able to fight against
them, and shall drive them out. And ' God ' said unto 12
Balaam, Thou shalt not go with them ; thou shalt not curse
the people : for they are blessed. And Balaam 'rose up in 13
the morning,' and said unto the princes of Balak, Get you
into your land : for Yahweh ' refuseth to give me leave ' to
go with you. And the princes of Moab rose up, and they 14
went unto Balak, and said, Balaam refuseth to come with us.
And Balak sent yet again princes, more, and more honor- 15

16 able than they. And they came to Balaam, and said to him,
Thus saith Balak the son of Zippor, Let nothing, I pray
thee, hinder thee from coming unto me. [And Balaam
answered and said, What Yahweh saith unto me, that will I
19 do]. Now therefore, I pray you, tarry ye also here this
night, that I may know what Yahweh will speak unto me
20 more. ' And God came unto Balaam at night,' and said
unto him, If the men be come to call thee, rise up, go with
them ; but only the word which I speak unto thee, that shalt
21 thou do. So ' Balaam rose up in the morning,' and went
36 with the princes of Moab. And when Balak heard that
Balaam was come, he went out to meet him unto Ir of Moab,
which is on the border of Arnon, [a city] which is ' in the
37 utmost part of the border.' And Balak said unto Balaam, Did
I not earnestly send unto thee to call thee ? wherefore
38 camest thou not unto me ? And Balaam said unto Balak,
Lo, now I am come unto thee : have I now any power at all
to speak anything ? the word that ' God ' putteth in my
40 mouth, that shall I speak. And Balak sacrificed oxen and
sheep, and sent [portions] to Balaam, and to the princes that
were with him.

THE ORACLE AGAINST ISRAEL.

41 And it came to pass in the morning, that Balak took Balaam, and brought him up unto Bamoth Baal (*i. e.* " High
places of Baal ") and he saw from thence the utmost part of
23—1 the people. And Balaam said unto Balak, ' Build me here
seven altars, and prepare me here seven bullocks and seven
2 rams.' And Balak did as Balaam had spoken ; and ' offered
on every altar a bullock and a ram,' and he said unto him, I
have ' prepared the seven altars, and I have offered up a bul-
3 lock and a ram on every altar.' And Balaam said unto
Balak, Stand by thy burnt offering, and I will go ; peradventure Yahweh will come to meet me : and whatsoever he
4 sheweth me I will tell thee. And he went to . . . .* And

* The translation " a bare height " usually adopted here is unknown to the
versions and open to much doubt, if not inadmissible. The text is probably
corrupt.

'God' met Balaam, and put a word in Balaam's mouth, and 5
said, Return unto Balak, and thus thou shalt speak. So he re- 6
turned unto him, and, lo, he was standing by his burnt offering, he, and all the princes of Moab. And he took up his 7
oracle, and said,

> From 'Aram' hath Balak brought me,
> The king of Moab from the mountains of the East :
> Come, curse me Jacob,
> Yea come, taunt Israel.
> How shall I curse, whom God hath not cursed?   8
> And how shall I taunt, whom Yahweh hath not
>   taunted?
> For from the top of the rocks I see him,   9
> And from the hills I behold him :
> Lo, it is a people that dwell alone,
> And reckoneth itself not of the nations.
> Who can number the dust of Jacob,   10
> Who can count the myriads of Israel?
> Let me die the death of the "righteous," (*Yesharim*) †
> And let my succession be like his !

And Balak said unto Balaam, What hast thou done unto 11
me? I took thee to curse mine enemies, and, behold, thou
hast blessed them altogether. And he answered and said, 12
Must I not take heed to speak that which Yahweh putteth
in my mouth? And Balak said unto him, Come, I pray thee, 13
with me unto another place, from whence thou mayest see
them all, and curse me them from thence. And he took 14
him into the field of Zophim, ("Watchers") to the top of
Pisgah, and 'built seven altars, and offered up a bullock and
a ram on every altar.' And he said unto Balak, Stand here 15
by thy burnt offering, while I meet [Yahweh] yonder. And 16
Yahweh met Balaam, and put a word in his mouth, and said,
Return unto Balak, and thus shalt thou speak. And he 17
came to him, and, lo, he stood by his burnt offering, and the
princes of Moab with him. And Balak said unto him, What
hath Yahweh spoken? And he took up his oracle, and said, 18

---

† Probably a play upon the stem. of Israel, *yisrael*, like "Jeshurun" *yeshurun*.

Rise up, Balak, and hear ;
Hearken unto me, thou son of Zippor :

19   God is not a man, that he should lie ;
Neither the son of man, that he should repent :
Hath he said, and shall he not do it ?
Or hath he spoken, and shall he not make it good ?

20   Behold, I received [commandment] to bless,
And have blessed, and I cannot reverse it.

21   Iniquity is not seen in Jacob,
Nor is trouble to be seen in Israel :
Yahweh his God is with him,
And royal acclamations are [heard] in their midst.

24   Behold, the people riseth up as a lioness,
And as a lion doth it lift itself up :
He lieth not down till he eat of the prey,
And drink the blood of the slain.

25   And Balak said unto Balaam, Neither curse them at all,
26   nor bless them at all.   But Balaam answered and said unto
Balak, Told not I thee, saying, All that Yahweh speaketh,
that I must do?   [And Balaam rose up and returned to his
place.   And Balak also went his way.]

ISRAEL'S IDOLATRY WITH BAAL-PEOR.

25—1a, 3   So Israel abode at Shittim.   And Israel joined himself unto Baal-peor ; and the anger of Yahweh was kindled
5   against Israel.   And Moses said unto the 'judges' of Israel,
Slay ye every one his men that have joined themselves unto
Baal-peor.

THE INHERITANCE OF REUBEN AND GAD.

32—1   [Now the children of Reuben and the children of Gad]
had a multitude [of cattle].   And when they saw the land
of Jazer, and the land of Gilead, that, behold, the place was
16   a place for cattle, they came near unto [Moses], and said,
We will build 'sheepfolds' here for our cattle, and cities for
17   our 'little ones' : but we ourselves will be ready armed to go
before the children of Israel, until we have brought them

unto their place : and our 'little ones' shall dwell in the
fenced cities because of the inhabitants of the land. [And
Moses said unto them] Build you cities for your 'little 24
ones' and 'folds for your sheep'; and do that which hath
proceeded out of your mouth. So Moses gave unto them 33
[the land of Gilead and the land of Jazer.] And the children 34
of Gad built Dibon, and Ataroth, and Aroer : and Atroth- 35
shophan, and Jazer, and Jogbehah ; and Beth-nimrah, and 36
Beth-haran : fenced cities, and 'folds for sheep.' And the 37
children of Reuben built Heshbon, and Elealeh, and Kiriathaim ; and Nebo, and Baal-meon, and Sibmah : and gave 38
other names unto the cities which they builded.

DEUTERONOMY. (Heb. "Words of Moses.")

The Covenant in the Plain of Shittim. Moses gives Israel the Statutes and Judgments of God.

[Then Moses gathered all the people together (**Jos. 24**—1)
and called for the elders of Israel, and for their heads, and
for their judges, and for their officers, and they presented
themselves before God. And Moses said unto the (**Dt. 5**—1ff)
people, Behold, Yahweh our God made a covenant with us
in Horeb, and spake to you out of the mount Ten Words ;
and he wrote them upon two tables of stone and gave them
unto me. But ye were afraid, when ye heard the voice of
Yahweh, and ye said unto me, Go thou near and hear the
words of Yahweh and speak unto us what Yahweh saith, and
we will hear it and do it. And Yahweh heard the voice of
your words, and he said unto me, They have well said all
that they have spoken. Go, say to them, Return ye to your
tents. But as for thee, stand thou here by me, and I will
speak unto thee the statutes and the judgments which thou
shalt teach them, that they may do them in the land which I
give them to possess it. So I went up into the mount (**Dt. 9**—9)
unto Yahweh, to receive the tables of stone, even the tables
of the covenant which Yahweh made with you, and I abode

(10) in the mount forty days and forty nights. And Yahweh delivered unto me the two tables of stone written with the
(15—17) finger of God. So I turned and came down from the mount, and the two tables of the covenant were in my two hands. And I looked, and, behold, ye had sinned against Yahweh, ye had made you a molten calf. And I took hold of the two tables and cast them out of my two hands and
(21) brake them before your eyes. And I took your sin, the bull that ye had made and burned it with fire, and stamped it, grinding it very small, and I cast the dust thereof into
(10—10f.) the brook that descended out of the mount. And I went up and fell down before Yahweh forty days, as at the first, and Yahweh hearkened unto me and would not destroy you. And he made a new covenant with us and sent an angel before you to bring you in unto the land which he
(1—6-8) promised you. And he said unto me, Ye have dwelt long enough in this mountain; turn you, and take your journey and go to the hill country of the Amorites. Behold I
(9—18) have set the land before you, go in and possess it. And I spake unto you at that time saying, I am not able to bear you alone. Take you men according to your tribes, and I will make them heads over you. So I took the heads of your tribes, wise men and known, and made them heads over you, captains of thousands and captains of hundreds, and captains of fifties, and captains of tens, and officers. And I charged your judges, saying, Hear the causes between your brethren, and judge righteously between a man and his brother, and the stranger that is with him. Ye shall not respect persons in judgment. Ye shall hear the small and the great alike; ye shall not be afraid of the face of man; for the judgment is God's: and the cause that is too hard for you ye shall bring unto me and I will hear it.
(19—46) So we journeyed from Horeb by the way to the hill country of the Amorites and we came to Kadesh. And ye came near unto me and said, Let us send men before us that they may search the land for us, and bring us word again. So I took twelve men of you, one man for every

tribe, and they turned and went up into the mountain country, and came unto the valley of Eshcol and searched it out.
And they took of the fruit of the land and brought it unto
us and brought us word again, saying, It is a good land
which Yahweh giveth unto us. But ye would not go up,
but rebelled against Yahweh, and said, Yahweh hath brought
us up to deliver us into the hand of the Amorite to destroy
us. And Yahweh was angry and said unto me, Surely not
one of these that have rebelled against me shall see the land;
turn you and take your journey into the wilderness by the
way to the Red Sea. Then ye answered and said unto me,
We have sinned against Yahweh, we will go up and fight as
he commanded us. And ye girded on every man his weap-
ons and deemed it a light thing to go up into the mountain
country. And Yahweh said unto me, Say unto them, Go
not up, nor fight ; for I am not among you ; lest ye be smitten before your enemies. But ye rebelled against the word
of Yahweh and went up into the mountain. And the Amorite which dwelt in that mountain came out against you, and
chased you as bees do, and beat you down in Seir even unto
Hormah. And ye returned and wept before Yahweh, but he
hearkened not. So ye abode in Kadesh many days.

Then we turned and took our journey into the wilder- (2—1)
ness by the way to the Red Sea, as Yahweh had spoken unto
me : and we compassed mount Seir many days and went up
through the wilderness of Kedemoth. And I sent (26—37)
messengers out of the wilderness of Kedemoth unto Sihon
king of Heshbon with words of peace, saying, Let me pass
through thy land. But Sihon king of Heshbon would not
suffer us to pass by him, but came out against us, he and all
his people unto battle at Jahaz. And Yahweh delivered
up the Amorites before us and we possessed their land.
And I gave the land for an inheritance unto the chil- (3—12ff.)
dren of Gad and Reuben, and commanded them saying, Ye
shall surely pass over with your brethren until Yahweh have
driven out the Amorite from before you. Afterward shall ye
return hither unto your possession.]

27—17 Remember what Amalek did unto thee by the way,
18 when ye came out of Egypt, how he met thee by the way
and smote all that were feeble of thee, and ' feared not God ';
19 therefore it shall be, when Yahweh hath given thee rest from
all thine enemies round about, that ye shall blot out the
remembrance of Amalek from under heaven.

(23ff.) [And Moses said unto all the people, Behold, we stand
18 here before Jordan, and Yahweh hath said unto me, Thou
shalt not go over this Jordan , now therefore hearken, and
I will speak unto you the statutes and the judgments which
19 Yahweh gave unto me in mount Horeb to teach you, that ye
might do them in the land whither we go over to possess it.]

The Book of Judgments.

(Ex. 21—1) And [Yahweh said unto me] These are the judgments which thou shalt set before them.
2   If thou buy an Hebrew slave, six years he shall serve : and
3 in the seventh he shall go out free for nothing. If he come
in by himself, he shall go free by himself : if he be ' mar-
4 ried,' then his wife shall go free with him. If his master
give him a wife, and she bear him sons or daughters ; the
wife and her children shall be her master's, and he shall go
5 free by himself. But if the servant shall plainly say, I love
my master, my wife; and my children ; I will not go out free ;
6 then his master shall ' bring him unto God,' and shall bring
him to the door, or unto the door post [of the sanctuary] ;
and his master shall bore his ear through with an awl ; and
he shall be his slave forever.
7   And if a man sell his daughter to be a ' maidservant,' she
8 shall not go free as the menservants do. If she please not
her master, and he hath not cohabited with her, then shall
he let her be redeemed : to sell her unto a strange people
he shall have no power, seeing he hath dealt deceitfully
9 with her. And if he espouse her unto his son, he shall deal
10 with her after the manner of daughters. If he take him
another [wife], her food, her raiment, and her duty of mar-
11 riage, shall he not diminish. And if he do not these three

CIRC. 750 B. C. 353

unto her, then shall she go free for nothing, without money.

He that smiteth a man, so that he die, shall surely 12 be put to death. And if a man lie not in wait, but 'God' 13 deliver [his enemy] into his hand ; then he shall flee to mine altar. But if a man come presumptuously upon his neigh- 14 bor, to slay him with guile ; thou shalt take him from mine altar, that he may die. And he that smiteth his father, or 15 his mother, shall be surely put to death. And he that steal- 16 eth a man of the children of Israel,* whether he have sold him or he be found in his hand, he shall surely be put to death.

And if men contend, and one smiteth the other with a 18 stone, or with his fist, and he die not, but keep his bed : if 19 he rise again, and walk abroad upon his staff, then shall he that smote him be quit : only he shall pay for the loss of his time, and shall cause him to be thoroughly healed. But if 23 any mischief follow, then thou shalt give life for life, eye for 24 eye, tooth for tooth, hand for hand, foot for foot, burning 25 for burning, wound for wound, stripe for stripe. And if 22 men strive together, and hurt a woman with child, so that her fruit depart, and yet no mischief follow : he shall be surely fined, according as the woman's husband shall lay upon him ; and he shall pay for the miscarriage.

And if a man smite his bondman, or his 'bondwoman' 20 with a rod, and he die under his hand ; he shall surely be punished. Notwithstanding, if [the slave] linger a day or 21 two, he [the master] shall not be punished : for he [the lost slave] is his money. And if a man smite the eye of his 26 bondman, or the eye of his 'bondwoman,' and destroy it ; he shall let him go free for his eye's sake. And if he smite out 27 his bondsman's tooth, or his 'bondwoman's' tooth ; he shall let him go free for his tooth's sake.

And if an ox gore a man or a woman, that they die, the 28 ox shall be surely stoned, and his flesh shall not be eaten ; but the 'owner' of the ox shall be quit. But if the ox were 29

* So LXX.

wont to gore in time past, and it hath been testified to his
'owner,' and he hath not kept him in, but he hath killed a
man or a woman ; the ox shall be stoned, and his 'owner'
30 also shall be put to death. If there be laid on him a ransom, then he shall give for the redemption of his life what-
31 soever is laid upon him. Whether he have gored a son, or
have gored a daughter, according to this judgment shall it
32 be done unto him. If the ox gore a bondman or a 'bondwoman'; he shall give unto their master thirty shekels of
silver, and the ox shall be stoned.

33   And if a man shall open a pit, or if a man shall dig a pit
34 and not cover it, and an ox or an ass fall therein, the
'owner' of the pit shall make it good ; he shall give money
unto the 'owner' of them, and the dead [beast] shall be
his.

35   And if one man's ox hurt another's, that he die ; then
they shall sell the live ox, and divide the price of it ; and
36 the dead also they shall divide. Or if it be known that the
ox was wont to gore in time past, and his 'owner' hath not
kept him in ; he shall surely pay ox for ox, and the dead
[beast] shall be his own.

22   If a man shall steal an ox, or a sheep, and kill it, or sell
it ; he shall pay five oxen for an ox, and four sheep for a
sheep. If he have nothing, then he shall be sold for his
4 theft. If the theft be found in his hand alive, whether it be
ox, or ass, or sheep ; he shall pay double. If the thief
2 be found breaking in, and be smitten that he die, there
3 shall be no bloodguiltiness for him. If the sun be risen
upon him, there shall be bloodguiltiness for him : he
should make restitution.

5   If a man shall cause a field or vineyard to be eaten, and
shall let his beast loose, and it feed in another man's field,
he shall make restitution according to the yield thereof from
his own field ; but if it eat the whole crop,* he shall make
restitution of the best of his own field, and of the best of
his own vineyard.

* So LXX.

If fire break out, and catch in thorns, so that the shocks **6** of corn, or the standing corn, or the field, be consumed ; he that kindled the fire shall surely make restitution.

If a man shall deliver unto his neighbor money or stuff to **7** keep, and it be stolen out of the man's house ; if the thief be found, he shall pay double. If the thief be not found, then **8** the 'master' of the house shall 'come near unto God,' [to determine by the sacred lot] whether he have not put his hand unto his neighbor's goods. For every matter of tres- **9** pass, whether it be for ox, for ass, for sheep, for raiment, [or] for any manner of lost thing, whereof one saith, This is it, 'the cause' of both parties shall 'come before God ;' he whom 'God' shall condemn [by the sacred lot] shall pay double unto his neighbor.

If a man deliver unto his neighbor an ass, or an ox, or a **10** sheep, or any beast, to keep ; and it die, or be hurt, or driven away, no man seeing it : the oath of God shall be between **11** them both, whether he hath not put his hand unto his neigh- bor's goods ; and if the 'owner' thereof shall accept it, he shall not make restitution. But if it be stolen from him, he **12** shall make restitution unto the 'owner' thereof. If it be **13** torn in pieces [by wild beasts and he can] bring it for wit- ness, he shall not make good that which was torn. And if **14** a man borrow [an animal] of his neighbor, and it be hurt, or die, the 'owner' thereof not being with it, he shall surely make restitution. If the 'owner' thereof be with it, he **15** shall not make it good : if it be an hired thing, [the loss] is included in its hire.

And if a man entice a virgin that is not betrothed, and **16** lie with her, he shall surely pay a dowry for her and take her to wife. If her father utterly refuse to give her unto **17** him, he shall pay money according to the dowry of vir- gins.

Thou shalt not suffer a sorceress to live. **18**

Whosoever lieth with a beast shall surely be put to death. **19**

And he that curseth his father, or his mother, shall **21—17** surely be put to death.

22—20 He that sacrificeth unto any god, save unto Yahweh
21 only, shall be devoted. And a stranger shalt thou not wrong,
neither shalt thou oppress him :

25 If thou lend money to any of my people with thee that is
poor, thou shalt not be to him as a creditor ; neither shall ye
26 lay upon him usury. If thou at all take thy neighbor's
garment to pledge, thou shalt restore it unto him by that the
sun goeth down :

28 Thou shalt not blaspheme 'God,' nor curse a ruler of thy
people.

23 Thou shalt not take up a false report : put not thine hand
2 with the wicked to be an unrighteous witness. Thou shalt
not follow a multitude to do evil ; neither shalt thou turn
3 aside after a multitude to wrest judgment: neither shalt thou
favor a great man* in his suit.

4 If thou meet thine enemy's ox or his ass going astray, thou
5 shalt surely bring it back to him again. If thou see the ass
of him that hateth thee lying under his burden, thou shalt
forbear to leave him in the lurch, thou shalt surely help him
to release it.

6 Thou shalt not wrest the judgment of thy poor in his suit.
7 Keep thee far from a false matter ; and the innocent and
righteous slay thou not : neither shalt thou justify the wicked.
8 And thou shalt take no gift : for a gift blindeth them that
have sight, and perverteth a righteous cause.

THE STELAE OF THE LAW, AND THE ALTAR AT EBAL.

Dt. 27—1 And Moses commanded 'the elders of Israel,'
4 saying, It shall be when ye are passed over Jordan that thou
shalt 'set thee up great stones' in mount Ebal and shalt
5 whitewash them with whitewash. And thou shalt 'build there
an altar' unto Yahweh, an 'altar of stones :' thou shalt 'lift
6 up no iron [tool] upon them.' Thou shalt build the altar of
Yahweh of 'unhewn stones': and thou shalt 'offer burnt
7 offerings thereon, and sacrifice peace offerings,' and shalt

* So Kautzsch (assuming Dt. to be a corruption from GDt.?).

eat there. And thou shalt write upon the stones all the 8
words of this law very plainly.

THE CHARGE TO JOSHUA.

And Yahweh said unto Moses, Behold, thy days **Dt. 31**—14
approach that thou must die : call 'Joshua,' and 'present
yourselves in the Tent of Meeting,' that I may give him a
charge. And Moses and Joshua went, and 'presented themselves in the Tent of Meeting.' 'And Yahweh appeared in 15
the Tent in a pillar of cloud : and the pillar of cloud stood
over the door of the Tent.' And he gave Joshua the son of 23
Nun a charge, and said, Be strong and of a good courage :
for thou shalt bring the children of Israel into the land
which I sware unto them : and I will be with thee.

MOSES' DEATH.

So Moses 'the servant of Yahweh' died there in the **Dt. 34**—5
land of Moab : but no man knoweth of his sepulchre unto
this day. And there hath not arisen a 'prophet' since in 10
Israel like unto Moses, whom Yahweh knew 'face to face.'

(THE) EXODUS.

NAMES OF ISRAEL'S SONS. GENEALOGY OF LEVI.

1 Now 'these are the names' of the sons of Israel, which
2 came into Egypt; 'every man and his household' came with
3 Jacob. Reuben, Simeon, Levi, and Judah; Issachar, Zebu-
4 lun, and Benjamin; Dan and Naphtali, Gad and Asher.
5 And all the 'souls' that came out of the 'loins' of Jacob
were seventy 'souls': and Joseph was in Egypt already.

6—16 And 'these are the names' of the sons of Levi 'accord-
ing to their generations';
Gershon, and Kohath, and Merari:
'And the years of the life of Levi were 137 years.'

17 'The sons of ' Gershon:
Libni and Shimei, according to their families.

18 'And the sons of ' Kohath;
Amram, and Izhar, and Hebron, and Uzziel:
'And the years of the life of Kohath were 133 years.'

19 'And the sons of ' Merari; Mahli and Mushi.
'These are the families' of the Levites 'according to
their generations.'

20 And Amram took him Jochebed his father's sister to
wife; and she bare him Aaron and Moses: 'and the years
of the life of Amram were 137 years.'

21 'And the sons of ' Izhar; Korah, and Nepheg, and
Zichri.

22 'And the sons of ' Uzziel; Mishael, and Elzaphan, and
Sithri.

23 And Aaron took him Elisheba, the daughter of Amminadab, the sister of Nahshon to wife; and she bare him Nadab
and Abihu, Eleazar and Ithamar.

24   'And the sons of' Korah; Assir, and Elkanah, and
Abiasaph ;
     'These are the families' of the Korahites.

25   And Eleazar Aaron's son took him one of the daughters
of Putiel to wife ; and she bare him Phinehas.
     'These are the 'heads of the fathers'' [houses] of the
Levites 'according to their families.'

THE BONDAGE OF EGYPT. ISRAEL'S CRY TO GOD.

1—7   And the children of Israel 'were fruitful, and increased
abundantly, and the land was filled' with them.

13   And the Egyptians made the children of Israel to 'serve
14 with rigor '; and 'made their lives bitter' with hard bondage, all their bond service, wherein they made them 'serve
with rigor,' and the children of Israel sighed by reason of
the bondage, and they cried, and their cry came up unto
2—24 'God' by reason of the bondage. And 'God' heard their
groaning, and 'God' 'remembered' his covenant with Abra-'
25 ham, with Isaac, and with Jacob. And 'God' saw the children of Israel, and 'God' took knowledge. . . . .

GOD'S REVELATION OF HIS NAME YAHWEH. MOSES SENT TO
DELIVER ISRAEL.

6—2   And 'God' spake unto Moses, and said unto him, I am
3 Yahweh : and I appeared unto Abraham, unto Isaac, and
unto Jacob, as ' El Shaddai ' but by my name Yahweh I was
4 not known to them. And moreover I 'established my
covenant' with them, to give them the land of Canaan, the
5 land of their 'sojournings,' wherein they 'sojourned.' And
now also I have heard the groaning of the children of
Israel, whom the Egyptians keep in bondage ; and I have
6 'remembered my covenant.' Wherefore say unto the children of Israel, 'I am Yahweh,' and I will bring you out from
under the burdens of the Egyptians, and I will rid you out
of their bondage, and I will redeem you with a stretched out
7 arm, and with great 'judgments ': and I will take you to
me for a people, and I will be to you a God: and 'ye shall

know that I am Yahweh your God,' which bringeth you out
from under the burdens of the Egyptians.　And I will bring　8
you in unto the land, concerning which I ' lifted up my hand '
to give it to Abraham, to Isaac, and to Jacob ;　and I will
give it you for an heritage : 'I am Yahweh.'　And Moses　9
spake so unto the children of Israel : but they hearkened
not unto Moses for discouragement and for cruel bondage.

　　And Yahweh spake unto Moses saying, Go in, speak unto 10
Pharaoh king of Egypt, that he let the children of Israel go 11
out of his land.　And Moses ' spake before ' Yahweh, saying, 12
Behold, the children of Israel have not hearkened unto me ;
how then shall Pharaoh hear me, who am of uncircumcised
lips ?

AARON APPOINTED MOSES' PROPHET TO PHARAOH.

　　And Yahweh said unto Moses, See, I have made thee a　7
god to Pharaoh : and Aaron thy brother shall be thy prophet.
Thou shalt speak all that I command thee : and Aaron thy　2
brother shall speak unto Pharaoh, that he let the children of
Israel go out of his land.　And I will make Pharaoh's heart　3
'strong' and multiply my signs and my wonders in the land
of Egypt.　But Pharaoh will not hearken unto you, and I　4
will lay my hand upon Egypt, and bring forth my ' hosts,'
my people the children of Israel, out of the land of Egypt
by great ' judgments.'　And the Egyptians ' shall know that　5
I am Yahweh,' when I stretch forth mine hand upon Egypt,
and bring out the children of Israel from among them.　And　6
Moses and Aaron did so ; 'as Yahweh commanded them, so
did they.'　' And Moses was fourscore years old, and Aaron　7
fourscore and three years old,' when they spake unto
Pharaoh.

THE WONDERS OF EGYPT.　FIRST WONDER.　AARON'S ROD TURNED
TO A REPTILE.

　　And Yahweh spake unto Moses and unto Aaron, saying,　8
When Pharaoh shall speak unto you, saying, Shew a wonder　9

for you : then ' thou shalt say unto Aaron, Take thy rod,'
and cast it down before Pharaoh, that it become a ' reptile '
10 (Heb. *tannin*, any large reptile ; and so in vv. 10, 12).　And
Moses and Aaron went in unto Pharaoh, ' and they did so,
as Yahweh had commanded ' :　and Aaron cast down his rod
before Pharaoh and before his servants, and it became a
11 ' reptile.'　' Then Pharaoh also called for the wise men and
the sorcerers : ' and they also, ' the magicians ' of Egypt, did
12 in like manner with their ' enchantments.'　For they cast
down every man his rod, and they became ' reptiles ': but
13 Aaron's rod swallowed up their rods.　And Pharaoh's heart
was ' strong,' ' and he hearkened not unto them ; as Yahweh
had spoken.'

SECOND WONDER.　THE WATERS OF EGYPT TURNED TO BLOOD.

19　' And Yahweh said unto Moses, Say unto Aaron, Take thy
rod, and stretch out thine hand over the waters of Egypt,
' over their rivers, over their canals, and over their pools,
and over all their ponds of water,' that they may become
blood ; and there shall be blood throughout all the land of
Egypt, both in vessels of wood and in vessels of stone.
20 ' And Moses and Aaron did so, as Yahweh commanded ' :
22 and the blood was throughout all the land of Egypt.　' And
the magicians of Egypt did in like manner with their
enchantments ' : ' and Pharaoh's heart was strong, and he
hearkened not unto them ; as Yahweh had spoken.'

THIRD WONDER.　FROGS.

8—5　' And Yahweh said unto Moses, Say unto Aaron, Stretch
forth thine hand with thy rod ' ' over the rivers, over the
canals, and over the pools,' and cause frogs to come up upon
6 the land of Egypt.　And Aaron stretched out his hand over
the waters of Egypt ; and the frogs came up, and covered
7 the land of Egypt.　' And the magicians did in like manner
with their enchantments,' and brought up frogs upon the
land of Egypt.　' But Pharaoh's heart was strong and he
hearkened not unto them ; as Yahweh had spoken.'

FOURTH WONDER. THE SAND TURNED TO LICE.

' And Yahweh said unto Moses, Say unto Aaron, Stretch out 16
thy rod,' and smite the dust of the earth, that it may become
sand-flies, throughout all the land of Egypt. 'And they did 17
so ;' and Aaron stretched out his hand with his rod, and
smote the dust of the earth, and there were sand-flies upon
man, and upon beast ; all the dust of the earth became
sand-flies throughout all the land of Egypt. 'And the 18
magicians did so with their enchantments' to bring forth
sand-flies, but they could not : and there were sand-flies
upon man, and upon beast. Then 'the magicians' said 19
unto Pharaoh, This is the finger of God : 'and Pharaoh's
heart was strong, and he hearkened not unto them ; as
Yahweh had spoken.'

FIFTH WONDER. SOOT PRODUCING BOILS. THE MAGICIANS FLEE.

' And Yahweh said unto Moses and unto Aaron,' Take to 9—8
you handfuls of soot of the furnace, and let Moses sprinkle
it toward the heaven in the sight of Pharaoh. And it shall 9
become small dust over all the land of Egypt, and shall be
a boil breaking forth with blains upon man and upon beast,
throughout all the land of Egypt. And they took soot of the 10
furnace, and stood before Pharaoh ; and Moses sprinkled it
up toward heaven ; and it became a boil breaking forth
with blains upon man and upon beast. And 'the magicians' 11
could not stand before Moses because of the boils ; for the
boils were upon 'the magicians,' and upon all the Egyptians.
' And Yahweh made the heart of Pharaoh strong and he 12
hearkened not unto them ; as Yahweh had spoken unto
Moses.'

PREPARATIONS FOR THE FINAL STROKE. THE LAW FOR THE FEAST OF PASSOVER

' And Yahweh spake unto Moses and Aaron' in the land 12
of Egypt, saying, This month shall be unto you the begin- 2
ning of months : it shall be the 'first month' of the year

3 to you. Speak ye unto 'all the congregation of Israel,' saying, In the 'tenth' [day] of this month they shall take to
them every man a lamb, 'according to their fathers' houses,'
4 a lamb for an household: and if the household be too little
for a lamb, then shall he and his neighbor next unto his
house take one 'according to the number of the souls;'
'according to every man's eating' ye shall make your count
5 for the lamb. Your lamb shall be without blemish, 'a male'
of the first year: ye shall take it from the sheep, or from
6 the goats: and ye shall fatten it until 'the fourteenth day'
of the same month: and 'the whole assembly of the con-
7 gregation of Israel' shall kill it at even. And they shall
take of the blood, and put it on the two side posts and on
8 the lintel, upon the houses wherein they shall eat it. And
they shall eat the flesh in that night, roast with fire, and un-
9 leavened bread; with bitter herbs they shall eat it. Eat not
of it raw, nor sodden at all with water, but roast with fire;
its head with its legs and with the inwards thereof together.
10 And ye shall let nothing of it remain until the morning;
but that which remaineth of it until the morning ye shall
11 burn with fire. And thus shall ye eat it; with your loins
girded, your shoes on your feet, and your staff in your hand:
12 and ye shall eat it in haste: it is Yahweh's passover. For
I will go through the land of Egypt in that night, and will
smite all the firstborn in the land of Egypt, both man and
beast; and against all the gods of Egypt I will 'execute
13 judgments': 'I am Yahweh.' And the blood shall be to
you for a token upon the houses where ye are: and when I
see the blood, I will "pass over" (*pasach*) you, and there
shall no plague be upon you for a destroyer, when I smite
14 the land of Egypt. 'And this day shall be unto you for a
memorial, and ye shall keep it a feast to Yahweh': 'throughout your generations ye shall keep it a feast by an ordi-
15 nance for ever.' Seven days shall ye eat unleavened bread;
even the first day ye shall put away leaven out of your
houses: for whosoever eateth leavened bread from the first
day until the seventh day, 'that soul shall be cut off from

Israel.' And in the first day there shall be to you 'an holy 16 convocation,' and in the seventh day ' an holy convocation '; no manner of work shall be done in them, save that which every man must eat, that only may be done of you.

The Law for the Feast of Unleavened Cakes.

And ye shall observe the [ordinance as to] unleavened 17 cakes ; for in ' this self-same day ' have I brought your ' hosts ' out of the land of Egypt : therefore shall ye ' observe this day throughout your generations by an ordinance forever.' In the ' first ' [month], on the fourteenth day of 18 the month at even, ye shall eat unleavened cakes, until the one and twentieth day of the month at even. Seven days 19 shall there be no leaven found in your houses : for whosoever eateth that which is leavened, ' that soul shall be cut off from the congregation of Israel,' whether he be a sojourner, or one that is born in the land. Ye shall eat nothing leav- 20 ened ; in all your habitations shall ye eat unleavened cakes.

And the children of Israel ' went and did so ; as Yahweh 28 had commanded Moses and Aaron, so did they.'

Yahweh Smites the Firstborn of Egypt. The Law of the Firstborn, and the Exodus.

[And Yahweh passed through the land of Egypt (Vv. 12f.) that night and smote all the firstborn in the land of Egypt, both man and beast ; and against all the gods of Egypt he executed judgments ; but he passed over the houses of the children of Israel, where the blood was placed for a token. And on the morrow the whole congregation of (**Num. 33—3f.**) the children of Israel went forth by their hosts. On the fifteenth day of the first month, they journeyed from the land of Rameses and encamped in Succoth ; on the morrow after the passover the children of Israel went out with an high hand in the sight of all the Egyptians, while the Egyptians were burying all their firstborn which Yahweh had smitten among them].

And Yahweh spake unto Moses, saying, ' Sanctify unto **13**

2 me' all the firstborn, whatsoever openeth the womb among
the children of Israel, both of man and of beast : it is mine.

12—40 Now the 'sojourning' of the children of Israel, which
they 'sojourned' in Egypt, was four hundred and thirty
41 years. So it came to pass at the end of four hundred and
thirty years, 'even the self-same day' it came to pass, that
all the 'hosts of Yahweh' went out from the land of Egypt.

THE ORDINANCE OF THE PASSOVER.

43 And Yahweh said unto Moses and Aaron, 'This is the ordinance' of the passover : there shall no alien eat thereof :
44 but every man's servant that is bought for money, when
45 thou hast circumcised him, then shall he eat thereof. A so-
46 journer and an hired servant shall not eat thereof. In one
house shall it be eaten ; thou shalt not carry forth aught of
the flesh abroad out of the house ; neither shall ye break a
47 bone thereof. 'All the congregation of Israel' shall keep
48 it. And when a stranger shall sojourn with thee, and will
keep the passover to Yahweh, let all his 'males' be circumcised, and then let him come near and keep it ; and he shall be
as one that is born in the land : but no uncircumcised person
49 shall eat thereof. 'One law shall be to him that is homeborn, and unto the stranger that sojourneth among you.'
50 'Thus did all the children of Israel ; as Yahweh com-
51 manded Moses and Aaron, so did they.' And it came to
pass the 'self-same day,' that Yahweh did bring the children of Israel out of the land of Egypt 'by their hosts.'

THE CROSSING OF THE RED SEA.

13—20 'And they took their journey from Succoth and encamped in Etham,' in the edge of the wilderness.

14 'And Yahweh spake unto Moses, saying, Speak unto the
2 children of Israel, that they' turn back and encamp before
Pi-hahiroth, between Migdol and the sea, before Baal-
4 zephon : over against it shall ye encamp by the sea. And
I will 'make' Pharaoh's heart 'strong' and he shall follow
after them ; and I will 'get me honor' upon Pharaoh, and

upon all his ' host ' ; and ' the Egyptians shall know that I am Yahweh.' ' And they did so.' And Yahweh ' made ' the 8 heart of Pharaoh king of Egypt ' strong ' and he pursued after the children of Israel : while the children of Israel went out ' defiant.' So the Egyptians pursued after them, 9 ' all the horses [and] chariots of Pharaoh, and his horsemen, and his army,' and overtook them encamping by the sea, beside Pi-hahiroth, before Baal-zephon.

' And Yahweh said unto Moses, Speak unto the children 15 of Israel, that they ' go forward. And stretch out thine 16 hand over the sea, and divide it : and the children of Israel shall go into the midst of the sea on dry ground. ' And I, 17 lo, I will make the hearts ' of the Egyptians ' strong,' and they shall go in after them : and I will ' get me honor upon ' Pharaoh, and upon all his host, upon his chariots, and upon his horsemen. And the Egyptians ' shall know that I am 18 Yahweh,' when I have ' gotten me honor upon ' Pharaoh, upon his chariots, and upon his horsemen. So Moses 21 stretched out his hand over the sea, and the waters were divided. And the children of Israel went into the midst of 22 the sea upon the dry ground : ' and the waters were a wall unto them on their right hand, and on their left.' And the 23 Egyptians pursued, and went in after them into the midst of the sea, ' all Pharaoh's horses, his chariots, and his horsemen.'

And Yahweh said unto Moses, Stretch out thine hand 26 over the sea, that the waters may come again upon the Egyptians, ' upon their chariots, and upon their horsemen.' So 27 Moses stretched forth his hand over the sea, and the waters 28 returned, and covered the chariots, and the horsemen, even all ' the host ' of Pharaoh that went in after them into the sea ; But the children of Israel walked upon dry land in the 29 midst of the sea ; ' and the waters were a wall unto them on their right hand, and on their left.'

THE WILDERNESS OF SIN. FROM THE RED SEA TO SINAI.

So they journeyed from the [Red Sea], and ' all the **16**—1 congregation of the children of Israel' came unto the wilderness of Sin, 'on the fifteenth day of the second month' after their departing out of the land of Egypt.

17 'And all the congregation of the children of Israel journeyed from the wilderness of Sin, by their stages, according to the commandment of Yahweh,' and pitched in Rephidim.

19—2b 'And they journeyed from Rephidim and pitched in the wilderness of Sinai.' 'In the third month after the children of Israel were gone forth out of the land of Egypt, the same day came they into the wilderness of Sinai.'

THE TEN WORDS OF THE TESTIMONY.

(15—16) [And the glory of Yahweh appeared upon mount Sinai in a thick cloud, and Yahweh spake out of the cloud these words in the hearing of all the people.

I am Yahweh thy God, which brought thee out of the land of Egypt, out of the house of bondage.

Thou shalt have none other Gods before me. Thou shalt not make unto thee a graven image nor the likeness of any form that is in heaven above, or that is in the earth beneath, or that is in the water under the earth : thou shalt not bow down thyself unto them, nor serve them : for I Yahweh thy God am a jealous God, visiting the iniquity of the fathers upon the children, upon the third and upon the fourth generation of them that hate me ; and showing mercy unto thousands of generations, of them that love me and keep my commandments.

Thou shalt not invoke the name of Yahweh thy God upon a falsehood ; for Yahweh will not hold him guiltless that invoketh his name upon a falsehood.

Remember the Sabbath day to sanctify it. Six days shalt thou labor, and do all thy work : but the seventh day is a sabbath unto Yahweh thy God : in it thou shalt not do any work, thou, nor thy son, nor thy daughter, thy manservant, nor thy maidservant, nor thy cattle, nor thy stranger that is

20—11 within thy gates] : for in six days Yahweh made heaven and earth, the sea, and all that in them is, and rested the seventh day : wherefore Yahweh blessed the sabbath day, and 'sanctified it.'

[Honor thy father and thy mother that thy days may be long upon the land which Yahweh thy God giveth thee.

Thou shalt do no murder.

Thou shalt not commit adultery.

Thou shalt not steal.

Thou shalt not bear false witness against thy neighbor.

Thou shalt not covet thy neighbor's house, thou shalt not covet thy neighbor's wife, nor his manservant, nor his maid-servant, nor his ox, nor his ass, nor anything that is thy neighbor's].

MOSES ON MOUNT SINAI. THE TABLES OF THE TESTIMONY AND PATTERN OF THE TABERNACLE.

[And Yahweh said unto Moses, Come up unto me into the mount and I will give thee the tables of stone which I have prepared for a testimony unto the people, and will show thee the pattern of the sanctuary which ye shall build me]. So Moses went up into the mount. Now the cloud had 24—15 covered the mount and the 'Glory of Yahweh' abode upon 16 mount Sinai, and the cloud covered it six days : and the sev-enth day he called unto Moses out of the midst of the cloud. And the appearance of the 'Glory of Yahweh' was like 17 devouring fire on the top of the mount in the eyes of the children of Israel. And Moses entered into the midst of 18 the cloud.

*　　*　　*　　*　　*　　*　　*　　*

In chapters xxv.-xxvii. follows an elaborate specification of the tabernacle and its furniture in detail, which Moses is directed to construct. In chapters xxviii f. an equally elaborate description of the garments and other preparations and paraphernalia required for inducting Aaron and his sons into the priest-hood. Chapter xxx. gives directions for the altar of incense, the half-shekel poll-tax for the sanctuary, the brazen laver, the holy oil and incense. Chapter xxxi. 1-17 appoints the workmen for the construction, and enjoins strict observance of the Sabbath. We resume the story where the interview of Moses on the mount is at an end.

*　　*　　*　　*　　*　　*　　*　　*　　*　　*

31—18 So he gave unto Moses, when he had made an end
of talking with him upon mount Sinai, the two 'tables of
32—15 the testimony'; and Moses turned, and went down from
the mount with the two 'tables of the testimony' in his
hand, tables that were written on both their sides; on the
one side and on the other were they written.

*　　*　　*　　*　　*　　*　　*　　*

In chapters xxxiv. 29–xl., the entire book of Leviticus, and the first ten
chapters of Numbers, follows the nucleus of the Priestly Lawbook, relating
how upon Moses' descent from Sinai the Tables of the Testimony were
deposited in the Ark, and how the Tabernacle was erected and dedicated, and
its service inaugurated as prescribed by Yahweh Then follows the fundamental priestly and ceremonial law (P¹), incorporated in P², which forms the
kernel of Leviticus. The opening chapters of Numbers are occupied with the
census, appointment of the Levites and their duties; chapters v. and vi., with
miscellaneous Levitical laws (uncleanness, guilt offerings, ordeal of the water
of jealousy, nazirite vows, Aaronic benediction) devoid of connection with the
narrative; chapter vii. with the dedication gifts of the 12 princes (all exactly
alike), chapter viii., with the making and lighting of the candlestick, and
Aaron's wave-offering of the 22,000 Levites. Chapter ix. gives a supplementary Passover ordinance and prescription of the order of march according to
the sign of the cloud and Glory. Ch. x. 1–10 provides for silver trumpets.

*　　*　　*　　*　　*　　*　　*　　*　　*　　*

NUMBERS. (Heb. "In the Wilderness.")

Departure from Sinai. The Wilderness of Paran.

10—11 And it came to pass in the 'second year,' in the 'second month,' on the 'twentieth day of the month,' that the
cloud was taken up from over the 'Tabernacle of the Testi-
12 mony.' And the children of Israel set forward 'according
to their journeys' out of the wilderness of Sinai; and the
12—16b cloud abode in the wilderness of Paran. 'So they
pitched in the wilderness' of Paran.

Manna and Quails.

Ex. 16—2 And 'the whole congregation of the children of
Israel' 'murmured against Moses and against Aaron in the

wilderness : and the children of Israel said unto them, 3
' Would that we had died by the hand of Yahweh ' in the
land of Egypt, when we sat by the flesh pots, when we did
eat bread to the full ; for ye have brought us forth into this
wilderness, to kill this ' whole assembly ' with hunger.
' And Moses said unto Aaron, Say unto all the congregation 9
of the children of Israel,' Come near before Yahweh, for he
hath heard your ' murmurings.' And it came to pass, as 10
' Aaron spake unto the whole congregation of the children
of Israel,' that they looked toward the tabernacle, and, behold, ' the Glory of Yahweh appeared in the cloud.' And 11
Yahweh spake unto Moses, saying, I have heard the ' mur- 12
murings ' of the children of Israel ; speak unto them, saying,
At even ye shall eat flesh, and in the morning ye shall be filled
with bread ; ' and ye shall know that I am Yahweh your God.'

And ' Moses and Aaron said unto all the children of Israel,' 6
At even, then ye shall know that Yahweh hath brought you
out from the land of Egypt : and in the morning, then ye 7
shall see the glory of Yahweh ; for that he heareth your
murmurings against Yahweh, and ' what are we that ye murmur against us ?' And it came to pass at even, that the 13
quails came up, and covered the camp : and in the morning
the dew lay round about the camp. And when the dew 14
that lay was gone up, behold, upon the face of the wilderness a small flake, small as the hoar frost on the ground.
And Moses said unto them It is the bread which Yahweh 15
hath given you to eat ; an omer a ' head,' ' according to 16*b*
the number of your persons,' shall ye take it, every man for
them which are in his tent. And the house of Israel called 31
the name thereof Manna (Heb. *man*) : and it was like coriander seed, white ; and the taste of it was like wafers
[made] with honey. And the children of Israel did eat the 35
manna forty years, until they came to a land inhabited.

THE STORY OF THE SPIES.

And Yahweh spake unto Moses, saying, Send thou men, **13**
that they may ' spy ' out the land of Canaan, which I give 2

unto the children of Israel : of every 'tribe of their fathers'
3 shall ye send a man, every one a 'prince' among them. And
Moses sent them from the 'wilderness of Paran' 'according
to the commandment of Yahweh:' all of them men who were
4 'heads of the children of Israel.' And 'these were their
names' :

	Of the tribe of Reuben,	Shammua the son of Zaccur.
5	Of the tribe of Simeon,	Shaphat the son of Hori.
6	Of the tribe of Judah,	Caleb the son of Jephunneh.
7	Of the tribe of Issachar,	Igal the son of Joseph.
8	Of the tribe of Ephraim,	Hoshea the son of Nun.
9	Of the tribe of Benjamin,	Palti the son of Raphu.
10	Of the tribe of Zebulun,	Gaddiel the son of Sodi.
11	Of the tribe of Joseph,	Gaddi the son of Susi.
12	Of the tribe of Dan,	Ammiel the son of Gemalli.
13	Of the tribe of Asher,	Sethur the son of Michael.
14	Of the tribe of Naphtali,	Nahbi the son of Vophsi.
15	Of the tribe of Gad,	Geuel the son of Machi.

16 'These are the names' of the men which Moses sent to
'spy' out the land. And Moses called Hoshea the son of
17 Nun Joshua. And Moses sent them to 'spy' out the land of
21 Canaan. So they went up, and 'spied' out the land from
the wilderness of Zin unto Rehob, to the entering in of Ha-
25 math. And they returned from 'spying' out the land at the
26 end of forty days. And they went and came 'to Moses, and
to Aaron, and to all the congregation of the children of Israel,' unto 'the wilderness of Paran,' and brought back word
32 unto them, and unto 'all the congregation.' And they
brought up an 'evil report' of the land which they had
'spied' out unto the children of Israel, saying, The land,
through which we have gone to 'spy' it out, is a land that
[for barrenness] eateth up the inhabitants thereof ;

REBELLION OF THE PEOPLE AT THE SPIES' REPORT. CONDEMNA-
TION TO FORTY YEARS OF WANDERING.

14 And 'all the congregation murmured against Moses and
against Aaron :' and 'the whole congregation' said unto

them, 'Would God that we had died in the land of Egypt'! or 'Would God we had died in this wilderness!' 'Then 5 Moses and Aaron fell on their faces before all the assembly of the congregation of the children of Israel.' And Joshua 6 the son of Nun and Caleb the son of Jephunneh, which were 7 of them that 'spied' out the land, rent their clothes: and they spake unto 'all the congregation of the children of Israel,' saying, The land, which we passed through to 'spy' it out, is an exceeding good land. But 'all the congrega- 10 tion' bade stone them with stones. 'And the Glory of Yah- weh appeared in the Tent of Meeting unto all the children of Israel.'

'And Yahweh spake unto Moses and unto Aaron,' saying, 26 How long [shall I bear] with this evil 'congregation,' which 27 'murmur against me? I have heard the murmurings of the children of Israel, which they murmur against me.' Say 28 unto them, As I live, saith Yahweh, surely as ye have spoken in mine ears, so will I do to you your carcases shall fall 'in 29 this wilderness'; and all that were numbered of you, accord- ing to your whole number, 'from twenty years old and up- ward,' which have 'murmured' against me, surely ye shall 30 not come into the land, concerning which 'I lifted up my hand' that I would make you dwell therein, save Caleb the son of Jephunneh, and Joshua the son of Nun. After the 34 number of the days in which ye 'spied' out the land, even forty days, for every day a year, shall ye 'bear your iniqui- ties,' even forty years, and ye shall know what the revoking of my promise is. 'I Yahweh have spoken,' surely this will I 35 do unto all this 'evil congregation,' that are gathered together against me: in this wilderness they shall be consumed, and there they shall die. And the men, which Moses sent to 36 'spy' out the land, who returned, and made 'all the congrega- tion' to murmur against him, by bringing up an 'evil report' against the land, even those men that did bring up an 'evil 37 report' of the land, died by 'the plague' before Yahweh. But Joshua the son of Nun, and Caleb the son of Jephunneh, 38 remained alive of those men that went to 'spy' out the land.

THE MUTINY OF KORAH. AN ATTACK UPON THE EXCLUSIVENESS
OF THE PRIESTHOOD.

16—1-2   Now Korah the son of [. . .] took two hundred and
fifty 'princes of the congregation,' 'called to the assembly '
3 and they 'assembled themselves together against Moses and
against Aaron,' and said unto them, Ye take too much upon
you, seeing 'all the congregation' are 'holy,' every one of
them : wherefore then lift ye up yourselves above 'the as-
8 sembly of Yahweh'? ye take too much upon you, ye sons of
4 Levi. And when Moses heard it, he 'fell upon his face' :
5 and he spake unto Korah and unto all his 'company,' saying,
In the morning Yahweh will shew who are his, and who is
'holy,' and will cause him to come near unto him : even him
whom he shall choose will he cause to come near unto him.
6 This do ; take you 'censers,' Korah, and all his 'company ';
7 and put fire therein, and put 'incense' upon them before Yahweh to-morrow : and it shall be that the man whom Yahweh
18 doth choose, he [shall be] 'holy' : So they took every man
his 'censer,' and put fire in them, and laid incense thereon,
and stood at the door of the Tent of Meeting with 'Moses
19 and Aaron.' And Korah 'assembled all the congregation'
against them unto the door of the Tent of Meeting : 'and
the Glory of Yahweh appeared unto all the congregation.'
20   'And Yahweh spake unto Moses and unto Aaron,' saying,
21 'Separate yourselves from among this congregation, that I
22 may consume them in a moment.' 'And they fell upon their
faces,' and said, O God, the 'God of the spirits of all flesh,'
shall one man sin, and wilt thou be wroth with 'all the con-
23 gregation'? 'And Yahweh spake unto Moses, saying,
24 Speak unto the congregation,' saying, Get you up from about
27 'the Tabernacle of Yahweh.' So they gat them up from 'the
35 Tabernacle of Yahweh' on every side. And fire came forth
from Yahweh and devoured the two hundred and fifty men
that were offering the 'incense.'

RENEWED MURMURINGS AND PLAGUE. THE BUDDING OF AARON'S ROD A TOKEN OF YAHWEH'S CHOOSING OF THE AARONIC PRIESTHOOD.

But on the morrow 'all the congregation of the children 41 of Israel murmured against Moses and against Aaron, saying,' Ye have killed the people of Yahweh. And it came to 42 pass, when 'the congregation was assembled against Moses and against Aaron,' that they looked toward the Tent of Meeting : and, behold, the cloud covered it, 'and the Glory of Yahweh appeared.' And Moses and Aaron came to the 43 front of the Tent of Meeting. And Yahweh spake unto 44 Moses, saying, 'Get you up from among this congregation, 45 that I may consume them in a moment.' 'And they fell 46 upon their faces.' And Moses said unto Aaron, Take thy 'censer,' and put fire therein from off the altar, and lay 'incense' thereon, and carry it quickly unto 'the congregation,' and 'make atonement' for them : for there is wrath gone out from Yahweh ; the 'plague' is begun. And 47 Aaron took as Moses spake, and ran into the midst of 'the assembly '; and, behold, 'the plague' was begun among the people : and he put on the 'incense,' and 'made atonement' for the people. And as he stood between the dead and the 48 living 'the plague' was stayed. Now they that died by 'the 49 plague' were fourteen thousand and seven hundred, besides them that died about the matter of Korah. So Aaron 50 returned unto Moses unto the door of the Tent of Meeting : and 'the plague' was stayed.

'And Yahweh spake unto Moses, saying, Speak unto the **17**—2 children of Israel,' and take of them rods, one for each 'fathers' house,' of all their 'princes according to their fathers' houses,' twelve rods : write thou every man's name upon his rod. And thou shalt write Aaron's name upon the rod 3 of Levi : for there shall be one rod for each 'head of their fathers' houses.' And thou shalt lay them up in the Tent 4 of Meeting before 'the Testimony,' where I meet with thee. And it shall come to pass, that the man whom I shall choose, 5 his rod shall bud : and I will make to cease from me 'the

murmurings of the children of Israel, which they murmur
6 against you.' And Moses spake unto the children of Israel,
and all their 'princes' gave him rods, for each 'prince' one,
'according to their fathers' houses,' even twelve rods : and
7 'the rod of Aaron' was among their rods. And Moses laid
up the rods before Yahweh in the 'Tent of the Testimony.'
8 And it came to pass on the morrow, that Moses went into
the 'Tent of the Testimony'; and, behold, the 'rod of
Aaron' for the house of Levi was budded, and put forth
9 buds, and bloomed blossoms, and bare ripe almonds. And
Moses brought out all the rods from before Yahweh
unto all the children of Israel : and they looked, and
10 took every man his rod. And Yahweh said unto Moses,
Put back 'the rod of Aaron' before the 'Testimony,' to be
kept for a token against the children of rebellion ; that thou
mayest make an end of 'their murmurings against me,' that
11 they die not. 'Thus did Moses : as Yahweh commanded
him, so did he.'
12   And the children of Israel spake unto Moses, saying, Be-
13 hold, we perish, we are undone, we are all undone. Every
one that cometh near, that cometh near unto the Tabernacle
of Yahweh, dieth : shall we perish all of us ?
18   And Yahweh said unto Aaron, Thou and thy sons 'and thy
fathers' house' with thee shall 'bear the iniquity' of the
'Sanctuary' : and thou and thy sons with thee shall 'bear the
2 iniquity' of your priesthood. And thy brethren also, the
tribe of Levi, the tribe of thy father, bring thou near with
thee, that they may be "joined" (*lavah*) unto thee, and minister unto thee : but thou and thy sons with thee shall min-
3 ister before the 'Tent of the Testimony.' And they shall
keep thy charge, and the charge of all the Tent : only they
shall not come nigh unto the 'vessels of the Sanctuary' and
4 unto the altar, that they die not, neither they, nor ye. And
they shall be "joined" unto thee, and keep the charge of the
Tent of Meeting, for all the service of the Tent : 'and a
5 stranger shall not come nigh unto you.' And ye shall keep
the charge of the Sanctuary, and the charge of the altar:

that there be wrath no more upon the children of Israel. 'And I, behold, I ' have taken your brethren the Levites 6 from among the children of Israel : to. you they are a gift, given unto Yahweh, to do the service of the Tent of Meeting. And thou and thy sons with thee shall keep your 7 priesthood for every thing of the altar, and for that within the veil ; and ye shall serve : I give you the priesthood as a service of privilege : 'and the stranger that cometh nigh shall be put to death.'

*   *   *   *   *   *   *   *

The rest of chapter xviii. is devoted to prescription of the priests' dues. Chapter xix. has no relation to the context, but presents the law of purification in case of various defilements from dead bodies.

*   *   *   *   *   *   *   *

MERIBAH-KADESH. WATER FROM THE ROCK.

'And the children of Israel, even the whole congrega- 20 tion, came into the wilderness of Zin in the first month of the fortieth year.' And there was no water for ' the congre- 2 gation : ' 'and they assembled themselves together against Moses and against Aaron,' and spake, saying, 'Would God that we had died ' when our brethren died before Yahweh ! And why have ye brought ' the assembly of Yahweh ' into 4 this wilderness, that we should die there. 'And Moses and 6 Aaron went from the presence of the assembly unto the door of the Tent of Meeting, and fell upon their faces : and the Glory of Yahweh appeared unto them.' And Yahweh spake 7 unto Moses, saying, 'assemble the congregation,' thou, and 8 Aaron thy brother, and speak ye unto the rock before their eyes that it give forth its water, and thou shalt bring forth to them water out of the rock. So shalt thou give 'the congregation' drink. [And Moses and Aaron spake before Yahweh] and said, Shall we indeed bring them 10b forth water out of this rock ? And Yahweh said unto Moses and Aaron, Hear me, ye rebels ; forasmuch as ye believed 12 not in me, to ' show my " holiness " ' in the eyes of the children of Israel, therefore ye shall not bring ' this assembly '

8 into 'the land which I have given them.' [And unto Moses
he said], Take thou the rod [which is before me, and smite
9 the rock with it and the waters shall come forth]. So Moses
took the rod from before Yahweh as he commanded him.
'And Moses and Aaron gathered the assembly together'
11 before the rock. And Moses lifted up his hand, and smote
the rock with his rod twice : and water came forth abund-
13 antly, and the 'congregation' drank. These are the waters
of Meribah [of Kadesh] ; because the children of Israel
"strove" (*rib*) with Yahweh, and he "showed himself holy "
(*kadesh*) among them.

DEATH OF AARON.

22   'And they journeyed from Kadesh : and the children of
Israel, even the whole congregation, came unto mount
23 Hor.' 'And Yahweh spake unto Moses and Aaron' in
mount Hor, by the border of the land of Edom, saying,
24 Aaron shall be 'gathered unto his people :' for he shall not
enter into 'the land which I have given unto the children of
Israel,' because ye 'rebelled against my word' at the waters
25 of Meribah. Take Aaron and Eleazar his son, and bring
26 them up unto mount Hor : and strip Aaron of his garments,
and put them upon Eleazar his son : and Aaron 'shall be
27 gathered [unto his people],' and shall die there. 'And
Moses did as Yahweh commanded :' and they went up into
28 mount Hor 'in the sight of all the congregation.' And
Moses stripped Aaron of his garments, and put them upon
Eleazar his son ; and Aaron died there in the top of the
mount : and Moses and Eleazar came down from the mount.
29 And when 'all the congregation' saw that Aaron was dead,
'they wept for Aaron thirty days,' even all the house of Israel.

FROM HOR TO NEBO.

21—4   'And they journeyed from mount Hor [and pitched in'
.   .   .   .
10 'And the children of Israel journeyed, and pitched ' in Oboth.
11 '.And they journeyed from' Oboth, 'and pitched at' Iye-

abarim. 'And the children of Israel journeyed, and pitched 22—1
in ' the ' plains of Moab beyond the Jordan ' at Jericho.

THE CORRUPTION OF ISRAEL THROUGH THE COUNSEL OF BALAAM. THE PLAGUE TURNED AWAY BY PHINEHAS.

[And while Israel abode in the plains of Moab the elders
of Moab took counsel with the elders of Midian how they
might destroy the people. And the elders of Midian sent
unto Balaam the son of Beor to the land of the children of
Ammon, and he gave them counsel saying, Give your daughters unto the children of Israel in marriage and let your
people mingle with theirs, for Yahweh their God is a jealous
God. He will not suffer them to mingle with the nations
round about. Thus shall ye bring enmity from Yahweh
upon Israel. And the counsel pleased the elders of Moab
and the elders of Midian, and they did so. And it came to
pass when the children of Israel were gone in to the daughters of Midian that Yahweh sent a plague into the camp and
the people died]. And, behold, one of the children of Is- 25—6
rael came and brought unto his brethren a Midianitish
woman ' in the sight of Moses, and in the sight of all the
congregation of the children of Israel,' while they were
weeping at the door of the Tent of Meeting. And when 7
Phinehas, the son of Eleazar, the son of Aaron the priest,
saw it, he rose up from the midst of the ' congregation,' and
took a spear in his hand ; and he went after the man of 8
Israel into the inner room, and thrust both of them through,
the man of Israel, and the woman through her belly. So
' the plague was stayed ' from the children of Israel. And 9
those that ' died by the plague ' were twenty and four thous-
and.

And Yahweh spoke unto Moses, saying, Phinehas, the 10—11
son of Eleazar, the son of Aaron the priest, hath turned my
wrath away from the children of Israel, in that he was jealous with the jealousy I myself show among them, so that I
' consumed ' not the children of Israel in my jealousy.
Wherefore say, ' Behold, I give unto him my covenant of 12

13 peace': and it shall be 'unto him, and to his seed after
him,' the 'covenant of an everlasting priesthood'; because
he was jealous for his God, and 'made atonement' for the
14 children of Israel.   Now the name of the man of Israel
that was slain, who was slain with the Midianitish woman,
was Zimri, the son of Salu, a 'prince of a fathers' house'
15 among the Simeonites.   And the name of the Midianitish
woman that was slain was Cozbi, the daughter of Zur; he
was 'head of the people of a fathers' house' in Midian.
16-17   And Yahweh spake unto Moses, saying, Vex the Midianites, and smite them : for they vex you with their wiles,
wherewith they have beguiled you.

[THE WAR WITH MIDIAN].

(31—1-54)   [So Moses chose out men and sent them to smite
the Midianites, and they destroyed them so that there re-
. mained not one, and devoted their cities ; and they returned
to Moses to the camp].

THE INHERITANCE OF GAD AND REUBEN.

32   Now the children of Reuben and the children of Gad
2 had a multitude of cattle : and they came and spake ' unto
Moses, and to Eleazar the priest, and unto the princes of the
4 congregation,' saying, the land which Yahweh ' smote before
the congregation of Israel,' is a land for cattle, and thy servants have cattle.   [Let us now receive our inheritance on
18 this side Jordan].   We will not return unto our houses,
until the children of Israel have 'inherited every man his
19 inheritance.'   For we will not inherit with them on the
other side Jordan, and forward ; because 'our inheritance'
is fallen to us on this side Jordan eastward.
28   So Moses gave charge concerning them 'to Eleazar the
priest, and to Joshua the son of Nun, and to the heads of
the fathers' [houses] of the tribes of the children of Israel.'
29 And Moses said unto them, If the children of Gad and the
children of Reuben will pass with you over Jordan, 'every
man that is armed to battle,' before Yahweh, and the land

shall be subdued before you ; then ye shall give them the
land of Gilead ' for a possession ' : but if they will not pass 30
over with you armed, they shall have 'possessions' among
you in the land of Canaan. And the children of Gad and 31
the children of Reuben answered, saying, As Yahweh hath
said unto thy servants, so will we do. We will pass over 32
armed before Yahweh into the land of Canaan, and ' the
possession of our inheritance ' [shall remain] with us beyond
Jordan. So Moses gave them the land [of Gilead] ' accord- 33
ing to the cities thereof with [their] borders, even the cities
of the land round about.'

PREPARATION FOR MOSES' DEATH. HE RECEIVES DIRECTION TO APPOINT JOSHUA IN HIS STEAD.

And Yahweh said unto Moses, Get thee up into this **27**—12
mountain of Abarim, and behold ' the land which I have
given unto the children of Israel.' And when thou hast seen 13
it, thou also ' shalt be gathered unto thy people,' as Aaron
thy brother was gathered : because ' ye rebelled against my 14
word ' in the wilderness of Zin, in the strife of the ' congregation,' to ' sanctify me ' in the matter of the waters ' before
their eyes.' (These are the waters of Meribah of Kadesh in
the wilderness of Zin). And Moses spake unto Yahweh, 15
saying, Let Yahweh, 'the God of the spirits of all flesh,' ap- 16
point a man over the ' congregation,' which may go out
before them, and which may come in before them, and 17
which may lead them out, and which may bring them in ,
that ' the congregation of Yahweh ' be not as sheep which
have no shepherd. And Yahweh said unto Moses, Take 18
thee Joshua the son of Nun, a ' man in whom is the
spirit,' and lay thine hand upon him ; and set him be- 19
fore ' Eleazar the priest, and before all the congregation ' ;
and give him a charge in their sight. And thou shalt put 20
of thine authority upon him, that ' all the congregation of
the children of Israel ' may obey. And he shall stand be- 21
fore ' Eleazar the priest,' who shall inquire for him ' by the
oracle of the Urim,' before Yahweh : ' at his word ' shall

they go out, and 'at his word' they shall come in, both he,
and all the children of Israel with him, even 'all the
22 congregation.' 'And Moses did as Yahweh commanded him ' :
and he took Joshua, and set him 'before Eleazar the priest,
23 and before all the congregation' : and he laid his hands upon
him, and gave him a charge, 'as Yahweh spake by the hand
of Moses.'

——————◆——————

DEUTERONOMY. ("Words of Moses.")

Death of Moses.

34   So Moses went up 'from the plains of Moab' unto mount
5 Nebo, [and died there] 'according to the word of Yahweh.'
7 'And Moses was an hundred and twenty years old when he
died': his eye was not dim, nor his natural force abated.
8 'And the children of Israel wept for Moses in the plains of
Moab thirty days ' : so the days of weeping in the mourning
9 for Moses were ended.   And Joshua the son of Nun was
'full of the spirit of wisdom' ; for Moses had laid his hands
upon him : and the children of Israel hearkened unto him,
and 'did as Yahweh commanded Moses.'